Christoph Marx
The Anxieties of White Supremacy

Africa in Global History

Edited by
Joël Glasman, Omar Gueye, Alexander Keese and
Christine Whyte

Advisory Board:
Joe Alie, Felicitas Becker, William Gervase Clarence-Smith, Lynda Day,
Scholastique Diazinga, Andreas Eckert, Babacar Fall, Toyin Falola, Matt Graham,
Emma Hunter, Erin Jessee, Isabella Kentridge, Colleen Kriger, Kristin Mann,
Patrick Manning, Conceição Neto, Vanessa S. Oliveira, Lorelle Semley,
Ibrahim Sundiata

Volume 8

Christoph Marx

The Anxieties of White Supremacy

Hendrik Verwoerd and the Apartheid Mindset

Translated by
Ulrike Kistner

DE GRUYTER
OLDENBOURG

First published in German © by De Gruyter Oldenbourg, Walter de Gruyter GmbH, Christoph Marx, Trennung und Angst. Hendrik Verwoerd und die Gedankenwelt der Apartheid, Berlin/Boston, 2020.

ISBN 978-3-11-221416-9
e-ISBN (PDF) 978-3-11-078731-3
e-ISBN (EPUB) 978-3-11-078735-1
ISSN 2628-1767

Library of Congress Control Number: 2023941011

Bibliographic information published by the Deutsche Nationalbibliothek
The Deutsche Nationalbibliothek lists this publication in the Deutsche Nationalbibliografie; detailed bibliographic data are available on the internet at http://dnb.dnb.de.

© 2025 Walter de Gruyter GmbH, Berlin/Boston
This volume is text- and page-identical with the hardback published in 2024.
Cover image: Statue of Verwoerd in Bloemfontein (removed in 2004). Photo: Christoph Marx
Typesetting: Integra Software Services Pvt. Ltd.
Printing and binding: CPI books GmbH, Leck

www.degruyter.com

Contents

Abbreviations —— IX

Introduction —— 1
    Sources —— 17
    Structure of the Book —— 18

Principles —— 21

Sharpened Thoughts – Blunted Feelings —— 50
    The Double Task: Verwoerd's MA Dissertation —— 63
    Verwoerd's Thesis —— 71

Trajectories —— 84
    Post-Doctoral Studies in Germany —— 84
    Sojourn in the US, 1927 —— 98
    Professor Verwoerd —— 100
    Childhood Psychology —— 100
    Ethnopsychology and Theories of Civilisational Stages —— 109
    Apartheid and Development —— 118

From Sociology to Social Policy —— 126
    Commitment to the 'Poor Whites' —— 126
    Transitioning into Politics —— 138
    Verwoerd as Intellectual —— 155

Propaganda —— 160
    The Journalist —— 160
    Propaganda Techniques —— 168
    Verwoerd as Orator —— 174
    Logic as Rhetorical Device —— 179

Organised Unity of the "Volk" —— 188
    'Unity of the People': Organised Nationalism —— 190
    The Outbreak of the War and the Failure of "Hereniging" —— 193
    The Afrikaner Broederbond —— 195
    The Struggle against the *Ossewabrandwag* —— 206
    The Post-War Period —— 215
    "Hereniging" —— 217

Chaos and Order —— 222

Difference and Purity —— 241
    Verwoerd's Antisemitism —— 261

Apartheid —— 271
    From Concept to Plan: The Sauer Report —— 276
    Minister Verwoerd's Concept of Apartheid —— 278
    Urban Apartheid —— 301
    Bantu Education —— 308

Knowledge and Epistemologies of Ignorance – Justifications of Apartheid from the Human Sciences —— 316
    Ethnopsychology (*Völkerpsychologie*) —— 317
    Ethnology —— 322
    History —— 339

'Homelands' —— 347
    Prime Minister Verwoerd —— 347
    The Homeland Policy —— 350
    The Republican on the Path to Victory —— 358
    From Cultural Nationalism to Nation-Building —— 378
    South Africa and the Global Racial Conflict —— 384

Repression and Control —— 394
    Repression against Political Opponents —— 395
    Dealing with the Press —— 405
    Refusal to Engage in Dialogue —— 406
    Conflicts with the English Churches —— 409
    Indians and Coloureds —— 416

Modernisation —— 438
    The Orange River Dam —— 458

The Breath of Death —— 469
    'The Breath of Death' —— 486

Conclusion —— 497

Bibliography —— 505

Literature —— 509

Name Index —— 571

Location Index —— 575

Subject Index —— 577

Abbreviations

AB	Afrikaner Broederbond
ANC	African National Congress
AP	Afrikaner Party
DRC	Dutch Reformed Church (=NGK)
FAK	Federation of Afrikaans Cultural Associations
FAV	Family Archive Verwoerd
HNP	Herenigde Nasionale Party (Re-united National Party)
IfZ	Institut für Zeitgeschichte/Institute for Contemporay History (Munich)
ISCOR	Iron and Steel Corporation
NA	National Archives (Pretoria)
NAD	Native Affairs Department
NGK	Nederduits Gereformeerde Kerk (=DRC)
NHK	Nederduits Herformde Kerk
NP	National Party
NRC	Natives Representative Council
OB	Ossewabrandwag
PAC	Panafricanist Congress
PV	Persoonlike Versameling/Private Collection
RDM	Rand Daily Mail
SABRA	South African Bureau of Racial Affairs
SAIRR	South African Institute of Race Relations
UA	University Archive
UNISA	University of South Africa
UP	United Party
UR	Uitvoerende Raad/Executive Council
US	University of Stellenbosch, J. Gericke-Library, Documents Section

Introduction

> Now you would not think to look at him
> But he was famous long ago
> For playing the electric violin
> On Desolation Row
>
> *Bob Dylan*

In the early afternoon of September 6, 1966, after a lunch break, members of the South African Parliament convened for a meeting in the Chamber. Prime Minister Hendrik Verwoerd had just arrived. He had already taken his seat on the government bench and was busy reading some documents, when a parliamentary messenger pushed his way past the MPs who were gathering in their numbers. He hurried towards the government bench and, before anyone could react, he overpowered the Prime Minister and killed him with four knife stabs.

In the history of the twentieth century, which is not exactly lacking in dramatic assassinations, the fatal attack on Hendrik Verwoerd is one of the most spectacular, and at the same time, one of the most symbolically laden: at the height of his power, the Prime Minister of the apartheid state was killed literally in the seat of power – archaically, as it were. This act ended a life that his followers, until then, had celebrated as a success story, while his opponents saw it as an escalating trajectory of misguided and ideologically misleading politics.

The diametrically opposed estimations of the man and the tracks set by him, are also reflected in the assessments of his role internationally: To his followers, he was a 'man of granite' who stood firm against external pressures, and who never tired of presenting racial segregation as a 'fair deal' to an uncomprehending international public. To his opponents, on the other hand, he was an unbending dogmatist; it was precisely this intransigence that side-lined South Africa from the international political arena. Thus, from the perspective of the international community, Verwoerd's political course had made a pariah of the country – a status deemed extremely perilous, especially when considered in the context of the East-West conflict. While the regime led by Verwoerd was obsessively anti-communist, the black opposition took up an increasingly active social-revolutionary stance. As a result, the internal political contradictions attained ever more sharp and toxic dimensions; by the end of the 1980s, a solution seemed impossible.

From Verwoerd's perspective, however, the role of South Africa within international politics was more complex. He had made of the South African state a regional-imperial actor, with the aim of securing a permanent hegemonic status within a constellation of economically weak neighbouring states, thus creating a counter to the isolation from international relations in a broader context (which Verwoerd considered to be a short-term scenario anyway). As soon as the successes of racial segregation would be recognised, he opined, the criticism would subside, and South Africa would be able to once again take its rightful place as recognised international player. This turned out to be a gross miscalculation, for even Verwoerd's successors who implemented all manner of strategies to end South Africa's isolation while retaining apartheid, failed dismally.

By no means did the assassination of Verwoerd end apartheid, which persisted through more than two decades after the event. But in a certain sense, the apartheid state lost its motive force in the person of the politician who had sought to implement racial segregation with determination and unscrupulousness, who had propagandistically justified it and who had trivialised, played down, denied and obscured the devastating consequences for the majority of the population. Verwoerd excelled in propagandistic contortions, presenting a monstrous politics of inequality and injustice in the light of justice, and conveying this in a convincing way; to this day, it is not clear whether and how far he himself believed in it.

Hendrik Verwoerd (1901–1966) was without doubt the most dynamic politician in South Africa in the twentieth century. During the eight years in which he presided over the Ministry of Native Affairs, he re-engineered state and society on the model of apartheid. A further eight years in office as Prime Minister saw fundamental changes in the status of South Africa in international relations; having been declared a Republic in 1961, South Africa left the Commonwealth. At the same time, Verwoerd instituted an interventionist state that made its appearance at the most diverse sites of planning and co-ordination. The ripple effects of the grand projects initiated by the apartheid state are palpable right up to the present day. It may come as a surprise that before entering national politics, Verwoerd was an academic. His understanding of science and his training as a psychologist will be moved into focus for the first time in this book. As a scholar with a doctoral degree in psychology and after 1932, as professor of sociology, he was particularly interested in white poverty. His engagement in this field was underpinned by a radical form of cultural nationalism; having been born into an Amsterdam-based family identifying with the struggle of the Afrikaners, Hendrik Verwoerd gave fanatic expression to this identification. The assassination of Verwoerd in September 1966 presented a break insofar as the dynamic development of apartheid that had been enthusiastically embraced by his supporters stalled, and security concerns moved centre stage instead. Confronted with international isolation and since the 1970s also with increasingly powerful internal and external opposition, the state went on the defensive. Verwoerd represents the triumphalist Afrikaner nationalism and the politics of apartheid that he spearheaded. The focus of this book is not so much the active politician though, but the intellectual world of Verwoerd – the ideas, conceptions, and values that he held and shared with most of his fellow Afrikaans-speaking nationalist intellectuals and politicians. Although Verwoerd himself was anything but an anxiety-ridden person, his politics was marked by anxiety – anxiety over the cultural take-over and demise of the Afrikaner people, over the loss of identity, and over 'racial mixing'. This anxiety is what gave rise to the politics of segregation and self-isolation.

When Henry Kenney's biography of Hendrik Verwoerd appeared, reviewers began to realise how fleeting was the memory of the former Prime Minister who had dominated politics in that country like no one else; by 1980, the year in which the biography appeared, he was largely forgotten.[1] Despite the fact that a few tributes paid to him by his peers remained in circulation for a while, the memory of this statesman faded in South Africa soon after his death; internationally, however, it remained alive. In a survey conducted in Bloomington, Indiana, Verwoerd was named, ahead of Idi Amin,[2] as number five of "the most abhorrent despot of all times". Until then there were only two biographies, one of which, penned by English-language left-liberal politician and trade unionist Alexander Hepple, appeared in 1967 shortly after Verwoerd's death; the second one, an uncritical hagiography, appeared in 1974, authored by his old companion and admirer G. D. Scholtz. The third biography, that written by economist Henry Kenney, remained for many years the last among the life stories of the man who attained the epithet of "the architect of apartheid", as he was named by the author of that book. In common parlance, the politics of apartheid was associated, *tout court*, with the name of Hendrik Verwoerd. Even more puzzling would it seem that no one bothered with this figure in all the years until the abolition of apartheid in 1994.[3]

It took a while for renewed interest in Verwoerd to arise. In 2009, a biography of Verwoerd was published in French, authored by political scientist Pierre-Olivier Sabalot. In South Africa, too, we can anticipate a number of investigations, including biographical ones.[4] In 2012, Hermann Giliomee published a brief biography in which Verwoerd appears in an astonishingly mild light; since it is not based on independent research, however, it does not yield any remarkable new insights.[5] Verwoerd's grandson Wilhelm, himself a member of the African National Congress (ANC), engaged with the political inheritance of his grandfather

---

1 *Sunday Times*, 7.9.1980; *Eastern Province Herald*, 18.10.1980.
2 Eckel 2015: 410.
3 Froneman (2013) provides a comprehensive overview of the publications on Verwoerd.
4 Giliomee (2012a) provides a detailed portrait of Verwoerd.
5 Giliomee 2012c.

in an intensely personal and reflective way. The book, which appeared in 2018, does not pose as a scholarly contribution to research on Verwoerd, though.[6]

The long period of disinterest in the person of Verwoerd becomes explicable if we consider the changes in South African historiography in predominantly English-language publications. 'Big-men-making-history' biographies had been thoroughly discredited, and perfectly understandably so. But more importantly, ever since the late 1960s, South African critical historiography moved into a completely different direction. Social history as 'history from below' became the motto of the new historiography. It set itself the task of researching the history of those who had been made the objects of administrative policies, with the aim of returning to Africans the position of subjects and agents of their own history. This approach broadly dovetailed with tendencies in postcolonial studies seeking to make the agency of the colonised the focus of investigation. This change in perspective generated a multiplicity of empirically and theoretically inspiring studies; they were methodologically innovative insofar as they opened the most diverse forms of oral history and new approaches to the sources and the value of history from below in unearthing and analysing experiences of exploitation and oppression. After the end of apartheid, this tendency persisted, but now with extended perspectives that took on board the apartheid state itself. Due to the long period of disinterest in state departments and functionaries, historical investigations had not identified the persons of the perpetrators, simply referring to them by their official designations as 'the Prime Minister' or 'the Undersecretary of State', instead. In short, as Deborah Posel pertinently remarks, the state was a kind of "black box" about whose internal workings one could hardly ascertain anything.[7] New interest focused on the apartheid state could no longer rest content with representing the latter as a faceless, dark power manipulating the living conditions of black people from behind the scenes; instead, it focused very concretely on the state, its institutions, and the actions of its politicians and officials.

The change or rather, extension, of perspective was ultimately inspired by the work of the South African Truth and Reconciliation Commission that did identify state actors as individuals. Instead of an anonymous state machinery, the Commission was tasked with searching out the crimes and criminals, and dragging them into the light of the public, with the aim of preventing a repetition of the dark age of repression in future.

However, as early as 2003, journalist and apartheid-opponent Terry Bell summarily criticised the Truth Commission in his book entitled *Unfinished Business*. He

---

6 W. Verwoerd 2018.
7 Posel 1988: 19.

pointed out that the TRC's terms of reference were limited to investigating only the violence of apartheid. Apart from the personalisation of history and the focus on the perpetrators, this limited brief set an arbitrary cut-off point, namely the Sharpeville Massacre of 21 March 1960. What remained obscured as a result, was the entire pre-history of this event, which could have contributed to illuminating the systemic character of apartheid and the long-standing continuities of violence, unfreedom, and exploitation.[8] This applied, to a large extent, also to the impact of the directions set and ideologically-politically consolidated by the statesman who was frequently named "the architect of apartheid": Hendrik Verwoerd.

What was apartheid? In Europe and North America, it tended to be thought of as mere reaction, both reactive and reactionary – that is, as an atavistic attempt to save the colonial order or worse, as re-edition of national-socialist racial fanaticism. What was overlooked in this characterisation was the fact that apartheid was not primarily an expression of an underlying racial ideology of a kind that historians to this day are battling to explain. The historical significance of apartheid lies in the fact that it was a gigantic social experiment. It was supposed to disentangle a society that was becoming integrated in a process impelled by spurts of industrialisation. Instead of promoting the development of a class society, it was supposed to install vertical spatial segregation. Social antagonisms were re-interpreted as ethno-cultural divisions – South Africa experienced its own 'cultural turn' decades before that registered in the human sciences in the West. Instead of a social division of labour, segmentation was enacted to create territorially segregated so-called 'nations'. At the same time, the modernisation drive was to be taken further. Apartheid did not, in fact, act as a brake on modernisation; on the contrary, it was decidedly and energetically accelerated. Apartheid is one of the gigantic, horrific social experiments of the twentieth century; it is characterised by a voluntarism and confidence in planning and technical feasibility, by an idea of the disposability of human resources, and by ruthless exploitation of natural resources comparable to similar experiments in other regions of the world.[9] Totalitarian regimes under Hitler and Stalin come to mind, but there are numerous other examples that may have been less bloody, but in most cases turned out to be economically and socially devastating.[10]

It is precisely for this reason that historians sought to draw comparisons in trying to find out where the ideas of apartheid came from. An extraordinarily obstinate myth traces the origins of apartheid to national-socialist Germany. In the

---

8 Bell/Ntsebeza 2003: ch. 2; see also Marx 2004: 115; Marx 2006: 158; Marx 2007: 80.
9 Hobsbawm 2011: ch. 4.
10 Scott 1998.

polemics of political exiles registering superficial similarities between the Nuremberg Laws and the prohibition of mixed marriages in South Africa,[11] we often find the notion that apartheid was a South African version of fascist rule. This was a view put forward by a minority, though; no serious historian or social scientist has paid much heed to it. But what can be confirmed is the affinity with right-wing extremist and antisemitic attitudes held by many Afrikaner nationalists and some English-language and Black South Africans. During the period of World War II, some organisations subscribed to fascist organisational forms; *Ossewabrandwag*, for instance, became a right-wing extremist mass movement. Whether it was fascist models of order that constituted the bedrock of apartheid, however, is an entirely different question that can be clearly ruled out. It is clear that national-socialist racism inspired racial segregation policies in South Africa only to a very limited extent. Apartheid, rather, is a South African phenomenon born out of a form of colonial racism typical of settler colonies. But unlike other settler colonies, it promoted an image of future-oriented modernisation and became ever more radical in its social and political ambitions.

In his history of foreign policy under John Vorster, Jamie Miller dates South Africa's modernisation to the period of office of this Prime Minister. His characterisation of Verwoerd as a crude representative of traditional and outmoded organisational forms, who founded his politics on the nationalist articles of faith of the 1940s,[12] is misguided. Verwoerd's policy of apartheid was the attempt to mobilise vastly extended state functions to fundamentally restructure South African society according to the principles of racial segregation, and to extend comprehensive planning also to the economy. It is no co-incidence that gigantic projects of industrial modernisation fell into the period of Verwoerd's premiership. During his term of office as Minister (1950–1958) and Prime Minister (1958–1966), the South African state increasingly assumed the character of a total state, reaching into the lives of its inhabitants, to redirect and manipulate them.

The man who stood at the helm of the state during the period of apartheid, and who decisively and ruthlessly sought to push through this experiment of radical racial segregation against all odds, is the subject of this book. This does not mean that he was the sole originator of the ideas underlying it, for Verwoerd was not a creative thinker;[13] there is not a single concept of apartheid that he came up

---

11 Mzimela 1983: 25ff see also Bunting 1986: ch. 9. Simson (1980) calls Afrikaner nationalists Afrikaner fascists, without providing an explanation that could justify this designation.
12 J. Miller 2016: 39, 51, 146.
13 That is why it would be misleading to call him "the greatest of the apartheid theoreticians" (M. de Villers 1990: 305); being hostile to theory, Verwoerd himself would not have accepted this epithet.

with. His talent showed itself, rather, in the systematisation of previously divergent ideas: he crafted an agglomeration of ideas and plans of reform and racial segregation in different social spheres into a closed, argumentatively coherent system. In this way, he could create the impression that apartheid was a policy cast in one mould, a rationally thought-through set of policies for the future. That is what makes it worthwhile to deal with his thinking and with his intellectual trajectory. Precisely because he did not provide the most important ideas, but only re-worked and developed them, he became a figurehead for those who promoted Afrikaner nationalism and elevated it to the dominant political force. That is why this book follows a biographical approach, embedded in the social history and the history of ideas of Afrikaner nationalism.

From the 1970s to the 1990s, South African critical-historical research, with contributions from social anthropologists, sociologists, archaeologists and literary theorists, was exercised by the question as to how to understand apartheid in the context of South Africa's development into a modern industrial society. In addressing this question, two directions emerged.[14] While conservative-liberal historians and economists understood apartheid as an atavistic, reactionary ideology standing in the way of the unfolding of the productive forces, and for that reason doomed to become counter-productive and outmoded, Marxist-inspired historians and social scientists saw it exactly the other way round. According to the latter, apartheid was functional to capitalism; under the specific conditions prevailing in South Africa, it was this political order that proved particularly conducive to capital. This is how Harold Wolpe, specifically, interpreted the homeland policy; with this interpretation, he set the standard for an entire generation of social historians and political economists, persistently urging them to adhere to it.[15] The scholarly controversy clearly amounted to a political stance on apartheid. Radical historians, in particular, stood in opposition to racial segregation. It must be pointed out, though, that they often cast the 'liberal' position in generalising terms serviceable to their own aims of distancing themselves from it all the more emphatically.[16] Some arrogant statements against so-called 'conventional wisdom' were wielded particularly by young historians to attain definitional power. Over several decades, the radical interpretation could establish itself as the hegemonic one, due not least to excellent empirical research and innovative methods.

---

[14] Saunders (1988). For an account that includes Afrikaans–language historiography to a greater extent, see Smith (1988).
[15] Wolpe 1972; see also Friedman 2015: 113–115 on the intolerant and authoritarian stance frequently taken by Wolpe.
[16] See Lipton 2007: ch. 2; see also Lever 1978: 91–97.

With the demise of apartheid, the erstwhile divergences in historical scholarship lost their *differentiae specificae*. The economic history of South Africa penned by Charles Feinstein – who cannot be counted among conservative-liberal economic historians -, for instance, demonstrates by way of empirical evidence, how apartheid did in fact impede economic development.[17] Deborah Posel has provided a much more differentiated account of apartheid, focusing not only on intentions and aims of historical actors, but also on the non-intended consequences of their actions[18] and the learning processes that these generated; in this way, she could dissolve the either-or dichotomy that had dominated the scholarship up to that point.[19] Her conclusion that "the relationship between the state and particular capitalist interests must be addressed as an empirical, rather than as a theoretical, question"[20] was particularly generative. In this way, she could demonstrate that Verwoerd's influx control policy apparently had unintended consequences: it meant that Africans born in the city, and some others, were exempt from influx control regulations, and could therefore refuse to accept any kind of job. This is but one aspect of apartheid policies, albeit an important one. The question that it raises, is whether one can draw conclusions from this for the entire set of apartheid policies, and for the political positions and aims of Verwoerd in particular.

Three studies appeared in the 1990s, which dealt with the implementation of apartheid policies, more or less centred on Verwoerd. All three of them characterise him as a pragmatist. This view has become the established one, cited as such in several other publications.

From Verwoerd's rejection of the Tomlinson Report, historian John Lazar infers that he was not a "possessed ideological visionary",[21] but a pragmatist – without, however, providing any evidence from the sources. In Verwoerd's case, a flexible tactical attitude, and sometimes even sheer opportunism, is frequently mistaken for pragmatism. The deduction of politics from fundamental principles, as we see it in the case of Verwoerd, rather, shows that he was not in the least bit partial to American pragmatism of the kind formulated by William James or John Dewey.

John Lazar distinguishes between purists and visionaries on the one hand, whom he sees located primarily in the nationalist *Broederbond*-inspired intellectual forefront of apartheid – the South African Bureau of Racial Affairs (SABRA) and related institutions -, and the supposed pragmatist politician Verwoerd, on

---

17 Feinstein 2005: 190–193.
18 Posel 1997: 16.
19 Ibid., 8–22.
20 Ibid., 21.
21 Lazar 2001: 383–84.

the other. While Afrikaner intellectuals were aiming for thoroughgoing racial segregation, Verwoerd would have paid lip service to this goal, while at the same time envisaging a continuation of apartheid exploitation and oppression. As pertinent as this distinction is on empirical grounds, the contrast between purism and pragmatism is questionable. For Verwoerd's reaction to the SABRA line–touting Tomlinson Report, commissioned in 1956 by the apartheid state and named after its chairperson Tomlinson, shows that it was in fact Verwoerd who represented the 'pure' doctrine, while Tomlinson pleaded for a pragmatic approach. Verwoerd considered investment into homeland infrastructures as irresponsible compromise and dilution of his policies, which is why he counterposed it with the model of 'border industries', to ensure that whites could only invest in "white South Africa". In the end, he sacrificed the feasibility of the implementation of apartheid to the purist doctrine of apartheid. This was clearly recognised by Frederick Tomlinson himself, as well as some of his contemporaries who showed some level of insight. Verwoerd was precisely not a pragmatist, but a politician whose room for manoeuvre was limited by his own dogmatism. "It was clear that compromises had no place in his scheme of things."[22] Permanent anxiety over creating precedents that would lead to a relaxation of racial segregation even in minor areas of social life, was stoked by his conviction that these would unleash an avalanche ending in black majority rule. This provides an indication that Verwoerd's political thinking and his peculiar logic would merit closer investigation, on which this book proposes to embark.

The image of the pragmatist Verwoerd nevertheless persisted. Deborah Posel joined John Lazar in stipulating it, generalising from the implementation of influx control – the subject of her doctoral thesis – to Verwoerdian politics *tout court*.[23] She correctly assumed, on the basis of empirical evidence, that the nationalist camp was not nearly as closed as it had always appeared to be, and that Verwoerd, in his position as Prime Minister, had to strike compromises between different interest groups within his party, as well as within the economy.[24] This, of course, is the case for every politician in a prominent position, and therefore does not in itself say anything about the character of the man.

In her pathbreaking book entitled *The Making of Apartheid, 1948–1961*, Posel rejects previously prevailing views that the National Party (NP) had simply put into effect an established legislative blueprint and implemented apartheid poli-

---

[22] Meiring 1990: 39.
[23] For a critique of this view, see Evans 1997: 58; on the Native Affairs Department's distrust of market forces, that is, capitalism, see ibid., 65.
[24] Terreblanche (2012: 321) is more cautious; he views Verwoerd as a hardliner, who proceeded pragmatically only when he saw no other way.

cies on a 1:1 basis. This view is explicable: where on earth could such an implementation of a complete programme have ever happened? Nevertheless, it is doubtful whether the concessions made to the economy, regarded as temporary by Verwoerd himself, can be interpreted as indications of a pragmatic attitude. Like every other politician, Verwoerd was interested in holding onto and consolidating his position of power, and for that reason, had to make concessions to particular interest groups. According to this reasoning, every politician, even an orthodox communist like Lenin, could be labelled a 'pragmatist'. Lenin provides an especially instructive example, for he understood the New Economic Policy of the early 1920s and its return to capitalist relations as a temporary compromise not in any way detracting from the socialist aims that he consistently and persistently pursued.

Even more resounding was the favourable reception of a piece of revisionist historiography – a 1992 essay dealing with a stage of Verwoerd's life that had not received much attention in the extant biographical literature. That is what accounted for the fact that American environmental scientist Roberta Miller's assessment of Verwoerd's early career could entrench itself so firmly – despite evidence to the contrary provided by the sources. Apart from this essay, Miller had not extensively dealt with aspects of South African history; all the more puzzling is the influence of this publication, cited approvingly in every study on Verwoerd without any effort taken to scrutinise Miller's sources.[25] Because of its great resonance in the literature on the subject, I would like to look at this essay a bit more closely.

Adopting the above-mentioned revisionist approach, Miller set about to replace the traditional image of Verwoerd with an entirely new and surprisingly different one. It is not clear what her motives were for painting a picture that effectively rehabilitates Verwoerd. These were her central theses:

1. Before 1937, Verwoerd was not a nationalist; instead, he supported the move initiated by Hertzog, to seek a rapprochement with English-speaking sections of the population. Miller rebukes extant scholarship on the subject for selective use of the sources, pointing out that "[Verwoerd] is often quoted out of context to demonstrate the connections between his earlier and later beliefs."[26] Miller herself does not escape the charge of selectivity, for her allegation is not substantiated by a single example. As this book will show, the contrary is the case: Miller

---

25 See for instance Ally/Mooney/Stewart 2003: 76, 83; also Seekings 2008: 527; Giliomee 2012b: 73–74; and Teppo 2004: 107.
26 R. B. Miller 1993: 636. On his alleged support for Hertzog's Two-Stream Policy, see ibid., 637.

adduced only scattered pointers that apparently support her contentions but ignored others. The overwhelming evidence demonstrating that Verwoerd was an Afrikaner cultural nationalist, was simply ignored by her. Verwoerd himself repeatedly and emphatically stated: "Ever since I was a child, I was a Nationalist and Republican, initially probably because this was the spirit prevailing in my parents' home, and later, because during my years at school and as university student and lecturer, I became more and more convinced that South Africa had to become a Republic, as a precondition for solving the problems of this country."[27] This is what Verwoerd himself states; written as it is, from hindsight, it could admittedly be seen to smooth over some of the earlier developments. Yet in my reconstruction of Verwoerd's nationalism in chapter one, I will show that his self-portrayal is correct, while Miller's is not.

While Miller's essay was favourably received, another study that refutes her arguments with good reason, has hardly received any attention in the literature on Verwoerd. South African communication studies scholar Johannes Degenaar Froneman tracked Verwoerd's political activities during the time of his studies at the University of Stellenbosch, by means of minutes of student council meetings, as well as other contemporary publications. These archival documents clearly reveal Verwoerd's commitments to an exclusive Afrikaans cultural nationalism.[28] In his correspondence with Miller, South African sociologist Dian Joubert, too, expressed his reservations about her pronouncements. It was especially her contention that before 1937, Verwoerd was not a nationalist of the exclusive Afrikaner-nationalist kind, that raised Joubert's misgivings.[29]

However, Miller's contention that Verwoerd went to Germany to further his studies for professional rather than ideological reasons, is correct.[30] To take Verwoerd's activities during and after the Conference on the 'Poor White Problem' held in Kimberley in 1934, as evidence for his "vigorous attempts to forge an alliance between English and Afrikaner social welfare activities", is not pertinent, because the conference had not been initiated by Verwoerd, but by the churches intent on establishing such a collaboration. Thus, the co-operation envisaged does not justify any conclusions about Verwoerd's nationalist convictions.

---

27 Verwoerd 1966: 5.
28 Froneman 2000: 400, 408–409.
29 SU 231, H.F. Verwoerd Collection, Letter by Dian Joubert to Roberta B. Miller, 4.12.1992, p. 4; see also Sabalot 2009: 32.
30 R. B. Miller 1993: 638.

2. Miller insists that Verwoerd was not a racist, that his views "on race were more liberal than those of many sociologists of his time".[31] Indeed, there is only one instance in his lectures on sociology picked up by Miller, in which he expresses himself cautiously on biological race theories. However, in his sociological lectures, he showed himself to be sceptical rather than negative as far as biological racism is concerned. Throughout his life, he concerned himself with theories of race and entertained close friendships with persons upholding biological racism. For him, it was not so much a matter of innate capabilities such as intelligence, as it was a matter of the 'barbaric' condition of Africans and their radically different culture; so he could afford to be sceptical without thereby becoming less ethnocentric or racist. Even during his youth did he express a deep aversion to miscegenation and cohabitation of whites and coloureds in the same suburbs. His racism came to the fore particularly in his attitude toward coloureds, who are not exactly culturally distinct from whites; in this case, his negative attitude towards coloureds could only have been based on the presumption of biological markers of distinction, namely skin colour, as reason for advocating segregation.

3. Miller thinks that the later policies of Verwoerd cannot be considered as designs for social engineering, because there is nothing to be found in his speeches or in his writings that indicates any dealings with the American literature on social engineering or scientific management.[32] This reasoning is strange; Verwoerd did, in fact, bring in policies and procedures clearly in line with social engineering. This is how he approached the field of sociology; and the apartheid policies that he pursued at a later stage did essentially amount to social engineering, even if he himself never used this term. Equally incorrect is the contention that Verwoerd did not seek to expand the state's sphere of activities.[33] On the contrary: he sought to extend the powers of the state over welfare organisations, as his draft for an ordinance and his ideas on the role of the state proclaimed in a keynote address to the Congress of Kimberley in 1934 clearly show.

4. Miller characterises Verwoerd as a statesman thinking and acting pragmatically, rather than dogmatically or doctrinally. Instead of ideological fanaticism, Miller sees careerism as the force driving him: "he was, however, clearly ambitious, energetic, pragmatic, and opportunistic."[34] South African sociologist Dian

---

[31] Ibid., 648; other sociologists are not named. On the subsequent page, however, she explicitly states that in his introductory lecture, Verwoerd "discussed the South African native population and the issue of differences among the races at great length".
[32] Ibid., 641.
[33] Ibid., 656.
[34] Ibid., 637.

Joubert also rejects this idea, reprimanding Miller: "Accusations of opportunism and unprincipled behaviour are not substantiated by your material – and cannot be taken seriously in a historical and sociological analysis."[35]

Among contemporaries, there is overriding consensus that Verwoerd was a dogmatist through and through – liberal opposition politician Helen Suzman spoke of his "doctrinaire approach"[36] -, which indicates that Miller's characterisation of Verwoerd as pragmatist is simply absurd.[37] Suzman even admitted that Verwoerd's fanaticism and sense of mission made him "the only man who has ever scared me stiff".[38] Journalist Piet Meiring, who had accompanied Verwoerd over the years, wrote: "Dr Verwoerd did not readily allow anyone with a different opinion to derail him. I have never met anyone more convinced of his own thinking and his own cause, and less prepared to concede a point to an opposing argument or standpoint."[39] Having listened to a "45–minute lecture", US ambassador Philip Crowe (1959–1961) noted his impression: "He is a fanatic with a fanatic's absolute faith in his own righteousness."[40]

The contrast between dogmatism and pragmatism pervades the assessments of Verwoerd; his grandson Wilhelm Verwoerd suggested considering him a pragmatic ideologue, that is, a politician pursuing clear principles and an unambiguous, systematically elaborated programme, while remaining flexible when it came to short-term decisions on particular issues.[41] In this case, the designation of 'pragmatism' is misleading; what is meant in characterising Verwoerd as a tactically skilled politician making decisions on a case-by-case basis, is not pragmatism, but a flexible manner of proceeding. American philosopher William James describes pragmatism as a goal-directed or problem-solving approach not deduced from fundamental principles: "The attitude of looking away from first things, principles, 'categories', supposed necessities; and of looking towards last things, fruits, consequences, facts."[42] In terms of this definition, it becomes clear that Verwoerd was anything but a pragmatist; on the contrary, he was a statesman who deduced his aims from abstract principles. Prominent Afrikaans-speaking journalist Piet Cillié describes

---

35 231 H.F. Verwoerd Collection, Letter by Dian Joubert to Roberta B. Miller, 4.12.1992, p. 7.
36 Lewsen 1991: 71.
37 Dubow (2014: 293) presents a much more differentiated assessment.
38 Suzman 1994: 65.
39 Meiring 1973b: 124.
40 LaFantasie 1992: 732; Dok. 337, Telegram from the Embassy in South Africa to the Department of State, 27.4.1959.
41 W. Verwoerd 1994: 214–215.
42 James 2007: 29.

Verwoerd in terms of a particular style of politics, rather than in terms of a scholar's understanding of politics: "Verwoerd was a man of the idea, at home in the world of concepts, blueprints, and comprehensive long-term plans."[43] Some contemporaries promoted this image of an unworldly academic. Horace Flather, then editor of the Johannesburg-based daily newspaper *The Star*, for instance, describes him thus: "He was soft-spoken and arrogant, an academically brilliant scholar with no experience of people except his own small community. A man imprisoned in the ivory tower of Nationalist thought and experience. A man to whom the outside world had little meaning."[44] But flexible he was, since he always had his electorate in mind and was prepared to strike temporary compromises whenever he saw his power base in jeopardy.

Although Miller's theses lack plausibility and contradict all evidence provided by Verwoerd's contemporaries, no one has so far taken the effort to check her sources. As early as 1994 did Wilhelm Verwoerd, the oldest son of Hendrik Verwoerd, publish a response to Miller's theses in an article in the daily *Die Burger*, rebuking (albeit for reasons different from those presented here) Miller's contention that Verwoerd was a pragmatist.[45] In fact, Verwoerd was exactly the ideological dogmatist and fanatic that his contemporaries describe. His tendency to reduce social problems and political solutions in the country to two, namely either his version of apartheid or, alternatively, the demise of the white population, deprived him of any flexibility, and of exactly those pragmatic courses of action that have frequently been attributed to him ever since Miller's article appeared.[46]

In contrast to Miller's caution against stipulating a continuity between the politics of the later Verwoerd and his youthful visions – for which she does not offer any substantiation or plausible developmental-psychological theories –, this book argues that Verwoerd was ideologically consistent throughout his life. The latter perspective dovetails with psychological insights into the tracks set during his childhood and youth, and persisting throughout his life, rather than with Miller's implausible notion of the peculiar turn from a 36-year-old liberal scholar to a radical politician. The absence of an explanation for any sudden change of mind in 1937 remains the weakest point of Miller's essay.[47]

Miller's contentions are cited all around in the literature, because her essay was published at a time when there was hardly any research on Verwoerd anymore, and when an investigation of his ideas and actions had not yet passed from

---

[43] Cillié 1980: 19.
[44] Flather 1977: 172.
[45] W. J. Verwoerd, Hendrik Verwoerd was alles behalwe 'n pragmatikus, *Die Burger*, 3.11.1994.
[46] See for instance Davie 2015: 163.
[47] R. B. Miller 1993: 660–661.

political scientists to historians. That is why many of her readers were prepared to accept her implausible theses, albeit with some reservations palpable in some of the reviews. Other publications, even those providing much clearer analyses of Verwoerd's thinking, went almost entirely unrecognised – even though they were ahead of their times in identifying him as technocratic moderniser, thereby paving the way for new interpretations. A clear-sighted article on the foundations of Verwoerd's thinking was published by South African philosopher Johannes Jacob Venter in the journal *Koers*; in contrast to Miller's essay, this article hardly received any attention, even though it was a much more apt characterisation of Verwoerd's thinking.

Venter presented an analysis, according to which Verwoerd was a positivist rooted in nineteenth-century ideas of progress; his stance showed a lack of self-reflection and empathy for those on the receiving end of his political actions.[48] In putting forward this argument, Venter focuses on three "basic concepts" of Verwoerd – namely, rationality, the ideal of a republic for the Afrikaner people, and his views on 'development'. For Venter, Verwoerd was a politician who was convinced of having found a panacea for South Africa's problems – and he pursued it with a semblance of rationality, disregarding emotional or affective impulses of any kind. He sees the roots of Verwoerd's thinking in positivism, which would rule out any possible influences of German idealism on his world view: "He tended towards totalitarian social planning on the basis of a few principles ... which is reminiscent of the technocratic social engineering tradition related to positivism."[49] This characterisation coincides to some extent with my own findings, as does the importance of nationalism and republicanism in Verwoerd's thinking highlighted by Venter. I would not attribute Verwoerd's nationalism so unambiguously to the tradition of the Enlightenment, however; on the whole, I would not find a derivation of nationalism from a narrowly conceived history of ideas very convincing.[50] As far as Venter's third concept – that of 'development' – is concerned, it seems to me that Venter does not distinguish sufficiently clearly

---

48 J. J. Venter 1999; on Venter's article, see also Froneman 2013: 8–10.
49 J. J. Venter 1999: 417.
50 One does not have to be an intellectual, nor even especially bright, to tout a nationalist cause. Seeking the roots of nationalism in certain philosophical ideas does not, in my opinion, yield particularly fruitful insights. It would be much more productive to consider historical and social processes soliciting a need, across broad sections of the population, for what can be described as national identifications. For this reason, too, I find the social–anthropological model put forward by Gellner (1998) more convincing than the reconstruction offered by Anderson (2006). The latter hardly pays any attention to actually operating mass media like radio, television, and tabloid press; instead, it thinks of nationalists as imagined community of readers of elite bourgeois print media.

between what, in the case of Verwoerd, is propaganda and what are actual concepts. It is especially the rejection of the Tomlinson-Report that raises doubts as to whether Verwoerd ever seriously envisaged developing the 'native reserves' into industrial societies; what comes to mind are his relativising statements, frequently reiterated, casting doubt on the very capability of black people to act as agents of social development. While the statements of philosopher Danie Goosen may say something about the applicability of Derrida's approaches, they do not provide an analysis of Verwoerd's thoughts and actions, as Goosen himself admits.[51] Something similar can be said about the highly associative and hardly analytical essay by psychologists Truscott and Smith, which does not contribute much to an understanding of Verwoerd's thinking.[52]

The fact that Hendrik Verwoerd was a psychologist and that he had set off on an academic career before embarking on a political one, repeatedly finds mention in studies on the history of psychology and on the biography of Verwoerd. Apart from some sporadic comments, this aspect has hardly met with more sustained research interest, though.[53] Apart from Miller and Froneman, no one has hitherto found it worth investigating Verwoerd's academic career more closely, and systematically connecting it with his political thinking. That is the task that this book sets itself. This slant makes of the book no conventional biography; it is not my aim to narrate the life history of Verwoerd, but to investigate the ideas and ideologies at the base of his politics. This does not amount to recalling his political actions as party functionary, Minister and Prime Minister. These aspects will be touched on only insofar as his political praxis reveals some of the concepts and ideas underlying it. Nor will his private life come into focus here, even if the portrayal of the private person and the family man in the context of his politics was a popular trope used by the regime to demonstrate the moral fibre of his politics.[54]

---

[51] Goosen 1996: 121.
[52] Truscott/Smith (2016: 251–252) overestimate the applications of electrical current in Verwoerd's laboratory experiments; moreover, they seek to establish continuities with later apartheid policies that are not plausible or empirically validated.
[53] It was mentioned briefly by Louw (1986: 84); also Foster 1991a: 16; Foster 1991b: 205; Foster 2008: 99. See also Marx 2011a. Less informative on Verwoerd is Pfaffe 1987: 67f.
[54] This pertains especially to the compilation of photos that appeared briefly after Verwoerd's death (Hefer/Basson 1966).

Sources

The major source for the investigation presented in this book is the collection of papers of Hendrik Verwoerd, held in large part by the Archive for Contemporary Affairs at the University of the Free State in Bloemfontein. Apart from the political correspondence of Verwoerd on the most diverse topics, it consists of manuscripts of speeches, newspaper clippings, as well an entire bundle of handwritten notes on his psychological studies. A smaller collection of papers, consisting mostly of typewritten lecture notes, as well as his two Master's dissertations and his doctoral thesis, are to be found in the Gericke Library of Stellenbosch University. Official documents dating back to Verwoerd's time as Minister and Prime Minister are kept in the National Archives in Pretoria; however, due to the woeful conditions prevailing in this Archive, they were only accessible in parts. Wilhelm Verwoerd, the oldest son of Hendrik Verwoerd, kindly offered me access to the family archive established by him.[55] In addition to these archival holdings most important for my purposes here, there are collections assembled by colleagues and friends of Verwoerd's; among these collections, that of his long-serving private secretary Fred Barnard in Bloemfontein proved to be of particular importance. The Archive of the Broederbond and the Archive of the United Party in Pretoria yielded important insights into Verwoerd's role in organised nationalist circles. Archives of various universities in Germany provided clarifications of questions related to the history of psychology. Archives consulted in the course of my research for this book are listed in the Appendix.[56]

Of the published sources, the collected speeches of Verwoerd's until 1963 were particularly interesting for the investigations of this book; they were compiled by the Institute for Contemporary History in Bloemfontein, which is no longer in existence.

---

[55] In addition, I would like to thank Bas Kromhout, who generously provided materials for my perusal.
[56] The footnotes only indicate archival classifications, not the names of the archives themselves, which are listed in the Appendix. Afrikaans-language citations are rendered as per the translator's (English) translations.

Structure of the Book

The chapters of this book, thirteen in all, track the life of Verwoerd chronologically; but they are also thematically structured, to show the continuity and ideological consistency of his thinking. The individual chapters present a chronological development of the thematic fields.

The first chapter deals with Verwoerd's harping on principles, often referred to as 'dogmatism' by his contemporaries. The three subsequent chapters take up themes that were of academic interest to Verwoerd, namely the psychological separation of thought and affect, the malleability of feelings, and developmental psychology. These influenced his political thinking at a later stage, and that is why subsequent chapters repeatedly return to his early formations; the aim is to show how the politician's penchant for order and control can be traced back to the conceptualisations of the young psychologist, as chapter 7 demonstrates in some detail by way of an example.

Chapter 2 investigates Verwoerd's psychological training and his study of thinking (introspectively) and feeling (in the laboratory), all the while seeking to distinguish them from each other. These academic pursuits became formative for his later career, in particular for his propagandistic pronouncements, and for his self-presentation as public speaker. Chapter 3 deals with developmental psychology. During his sojourn in Germany during the 1920s, Verwoerd became acquainted with psychology in two of its sub-disciplines – namely child psychology and ethnopsychology -, brought together under the umbrella of developmental psychology by some of the leading psychologists at the time, with whom Verwoerd came into contact. Verwoerd's view of the black population in South Africa was decisively influenced by concepts of developmental psychology, from which he drew important 'insights', as evinced in his lecture notes and theses submitted for postgraduate degrees in 1922.

Chapter 4 describes and probes his 1932 turn from psychology to sociology, indicating the transition toward a political career. Verwoerd's concern with poverty among whites in South Africa is one of the major and important lines of continuity in his biography; more than anything else, this is what explains his pursuit of a political career. Chapter 5 shows in some detail how his turn to politics was related to a journalistic career as editor of the nationalist daily *Die Transvaler* between 1937 and 1948. Verwoerd turned the newspaper into a propaganda outlet for the NP; it is his position as editor that facilitated his rise to the top echelons of the party in the Witwatersrand and in the Transvaal Province, in close collaboration with J. G. Strijdom, chief of the party in that province.

During these years, Verwoerd was politically socialised in the circles of the secret organisation, the Afrikaner Broederbond (AB), which was a formative influence for him, just as he himself influenced the direction of the Bond during the ten years of his membership of its Executive Council. His activities in the AB were closely related to acrimonious internal conflicts within the nationalist camp, within which Verwoerd consistently took an openly dogmatic stance. The idea of "unity of the people" (*volkseenheid*) within the National Party and the Broederbond is the subject of chapter 6.

The time of the Fusion government was marked by the initial weakness of the "Purified" NP during the 1930s, by white poverty, the impact of the world economic crisis, and the imminent dissolution of cultural nationalist identities in General Hertzog's fusion politics. Like many of his contemporaries, Verwoerd experienced these developments as crisis, also commonly referred to as 'chaos', which he sought to counteract with his orderly schemes. A preoccupation with control and order, as chapter 7 argues, characterised not only the individual psyche of Hendrik Verwoerd, but the apartheid state as a whole.

Chapter 8 investigates Verwoerd's racism and his preoccupation with difference, that is, with establishing clear distinguishing features, corresponding to notions of ethnic and racial purity. Chapter 9 analyses the fundamental ideas of apartheid and the ways in which Verwoerd justified them in his arguments – predominantly through the presentation of apartheid policies as if they were part of a system designed from the start to re-model South African society. Chapter 10, on the other hand, outlines apartheid in terms of a history of ideas, showing it up as a "regime of ignorance", as it was based to a surprisingly large extent on a lack of knowledge plastered over by the Afrikaner political elite's ambitions to exercise total control, by data-gathering, and by the pretence of superior knowledge.

Chapter 11 homes in on the consequences of Verwoerd's nationalism for political practice. At issue is his central aim of creating a white nation state, through embarking on the policy, transforming the state into a republic, and leaving the Commonwealth (while highlighting the alleged involuntary nature of the latter step). Chapter 12 elucidates the significance that political and definitional power held for Verwoerd, analysing his attitude to repression and democracy through various examples and incidents during his term of office as Prime Minister. It is especially his politics regarding the coloured population that gave rise to tensions in the Party in the 1960s; throughout, Verwoerd managed to assert his authority through punitive measures designed to intimidate and exclude individual dissenters.

Chapter 13 is devoted to the last phase of Verwoerd's term of office, after the constitutional arrangement of the state had been completed according to his designs. During the same time period, from 1961 onwards, large-scale economic and military upgrading plans were designed to secure 'his' nation state. Paradigmatic for these and related developments is the massive dam project on the Orange River, which later was to be named after Hendrik Verwoerd. Such projects are indicative of the understanding of politics that Verwoerd sought to present. The last chapter gets to Verwoerd's assassination on 6 September 1966, but more importantly, it focuses on the consequences of the obsession with control, orderliness and repression for the cultural vitality and survival of Afrikanerdom.

Verwoerd is one of the great perpetrators in the age of extremes, even if he did not manage to reach the heights of totalitarian achievements of a Hitler, a Stalin, or a Mao. Apartheid was not a regime that can be equated with national socialism or Stalinism. On the other hand, it is comparable with these and other regimes insofar as they are characterised by extended powers of the state. Verwoerd can be counted among those who approached major political tasks through setting them on scientific foundations; with his grandiose plans, he aimed to restructure state and society, irrespective of the violation of human and civil rights wrought in the process. Apartheid is one of the failed utopias of the twentieth century; like many others, it was pursued with the promise of religious or quasi-religious salvation.[57]

---

[57] A. Venter (2011: 538) correctly views apartheid as a secular salvation ideology like national socialism and communism.

Principles

For the white, Afrikaans-speaking section of South Africa's population, the Anglo-Boer War (1899–1902) held a significance similar to that of World War I for European societies. It was the primal catastrophe. Indeed, the emergence and radicalisation of Afrikaner nationalism and the politics of apartheid can be explained as response to the trauma of a lost war. The Anglo-Boer War was not a material battle comparable to World War I; nevertheless, the scorched earth policy pursued by the British to rout Boer guerrilla fighters, wrought massive devastation. The internment of thousands of women and children exacted a death toll of up to 26 000 persons. The Afrikaners saw themselves reduced to a defeated, humiliated and disempowered people in their own country. In their eyes, the war of aggression unleashed by Great Britain, with the overwhelming resources of Empire, against the small Boer Republics was unjust.[1]

The anglicisation policies of Governor Lord Milner added fuel to the flames of the resentments and vengeful feelings brewing in the Afrikaans-speaking sections of the population after the lost war. Milner sought to use the education system to culturally assimilate young Afrikaners with the aim of integrating the conquered colonies into the British Empire. Different forms of Afrikaner nationalism arose in response. In the face of Milner's politics, it was not surprising to find a decidedly cultural-nationalist orientation developing alongside constitutional revisionism from the start. The latter was primarily geared to the re-establishment of political sovereignty in the form of a republic. Nicholas Diederichs, an influential figure in the Afrikaner nationalist movement, defined nationalism exclusively in cultural terms:

> What makes a person into a member of a nation is the adoption of the language, but especially of the culture and the spiritual values of this nation. A nation is a nation by virtue of the fact that its members stand for the same spiritual values, that they feel connected to each other through a common sense of a calling and through faith in the invisible bonds connecting them to each other.[2]

After the War and the unification of the four colonies in the Union of South Africa in 1910, two rival conceptions of nationhood emerged in South Africa; both were racially based and excluded the black majority from the national community. The kind of nationalism represented by the first Prime Minister of the Union, Louis Botha (1910–1919) and his South African Party, was a conciliatory nationalism aim-

---

[1] Marx 2015c.
[2] Diederichs 1975: 1.

ing to bring together the opposing camps of the Anglo-Boer War in a white nation. It was a voluntarist kind of nationalism appealing to whites individually, to decide to become members of the nation. Contrasting and rivalling this type of nationalism was the cultural nationalism of the Afrikaners, which emerged shortly after the War. Membership of the cultural nation was not left up to the decision of individuals; instead, it was allocated on the basis of supposedly objective criteria such as language, religious denomination, history and culture of one of the two white groups, namely the Afrikaner nation or the English-speaking section of the population. While the conciliatory nationalism of Botha aspired to be a nationalism based on citizenship – albeit racially exclusive –, Afrikaner cultural nationalism subjected the individual to the nation.

Ever since the establishment of Union, Minister of Justice James Barry Munnik Hertzog had drawn attention to himself for touting nationalist rhetoric and polarising the political landscape. Historian Lindie Koorts characterised him "as diplomatically skilled as an army tank and as subtle as a cannon", adding, "he did not flinch from name-calling, and launched personal attacks on his opponents".[3] Prime Minister Louis Botha excluded him when he formed a new cabinet in 1912, on account of his provocative speeches that posed an affront to English-speaking politicians in government. Hertzog made good use of his time until the outbreak of World War I, to build up his political profile; he stopped short of forming a party, though, opting to wait for an opportune moment instead. This moment came with the outbreak of World War I in August 1914, followed by an armed rebellion on the part of sections of the Afrikaner population in the Northern Free State and in Southwestern Transvaal protesting South Africa's involvement in the War of Empire, and aiming to restore the old Boer republics. The rebellion was crushed by government troops within a short time span; for his part, Hertzog utilised the extensive discontent vis-à-vis government, and formed a new party. While this party claimed to have representation on a national basis, it initially consisted of loyal adherents of the Orania Unie – a party confined to his home province, the Orange Free State. Attorney Tielman Roos founded a similar movement in the Transvaal. At a Congress in Bloemfontein held from 7th to 9th January 1914, the new National Party was launched, designed to cover South Africa as a whole.[4] The NP in the Cape Province needed a bit more time for building a party organisation, which then proved to be more stable, accompanied as it was by the establishment of a press loyal to the Party. Along with the collegial and consensus-building leadership style of provincial party chief Daniel Malan, this

---

3 Koorts 2014: 93.
4 M. P. A. Malan 1964: 11–20.

combination was to secure a sustainable, much more coherent and effective party structure for the NP in the Cape Province.⁵ Organisationally, the National Party remained an association of four largely autonomous provincial parties held together by a federal council and the person of *"hoofleier"* [chief leader] Hertzog. In this way, regional traditions could be optimally integrated and sustained. Like the clientelistic traditions of the two erstwhile Boer republics, this meant that the party was extremely heterogeneous, though. While republican structures, albeit oriented towards local leadership, predominated in the North, the National Party in the Cape Province tended towards cultural nationalism.⁶ In the Transvaal, cultural nationalism also featured, especially where it was inspired by the second Afrikaans language movement,⁷ by private schools geared to upholding 'Christian National Education', and a gradually emerging nationalist movement in industrial cities like Johannesburg. But this nationalist movement only became organised from 1918 onwards within the Afrikaner Broederbond, while it remained marginal in the Party for a long time.

The Anglo-Boer War had spawned movements in solidarity with the Boers in many European countries, especially in the Netherlands. An enthusiastic follower was Wilhelm Verwoerd (1874–1961) from Bodegraven near Amsterdam who, together with his wife Anje Strik (1873–1940) attentively followed the events of the war in distant South Africa.⁸ Verwoerd came from a humble background; the peasant family hailing from the area between Utrecht and Leiden can be traced back to the sixteenth century.⁹ The ancestry of his wife came from rural Vriesland; this explains Hendrik Verwoerd's second name which is uncommon in South Africa. Frens is the Friesian version of Francis.¹⁰ Wilhelm Verwoerd, who can be described as a conservative, had worked his way up from shop assistant to share-owner of a grocery store in Amsterdam. He and his wife felt a close affinity with the Boer people, to whom they considered themselves related. The assistance

---

5 Marx 2012: 193–194; Korf (2010: 144) points out that the founders of the newspaper were all related to each other, and all hailed from the NP stable in Cape Town and Stellenbosch. Willy Hofmeyr was the driving force behind Malan's early political career (ibid., 164).
6 Marx 2008: 152–153.
7 I. Hofmeyr 1987. The first language movement in the late nineteenth century was confined to the Western Cape, with only few indications of a nationalist orientation. For Malan's membership of the Afrikaanse Taalgenootskap, see Koorts 2014: 56; see also 61.
8 On the background of the family, see Terblanche 2001a: 219–220.
9 Pama 1967: 80. The name 'Verwoerd' comes from 'Woerd', designating a river bank. Wilhelm Verwoerd was born in Nieuwer Amstel south of Amsterdam.
10 The name would have had to be Frens, but Verwoerd's father, who was not proficient in Friesian, had spelled the name incorrectly – as 'Frensch' – when it was entered into the birth register (FAV 2.2.6, Letter by Wilhelm Verwoerd to Wilhelm Verwoerd jun. 20.2.1959).

they rendered went beyond verbal solidarity. They took it as far as accommodating "Afrikaners who had wound up in Europe in their home; and they were fully occupied with organisational work and collection of donations for the Afrikaner cause".[11] Solidarity with a people defeated by a materially incomparably superior British Empire in the course of an unjust war and staunch resistance, was one of two main reasons that moved Wilhelm Verwoerd and Anje Strik to emigrate to the Cape Colony in 1903, where they were naturalised on 12.1.1909.[12] Their son Hendrik remembers his father's attitude at the time: "He immediately immersed himself in the Afrikaner community, even though the Cape Colony at the time was predominantly English in character."[13] Apart from political sympathies, there was also a religious influence that motivated the father's decision to emigrate; for he was a follower of the strict Calvinist church of Abraham Kuyper, which had split from the Reformed Church of the Netherlands in 1886.[14] Having combined his political sympathies with his religious convictions, he had long held the wish to work as Christian missionary among whites. Hendrik Verwoerd was born on 8 September 1901 in Amsterdam as second son of Wilhelm Verwoerd and Anje Strik.[15] Having arrived in South Africa as a two-year old child with his parents and his older brother, he was an immigrant here.[16] Together with his older brother Leendert, who was named after Wilhelm's father, Hendrik attended the

---

[11] W. J. Verwoerd 1990: 3.
[12] FAV 2, Letters of Naturalization. W.J. Verwoerd had three brothers and one sister living in the Netherlands. He maintained contact with them only sporadically (FAV 2, Letter of W.J. Verwoerd to his brother and sister, 22.11.1938. FAV 2.2.2, notices of the deaths of the mother and relatives of the father). One of the brothers, Hendrik Verwoerd, owned a printing press in Lisse (between Leiden and Haarlem) that published the journal *Ons Weekblad*. It was in this journal that W. J. Verwoerd published his 'Brieven uit Zuid-Afrika' [Letters from South Africa] of 8.10. and 1.12.1932, and of 27.5., 22.7. and 26.8., with information on the region. As late as 1940, he campaigned for pensions for Boer War veterans within his circles (FAV 2.2.5, Letter by W.J. Verwoerd to H. F. Verwoerd, 10.12.1949). Information on the house in which Verwoerd was born, and memories of the emigration of the Verwoerds, were provided by a former neighbour in a letter to the editor of *Huisgenoot* magazine (see T. Veraar-Schwarwäler (Amstelveen), 'Dr. Verwoerd – 'n Herinnering', *Die Huisgenoot*, 3.2.1967).
[13] FAV 2.3, H.F. Verwoerd, biographical notes on his father.
[14] Verwoerd was christened on 24.9.1901 in the Raamkerk which is no longer in existence today. It was one of the so-called Doleantiekerken built after the split (FAV 2, note on Verwoerd's christening).
[15] FAV 2, birth certificate H.F. Verwoerd. Parents' marriage certificate of 21.9.1898. On the family history of the mother, see Pos 1967: 121–122.
[16] FAV 2, ticket for the steam liner Goorkha of the Union Castle Line. According to the date on the ticket, the family departed from Southampton on 24 October 1903 and arrived in Cape Town on 18.11.1903 (ibid., immigration form).

German Lutheran school in Wynberg between 8 October 1907 and 12 December 1913; he left the school after having completed Grade 5 [Standard III].[17]

In 1913, Wilhelm Verwoerd, who was running a small construction company in Wynberg,[18] was offered the position as temporary assistant in the reformed mission in Bulawayo, (then) Rhodesia. In Rhodesia, he worked among the Boer settlers. His job was to persuade those who had left the reformed church for other denominations, to return to the church on which they had turned their backs.[19] Like his brother Len, Hendrik attended Milton High School in Bulawayo between January 1914 and April 1917; he completed Grade 10 [Standard VIII] there, attaining the Junior Certificate issued by the University setting the examinations, namely the University of the Cape of Good Hope.[20]

On the occasion of a visit to Cape Town in 1915, his father came into contact with the newly formed NP, and returned to Bulawayo a committed nationalist; "ever since then, and for the rest of his life, he never wavered from his staunch nationalist stance".[21] Hendrik performed very well at school, winning several book prizes; in the course of a competition, he was awarded a Beit Scholarship for the best academic achievement of his school,[22] and fifth best in Rhodesia in 1915. He was able to take up the scholarship only after his return to South Africa in 1917. He showed talent particularly in mathematics, for which his report at-

---

17 H. G. Maritz, 'Ons bring hulde . . .', *Jongspan* n.d. Copy with covering letter from Maritz to E. Verwoerd of 1.9.1995 in FAV 4.2.2. Verwoerd himself states in a *curriculum vitae*, handwritten in German (FAV 4.3.2) that he attended the German School in Wynberg between January 1908 and December 1912, and subsequently – from 1913 – the Wynberg High School for Boys. Three reports of Verwoerd's from the Wynberg High School for Boys have been preserved (FAV 4.2.1, Reports dated 20.6., 27.9. and 12.12.1913). The last of these reports marks his completion of Grade 7 [Standard V]. All of these reports name him as second–best student in his class, having achieved a percentage mark of 81 to 83,8%. His diligence is being judged "very satisfactory", and his general conduct somewhere between "very satisfactory" and "very good". His strength lay in arithmetic, Latin, and Dutch – see also the memoirs of his brother (PV 72/3), and Beukes, Report 'Ons kom nou in Wynberg' (pp. 6, 12). The teacher's surname was Bahlcke. Of the two brothers, Hendrik was the rebellious one (S. A. Verwoerd 1965: 21).
18 FAV 2.3, H. F. Verwoerd, biographical note on his father.
19 On Reformed Church's mission work in Bulawayo, see Hendrich 2011: 158, 160–161.
20 FAV 4.2.1, Junior Certificate exam questions.
21 FAV 2.3, H. F. Verwoerd, biographical note on his father. W. J. Verwoerd was also involved in the celebrations marking the centenary of the Great Trek in Brandfort in 1938 – see printed programme 'Besoek van die ATKV Ossewaens aan Brandfort, Maandag 24 Oktober 1938'.
22 At this stage, though, there were only c. 80 learners at the school. In 1916, Verwoerd achieved the second-highest marks in a class of six learners (FAV 4.2.1 Milton High School, Quarterly Report, 8.12.1916. FAV 4.2.1 Examination Card and exam questions for 'Henry French Verwoerd' [sic], 1915).

tested 'excellent' performance, with an achievement of almost 100% in some tests. His marks for French were noted as 'weak', however. Still, the verdict on his overall performance was "excellent work".[23] Like his older brother, he was a member of the cadet corps,[24] even though politically, he consistently opposed the British Empire, while his brother turned towards the British, and even served as major in the British Army during World War II.[25]

Afrikaners in Southern Rhodesia were a minority group generally despised, but also feared on account of their South African connections. They were often subject to arrogant and patronising treatment, and to marginalisation by the British-nationalist white settlers of the colony. Verwoerd himself experienced some of this while at school; he reports that "even as a child during World War I, [he] had a hard time at school".[26] The school principal tried his best to retain the gifted student when his parents returned to South Africa, but without success. It was probably Hendrik Verwoerd's identification with the Afrikaner rebels of 1914 that contributed to this decision, which would indicate that even at the age of thirteen,

---

[23] FAV 4.2.1, Milton High School, Quarterly Report 8.12.1916. He had achieved similar results in the preceding exams, as attested by the reports of 10.12.1915 and 22.9.1915.

[24] He was trained in heliograph and Morse signalling, and in the use of machine guns. The information in this paragraph is gleaned from a 1962 letter by E. Verwoerd to M. Cordell (Bulawayo): 'Reminiscences of School life at Bulawayo' (FAV 4.2.2, with covering letter to Cordell, 24.4.1962. Mai Cordell used this material for two articles – see *Cape Times Weekend Magazine*, 13.7.1963 and *Sunday Times*, 22.11.1964).

[25] ‚Dr. Len Verwoerd kyk terug', *Die Burger*, 14.7.1979. Len Verwoerd, born 14.7.1899, had also been a member of the Anglo Rhodesian Society. The outbreak of World War II led to an estrangement of the two brothers, which ended only in 1958, when Hendrik became Prime Minister (see also FAV 3.2, Len Verwoerd's memoirs of the War (in handwriting); PV 72/1, Invitation of Jan Smuts to Len Verwoerd and spouse to a military parade in honour of the King, 31.3.1947).

[26] FAV 4.5.1.4, Letter by Verwoerd to J.H. Labuschagne (Roodepoort), 17.7.1943 (see also W.J. Verwoerd 1990: 4 and Kenney 1980: 23). In 1960, Ernest Bluhm, an erstwhile fellow-learner, wrote to Verwoerd, reminding him that he himself could have been Verwoerd's predecessor as recipient of a Beit Scholarship in 1914 – a year before it was awarded to Verwoerd in 1915. But because of Bluhm's German family background, the School Board prevented him from writing the exam (PV 93/1/47/2/3, f. 172 Letter by Bluhm to Verwoerd, 4.2.1960). Verwoerd instructed his private secretary to reply and state: "He was interested to hear of your Rhodesian experiences." Upon his election as Prime Minister, he received a telegram from the Old Miltonians Association wishing him luck. *The Star* reported that two former learners at Milton remembered Verwoerd as "brilliant scholar"; he reportedly was a less impressive sportsman, but nevertheless "a charming boy" (*The Star*, 4.9.1958). John Nisper (?), another former fellow-learner, later based at the Salvation Army, congratulated Verwoerd in a letter dated 3.9.1958 (PV93/1/11/3). Verwoerd's own reserved attitude is contrasted by what his wife, who visited the school in 1970, notes: she was pleased to find that he had become known as "the most famous Old Miltonian" (55.K.V.16 (24) – Letter by Betsie Verwoerd to M. E. Rothmann, 23.8.1970).

young Hendrik was determined to take a political stand. He was openly committed to Afrikaner nationalism, which raised the ire of the principal and earned him a kick in the backside. His support for the rebels and the cause of Afrikaner nationalism became part of who he was; it would account for his habit of aggressively responding to attacks with counterattacks. To him, this was a matter of principle, which he staunchly defended regardless of the consequences.

His nationalist stance was clearly demonstrated in his refusal to take up the Rhodes Scholarship that had been awarded to him because of his excellent achievements at school.[27] It amounted to an openly expressed defiance of the legacy of Cecil Rhodes, enthusiastically revered by the British sections of the population as founder of the colony named after him. Even as school pupil, Hendrik Verwoerd, with his decidedly anti-British stance, appeared as a radical. When he became Prime Minister, a former fellow-student from Brandfort piped up, recalling the occasion when both were frantically awaiting the results of a by-election in Calvinia, in which "Dr Malan was competing with Senator Conroy and lost by 80 votes".[28] This incident shows how Verwoerd had been politicised even at a young age, identifying himself as Afrikaner nationalist.[29]

The family moved to Brandfort in the Orange Free State, where the father ran a religious bookshop and presided over the local NP structures for a while.[30] On his return, Hendrik found a situation that had, since the end of the South African War, split into different political camps. He grew up at the time of the establishment of the cultural-nationalist movement that was to become formative for him. It was this nationalism that exercised the earliest and most sustained influence on his political thought. He found a model in his father who consistently identified with the Afrikaners; ever since the formation of the NP in 1914, "he and his family never entertained a way of thinking other than a nationalist one".[31] Hendrik's parents changed their home language from Dutch to Afrikaans, even if the father never entirely lost his Dutch accent.[32] In February 1919 – with a couple

---

[27] FAV 4.2.1, Rhodes Trustee Prize for English 1915 won by Henry F. Verwoerd (Du Raan 1998: 19).
[28] PV 93/1/11/5, Letter by J.F.J. van Rensburg to Verwoerd, 5.9.1958.
[29] "Objectively viewed, many of the values held by grown-ups – values influencing their life style and their decisions to a large extent – tend to be values attained during their childhood, which are not always in the best interest of society." (Hutschnecker 1975: 232).
[30] PV72/3, Report by Beukes on trip to Brandfort with Len Verwoerd. His father was known in the Orange Free State not only as Calvinist preacher, but also as political orator (S.A. Verwoerd 1965: 43, 48).
[31] FAV 4.5.1.4, Letter by Verwoerd to J.H. Labuschagne (Roodepoort), 17.7.1943.
[32] Even as late as 1940, his mother composed her letters in a curious mix of Afrikaans and Dutch (FAV 2.2.7, Letter by Anje Verwoerd to Lucie Cloete, 13.7.1940).

of months' delay due to the Spanish Influenza –,³³ Hendrik completed his final exams in Brandfort, where he had spent the last years of his schooling. For his excellent results, he was awarded a prize.³⁴ Immediately afterwards, he started his studies, for which he returned to the Western Cape – this time to Stellenbosch. In the previous year, Victoria College in Stellenbosch had been granted university status; it was to become a bastion of Afrikaner nationalism and NP elite training ground for decades to come. Because Hendrik's father did not have the means to pay the fees, he had to borrow money, and apply to the university several times for a reduction of tuition fees for his son; without it, he would not have been able to make it possible for "the promising young man" to study at University.³⁵ Verwoerd writes about his time there in retrospect: "Myself and others who were with me during this time recall decisive elections even after forty years; and we remember how students and professors of Stellenbosch University made common cause in participating [in these elections], publicly and uniformly expressing their Afrikaner identity, irrespective of the attitude of the majority of academics who, at the time, would have been hostile [to the action of the students]."³⁶

Verwoerd soon distinguished himself in Stellenbosch as brilliant and promising student.³⁷ Within the context of cultural-nationalist mobilisation, the University itself had been set up as Afrikaans-language competitor of the University of Cape

---

33 Verwoerd and his parents fell ill with the Spanish Influenza, which turned out to be temporarily life-threatening for Hendrik (see H. J. L. Cloete, 'My herinneringe aan 'n geliefde broer', *Die Huisgenoot*, 8 September 1967).
34 FAV 4.2.1, Documents related to the exam on 10.10.1918 and reports of 1917 (higher division) and 1918 (highest division), both in the second class (with 50% of attainable points). In addition, he submitted himself to an exam in Afrikaans, set by the Saamwerk Unie van Natalse Vereniginge. Among the examiners was E. G. Jansen who, some decades later, was to become predecessor of Verwoerd as Minister for Native Affairs; and Jansen's wife Mabel. With 80% of attainable percentage points, his result was in the first class (Report issued by the Saamwerk Unie, 1918). His older brother wrote the final exam at the same time; beforehand, he had already worked for four years as teacher at a rural school. Len Verwoerd took up his academic studies only in 1923. He was appointed as lecturer and professor at the University of Stellenbosch, and remained affiliated to that university for a long time (see FAV 421, Junior Matrikulatie, Eerste Prijs toegeken aan Hendrik French [!] Verwoerd, December 1917; see also Marikulatie–Certifikaat, 22.3.1919).
35 FAV 2.2.1, Letter by W.J. Verwoerd to ds. D. J. Botha, 12.2.1919 and 20.2.1919; also UA Stellenbosch, personnel file Verwoerd, Letter by W. J. Verwoerd to the Registrar, 28.3.1919 and reply by the Registrar, 8.5.1919 informing W.J. Verwoerd that his son had been awarded a scholarship (Letter by W.J. Verwoerd to Registrar, 10.5.1919 and reply by the Registrar, 14.5.1919).
36 PV93/1/47/2/6, f. 183, Letter by Verwoerd to Thom, 28.9.1960.
37 FAV 4.3.1, Academic record of H.F. Verwoerd, according to which it was only in the first year of study that he received a B in History; otherwise, for all other subjects throughout his studies, he consistently received an A. The questions for his exam at the end of the first year of studies (December 1919) are accessible (FAV 4.3.1).

Town established at the same time; the former was to position itself along nationalist lines as expressly Afrikaans-language institution, right into the twenty-first century.[38] Even though cultural nationalism met with great sympathies among the professors – bearing in mind that the language question had given rise to the establishment of the University in the first place[39] –, there were still numerous English-speaking academics teaching there in the 1920s. In the first years of the University's existence, Dutch was still the official language; a commitment to Afrikaans and cultural-nationalist ideas were therefore not widely held at the time, unlike during the apartheid years; one can therefore assume that they indicated a dedicated engagement on the part of their adherents. The students celebrated the Boer War generals and rebels of 1914 when they came to town on 19 April 1920.[40] The Students' Council promoted the use of Afrikaans in church services,[41] and refused to work together with the English-oriented National Union of Students.[42] In November 1921, it reached agreement with the University Council on the naming of a new student residence, on condition that the English first name John would be elided from the name of Murray House;[43] but soon after, the name '*Dagbreek*' ['Dawn'] caught on, and it is under this name that the house is known to the present day.[44]

Verwoerd's academic teacher Raymond Wilcocks was Head of the Psychology Department – the only department at the University in which lectures were held in Afrikaans at the time.[45] This, and an interest in the 'poor white' problem, may have contributed to Verwoerd's decision to study Psychology. In his first year of study, Verwoerd had become acquainted with the poor white neighbourhoods of Cape Town. This experience impressed him deeply, so much so that the struggle

---

[38] Boucher 1973: 132–138. For developments after apartheid, see the one-sided report by Kapp 2013.
[39] P. S. du Toit 1966b: 65.
[40] Du Raan 1998: 22–23. Students under the age of 21 were granted voting rights only in 1929.
[41] UA Stellenbosch, Minutes of Student Council meetings, f. 43, 12.10.1922. On this occasion, it was not a matter of the division between English and Afrikaans, but of replacing Dutch with Afrikaans as "people's language" [*volkstaal*] (see Verwoerd 1924c: 3).
[42] UA Stellenbosch, Minutes of Student Council meetings, f. 45, 30.10.1922. For further examples of Verwoerd's early commitment to nationalism, see Froneman 2000. For the activities of the Student Council, see the overview provided by Du Raan 1998: 41–43.
[43] UA Stellenbosch, Minutes of Student Council meetings, f. 24, 15.11.1921.
[44] Booyens/Oosthuysen 1971: 9, 14, 30–31. Verwoerd was one of the first students to move into the newly built residence 'Dagbreek' (ibid., 16, 36; see also J.D.J. Hofmeyr's reminiscences, idid., 91–93; P.S. du Toit 1966d: 205).
[45] For the use of Afrikaans as medium of instruction in the Department, see M. Scholtz 2002: 2–3. In the newly instituted subject of 'Bantu Studies and Ethnology', it was Werner Eiselen who taught in the Afrikaans language from the start (Bank 2015c: 182).

against white poverty became a life-long commitment for him – as evinced in the publication of his first article in a student newspaper.[46]

Soon afterwards, he once again showed his political colours in refusing to accept the Abe Bailey Scholarship[47] awarded for excellent achievements after attaining his MA degree. The reason for his refusal, he stated, was that, "as a matter of principle, he did not wish to study with any money from Bailey and also did not wish to study in England". Abe Bailey was a South African mining magnate loyal to Britain, who tied the scholarship to the condition of studying in Britain. Verwoerd, in contrast, boasted of being the first Afrikaans-speaking student to have studied at South African universities continuously up to doctoral level, without having ventured abroad.[48]

He wrote the three dissertations for his academic degrees in Afrikaans. While that was less significant for his two Master's dissertations, as this was becoming common practice at universities, the choice of language for his doctoral thesis was an act of nationalist commitment. A thesis in Psychology was a contribution to internationally oriented research. In composing it in Afrikaans and publishing it in a local university-based, Afrikaans-language series, he decidedly renounced an international reception of his research findings. In fact, the thesis which did, after all, win high accolades at Stellenbosch University, did not solicit any recognition from international psychological researchers investigating the emotions, and the relation between emotions and cognitive processes; it went down unnoticed. To an ambitious young academic like Verwoerd, who aspired to an academic career at this time, the lack of an international reception of his research could not have been a matter of indifference. His decision to adopt the Afrikaans language for his scientific research could not have stood for anything but a commitment to nationalism.

In July 1922, Verwoerd was voted onto the 16-member Students' Council,[49] of whom his wife-to-be, Elizabeth 'Betsie' Schombee, was already a member.[50] The atmosphere among students was racially charged, as manifested in a series of demands and actions against coloureds.[51] In a meeting held on 17 August 1922, the Student Council criticised the University Council for inviting "[African] American

---

46 Verwoerd 1920.
47 FAV 4.3.2, *Curriculum Vitae*, handwritten in German.
48 W.J. Verwoerd 1990: 4–8. On two occasions during the 1930s, Verwoerd rejected the award of British medals in recognition of his work for poor whites (ibid., 6–7).
49 UA, Minutes of Student Council meetings, f. 30, 17.8.1922.
50 Ibid, f. 27, 27.5.1922.
51 Du Raan 1998: 23.

... Max Vergan" to present a lecture to students.[52] Verwoerd was elected Chairman of the Council on 17 August 1922.

From 2 November 1922 onwards, he acted as chairman of the Students' Council (and member of a standing committee on finances);[53] he officiated in this capacity until beginning of December 1923.[54] He made his imprint as new chairman in the institution of numerous commissions; his penchant for systematisation and hierarchisation made itself felt even at this early stage. With his taking of office, the minutes of meetings became more voluminous – not so much because of their detailed nature, but because of the fact that the Council took on more issues than before.[55] However, in May 1923, there was a discussion on whether Verwoerd, who in the meantime had been appointed in a paid position as assistant in Psychology, would still be entitled to full voting rights as student representative; in his case, the question was decided in the affirmative.[56]

Whether it was Verwoerd who took this initiative, is not clear; but it is nevertheless remarkable that in 1922, the Student Council turned to those local firms that refused to advertise in the student newspaper, noting "that they also have to take into account our interests as students".[57] As Verwoerd later reported triumphantly, the threat issued to these firms that they would "face a dark future", had shown "the desired effect".[58] In the same year, Dutch was ditched, and Afrikaans adopted as official language of the Students' Union.[59] "With a humorous face and a most winsome smile", Chairman Verwoerd greeted the audience of an alumni-meeting in Afrikaans – not in Dutch.[60] A year later, he announced that the Cape

---

52 UA Stellenbosch, Minutes of Student Council meetings, f. 30, 17.8.1922. It concerned Max Yergan, who visited Fort Hare in the 1930s (Williams 2001: 101).
53 UA Stellenbosch, Minutes of Student Council meetings, f. 46, 2.11.1922. Verwoerd was also a member of the Graduate Day-Commission as well as a member of a commission for ceremonies. In a move clearly designed to highlight the role of the Chairman, Verwoerd had pointed out that "it is desirable to stand up when [he] is being addressed". A corresponding motion was accepted (f. 48). On Verwoerd's reforms concerning graduation ceremonies, see Du Raan 1998: 64.
54 The three board members refused to accept a monetary gift from the Council after the end of their term of office; still, the Council thanked them for their good work (UA, Minutes of the Student Council meetings, f. 75, 6.12.1923).
55 UA Stellenbosch, Minutes of Student Council meetings, f. 50, 26.3.1923.
56 Ibid., f. 58, 29.5.1923.
57 Ibid., f. 64, 14.8.1923.
58 Verwoerd 1924c: 4.
59 Due to the fact that the exact date could not be established, it is not clear whether this was implemented during or after Verwoerd's term of office as chairman (see Pieter Kapp, 'n Bron van Welbehae', University Stellenbosch 2004: 12).
60 *De Zuid–Afrikaan, verenigd met Ons Land*, 29.5.1923. The newspaper report is written in English, the speech of Verwoerd, presented *verbatim*, in Afrikaans. The description of Verwoerd in

Orchestra had responded to his letter with a decision not to play the British national anthem (which at the time was still the official South African national anthem) in future.[61] Among his nationalist initiatives was setting up an office to train students as public speakers; in lecturing on all possible themes, he thought, they would promote the spread of Afrikaans.[62] In addition, the public speakers-in-training would contribute to the "intellectual and ethical development of our people".[63] Verwoerd himself was active in the debating society of the University and, together with his team, embarked on a tour that took him to Kroonstad (among twelve other locations), where he was hailed by the local press as "leading speaker" and "brilliant scholar".[64] His participation in a debate with two Oxford students on free trade saw him opposing free trade; while his stance did resonate in the press, the assembly passed a resolution with two-thirds majority in favour of free trade. Verwoerd's appearance was obviously not sufficiently convincing to win the majority over to his position.[65]

In an official report of 1924, Verwoerd accounted for his activities during his term of office. While the editor of the student paper made a point of the Student Council's heightened level of activity during this time, Verwoerd used the opportunity to castigate the students of his university, over nearly two pages, for their "lack of responsibility and deadly complacency". The highly committed student that he was, confronted with the "thanklessness of any representative task", he saw himself entitled to reprimand his fellow-students in indignant tones. "Our utmost efforts notwithstanding, we often had to counter a general apathy and lack of interest on the part of our student organisations, which amounted to nothing less than defiance."[66] Still, the extent to which he conceived of students as 'community', is noteworthy: "Every individual has to enter into lively contact with the student body as a whole." Only in that way would it be possible to live to the full

---

largely flattering terms is taken from an article that appeared in the *Cape Argus* on the same day.
61 UA, Minutes of the Student Council meetings, ff. 68–69., 11.9.1923.
62 Verwoerd, 1924b: 37. He concluded his argument with the following programmatic statement: "We will help with the development and especially with the dissemination of Afrikaans–language science in a broader sense. We will help to fulfil the justified demands of our disadvantaged compatriots, affording them opportunities for further development and extension of their horizons. We will be faithful! [*Ons sal handhaaf!*]".
63 Verwoerd 1923.
64 *Kroonstad Times*, 30.1.1925. But his allegedly outstanding appearances were not mentioned in the Jubilee edition of the Debating Society that appeared in 1926 (Blignaut 1926).
65 *Cape Times*, 15.8.1924. See also the report by P.H.L., 'Oxfordse Studente op Stellenbosch', *Die Stellenbosse Student* 25 (6), 1924, pp. 188–189.
66 Verwoerd 1924c: 5.

within a "purely student-like atmosphere" while at the same time "already learning about the challenges of governing oneself in the true sense".[67]

Added to this was a similar reproach expressed in the first article of Verwoerd's, published when he was 18 years old, in the student magazine of the University of Stellenbosch. In the sharpest of terms, he accused the "so-called patriots", meaning the NP followers, of a lack of commitment and attention to the plight of the poor whites. The reprimand arose from his dismay over the lack of dedication to 'the community'.

Some journalists and peers asked themselves whether Hendrik Verwoerd's intense nationalism was a kind of overcompensation for the fact that he was not born a South African, but came to this country as an immigrant.[68] There were continuous allusions to this fact, or even reproaches openly expressed by members of the opposition and the English-language press.[69] These impelled him to respond in his own right, soon after he was elected Prime Minister. In front of the Senate, he pointed out that a sense of belonging does not arise from the place of one's birth, but from what one believes in and acts upon. Journalist Jan van Rooyen, a close acquaintance of Verwoerd's, thought him to be particularly "sensitive" on this point, having had to wrest a concession from him to be able to mention his background in writing up a biographical sketch for van Rooyen's newspaper.[70]

A more subtle argument was put forward by Piet Cillié, long-serving chief editor of the daily *Die Burger*, after Verwoerd's assassination. Cillié had tracked Verwoerd's career with critical sympathy. In mentioning Verwoerd's Dutch family history, he said, he was wondering whether the radical stance of some politicians could be explained by the fact that they came from remote areas or immigrant backgrounds, driving them to overcome the perceived stigma through taking extremist positions. As examples, Cillié adduced Napoleon hailing from Corsica, Hitler from Austria, Stalin from Georgia, and Verwoerd from the Netherlands.[71] Indeed, this form of nationalism becomes explicable if we consider it as an attempt at essentialising the periphery, and at moving the margins closer to the

---

67 Ibid., 8.
68 For instance J. Basson 2006: 102, 136–137; see also Meiring 1990: 2, 5.
69 In an address presented in the US, Verwoerd-critic and businessman Anton Rupert spoke of the Prime Minister as "that apostle of apartheid born in Amsterdam" (B. M. Schoeman 1982: 13). For an example from the conservative camp, see Barnard/Marais 1982: 109.
70 J. J. van Rooyen 1971: 28. Similarly Cillié 1980: 53 and Mouton 2002: 55. Significantly, Verwoerd's place of birth is not mentioned in a History of the NP in the Transvaal published in 1964 (Mulder/Cruywagen 1964: 93). For further examples, see Terblanche 2001: 130.
71 Cillié 1980: 54–55; see also Meiring 1987: 13; and I. L. de Villiers 2009: 130.

more securely established centre. The new emerges from the frontiers, the insecure margins; it attempts to overcome its marginality through outdoing the established centre.[72]

Verwoerd clearly played an active role in the radicalisation of nationalism. The older historiography represented by historians such as Hepple, Kenney and (painting Verwoerd in a positive light) Scholtz described Verwoerd as dogmatist, whose intransigent and uncompromising attitude was based on his firm belief in racist doctrines, and on his nationalist convictions. This idea was subsequently questioned. American environmental scientist Roberta Miller maintains that Verwoerd was a pragmatist, who miraculously turned around in 1937, to pursue an uncompromising political course.[73] Her selective reading of the sources makes her arguments less than credible. Verwoerd himself stated that "due to his upbringing and his world view, he has only ever been Afrikaner and nationalist".[74] Like other nationalists, Verwoerd worked from the assumption that his political role should be aimed at the "survival" of the Afrikaners. "It is the basic fact of our political philosophy, and that is how to preserve South Africa for the white people."[75]

In a book published in 1975, South African sociologist Dunbar Moodie maintained that young Afrikaans-speaking intellectuals, including Verwoerd, were influenced by their encounter with German nationalism during their studies in Germany, and that this would explain the radicalisation of Afrikaner cultural nationalism after 1934.[76] There were, in fact, numerous Afrikaner intellectuals who studied in Germany. Owing to his highly rated PhD thesis completed in 1924, Verwoerd was awarded a scholarship of 150 pounds over three years, to be able to further his studies abroad.[77] Equipped with the necessary financial means, he went to Germany for three semesters. But even the fact that persons with such diverse ideological orientations as A. L. Geyer or H. B. Thom, Andries van der Walt or Cornelis de Kiewiet completed their doctoral studies under the supervision of Friedrich Meinecke in Berlin, would caution against any hastily drawn conclusions. There is no evidence of a German cultural-nationalist influence on Verwoerd; and such evidence is not required to explain his nationalist commitments, as he had developed them long before his trip, and in the most radical

---

72 Schlögel 2004: 145.
73 R. B. Miller 1993: 660–661.
74 FAV 4.5.1.4, Letter by Verwoerd to J. H. Labuschagne (Roodepoort), 17.7.1943.
75 FAV 4.7.2.4.5, Speech at the Natal–NP Party Congress in Durban, 27.8.1963, p. 3; see also Froneman 2000: 399–400, 408–409.
76 T. D. Moodie 1975: 154.
77 UA Stellenbosch, Personnel File Verwoerd, Letter by Registrar to Verwoerd, 11.12.1924.

forms. The radicalisation of Afrikaner nationalism can be explained by reference to its own internal historical dynamics, rather than ideological transfers from Germany.

For Verwoerd, nationalism was more than simply an emphatic commitment to one's "own people"; for him, it was a matter of principle. Whereas humanity was an abstraction, it was the nation that was the quasi-natural unity: "A world without nationalism is not imaginable."[78] Internationally, apartheid was condemned as violation of fundamental values. In South Africa under the rule of the National Party, human rights and basic civil rights such as freedom of movement, choice of the place of work, and political participation were systematically abrogated. The widely held and clearly expressed external view on the politics of racial segregation stands in marked contrast to the conviction, held by apartheid politicians, of its moral justifiability; they believed that apartheid made South Africa part of the Christian community with shared values. This self-assured attitude was bolstered by the deduction of apartheid from a set of basic principles that were resolutely implemented.

In his prolific speeches and writings, Verwoerd persistently and emphatically declared that his policies were based on principles that were consistently followed. His insistence on a principled stance became a trademark and character trait of Verwoerd's: "He is uncompromising when it comes to principles, indeed."[79] This is also the predominant impression of Verwoerd noted by contemporaries and historians: "For Verwoerd . . . apartheid was a political system based on clear and specific principles."[80] But by no means was the orientation along the lines of principles confined to his term of office as Minister and Prime Minister; it was what impelled him even in his youth, and subsequently in his positions as academic, journalist, and nationalist propagandist.

It would be important to clarify what Verwoerd understood by "principles", and what principles exactly he had in mind. A principle is a basic proposition from which all further rules are deduced. For the purposes of this investigation, we can distinguish between two kinds of principles: functional principles and principles guiding decisions or actions. A machine functions according to a certain basic principle; but this also applies to institutions such as public offices or the legal system. In the latter, the supra-individual context is of decisive importance, whereas the functional principles to which an individual official must ad-

---

[78] Verwoerd 1964a: 7.
[79] M. P. A. Malan 1964: 321. His son Wilhelm was convinced that this was to be explained by the influence of his academic teacher, Raymond Wilcocks (qtd. in Terblanche 2001: 233).
[80] Giliomee 2012a: 39. Scholtz also highlights the importance he placed on principles, from a young age (G. D. Scholtz 1974, vol. 1: 18, 09).

here, enjoy priority over actional principles determining the decision of the individual. Judges will have to act in accordance with prevailing laws; they would not be allowed to follow their own privately held notions of justice in reaching decisions.

Principles of action are based on values – on the decision to adopt those values from which actions emanate. "In willing them, we pose ourselves tasks that guide us and give us energy for deeds directed towards the realisation of aims."[81] The difference between actional and functional principles lies in the individual decision that is required for the former. Actional and functional principles can come into conflict with one another, as for instance in the case of a soldier who, having to heed the principle of command and obedience, is tasked with an action that goes against his innermost conviction, such as that of killing children.

When Verwoerd spoke about politics and the societal order, he re-defined actional principles as functional principles, that is, he negated the possibility that individual actions could be derived from a principled decision. In his understanding, principles were based on an incontrovertible truth that obviated any decisions, thus rendering human actions entirely functional. Political action guided by principles was not a matter of an *ad hoc* decision reached on the basis of an assessment of benefits and harms, but on an unquestionable knowledge of absolute truth. In an interview conducted in 1957 by journalist Rykie van Reenen, he could thus assert, "you see, that is why one never has any nagging doubt as to whether one could be wrong".[82] This is what explains the totalitarian hue of his politics – and we will come back to that.

In Verwoerd's understanding, a political decision would thus have to be based on truth and may not be taken to please anyone. A direct link can be established between Verwoerd's principled stance and his unbending matter of fact-style of politics pursued without consideration for the situation of persons at the receiving end of it. From principles he derived the 'factual' reasons for political and administrative decisions. Some of the examples adduced by Verwoerd in his MA dissertation on 'The double task' were to show that intentions considered less important were not allowed to interfere with the principle.[83] If the principle was the main reason for the action, there could be other, lesser reasons that could equally serve as guidelines for actions. But if a politician were to concede exceptions to certain measures, on grounds of personal considerations or empathy, he would give up on the principle stipulating the application of an equal yardstick to

---

81 Verwoerd 1922a: 16.
82 Qtd. in Terblanche 2001: 223.
83 Verwoerd 1922a: 12.

all. A functional principle for him was the legal principle of equal treatment for all, which he brought up whenever he rejected exceptional measures. This is what accounts for the inflexibility and bureaucratic ruthlessness that characterised his politics. But for him, this also implied that whites could not claim things for themselves that they were not prepared to grant to others. So, whites had to submit to apartheid in the same way as blacks, as for instance in the case the permission required to enter particular designated areas.

Even at a young age, Verwoerd concerned himself with the question of values. At the age of 21, he wrote an MA dissertation in Philosophy on 'The problem of values'. The beautiful, the good, and the true are the values that he identified as central aesthetic, ethical, and intellectual virtues. Reason and academic pursuits are not sufficient for the ability to make value judgements; for values pertain to the human being as a whole (14),[84] that is, the human being as social being. Ethics differs from the natural sciences: whereas the former develops a system of values, the latter only searches for causal relations (60).

Even if contradictions appear at the surface, there can be an underlying unifying principle. "The general principle can . . . represent the underlying unity, which facilitates ethical judgements on numerous issues." (61). Thus, all actions are attended or directed by values. Humans can share in the same values but embark on different courses of action in realising them. This does not mean, however, that they cannot all act according to an underlying principle, according to Verwoerd:

> That is why we do not seek the universal principle in different kinds of attitudes or issues, but in the aim that can inspire a multiplicity of situations, without having to limit oneself just to a few. The underlying principle can thus be called absolute . . ., in so far as its validity remains unchanged, despite the external difference between the value systems in which it finds expression. (76)

The value of any action derives from the further goal with which it is correlated. This implies that a value can be derived only from knowledge of the whole (76). This consideration is interesting in relation to Verwoerd's systematisation of apartheid as morally justifiable policy, which for him corresponds to the value of peaceful co-existence:

> The identity between the will to action and carrying out the action is what constitutes the ethical value. Thus it is not the action that is valuable, but the personality who realises the will to action in the action and who thereby realises itself. If we have learnt to compare the action before and after its realisation, we will see that the fulfilment of the willed action is indeed an absolutely valid value, for as soon as we become conscious of our own absolute

---

84 The following page references in brackets refer to the pagination of the MA dissertation.

value, 'esteem' is the only attitude we can assume vis-à-vis our actions. We conduct ourselves ethically, as soon as we carry out the action willed by ourselves. There is no particularist ethics; the only obligation is that of carrying out that action that you will for its own sake. The value of ethics is lost only when we negate ourselves, in not acting on decisions that we are actually affirming through our will.[85]

Verwoerd insists that all human beings have values along which they orientate themselves; that is why values are of primary normative significance for him: "All values are initially demands." (3)[86]

From the normative claim of a value held to be of general validity, Verwoerd derived a principle that was to direct action. In addition to functional principles with limited validity, which refer to a functional sphere such as the legal domain or the administration, Verwoerd (as early as 1922) postulated a universal fundamental principle, a *principium principiorum*, from which all other principles could be deduced. Which one could have fitted this description? Not democracy, for sure – he always thought of democracy as nothing more than lip service and vague reference to Western civilisation.[87] The fundamental principle that he never questioned, because it stood for him as fundamental truth about the world, was that of community – which had priority over the individual.[88] This idea recalls Rousseau's concept of the *volonté générale* – that collective will that is different from the sum of individual wills. Verwoerd set 'community' in a larger frame, without initially defining it in more specific terms. However, the context in which it appears indicates that what he had in mind were not necessarily smaller communities such as those of family or village, but a national community as community of shared values. He started from subjectively held values, in order then to get to supra-individual value-orientations from which he distilled the truth: "One

---

[85] Verwoerd 1922b: 38.

[86] Nevertheless, the MA dissertation does not clarify the relation between values and principles, or an underlying basic principle; nowhere is it concretised. On the one hand, he stated that values are attainable only in the particular, that is, in concrete form; on the other hand, his arguments remained at a level of abstraction that could not explain what such an underlying basic principle could be. As a result, many of his points remained diffuse. Verwoerd's conceptualisations remained too undefined and unreflective to be able to generate new insights – as he himself admits at the end of his dissertation: "But now we have to realise that we could contribute very little to the solution of the problem." (77).

[87] Roberts and Trollip interpreted the conflict between the NP and the OB as contestation over principles (1947: 179). Ever since the appearance of their book, the fable of Verwoerd as committed democrat was readily taken up by his apologists (see e.g. Terblanche 2001: 13).

[88] Verwoerd was not alone in upholding this tenet; the majority of Afrikaans–speaking cultural nationalists shared this view (see e.g. Keyter 1960:199–204).

can sacrifice one's life for love of one's people or the freedom of one's country."[89] Venter points out that Verwoerd never states in any precise terms what he actually means by "the people" [*volk*];[90] it clearly was an unquestionable unit for him, so unproblematic that he did not see the need to specify it. From "the people" [*volk*] or the nation, he deduced all other – secondary – fundamental principles, that is, the existence of different races, the inevitable conflict between ethnic groups, the central importance of family and descent.

Verwoerd postulated interdependence, since he saw the individual formed by the community; but the individual could, in turn, influence the community:

> Thus, the community is a unit with specific rights and obligations, and with similarly specific values emanating from the level of the unity of individuals. This is based on our understanding that even with all the differences in disposition, inclinations, and developmental possibilities, individuals are of the same kind in their essential being and their conditions of life. Human beings live and work together with others, and therefore their values cannot be purely individual; they become social, instead.[91]

From the idea that the nation was the most important value for every human being, Verwoerd deduced principles of action, such as that of securing the survival of "the people" [*volk*], biological and cultural. Other scholars, such as ethnologist P. J Coertze and sociologist G. Cronjé, agreed with him on this idea, insisting that "the human being" as such did not exist at all; human beings existed only in their concrete formation through the ethnic community.[92] The aim of sustaining a national community could therefore be realised only if principles of action would be implemented as consistently as if they were functional principles. From his understanding of the 'truth' that human beings could only realise themselves in communities, Verwoerd obtained a functional principle of human social life beyond the decisions of the individual. A commitment to the idea of nation was thus transformed from an ethical decision to an absolute necessity. That is how Verwoerd could come to view his own role as that of an executor of a principle, a kind of general manager of the world spirit; by the same token, he could deny,

---

89 Verwoerd 1922b: 59.
90 J. J. Venter 1999: 432.
91 Verwoerd 1922b: 59. P. J. Coertze (1979: 246) tries to explain 'community' through ethnological functionalism, which he manages to do only at the cost of logical cogency. The Leipzig 'holist' psychologists, especially Felix Krueger, believed that the individual would fully merge into the community (Geuter 1985: 63–68.; see also Prinz 1985: 108).
92 However, that did not stop them from waxing abstract on 'man' in their publications. Cronjé did so without any reference to the relevant research or literature on the subject (e.g. Cronjé 1964b, 1964c; see also E. F. Potgieter 1957: 129, for whom contact and communication only took place between communities, not between individuals).

with complete conviction, that the principle he invoked was based on an individual choice.

It was precisely the submission of the individual to the community that effectively implied the apartheid regime's denial of individual freedom and self-determination, as it was noted as early as 1957 by theologian B. B. Keet.[93] Moreover, this basic principle of Verwoerd's ran counter to the foundations of Western democracies, based as they are, on the idea of responsible autonomous decisions and free choice of the individual.

At the same time, Verwoerd's position implied the denial of the historical nature of ethnicity and nationhood; in Verwoerd's hands, these were treated as constants and as anthropological universals. That is how he could unproblematically project a contemporary understanding of the nation state back into the Middle Ages, and describe the dissolution of empires into nation states as a 'natural' process:

> Throughout history empires have fallen to pieces which sought to bind different national groups together even when they were ethnically related and with no colour differences involved and more so the greater the national or racial differences. Unceasing eternal strife within the multiracial state was often though not always succeeded by greater peace between them as national states and neighbours when they became independent.[94]

In Verwoerd's view, even the Roman Empire had to contend with national particularisms:

> Whenever account has been taken of national entities when creating new states, contentment has been the result. Is this not the lesson taught by the history of Southern and Eastern Europe? Was the Roman as well as other empires that came into being, not continually involved in internal strife and conflict and disorder until there was a separation and states were created? It is true that neighbouring states also fought one another, but there was never such a great degree of unrest and internal struggle, strife and hatred between states. After a conflict of interests, they often settled the matter between them and became allies.[95]

It was a matter of a fundamental historical law not requiring any further reflection, "that in contexts of different languages, views, and levels of civilisation, different nationalities live more happily in their own states than being dominated by one of them. Separation of different types is a law of nature. In that way, neighbouring states can live together in friendship more readily than under an attempt to force together what does not fit together."[96] In fact, Verwoerd de-

---

93 Keet 1957: 6–8.
94 PV 93/1/30/1/20, Letter by Verwoerd to J. A. Chambers, 17.9.1963, f. 158.
95 Verwoerd, Speech in the House of Assembly, 23 January 1962 (in Pelzer 1966: 660–689, 665).
96 PV 93/1/30/1/28, Letter by Verwoerd to J. Bogaards (Alkmaar, The Netherlands), 13.1.1964.

historicised and naturalised the nation state, elevating it to a timeless fundamental order of humankind. The politics of apartheid was seen to draw the consequences from the "lessons of world history", namely "that many wars and much internal disorder have been caused by attempting to force different racial groups, even of the same colour and stage of civilisation, into one political unit".[97] History was presented either as decline and chaos, or as a sequence of corrections continuously recalling to people the fundamental principle, and elevating ethnic units to the basis of their life in common.

A multi-ethnic unitary state was not feasible, according to this view; it was bound to lead to conflicts. This would occur all the more if these ethnic groups were also located on different civilisational levels, as he thought was the case in South Africa.

For Verwoerd, humanity was conceivable only in the form of ethnically segmented communities. Any appeals to and invocations of an inclusive humanity seemed to him to be sentimental and out of touch with reality; they were bound to dissolve established orders and hurtle towards chaos. Community, and the nation specifically, were notions implying differentiation between those who belonged and were included on the one hand, and those who were considered different and excluded, on the other. The nation could only be defined through a distinction from those who did not belong. On this understanding, sustaining the Afrikaner nation required segregation from those who were not included, like the English or the black majority. In Verwoerd's principle of community, that is, in the fundamental principle of his thought, segregation was of central significance from the start.

Because cultural nationalism was thought to have emanated from a principle, Verwoerd could state: "A people can never adjust its principle. A people can, however, assess or re-assess conditions."[98] The principle became concretised through the culture of a nation, and thus excluded the very possibility of a compromise that would have questioned cultural-nationalist presuppositions. Because Verwoerd deduced all actions from "principles", he became incapable of compromising.[99] The principle of the nation could be implemented politically only if its followers came together to form a party. That had already been one of the basic tenets of D. F. Malan: Bring together what, from innermost conviction, belongs together. Confronting Malan, Verwoerd stood for a more radical principle insofar as he prioritised objective "facts" over Malan's voluntarist "innermost convic-

---

97 PV 93/1/24/12, Declaration of the Prime Minister, 23.1.1962, f. 3.
98 PV 93/4/1/15, Verwoerd, undated notes or manuscript for a speech, n.d. ff. 13–15, 14.
99 This was attributed to him also by Meiring 1987: 144.

tion". The idea of the Party as embodiment of the nation would explain why Verwoerd so obstinately and uncompromisingly insisted on its principled orientation, "for it is the interest of the people [*volk*] (with the Party as instrument) that should be paramount, and thus has to form the bond."[100]

Throughout the notes of the young lecturer and after 1928 of the professor, there are numerous examples of psychological findings pertaining to contexts of white poverty and nationalism. In his Psychology MA dissertation on "the double task", he adduced examples taken from everyday life, including some directly linked to political issues – to be specific, to contradictory attitudes in politics. For instance: an Englishman writes about the Anglo-Boer war and the suffering of the Afrikaners. As a patriot, he maintains that the British did not know anything about the suffering of the Afrikaners.[101] English-speaking whites had a double loyalty, which is why they got entangled in contradictions. This also applies to Jan Smuts, whose politics served British interests, but who maintained that this was in the interests of South Africa as a whole.[102] For Verwoerd, any co-operation with politicians like Smuts who wanted to create an artificial white nation, or Hertzog, whose Two-Stream-Policy pursued the same aim with slightly different means, was unthinkable, as he considered their politics unprincipled.

For cultural nationalism, history was of central significance. Among its pivotal criteria, held to be objective givens, were language, religion, and background; in addition, collective experience was considered to be of major importance, which is why the nation, as historically developed organic unity, was thought to be "entirely independent of race".[103] Verwoerd's biographer G. D. Scholtz reduced this notion of 'nation' to the simple formula: "A people [*volk*] can, in short, be defined as spiritual unity."[104] Moreover, history was supposed to be the link between past and future; it was to secure the continuity of the nation biologically, and to connect present experience with visions for the future. In this way, present and future events could be placed in an overarching temporal context and meaningfully interpreted in the light of historical experience. With a view to constructing a meaningful context, history was understood not as the passage of homogeneous time, but as series of events promising the fulfilment of time. The limited perspectives imposed by salvation history minimised contingency or excluded it altogether.[105]

---

100 PV 93/1/30/1/4, Letter by Verwoerd to A. J. van der Merwe (Lichtenburg), 9.3.1959, f. 48.
101 Verwoerd 1922a: 12–13.
102 Ibid., 9–10.
103 231/2/1/2, Eerste Jaar Sociologie: Algemene Kursus, p. 39.
104 Scholtz 1974, vol. 2: 54.
105 Benjamin 2015: 90.

For Verwoerd, the reference to history served the aims of a self-assured nationalism, for history had been constructed as a meaningful framework, expressed in some deeply held convictions: The Afrikaners came to constitute themselves as a people in their own right in South Africa, which is reflected in the fact that they developed their own language. Their history was a unique history of suffering, with numerous biblical references and parallels to the history of ancient Judaism.[106] Their history was ordained by God – an idea expressed (in 1943) by long-standing chairman of the Broederbond J. C. van Rooy in the following terms: "God in His Eternal Wisdom has elected the Afrikaner Nation and ordained it to realise one or another idea of God, and to use it as his instrument to bring to fruition one or the other part of His Omniscient Plan on Earth."[107]

The fact that Verwoerd did not perceive the history of his people as purely coincidental sequence of events and developments, but as a kind of secular salvation process, was frequently expressed in his speeches at important national commemoration events. Shortly after the election that installed him as Prime Minister, he articulated his sense of mission within a nation of a special status:

> That is why we are building on the only rock of nations, namely the faith and the same helping hand which gave our forefathers the victory of Blood River. We are building in faith, we are building with power because we know that we have not been planted here aimlessly. . . . Why could they go through their wars of independence and, win or lose, yet survive as a nation? Why was this all given to us if there is no purpose in it? And I believe this to be the purpose – that we should be an anchor and a stay for Western civilisation and for the Christian religion. . . . Never before in history, at any rate the history of the past two thousand years, has the position of the white races been so perilous. They are in danger not because of their lack of knowledge or power, but on account of that which is going on in their own spirit: their inner weakening and wrong conception of what their task is on earth. . . . Perhaps it was intended that we should have been planted here at the southern point within the crisis area so that from this resistance group might emanate the victory whereby all that has been built up since the days of Christ may be maintained for the good of all mankind. May you have the strength, people of South Africa, to serve the purpose for which you have been placed here![108]

Through history, a cross-generational context was established, in which every individual was allocated their fixed place. Their right to exist was based on the fact that they belonged to a people [*volk*]: "For everyone, the story of the formation of his people is unique – that is his history in which he personally has a part

---

106 Walzer 1988; see also Marx 2008: 182–186.
107 FAV 4.5.2.4., Brochure for the 25th Anniversary of the AB 1943, Speech of Chairman J. C. van Rooy, p. 45.
108 Verwoerd, Day of the Covenant Address at Blood River, 16 December 1958 (in Pelzer 1966: 206–211, 210–211).

through his forebears whose blood is pumping in his veins. For him, this is the most important aspect; from it he derives not only knowledge – it involves his entire soul, steels his character, and grants him ideals for the future." The human being can live psychically and intellectually only through and for the nation. For Verwoerd, peoples were collective individuals, as each one of them had a special kind of genetic characteristic: "Every people of the world has its own particular nature. It is this character that enables it to realise itself and to live its life fruitfully."[109] He did not tire of continuously reminding his audiences of the priority of the community over the individual: "I say again that the merit which counts is not only the merit of the individual. . . . The merits of races and groups must also count. We who are White will stand, fight and win in Africa on the merits of our White community viewed as an entity."[110] Verwoerd viewed a people as an independent entity. For him, it was peoples, not individuals, who were the actual subjects of history; individuals, especially politicians, were simply the manging directors of the will of the people. The consequences of this way of thinking are not hard to grasp: peoples would need to maintain their identity and remain separate and distinct from one another. That is why he claimed that the apartheid policies he pursued amounted to nothing other than "follow[ing] the path of history and the way of nations".[111]

The crux of the cultural-nationalist creed was a mythicised history, described by Dunbar Moodie as "Civil Religion".[112] For political scientist Albert Venter, this is the reason for the divergence of the moral conviction and the ruthlessness of the implementation: "In the dreamworld of such a political ideology, modes of action considered senseless in the real world, are being presented as moral actions."[113] For Verwoerd, history was primarily the task of shaping the future, "in order that we may make of our future that which our past held out as a promise".[114] Despite his frequent invocations of the past, he was not really interested in history. It simply served him as a mandate for developing certain plans for the future. "Each generation must realize that the child is its continuation. It must dedicate all its thoughts and energy to those who are to follow."[115] He was capable

---

[109] FAV 4.5.2.7, Speech on Kruger Day, 10 October (no indication of the year, but in the 1940s).
[110] Verwoerd, Statement of Policy in the House of Assembly, 9.3.1960 (in Pelzer 1966: 340–369, 366).
[111] Scholtz 1974, vol. 2: 162.
[112] T. D. Moodie 1975.
[113] A. Venter 2011: 547.
[114] Verwoerd, Speech on Kruger Day, Pretoria 10.10.1959 (in Pelzer 1966: 313–318, 317).
[115] Verwoerd, Speech at the Inauguration of the Sunday School Buildings, Bloemfontein, 1.10.1959 (in Pelzer 1966: 299–312, 312).

of any kind of falsification of history, if it would allow him to project his own ideological precepts, styled as missions, back into the past – as he did with Paul Kruger, whom he credited with the same affect against 'liberalism' as the one held by himself. Kruger's antiliberal attitude, he argued, was not by the same token an indication of conservatism; on the contrary, Kruger himself was "progressive! He was progressive as a patriot, as the father of his people, as the creator of his nation's future within its own country. It is in this sense that we also want to be progressive, but not in any other sense."[116] In Verwoerd's notion of 'tradition', his self-image as moderniser became manifest.

His interest in history was always directed towards a practical, future-oriented goal. From the certainty offered to him by history cast as salvation history, he drew the confidence

> that we must enter the future full of courage and full of faith with the eye directed above, to Him who planted us here with a purpose. Let us believe that we are here to continue to exist and let us be ready with all the strength of our hearts, with all the strength of our minds, with all the power of our bodies, with all we possess, to offer whatever South Africa asks of us.[117]

Contingency would have been out of place in this scheme – which is why Verwoerd was always at pains to cast his long-term aims as inevitable results of realistic politics.

The experience of one's own suffering could now merge with the history of the suffering people. Ever since the first assassination attempt (at the latest), Verwoerd, the immigrant, felt even more connected with "the people": "A person who has suffered, and this is also true of a nation, should rather look to the future and press forward. If one is spared it is in order to fulfil further duties. Similarly, if a nation has been spared for centuries in a land of hardship but also of great promise, it too has a task to fulfil."[118]

History had made the nation into an actual community of a common fate – including immigrants like Verwoerd. As immigrant, Verwoerd defined the nation not by reference to descent, but as community with a shared socialisation. It is from this history of pain and suffering that he drew his energy and the certainty of having to cast his glance into the future. This is what explains the difference in the significance of nation and race in Verwoerd's thinking: race was not a com-

---

116 Verwoerd, Speech on Kruger Day, Pretoria 10.10.1959 (in Pelzer 1966: 313–318, 315).
117 Verwoerd, Speech on Union Jubilee, Bloemfontein, 31.5.1960 (in Pelzer 1966: 398–406, 406).
118 Verwoerd, First Speech after attempted Assassination, 20.5.1960 (in Pelzer 1966: 394–397, 396).

munity, but a categorical attribution, while nation stood for a vital community that alone could form identities.

Cultural nationalism related to apparently objective criteria such as membership of a language group, birth and descent, history and culture. Compared to these criteria, individual will and decision are much less important. That is why the National Party did not see it as its task to represent particular interests; on the contrary, it was thought to be a matter of course that a party "that was looking out for the concerns of the people [*volk*], often had to overrule the selfish wants of [particular] voters".[119] There was thus thought to be an overriding 'principal' interest that had priority over the interests of the voters; and this 'principal' interest was determined by the party leader rather than the voters or the majority.

An indication of the early stage at which this particularly radical and total version of nationalism had formed in Verwoerd's mind, is provided by a few short stories published in the popular magazine *Die Huisgenoot* in 1931. They appeared as an elaborated continuation of the collection of examples presented in his MA dissertation (in Psychology) on "the double task".[120] In these stories, too, the individual is confronted with a double task, where the two parts of the task are irreconcilable, forcing the individual to make a choice: either his individual happiness, or submission to the requirements and expectations of the community. The story entitled *'Die Lewensanker'* ['The Anchor in Life'] is skilfully structured; it elicits an expectation in the reader that is being disappointed through a radical turn in the end. It brings the readers face to face with a basic conflict behind the sentimental love story, suggesting that the decision taken in the story is what directly concerns every one of them. A young man and a woman, approximately seven years younger than him and from a neighbouring household, grow up together. The young man cares for the baby, plays with the little girl, and later helps her with her school tasks. She has a crush on him and is disappointed when she finds out that he is going out with another young woman. The two women become friendly with one another, but the young man and the 'other' woman get married and move to another place. Left behind, the young woman gives in to the solicitations of a young pastor. They get married, and she becomes active in his congregation. Having lost his wife to an illness, the friend of her youth comes to visit the pastor's family and sees his erstwhile neighbour again after a long time. It does not take long for him to realise that her marriage to the hypocrite and dunce of a pastor is an unhappy one. The woman spontaneously decides to elope

---

[119] Qtd. in Prinsloo 1979: 88. Principles were to be given priority over individual leaders, too (ibid., 96–97).
[120] see ch. 2.

with the love of her youth. Throughout the story, the reader is primed to believe that the two of them are destined for each other; their happiness seems to be geared to make for a happy end to the story. But then, as they are about to leave, she meets a woman from her congregation at the station; this woman draws her attention to the children, the sick and the elderly persons in need of her care. The woman momentarily turns around and decides to stay. To her friend, who stands aghast, she explains: "My understanding of responsibility means obeying the demands of the society in which I grew up, the framework of which makes it possible for us to live together in an orderly way in the first place." Conformism and submission to the community come to assume priority over autonomy and individual happiness; the double task can be met only through an either–or decision, as this case demands a principled decision.[121]

The lines of Verwoerd's thinking become even more clear in a story with a plot that runs counter to the one described above. As a trope for the kind of multi-ethnic sociality that he rejects, Verwoerd adduces a passenger liner on the way from Cape Town to Britain. The passengers hail from various European nations; in the course of a couple of weeks on board, they come into contact with one another and appear to form a community. But in Verwoerd's description, they are all borderliners: alcoholics, women with dubious pasts, a mentally ill person, etc. As the ship arrives in Britain and the passengers disembark, the pseudo-community falls apart; it becomes clear that a real communal bond never existed between them. "They are scattering with hardly a greeting, and without the least interest in what was going to become of each one of them."[122] This haphazardly assembled group of people of the most diverse nationalities cannot form a community; it is the opposite of what 'community' stands for – an 'organic community' characterised by solidarity and a fundamental sense of belonging together.

The people [*volk*] is the immortal collective body whose well-being necessarily overrides all particular interests. In this vein, he held forth in one of his Sociology lectures: "A family without children may be expedient for man and wife, but for the society and the people [*volk*] it means nothing."[123] Verwoerd's faith in progress, and his optimism about progress, crystallised in his concern for children and youth as integral parts of the nation:

> The future of the children is an incentive to effort not only in the home, but also for the nation and the state. . . . The desire to leave a better and more prosperous country to the

---

121 VEE [Verwoerd], 'Die lewensanker'. *Die Huisgenoot*, 8.5.1931, p. 45.
122 FAV 4.4.7, O. Nieuwenhuys [Verwoerd], 'Dwars–stromings'. Typescript, undated (presumably 1931).
123 231/2/2/2, 'Inleiding tot die Sociologie', p. 24.

next generation than you yourself inherited, is inspired in the state as in the home, by the fact that there are children, that there is a nation of the future.[124]

To be sure, he stated this from the experience as father of seven children; but what he essentially had in mind was the younger generation as the future nation: "Where there are children, anti-social traits such as selfishness and fear of people do not exist. The family, nation and the Church learn to live for their children, they learn to look to the future."[125] The task of the present generation was essentially that of laying the foundations for a "safe future": "Shall we, who today control the future of our state and of our nation, prove so faithful that our children in forty years' time may inherit and live to see a safe future, or shall we, because of weakness or selfishness or fear of what is trying to obtrude itself upon us, let them down?"[126] In order to secure a future for the children, the present generation would have to be prepared "to suffer hardship for the sake of our posterity." Only then shall we "ensure that they who come after us may be just as prosperous as we are because of what our forefathers did and suffered for us."[127] Children were an asset to the nation. Even a Sunday School building could become a monument to the nation, to the extent that it "pays tribute to the children of the present, but . . . will make the children of each generation realize that they are the nation of the future."[128]

Concern with children and their developmental possibilities was tantamount to a national service. Based on this idea, Verwoerd could interpret love for children in the light of integral nationalism, in contrast to a false individualism: "Love of a child destroys selfishness. It gives resistance to pain and fatigue."[129] Conversely, neglect of children was tantamount to "suicide, the suicide of a nation and a Church". If a people [volk] was not interested in the right upbringing of children, it was throwing away its future "which depends on people, not on beau-

---

124 Verwoerd, Speech at the Inauguration of the Sunday School Buildings, Bloemfontein, 1.10.1959 (in Pelzer 1966: 299–312, 302, 303). Even in his Sociology lectures as early as 1933, Verwoerd had underlined the importance of children as bearers of the nation's future (231/2/1/1, 'Inleiding tot die Sociologie', p. 119).
125 Verwoerd, Speech at the Inauguration of the Sunday School Buildings, Bloemfontein, 1.10.1959 (in Pelzer 1966: 299–312, 305: "The child is of the greatest importance both to the state and the church." (ibid., 302))
126 Verwoerd, Speech on Union Jubilee, Bloemfontein, 31 May 1930 (in Pelzer 1966: 398–406, 398, 399).
127 Ibid., 399.
128 Verwoerd, Speech at the Inauguration of the Sunday School Buildings, Bloemfontein, 1.10.1959 (in Pelzer 1966: 299–312, 299).
129 Ibid., 303.

tiful Church or state buildings, not on laws of Church or state".[130] For Verwoerd, as for most Afrikaner nationalists, the family was the basic unit of the nation, which 'organically' emerged from the family, and to which the submission of the individual to the community applied in equal measure.[131] J. J. Venter identified this totalitarian tendency in organic conceptions of society deriving behavioural norms from a descriptive metaphor.[132] The nation always enjoyed priority over the family, though: "Everyone will sacrifice himself for his family, but when the nation calls and national ideals are in the balance, he will pass the family by to listen to the voice of his country."[133] Youthful idealism was what would secure the future of the people [volk]: "Unselfish sacrifice, idealism and unreserved faith in the nation, and the abandonment of self-interest is characteristic of youth." These statements also reveal the perspective of the developmental psychologist: "For this reason reformers of society are often young people, but not always, since the characteristic of youth may be carried deep into adulthood."[134]

Verwoerd derived his thought and action from principles that to him stood firm as the truth. The principle that proved politically the most consequential and that determined his political activities and the politics of apartheid, in particular, was the absolute priority he accorded to the community over the individual, on the one hand, and over humanity, on the other.

---

130 Ibid., 309.
131 Apart from Verwoerd, sociologist Cronjé explicitly embraced such views.
132 J. J. Venter 1997: 94ff, referring to Verwoerd (98). For ethnologist P. J. Coertze, who was close to Verwoerd ideologically, man was only imaginable as ethnic being: "Anthropogenesis could only have proceeded along the path of ethnogenesis." (P. J. Coertze 1980: 86). Viewed in this way, ethnicity is posited as historical constant.
133 Verwoerd, Speech at the Inauguration of the Sunday School Buildings, Bloemfontein, 1.10.1959 (in Pelzer 1966: 299–312, 305).
134 Ibid.

Sharpened Thoughts – Blunted Feelings

Having completed his schooling, Verwoerd immediately started studying at Stellenbosch University. While the previous chapter described his activities, this chapter will focus on his academic career. Verwoerd's remarkable faith in logical reasoning and his renunciation of emotionally charged demagoguery are based on his rational convictions stipulating that feelings and thought must be kept separate from one another. His academic trajectory and his later career are closely connected with each other; for Verwoerd the politician, insights into action-orientations can be traced back to his dissertations at the University of Stellenbosch. The choice of this university was not a difficult one for a nationalist like Verwoerd, seeing that it was established as Dutch-language competitor to the English-language University of Cape Town, and later became the training ground for Afrikaner nationalists. An extension of its subject offerings had led to the expansion of the University of Stellenbosch shortly before attaining the status of a fully–fledged university, but especially in the process of attaining it in 1918. In that context, an institute for psychology was established, one of the first of its kind in South Africa, with Raymond William Wilcocks (1892–1967) as first professor appointed to that Institute in 1917.

Despite his English name, Wilcocks belonged to the Afrikaans–speaking section of the white population. He was born on 23 January 1892 in Vryburg (then Cape Colony, today North West Province) the son of pastor David Wilcocks and his wife Aletta van der Merwe. After completing his studies at Victoria College in Stellenbosch (later Stellenbosch University), he was awarded a scholarship that enabled him to study Philosophy and Psychology at the University of Berlin (1912–1917), where he obtained his doctorate in Philosophy in 1917. Having been classified as a citizen of an enemy country after the outbreak of World War I, he was not allowed to leave Germany; as a result, his subsequent attitude to Germany was more ambivalent than that of his germanophile student Verwoerd.[1] Wilcocks's academic teacher in Philosophy was Benno Erdmann, whose writings exercised a strong influence on him, as evinced by his dissertation.[2] He studied Psychology with Carl Stumpf, whose lines of questioning were formative for his

---

[1] Verwoerd's germanophile views found particularly clear expression in the editorials in *Die Transvaler* penned by him during World War II. In these articles, he emphasised the friendship between Germans and Afrikaners, while attacking British imperialism (*Die Transvaler*, 15.6.1942). On Wilcocks's biography, see A. B. van der Merwe 1987.
[2] Erdmann was professor of Philosophy at the Institute of Psychology at the Berlin University between 1909 and 1921 (Geuter/Hagemeier/Ash 1986: 17).

further research and whose interest in the psychology of feelings was to become influential even for Verwoerd's dissertation.³ In his doctoral thesis, Wilcocks dealt with a philosophical theme closely connected with Psychology, namely Epistemology;⁴ Wilcocks's main interest was Hegel's Philosophy. For many psychologists, Philosophy had been their primary discipline, which is what stood in the way of the establishment of Psychology as an independent discipline. What hampered the disciplinary anchoring of Psychology in equal measure, was its in-between status straddling natural sciences and humanities.⁵ Wilcocks's 84-page thesis entitled 'Zur Erkenntnistheorie Hegels in der *Phänomenologie des Geistes*' [On the Theory of Knowledge in Hegel's *Phenomenology of Spirit*], and written in German, was published in 1917 and then re-published in 1981. It was centrally concerned with the question exercising Kant and his successors, then posed and addressed anew by Hegel, as to "how it is possible for the subject, as pure thought, to know its accordance with something different to itself".⁶ Knowledge of the object as something different from the subject can succeed only if the object is grasped as being different from the subject, which in turn implies that the investigation of the subject is the decisive aspect, and has to be thought unconditionally.⁷ Starting from the identity of subject and object⁸ in turn, attention is being directed to Hegel's dialectical method and his logic,⁹ which is the actual object of philosophical cognition.¹⁰ Within a theory of knowledge, the philosophical subject searches not only knowledge about itself, but its absolute otherness, namely the object.¹¹ In thinking about its thinking, it "investigates itself and comes to know itself as object of itself."¹² This is what makes Philosophy the theory of knowledge of the concept.¹³ Philosophical truth is not the precondition, but the

---

3 Stumpf 1899; Stumpf 1928.
4 Hegel himself (2010: 517) distinguished Psychology as a preliminary stage from philosophical epistemology as such: "In Psychology, the stages preceding the understanding are *feeling* and intuition, and then *representation* generally."
5 For instructive comments on this, see Krueger 1913b: 254–259.
6 Wilcocks 1917: 9.
7 Ibid., 18–27.
8 Ibid., 14–15.
9 Ibid., 10–11.
10 Ibid., 14.
11 Ibid., 14.
12 Ibid., 14.
13 Ibid., 17–20.

result of the dialectical movement of philosophical conceptualisation.[14] What is decisive is the outcome of the dialectical development itself:

> Seeing that the beginning of the *Phenomenology* is understood to require dialectical mediation, Hegel does not start with the positing of a mere fact. . . . Seeing that Hegel similarly does not start with the fact of cognition of the appearing consciousness, but demands the dialectical mediation of this knowledge, the phenomenological investigation is an epistemological one.[15]

Wilcocks' thesis is devoted in large parts to the attempt at proving this. While his introductory remarks on Kant still display an affinity with Psychology, the main part of the thesis departs from this starting point in a move towards a genuinely philosophical topic. His interest in Philosophy was an abiding one,[16] even though this academic work subsequently gravitated more towards Psychology.

The field of his professorship in Philosophy at the University of Stellenbosch was designated as 'Logic and Psychology'.[17] He dealt intensively with both and came to exercise a lasting influence on his student Hendrik Verwoerd.[18] Logic became as foundational for Philosophy, as it did for the investigation of the psychic life of rational beings. As early as 1919, Wilcocks emphasised the importance that research held for him; he understood the role of the University in the sense of Wilhelm von Humboldt, as a site of teaching and learning combined.[19] During the first few years, Wilcocks focused on basic psychological research; only later did he turn his attention to applied psychology.[20]

---

14 Ibid., 17, 21. See also the extensive discussion of the logical problematic arising from the concept of dialectical negation and its sublation within the concept itself. Wilcocks elaborates the contradiction and the problematic within the framework of Aristotelian Logic clearly and in great detail (21–23). He explains how Hegel captures the problematic of the dialectical development of the concept and the traditional understanding of logic pertaining to the relation between understanding and reason (25–27); only the latter can "think the contradictory contents in unity" (26); see also ch. 3.
15 Ibid., 53.
16 See for instance his notes on Spinoza, in 77/13/1.
17 P. S. du Toit 1966a: 40. This was not an exception, since the first professorship established at UCT in 1920 carried the same designation (Foster 1991a: 1).
18 A. Boshoff 1993: 31. See for instance Wilcocks's essay (1923).
19 In 1919, Wilcocks announced: "What we want is not only a teaching university, but a research university – a researching university." (Qtd. in Du Raan 1998: 9–10).
20 In the 1930s, Wilcocks gradually withdrew from academic teaching and research. He authored the Psychological Report, volume two of the five–volume Carnegie Report that appeared in 1932. Subsequently, he became member and later chairman of the Commission of Inquiry Regarding the Cape Coloured Population (Wilcocks Commission) investigating the economic and social situation of coloureds (1934–1936), and member of the De Villiers–Commission on mixed mar-

During the first few years of the existence of the Psychology Department at the University of Stellenbosch, which bore the unmistakable stamp of its only lecturer, Raymond William Wilcocks, Hendrik Verwoerd was one of 30 students (from 1919 onwards). There are two reasons that could possibly explain his choice of the subject: even as a nineteen-year-old student, Verwoerd evidently showed an ardent interest in the 'poor white problem'. Psychology was instrumental in his pursuit of this interest and contributed to his understanding of applied science.[21] A second reason was the person of Wilcocks himself, who in no time had made himself a name as dynamic and innovative young professor at a fledgeling university. Only nine years his senior, Wilcocks exerted as powerful an attraction on young Hendrik Verwoerd as the subject itself, which under his headship developed into "one of the most important departments in the University".[22] The relation between the two soon became a collegial one, rather than a teacher–student relationship.[23]

Wilcocks did not only include Verwoerd as test subject in his close circle of colleagues, but also supported him as one of the most talented students.[24] That is why it is not surprising to find that many of the scientific interests pursued by Wilcocks are to be found in Verwoerd's work, too. This pertains especially to the keen reception of the Würzburg School of the Psychology of Thought [*Denkpsychologie*], and of the work of Otto Selz, which will be the subject of closer investigation in this chapter. Wilcocks never completely divorced Psychology from Philosophy; this is reflected also in the intellectual trajectory of Verwoerd, who similarly studied both subjects and chose for his MA dissertation in Philosophy a topic closely connected with a psychological problematic. But in contrast to Wilcocks, Verwoerd was not really philosophically minded. The orientation of the new Institute towards research conducted in Germany and the United States is not surprising, since these two countries were pioneering in the establishment of Psychology as a scientific discipline.

---

riages (1937–1939). Seedat/MacKenzie (2008) and Foster (2008: 99) provide an instructive overview of the history of psychology in South Africa, and of applied psychology in particular.

21 On the significance of the 'poor white problem' in the formation of Afrikaans-language psychology, see Böhmke/Tlali 2008: 136.

22 Verwey 1966: 255.

23 Wilcocks participated in hiking tours of students, see photographs in Hefer/Basson 1966: 21–22.

24 Wilcocks made his excerpts of psychological literature available to Verwoerd, for his perusal in the process of writing his PhD thesis (Verwoerd 1924a: 5).

After having attained the BA degree cum laude in 1921, Verwoerd completed his studies in 1922 with an MA degree,[25] followed by research toward his PhD. He wrote two MA dissertations, one in Psychology, and the other in Philosophy. Towards the end of 1924, he was appointed as assistant in Psychology for 1925: "My task was to assist with the practicals and with the lectures for second and third year students."[26]

In her influential article on Verwoerd's early career, Roberta Miller writes about his dissertations and the small number of articles published before his travels to Germany and the US, maintaining that "his work was technically and analytically unsophisticated". The development of Psychology in Germany as it decisively influenced Verwoerd and his doctoral supervisor Raymond Wilcocks merits much closer scrutiny than Miller is prepared to give it. In what follows, I would like to contribute to a better understanding of the history of psychology. Generalisations such as "German psychology had traditionally focused on basic research rather than the application of research"[27] tend to reduce the spectrum of psychological research going on in Germany at the time; there were, after all, important impulses emanating from this research for the development of applied psychology in the US – as was the case, for example, with the move of Hugo Münsterberg from Freiburg to Harvard.[28] Miller's generalisations thus neglect the powerful influence of German psychology on the history of psychology in the US, both in the initial years[29] and after 1933, when many Jewish academics sought refuge in the US. Neither do Miller's contentions contribute to an understanding of Verwoerd's psychology; she does not provide any evidence or further investigation to substantiate her contention that his short sojourn in the US was "far more important to his intellectual development than was his longer stay in Germany".[30] The reception of the Würzburg School of the Psychology of Thought [Denkpsychologie] in Stellenbosch was evident even in the exam questions to which Verwoerd had to apply himself. The first one of these questions was the following one: "Are thought processes me-

---

25 FAV 4.3.1, Exam Questions in Psychology and Philosophy, November 1922.
26 FAV, 4.3.2, Curriculum vitae, handwritten in German. UA Stellenbosch, personnel file, letter by Registrar to Verwoerd, 11.1.1924, offering Verwoerd a lecturing post for 1925, and reply by Verwoerd, 14.11.1924.
27 R. B. Miller 1993: 639 (both quotes).
28 Münsterberg 1997 and Galliker/Klein/Rykart 2007: 208; also Lück/Bringmann 2005.
29 Wundt's work had a particularly marked impact on the science of psychology in its formative stages, especially in Germany and in the US, since many of his students and assistants came from North America, where they themselves subsequently exerted considerable influence. For an instructive account of this, see Hoffmann/Deffenbacher 1992: 1–18. With respect to Applied Psychology, see Dorsch 1963: 36–38, 44.
30 R. B. Miller 1993: 640.

diated only through images? Substantiate your answer with your own experimental introspective findings."[31]

Psychology as academic discipline can be traced back to Wilhelm Wundt (1832–1920), who established the first Institute for Psychology globally in Leipzig in 1879. He supervised the work of 186 PhD candidates,[32] trained German and American psychologists, and conveyed to them his ideas on psychology as science. A trained physiologist, he understood psychology as a natural science methodologically based on experimentation, whose focus was to be that of perception. He established psychology as experimental science; initially he dealt primarily with fundamental questions in the Psychology of Perception, the impulse-response sequence, and the speed of reaction. Viewed from these perspectives, human perception is composed of the minutest of units, that is, psychic elements which, through association, are linked with each other to form larger units, that is, "psychic configurations" [*psychische Gebilde*].[33] In psychological research, perceptions were the indivisible basic units – akin to 'psychic atoms' that is, components of perceptions, experience, and action. Wundt was a proponent of a positivist methodology in psychological research: through measuring psychic elements, one would inductively arrive at psychic structures of higher orders.[34] The larger units that Wundt called "psychic structures" differed according to the number of the sensations and associations, that is, primarily in terms of the level of complexity they displayed. However, in contrast to English positivists, who considered perception as passive reaction to external stimuli, Wundt accorded great importance to human consciousness and will, as Danziger shows.[35] Association Psychology as it was still upheld by Wundt, can essentially be traced back to Aristotle.[36] In the early modern age, it was spelled out in detail and elaborated by John Locke, but especially by David Hume in his *Treatise of Human Nature*;[37] it persisted in various modifications right up to the time of early Experimental Psychology. While Wundt's idea of active apperception, of conscious reception, emanated from the German idealist tradition, it was attributed to an English tradition by American psychologists such as Titchener, as well as by Wundt's right-leaning Leipzig suc-

---

31 FAV 4.3.1, Exam Questions in Psychology, November 1922.
32 Tinker 1932: 630.
33 Wundt 1911: 18–28.
34 On Wundt's psychology, see Galikker/Klein/Rykart 2007: 196–209. On Wundts' rejection of applied psychology, see Meischner 2005: 40.
35 Danziger 1980: 78–82.
36 Aristotle 1995: 68–73.
37 Hume 1939: 19–20. Hume bases his epistemological scepticism on this. See also Steminger 1995: 155–56. For a general overview of Association Psychology, see Rohracher 1988: 282–293.

cessors in the circle of Felix Krueger. This deliberate misattribution served especially Krueger in distancing himself from Wundt, and to mark his own approach as a novel one.[38]

While perception had long held centre stage in Experimental Psychology, Wundt categorically declined to investigate the "higher" functions of the psyche, especially the actual processes of thinking going beyond perception and reflex-responses, through experimental methods, as experimental methods could not capture their complexity. He had thus drawn a clear, methodologically founded distinction between perception accessible to experimental investigation and 'higher' forms of mental processes.[39] Thought processes and cultural phenomena emerging from them, such as language, myths, or religion, could not be submitted to laboratory measurements; they could be analysed as complete 'products' only through methods germane to the humanities – which is what Wundt undertook in his inquiries into ethnopsychology [*Völkerpsychologie*].[40] The method he applied in ethnopsychology was an interpretive rather than an empirical one, according to Wallach.[41] In fact, Wundt himself never conducted field research; he assessed travel and research reports of other writers, without submitting the sources to rigorous scrutiny. Thus, Wundt's cultural psychology, especially his ethnopsychology, still displays a marked affinity with Philosophy, as was typical for psychology in Germany in its early stages.[42]

Despite the renown that Wundt enjoyed in Germany and internationally, the work of some of his students began to take different methodological and theoretical directions, even during his lifetime. While *Gestalt* psychologists proceeded to leave behind the theory of psychical elements and structures and thereby paved the way for the development of Cognitive Psychology,[43] Wundt's student Oswald Külpe set out on different paths. He turned toward the very field that Wundt had explicitly designated as inept for experimentation – namely the "higher" mental processes. Külpe who had been appointed professor in Würzburg in 1894, set new tracks, along with his colleague Karl Marbe. Under the name of the "Würzburg School", they embarked on experimental research with the aim of elucidating

---

[38] Guski–Leinwand 2007: 203.
[39] Wundt 1902:29–30; see also Wundt 1911: 127–28 and Meischner–Metge 2006b; and Schulz 2006: 179–183.
[40] Ernst Cassirer's *magnum opus*, *The Philosophy of Symbolic Forms* is largely based on Wundt's work, and develops the latter's ethnopsychology to form part of general philosophy.
[41] Walach 2009: 182.
[42] Thus Dessoir's history of psychology (1911) is founded on philosophy.
[43] Hartmann 1993: 6–7; see also Allport 1923: 612, n. 1.

thought processes.⁴⁴ Instead of reading off the results of higher mental processes from cultural phenomena, as Wundt had done, these processes were to be observed and analysed at the point of their formation.

Wundt took cognisance of Külpe's research with no small degree of apprehension, and all the more so, since Külpe and his colleagues in Würzburg recurred to the method of introspection. Self-observation and reporting on internal mental processes were procedures considered highly problematic by Wundt – and justifiably so, for the person directing the experiment would have to trust in the veracity of the processes reported by the subjects involved in the experiment, and in the adherence to the rule not to alter the findings in retrospect. In fact, introspection did not meet his ideal of a scientific psychology adhering to any degree of precision; too great was the risk that the results could be subjectively distorted.⁴⁵ Only a laboratory-based experimental set-up allowing for the replicability and control of the procedures and results met Wundt's idea of scientificity.

The psychologists of the Würzburg School were fully aware of Wundt's misgivings; they were at pains, especially during the initial period, to formulate the introspective method to allow for as much methodological transparency as possible. Only gradually did Psychology of Thought [*Denkpsychologie*] detach itself from Association Psychology; but subsequently, Psychology of Thought developed a potential for innovation that enabled it to break through the Aristotelian frame.⁴⁶

Gradually, the task became central in the set-up of the experiment, and along with it, inevitably also the willingness of the test subject to solve the task. In the process, the subject can direct his/her thought in a way that would not have come into consideration in Association Psychology.⁴⁷ Külpe himself claimed on behalf

---

44 See the brief overview by Mack (2005).
45 Hammer 1994: 39. A psychologist who resolutely opposed Wundt's methodological distinction between basic and higher-level psychic processes was Karl Bühler (1999a: 226). Narziß Ach, another member of the Würzburg School, intensely engaged with the problematics of introspection, became convinced that it could yield feasible results (Ach 1999: 121). This did not apply to lines of thought arising from the will, though (ibid., 122–125; also 128). Karl Bühler went a step further, in moving the task itself into the centre of his methodological-theoretical considerations, especially since it entailed a division of labour between the person directing the experiment and the test subject, and thereby facilitated methodically reflective introspection (Bühler 1999b: 159, 162–164).
46 While previous experiments conducted by Mayer and Orth within the context of Association Psychology did not pose a task to their test subjects (Mayer/Orth 1999: 69), they did come to the conclusion that conscious processes were not always related to representations – as had hitherto been assumed (Aristotle 1995: 79). But what should not be overlooked is the fact that Max Wertheimer, too, dealt with productive thinking, albeit from the perspectives of *Gestalt* Psychology (Fitzek 1996: 187).
47 Marbe 1999: 86–90.

of the Würzburg School to have demonstrated the imageless nature of thinking in scientifically consequential ways;[48] with this claim, he started the process of divorcing himself from Association Psychology.[49]

Along this path, the Würzburg psychologists discovered a new basic psychic unit – no longer the psychic element in the sense in which Wundt had conceptualised it,[50] but thought itself. In a certain sense, it was the correlate of the *Gestalten* of Berlin-based *Gestalt* Psychology (though the latter remained confined to perception and cognition, not extending to actual thought processes). According to Bühler, decisive for the Würzburg School are the laws[51] determining thinking. The construction of analogies is the fundamental operation of thought; analogies determine the formation of laws.[52]

When Külpe moved to Bonn in 1909, he encountered Otto Selz who studied there at the time. It was Otto Selz who made the actual breakthrough to the Psychology of Thought, with the elaboration of the respective methods, and the interpretation of the research findings. In the course of a number of experiments, he discovered the law-like systematicity of human mental activity, through which he could move beyond Association Psychology. Selz published his research findings in two volumes, the first of which is the thesis he submitted for his habilitation, while the second one (due to World War I) appeared in print only ten years later.[53]

In his experimental set-up, Selz – like most of the other proponents of the Würzburg School – foregrounded the task to be addressed by the test subject. This meant that the person directing the experiment posed a task to the test subject, who then had to address that task, while the time taken to address the task was being measured. The solution to the problem posed in the task was less im-

---

48 Külpe 1999: 47–50. See also Verwoerd's observation claiming that his own thinking was largely imageless (Verwoerd 1924a: footnote in handwriting on p. 238): "This may be related to the fact that images arise for me mostly in connection with emotionally charged contents; they do not arise in connection with experiments *à la* Bühler or with forcibly imposed states of consciousness – in none of these do emotionally charged contents present themselves." However, this is contradicted by others noting that Verwoerd visualised his political conceptions through drawings. Thus, J.J. van Rooyen (1971: 60) remarked: "He liked to expound his thoughts through sketches on pieces of paper [in front of him] on the table. It was as if this [practice] got his thoughts flowing, and made things clearer to his interlocutors." See also Barnard 1967: 33f.
49 Külpe 1999: 53.
50 Bühler 1999b: 181–184.
51 Ibid., 185–187.
52 Ibid., 188. See also Hofstadter/Sander 2014.
53 Selz 1913 and 1922; also Seebohm 1970: 144–45.

portant than the path embarked on in the thought process.⁵⁴ That is why introspection proved to be decisive: the test subjects would report on the internal mental processes in searching for a solution to the problem posed. The tasks posed by Selz show the affinity of the Würzburg School with the procedures of formal logic.

Test subjects would be given the task⁵⁵ to search for a concept that was different from, but could be logically co-ordinated with, a so-called stimulus word, that is, a term designating a concrete object. As a logical co-ordinate, they could choose either a superordinate or a subordinate term, or a semantically correlated term; alternatively, they had to define the stimulus word. Selz distinguished the temporally-spatially more comprehensive⁵⁶ whole [*das Ganze*] from the conceptually more comprehensive superordinate [*das Übergeordnete*], and analogously, the temporally-spatially subordinate (the part) from the conceptually subordinate, respectively. If the given stimulus word was 'tree', the whole would be 'forest' or 'garden', while the superordinate concept would be 'plant'. The part in this example would be 'branch' or the 'leaf', while the subordinate concept would be 'beech tree' or 'fir'. A semantically correlated term would be 'blade of grass'.

From these conceptual elements, Selz formed an increasingly complex theory of thought processes, and of errors in thought, which can be considered among the monuments of psychological research in the first half of the twentieth century.⁵⁷ It was innovative in replacing the notion of thinking as a reactive process occasioned by external stimuli with an explanation that could account for thinking as a process influenced by will and determined by tasks.⁵⁸

Selz replaced the concept of reproduction by that of reaction. On the basis of his empirical research, he concluded that it is not undirected associations that act as stimuli in the brain, but that a reaction is directly and clearly triggered by external stimuli. According to his findings, "an ordered intellectual process represents a closed chain of intellectual operations, the sequence of which is tied to certain definitive triggering conditions, as is the case with partial operations of a composite movement".⁵⁹

---

54 Ter Hark 2003: 469.
55 These tasks and their results are explicated and analysed in detail by Selz in the extensive second section of his book on the psychology of productive thinking and error (1922).
56 According to Selz, thinking processes dealing with the relation of part to whole generate visual representations – which is what distinguishes his conceptualisation from the ideas of the Würzburg School.
57 Humphrey 1951: ch. 5, esp. p. 149. On the impulses of Selz's work for research, see the contributions on musical creativity, on playing chess, and on informatics in Frijda 1983.
58 Selz 1913: 119–122, Seebohm 1971: 3, 7.
59 Selz 1922: ix.

Selz's shift in perspective towards the thinking subject as agent is reflected in his formulations: instead of a 'process', he spoke of an 'operation',[60] since the task required the will for its solution. The stimulus word changed a task formulated in general terms, such as the task to identify the superordinate concept, into the task to identify a *specific* superordinate concept. Thus, the thinking operation became a determinate operation insofar as it was directed toward an aim that, for Selz, was 'cognition'.[61]

The attempt at finding a concrete solution was only possibly by recourse to general principles, that is, laws of thinking.[62] The test subject would schematically anticipate the structure to be completed in analogy to thinking operations proceeding in a similar way.[63] If this method failed, it would move to a different method of finding a solution; Selz analysed such a move in detail and formulated it in terms of the laws of thinking. Schematic anticipation became a pathbreaking method distinguishing his approach from that of Association Psychology for which determinate laws of thinking did not play any role.[64]

This theory allowed Selz to explain errors; on the basis of his experimental series, he could show by way of concrete examples that mistakes always occurred when aspects of anticipation remained ineffective, as would happen in the events of disturbances or distractions.[65] But mistakes did not inevitably lead to failures of experiments; controls in thinking operations could set in that "would, on the basis of reflexive co-ordination, potentially link up with any attempt at a solution, draw attention to contradictions between the task and the solution, and bring about the corresponding correction of the initial solution".[66]

This is how Selz demonstrated that deductive and inductive syllogisms were already inherent in fundamental thinking operations. The Würzburg School did, in fact, manage to bridge the gap between psychology as "the way of knowing the soul" and logic. It could achieve this insofar as it underlined the nonvisual character of thought processes on the one hand, while elaborating the close connection between concrete and abstract aspects, and between particular problematics and generalisable methods on the other. In this way, it could demonstrate the interac-

---

60 Selz 1991b: 139–40; also Seebohm 1970: 82.
61 Selz 1913: 154. See also Verwoerd 1924a: 222.
62 Selz 1913: 69–70.
63 Hofstadter/Sander 2014 showed similar results, albeit through the application of an entirely different methodology.
64 Selz 1924a: 14.
65 Selz 1922: 11, 54–55; Selz 1924a: 15.
66 Selz 1924a: 14; Selz 1913: 261–272; Selz 1922: 606.

tion of individual case and general law, of particular fact and concept formation in the sense of psychic laws.

What pertained to the complementary conception of complexity, that is, to reproductive thinking, applied equally to actual innovative, productive thinking generating new solutions. In this case, too, it entailed a determined thinking operation, as the general method directing the schematic anticipation was known.[67] In the concrete operation, composite solutions tended to be the decisive ones;[68] they would combine methods in a modular way. This procedure resonated with Verwoerd's way of thinking; he considered the idea important for decision-making.[69] In a footnote in his dissertation he referred to a lecture presented by Wilcocks in 1920, indirectly recalling Selz, for whom anticipation was an important step in thinking operations.[70]

Selz emphasised that "the constant lawlike co-ordinations of mental operations and the return of the similar triggering conditions form the precondition for the development and the emergence of new operations and new mental products". He thought of evolution in analogy to basic Darwinist principles; however, cultural development had no *telos* for Selz. Through the methods he elaborated and applied, he brought psychology into close proximity with biology.[71] Karl Popper, who recognised the importance of Selz's work early on, considered it more apt than the experiments of the Berlin *Gestalt* psychologists in the circle of Köhler, who sought to link up with the science of Physics.[72]

While Association Psychology started from the reproduction of representations [*Vorstellungen*], Selz emphasised that a routine actualisation of the problem-solving method [*Mittelaktualisierung*] could yield new 'products', since the tried and tested methods would be applied to ever new materials and would thereby become innovative.[73] Verwoerd's orientation along the lines of Selz's methods is evinced in the notion that emotional sensation was intense when intellectual content was anticipated and actually set in. In cases of mere updating of knowledge [*Kenntnisaktualisierung*], only a weak emotional sensation was registered.[74] Selz's theory could, in fact, explain intellectual progress and learning processes in a way that Association

---

67 Selz 1922: 492.
68 See for instance Selz 1913: 165–66.
69 Verwoerd 1924a: 271, 273.
70 Ibid., 270.
71 Selz 1924a: 31.
72 Popper 1928: 19; Köhler 1927; see also Selz 1991d: 174.
73 Selz 1991c.
74 Verwoerd 1924a: 104–05.

Psychology could not.[75] But what he failed to take up, was the question as to the cultural relativity of his research findings, that is, the question as to whether the intellectual operations described by him were valid only for a specific cultural realm, or whether they were universally valid anthropologically.

Selz had been firmly embedded in the scientific community in Germany – until the Nazi regime forced him into retirement in 1933. As German Jewish scientist, Selz had to flee Nazi Germany. He went into exile in the Netherlands, where he found a few students and followers in the late 1930s. Yet his influence remained confined to German-speaking countries.[76] All the more astonishing is it that he did not only receive attention, but advanced to a leading light in Psychology – and that in Stellenbosch, of all places. This was owed to Wilcock's keen interest in searching for the epistemological foundations of Philosophy in Psychology. This explains the zeal with which he took cognisance of and elaborated the work of the Würzburg School, and especially of Selz. The University of Stellenbosch had one of the first psychological laboratories – a facility with which Wilcocks had become acquainted while in Germany.[77] This allowed him to engage with the research of the Psychology of Thought [*Denkpsychologie*] not only passively, but critically and actively.[78] In a 1925 edition of the *American Journal of Psychology*, he published an essay mounting a comprehensive critique of Külpe, based on his own empirical research.[79]

Selz had deeply impressed Wilcocks – so much so that Wilcocks wrote him a letter dated 26 August 1925 (that is, before Verwoerd's sojourn in Europe), expressing the appreciation and esteem in which he held Selz:

> I would like to take this occasion to express my sincerest thanks and my deep admiration for your great achievements in the field of the Psychology of Thought. I have long held the

---

75 Selz 1922: 682–83.
76 While Selz's theory caused a stir in professional circles, its reception remained limited. The scant reception of his work is undoubtedly owed to his tragic life story. Selz was appointed professor for Philosophy, Psychology, and Educational Theory at the Commercial College of Mannheim, the precursor to the University; between 1929 and 1930, he served as Rector of this institution. Because of his Jewish background, he was forced into retirement in 1933. After a brief period of detention in Dachau concentration camp in 1938, he decided to emigrate to the Netherlands in 1939, where he lived in precarious circumstances. After the German invasion of the Netherlands, Selz was arrested in 1943 and murdered in Auschwitz on 27 August 1943 (Métraux 2005; also Beckmann 2001: 8–17).
77 At this time, when Verwoerd conducted his experiments, it was situated in the Ou Hoofgebou of the University (University of Stellenbosch 1960: 6; see also M. Scholtz 2002: 30; D. J. Kotzé 1966: 475).
78 Wilcocks's terminology clearly reveals his close engagement with Selz's work (Wilcocks 1928b: 51).
79 Wilcocks 1925.

wish to do so, and to let you know that even in this part of the world remote from yours, your work is not only not unknown to, but held in high esteem by, scientists of the Afrikaner people – to whom I belong – at a newly established facility. For many an inspiration in my own research work, I also owe you a debt of deep gratitude.[80]

In 1928, Wilcocks published two further essays in which he engaged intensely and critically with Selz's major works.[81] Among the test subjects in Wilcocks's experiment were J.C. Conradie and Verwoerd, whose introspective reports are cited in Wilcocks's essays. Yet Wilcocks remained within the paradigm of Association Psychology and confused association–psychological arguments with Selz's theoretically completely different approach centred on determined thinking operations.[82]

This is instructive insofar as it significantly elucidates the proximity of Wilcocks's understanding of psychology to that of Verwoerd; in paraphrasing Selz's position in his lectures, Verwoerd, too, remained caught within Association Psychology.[83] Association Psychology was also the framework of Verwoerd's MA dissertation. Verwoerd's disinterest in scientific theories meant that what was novel about Selz's theory escaped him. While the critics, notably Piaget, reproached thought psychologists for neglecting feelings to a large extent,[84] Verwoerd was motivated by his reading of Selz's work to draw a clear distinction between thoughts and feelings, and to probe their interactions in his dissertation.

The Double Task: Verwoerd's MA Dissertation

Verwoerd was inspired by Wilcocks's interest in the Würzburg School's Psychology of Thought. Even though he freely chose the topic for his MA dissertation, the influence of the Psychology of Thought was clearly evinced in the method he applied. However, his argumentation remained within the framework of Association Psychology. At the time, he did not as yet know the second, decisive volume of Selz's pathbreaking study.[85] In his MA dissertation in Psychology, which he submitted in 1922, the 21 year old student dealt with a specific problem situated

---

80 UB Mannheim, Otto Selz Collection, K–019–1, Letter by R. W. Wilcocks to Otto Selz, 26.8.1925.
81 Wilcocks 1928a: 47–50. On Verwoerd's role in the experiment, see ibid., 33; and Wilcocks 1928c: 280, 298, 304, 311–312, 315–316.
82 Wilcocks 1928a: 41.
83 PV 93/3/1/33/4, four-page text of Verwoerd's without title, starting with "The objections of Selz are shattering . . .".
84 Hammer 1994: 73.
85 He was familiar with Selz's book as early as 1925; in a lecture, he discussed Selz's findings in detail; and his thesis, too, contains unmistakable traces of Selz's work.

within the Psychology of Thought, namely that of the double task. In the Introduction, Verwoerd noted that the notion of a task had already been closely investigated. The task was what structured and ordered thinking – with this tenet, he referred to the findings of the Würzburg School. In the choice of his research topic, he started from the observation that everyday life frequently poses dual tasks not reducible to the combined demands of two separate tasks (1).[86]

The choice of this topic points to Verwoerd's interest in applied sciences, underlining the relation of the topic to everyday situations.[87] People continuously encounter double tasks in everyday life, they are ubiquitous, as illustrated by the numerous examples introduced in the beginning. Verwoerd's analysis went beyond thinking processes as conceived of by the Würzburg School: he investigated not primarily the thinking structures, but the problems in solving concrete tasks. That means that he did not conduct basic research in Psychology – as Selz did – but applied research. Verwoerd's research was directed toward results, not so much toward methods. Central to his investigation was the way in which the test persons solved their tasks, rather than the thinking processes underlying the solution, or mobilised in the process of finding the solution (53–78).

In his Introduction, Verwoerd adduced numerous examples from everyday life. Yet he maintained that they served heuristic purposes, showing what was meant by 'the double task', and how exactly the question was posed (6). The double task was not reducible to a general model – at most, there were different weightings between parts of the task. Neither was there a uniform connection between the parts of the task; it depended to a large extent on the solution of the task. To open the entire spectrum of what fell under the definition of a double task, he required thirteen examples in total. He told of a game of checkers with his father, whom he usually beat at this game, but whom he wanted to let win without him noticing. As it turned out, his father did win the game because the son [Hendrik Verwoerd] himself was distracted and therefore made mistakes. Beyond this, he could – in contrast to other games – not remember all the moves; contrary to expectations and intentions the double task made him lose the game.

An artist was intent on painting a beautiful picture, while at the same time representing nature. He tried to bring out the beautiful in nature by idealising it. Thus, he modified the task in order to fulfil a different one. Carrying out a double task was not always successful; in many cases, the person was aware of the task

---

86 The numbers indicated in brackets in this section refer to the pagination of Verwoerd's MA dissertation.
87 This could possibly have been in response to the scepticism with which many of the laboratory experiments were eyed, for reasons of allegedly being out of touch with reality (see Bartlett 1929: 7).

as a whole but fulfilled only a part of it. Verwoerd illustrated his through an example of a man who was not a strong swimmer but was intent on rescuing a child from drowning. At the same time, for the sake of his own family, he was not willing to risk his life. Therefore, he ran to get help (double task), whereas otherwise he would have tried to rescue the child by himself (simple task) (8). There were other cases besides, in which the result did not correspond to either one of the two individual tasks, but only to the double task. This could be due to the fact that tasks were in conflict with one another, even as they were combined in a double task. Mr A was a member of the board of two associations. One of them suggested something that would have harmed the other one, inducing Mr A to try and reconcile the interests of the two associations with each other. He abstained from voting, that is, he did not achieve a result for one of the two tasks, but only for the double task. In this case, it was a matter of a clear conflict of interest – a topic that Verwoerd had to face repeatedly in the course of his political career. At times, this could even entail a 'double bind', that is, two irreconcilable partial tasks which preclude the very possibility of arriving at a solution.[88] It would be impossible, by definition, for an irresolvable conflict to bring about a result. Two persons asked a third one to write a letter in their names. Each one of them addressed the same person, but the two letters made stipulations contrary to each other. The writer composed the letters with the vague sense that they were contradictory and decided to forget about the whole thing. In this case, the contradiction was embedded in the double task itself, which led to a neutralisation of the task (as it was with the person sitting on the board of two associations): the result was that it was forgotten (8f.). However, in other cases, and not infrequently, the double task induces an attempt to reconcile the two partial tasks with each other. At times, one of the partial tasks included the other one, even though it was different; and on occasion, one of the partial tasks was entailed by the other one. This is how one part of the double task could open the way for the realisation of the other one.

While he was professor, Verwoerd wrote some short stories under a pseudonym; they were published in the popular magazine *Die Huisgenoot*. In their construction, they closely resemble the examples 'from everyday life' adduced in his MA dissertations, some of which deal with 'double tasks'. Thus, in one of the stories a young woman comes to grief because she loves a man with whom she could not have children because of a congenital condition – which made her marry another man in order to start a family.[89]

---

[88] Bateson 2011: 276–283.
[89] Gerrie Bruno [Verwoerd], 'Gedoemde liefde', *Die Huisgenoot*, 1.4.1932: 39, 51.

Verwoerd's handwritten Psychology MA dissertation of 164 pages is divided into two parts – an Introduction outlining the problematic to be investigated and a research programme, and a longer main part describing the corresponding experiment and analysing the results. This was Verwoerd's first experiment, for which he could rely on relevant experiences (156), even though he had gathered them in the capacity as a test subject in the experiments conducted in collaboration with his professor Raymond Wilcocks. For Verwoerd, the double task was not simply the simultaneous posing of two different tasks; rather, the two partial tasks were closely connected with one another in such a way that the solution to the one was not possible without the other one. But this also meant that both partial tasks were vying simultaneously for the attention of the test subject, constantly stirring up the inclination to get them mixed up (19).

At times, test persons tried to merge the double task into a single one, which generated errors in reasoning, because they could not actually be reconciled (154). It became clear "that the parts of a double task influence one another, and that errors in reasoning can easily occur insofar as the double task necessarily causes a lack of critical reasoning to a much larger extent than other states of consciousness" (124). It was in the nature of the double task "to make us less capable of judging" (126).

In the second last chapter of his MA dissertation, Verwoerd engaged with Ernst Westphal's reference work on principal and secondary tasks. He had become acquainted with it only after completing his own test series (140).[90] Some of his findings seemed to correspond exactly to those of Westphal, while others showed exactly the opposite. Verwoerd explained this by referring to the difference in the respective problem statements: Westphal investigated tasks subordinated to one another, which is why the secondary task was solved only after the solution to the principal task had been stated. The double task, in contrast, consisted of two single tasks integrally related to each other (72, 140, 142–143): "Through their interrelation the single tasks become organically connected, and lead to an action with a specific structure." (141)

The thinking process was the precondition for the solution of the task. Verwoerd asked about "the role that the double task played in thinking as cause for an action. The thinking process is not directed by the task as such, in the sense of a purely mental operation tackling a question or a problem, for it is directed to an action and therefore directs only those processes of consciousness that are directly or indirectly related to the carrying out of the action." The double task was related to intellectual processes and to the will. But Verwoerd was interested

---

90 Westphal 1911.

above all in the consequences for human action, less in thinking as such. He took up the determining tendencies that the Würzburg psychologists had identified as essential aspects of thinking processes. A task had to be willed, it amounted to nothing other than setting a goal (16–17). The thinking process pertained to considerations toward realising the singular tasks within the framework of the double task; "their direction is determined by the measure of force operating behind each of its parts". Thus, it was a matter of measuring the exertions of will, rather than developing a theory of thinking processes – which corresponded to Verwoerd's pronounced voluntarism.

The actual experiment consisted of two different test series, whereby the initially presented spectrum of what fell under the double task, was reduced to two cases. Verwoerd conducted the experiments with two test subjects (29) whom he designated with the initials R.W. and J.C.[91] His lack of experience manifested itself in the fact that he arranged two entirely different test series. He even explicitly admitted his "complete ignorance as to how such an experimental investigation should be approached, and how the material should be processed and systematised" (156). In the process he used a Ranschburg device, with syllables printed on cards. Technical problems disrupting the process of the experiment frequently led to modifications. Moreover, they caused confusion among the test persons who were frequently distracted, unable to concentrate on complicated tasks. In fact, the set-up he devised for the two test series was overly complex. As a result, the test subjects committed numerous mistakes, which then had to be analysed in an exceedingly laborious process. In writing his résumé, Verwoerd was highly self-critical; he openly identified the weaknesses of the study which were, in fact, evident (157). Nevertheless, there were some observations that seemed to have been important to him. If test subjects reported having thought of the task in visual terms, but without sensory representations, it was a matter of "the type to which this person belonged [!]" (160). The interference of sensory representations was thus to be considered dependent on the person of the test subject, rather than a general problem. While others noticed that Verwoerd represented his thoughts to himself and others through sketches, he personally counted himself among imageless thinkers: "I tend to think abstractly, but to become clear in my own mind and elucidate my thoughts, I have made it a habit to represent my thoughts concretely, as far as possible."[92] In cases where a test subject was aware

---

91 R. W. stands for R. W. Wilcocks, supervisor of his PhD thesis; J.C. stands for J.C. Conradie, a fellow student.
92 "When I . . . heard for the first time that my sister had undergone surgery, I thought of the risks that this posed, and of the hospital, and the anxiety of my parents, and other things. It became clear to me that I wanted to know how things would continue from here . . . and in my

of the task, the task would be executed more expeditiously, more assuredly, and largely without problems. The capacity to pay close attention dispelled anxiety and fear and generated more confidence. It was not the double task itself, but its content and scope that caused difficulties.

The use of meaningless syllables was meant to direct close attention to what was considered essential, namely the correct execution of the double task. Meaningless syllables were supposed to exclude any association with known words and concepts as far as possible; the method can be traced back to German psychologist Hermann Ebbinghaus, who applied it in his investigation of the workings of memory.[93] In the first experimental set-up (Series A), the test subjects had to find words rhyming with meaningless syllables, and invert others so as to be able to read them back to front. This was the first part of the task. The second part of the task consisted in the irregular sequence of rhyme or inversion (21). The test subjects found it difficult to memorise the sequence, which accounts for the fact that most of the mistakes occurred in this particular series. Verwoerd overtaxed the test subjects with the second part of the task; the sequence entailed primarily a test of memory, rather than a test of thinking processes.

The test subjects found Series B less difficult to deal with. This experiment was very similar to the experiments of the Würzburg School, especially the test series that had afforded Otto Selz (in Bonn in 1910) the empirical material for developing his theory of thinking processes. The person conducting the experiment would give the test subject a piece of paper with two words written on it – for instance, Human Being – Socrates. In response, the test subject had to offer one term that was simultaneously subordinate in relation to the first, and superordinate in relation to the second term – for instance, Man – Greek. The test subject was thus given a double task, namely, to find the superordinate term, and the subordinate term, where both parts of the task would have to lead to the same answer. This structure was simultaneously designed as control, for the test sub-

---

mind, I went through the period immediately preceding this situation. I could not come up with any images, and yet I was fully apprised of the whole situation in all details. Later I caught myself out on several occasions thinking about the case, but with waning anxiety; it was not only that I did not register any images, but also that I thought of the situation in vague and much more general terms. I did not actually become fully aware of the anxiety of my parents, the rushed admission to hospital, their own pain, and the risk, etc. (When I did become aware of it and the details appeared in my consciousness, the anxiety returned.) Later, the situation became less personal, in other words, it was as if I thought incidentally that someone was undergoing surgery, with a vague impression that I had something to do with the situation in one way or another." (Verwoerd 1924a: 235, n. and example 236).

93 Boring 1929: 380–381. Verwoerd's experimental set-up clearly resembled that of Narziß Ach, who worked with meaningless syllables in investigating thinking processes (Ach 1999: 128–129).

ject knew that there was an answer that would address both parts of the task, which is why she or he could check the correctness of the concept in both directions (26).

Although the two experiments complemented each other, the discrepancy in the degree of complexity of the tasks was evident from the start. In numerous instances in series A, test subjects found it hard to remember the actual task (32). In the process of introspection, they got bogged down with the difficulties presented by individual syllables in test series A, and therefore neglected the double task (27).

Verwoerd interpreted the results in the context of Association Psychology, whereas the Würzburg School had distanced itself from the fundamental tenets of Association Psychology (including its uptake in the Constellation Theory of G.E. Müller).

> It seems as if contents associated with a specific stimulus word are being reproduced, which do not directly address the task, but indirectly lead to an answer referring to the task, where the latter is immediately recognised as correct by the test subject. It thus seems as if the task is in the background of consciousness and generates a series of reproductions which allow for the recognition of the correct answer as soon as it appears. (77)

After all, the execution of the task is being influenced by feelings; anxiety and insecurity evoked through confusion and other influences could compromise the experiment (102).

Interestingly, Verwoerd presumed the 'unconscious' working of the double task in cases where the task did not command the attention of the test subject and was yet correctly solved (60). He explained this by reference to the determining tendency of the double task, which he did not investigate further. Instead, he elevated attention itself to the central factor. "This shows that under certain circumstances, it is necessary for the double task to occupy an absolutely dominant position; even the slightest distraction of attention can at times be sufficient to impair or diminish the execution of the task." (62) The double task impels the test subjects to immediately proceed to its execution – more so than a simple task would; this is why a test subject would often say something even though he or she knew it to be false (66).

Based on the empirical results of Series B, Verwoerd came to the conclusion that errors in thought in everyday life do not depend so much on whether at issue is a double or a single task, but on the content of the task (67). What often happens in that case, is that one part of the task is predominant in consciousness, even though the task had been consistently approached as a double one; this did not mean, though, that the dominant part of the task would direct the test subject to the correct answers (70). "It therefore seems difficult to keep one's attention directed to a double task as a whole if the latter has several contents where one task differs from another by its respective scope." (71)

Added to the determining tendency was the anticipation of the answer in cases where some prior knowledge was present already.[94] In that case, the answer of the test subject would be checked for its correctness (82); it could easily happen that a false judgement would be followed by further false answers (83). A state of confusion would set in if the task had not been clearly recognised, that is, if one part of the double task had been forgotten (104–105), as in the case where different contents of consciousness were in conflict with each other, rendering the co-ordination of parts of the double task impossible (106), or in the case where related feelings interfered, as for instance anxiety over addressing the task correctly (107). Anxiety and mistrust, in general, had the effect of impeding thinking processes, so that "attention would be wholly engulfed by a wave of feelings while thoughts still attempt to attain validity" (109). Contradictory thoughts alone were not sufficient to create confusion – they would have to be linked with feelings (111).

Towards the end of his dissertation (ch. 9), Verwoerd elaborated on the role of the double task in the process of committing errors in thought and deceiving oneself. Missing or fading attention, as well as prejudices, could lead to errors in thought, to which the double task itself could have contributed if it was too arduous or lengthy. (116–139) Concentrating on one part of the task could mean overlooking minor differences (119). Haste and lack of critical attention to one's own answers could result in mistakes. It must be pointed out, though, that Verwoerd's explanations display a tendency to criticise persons rather than analysing their thinking processes (120–123). Personal judgements become apparent in some of Verwoerd's formulations, for instance: "Here again, the sense of not being able to carry out the task leads to a lack of critical awareness, rendering test subjects incapable of recognising mistakes in their thinking processes and their answers." (123)

Self-deception could be related to unconscious wishes; alternatively, there may have been a confusion of part and subordinate concept, for instance in cases where a preceding task was mistakenly repeated and test subjects deceived themselves about it (137). It is noticeable that Verwoerd drew a clear distinction between mistakes and self-deception, for the latter was only an unacknowledged mistake; here again Verwoerd's tendency to judge the test subjects comes to the

---

[94] Selz 1913: 117–122.

fore. As the previous examples drawn from everyday life had shown, ambiguous situations, in his view, were bound to lead to self-deception.[95]

Verwoerd's MA dissertation showed the influence of Psychology of Thought to which Wilcocks had introduced him. While it motivated him to analyse thinking processes more closely, he always did so with a view to practical applications. All the while, though, his preoccupation with principles overshadowed the double task; indeed, the double task could result in the loss, or the watering-down of principles. Verwoerd's interest in the double task in everyday life, which had motivated his study in the first place, led him to re-affirm hard and fast principles as guidelines for his own thought and action in everyday life, despite the frequent occurrence of double tasks. He underlined this also in discussing the "double task" in a review of the volume on economic conditions that Grosskopf contributed to the Report of the Carnegie Commission.[96]

Verwoerd's Thesis

At the age of 23, Verwoerd obtained his PhD with a thesis supervised by his mentor Raymond Wilcocks at the University of Stellenbosch.[97] His MA dissertation in Philosophy on the problem of values already had a few things to say about the role of feelings, which became the subject and focus of his PhD thesis. In his laboratory investigations, he sought to identify different factors as variables and elucidate their interaction and impact. With more than 300 pages, it was unusually bulky for its time (the 1920s), which is largely due to the fact that it was based on a whole series of experiments whose structure and methodology he outlined in detail and whose results, gleaned from introspection, he documented and cited diligently. Inquiry into feelings had been a prominent theme in Experimental Psychology of the 1920s, and even in the preceding decades. The interest of researchers at the time was directed to the measurability of feelings, as well as the relation of feelings to thinking processes. In the meantime, Verwoerd had also become acquainted with the work of Selz. In engaging with the results demon-

---

95 Even at a much later stage, in 1936, Verwoerd noted that matrons of residences for poor white children shouldered a double task which they did not usually manage to fulfil (Verwoerd 1937b: 96).
96 *Die Burger*, 28.12.1932.
97 FAV 4.3.1., copy of PhD certificate of 10.12.1924. Numbers indicated in brackets in this section refer to the pagination of Verwoerd's PhD manuscript.

strated in that work on several occasions, he adopted Selz's clear separation of feelings from thoughts.[98]

Like his MA dissertation on the double task, Verwoerd started from the everyday observation that emotional sensations fade under certain conditions, to the point of unrecognisability, even though their causes continue to be operative (3). This provides an indication that he was primarily interested in his experiment's applicability to and relevance for everyday life.

The term '*gemoedsaandoening*' that can be translated into English as 'emotional sensation', would first have to be defined. Indeed, in the literature of Verwoerd's time, we do not find generally recognised and clearly defined concepts related to 'emotion', 'emotional sensation', etc. He did distinguish different subcategories, though: in accordance with Alfred Lehmann,[99] he explained sensory reactions by reference to external stimuli and reduced emotional sensations to pleasure and unpleasure [*aangenaamheid en onanangenaamheid*]. He followed Lehmann in differentiating emotional sensations from feelings; for Lehmann, the concept of emotional sensation comprised the entire spectrum of emotions like anger, agitation, etc.[100]

Verwoerd's critical discussion of the state of research reveals his own approach and line of questioning. He reviewed the work of a wide range of authors, mainly US–American and German researchers, and identified problems and gaps in their treatment of the topic (10–15). In a note inserted in handwriting at the end of the chapter, he referred to a study by Kurt Lewin dealing with a similar problematic (76).[101]

---

[98] Selz was not so much concerned with separating emotions from thoughts as with not including emotions in his analysis of thinking processes.

[99] Lehmann 1914.

[100] He did not share the commonly held assumption that there are composite emotions – this notion had already been refuted by Saxinger 1902: 394–398. Wundt himself made some clear distinctions even in his early work (Wundt 1862: 445–451). The intensification or attenuation of emotions on the basis of contrasting perceptions and emotions had been discussed previously by Wirth (1898: 74–81), whose work is mentioned in the bibliography of Verwoerd's thesis. These discussions moved within the framework of Association Psychology (for instance 58, 62); they were rendered obsolete by the insights of *Gestalt* Psychology, which did not hold any interest for Verwoerd.

[101] The reference is to Lewin 1922. Lewin devised methods for generating emotions that were similar to those applied by Verwoerd. Lewin worked for some time at the Institute for Applied Psychology which was an institution independent from the Psychological Institute at the University with Otto Lipmann as director. There is a possibility that Verwoerd may have met him during his sojourn in Berlin.

Emotional sensations arise consequent upon ideas or judgements connected with the mental or material interests of the person concerned. Composite intellectual contents such as jokes, sad stories, etc. trigger emotional sensations in the same way as awareness of an actual event or the memory thereof. Ideas, but also the execution of tasks posed to the person concerned, are accompanied by emotional sensations. In his experiment, Verwoerd considered different circumstances such as these, in order to be able to investigate a wide spectrum of emotional sensations (32–33).

The investigation of feelings under laboratory conditions proved difficult because it had to rely on conditions to be kept constant, to be able to verify and reproduce the experiment. The circumstances and causes of blunting upon repetition, as well as the different conditions, were of interest to him. Emotional sensations get blunted in some instances but not in others – there was no satisfactory explanation for this difference (6–7). To be able to observe this under controlled conditions it is important to work out a reliable method of evoking feelings under laboratory conditions, to reproduce them, and to be able to monitor and measure the blunting effect in this context. The laws of Association Psychology would lead one to expect that emotional sensations would, upon repetition, occur with equal or heightened intensity, and not be subject to blunting (6). Verwoerd was intent on keeping the circumstances triggering emotional sensations constant, in order to be able to locate variables he called blunting factors. However, his searches started from an unstated presupposition: the cause for blunting was not so much to be sought within the sensations themselves, but in factors in the environment that could be manipulated in corresponding ways. It was only on this condition that an experimental situation could be set up, since the psychological experiment was based on manipulable conditions. This explains why Verwoerd's contemporaries considered him a behavourist.[102]

The 'constancy in surrounding stimuli' was the invariant necessary for measuring and assessing the variables (36). The stimulus was triggered by a particular element in consciousness, through which the test subject would become aware of a certain event or goal. A circumstance of a stimulus was defined by him as a "circumstance or event that, in becoming conscious, would act as causative antecedent for the emotional sensation" (36). Awareness of the circumstance of a stimulus would have to be present for an emotional sensation to arise (35). There were cases in which the person was conscious of the identical object or event, and the surrounding conditions were constant, but the emotional sensation was less intense, or did not arise at all. This was a case of blunted emotional sensation

---

[102] I. L. de Villiers 2009: 132.

(37). The question arose as to which disrupting factors were counteracting the emergence of emotional sensations in cases where the circumstance of the stimulus was present and the triggering of an emotional sensation could therefore be expected. Verwoerd did observe that an emotional stirring, once blunted, could recur in intensified form at a later stage (40).[103]

Verwoerd engaged with these questions and experiments between 16 April and 16 November 1923. Every one of the test subjects was involved in the execution of this experiment – twice a week over a period of four to five months in total. Every session lasted between 30 and 45 minutes, and was carried out in regular intervals – meaning that there were breaks of three to five days between the experiments for the respective test subjects who were instructed not to think about the experiment during the intervening periods (48). Similarly to his MA dissertation, the PhD thesis took up the issue of introspection under experimental conditions. Introspection and the corresponding reports by test subjects were measured with a stop watch. Test subjects were instructed to concentrate on their emotional sensations and the attendant intellectual contents during the process of introspection and reporting (47). In total, there were five different experiments designed to investigate emotional sensations according to function, content, memory, and experience (46).

In Series 1, the person directing the experiment instructed test subjects to transpose themselves into particular emotional states – such as rage, shame, anger, and contentment (50). Test subjects were to think of the constancy of surrounding stimuli that was supposed to generate the respective emotional state; after 10–15 seconds, introspection was to follow. Some test subjects were presented with the stimulus words in the same sequence, others in alternating albeit previously determined sequence. The number of repetitions of the stimulus words was found to be sufficient to register a blunting effect with simultaneous awareness of the constancy in surrounding stimuli (50).

Verwoerd noted critically, that the person directing the experiment had too little control; whether the stimulus word always appeared in the same context was not clear (51). Still, Series 1 was important for purposes of preparation, and of directing attention to different emotional sensations, that is, it had primarily heuristic function. In Series 2, test subjects were given certain words that created constant surrounding stimuli in their minds. Test subjects were then asked which emotional sensation the subsequent word evoked (53). Conditions remained constant due to the fact that the stimulus words always followed the same sequence;

---

[103] This is what had occupied him even in his MA dissertation on the topic of values (Verwoerd 1922b: 50).

only occasionally a new word was inserted so as not to make the expectations all-too predictable.

In Series 3, the person directing the experiment repeatedly read out jokes aloud. "The jokes were of average quality and evoked emotional sensations of average intensity. Some particularly vulgar jokes were inserted in order to cause the test subject to develop a sense of shame in sympathy with the person directing the experiment – a phenomenon also observed in everyday life." (56) Due to manifold intellectual contents, the emotional sensations turned out rather weak. The long duration of the introspective phase, and the high number of intellectual contents had an adverse effect on the introspection. What was noted positively, however, was the fact that "it is possible to recognise a natural, albeit complex process under experimental conditions" (57).

In Series 4, test subjects were enjoined to solve the same problem over and over again – or rather, the contents varied, but the method of the solution to the problem remained the same (57); alternatively someone was repeatedly presented with the same problem in order to repeatedly come up with the same solution. In this case, the conditions changed because the solution did not take long to figure out (58). The person directing the experiment would emphatically assess the results as correct or incorrect (58). If test subjects failed in providing the solution, they were told the correct answer, so that they could state the latter upon repetition of the same task; in this case, failure was frequently programmed into the exercise by the person directing the experiment (59). The anticipated emotional sensations were rage and disappointment. They proved to be explicit and intense because test subjects were keen to find the solution. The experiment was useful for investigating blunting effects, even if the person directing the experiment found it hard to control it, and did not always receive the required information about important aspects of introspection. In a simple procedure, this test series produced emotional sensations typical of everyday life and the results were deemed important in many instances.

The last series was the most complex one, and was conducted with laboratory devices then available. Verwoerd utilised the possibilities offered to him by the psychological laboratory (60) established by Wilcocks in today's 'Ou Hoofgebou' in Stellenbosch. In the process, he reverted to procedures that had previously featured in his MA dissertation, and were frequently used by psychologists at the time. In this case, the tasks were experimentally produced by a Ranschburg device displaying colour cards (or senseless syllables) in different sequences and combinations in rapid succession. Verwoerd wanted to make sure that the experiment would proceed as smoothly as possible; this meant that test subjects had to concentrate on the coloured discs. If the disc had skipped, test subjects would have responded by activating the reaction key (that is, a switch). The person directing the experiment would then assess whether the reaction was correct or incorrect, and the phase of introspection would follow. The sequential presentation of discs was aimed at allowing test subjects to render correct answers, and to create the impression of having performed well in fulfilling the task. This impression was created because of in-built sources of error, which were yet recognisable as such by the test subject. This way, the test subject could conclude that she or he had successfully managed to bypass 'traps', which in turn generated an elated feeling of satisfaction. After a few repetitions of the exercise, however, this emotional sensation became blunted (64).

Test subjects had to fulfil a particular task, which to a large extent entailed reaction tasks. But emotional sensations were evoked through the addition of various external conditions, for instance sanction by punishment in cases where the task was not executed correctly. This is what evoked intense emotional sensations that could be observed to become blunted with repetition.

Another task with coloured discs consisted in making test subject react upon particular colour combinations. The combination appeared regularly, thus lulling the test subject in the expectation of reliability, only to surprise her or him with a false combination (65). An emotional sensation of satisfaction upon a reaction judged "correct", and of disappointment upon a reaction judged "incorrect" could be registered; and in this case, too, repetition produced blunting effects.

In a further series within the experiment, test subjects would be informed that a certain sequence of colours would incur punishment, even though they themselves did not have to respond to anything; thus, test subjects were given to understand that they could not, on their own accord, either cause or prevent the punishment (67). In this way, fear and anxiety were to be generated. The process of introspection was to follow immediately, since the feeling of fear subsided as soon as test subjects felt that they had managed to survive the punishment. A similar sense of relief was noted when a lighter punishment followed upon a couple of severe punishments (67). In a further series involving colour combinations, a trap had been set, for one colour combination, marked as an incorrect one, had followed upon a correct one (68). In a further variant, the person directing the experiment was punished for a mistake committed by the test subject through the administration of an electric current. Compassion for the innocent person directing the experiment, as it had been evoked in other experiments, soon became blunted (69). The aim of the experimental set–up was not to find the correct solution, but to generate and measure various feelings within the parameters of the experiment.

The laboratory experiment consisted of a considerable number of test series; according to Verwoerd, it fulfilled the requirements for a good psychological experiment (73). It proved successful insofar as it managed to evoke different emotional sensations even after the test subjects had found out about the purpose of the experiment. Through the use of senseless material, concrete intellectual contents could be excluded to a large extent. "Apart from that, the person directing the experiment could, by and large, control even the conscious processes attendant upon emotional sensations, by means of the deliberate deployment of senseless materials, and by means of the task, and of punishment." (74) Having learnt from his own experiment that the results achieved by means of the Ranschburg device were valid, as opposed to others that were less trustworthy, Verwoerd convinced himself of the advantages of such devices. This explains why, during his visit to Germany, he was rather disparaging about the tendency to opt for "paper and pencil" tests or to trust the intuition of psychologists, while heaping praise on studies making use of measuring devices.[104]

In his assessment, Verwoerd developed a comprehensive case study method, testing the different variables in ever new combinations with a view to finding out about the blunting effect to which they were subject. He could assess their significance on the basis of experimentally generated data. The question he posed in the Introduction, as to whether any general rules could be found that would explain differences in the pace of blunting, was answered in the negative, as there were too many different factors involved, and therefore the results were too variegated. Other factors to be considered were differences in temperament between different persons (208–209). In a remarkable Conclusion, circular albeit tentatively formulated, Verwoerd stated: "An analysis of the absence or presence of these blunting factors indicates causes for the intensification or blunting of the respective emotional sensation" (310). In other words, the blunting factors were the causes of the blunting.

Interpreting his findings, he started with the constant of surrounding stimuli and their impact on the process of blunting. Initially, he found that the resulting awareness turned out differently, without, however, considering the question, if there were constant surrounding stimuli in the first place (77). If this were not to be the case, one of the central premises would be in question, namely that this would not be a matter of a fixed measure for the assessment of other factors, but of an additional variable. Blunting was said to occur when an emotional sensation became attenuated due to diminished awareness of the constant surrounding stimuli. Verwoerd adduced a telling example from everyday life in South Africa:

> Upon the first setting of the stimulus word, the test subject D. . . . thought of a [black worker] making trouble on his parents' farm. This caused quite a strong reaction of anger.

---

[104] FAV 4.3.2, Diary of the trip, entry on the Winter Semester 1926/27. See also Ash 2005: 100.

He noticed that he was tensing his jaw bones, that he was blushing, and that his chest was tightening. When he was given the set word for the third time, he only vaguely thought of the [black worker], and retained only a dim memory of the circumstances that had previously been the focus of his attention. No strong anger arose. (78)

Intellectually multifaceted contents tended to be consciously retained; but when these contents no longer displayed variation, the emotional sensation became blunted (80). The same applied to books, but in this case Verwoerd obviously spoke of his own experience in mentioning Aristotle's *Ethics*, whose multifaceted contents could sustain a sense of enjoyment. If, however, scholarly work was only mechanically executed, the surrounding stimuli were not consciously registered to the same degree (81). Verwoerd referred to the observation by Ebbinghaus that known objects do not attract the same attention as new things. If the surrounding stimuli are sufficiently familiar not to be consciously recognised, blunting is more likely to take effect (82). The law of attention to distinction[105] formulated by Selz explains why the new or unknown often attracts attention. It means that feelings depend on new stimuli and impressions, which is what holds implications for the psychology of advertising, and for Verwoerd's later propaganda methods.

The idea that disciplining contributes to blunting of feelings was clearly significant for Verwoerd: in this view, habituation to surrounding stimuli leads to attenuation of intellectual engagement and along with it, of emotional sensation (231). The tension attendant upon decisions, in contrast, was favourable to the emergence of emotional sensations (272). Correspondingly, the attenuation or disappearance of a decision resulted in a blunting of emotional sensation (274–275). "An emotional sensation thus gets blunted as soon as the tension is diminished, provided that emotional sensation depends on tension." (278)

What could stabilise emotional sensation, apart from intellectual contents, was a general mental attitude [*geestesstelling*] (99). "There are certain persons who rather consistently think along the same lines and in the same way. Insofar as their emotional sensations are determined by their mental attitudes, they will not become subject to blunting." (100) This was an instructive pointer to the influence of character on emotionality.

In the subsequent chapter, Verwoerd turned to the theme of reproduction and blunting – that is, to situations in which only what was previously known, and nothing new, was registered. This could occur in three ways: either as direct experience of a reproduction, or as memory of an experience, or as imagined event related to dispositions and associations (106). Accordingly, routinisation meant diminished feelings: "In actual fact, all cases of habituation or familiarisa-

---

[105] Selz 1922: 495–496.

tion, as well as mechanical actions that involve blunting effects, are cases of associations and dispositions that are newly developing, or of existing associations and dispositions that are being reinforced." (110)

Contents could influence emotional sensations, including (in most cases) value judgements (167). Judgements would, in most cases, arise spontaneously, and exercise a strong influence on emotional sensations, but only where it was a matter of a strongly held conviction (168). "The emotional sensation apparently is all the more intense, the more clear and decisive the judgement is." (171) Convictions or doubts making themselves felt in the process were more important than the truth of the judgement, while the absence of value judgements was deemed to contribute to blunting (174).

How does this investigation relate to Verwoerd's later political activity? Can any connections be drawn at all? If so, is it a matter of direct or indirect connections, major or subsidiary ones? The electrical current, which Verwoerd imposed on himself and his test subjects as 'punishment', would appear at first sight as hallmark of an authoritarian temperament; they point to some horrifying practices in South African psychiatry under apartheid.[106] Yet the references to such practices tend to pick up issues on the side lines; they do not get to the crux of the matter.[107] The literature does not tire of noting the title of Verwoerd's thesis, but never bothers to examine what it actually meant for his politics. This can be taken to indicate that no one has bothered to actually read the thesis and to probe its references and links to broader debates and political–ideological contexts. Interpreting the blunting of emotional sensations as part of an experiment in dulling human feelings for purposes of heightened exploitation of human labour power, would be absurd. Moreover, there are no indications that Verwoerd ever reverted to such considerations. Miller maintains that Verwoerd's writings showed a visible improvement after his sojourn in Germany, whereas the thesis was "unsophisticated". It is important to note though, that Miller refers to only one article published at a later stage in the *American Journal of Psychology*, which presents only an excerpt from the thesis.[108]

More explicit in this respect are the statements made at a later stage, in which Verwoerd expresses concern about boxing matches among whites watched by blacks "whose respect for whites diminishes or becomes blunted in matches in which whites participate. This may have a deep and dangerous impact on their minds."[109] Moreover, he frowned upon the sympathy of "liberalists" with banned

---

[106] Lambley 1981, ch. 3; see also Kistner 2014: 90–96; and Swartz 2008.
[107] That applies especially to Truscott/Smith 2016.
[108] R. B. Miller 1993: 638–39.
[109] PV 276/I/27/8/1, Letter by Verwoerd to C. R. Swart (Minister of Justice), 16.6.1956.

persons, whom they visit at the sites to which the banning orders restrict them. Simultaneously assuaging his misgivings, he presumed that "this interest will subside after a short time, as it happened in other contexts."[110]

In his research, Verwoerd did not only separate feelings and thoughts to be able to measure them, respectively; he understood them to be contrary to each other, since intellectual activity could lead to blunting of feelings for as long as it did not consider their causes – namely, the surrounding stimuli.[111] Yet he could not establish a clear connection in the sense that an increase in thoughtful activity would lead to a corresponding decrease in feelings. An important additional consideration concerned the temporal factor in the blunting *qua* process. To Verwoerd, this was decisive, since his research – from which he drew key insights for his political actions – had opened his eyes to the inconsistency and unreliability of feelings. However, Verwoerd made the mistake common among scientists of the time: through their definitions, classifications, and delimitations, they created entities of their design, as if they were objective givens.[112] Only if one believes that thoughts and feelings are clearly distinguishable, can one treat them as opposites, as Verwoerd did. Seeing that his academic teacher Wilcocks had studied with Carl Stumpf, it was possibly Stumpf's indirect influence that had led Verwoerd to treat intellectual and affective states as being fundamentally different.[113] But actually his research was aimed at the verification of certain previously determined fundamental presuppositions stipulating that feelings were different from thoughts and could be categorically distinguished from each other. The holistic psychologists of the Leipzig School around Felix Krueger were presumably more versatile in this respect, their fuzzy terminology notwithstanding: instead of separating feelings and thoughts, they stipulated diffuse complex qualities.[114]

---

110 FAV 4.6.1.3, Letter by Verwoerd to J.F. Malan, Vryburg Farmers' Union, 5.9.1956.
111 The distinction appears earlier, in his MA Dissertation on the topic of values: "Feeling as emotion can initially be considered as value judgement, but it is actually an effect produced not by the conscious self, but by the organism or the unconscious part of the mind." (Verwoerd 1922b: 55).
112 For an analogous case in racial science, see Etzemüller 2015a: ch. 17.
113 Reisenzein 2003: 106; see also 108. In his PhD thesis, Verwoerd leaned heavily on Lehmann, whose approach was entirely different from that of Stumpf (Verwoerd 1924a: 122).
114 Krueger 1926: 118ff; Krueger 1953b and 1967. Instead of *Gestalten*, Krueger defined primary perceptual phenomena as "complex qualities" – diffuse, quasi–multidimensional perceptions. Research interest was directed to these "complex qualities" within which rational thoughts were thought to take place. But the Leipzig School did not develop a clear research strategy. Only the blunting of feelings was considered experimentally demonstratable (Krueger 1931: 22). It stands to reason that this idea could have arisen in a conversation with Verwoerd.

Verwoerd consistently refrained from demagoguery targeting feelings; it was clear to him that this would not make for sustainable mobilisation. All the observations on Verwoerd as orator are unanimous in noting that he was always eager to present a logically watertight argument. He argued instead of whipping up emotions. "He is no orator, and yet he has a compulsive, persuasive way of talking. His power comes from the unshakeable conviction that he is doing the right thing for everyone."[115] In a speech advocating the Republic, Verwoerd made this explicit: "To achieve unity in South Africa there must be a republic. But also to solve our colour problems, there has to be a republic. The reason for this is the following: I am trying to play on your reasoning powers not on your emotions."[116] This is what quite accurately describes the form of his political argumentation, which was geared toward logical closure. As late as 1959, he professed to his opponent L.J. du Plessis that he had decided "to put all personal feelings aside and only to live and work for the best of our *volk*".[117] From this, he even derived certain essential leadership qualities: "We will not allow reason to abandon us, for a leader concerned about his people [*volk*] cannot govern if driven by emotions or resentment."[118] His distrust of emotional stirrings and their fickleness had an empirical basis in the findings he had presented in his thesis. "He would not allow himself to be guided by feelings. Powerful surges of popular sentiment were suspect to him."[119] In an obituary, Verwoerd praised J.G. Strijdom's rational and considered ways, contrasting him with "Mr Werth, man of genteel sensibility", who was inclined to give in to momentary feelings. "Advocate Strijdom and others were fully occupied with appeasing him, until his sober judgement could reassert itself."[120]

Feelings attended by values and ideals were something else, but these had been excluded from Verwoerd's investigation. His philosophical MA dissertation attests to the fact that he could positively acknowledge these.[121] His commitment to the nation was heartfelt and his speeches invoking national values were full of pathos.

Feelings could be manipulated, as Verwoerd's experiments had amply shown. After all, his discovery that it was possible to artificially generate feelings under

---

115 Pearson Phillips, 'When I Saw Verwoerd's Smile', *Daily Mail*, 8.3.1961.
116 Verwoerd, Speech at Meyerton, Transvaal, 26 March 1960 (in Pelzer 1966: 374–387, 383).
117 PV 93/3/1/24 f. 81, Letter by Verwoerd to du Plessis, 6 August 1959.
118 Qtd. in G. D. Scholtz 1974, vol. 2: 149.
119 W.J. Verwoerd 1990: 7.
120 FAV 4.6.2.3, Verwoerd, Huldeblyk aan adv. J.G. Strijdom, p. 2. The name of Werth refers to the NP politician A. J. Werth (1880–1948).
121 Verwoerd 1922b: 44–49.

controlled laboratory conditions was sufficiently important to impel him to repeat it 1926 in Leipzig with more modern equipment and different lines of questioning; he announced his findings in English to an international audience.[122]

Not only feelings could be manipulated, but also thoughts. The shrewd manner in which Verwoerd anticipated the thoughts of his test subjects and integrated them into his test series indicates that it was not only feelings that he deemed manipulable.

It is noteworthy that these considerations were not affected by racial differentiations; at this stage, Verwoerd had no intention to manipulate the black section of the population in any particular way. In accordance with the views of racial theorists like J.D.J. Hofmeyr, he assumed that they were in any case primarily governed by affect, and therefore easily manipulable. He did not consider them endowed with rational capacity and intellectual contents that were separable from attendant emotional sensations through blunting. That is why he accorded University apartheid a prophylactic function guarding against what would otherwise become an increasingly attenuated "aversion to miscegenation"[123] presumed inherent to black students. In this view, blacks were considered to be dominated by emotional surges potentially triggering uncontrolled violence. Unrest was blamed on whites opposing apartheid, who accused the government of "dishonesty and injustice"; this was bound to "leave an impression on the mind of the natives".[124] Verwoerd considered whites to be civilised and therefore amenable to logical thinking, while he saw blacks as following their feelings in uncontrolled ways. He attributed the capacity to separate feelings and thoughts to the white population; but he did not want to present the latter as insensitive to the suffering of others. He considered whites civilised and thereby amenable to rational arguments. On the basis of the parallelism of child psychology and ethnopsychology and their combination in developmental psychology, we can surmise how he viewed the black population when he drew a connection between overly intense emotionality and proneness to youth criminality.[125] In his speeches, Verwoerd repeatedly and emphatically stated that in interactions between individuals and peoples, it would be best to "let them speak themselves", rather than "letting their emotions speak for them". He went as far as stipulating this as a principle: "What

---

[122] Verwoerd 1926: 371.
[123] Qtd. in G. D. Scholtz 1974, vol. 2: 142.
[124] Qtd. in ibid., 128.
[125] 231/2/3 Socio-psigologie van misdaad, 41. See also ibid., 43, where Verwoerd finds that a successfully completed action brings emotional satisfaction, which in turn leads to the repetition of the action.

is important is not the wish of your feeling, but that which your understanding tells you is in the best interest of South Africa."[126]

From Verwoerd's academic activities, we can discern many links to the political pathways he embarked on at a later stage; this pertains to both the contents characterised by an orientation toward 'community', and his approach in general, especially his insistence on the separation of logical reasoning and feelings, which is what distinguished the form of his propaganda from sheer demagoguery.

---

[126] FAV 4.7.2.4.5, Transcript of a speech in Florida 1963, p. 1, second quote p. 8.

Trajectories

Post-Doctoral Studies in Germany

After the successful completion of this PhD (1924), Verwoerd obtained a scholarship and spent a period of three semesters in Germany (1926/27), and cut short to three months (October to December 1927) in the US. Upon his return to South Africa, he started his academic teaching career in January 1928, with an appointment in a newly created professorship for Applied Psychology and Psychotechnics at his *alma mater*.[1] The main purpose of his sojourn in Germany was to find out about the most recent developments in international psychology, as he had long held ambitions for an academic career. From his diary (which has been preserved) documenting his experiences in Leipzig and Hamburg at the time, it becomes clear that his interest was almost exclusively focused on applied psychology.[2] In Germany this field of research, also known as Psychotechnics, experienced a boom after World War I, when psychological criteria were applied on a large scale, in processes of qualitative changes to workplace organisation, and hiring of employees selected on the basis of psychological assessments.[3] That is why it was not coincidental that Verwoerd chose institutions in Germany to further his studies. His publications, too, reflected this interest, dealing, as they did, specifically with job

---

[1] P. S. du Toit 1966c: 81. A pamphlet of the NP in 1958 claimed that Verwoerd had spent time studying in England (M. P. A. Malan 1958: 1045) – possibly an attempt to woo English-speaking voters.

[2] R.B. Miller (1993: 639) maintains that German psychology had "traditionally" focused on basic research, without noticing that German and American psychology were similar in their applied approach. Moreover, she relies on anachronistic literature from 1966. She argues that after the "extent of these visits" to American research institutions, "it is possible that some of Verwoerd's growing statistical sophistication came from his American rather than his German experience" (640). But Verwoerd spent one and a half years in Germany and hardly three months in the US, where he paid only brief visits to the research institutions. Even for "statistical sophistication" no evidence of any kind is being provided. The fact that theoretical works published in the German language did not leave any traces in Verwoerd's thought was owed to his anti–theoretical stance; it does not demonstrate that his stay in Germany was less formative for him and his understanding of scientificity than the cursory visits to American laboratories. On the differences between German and American psychology, viewed from perspectives of the sociology of knowledge, see Danziger 1979: 34–38.

[3] On Psychotechnics and its initial stages, see Killen 2007: 50; also Schönpflug 2004: 388–392.; and Moede 1920: 307–08. On the military background, see also Rothe 2013: 2–5. As early as 1929, Felix Krueger thought that Psychotechnics was becoming "overly widespread" (Krueger 1929b: 158). On the interest that it garnered in South Africa, see Livie–Noble 1922: 448.

aptitude testing.[4] The value of introspection whose importance for the psychology of thinking and feeling he had explicitly highlighted, applied also to the psychology of advertising – or so he thought.[5] With respect to his further career, the influences of basic psychological research and theory formation are equally noteworthy. In his own lectures from 1928 onwards, he also dealt with the fundamentals of Cognitive Psychology as he had become acquainted with it in Germany.

The claim that Verwoerd was politically influenced during his sojourn in Germany has been in circulation for a long time. As early as 13.8.1958, an article in the *Cape Times* speculated: "He is bringing to South Africa authoritarian philosophy which led Germany and Italy to ruin."[6] Possibly still under the influence of South African propaganda during World War II, some writers were quick to seek the origins of apartheid in Germany.[7] Sociologist Dunbar Moodie developed this supposition into a coherent argument. In his book *The Rise of Afrikanerdom*, he put forward the idea that quite a number of young Afrikaans-speaking intellectuals had studied in Germany in the 1930s, and had been contaminated with what he called neo-Fichteanism, that is, a radical nationalism attributed to the philosopher Johann Gottlieb Fichte. Among them he explicitly counted Verwoerd. However, he failed to empirically prove this influence, which did not prevent generations of historians from taking over this claim without question.[8] No evidence for Moodie's contention can be found, because the sources are telling only about Verwoerd's academic interests, leaving a blank as far as his political activities, discussions or readings are concerned. It is remarkable that authors analysing nationalism are themselves constructing national categories such as the 'German' influence, rather than questioning them. This is what accounts for the fact that numerous studies on this subject remain caught in the immanence of their own approaches.

Verwoerd spent one semester each at the Psychological Institutes of three German universities – Leipzig (20 April to 26 July 1926), Hamburg (23 October 1926 to 18 February 1927), and Berlin (28 April to 8 August 1927). He was drawn to these universities primarily because they specialised in applied psychological research.[9] At the same time, he visited numerous non-university institutions in Berlin and in

---

4 Verwoerd 1928a: 508–09.
5 Verwoerd 1928c: 469–70.
6 Qtd. in *Skietgoed* 3, 1958/59, 30.9.1958, 1046.
7 For instance with regard to the education system (Tabata 1980: 34, 40): "Dr Verwoerd seems to have steeped himself, nay, soaked and nourished himself in the spiritual cultural stuff of National Socialist education."
8 T.D. Moodie 1975: 154; see also Furlong 1991: 80. On the uptake of this idea, see also Terreblanche 2012: 301. Similar insinuations were circulating even earlier (Troup 1975: 318).
9 For an overview of Applied Psychology (Psychotechnics) during the period after World War I in Germany, see Geuter 1988: 88–99.

the Netherlands, which developed and conducted aptitude tests.[10] It is noteworthy that Eugen Fischer's Kaiser-Wilhelm Institute for Anthropology, Human Genetics and Eugenics was not among them, considering that its Division for the Psychology of Heredity was established only in 1935.[11]

At the beginning of his stay in Germany, even before venturing to Leipzig, Verwoerd attended lectures (between January and March 1926, during the Winter Semester of that year) by Professor Moede at the Technical College and the Business College (today's Technical University) in Berlin-Charlottenburg on 'aptitude tests and career analysis', as well as industrial and advertising psychology.[12] Apart from that, he attended – as observer – laboratory practicals in Applied Psychology, for instance an aptitude test administered to 15 year old apprentices in the metal industry; on this occasion, he familiarised himself with the specialised testing equipment.[13]

Moreover, he encountered humanities-based Psychology in two courses on Child Psychology presented by Eduard Spranger at the Friedrich Wilhelm University in Berlin.[14] At the Charité (on 27.2.1926), he visited the ward for psychopathic children. Specially trained observers were instructed to diagnose the condition of the children, to then decide on forms of therapy to be applied by the parents. Between 2 and 6 March 1926, he looked in on vocational aptitude testing for artisans and workers carried out at the testing centre in the Prussian Employment Office in Berlin. He found that the young test subjects were being treated too severely and "in too schoolmarmish a manner", "with threats of being sent home when not sitting still". He was similarly critical of the actual testing methods which risked fostering "routinised perception"; to counter these, he advocated "psychologically trained insight", especially seeing that persons directing the experiment were "more prone to rely on quantitative data than they would like to admit".[15] Before venturing to Leipzig, he paid a visit to Amsterdam, the city of his birth

---

10 He also participated in the 8th International Psychological Congress in Groningen, and obtained a report on a hypnosis experiment conducted during the Congress (Van Loon/Thouless 1926). He is supposed to have also visited his relatives in the Netherlands during this time (Terblanche 2001a: 231).
11 On the focus on typological characterology, see Ash 2003: 215.
12 FAV 4.3.2, *Curriculum vitae* handwritten in German. Verwoerd's travel document contains an official registration in Leipzig dated 17. (or 7.) 5.1926. On Moede, see Geuter/Hagemeier/Ash 1986: 19.
13 FAV 4.3.2, Verwoerd's Diary on his studies 1926/7, pp. 1–2.
14 Ibid. On Moede, see also Eckhardt 1998: 26–27.
15 FAV 4.3.2, Verwoerd's Diary on his studies 1926/7, pp. 3–5. During the summer of 1927, Verwoerd and his wife, together with a professor who unfortunately is not mentioned by name, visited a prison, in order to take a look at inmates of the ward for the mentally ill (FAV 4.3.2, Letter by E. Verwoerd to her parents and sisters, 6.7.1927).

(12 April 1926). Having been taken around the Municipal Psychology Laboratory of Dr G. van Wagenburg, he showed himself impressed by its modern equipment. Three days later, he visited the psychotechnical laboratory of Dr F. J. Brugmans, which was equipped with several devices of a kind that Verwoerd had not previously encountered – similarly to the laboratory of the University, which he also visited. Brugmans invited him to an international Psychology congress in Groningen, in which he actually participated in September 1926.[16]

In the 1920s, the discipline of Psychology found itself in murky waters. It was a time of basic research which generated new approaches and explanations; and new schools of thought emerged, which were competing with each other. The intense competition in basic research turned out to be conducive to innovation, with the elaboration of scientific paradigms. During this time, Cognitive Psychology developed its most advanced form, namely *Gestalt* Psychology, whose academic home was the University of Berlin.[17] At the same time, Applied Psychology, at the time also known as Psychotechnics, became an independent sub-discipline without, however relinquishing its links with basic research.[18] Numerous psychological institutes worked with both, even if they were separated institutionally through the establishment of an independent division of Applied Psychology, as it happened in Berlin.[19] Numerous researchers were active in both branches of Psychology. Probably the most prominent and productive scientist embracing both branches was William Stern in Hamburg, with whom Verwoerd studied for one semester.

In Leipzig, Verwoerd got to know the biggest and oldest psychological institute. "For tutorials on psychopathological or ethno-, social- and cultural psychological topics, specially trained teaching staff are being deployed on a regular basis – that

---

[16] PV 93/1/11/7, Letter by Dr Robert H. Thouless, Corpus Christi College, Cambridge, to Verwoerd, 9.9.58. Thouless introduced himself as a psychologist who had made the acquaintance of Verwoerd in Groningen. "I have since followed your political career with interest – not, of course, always with complete agreement. You are, I think, the first psychologist to have become a Prime Minister and that is a matter for congratulation. I have always believed that those trained in scientific psychology have something to give the world of affairs in the way of a wiser and more understanding organisation of international affairs, and I look forward to seeing your contribution as a psychologist to international understanding."
[17] Ash 1998: 2, 11–12, 60, 198; see also Metzger 1970; Metzger 1986: 101–105; and Sprung 2005. Leichtman (1979: 57–60) makes the point that *Gestalt* Psychology opposed positivism.
[18] See the brief overview in Chestnut 1972: 781, among other things on the Institute at the Technical University in Charlottenburg, where Verwoerd initially studied with Moede.
[19] Frensch/Krause/Wandke/Zimmer/Markner/Franke 2000: 8.

is, medical doctors, ethnologists, religious studies scholars, and others."[20] That is what accounts for the fact that Verwoerd's attendance registers also contain names of scientists who did not hold lectureships at the Institute for Psychology. Thus, he participated in two tutorials conducted by Prof Richard Pfeifer (1877–1957) who had obtained a doctorate in Medicine as well as in Psychology, and conducted tutorials in his capacity as psychiatrist, on 'The psychopathology of the child and the young adult', and on 'Psychological Therapy and Hypnosis'. In addition, he attended the tutorials of legal scholar Prof Franz Exner (1881–1947) on 'Basic Principles of Criminal Psychology', as well as those of medical doctor Prof August Döllken on the same topic,[21] which was to occupy him further in South Africa, as it was related to his pronounced interest in 'poor whites'. He attended a lecture by the director of the Institute, Felix Krueger, apparently only out of politeness; the interlocutors who were important to him were child psychologist Hans Volkelt and director of the Division of Applied Psychology, Otto Klemm.

In 1923, Otto Klemm (1884–1939) obtained the first professorship for Applied Psychology in Germany. Verwoerd was somewhat disappointed to find that the laboratory was "not specifically equipped for Psychotechnics".[22] During his time in Leipzig, he could study the different devices in more detail, and conduct some of his own experiments.[23] He also volunteered to act as test subject, but found the courses in Psychotechnics insufficiently elaborated. Psychotechnics was only one of several themes in various courses, and was mentioned only in the sidelines of colloquia and practical sessions. "It looks to me like a big waste of time." Besides, noted Verwoerd, Klemm tended to lose the thread amid a lot of detail, so "that one cannot gain comprehensive and in-depth knowledge in the laboratory, not even with regard to Psychotechnics. – The whole atmosphere is one of much ado, much of talk, and much of a waste of time!" Nevertheless, there were numerous references to professional practice; Klemm's division worked together with indus-

---

20 UA Leipzig. Philosophische Fakultät, Nr. B1/14: 37, vol. 1 (microfilm no. 1205), Psychologisches Institut 1911, 1925, 1931–1941, brochure ‚Psychologisches Institut und Staatliches Forschungsinstitut für Psychologie bei der Universität Leipzig', p. 4. In another instance (p. 6), it is stated: "Membership is usually granted only to those who have already engaged scientifically with psychology and its most important cognate disciplines. An appointment with the Director is a requirement, as is participation in the inaugural session of the semester. Candidates need to contact the relevant lecturers and supervisors of independent research projects."
21 Entries to this effect can be found in the course registration record book (no. 908) of the University of Leipzig (FAV 4.2.3).
22 FAV 4.3.2, Verwoerd's Diary on his studies 1926/7, entry on the Summer Semester 1926.
23 In one of his few publications, Verwoerd expressly thanks Krueger and Klemm for affording him an opportunity to use the devices of the Leipzig Institute for his research (Verwoerd 1928a: 495).

try as well as the Employment Office, so for instance in the selection of suitable applicants for particular jobs. Verwoerd was given the chance to conduct and score tests by himself.

More than anyone else, Hans Volkelt (1886–1964) contributed to make Holistic Psychology accessible to empirical research. He was the son of then renowned German philosopher Johannes Volkelt (1848–1930), had studied with Wundt, and later became assistant to Krueger and leading exponent of the latter's Holistic Psychology. He specialised in child and developmental psychology and made himself a name in this field as one of the leading and most innovative researchers.[24]

His writings on Child and Developmental Psychology are analytically clear, meeting standards of scientific writing, and yet accessible to readers not adept in Holistic Psychology. Where Volkelt dealt with the latter, however, his writing style became unclear and highfalutin, similar to that of Krueger's writings.[25] Still, where he managed to separate ideological commitments from empirical research, also in stylistically manifest ways, Volkelt could facilitate practical applications of Holistic Psychology.

Among the teaching sessions Verwoerd visited, two sets of tutorials taught by Volkelt are particularly significant. Volkelt conducted them alternating fortnightly, under the titles of 'Progressive steps in the development of Experimental Psychology of the child and the young adult', notes of which are still available, and 'Early forms of religion in children and indigenous peoples'; for the case of the latter, it is noted that it deepened insight into specific problems observed in children.[26] This shows that child psychology and ethnopsychology were closely interwoven – and I will come back to this connection further down the line.

About what Verwoerd did in Leipzig beyond his academic activities, we do not know anything;[27] and so Moodie's contention can be probed only with regard to Verwoerd's studies. Felix Krueger did call the Psychological Institute directed by him an "ethno-nationalist populist cell" [*völkische Zelle*], but this cannot be taken to attest to a political influence on Verwoerd. An exception may be found in the encounter with Karlfried Graf Dürckheim-Montmartin who, coming from an impoverished aristocratic family and harbouring a right-wing extremist mind-

---

24 See Hansen 1960: 81–83; also Volkelt's notes in the Volkelt Collection, Box 26, Child Psychology.
25 See for instance Volkelt 1962.
26 Volkelt Collection, Box 33, rough notes 22, Progress in Experimental Psychology with children, Summer Semester 1926. See also Volkelt's research report documenting the research projects introduced in the tutorials, as well as his own investigations at the time (Volkelt 1926).
27 Betsie Verwoerd first came to Germany when her husband had already left Leipzig (A. Boshoff 1993: 26).

set from an early age, had participated in crushing the Munich Soviet Republic.[28] Together with Volkelt, he later held strong sympathies for National Socialism; he joined the NS Teachers' Association as early as 1 October 1933.[29] He studied Psychology and worked as unpaid assistant in the Leipzig Institute during the time that Verwoerd spent there. Even though Verwoerd did not attend any academic sessions with Dürckheim, they must have known each other, since Dürckheim presented the introductory lectures.[30] A few years later, they met again, when both of them participated in the international congress of the New Education Fellowship in South Africa.[31]

The Leipzig Institute under Krueger did not only accommodate itself to the new regime after 1933; some of its members openly welcomed the seizure of power by the national socialists.[32] Having previously distinguished himself within the German ethno-nationalist right wing, Krueger was appointed rector of the University, but the NS-regime forced him to resign because he allegedly called

---

28 Dürckheim–Montmartin 1995: 26–29 and Wehr 1988: 76.
29 Bundesarchiv (formerly Berlin Document Center), personnel file Graf von Dürckheim-Montmartin, membership no. 229796. The file contains a memo by Dürckheim written from Tokyo, dated 2 July 1940 and addressed to Hanns Johst, in which the former advocates the intensification of national socialist propaganda to be directed at Japan as ally. Friedrich Sander, too, attested to the compliance (in principle) of the Leipzig Institute with National Socialism.
30 Dürckheim–Montmartin 1995: 34–35.
31 Unfortunately, the family of Dürckheim debars anyone from accessing the collection of papers of Graf von Dürckheim-Montmartin (e-mail from Dr Paul Warmbrunn, Landesarchiv Rheinland–Pfalz, Speyer, 20.7.2011). That is why it was not possible for me to look at the diary he kept of his travels in South Africa in which his biographer says, he carefully noted all encounters. Dürckheim contributed three chapters on national socialist theory of education to the conference proceedings; Verwoerd, who at the time already had a position in Sociology, is said to have contributed a discussion paper on poor whites (Malherbe 1937: 357). On other activities pursued in South Africa by Dürckheim on behalf of the NS regime, see Saron 1940: 2–3; Hagemann 1989: 83–90 and Wehr 1988: 124ff; on the Congress of the New Education Fellowship, see Dubow 2006: 228–234 and Boucher 1973: 188.
32 That applied to Friedrich Sander, for instance, whose role I will not further investigate here, as Verwoerd did not have any close dealings with him (Thiermann 136–37); it also applied to Albert Wellek, who started working at the Institute only towards the end of the 1920s. After the War, Wellek spread legends about the Institute's alleged distanciation from the NS; and he was at pains to delete any hint of his own closeness to the NS regime from his autobiography. Among psychologists, it was Wellek who, in his position in Mainz after World War II and in his role as influential functionary of the Association, most ardently argued for the continuation of the Leipzig School of Holistic Psychology (Wellek 1972: 363–366).

Heinrich Hertz and Baruch de Spinoza "noble Jews" in a public address.[33] He left the university a few years later, officially for health reasons, taking early retirement. Yet he cannot be counted among the victims of National Socialism; in 1933, when Jewish colleagues like William Stern lost their leading positions in professional psychological associations, he used the opportunity to fill these with his own disciples.[34] In contrast to Wolfgang Köhler in Berlin, Krueger never said even a word to express his regret or solidarity with those psychologists who had to relinquish their positions and go into exile.[35] But the reason why the Leipzig School of Holistic Psychology could not be revived after the War, was to be found in its scientific sterility. Krueger's opportunism and his sycophantic attempts to cosy up to the NS-regime were not the main reasons for its decline.[36]

From the beginning of the 1920s, Felix Krueger's Holistic Psychology had progressively turned away from Experimental Psychology; it branded itself as irrationalist holistic philosophy centred on the idea of 'community' [*Gemeinschaft*], displaying an affinity to ethnonationalist thinking from early on.[37] Decisive for

---

33 Geuter 1980: 41–42. On his activities as philosopher, see Tilitzki 2002: 523–524; and for a portrait of Krueger, see Tilitzki 2002: 527–532 and Thiermann 1981: 108–111. This address was often adduced with the aim of rehabilitating Krueger after the War. Krueger's alleged pro–Jewish stance is contradicted by the fact that, after his resignation from the position as Rector, vocal antisemites such as his Marburg colleague Erich Jaensch defended Krueger against the national socialists by pointing to Kruegers antisemitic stance (see ibid., 139–142). Having been sent into retirement involuntarily, Krueger's student Rudert spoke up for his teacher: "Unlike most professors, his life's work was a constructive one in the national-socialist sense. To be specific, he is one of the few professors who even before 1933 decisively declared his commitment to antisemitism." (Personnel file Krueger, Document 110 of the Psychological Institute, Memo by Deputy Director Rudert to his colleague Lenk, 21.6.1944). It is also worth noting how Krueger, in his call for the 15th Congress of the German Association for Psychology, affirmed the racism of the regime even after his resignation; and how he cloaked this in pompous pseudo-erudition (Krueger-Collection 17, f. 8 (4 pp.). Congress Correspondence no. 26, 27.6.1936). On Krueger's initial cosying–up to the NS regime, see Ash 1998: 342–343.
34 Still, Stern was elected Chairperson of the German Association for Psychology in 1931; but Krueger did not even dignify his predecessor with any mention during the Leipzig Conference of 1932 (Lück 1991: 410–11).
35 Ash 2002: 239–242, and even more clearly so in light of the anticipatory obedience of the Leipzigers (see Ash 2004: 111; see also Geuter 1988: 102–103; on Köhler, see Jaeger 1993: 221–222).
36 To my knowledge, there was, apart from the rear-guard battles conducted by Wellek in 1950 and a couple of others in more recent times, only one attempt to resurrect Holistic Psychology, namely that of Eichstätt-based psychologist Plaum (1989, 1993, and 1996, as well as the response of Prinz 2000).
37 Vorwerg 1979: 25. For a contemporary critique of holistic approaches, see Selz 1991a; Guski–Leinwand (2007: 75–78) points to the congruity between Krueger and H.S. Chamberlain. On Krueger's biography, see ibid., 169–191.

the independent path of the Leipzig School was the inclusion of feeling, which Krueger was soon to declare as most important task for psychological research.[38] Instead of *Gestalten*, he posited primary perceptual phenomena, which he called "complex qualities" – diffuse, quasi-multidimensional perceptions within which rational thoughts move. But owing to their near-complete dependence on the surrounding feelings, they were hardly accessible to empirical research.[39]

Holistic Psychology increasingly rested content with the idea that experiences are centred on highly complex feelings that cannot actually be grasped analytically. It lost the capacity for conducting empirically productive research, and degenerated into intellectually vacuous formulae.[40] Instead, it pontificated upon its ideological commitments. The move away from Wundt's elemental psychology was associated with a general rejection of 'Western' empiricism, while German thinking was supposedly directed to organically grown units, holistically understood.[41] Krueger promoted an irrationalism inspired by a Philosophy of Life [*Lebensphilosophie*], which manifested itself in his personal *habitus* and the search for a holistic 'synthesis'. He epitomised what Fritz Ringer called "German mandarins", that is, the status-conscious and conservative professoriate submissive to authority: "One can ask oneself whether the writings of some German psychologists of the time are anything more than ideological responses to freely construed

---

[38] The notion of feelings thematised in Verwoerd's thesis, is an entirely different one: he considered them isolatable and artificially generatable phenomena, measurable and manipulable. This is in direct contradiction to the concepts of "complex quality" and "the whole of experience" which emphasise precisely the diffuse and the unmeasurable (Krueger 1926a: 118–121. and 1953b: 146–149.).

[39] Wellek 1950: 6. Philosopher Ernst Cassirer has pointed to this problematic, albeit from within a different context: "Feeling can join anything with anything; hence it provides no adequate explanation for the grouping of *specific* contents into *specific* unities." (Cassirer1980: 294). Felix Krueger was strongly influenced by *Gestalt* Psychology, even as he persistently tried to present his own version as an original approach. He felt the pressure of intense rivalry with *Gestalt* Psychologists, which is why the holistic approach displays some level of one-upmanship, based on its claim that *Gestalt* Psychology's approach represented only one step in the right direction, which was fully elaborated and perfected by the Leipzig psychologists in the form of a psychological and philosophical explanation of psychic phenomena (see for instance the patronising statements by Krueger on the Berlin *Gestalt* psychologists – Krueger 1926a: 92, 93, n. 1; Krueger 1926a: 103; Krueger 1948: 35). The rivalry was a one–sided affair – that is, *Gestalt* psychologists did not perceive Krueger as serious competitor (see also Harrington 2002: 233–240).

[40] This becomes particularly clear in Krueger 1929a: 20, 25; see also Thiermann 1981: 153.

[41] Krueger 1915: 45–47; see also Geuter 1980: 37–38; Krueger tried to relativise Kant's Enlightenment-rationalist orientation, in order to assimilate it to the German–national casting of the history of ideas as he wanted to see it (see Krueger 1953a: 164–168; Krueger 1931: 6–7; see also Volkelt Collection, Box 18: Holistic Psychology, Notes and Drafts: From Association Psychology to Holistic Psychology).

castings of misguided positivistic conclusions. The exclusively programmatic aspect of many of the writings does actually convey this impression."[42] In this context, it is noteworthy that Krueger omitted the designation 'experimental' from the name of Wundt's institute, calling it simply 'Psychological Institute'.[43]

One would have expected that the Holistic Psychology of the Leipzig School, with its openness toward ethnonationalist ideas, would have resonated with Verwoerd, since it closely corresponded to his own thinking.[44] Verwoerd jotted down impressions of scientific research subjects that he found important for his own research and teaching, but there are no traces of Holistic Psychology to be found in his notes, even though he attended Krueger's lecture 'Introduction to Psychology'. The theoretical edifice of Holistic Psychology clearly did not convince or impress or even interest him. Even in his diary, he does not mention Krueger and his academic teaching, directing his attention exclusively to psychotechnical work instead.[45] Rather than pursuing aspects of Holistic Psychology, he focused on three other fields, namely Child or Developmental Psychology, Ethnopsychology, and Characterology.

Apart from Klemm's laboratory, Verwoerd visited non-academic institutions, such as the Psychotechnical Division of the Leipzig Employment Office, whose director was not a psychologist. The latter could only administer the existing tests, while relying in his assessment on common sense about human nature. Verwoerd was critical of the fact that in his capacity as adviser of the Division, Klemm effectively supported practices that judged test subjects on the basis of common knowledge of human nature rather than evidence gleaned from test results.[46] This is what ran counter to his own positivistic understanding of scientificity.

Having spent a semester in Leipzig, Verwoerd ventured to Hamburg, where his fiancée joined him. They got married there on 7 January 1927. The director of the Hamburg Institute, William Stern (1871–1938), was one of the most influential psychologists in Germany in the 1920s; his comprehensive work opened new perspectives in various disciplines. He came from an old Berlin Jewish family. After

---

[42] Ringer 1969: 382, with reference to Krueger; on holism as key concept of the conservatives, see 387–395. It is not surprising to find a letter from Ernst Jünger to Krueger affirming this stance (AU Leipzig, Krueger Collection, 13, f. 56: Letter by Jünger to Krueger, 10.9.1929; see also Vorwerg 1979: 25).
[43] UA Leipzig, Philosophische Fakultät, no. B1/14: 37, vol. 1 (microfilm no. 1205), Psychologisches Institut, 1911, 1925, 1931–1941, 10.7.1925, Letter by Ministerium für Volksbildung (von Seydewitz), Dresden, to Director of the Psychological Institute.
[44] See the contribution by Dürckheim–Montmartin 1954 and Krueger 1953a. On Holistic Psychology see also Wellek 1954: 15–20; Geuter 1985: 60–65; and Prinz 1985: 99–103.
[45] FAV 4.3.2, Diary of Verwoerd on his studies 1926/27, entry on Summer Semester 1926.
[46] Ibid.

studies in Psychology and Philosophy, he obtained his PhD under the supervision of Moritz Lazarus. Like many other psychologists at the time, he vacillated between natural-scientific and humanities-based approaches, while attempting to integrate them.[47] Having completed his habilitation with Hermann Ebbinghaus whom he had followed from Berlin to the University of Breslau, he worked there as extraordinary lecturer for 19 years, and then as professor for educational theory. In 1916, he was appointed professor of Philosophy in the 'General Lecturing Programme' in Hamburg, which was the precursor of the University in that city.[48] Stern himself played an important role in establishing the University in 1919. Since he was more devoted to psychology, he saw to the appointment of another philosopher – Ernst Cassirer –, with whom he subsequently worked together closely.[49] Cassirer's major work *The Philosophy of Symbolic Forms* was clearly influenced by contemporary psychology, namely that of Stern's. In some respects, it represented a more systematic and philosophically elaborated development of Wundt's ethnopsychology, along with a neo-Kantian epistemology based on symbolic forms.

Stern's research was centred on personhood[50] and hence he postulated a developmental psychology focused on the child. To him, experiments could only yield partial truths on partial aspects. The interpretation and integration of the results that Stern sought to achieve, situated his work in close proximity to Philosophy and the Humanities: "Sternian philosophy is strictly anti-mechanistic."[51] Considering that he was intent on specifying the spectrum of variation within a differentially elaborated psychology, his interest in social deviancy does not come as a surprise.

---

47 Lück 1991: 408–09. On Stern's biography, see also Lück 1990: 39–41. Probst and Bringmann (1993:3) speak of a pluralism of methods (see also Schmidt 1991; Schmidt 2005).
48 The long period during which Stern worked as extraordinary lecturer and professor in Breslau is clearly in large part due to his Jewish background, for he had long attained international renown; in 1909, at the age of only 38 years, he was awarded an honorary doctorate, along with Sigmund Freud and C.G. Jung, by Clark University. The award took place on the occasion of a conference attended also by Franz Boas. At the time, the rector of Clark University was Stanley Hall, himself a child psychologist and author of an influential book on adolescence taken up by Verwoerd. There is a good chance that the award of the honorary doctorate to Stern was due to the direct influence of Stanley Hall (Bühring 1996: 52–59). On Stern's biography, see Schmidt 2005; on the predecessor institutions see also Probst/Brinkmann 1993: 5–6. On the circumstances surrounding the appointment of Stern, see ibid., 8.
49 Lück 1991: 410; see also Bühring 1996: 116.
50 Sichler 1998: 73.
51 Bittner/Deutsch 1990: 61–62. Moser (1991: 490) insists that in Hamburg, psychologists were not enjoined to align themselves with either natural-scientific or humanities–based psychology.

Having given much thought to the topics of crime and punishment,[52] Stern attended court proceedings as expert on social deviancy. Apart from Hugo Münsterberg, who had left for Harvard as early as 1892, Stern was one of the first psychologists to apply his scientific research to the social field. As former professor in Educational Theory, he offered teachers an opportunity to further their studies, and developed methods for researching and promoting talent.[53]

According to entries in his study diary, the South African visitor attended only four courses between 9 November 1926 and 16 February 1927 – three of them with Stern himself. The entries in the study diary do not specify what kind of courses these were. 'General Psychology' could have been one of the lectures, while 'Instructions for psychological work and work with young adults' and 'Lessons on the Psychology of Puberty' would have been tutorials or seminars.[54] Apart from these sessions, Verwoerd looked at tests for police drivers, and sought to get an impression of forensic psychology. In January 1927, he visited the training centre in the dockyard of Blohm and Voss, where he observed the testing of applicants. An engineer by the name of Beinhoff, a "typical schoolmaster" presiding over the training centre and conducting the tests, "appeared not to have had any psychological training", despite having attended courses at the Hamburg Institute, whose tests he administered. He rejected the use of devices for tests, and did "everything with paper and pencil, as it were".[55] Instead of accurately calculating the test results, Beinhoff trusted his own judgement, allowing "subjective elements to creep in. Here again we see a deviation from strictly mathematical calculations applied by Moede, in the sense of subjective judgement", as Verwoerd had been able to observe it before in Leipzig.

In April 1927, Verwoerd travelled from Hamburg to Dresden to visit the Psychotechnical Institute of the Technical College Dresden; here, too, he found that testing equipment was not extensively used. In this case, this was due more to financial constraints than to aversion; the shortage of funding was also evident in the lack of space in the Institute. For children, members of the Institute deemed the written tests more suitable than the apparently exact results produced by the measuring

---

52 See his elaborations on the credibility of children as witnesses in court (Stern 1928a: 221–22; see also Bühring 1996: 147–150; and Moser 1991: 491). See also Schmidt 1994: 13–16.
53 Stern 1931: 205–207; see also Bühring 1996: 143–151; and Moser 1991: 491. See also Schmidt 1994: 13–16.
54 During the time that Verwoerd spent in Hamburg, Stern's interest in and engagement with the psychology of adolescence and research on puberty had reached its peak. Allport (1968: 323) sees this interest spanning the period between 1925 and 1928.
55 FAV 4.3.2, Diary of Studies Abroad, entry on Winter Semester 1926/7 in Hamburg.

devices.[56] Instead of being inspired by the German psychologists' adherence to their experiential knowledge to reflect on the use of devices and apparently objective testing procedures, Verwoerd criticised their methods as inadequate. This is indicative of Verwoerd's positivistic understanding of scientificity.

Apart from the Hamburg Institute, the Berlin Institute for Psychology was one of the most renowned in Germany, because Carl Stumpf (1848–1936) had been Professor of Philosophy and Psychology here for a long time (between 1894 and 1920). His successor, Wolfgang Köhler (1887–1967), took over in 1920; Köhler had made a name for himself with this psychological research on chimpanzees conducted during World War I at the Anthropoid Research Station on Tenerife.[57] Besides Köhler, another prominent proponent of *Gestalt* Psychology, Max Wertheimer, worked in Berlin between 1916 and 1929. This constellation became known as the Berlin School; and *Gestalt* Psychology was essentially associated with the University of Berlin.[58] Being averse to theory, Verwoerd was not the least bit interested in *Gestalt* Psychology, nor even in Krueger's holism; there is no trace of either to be found in his lectures and notes. Verwoerd was primarily interested in Psychotechnics, and therefore sought closer collaboration with Otto Lipmann (1880–1933)[59] and Hans Rupp (1880–1955) in their Division for Applied Psychology (established in 1922) than with the *Gestalt* psychologists at the Institute for Psychology in the Berlin Palace.[60] Lipmann had developed a distinct kind of psychotechnics that he called Industrial Psychology [*Arbeitspsychologie*]; he considered adjustment of work environments to workers more important than aptitude tests.[61] It is especially with regard to Verwoerd's sojourn in Berlin that the speculations of some scholars are running wild. Based in Berlin were scien-

---

56 Ibid., entry on semester vacation 1927.
57 Köhler 1917.
58 Apart from that, there was the lesser-known Graz School of *Gestalt* Psychology (Fabian 2005).
59 At the beginning of the century, Otto Lipmann had collaborated closely with William Stern while the latter was in Berlin. In the immediate aftermath of the War, and then again between 1923 and 1925, Kurt Lewin worked together with Hans Rupp on issues in industrial psychology [*Arbeitspsychologie*] (Sprung/Brandt 2003; Lück 2001: 111). See also Guski–Leinwand 2007: 218–221.
60 FAV 4.3.2, Diary of Studies Abroad. The only diary entry concerning Berlin is a heading, "Somersemester 1927. Psigotegn. Inst. Uniw. Berlyn – Rupp", with nothing following it. (see also ibid. Friedrich Wilhelm–University, Berlin. Registration book of Verwoerd's lecture attendance: Prof Köhler: Principal Problems in Psychology [*Hauptprobleme der Psychologie*], Prof Rupp: Psychotechnics [*Psychotechnik*] and Psychotechnical Exercises [*Psychotechnische Übungen*]. Dr Birnbaum: Psychopathology of Crime [*Psychopathologie des Verbrechens*]; Prof Lipmann: Selected Chapters from Sexual Psychology [*Ausgewählte Kapitel aus der Sexualpsychologie*]. See also Geuter/Hagemeier/Ash 1986: 18.
61 Lipmann 1926: 8, 11.

tists and institutions that later became directly or indirectly associated with NS-ideology and its racial science. Thus, it comes as no surprise that time and again, statements circulated, claiming that Verwoerd had met Eugen Fischer in Berlin, or even worked together with him.[62] However, there is no evidence of an encounter or even co-operation with Fischer and other racial theorists and eugenicists; nor is this contention plausible, because at the time, Verwoerd was registered at the University. There are no indications of any contacts with the Kaiser Wilhelm Institute for the Psychology of Heredity.

The main contacts of Hendrik and Betsie Verwoerd were South Africans who had come to Berlin to further their studies, or for other reasons. Betsie Verwoerd named them as Meiring Naudé, Hendrik Kotzé Muller, W. P. de Villiers (who was later appointed professor at the University of Pretoria), and Dr A. J. H. van der Walt and his wife. Van der Walt had studied History in Berlin and completed his PhD under the supervision of Friedrich Meinecke; at a later stage, he was to play a key role in the establishment of the University of South Africa as distance learning institution.[63] Shortly after Verwoerd's arrival, van der Walt and his wife returned to South Africa.

Besides these persons in the social circle around the Verwoerds in Berlin, there was Oskar Hintrager, who acted as mentor and host. During the South African War, he had fought on the side of the Afrikaners. Following his legal studies, Hintrager (1871–1960) worked in the German colonial administration, and moved through the ranks to take over the position as Deputy Governor of South West Africa.[64] After the War, he occupied various positions in the administration, while keeping an open house for South Africans living in Berlin; once a month, he would invite them to his home for sociable evenings.[65]

Hintrager was a zealous German nationalist, but a national socialist he was not; it may have even been very opportune for him to be able to retire in December 1933. Of any connections of Verwoerd or other South Africans with national socialist circles or racial anthropologists, nothing is known. Nor is it known whether Hintrager, himself a proponent of colonial racial segregation, entertained such connec-

---

62 For instance, Q. Smith 2016: 341; similarly unsubstantiated claims on Verwoerd's sojourn in Leipzig are to be found in Burke 2006: 118.
63 Boucher 1973: 218–219, 286–290.
64 His sympathy for the Boers dated back to the time when he volunteered to fight on the side of the Boers during the South African War (see Bundesarchiv N1137/1, newspaper report on his orders in *Hamburger Nachrichten*, 27.6.1905.
65 *Allgemeine Zeitung* (Windhoek), 29.11.1930. The Verwoerds rented a room at Savignyplatz (A. Boshoff 1993: 27).

tions.⁶⁶ According to all available evidence, there are no indications that Verwoerd concerned himself with German politics during his stay in Berlin; or that he cultivated relations with racial anthropologists, right-wing extremists, and national socialists. Statements claiming that he had imbibed a radical form of nationalism in Germany, to then transfer it to South Africa, cannot be empirically validated, but neither can they be refuted. As has been demonstrated in the first chapter, this question is moot, as Verwoerd had shown himself to be a fanatical cultural nationalist from early on.

Sojourn in the US, 1927

Verwoerd's visit to the US was exclusively devoted to applied psychology. He stayed mostly in New York and Boston,⁶⁷ from where he undertook shorter trips to institutes along the East Coast. He gathered questionnaires and research materials for aptitude tests and for the optimisation of work processes. In his capacity of professor at Stellenbosch University, he would conduct regular lectures on industrial psychology, covering advertising as well as the training of salespersons, for which his American experience was to him well. This included a manual on selection processes of 'salesmen' of the Bureau of Personnel Research of the Procter and Gamble department store chain in Cincinnati, at the time considered pioneers in advertising and marketing, as well as brand management. This manual was divided into two parts: the first part, a general guideline on how to conduct interviews and subsequent selection, was followed by a second part explaining additional testing procedures.⁶⁸ To the extent that this manual provided an inventory of recruitment, training, and deployment of salespersons, and took into account aspects like word-of-mouth information-sharing in the recruitment of suitable applicants, it methodologically surpassed the standardised tests.⁶⁹ But it also contained precise information, based on empirical values, on the design of job advertisements as well as the various forms of job interviews.⁷⁰

Ever since the days of William James and Hugo Münsterberg, Harvard was one of the universities at which psychological research was accorded a prominent

---

66 A. Boshoff 1993: 28. Apparently, Hintrager was more interested in social support for South Africans and sociability, as reflected also in Betsie Verwoerd's memories of frequent visits to the opera, which were memorable and novel experiences for the couple.
67 FAV 4.3.2, letter by E. Verwoerd to Annie Schoombee (?), New York, 29.1.1927.
68 PV 93/1/52/2, Bl. 7–25, Investigation (cover page is missing), pp. 13–17.
69 Ibid., p. 2.
70 Ibid., pp. 3–11.

place. Verwoerd went to see Dr Dearborn at the Wells Psychopathic Hospital that was affiliated to the University's Psychology Department; he also visited the Judge Baker Foundation in Boston. He made contact with the Yale Psycho-Clinic and, further south, with the University of Pennsylvania. There he also visited Dr Murphy at the Psycho-Clinic.

In addition to vocational aptitude tests, Verwoerd was interested in test procedures for children, such as the tests designed by Caroline and Garry Myers,[71] who had worked extensively on educational and psychological issues in primary education. The Yale Psycho-Clinic tests on young children[72] conducted under the directorship of Arnold Gesell, as well as the Detroit Kindergarten Test,[73] and the Dearborn Group Test of Intelligence (Harvard),[74] were based on empirical data about the behaviour of young children. At the Judge Baker Foundation, Verwoerd was particularly interested in the 'Silent Reading Test' for school children;[75] the same interest captivated him at the Institute for Juvenile Research in Chicago, which he visited around Christmas time.[76] In addition to research focused on young children and adolescents, the Yale Psycho-Clinic[77] and the Psychopathic Hospital (Psychological Laboratory) affiliated to Harvard's Psychology Department conducted general assessments of persons with behavioural problems.[78]

During his stay in the US, Verwoerd was informed that a newly instituted professorship in Applied Psychology had been advertised at Stellenbosch University. The telegram by which he applied for this position was addressed to his doctoral supervisor Wilcocks and consisted of exactly four words: "Herewith apply psychology post".[79] His appointment in this post can be read as a clear indication that it had been tailor-made for him, and that arrangements to this effect may even have been made before his departure. What could have explained the decided focus on applied psychology during his trips to Germany and to the US, if

---

71 PV 93/1/52/2, f. 47, The Myers Mental Measure.
72 Gesell 1926.
73 PV93/1/52/2, f. 31, Detroit Kindergarten Test, Individual.
74 PV 93/1/52/2, f. 38–40., Games and Puzzles, as well as Games and Picture Puzzles, and Kuhlmann Supplement. In South Africa, intelligence tests were standardised by mostly Paul Skawran (who was of German background and collaborated with Wilcocks – Skawran 1929: 28, 30; Skawran 1930) and M L Fick, who had studied at Harvard (J. Louw 1986: 76; Dubow 1991: 154).
75 PV 93/1/52/2, f. 1, Silent Reading Test, Shimberg–Meehan, Judge Baker Foundation, Boston.
76 PV 93/1/52/2, f. 50, Outline for Recreation Interview, 8 years and younger. He had taken along related material also from German (f. 86, Psychotechnical Aptitude Tests, Higher Education Institutions, Leipzig). On the dates of his visits to Chicago, see E. Verwoerd 2001: 43.
77 PV 93/1/52/2, f. 32, Observation of Adjustment; ff. 32–37, Introductory Report.
78 PV 93/1/52/2, f. 37, Record Sheet for School Tests.
79 UA Stellenbosch, Personnel File Verwoerd, Telegram 28.11.1927.

not the realistic prospect of a career in this field? He did not have to wait long for a response. On 6 December 1927, the University Registrar confirmed Verwoerd's appointment as professor, which he had already announced to him telegraphically beforehand.[80] Verwoerd became a professor at the age of 26 years, which was unusual but not unprecedented in Stellenbosch.[81]

Professor Verwoerd

Verwoerd returned from the US to Stellenbosch earlier than planned, to start teaching at Stellenbosch at the beginning of 1928. Psychology of personality was one of the main themes that he dealt with in his lectures and in some of his writings. He started by introducing developmental psychology, from which he developed a typology of different characters. Specific characters start taking shape in early childhood, he surmised. Like his Hamburg teacher Stern, Verwoerd combined developmental and differential psychology; the latter found its way into ethnopsychology. His statements shed light on whether he accorded greater importance to hereditary or to environmental factors, and to what extent his conception of ethnic differences played into his typologies.

Childhood Psychology

Verwoerd's Psychology course for second year students dealt with "the human personality", covering the psychological development from childhood to adulthood, for which Verwoerd foregrounded Stern's and Koffka's books on child psychology as recommended readings for students.[82] In addition, he encouraged students to familiarise themselves with differential psychology identifying and

---

[80] UA Stellenbosch, Personnel File Verwoerd, letter by Registrar to Verwoerd (c/o South African Trades Commissioner, New York), 6.12.1927. On 6 January, Verwoerd accepted the position, and informed the University about this planned return to South Africa (ibid., letter by Verwoerd to Registrar, 6.1.1928).

[81] Jurist Izak van Zyl Steyn, for instance, was appointed professor at the age of 25; he passed away five years later (obituary in *Die Burger*, 9.5.1935). Verwoerd attended the funeral as pallbearer.

[82] Some of the titles appeared in 1929, which suggests that Verwoerd conceptualised and presented this lecture in his position as professor, after returning from his sojourn abroad. Stern and Koffka are mentioned in PV93/1/33/3, f. 64, Oorsake van individuele verskille in kinder pers., p. 11.

characterising different personality types.⁸³ Following these authors, Verwoerd maintained that one could only understand the world of the child through the child's own yardsticks. He followed his Hamburg teacher in dividing childhood and adolescence into three phases, each lasting about six years.⁸⁴ While Hans Volkelt was the expert on child psychology in Leipzig,⁸⁵ the work of Professor William Stern had made Hamburg a centre for the psychology of childhood and adolescence – in a sense the first port of call in Germany for someone like the young scholar from South Africa with a special interest in this field.

Stern was one of the most versatile and influential psychologists of the 1920s and 30s, a pioneer in numerous fields, and author of standard works.⁸⁶ His holistic psychology focused on the human personality. His approach, pathbreaking for the psychology of the first years of life, was honed by the documentation of observations over many years, undertaken jointly with his wife Clara, of the development of their own children Hilde, Günther,⁸⁷ and Eva. The diarised notes were subsequently evaluated in his writings. His influence on Verwoerd can be gauged from the fact that the latter, together with his wife, composed a similar diary about his son Wilhelm (born in 1929), which did not, however, develop into a study.⁸⁸

In 1914, Stern presented his work *Psychology of Early Childhood*. Being hailed (until the publication of Piaget's work) as the most important study on the subject, it stood as a milestone for a long time. The central thesis of this book, which was quite novel at the time, was that children should not be psychologically evaluated by the standards of adults; children were not simply deficient adults.⁸⁹ That ex-

---

83 The Yearbook of the University of Stellenbosch for 1930 (p. 131) contains the contents of the lecture. In addition, Verwoerd presented standardised lectures on business psychology and forensic psychology, among other things, in each year of his academic career (see Yearbooks 1928: 218; 1929: 167–168; 1931: 136).
84 PV 93/1/33/3, f. 217, 'Die Psiegiese Persoonlikheid van die Kind', handwritten notes, p. 1.
85 Volkelt provided inspiration for further works on child psychology, for instance Rüssel 1943: 105–106.
86 According to Allport (1968: 322), he wrote all of his path-breaking works in a time period of seven years at the beginning of the twentieth century.
87 Stern's son Günther (1902–1991) became famous as a philosopher under the journalistic pseudonym of Günther Anders; between 1929 and 1937, he was married to Hannah Arendt.
88 FAV 4.3.2, Diary entry in the handwriting of E Verwoerd, on Wilhelm Verwoerd, January – November 1930. In 1938, E Verwoerd kept a similar diary, noting her observations of her two year-old daughter Elsabet, without intending to attain insights into child psychology. See also FAV 4.4.2 for other parts of the diary of E Verwoerd, noting observations about her son Wilhelm during the years 1929 and 1931.
89 Stern 1928a: 249. Regarding colours and shapes, see p. 369; regarding the central concept of 'striving', see pp. 393–394; see also Hansen 1960: 32–33.

plains why, right at the outset of his book, Stern pleaded for developing new perspectives on what appeared to be familiar.[90] While the intelligence quotient is attributable to Stern, he distanced himself from IQ-tests schematically applied under the assumption that the IQ represents a trait and not a potential.[91] Stern believed that such applications of IQ tests did not do justice to the human personality,[92] which is why he characterised his own distinct approach as "critical personalism".

The experiences of small children are not based on passive reception of stimuli, but on self-activity. "Children do not acquire most of the skills through imitation of what is expressly demonstrated to them, but through continuous involuntary accumulation of impressions, which are projected outwards again in a similar way."[93] Based on the expectations of children he formulated a general law of development: "References to the future are grasped by consciousness earlier than references to the past."[94] Confrontation with the unknown, for instance with strangers, triggers learning processes: "for just as feelings of familiarity belong to mnemic processes, so feelings of strangeness impel learning processes."[95] He also noted active processes of acquisition, for instance those involved in language learning, while pointing out that the first linguistic utterances were not single words, but whole sentences.[96] Stern's "convergence theory" stipulates that inherited disposition and environmental influences come together in the development of the child.[97]

Alongside Stern, Leipzig-based researcher Hans Volkelt was the most important German figure in the psychology of child development in Germany at the time. Holistic psychology afforded him the possibility of developing his own methodology, which departed from Wundt's elemental psychology.[98] Volkelt maintained that it was not the number of perceived elements that increased as the child grew up, which then coalesced in the brain to form sensations, but rather that a diffuse, ho-

---

90 Stern 1982a: 2.
91 On the methodological problems of IQ tests, see Chorover 1982: 64, 82; also Gould 2016: 161–170.
92 For methodological objections, see Stern 1911: 92ff; also, with regard to child psychology, Stern 1928a: 378ff; Stern 1931: 192–193; Schmidt 1994: 16–17. On the rejection of mechanistically applied testing procedures by the Hamburg-based child psychologists, see Moser 1991: 492; see also Allport 1968: 323.
93 Stern 1928a: 67.
94 Ibid., 84.
95 Ibid., 105.
96 Ibid., 12; see also Cassirer 1956: 27, 280–281.
97 Remplein 1962: 38.
98 Volkelt 1954: 2–5.

listic impression stood at the beginning (complex quality), to then become more and more differentiated as the child developed. The process of human maturation was reflected in the fact that complex qualities were being dissolved through experience and mental activity or were channelled into more structured pathways.[99] In this sense, holistic psychology, unlike Berlin Gestalt Psychology, was oriented more fundamentally and more clearly towards development.

Verwoerd's leaning towards Stern (and Volkelt) can be seen not only in his emphasis on scale relativity, but also in the fact that what for him was pivotal were not particular abilities or aspects like memory, perception, imagination, but the whole personality of the child. Stern's personality psychology combined two strands – developmental psychology on the one hand, and differential psychology on the other. In taking up Stern's psychology of childhood, Verwoerd sought to determine the general characteristics of the child's psyche, while simultaneously showing up the differences accounting for different personality types in children.

Within the framework of his lectures of developmental psychology, Verwoerd pursued the question as to the extent to which learning processes were genetically preformed. In his discussion of hereditary dispositions, the focus of his attention becomes clearly recognisable, even at this early stage – namely deviant behaviour and juvenile delinquency. Popular opinion tended to regard much of manifest behaviour as "innate", he pointed out; the idea of hereditary characteristics was pervasive in the literature on developmental psychology. Without referring to any particular author, Verwoerd noted that at least some heed was given to "external circumstances" as "character-forming influences, the kind of susceptibility to influence characteristic of the child's mind".[100] Lay persons deemed innate characteristics more important than environmental influences, which is what Verwoerd considered an easy excuse for educators' own failures, for it sent them searching for inherited dispositions at the first signs of deviant behaviour on the part of the child. Verwoerd, in contrast, sought the reason why late-born children often developed differently from their older siblings, not in hereditary disposition, but in the changing attitude of the parents, as for instance in the tendency for parents to become less strict. This is what led him to the following conclusion: "Among the multiple influences based on experiences, inherited factors have a relatively minor role, only to make us realise that the innate basis of the personality opens hundreds of possibilities for development. And the different di-

---

99 On Volkelt's child psychology, see Hansen 1960: 81–84.
100 PV 93/1/33/3, f. 74. 'Oorsake vir individuele verskille in kinder pers.', p. 1, dated 16 June, with a further notation of date in pencil on the same page, indicating that the year is 1929. He similarly emphasised environmental influences in his lecture 231/2/3, 'Socio–Psigologie van misdaad', pp. 8–9.

rections of development give us the different personalities."[101] For Verwoerd, it was the social context that became the decisive factor, for the child learnt from an early age that as an individual it was dependent on community.[102]

Verwoerd's lectures turned into a plea for the preponderance of environmental influences over inherited characteristics, with which he linked his criticism of a widespread attitude toward Afrikaner families deemed socially problematic. Adducing various examples, such as learning to walk or learning to speak, he showed how children growing up normally could reconcile the recognition accorded to them by the community with their own desire for recognition,[103] if they received praises and rewards for their achievements. However, "a conflict between the desire for recognition and a sense of community can arise . . . if children are made to doubt their abilities or aptitudes."[104] From as early as the age of two, the desire for recognition manifests itself in their wish to be like adults:

> All experiences of children during this period have an influence on the personality ideal. Thus, for instance, a child who is the centre of attention, being pampered by all around and growing up in a home where a sickly, weak mother is treated with kid gloves by a capable father, can develop a personality ideal not oriented toward the father's powerful role, but toward the prerogatives arising from the weakness of the mother.[105]

Demonstrative weakness can be a way of gaining power over others. When a child adopts such behaviour, she or he stands to develop an egoistic personality type.[106]

Verwoerd called this path toward a "personality ideal" the "guideline" [*rigtingslyn*] that is, however, not consciously followed. "A healthy development of a child is one that is guided by achievements in such a way that it moves in the direction of his or her later task in life. Every achievement of this kind does not only satisfy the desire for recognition, but it also reinforces contact with the community and adaptation to the environment."[107] If children do not take the path of self-assertion [*selfhandhawing*], this is the result of a development that makes them doubt their chances of success and discourages them. Children may react to this by

---

[101] PV 93/1/33/3, f. 74, 'Oorsake vir individuele verskille in kinder pers.', p. 1.
[102] Verwoerd dealt with Alfred Adler's individual psychology, referring especially to the latter's seminal essay (Adler 1978). On the social environment as principal factor in youth delinquency, see 231/2/3, 'Socio-psigologie van misdaad', pp. 14–20.
[103] In another manuscript, Verwoerd commented on the formation of the will in children and young people (PV 93/1/33/3, f. 30, 'Onderlinge Verskille', pp. 8–9).
[104] PV 93/1/33/3, f. 73, 'Oorsake vir individuele verskille in kinder pers.', pp. 2–3.
[105] Ibid., p. 3.
[106] Ibid., 5; see also 231/2/3, 'Socio–psigologie van misdaad', p. 17.
[107] PV 93/1/33/3, f. 72, 'Oorsake vir individuele verskille in kinder pers.', p. 3.

over-compensating, putting themselves under massive pressure to succeed; and instead of taking pleasure at their own achievements, they develop ambition [*eergierigheid*]. This is what Verwoerd considered a misguided development, since the individual desire for recognition took on traits inimical to the community, as soon as an individual child sought only to outdo others. In that case, achievement was not sought for the satisfaction that it brings, but as means to an end, namely for the purpose of garnering praise.

In Verwoerd's view, the parental home and the method of purposeful education were decisive.[108] In the attempts of parents to break the will of the child, he could only see signs of parental weakness. For the child, this meant a sense of humiliation that was bound to misdirect her or his will to achieve – the child would not be able to become independent.[109] The same was true for the completely conforming child who only wanted to solicit praise from the parents, or for the pampered child, who was relieved of every expectation to achieve.[110]

Verwoerd practiced psychology as a science oriented toward everyday life, which is why he translated his findings into a short story published pseudonymously in 1931 in the weekly *Die Huisgenoot*. Adducing the example of a young man brought up from childhood not to attain independence, he showed how a lack of support for the development of an individual causes his failure in life. A child who does not experience freedom in her or his development but is bullied by the father even in childhood play, will not become an independent adult. However, this was not about the contrast between individual happiness and the expectations of the community, but about the fact that a person could not even find a place in society that would enable her or him to act in conformity with the community.[111] The situation described here was structurally similar to that of poor whites who were also prevented by social circumstances from becoming useful members of a national community. Only when they can attain a rightful place, can the choice between individual happiness and subordination to the community arise.

The specific family constellation, for instance the presence of younger siblings,[112] could exert a strong influence on individual development, as could gender. In the case of gender, however, Verwoerd put forward an astonishingly relativising argument:

---

108 Ibid., p. 5.
109 Ibid., p. 6.
110 Ibid., pp. 6–7.
111 O. Nieuwenhuys [Verwoerd], 'Die Slagoffer'. *Die Huisgenoot*, 19.6.1931, pp. 37, 43, 45.
112 PV 93/1/33/3, f. 67, 'Oorsake vir individuele verskille in kinder pers.', p. 8.

> In our culture [!], the notions of 'masculinity' and 'superiority' largely coincide, while 'surpassing' is the personality ideal of every girl and every boy. For as long as there are no other discouraging factors, the boy is not being hindered in this, whereas the girl is to a large extent. It is gender that is the underlying factor in the discouragement [of girls]. At some stage, a girl learns that she belongs to that part of humanity that is not destined for the achievements esteemed as the greatest and most valuable. She learns that she is destined for limited development only, but nothing more.[113]

Although Verwoerd showed a clear understanding of gender dynamics, he did not by any means advocate the emancipation of women; in a cunning argumentative twist, he affirmed male leadership roles instead. Even if puberty were to occur earlier, as it did in the case of girls, he conjectured, intellectual development would not have advanced sufficiently to be able to process the insecurity and the emotional upheavals of this stage of life. The boy who undergoes this process at a later stage, is intellectually more mature, and can use the time to reflect on fundamental questions "emanating from his experiences of that time, including, for example, questions about himself and his relation to society, life, the world, and God, etc."[114] Despite his emphasis on individual deviations, Verwoerd developed a general picture of gender differences:

> It is the case, however, that girls' earlier maturity contributes to the fact that their interest (like that of precociously developed boys) is more strongly directed toward other persons and their respective emotional lives from early on, while the interest of boys (like that of late bloomers among girls) is more strongly directed toward factual issues, and toward intellectual problems and subjects.[115]

The conclusion that a girl is inclined toward other persons and is "steeped in their emotions"[116] is possibly related to a new reading of Eduard Spranger, whose ideas on character types Verwoerd took up in his lectures – to the effect that "social man" tends to be a woman, while the remaining five character types are imbued with 'male' traits. This would imply that women correspond to only one character type and are thus less differentiated than men.

In addition to gender differences, Verwoerd addressed social differences, as well as the contrast between city and country, which accounted for the fact that children living in cities become intellectually active at an earlier age. The risk of intellectual stunting pertained particularly to children living in rural areas, who lacked the required incentives, which is why "a purely instinctive primitive devel-

---

113 Ibid., p. 10.
114 PV 93/1/33/3, f. 21, 'Onderlinge Verskille', p. 1.
115 Ibid.
116 Ibid.

opment would take place in the less intellectually active rural child of the same age".[117] Finally, Verwoerd spoke to the wider social environment, highlighting poverty as a significant factor in preventing children from developing self-esteem.[118]

According to Verwoerd, puberty was the most important and consequential step in human development. Anyone investigating it could only try to understand the significance of this momentous transformation with empathy, and by recalling one's own youth.[119] For him, there was much to suggest that during this period of life, the imagination and abstract thinking tended to diverge, to be brought back together again only in post-puberty.[120]

Regarding puberty, Verwoerd presented biologically based arguments, drawing comparisons with the attainment of sexual maturity in animals and pointing to the close connection between physical sexual maturity and certain psychic developments in humans. "In addition, the process of reaching maturity is accompanied by an internal and an external restlessness catapulting the individual out of his self-sufficiency and quiescence; he will have to become aware of the need for complementarity – the ego will open itself to another person."[121] This person may be an older person fulfilling the role of a mentor, in which case the attachment would not be sexually motivated, but represented a transitional phase characterised by an undifferentiated inclination of the child, and the insecurity of the pubescent.[122] In a sense, the will had to be re-built and re-aligned during puberty: "That is why the school is obliged to expose 12 to 13 year old girls and 14 to 15 year old boys to the best of personalities, people who can perform actions and thereby serve as role models."[123] Physical maturity would have to be accompanied by cultural maturity oriented toward the community if cultural continuity is to be safeguarded.

Verwoerd's elaborations on puberty contained elements of what he had learnt in Leipzig. On 26 June 1926, while Verwoerd was still there, Volkelt had presented his inaugural lecture in Leipzig. In this lecture, he emphasised the special

---

117 Ibid., p. 3.
118 PV 93/1/33/3, f. 66, 'Oorsake vir individuele verskille in kinder pers.', pp. 9–10.
119 PV 93/1/33/3, f. 37, 'Die psigiese persoonlikheid v.d. Jeugdige en Najeugdige', p. 2; see also PV93/1/33/3, f. 32, 'Onderlinge Verskille', p. 6; on religion in the life of young people, see ibid., f. 27, p. 11.
120 PV 93/1/33/3, f. 29, 'Onderlinge Verskille', pp. 9–10.
121 PV 93/1/33/3, f. 36, 'Wat is puberteit?', p. 1.
122 PV 93/1/33/3, 'Onderlinge Verskille', p. 5; PV 93/1/33/3, f. 36, 'Wat is puberteit?', p. 3.
123 PV 93/1/33/3, f. 29, 'Onderlinge Verskille', p. 9; see also PV 93/1/33/3, f. 17, Wat het ons gedurende die Bespreking v.d. Kinder, Jeugdige en Najeugdige persoonlikheid bereik wat prakties bruikbaar is? Manuscript, p. 3.

nature of puberty and adolescence as distinct phases in a person's life and underlined their immense importance for the further course of life. In this respect, he moved within the same interpretive framework as child psychology. With child psychology, he shared the non-teleological approach to child development, as opposed to a retrojection taking the 'grown' adult as a starting point. Instead, Volkelt's child psychology emphasised the open nature of development, as well as the completely different forms of children's perception, logics of action, and learning that fundamentally distinguished them from those of adults.[124]

Verwoerd also highlighted the extent to which puberty could be a phase of reorientation, a sort of biographical exclave that could not be dealt with by the usual standards that applied to psychological development in other stages of life. This was to become important for his own conclusions regarding the theme of juvenile delinquency to which he was going to turn in his capacity as sociologist in the years that followed.[125]

As far as criminal offences were concerned, Verwoerd opined, one could hardly speak of such in the case of children; it was rather a matter of gradual misconduct. Here, too, it was true that punishments that did not take personality development into account, tended to bring about even more grave consequences. Certain aspects such as lying on the part of children, were frequently dramatized, when in fact such conduct stemmed from the nature of childhood. Regarding juvenile delinquency, Verwoerd pleaded for prevention instead of punishment. Knowledge of the personality traits of the juvenile was important for the psychology of criminality, because it helped to understand the motivation for the deed, and to prevent him from slipping into crime.[126] These remarks seem astonishingly enlightened, especially when considering the authoritarian approach of the later Verwoerd as politician who responded to youth cultures of the 1950s and 1960s by relying on repression rather than understanding. The fact that he did not even apply his findings to black youth, once again attests to his racism.[127]

---

124 Volkelt Collection, Box 10, Inaugural Lecture (various handwritten and corrected versions).
125 231/2/3, 'Socio–psigologie van misdaad', pp. 30–32.
126 PV 93/1/33/3, f. 18, Wat het ons gedurende . . ., p. 4. On children lying, see also Hansen 1960: 199–104.
127 See also Smit 1989: 240.

Ethnopsychology and Theories of Civilisational Stages

For Verwoerd, the relativisation of evaluation standards was not limited to the developmental psychology of the individual; following ethnopsychological precepts, he extended it to collectives cast in the mould of cultural essentialism.[128] To elucidate this, we need to look back at Verwoerd's experiences in Leipzig, and at developments in psychology in Germany. In fact, in the late nineteenth century, the two young sciences of ethnology and psychology, both strongly inflected by positivism, were methodologically and theoretically very closely related and mutually influential.[129] With the intensification of research travel to regions outside of Europe, and with growing awareness, since the eighteenth century, of the respective cultures, cultural-evolutionist stage-theories became prevalent. These theories assumed a civilisational disparity, which was then arranged in evolutionist sequence, suggesting that so-called primitive societies were the living remnants of earlier stages in the development of human civilisation. Nineteenth century social theorists designed different stage models variously based on the criterion of technical development. Authors as diverse as Tylor, Spencer, Fraser, Morgan, Marx and Engels, Wundt, Lamprecht or Breysig related these stages to family structures, societal forms, or economic modes of production. These stage theories were unmistakably Eurocentric, since the theorists made their own cultures the yardsticks by which to measure all others, which would consequently appear deficient. They were thus able to postulate a hierarchy of distinct stages of development in which they positioned cultures around the world.

Ethnopsychology in the form in which Wundt had developed it early on, and which he had always understood as integral part of his work in psychology,[130] was characterised by several additional approaches and explanatory patterns. Wundt gave a special twist to theories of civilisational stages by positing a parallel development of ascending civilisation and progressive individual-psychic stages. He outlined three distinct stages of "primitive" peoples, of totemism and of the era of

---

128 Volkelt Collection, Box 6: Notes 'What is psychology of culture [*Kulturpsychologie*]?'.
129 On German ethnologists interested in psychological issues, see Staeuble 1992: 146; also Marx 1988: 211–215. On conditions in Leipzig, where psychology and ethnology influenced each other in taking up the historical approaches of Karl Lamprecht (see Bruch 1995: 265; also Chickering 1995: 238–242.).
130 Jüttemann 2006: 17–20; Volkelt 1922: 7–8, 17; see also Oelze 1991. On the explanatory models of Steinthal and Lazarus preceding Wundt's ethnopsychology, see Graevenitz 1999; on Hellpach's own version, see Stallmeister/Lück 2006: 119–121; also Guski–Leinwand 2007: 130–131. However, contrary to initial plans, ethnopsychology was never institutionalised in Leipzig (see Meischner–Metge 2006a: 132). Danziger (1983: 307–310) highlights ethnopsychology's methodological proximity to experimental psychology.

heroes and of gods, understood as evolutionary antecedents of mature civilisation, in analogy to individual-psychic developmental stages.[131] The main problem of ethnopsychology, however, was the unquestioned assumption of "peoples" as basic units, posited as fixed reference point of all transformations and changes.[132] Krueger produced a reinforced version of such folk psychology to the extent that he made the 'folkish' orientation pivot on 'community' as the highest value, as opposed to 'society'.[133]

For his searches on "psychogenesis", the genesis of the human psyche, Wundt thought that ethnopsychology would yield the most promising insights, for "the child of cultured people is surrounded by influences that can never be separated from that which spontaneously arises in the consciousness of the child itself. In its consideration of the various stages of mental development still discernible in human life forms today, ethnopsychology, in contrast, takes us along a path of true psychogenesis."[134] For ethnopsychology, the "primitive" was not, as it was for ethnology, "the originary according to the genealogy of peoples", but a stage in mental development, universally conceived.[135] But as an old-school liberal, Wundt vehemently rejected the racist idea that deficient intelligence accounted for the low level of culture of the so-called "primitives".[136]

While Wundt was decidedly cautious in developing hypotheses concerning psychological fundamentals, he displayed no such inhibitions regarding ethnopsychology. Contrary to his psychological research, his ethnopsychological research was not experimentally oriented, since he was of the opinion that 'higher' psychic processes, moreover processes involved in the psychology of community life, could not be captured by laboratory experiments.[137] He operated rather like a classical armchair scientist, that is, he relied on second and third hand knowledge

---

131 Wolfradt 2009: 187. In developing his sequence of stages, Wundt is clearly indebted to Giambattista Vico (Vico 2017: 29–30, 492–505). It is significant that Otto Klemm, a student of Wundt's, wrote his PhD thesis on Vico as ethnopsychologist (see Klemm 1911: 118; see also Loosch 2008: 71).
132 See for instance Hellpach 1954: 32–36. Verwoerd was familiar with Hellpach's writings, and the latter's elaborations on race and peoples; Hellpach posited 'race' as an unproblematic unit.
133 Wellek 1953: 45, 48. On the contradistinction of 'community' and 'society', borrowed from Tönnies and raised to the level of the 'folkish' [völkisch], see Wellek 1953: 53; also Meischner/Eschler 1979: 94.
134 Wundt 1913: 4.
135 Ibid., 6.
136 Ibid., 109–115. On Wundt's political engagement within the framework of workers' associations of the 1860s, see Bebel 1910: 114.
137 Vorwerg 1984: 66–67; also Graumann 2006: 59–60; see also Eckardt 1998: 19. See also Engstrom 1997: 167–168. Wundt thought that interpersonal communication was not accessible to psychology (see Zitterbarth 2006: 110).

as empirical basis of his hypotheses, without critically interrogating the patterns in the observations noted by explorers, missionaries, and field researchers whose writings he reviewed. Rather, he took these reports at face value and erected entire explanatory edifices on them.

Wundt's pupil Felix Krueger, with whom Verwoerd studied in 1926, combined ethnopsychology, the psychology of childhood and adolescence, and animal psychology in the concept of developmental psychology.[138] He had introduced the concept of holistic psychology "into Wundt's school, at first primarily through his experimental work in sound psychology (since 1904) and not least also through his lectures and tutorials on the psychology of primitive cultures".[139] In the process, he had gauged the level of civilisational development on the basis of attitudes to work, linking the former to the detachment of thought from magical causality.[140] In this way, Krueger succeeded in bending Wundt's theses on civilisational development in such a way that he could connect them with developmental psychology.[141] Within this schema, a people learns, like a child, to differentiate and structure diffuse complex qualities. "Psychic as well as cultural development progresses steadily from primitive wholeness, to less primitive wholeness, which means, among other things, more structured wholeness."[142] Differentiation thus became the criterion of development, which applied in an analogous way to peoples, for according to Wundt, "primitive" cultures were characterised by a low level of differentiation not only in cultural resources, but also in their patterns of perception. "Primitives" were thus like children, an idea that corresponded to widespread colonialist assumption also shared by Verwoerd;[143] in Krueger's view,

---

[138] Beuchelt 1974: 25–28. On pertinent research conducted in Krueger's institute, see Beuchelt 1974: 42; also Thiermann 1981: 87; and Wellek 1950: 18f. On the relation that Krueger construed between child psychology and ethnopsychology, see Schubeius 1990: 249. Krueger is said to have succeeded Wundt because he promised to continue with Wundt's ethnopsychological studies (see Hammer 1995: 34; also Wolfradt 2009: 189). Wundt himself was not enthusiastic about Krueger's appointment (see Guski–Leinwand 2007: 124, n. 141).
[139] Volkelt 1962a: 3, n. 1. Volkelt surmised "that the main developmental tendencies across widely diverging groups, such as children and primitive peoples show astonishing correspondences" (1962a: 7).
[140] Krueger 1913a: 260–261.
[141] On this, see especially Krueger 1915: 104, 167ff; and his critique of Wundt (Krueger 1915: 200ff). Wundt himself rejected the idea that developmental psychology constituted a comprehensive approach (see Mack/Kressley-Mba/Knopf 2006: 70; see also Meischner-Metge 2006b).
[142] Krueger 1926a: 75; see also Buss 1934: 55.
[143] There are indications that such-like assumptions have not been dispelled by any means – see for instance the direct comparisons between 'primitives' and children in Hallpike 1990: ch. 4 and Dux 1990: ch. 4.

"primitives" were more oriented toward emotional responses, whereas civilised people were more intellectually oriented.[144] Krueger's ethnopsychology differed from Wundt's stage theory in one respect, however: Krueger qualified ethnopsychology as "differential ethnopsychology", meaning that peoples were evaluated not only on the basis of their different level of development, but also on the basis of fundamental differences. This entailed the possibility that two peoples of the same level of development could still display major differences. Krueger was primarily concerned to determine the specificity of the German ethnic soul ['*Volksseele*'].[145] The role of ethnopsychology during Krueger's time in Leipzig is easily overlooked, due to the fact that he himself and his students did not publish much within this field.[146] However, its role in teaching should not be underestimated – it is likely that the teaching of ethnopsychology in Leipzig exercised a lasting influence on Verwoerd.

Apart from Krueger, it was Volkelt in particular who devoted himself to Wundt's ethnopsychology time and again in numerous courses.[147] In the summer semester of 1926, Verwoerd participated in one of the accompanying tutorials titled 'Early Forms

---

144 Krueger 1940: 47. This 'insight' was also disseminated by Afrikaans-speaking ethnologists (J. F. Eloff 1959: 56).
145 Guski-Leinwand 2007: 85; on the possibility that Wundt's later writings were manipulated, see Guski-Leinwand 2007: 92: n. 99. See also Krueger's appropriation of Wundt for his own German–nationalist positions, see Krueger 1922: 43–44; also Klemm (1922: 106), who sees the departure from experimental psychology under Krueger dating back to Wundt.
146 Krueger (1915) is an exception.
147 Krueger Collection, 8, 'Magical Factors in the first development of human labor' (1913). This text, as well as 3 (collection of notes on the topic of 'taboo'), indicates a direct connection to Wundt's theses. Krueger's personnel file contains a note dated 30.6.1909: "Ever since his return from America, he added well-attended lectures on the psychology of primitive peoples to his lecturing schedule." (UA Leipzig, Phil. Fac., microfilm no. 1272, personnel file 664, Felix Krueger, Doc. 18, personnel files 410, 455, 664, from 1891 to . . .). In the context of his appointment in 1917, it is noted that "after he had returned to Leipzig, he continued working at the psychological Institute, and simultaneously conducted a course on ethnopsychology at Lamprecht's Institute for Cultural and Universal History" (ibid., doc 28). In another document, it is noted that "Krueger resolutely maintained that research into cultures in general found itself at a turning point, and that from now on, it would have to engage much more with methods and problems of 'developmental psychology' than it has in the past" (Doc. 36, Würzburg, Volkelt Collection, Box 8, Ethnopsychology; Box 14, Psychology IV, 'Four Lectures on Ethnopsychology', as well as manuscripts of 1921/1922 lectures: Introduction to Ethnopsychology and various other notes on Ethnopsychology, of different dates). Volkelt referred to the same ethnological researchers and examples as Wundt. (Box 21: Tutorials on Art and Ethnopsychology, as well as Boxes 23 and 24 on Ethnopsychology and Art and Religion of the Primitives; Box 29, Rough Notes 6, lectures on Wundt's Ethnopsychology – clearly the lecture notes taken by Volkelt when he was a student).

of Religion in Children and Primitive Peoples'.[148] At the time, Volkelt stated: "The experimental method for the study of young children should be guided not so much by special hypotheses as by the theory of primitive consciousness, which has been validated through numerous sources, including ethnopsychological ones."[149] As early as 1925, the Institute issued a 'self-portrait', describing its approach as follows:

> The research field that Wundt termed 'ethnopsychology' has now been firmly integrated into the Institute's research and teaching. Nearly all questions are being addressed from the point of view of genetic comparison. The psychology of the childhood and adolescence – not explicitly referred to by Wundt – is the current focus of the Department of Developmental Psychology. Experimental and ethnological methods are working hand in hand here towards the goal of a theory of primitive consciousness and mental development.[150]

In one of his own contributions, Volkelt stated their interrelation even clearer by pointing to the importance of genetic connections:

> They run through individual life, from the psychology of the embryo to that of old age, as through the life of a people, from the most deeply 'primary-primitive' . . . tribes – not in a linear fashion, but in innumerable branches and ramifications – to the highest levels of culture, from the plant through the animal kingdom right up to the level of man. Moreover, it is astonishing to observe that the main lines of development in far-flung regions often coincide, as for instance in children and primitive peoples, in animals and children.[151]

Just as the understanding of children's drawings as 'expression' of the child's psyche, and not as life-like reproductions of outer appearances,[152] can be seen as a step forward in child psychology, one had to relativise one's own standards, otherwise one would not be able to understand magical thinking among "primitive" peoples.

As far as the belief in magic is concerned, it arises from what elicits "fear and fright", and not from causal thinking: "Causality in our sense of the term does not exist for primitive man."[153] According to Volkelt, one cannot measure so-called primitive peoples by the yardsticks of cultures at a later stage of development, but only by their own 'logic' in the context of their own natural philosophy and

---

[148] Unfortunately, no notes of this tutorial are available.
[149] Volkelt 1926: 13, 48–55.
[150] UA Leipzig, Psych. Inst., Brochure, p. 5.
[151] UA Leipzig, Psych. Inst. Literary Reports on Philosophy, Issue 6, 1925, p. 17.; see also Volkelt 1925: 18.
[152] See also Marx 2013: 107–108; also Remplein 1962: 303.
[153] Wundt 1913: 92–93. On causal thinking of children, see Hansen 1960: 185–186, 217–222.

the norms of their own ethics.[154] The problem was that ethnopsychologists did not have the faintest knowledge of these standards and norms; they existed only in their imagination. This kind of interpretive psychology of Volkelt's design overcame Wundt's ethnopsychology by appearance only; it did not actually break away from the latter's ethnocentrism.

Volkelt explained the religious beliefs and practices of primitive peoples by reference to the lack of causal thinking, and to an affective response to certain phenomena like illness and death.[155] This clearly shows an affinity to Levy-Bruhl's idea of the "prelogical mentality", indicating, in turn, the wide dissemination of such views in the early twentieth century.[156] For it was not only the right-wing Leipzig psychologists who construed a parallel development of "primitive peoples" or "peoples close to nature" and children; rather, this notion had attained doctrinal status among early twentieth century psychologists in general, independently of their respective political orientation. Even progressive psychologists such as Stern and Koffka equated child development, or the development of forms of perception in children, with those of "primitive" peoples.[157] This implied that the latter lacked creativity, and the capabilities of innovation and logical combination.[158] Assessments of this kind are to be found, to a significant extent, in Verwoerd's conjectures on the developmental capacity of "the Bantu". The problematic nature of ethnopsychology as a field of scientific inquiry can be gauged from the statements on the supposed immaturity of Africans, on the lack in capabilities at the current state of their development, etc., which largely coincided with popular prejudices.[159] Once

---

154 Wundt himself construed a close connection between the thinking of 'primitives' and child psychology: Wundt 1914: 145–149.

155 Volkelt Collection, Box 17, 'Art and Ethnopsychology', III, 1, 'Phenomenol. of primitive naturalness and Phenomenology of the Gap', and various notes (unpaginated). In a different part of the same collection of notes, it says: "A notable moment of individual-causal process, which itself can be an individual causal process. But the missing moment at earlier stages is certainly not in consciousness; in consciousness is only the realisation that *something* is missing: at a very primitive level: *strangeness*; or – at a higher level – also the kind of thing that is missing: *unnaturalness*." (see also Box 23 with numerous notes on "the gap" and forms of perception in 'primitives' in contrast to 'us'.)

156 Lévy–Bruhl 1923: 26–33, ch. 11; Holloway 1964: 24, so for instance also Le Bon 1908: 43, 46, 81; on Le Bon, see Hannaford 1996: 337–340.

157 Stern 1911: 104–105; see also Koffka 1921: 1–2; and Wertheimer 1967: 151–155 (but much more differentiated in Wertheimer).

158 Koffka, 1921: 253: The world of children and that of 'primitives', he states, is not logically, that is non-contradictorily, structured.

159 Koorts 2014: 202-2-3. On this, see the widespread nature of such ideas among members of the white elite in South Africa: over 70% of persons interviewed compared Africans with children (Adam 1971: 80, 82).

again, we are dealing with a circular argument: the researcher arbitrarily determines primitiveness and proceeds to develop criteria from this determination by which he then proves it.

What had transpired from Volkelt's Leipzig seminars was reflected in a statement of Verwoerd's, which can serve as an example: "Characteristic of children's play is the fact that inanimate objects are perceived by them as animate and conscious."[160] Meanwhile the child cannot as yet distinguish between alive and lifeless; thus, it does not, on the basis of its own consciousness as living being, transfer this attribute to lifeless objects, but rather, "primitive man and the child originally perceive the object as living, and only at a later stage does the distinction between alive and lifeless arise".[161] If one were to pursue this parallel further, and replace 'the child' with 'the primitive', one can glean, albeit indirectly, Verwoerd's perspective on South Africa's black population: "Here, then, we find a characteristic of the child's [and the 'primitive's'?] personality, namely a fixed, regular relation between the self in its whole being, to the whole of the anorganic, that is, also natural, world."[162] Entailed in this perspective is also the idea that the child does not as yet have a concept of time, and cannot connect the past or the future to the present.[163] However, Verwoerd underlines the idea that children grow up in a world controlled by adults, that they gradually adapt, oscillating between play and work.[164] The decisive difference between the world of children (and of the "primitives") and of the adults, according to Verwoerd, is the absence of logical thinking in the former. Since logic was of great importance to Verwoerd, the supposed absence of logical thinking implied a strong value judgement.

In his lectures, Verwoerd himself mentioned the "lack of coherence [*onsamehangendheid*] in the consciousness of children". Accordingly, adult consciousness was characterised by logic and consistency of thoughts, whereas supposedly childlike Africans had an incoherent consciousness not governed by logic.[165] Thus, assuming the ethnopsychological notion of an analogous development of children and peoples, he was able to declare nationalism a civilisational achievement. In an address on Dingaan's Day, a holiday by which the Afrikaners celebrated their victory over the Zulu as divine intervention, Verwoerd proclaimed:

---

160 PV 93/1/33/3, Verskynsels by die kind, handwritten note, p. 1.
161 Ibid.
162 Ibid.
163 Ibid., p. 2.
164 Ibid., p. 1.
165 PV 93/1/33/3, f. 15, 'Wat het ons gedurende die Bespreking . . .', p. 1.

> It is through days like these that we are lifted up, and we direct ourselves to a higher level of insight. In some respects, man is born an animal – self-centered in his physical needs and his striving for satisfaction. He is not interested in anything that does not concern himself, but he will have to be raised above this exclusive concern for himself. He will have to be guided toward a broader circle of ideas outside of himself, where he can forget his own paltry purposes and ascend to the aims of higher values – to become a person who, freed from the prison of his self, can participate in cultural life.[166]

The extent to which Verwoerd was directly influenced by ethnopsychology cannot be exactly determined, due to a lack of self-declaratory statements.[167] However, his political speeches abound with references to the supposedly low level of development of Africans, which he occasionally compared with that of children. A particular problem was bound to arise when elite groups themselves turned out to be misguided, not recognising the basic principles of their culture – as he diagnosed in the case of the black educated elite. In mentioning "a certain group of natives who steadfastly cling to their prejudices", he did not mean a tradition-bound tribal population in any sense, but the "so-called leaders" with their "selfish ambitions" who stood in the way of his politics.[168] The fact that they oriented themselves along the lines of Western civilisation instead of their own seemed to him a symptom of their immaturity in the sense stipulated by ethnopsychology. The fact remained that an internal differentiation assigning a higher level of development to a social elite, was dependent from the general level of development of the society as a whole. If it was at a barbaric level of development, one could not expect the educated elite to recognise its essential task, hence one did not have to, or would not even be able to discuss it with them. In this idea, the formula of Afrikaner nationalists, "apartheid and guardianship", found its ethnopsychological justification.

Verwoerd found that blunting of emotional sensations occurred in more "developed" persons, whereas uneducated persons remained fixated upon trivial matters and inanities. Moreover, judgements of more developed people were more variable, because they were more open to new views and ideas. This observation is interesting in that it could be applied also to ethnic and civilisational differences. Accordingly, less civilised people were thought to be more strongly guided by emotions because in their judgements, they followed customs and traditions rather than certain values. Civilised people, on the other hand, trusted their intellect, not

---

166 FAV 4.4.6, undated lecture notes.
167 But on a letter addressed to him by Arthur Leib from Hamburg, he highlighted the fact that the latter was an ethnopsychologist (PV 93/1/11/5, Letter by Arthur Leib to Verwoerd, 5.8.1958).
168 FAV 4.6.1.1, Letter by H. Jac. Rousseau (Pretoria) to Verwoerd, 14.11.1950; Verwoerd's reply, 7.12.1950.

so much as a matter of an inner attitude, but because their feelings were bound to get blunted at a faster rate, due to greater intellectual agility.[169]

Apartheid ideologists drew not only on stage theories, but also on cultural-relativist arguments for this policy, often even mentioning them in the same breath, even though they logically contradicted each other. Based on these stage theories, apartheid ethnologists in the circle of Eiselen and Coertze, as well as Verwoerd himself, developed a legitimation of apartheid policies: "the Bantu", to them, were not only less developed than the Europeans, but their culture differed fundamentally from that of the Europeans, and was therefore irreconcilable with it.[170] From this, they concluded that cultural interrelatedness would be detrimental for "the Bantu", making segregation in the form of apartheid the only answer. This once again placed difference – the basic principle of Verwoerd's thinking – at the centre of the argumentation. It cannot be ruled out that in formulating this idea, he drew on the differential psychology of his Hamburg teacher William Stern.

The aim of Stern's book entitled *Die Differentielle Psychologie in ihren methodischen Grundlagen* ('Methodological foundations of differential psychology') was to work out the differences between people, that is, between individuals as well as between groups of people. It was thus comparative by design – it set out to identify and analyse variabilities.[171] Stern was of the opinion that human development was determined neither exclusively by genetic make-up nor exclusively by environmental factors, but by both.[172] In the course of its development, the human personality was exposed to numerous environmental influences, through which certain genetic dispositions would be allowed to develop, or would be diverted or hindered.[173] Differential psychology led to a psychology oriented towards the individual, which was supposed to account for differences between personalities.

Apartheid ideologists repeatedly made use of politically and philosophically quite different findings, which they transferred from their respective intellectual contexts to that of racial segregation.[174] The basis for the cultural-relative arguments on Africans that Verwoerd developed at a later stage, possibly stem from

---

169 Verwoerd 1924a: 100–105. See also Lehmann 1914: 381–384.
170 Barnard 1967: 47: "Because the Bantu is 'different', he has to be treated differently, without diminishing his value as a human being."
171 Stern 1911: 55; for references to characterology and other approaches, see ibid., 150–154.
172 Ibid., 72–75, 270; see also 1928a: 26–27, 31.
173 Bittner/Deutsch 1990: 61.
174 See M. Sanders' (1999: 614–617) analysis of van Wyk Louw's adoption of the ideas of liberal philosopher Hoernlé, and of the ways in which the former distorted these and (ab)used them for his own cultural–nationalist argumentation.

differential psychology and cultural-relativist ethnology. "Primitive" peoples were thought to be located at the developmental stage of small children, to whom one could not apply the standards of adults or whites. At the same time, they underwent a different development that made them incomparable. The contradiction inherent in these views was never articulated, and most likely never even picked up.

Apartheid and Development

For Verwoerd, the essential difference between whites and blacks did not consist in the notion that the one group was culturally more highly developed than the other, but in psychological factors that were supposed to explain why that was the case. External circumstances like climate were not sufficient to explain differences in the pace of development; Verwoerd thought "that the pace of development was determined not so much by external factors, but by psychological susceptibility at different stages."[175] Africans did not simply have to catch up, but their development would have to take cultural specificities into account. From observations deemed 'empirical', that whites in his opinion were more highly developed in essential respects, Verwoerd derived, by way of a circular argument, the justification for the estimation of their developmental prospects. Thus, as early as 1922, in his MA dissertation, Verwoerd noted that "not everyone can attain the higher values, for human nature presents different degrees of values and capabilities to realise them". This applied not only to individual but also to collective differences: "primitive man seeks his values in pleasure and deeds, which an intellectual civilisation holds in rather low esteem".[176]

Ethnopsychologists maintained that "primitive" peoples not only resembled children, but that they were childlike – their overall cognitive abilities and the forms of their cultural expressions were those of children. Children have to be guided by grown-ups, and by analogy, this equally applied to childlike civilisations. That is why Verwoerd, talking about self-governing structures at a later stage, could say: "It follows logically that depending on the degree to which the possibilities of the mind, the initiative and the sense of responsibility of the Bantu develop", a gradual withdrawal of whites from administration can be envisaged.[177] In many of his speeches, specifically in those mentioning the homeland

---

[175] G. D. Scholtz 1974, vol. 1: 299. This is where Verwoerd's training as psychologist, and possibly his immersion in 'ethnopsychology' at the Institute of Felix Krueger in Leipzig, is borne out.
[176] Verwoerd 1922b: 1–2.
[177] Hansard, 25.5.1956, col. 3993f.; see also col. 4021.

policy, Verwoerd referred to psychological factors that had to be taken into account in properly gauging the developmental possibilities.

Thus, he always emphasised the profound cultural differences between blacks and whites: "Between the white and black people there exists an enormous difference in character and attitude to life [*"die grootste verskeienheid van karakter en van uitkyk"*], and therefore also an enormous difference in their ideals and interests." Apart from skin colour, which he considered an important factor, there were differences in "religion, level of civilisation, customs, geographical location, etc."[178] In his justification of apartheid, the term *'beskawing'* ('civilisation') was key.[179] The difference between barbarism and civilisation was adduced again and again as a reason why living together in one state and in one society was impossible in the case of people with such a great "psychological variety of abilities among the various race groups in the country",[180] and why the only solution was to be found in segregation. Living together would mean forcing people together, resulting in multiple conflicts[181] that would threaten the civilisational status of whites. "It is as unlikely that it will be possible to hold together the Whites and the Bantu in peace and free of strife in one multi-racial unit as it is to do so in the case of Black nations in other parts of Africa or as it is to throw together Xhosa, Basuto and Zulu without conflict into one communal entity."[182]

In an address to the South African Academy of Arts and Sciences in June 1964, Verwoerd set out his ethnopsychological assessments of "the Bantu" with particular clarity:

> It is often thought that the Bantu are suitable for any kind of work needed in society. . . . But those of us who are dealing with them and are thoroughly acquainted with them, know that this is not the case. Those who want to study the history, also know that this is not the case; they know that there are differences between one person and another. This does not mean that one wants to brand some as inferior compared to another group that is considered superior; but people are simply not the same. Different races are not simply of the same kind. In our own Bantu areas we have found out that for eighty years now, we have

---

178 PV 93/4/1/9, Address to the 1963 ATKV Congress, ff. 172–187, 183.
179 But Verwoerd could not provide an answer to the question that a member of the Federal Council had posed to him – namely what exactly he understood by 'Western civilisation' (PV 54/2/5, Minutes of the Federal Council of the NP, 7.6.1965, TOP 6, p. 2).
180 Verwoerd, Annual Congress of the Afrikaans Trade Institute, Pretoria, 19.9.1961 (in Pelzer 1966: 611–628, 625).
181 "Like all other countries of the world, South Africa has its problems, even if they are distinct from those of others in revolving around the great difference between white and black, civilised and uncivilised." (PV 93/1/30/1/23, letter by Verwoerd to H. Axt, Munich, 22.1.1964, f. 68, originally in German).
182 Verwoerd, House of Assembly, 23.1.1962 (in Pelzer 1966: 660–689, 665f.).

been trying to make ordinary good farmers out of them, but this has not been achieved by most of them, due to certain character traits [among them].

Apart from external circumstances, it was particularly "human psychology, the psychology of the Bantu, that counteracts capability, initiative, and drive". This was bound to become a problem not only for the South African homelands, but throughout Africa as a whole. "The world which, in considering the development of Africa and Asia, does not take account of the psychology of the people with whom it is dealing, thinking that it can make everyone work like Westerners, with the same methods and the same goals, is thus committing a grave mistake, slowing down rather than promoting the development of these countries."[183] The reference to "psychological factors" did not simply mean cultural differences, but the underlying mental developmental steps and skills.

The psychologically based civilisational differences were said to be reflected in economic development:

> In South Africa there was at the same time a Bantu community lagging behind that development. That community remained behind at a subsistence economy and practically continued to supply only unskilled labour. If our economy is to flourish in the future then the standpoint is that (even if the pace is slower than that elsewhere because of the psychological deficiencies as well as shortcomings in management, ability and capital wealth) those communities must be developed in one way or another, on similar lines to benefit sufficiently the whole of South Africa's economy.[184]

That is, Verwoerd noted, why it was important to realise that "the development of backward nations with their psychological outlook is no easy matter as current history elsewhere in Africa shows".[185] Apartheid, in contrast, would set economic development of "the Bantu" in motion, "which is right in every stage according to their ability and which, within their own circle, is at a pace which is psychologically suitable for them".[186]

In fact, for him, blacks were not even capable of continuing to build on what whites in Africa had put in front of them: Africa's "psychological problems" lay in the fact that "the Native's idea of 'freedom', also in Central Africa, is not to work hard for one's independent existence, but that after 'freedom' you need not work any more, because you will inherit that which the White man built up there! That

---

183 PV 93/4/1/10, ff. 81–96. Verwoerd's address to the Akademie vir Wetenskap en Kuns, 27.6.1964, p. 11.
184 Verwoerd, Annual Congress of the Afrikaans Trade Institute, Pretoria, 19.9.1961 (in Pelzer 1966: 611–628, 624).
185 PV 93/1/30/1/30, Letter by Verwoerd to Mrs E.M. Gould, Pietersburg, 9.9.1965.
186 Verwoerd, Annual Congress of the Afrikaans Trade Institute, Pretoria, 19.9.1961 (in Pelzer 1966: 611–628, 625).

is often the idea of freedom or 'Uhuru'."[187] In contrast to black's expectation of being given the goods of life, whites had posed challenges for themselves, and overcome difficulties, which is one of the reasons for their civilisational progress: "We become strong in mind and body only when we have difficulties to overcome, when we have hard work to do."[188] The most important character trait of the white man was his initiative: "It is his character, his initiative, and his other inherent qualities in the form of creative urge and intellectual capacity which have made the White man great."[189] Even after the South African War, whites had not given up: "When we were defeated, we did not stay lying down feeling sorry for ourselves, but got up and built anew and thereby worked miracles. From a wounded heart, a steely spirit has arisen."[190] His view of history was shaped by the idea of progress, progress was the measure of civilisation for him: "Literally everything which comes into being or which is ordered, only exists because man looks ahead. Throughout the centuries humanity has been building the world of the future. It has seldom been concerned with the present. Man is a rational and creative being because he looks ahead."[191] In his notion of civilisational differences, he was also influenced by the depth of time of Western civilisation, as he had experienced it to his amazement in Pompeii,[192] with which he contrasted Africans who were, in his opinion, still at the very beginning of their development, having achieved no cultural achievements comparable to those of the Romans.[193]

Even the otherwise little appreciated British Empire was considered proof of the creative power of the whites and as sign of the higher level of their civilisation: "It was possible by virtue of intellectual powers and because she [Great Britain] refused to abdicate from her duty and from her status."[194] The rule of a

---

187 Verwoerd, House of Assembly, 23.1.1962 (in Pelzer 1966: 660–689,680). See also PV 93/1/30/1/28, Letter by Verwoerd to E. Pots (Saldanha), 14.10.1964, f. 184. This remark of Verwoerd's is unintentionally comic, as it was especially Kenyatta who was preaching an ethics of hard work (Branch 2012: 9).
188 Verwoerd, Opening of the Hendrik Verwoerd Tunnels, 18.11.1961 (in Pelzer 1966: 636–641, 640).
189 Verwoerd, House of Assembly, 9.3.1960 (in Pelzer 1966: 340–369, 366).
190 PV 93/4/1/8, Message on the Vereeniging Monument, 17.1.1963.
191 Verwoerd, Inauguration of Sunday School Buildings, Bloemfontein, 1.10.1959 (in Pelzer 1966: 299–312, 302).
192 Verwoerd's wife wrote about the visit to the archaeological site, noting that both of them were astounded by "the high level that the art of painting had reached even in those days" (E. Verwoerd, 'Rome en Napels'. *Ons Kerk*, May 1927, pp. 328–329, 329). See also FAV 4.3.2, Letter by W. Verwoerd to E. Verwoerd, 14.2.1995.
193 Thus, notes from his earliest political speeches, held at a time when he was still appointed as professor, are titled, 'Emergence of civilised man from primitive man'.
194 Verwoerd, House of Assembly, 9.3.1960 (in Pelzer 1966: 340–369, 366).

comparatively small number of whites over the peoples of Asia could be explained psychologically: "The control of the future of civilization does not rest with numbers, but rests with those who have the strength of character, the knowledge, the initiative and the courage."[195] Progress in South Africa was assured because "the presence of the white nation of South Africa is a definite final guarantee."[196] It was the different level of civilisation that resulted in the superiority of the whites, which could only lead to "clashes" when living together in one state.[197] Territorial racial segregation was the consequence drawn from this ethnopsychological view.

Verwoerd gauged the level of civilisation by his idea of technological-material progress. Industrial society to him was the epitome of the West's high level of civilisation, and everything had to be done "to make South Africa a great agricultural country, a great industrial country, a great stronghold of civilisation!"[198] Conversely, blacks were not in a position "to govern this highly industrialised country, apart from the injustice that would be done to the white man if this land that he found empty three hundred years ago, were taken away from him in order to hand it over to the black man".[199] In his response to Macmillan's "Wind of Change"-speech, Verwoerd referred to the civilising achievements of the whites in Africa: "They are the people . . . who brought civilisation here, who made possible the present development of black nationalism by bringing the natives education, by showing them the Western way of life, by bringing to Africa industry and development, by inspiring them with the ideals which Western civilisation has developed for itself."[200]

---

[195] Verwoerd, 1820 Settlers' Trust Banquet, Johannesburg 27.4.1962 (in Pelzer 1966: 690–696, 690).
[196] Verwoerd, Opening of the Hendrik Verwoerd Tunnels, 18.11.1961 (in Pelzer 1966: 636–641, 640).
[197] PV 93/1/11/2, ff. 14–20, Radio speech upon election to Prime Minister, p. 4.
[198] Verwoerd, Opening of the Hendrik Verwoerd Tunnels, 18.11.1961 (in Pelzer 1966: 636–641, 639).
[199] PV 93/1/30/1/22, Letter by Verwoerd to Fr. Romanus Pally (Uznach, Switzerland), 14.12.1963.
[200] Verwoerd, Speech of Thanks to Mr Harold Macmillan, 3.2.1960 (in Pelzer 1966: 336–339, 338). Similarly the speech of Verwoerd, 'Uit Eenheid Krag: From Unity Strength.'n Dramatiese Voorstelling vir die Vyfde Verjaarsdag van die Republiek van Suid–Afrika in die Amfiteater van die Voortrekkermonument, Pretoria, op 31 Mei 1966 (PV 93/4/1/3, p. 20).

However, he also repeatedly expressed doubts as to whether "the Bantu" could really develop to the level of the whites,[201] and he expressed his conviction that the road to civilisational development would be a very long one. "If it is within the power of the Bantu, and if the territories in which he now lives can develop to full independence, it will develop in that way."[202]

In any case, the development of "the Bantu" had to start from the basics, that is, not starting with, or measured by, the small, educated elite, but with the broad mass of the population. Therefore, it was viewed as a matter of course "that the Bantu had to start at a low level. He is not psychologically prepared for the industrial world, and certainly not for the life of an entrepreneur to start on a grand scale." According to Verwoerd, that would not change in the coming decades, and that is why the "psychological mistakes committed in the process of developmental work in rural areas" should not now be repeated in industry. This was an educational task, which is why the government relied on the principle of self-help, in order to practice responsible management of financial resources. "That is why the Government is opposed to the large-scale establishment in the Bantu areas of White industries which will then have to be taken over by the Natives who are not yet capable of doing so."[203]

Helping people to help themselves implied guardianship, because "the Bantu" lacked initiative and stamina. Taking up his comparison of "the Bantu" with children – with very small children in this case –, he denounced the older dispensation "spoon feeding", propelling "the Bantu" into a mentality of dependence as he had previously diagnosed it for the case of "poor whites".[204] In his view, this was not a matter of oppression, but a matter of alignment with the nationalist creed

---

201 The aim of his government was "to let the Bantu act in accordance with his own capacity and create his own homeland. If he has the capacity to develop into his own independent nation, the government will not stand in his way." (PV 93/1/30/1/19, Letter by Verwoerd to D. T. van der Walt, 14.5.1963, f. 46) "But if development takes place, within the limits of the ability of the Bantu to govern himself . . ." (Verwoerd, No Confidence Debate, 27.1.1959, in Pelzer 1966: 216–247, 246).
202 Verwoerd, 'Bantu Self–government', Senate 20.5.1959 (in Pelzer 1966: 271–295, 278). The Afrikaans original version differs from the English one. The former (in English translation) reads as follows: "If the Bantu has the capacity for independence, and if the areas *donated to him for his emancipation – or rather, those areas that are already his own –* can develop to attain full independence, then this should come to pass." (see Pelzer 1963: 254–275, 260).
203 Verwoerd, Commission for the Development of Bantu Areas, 14.5.1956 (in Pelzer 1966: 102–123, 92–116; see also ''n permanente aparte blanke Suid–Africa' [n.d., 1960], p. 2 – in which Verwoerd presents arguments, different from those mentioned before, about the reasons why he was opposed to investment in the "homelands".
204 Verwoerd, 'Policy of the Minister of Native Affairs', June 20, 1955 (in Pelzer 1966: 86–101, 92–93). His wife expressed the view that the previous system of 'spoonfeeding' was responsible for the loss of self–respect among "the Bantu" (*Natal Daily News*, 23.1.1959).

that regarded all South Africans "as human beings with their own value, rights and legitimate aspirations, although they are at different stages of development and therefore have different capacities to meet the multiple obligations impinging today in relation to their own people".[205]

In any case, Verwoerd's policies were guided by the idea "that if one wants to lead a community to adulthood, one has to begin by using the talents and the skills available in that community. One has to build on its traditions and institutions".[206] For, as he had noted as early as 1922, "it is probably the case that primitive man regards habits as binding and that therein lies the beginning of a consciousness of moral obligation".[207] That is why, above all else, the pace of development had to be slowed down. "Naturally the psychology of our Bantu is an obstacle to speed, since South Africa cannot allow chaos as in the Congo to develop in the Bantu homelands."[208]

Verwoerd's insistence that the newly independent states of Asia and Africa could not be considered "adult",[209] did not signify the years of their actual existence, and not only their inexperience in handling bureaucratic apparatuses, but their immaturity in the sense derived from ethnopsychology. Even if he did not openly present arguments from biology, his racism is evident from his easy extrapolation from particular processes in a particular region on the continent, to general statements about the whole continent. He explained such developments not by reference to social causes, but to racial ones.[210]

For Verwoerd, there were not only immature peoples and nations, but also "unadult" states, especially in Africa and Asia, which nurtured "grievances and ambitions aimed at the Western nations".[211] In his PhD thesis, he noted that im-

---

205 FAV 4.7.1.5, Press statement released by Verwoerd, 22.11.1960.
206 Verwoerd, House of Assembly, 23.1.1962 (in Pelzer 1966: 660–689, 667; see also the heavy dose of scepticism expressed in the assessment of the future of Nigeria, in *Die Vaderland*, 15.4.1959).
207 Verwoerd 1922b: 60.
208 PV 93/1/30/1/26, Letter by Verwoerd to O.W. Grinaker, 9.7.1964.
209 Verwoerd, New Year's Message, 31.12.1961 (in Pelzer 1966: 654–659, 655).
210 Verwoerd was not alone in holding such views. This becomes clear from the statement on 'the native' by W. Carr, Manager of Non-European Affairs Department of the City of Johannesburg: "His gullibility and his tendency to mass hysteria can, in fact, lead to riots." (City of Johannesburg, 'Report of the Manager, Non–European Affairs Department for the Period 1st July 1956 to 30th June1957', p. 6).
211 Verwoerd, New Year's Message, 31.12.1961 (in Pelzer 1966: 654–659, 655). Similarly, his speech in Florida in 1963: As a "grown-up state", South Africa would not care about the reactions of other African states: "With time, they will learn, just as a child gradually learns, to get over its moods and tempers, and to attain self–mastery" (FAV 4.7.2.4.5, p. 8).

maturity and civilisational underdevelopment pertained to those cases in which politics was not conceived according to the standards of reason and logic but was driven by emotions. He saw the UN, in particular, with its growing number of Asian and African member states, as a kind of kindergarten for immature peoples who set the tone in that organisation. That is why he wondered "whether this overcrowded UN must not give way to a smaller body consisting of the really responsible nations of the world".[212]

To distract attention from their own shortcomings, Verwoerd stated, these "juvenile nations"[213] were eager to pillory South Africa. This also had consequences for their own behaviour in foreign policy: "Anybody who knows the native mind will know that help given without demanding proper respect from these Black States for South Africa will not have any desired result."[214]

What Wundt formulated as a theory of stages in the development of cognitive and intellectual qualities entailing their detachment from the natural, Verwoerd extended to social and political arenas. For him, Africans were not able to form complex societies; he considered the chiefdom as the form of political organisation adequate to their stage of development.

---

[212] Verwoerd, New Year's Message, 31.12.1960 (in Pelzer 1966: 429–433, 433).
[213] Verwoerd, New Year's Message, 31.12.1962 (in Pelzer 1966: 716–719, 716); in the original version, Verwoerd speaks of "duck-tailed nations" (Pelzer 1963: 667–670, 667).
[214] PV 93/1/30/1/29, Verwoerd to Harry E. Teifel, Johannesburg, 26.4.1965.

From Sociology to Social Policy

Commitment to the 'Poor Whites'

White poverty was not a new phenomenon, for social inequalities concealed behind the Boers' egalitarian self-image had been noted as far back as the 19th century. The impoverishment of large sections of the population after the devastation of the South African War aroused the attention of church circles.[1] In the meantime, it has been established that the rebellion of Afrikaners at the beginning of the First World War was carried out predominantly by impoverished whites.[2] For a long time, the churches and some welfare organisations tried to remedy the situation, but the issue was rarely addressed in public.[3] In the aftermath of the Great Depression, and a devastating drought persisting for a couple of years during the 1930s, white poverty assumed alarming proportions,[4] and consequently became politically and nationalistically charged, thus emerging as a 'problem' for the society as a whole. The existence of a large number of utterly impoverished whites called South Africa's racial order into question; it raised the spectre of demolishing the unquestioned respect for the supposed "higher level of civilisation" that whites enjoyed in the eyes of the black population. Research on white poverty in South Africa can be broadly divided into two fields:

1. Research on poverty itself: scholars have studied the topic extensively[5] – from the early work of William Macmillan[6] through the Carnegie Report to more recent research by historians and social scientists. Verwoerd's academic teacher R.W. Wilcocks was one of the authors of the *Carnegie Report on the Poor White Problem*, a comprehensive empirical study on white poverty, published in 1932 in five volumes; every one of the disciplines involved – medicine, economics, sociology, psychology, and education – contributed a

---

[1] Not least among them was clergyman D. F. Malan in 1917 (see Koorts 2014: 78–80); on his experiences in Graaff–Reinet, see Koorts 2014: 98–104).
[2] Grundlingh/Swart 2009: 25–30.
[3] The Women's Division of the NP dealt with that theme only briefly at its 1926 Congress in Graaff-Reinet (Nasionale Vroueparty 1927: 38).
[4] Minnaar 2013: 28, 36.
[5] W.M. Macmillan 1919, 1930.
[6] During the 1970s, excerpts were re-published (D. Joubert 1972, see especially the Introduction). The report of physician and poet Louis Leipoldt on his experiences as medical doctor in the Transvaal Lowveld is being unjustifiably neglected (Leipoldt 1988). He conducted the first intelligence tests on school–going children (J. Louw 1986: 74). As far as I could find out, Boehmke was the only one to address the topic of incest (1928: 84). For more recent research, see especially Morrell 1992.

study of its own, with Wilcocks as the author of the psychological report. At the instigation of educationist E. G. Malherbe, whose professional biography and positivist approach to science displayed astonishing parallels to Verwoerd's thought,[7] the Carnegie Foundation funded this project; the project was kickstarted with field research in 1929, continuing for most of that year, and concluding only in 1930.[8] Apart from church representatives, it was almost exclusively scientists from the University of Stellenbosch[9] who participated in the research, as well as a journalist, M. E. Rothmann, who was closely aligned with Afrikaner nationalism and its intellectual centre in Stellenbosch. Wilcocks was the only researcher among the four members of the Joint Board, and the supervisory board, whose members included educationist C. T. Loram, church minister A. D. Luckhoff, and politician F. S. Malan.[10] The work of the Commission facilitated the promotion of social scientists into the arena of policy formulation, for which Verwoerd himself served as paradigmatic case. Verwoerd was apparently not directly involved in the work of the Commission,[11] which entailed extensive travelling and wide-ranging investigations. Still, Verwoerd's change from psychology to sociology should be considered in the context of the Carnegie Commission, along with the introduction of sociology as scientific discipline in South Africa, replete with its positivist and quantifying orientation[12] emanating from the US. The Commission recommended scrapping the old age pensions for indigent poor whites, which had been introduced only a few years previously, and habituate them to hard labour instead; for a pension, so the argument went, was bound to be

---

7 Dubow 2001 and Fleisch 1995: 349–350, 353; on Wilcock's role in the Carnegie Commission, see ibid., 111; see also Giliomee 2003a: 346. Steensland (2013: 31–32) highlights the much more prominent role of Loram.
8 Malherbe 1973: 81, 84, 88; also Louw/Foster 1991: 64–65; also Dubow 2006: 7–8, 221–232. The Carnegie Corporation also contributed to the funding of the South African Institute of Race Relations (Brits 1994: 48). On the Carnegie Corporation, especially after 1945, see Unger 2009: 255–256, 261–264; also Steensland 2013: 26–35; and Bick/Rispel/Naidoo 2008: 167.
9 D.J. Kotzé 1966: 455–456.
10 Bell 2000: 491. Steensland (2013: 47ff) underlined Malan's powerful influence, especially as far as the role of church representatives in the Commission was concerned.
11 M.E. Rothmann's notes do not offer any insight into the work of the research team, which is why Verwoerd's participation cannot be conclusively established (55.M.3). Only Kapp (2013: 49) lists Verwoerd among the authors of the Report without, however, providing any evidence of his participation. Verwoerd himself praised his academic teacher Wilcocks as the one who "can, by right, be considered as director of the entire investigation" (*Die Burger* 30.12.1932). This was not the case; it was probably owed to Verwoerd's aversion against the actual initiator E.G. Malherbe, who belonged to a different political camp.
12 Groenewald 1987: 63–66; see also Lever 1978: 212.

understood as a right, which would only reinforce the mentality of dependence among poor whites.[13] Sociologist Geoffrey Cronjé who espoused concepts similar to those of Verwoerd, even went as far as stating that labour was a form of struggle, and the *"volk"* a labouring community, suggesting that he viewed the people as combative community.[14]

2. In addition, there is research dealing with the responses of the Afrikaner-nationalist elite and of South African politics more generally, to the 'poor white problem'. White poverty had the effect of radicalising members of the Afrikaner educated elite, and not least the scientists among them.[15] The politics of racial segregation and apartheid can be understood as an attempt at rehabilitating poor whites through granting them privileges in the labour market. Even more astonishing is it that there is as yet no critical study on Verwoerd, with his preoccupation with white poverty, as one of the most important protagonists of the politics of apartheid.[16] White poverty is key to understanding Verwoerd's political thought; it provides the biographical hinge between his academic career and his subsequent journalistic-political career.

Even from the beginning of his studies at the University of Stellenbosch in 1919, Verwoerd had been intensively engaged with the 'problem' of poor whites;[17] it is likely that it even influenced his decision to study psychology. Like many Afrikaans-speaking psychologists at the time, and during the following decades, he understood psychology as "service to the people", as practically applied science.[18] In his first publication which appeared in a student magazine, he complained about the lack of commitment on the part of self-confessed nationalists to those

---

13 Seekings 2008: 522–523. Nowhere did Verwoerd pronounce himself on state pensions.
14 Cronjé 1964c: 352, 354.
15 What is interesting is the fact that an economist within the nationalist camp held a decidedly anticapitalist position on the topic of white poverty (A. J. Bruwer 1934: 45). For his critique of the Carnegie Report, see A.J. Bruwer 1934: 238–269, and of the Kimberley Congress, 269. Cooper/Nicholas/Seedat/Stratman (1990: 2) consider the Carnegie Report to have set important tracks for taking psychology into the service of racial segregation.
16 The book by E. Theron (1970) is based on extensive source material, and is well informed, but it lacks the necessary distance to its subject–matter. That also applies to those sections of her autobiography that deal with Verwoerd (E. Theron 1983: 22–27).
17 Marx 2011a: 286–287. In a footnote of his thesis, Verwoerd noted: "The University lectures presented by Prof Dr R.W. Wilcocks in 1920 directed our attention to the fact that desires and wishes can be blunting factors." (Verwoerd 1924a: 239) The reference to the year indicates that Verwoerd continued to concern himself with the 'poor whites' even after publishing his article in the student newspaper.
18 Long/Foster 2013: 7.

"disdained in our midst", that is, the poor whites.[19] As a student, Verwoerd was so shocked at the conditions he met with in the slums of Cape Town that white poverty remained a persistent preoccupation for him, which exercised him even up to his time as member of Parliament. In fact, his thesis contains fictive examples of white poverty, based on his observations of "everyday life", that have nothing to do with his experiment:

> A poor white man, for instance, explained that he had had bad luck in his pursuits, and that he was facing impoverishment. He tried something else every time, and with every new venture he developed a strong desire to succeed. But to his great dismay, he experienced one failure after another, until he gave up. Having gone to so much effort without any results, he thought he should just let things go. He then went to work only for the sake of ensuring his survival, without any joy and without the urge to improve his situation. After once again losing his job, he had no emotional sensations left.

Since wishes were directed at fulfilment, emotional sensations became blunted as soon as the prospect of such wish fulfilment was becoming more remote.[20] To demonstrate the process of blunting in the most vivid terms, he adduced another example: "An impoverished white woman with a child crying in misery, showed no signs of sadness or love. She says that in the past, she always wanted the best for her child whenever it was hungry, but that she cannot obtain what she needs; experience had taught her that wishful thinking does not help". Alternatively, Verwoerd explained the process of blunting by direct reference to social degradation: "After a while, someone from a good background who has fallen down the social ladder to the point of landing in a slum, would no longer be ashamed of his filthy appearance and of the neglected environment."[21] This issue was of concern to him throughout.

In 1932, after four years of working in his capacity as Professor for Applied Psychology at the University of Stellenbosch, Verwoerd was appointed in a newly established professorship for Applied Sociology and Social Work. From 1930, he himself had undertaken the steps toward the establishment of this position that was tailor-made to his field.[22] In 1936, he declared that he would "devote [his]

---

19 Verwoerd 1920: 124.
20 Verwoerd 1924a: 259–260. For a change in the assessment, see 257.
21 Ibid., 4.
22 The first courses in the field of Social Studies had been announced as early as 1930 in *Social and Industrial Review* (vol. 9, no. 50, 5 February 1930: 54–55). The journal was edited by the Department of Labour. Before Verwoerd started in his position, C. W. Coulter, a "visiting professor" from the US, had taken over the training of social workers (P. S. du Toit 1966c: 82; see also D. J. Kotzé 1966: 476.). Ally/Mooney/Stewart (2003) provide an overview over the beginnings of Sociology in South Africa.

life" to the poor white problem.[23] "For him, there was no problem in the country that was of greater importance and urgency than the worrisome impoverishment and decline of his people."[24] In the process of urbanisation, many Afrikaners ended up in an English-speaking environment, which Verwoerd deemed to be to their disadvantage. That is why he considered the struggle for the abolition of cultural inequality in the cities an important precondition for the rehabilitation of poor whites.[25] To him, this was "closely related with their escape from poverty".[26]

Until 1932, Sociology at the University of Stellenbosch was taught by Professor of Philosophy N. J. Brümmer[27] and Professor of Educational Psychology J. J. Strasheim. But with the focus of Psychology shifting toward Psychotechnics, Sociology established itself as a discipline independent from that of Psychology. During the first few years, Verwoerd continued to teach Psychology, and only gradually began to devote himself to Sociology.[28] Addressing the Senate of the University, he had stated that he would agree to be a major participant in a new course to train social workers only on condition "that he would be put in charge of this new project".[29]

Initially, his new field of work was more like an extension of his previous teaching,[30] driven by his growing interest in a practical orientation towards public policy-making. During the years after 1932, he conducted research about the situation of poor whites, in which he related the findings of differential psychology to sociological questions, in order to develop an academic programme for the study of Social Work.[31]

---

23 Qtd. in E. Theron 1970: 53.
24 PV 117, f. 6, Notes, 'Dr Verwoerd, my professor tree tot die politiek toe', p. 1.
25 On this, see Stals 1986; see also Terblanche 1995: 159; Bottomley 2012: 61–80; Grundlingh 2005: 197; and with regard to Verwoerd, see 201.
26 Ibid., 2. See also Pauw 1946: ch. 8; M. E. Botha 1970: 184; Fourie/Stals 1978: 173–174; for a contrasting account, see Grundlingh 2003: 174, 182–186.
27 Brümmer had supervised Verwoerd's MA Dissertation in Philosophy and had himself held ambitions to ascend to the newly established professorship (FAV 4.4.3, Contents of Verwoerd's lectures).
28 Verwoerd 1932: 26.
29 UA Stellenbosch, Minutes of Senate Meetings, vol. VIII, 17.10.1930–12.8.1932, here December 1931, p. 232. According to Louw/Foster (1991: 67), Verwoerd had been participating in the capacity as psychologist in the training of social workers as far back as 1929.
30 231/2/1/1, 'Inleiding tot die Sociologie', pp. 5–6: "At the same time, there are occasions when we can, with psychological–experimental methods, gain reliable knowledge affording us an understanding of social life."
31 The first impetus for the professional training of social workers came from the Afrikaanse Christelike Vrouevereniging, in which M.E. Rothmann attained a leading position (Lambrechts 1957: 116); on early stages of her collaboration with Verwoerd, see 117–118.

He worked out a three-year cycle of Sociology lectures, in which the theme of poor whites featured prominently. This is also evident from the sequence of course components: 'Methods of sociological research' was followed by 'Socio-Psychology of Crime ['*misdaad*']', and 'Poverty and the Fight against Poverty'; even in the introductory courses for the first year of study, social conditions in South Africa were foregrounded, with a focus on juvenile delinquency.[32] For the second year of study, Verwoerd focused on "the entire problem of poverty", which was consolidated in the third year and extended, in the second half of that course, with lectures on history and current trends in Sociology. The extant lecture notes indicate that he did not develop any interest in sociological theory formation, and never engaged with it;[33] instead, his teaching remained confined to Applied Sociology for purposes of training social workers. "Instead of outlining the field of sociology theoretically, we outlined issues that indicated, in the most concrete terms possible, the sorts of phenomena, problems, and processes that we were going to be dealing with. As soon as one understands what is at issue, it is superfluous to give a vague definition which in any case would not be accepted by three quarters of the rest of the sociological profession."[34]

An American guest lecturer, C W Coulter, whose visit to Stellenbosch was financed by the Carnegie Foundation and who had temporarily accompanied the Commission on its travels in 1929, was apparently also involved, directly or indirectly, in putting together the sociological report of the Commission.[35] Verwoerd

---

[32] PV 93/1/29/2, Verwoerd, 'Ontwikkelinge in die studie van Sociologie aan die Universiteit van Stellenbosch' (n. d.), p. 3; see also Verwoerd 1932: 26–27. In addition, Verwoerd held numerous lectures and courses geared for a wider public; see, for instance, the programme of a lecture series held in April 1935 in Bloemfontein (PV 93/1/37/1, ff. 3–4; see also Wagner 1937: 10).

[33] His numerous notes and manuscripts do not give any indication that Verwoerd had read even one line of Max Weber, Emile Durkheim, or any other sociologist. His hostility to theory is what has clearly escaped Miller (see R. B. Miller 1993: 644).

[34] 231/2/2/2, 'Inleiding tot die Sociologie', p. 1.

[35] P. S. du Toit 1966c: 82. This is largely a matter of the fact that at the time, there were no academically educated sociologists in South Africa; upon the insistence of F.S. Malan, the clergyman J. R. Albertyn was entrusted with the sociological report, but he had to be assisted by two American consultants (Steensland 2013: 67–70). Coulter was a "visiting professor" in Stellenbosch, possibly he had been appointed in that capacity because of his research on an ethnic minority in a US-American city (Coulter 1920: 5, 7, 10), which highlighted the oppression, endured over years, and the resistance of a rural population against Russian domination, and the struggle for educational opportunities – all of which were themes that also applied to Afrikaners. On Coulter's contribution, see Louw 1986: 91. Apart from Coulter, agro–economist Dr K. Butterfield of Amherst College was involved (Malherbe 1973: 84–85). It is possible that H. Adler (1925: 27ff) provided a direct methodological model for the Carnegie Commission; the approach of the South African Commission resemble his serial tests administered to school-going children and children with behaviou-

maintained that a purely economic solution to the poor white problem in the sense of employment job creation could be meaningful only "if the accompanying social conditions" would also be addressed; to make this point, Verwoerd invoked the professional authority of this "famous American sociologist [that is, Coulter]". Well-educated social workers would be essential for implementing the recommendations of the Carnegie Report.[36] Following his visit to South Africa, Coulter's professional interest turned to the American family, to higher education institutions, to social relations in industry, to poverty and prisons in the US, as well as labour relations in central Africa (in 1931).[37] During his visit in Stellenbosch, he introduced his colleagues there specifically to empirical sociology with direct applicability to social issues, as it was taught in the US at the time. Like Verwoerd, who may have been influenced by him, Coulter lamented the dependency mentality of the poor, indirectly criticising the programme of the New Deal.[38] With regard to the establishment of the discipline of Sociology at universities, he advocated applied research.[39] In his public pronouncements, Verwoerd referred to this brand of American sociology as a model; what he had in mind were the startling investigations on the social conditions in particular cities or districts in the US.[40] In a speech shortly before his return to the US, Coulter listed American experiences, showing how the problem of white poverty in South Africa could be approached. The proposals largely corresponded to those that Verwoerd was to propagate shortly afterwards, with the zeal of a proselyte.[41] It is surely no coincidence that Verwoerd started preparing for the

---

ral problems. Several lecturers from Stellenbosch who were involved with the Carnegie Report – namely Wilcocks, Großkopf, and Bantu Studies scholar Engelbrecht – had been sponsored by the Foundation to spend their research leave in the US (*Stellenbossche Oudstudent*, 2, 1, 1932: 4, 37; see also Bell 2000: 492).

36 FAV 4.4.4, undated manuscript, Die opleiding en gebruik van geskoolde sosiale werkers en werksters, p. 1. But in the previous decades, Afrikaans–language organisations concerned with poor whites, had already trained their own social workers (Engelbrecht: 6–7). M. du Toit (1992: 10) highlights the nationalist orientation.

37 Coulter's work on US–American prisons (see Coulter 1958), and his review of forced labour (Coulter 1954), as well as his article on industrialisation in Central Africa (1935: 583, 588) indicate that he did not advocate segregation. Even long after his sojourn in South Africa, he wrote critical reviews, and generally expressed himself critically on South African politics, including racial segregation (Coulter 1943, 1953, 1958).

38 Coulter 1938: 23f.

39 Coulter 1934: 357, 362. Years later, he took a decidedly more conservative position (Coulter 1945: 436; see also R. B. Miller 1993: 643; and Groenewald 1987: 67).

40 Verwoerd takes this up in his lecture on poverty (231/2/4/1, 'Armoede en sy bestryding', p. 8–16; Verwoerd 1937b: 91).

41 Coulter 1930; see especially the listing on p. 6, which matched Verwoerd's approach, point by point, at a later stage.

establishment of the new Chair in Sociology and Social Work – which Coulter considered necessary – in 1930. None of the ideas that he came to advocate at a later stage were his own; instead, he used the list of various recommendations stipulated by Coulter and integrated them into a systematic programme that he was to pursue with characteristic dogmatism in the years that followed. Similarly, there was not a single conception of the later version of apartheid that could be traced back to Verwoerd. He was a thinker astonishingly lacking in creativity, but he had an unrivalled gift for systematisation in turning apartheid into a consistent political doctrine of salvation. In fact, this lent a different quality to the policy of racial segregation, as it was being turned from a bundle of rather conservative proposals into an overall idea for shaping the future, an integral transformation of South African society. The systematisation undertaken by Verwoerd turned apartheid into a comprehensive modernisation programme.

Verwoerd was as committed to a positivist method in sociology as he had previously been in psychology. He insisted "that gathering facts is always the starting point, which is why there have to be methods through which phenomena can be perceived and described in a very concrete, comprehensible way. Only when one has gathered the data can one proceed to their processing and derive laws and principles from them. If one has not collected sufficient data, or if one did not exercise due diligence in collecting the data, all theories will prove worthless."[42] In his methodology, too, he insisted above all on objective data collection, in which subjective perception was to be excluded; that is why he preferred to use particular instruments, rather than intuition.[43] From the abundance of data, he thought, it should be possible to derive general principles, that is, rules with a claim to general validity.[44] At the same time, he made a virtue of necessity, for his prior knowledge of the new subject he was teaching would have been very limited.[45] In Sociology, he distinguished two trajectories, depending on the thematic subject: on the one hand, there was the kind of sociology whose research subjects were "primitive" peoples, past and present; and on the other hand, the kind of sociology that investigated societal conditions of "civilised" peoples such as the

---

42 231/2/1/1, 'Inleiding tot die Sociologie', p. 3. That is why he announced the discussion of theories only for the third year of study (see also 231/2/2, 'Metodes van sociologiese navorsing', p. 13).
43 231/2/2, 'Metodes van sociologiese navorsing, pp. 16–27. However, in his opinion, not all instruments were suitable; Piorkowski's instrument measuring attention and fatigue, for instance, was insufficiently precise in his experience (Verwoerd 1928a: 495, 510; Verwoerd 1928b: 600–601).
44 Verwoerd 1929: 951.
45 Sooryamoorthy 2016: 16–21 on the early history of Sociology, which had to make do without any trained sociologists. The subject was established by cognate disciplines, first in Pretoria in 1931, and subsequently in Stellenbosch.

ancient Greeks and Romans.⁴⁶ He thus drew a clear dividing line between "primitive" and "civilised" peoples, denying the possibility that sociological studies of "primitives" could yield knowledge about the "civilised". For in the case of the "primitives", he thought, "all the rules [were] uniform"; they would become differentiated only in the process of civilisation.⁴⁷

Apart from individual references, his lectures, which were not very intellectually demanding, remained confined to social conditions in South Africa.⁴⁸ Even if Verwoerd was sceptical about biological race theories, the differentiation of various racial categories in South Africa held great significance for him, that is, he treated them as givens.⁴⁹ Most of his lectures were limited to a presentation of dates and facts on South African history, from which he drew conclusions for social policy, and for work practice specifically. Thus, he dwelt at great length on the family as the core unit of society while expressing alarm at the number of "mixed marriages".⁵⁰ This was to remain the only clearly stated eugenic theme; in his statements, the ethnocultural "purity" of the Afrikaner people carried more salience than the biological-racial "purity" of whites.

Even during his time as professor of Sociology, Verwoerd advocated biopolitical approaches to the co-existence of whites and coloureds; even though these were not yet fully elaborated at the time, they were clearly discernible. In this vein, Verwoerd published a short story in a 1931 edition of the popular weekly *Die Huisgenoot*. In this story, the narrator tells of a friendship with a man whose career he was supporting. This man falls in love with a woman who is being introduced to the narrator; the narrator takes an immediate dislike to her. But his friend is already making wedding plans, when he learns that the mother of his

---

46 231/2/1/1 'Inleiding tot die Sociologie', p. 2.
47 Ibid., p. 22.
48 Ibid., pp. 7–20. See also the structure 231/2/1/3, 'Opsomming van gebiede'; also 231/2/4/1, 'Armoede en sy bestryding', ch. 4, 'Die oorsake vir verarming in S.A.', pp. 21–49.
49 231/2/1/1, 'Inleiding to die Sociologie', pp. 8–9. The instance to which R. B. Miller (1993: 650) refers without, however, providing more detailed information, is 231/2/1/2, 'Eerstejaar Sociologie: Algemene kursus', pp. 22–28, where Verwoerd, taking up new research findings, questions the assumption of different brain sizes; he similarly expressed doubts about the contention of different capacities for sensory perception. He expressed skepticism and reservation regarding all assumptions of inheritance, especially regarding Lamarckian theses (p. 26); but in what is probably an implicit reference to Kretschmer and Hoffmann, he does concede the striking frequency of certain talents and capacities in certain families (p. 27).
50 231/2/1/1, 'Inleiding tot die Sociologie', pp. 30, 35: "The living conditions in the backyards are extremely unhealthy, especially in places where whites and Coloureds live together indiscriminately." This remained a constant theme for him (*Die Transvaler*, 20.1.1940: 'Nogeens gemenge huwelike').

bride-to-be is a coloured woman. He cannot cope with this revelation, which almost drives him mad. When his woman friend follows him expecting his love for her to trump social conventions, he sinks into utter despair and commits suicide.[51] Verwoerd's message was clear: social norms were more important than individual happiness, and love relations were subject to biopolitical and racial hygiene requirements; rigorously pursued racial segregation was a principle that took precedence over all others, including that of individual happiness. Apparently, to him, voluntary racial segregation was beyond question; he considered the "blunting of feelings about racial differences and one's own self-esteem" as symptom of the degeneration of poor whites.[52]

Even in his testimony before the Coloured Commission in Cape Town on 23 August 1937, he assumed that there were three population groups that were to be segregated, but formed part of a general problem. The core of that problem to him was the labour market, where blacks were displacing coloureds, while white skilled workers in turn were replacing coloureds, too. Even at that time, Verwoerd looked to territorial racial segregation as solution. His idea was that blacks should be held in reservations: "Native Affairs has got to start by making the possibilities for the natives better."[53] When asked whether whites moving from the countryside into the cities and taking over the jobs of coloureds there, should not be sent back to the countryside, he evaded the question. His only comment was that this was not possible. Instead, he pleaded for the inclusion of coloureds in welfare and social work programmes. The policies that had hitherto been focussed on poor whites could create new problems if the impact on coloureds was not integrated into the social welfare arrangements.[54] The basic features of apartheid were already becoming apparent; even at this stage, his arguments were aimed at developing an integrated overall programme that could solve problems all at once. This resulted from the interdependent nature of aspects of specific problems pertaining to population groups. What he envisaged was the separation of the three population groups; but if he wanted to succeed, he had to start from the advanced stage of their integration and their entanglement. He praised his

---

51 VEE [Verwoerd], 'Die enigste weg? (*Die Huisgenoot*, 13.2.1931: 57).
52 232/2/1/1, 'Inleiding tot die Sociologie', p. 103.
53 77.17.3, Coloured Commission, Evidence, vol. 3, p. 2543.
54 Ibid., 2541–2542; see also 231/2/4/2, 'Armoede en sy bestryding', pp. 17–18. In his lectures, too, he singled out the displacement of coloured labour in the labour market as cause of the impoverishment of coloureds; coloured labour was replaced by low–wage black labour from the Western Cape.

solution as salutary for all concerned: "I am looking for the benefit not of one only but of all the sections."[55]

Verwoerd's involvement in welfare work went beyond the University; he was a member of various committees in the Western Cape.[56] This was to the benefit of his students who received vocational training. While still in training, they were expected to venture into the poor neighbourhoods and conduct social science surveys to prepare them for the practical aspects of their profession. Verwoerd admonished them to pay particular attention to "the extent to which white and coloured recipients of charitable aid reside in the same neighbourhood". These and numerous other remarks by Verwoerd show that he held racist ideas and attitudes even at this stage and not, as Miller claims on the basis of a single reference, only from 1937 onwards.[57] After all, he supervised two PhD students,[58] three MA students, and taught twelve students in their third year of study (out of a total of 90 students).[59] Decades later, the woman who was to become the wife of John Vorster and who studied with Verwoerd, enthusiastically recounted the opportunities that he offered to his students: "He had an excellent arrangement with the associations in the Cape Province, which enabled us to undertake case studies." The students were required to submit three or four case studies each after the holidays.[60] In fact, the social workers he trained found employment in the welfare associations;[61] he always insisted that social workers should have a university education.[62] The students were expected to contribute to the work of local welfare associations, and at the same time help enforce Verwoerd's idea of replacing the short-term support measures that had been the norm until then, with long-term rehabilitation.[63] The way in which Verwoerd assigned research topics indicates his strategic planning of research. His own sister, for example, wrote her MA dissertation on 'The Single Mother as Beneficiary of Social Support' – a

---

55 77.17.3, Coloured Commission, Evidence, vol. 3, p. 2543.
56 E. Theron 1970: 13.
57 PV 93/1/29/2 Verwoerd, 'Ontwikkelinge in die studie van Sociologie aan die Universiteit van Stellenbosch', (n.d.), p. 4; see also R. B. Miller 1993: 650. Tayler (1992: 52–65), in contrast, points to Verwoerd's aggressive moves after the 1934 Kimberley Congress.
58 Erika Theron and O. J. M. Wagner. But only Wagner completed his studies with him (Wagner 1936), Theron completed hers after his departure, with Verwoerd's successor Wagner (Tayler 2010: 91, 100).
59 PV 93/1/29/2 Verwoerd, 'Ontwikkelinge in die studie van Sociologie' (n.d.), p. 1.
60 Jones/Muller 1986: 58–59.
61 FAV 4.4.1.2, Reference letter of Verwoerd's for Mrs R.H.J. Kotze, 21, 7.1936.
62 E. Theron 1970: 26, 28; see also Auret 1965: 39.
63 Theron/Stulting 1961: 26–28, 80–85.

topic pertaining to a group which was particularly affected,[64] being at risk of becoming dependent on emergency assistance.[65] He brought in his own students and graduates as persons uniquely qualified for the implementation of the measures he proposed, because they were the ones he had himself trained for the tasks, in line with his conception of an integrated rehabilitation strategy.

Verwoerd's more far-reaching ambitions were already indicated in his plan to establish an Institute for Social Research in Cape Town, which was to take on primarily co-ordination and steering functions for the charities operating there.[66] As early as April 1932, he sought to act on his plans in submitting a memorandum running into several pages to the Senate of his university, in which he proposed the establishment of such an institute in Cape Town; this institute was supposed to be affiliated to the Department of Sociology at the University of Stellenbosch. A resolution passed by the Senate supported this proposal.[67] Verwoerd wanted to make the approximately two hundred independent charitable organisations report to the new Institute to be established. He justified the need for co-ordination by drawing attention to the multiple co-existing burdens of unemployment, juvenile delinquency, and immorality weighing on impoverished families, which could not be addressed by organisations dedicated to any one of these social problems specifically. He pointed to already functioning institutes of this kind in the US as models.[68] On 3 June 1932, he submitted a similar paper to the Cape Town Charity Commission, in which he also cited the need for supervision and control as the rationale for founding the Institute; at the same time, he did not consider the need for administrative standardisation to be a priority.[69] In a manner typical

---

64 77.17.3, Coloured Commission, Evidence, vol. 3, p. 2541. In his statement before the Commission, Verwoerd mentioned the study "by one of my students".
65 In her study, Lucy Cloete investigated not only poor white, but also coloured single-parenting mothers (FAV 6, H. J. L. Cloete, 'Die alleenlopende Moeder as 'n ontvanger van liefdadigheid', MA Dissertation, Sociology, Stellenbosch, p. 5). The dissertation clearly shows the influence of her brother. She concludes that single-parenting mothers could not attain real independence, only a mitigation of the problems they faced (ibid., pp. 125–128).
66 Verwoerd 1932: 28. See also Verwoerd's criticism of the sociological part of the Carnegie Report which, in his opinion, lacked a detailed investigation of the welfare associations in the country (*Die Burger*, 11.1.1933). The overview of c 200 welfare organisations was possibly compiled by himself (see Manuscript 'Social Work in Cape Town', FAV 4.4.4, without indication of author's name; see also E. Theron 1970: 17–22).
67 *Die Burger*, 22.9.1932, Summaries and excerpts from the Commission's Report.
68 UA Stellenbosch, Senate meeting, 9.4.1932. Referring to related experiences in the US, Verwoerd stressed the need for co-ordination (see also Wannamaker 1925:1 – a text that Verwoerd had kept).
69 PV 93/1/19/1, Cape Town Charity Commission. Summary of Evidence, ff. 56–58, pp. 53–55: Professor Verwoerd, 3.6.1932.

for him, he immediately proceeded to specify the staffing requirements and the deployment of postgraduate students for work on specific issues.

Transitioning into Politics

As early as 1932, and perhaps even before, Verwoerd probably saw himself as more of a politician than a scientist; his push for developing a public profile underlines this just as clearly as his insistence on applicability indicates his understanding of science. Thus he legitimated his academic work by situating it in a bigger picture: "In time, therefore, it is not only a small group that will pick the fruits of this education, but the whole country."[70] In 1958, he confessed to his former colleague C.G.W. Schumann "[t]hat this work led to my present task was surely a work of Providence."[71]

In 1932, the Administrator of the Cape Province (1929–1939),[72] Johannes Hendrik Conradie, appointed Verwoerd as a member of a Commission of Inquiry into measures to be taken in Cape Town. Verwoerd's plea for rehabilitation rather than emergency relief was taken up in the Commission's report. In an article on a conference of women's associations in Bloemfontein in 1932, he was emphatic in stating that charity "destroyed lives" and "proved worse than ineffectual".[73] Real lasting improvement was possible only through a package of integrated rehabilitation measures,[74] which alone could sustainably lead poor whites back into the world of work and to a 'civilised' lifestyle. The Report pointed to the low wages of poor whites, in relation to which high rentals were disproportionate. As families often depended on a single income, a breadwinner's illness was enough to plunge an entire family into misery.[75] For sustainable rehabilitation, skilled workers would be needed – a measure that would be more costly, but would yield positive effects in the medium term. Among the measures to be taken, "labour colonies for those who do not want to work", that is, compulsory measures, were men-

---

70 PV 93/1/29/2 Verwoerd, 'Ontwikkelinge in die studie van Sociologie' (n.d.), p. 1.
71 PV 276/2/1/1/3, Verwoerd to C. G. W. Schumann (private), 22.9.1958.
72 Between 1951 and 1960, Conradie was Speaker of the House of Assembly.
73 Verwoerd, 'Liefdadigheid in die Weegskaal'. *Vrouewêreld, Die Huisgenoot*, 25.8.1933: 47.
74 Later on, he postulated the same for the black population: "I have already repeatedly pointed out that all the development services for the Bantu should form an organic whole. . . . Co–ordination of services will have the result that no longer will only one section be served and that the community will not be progressive in one respect and backward in another, but that it will progress as a whole and with regard to the community as a whole." (Verwoerd, Policy of the Minister of Native Affairs, June 7, 1954, in Pelzer 1966: 64–85, 84).
75 *Die Burger*, 21.9.1932.

tioned for the first time.[76] With most other authors and activists dealing with the problem of white poverty, Verwoerd shared the nineteenth century view of the civilising and salutary effects of hard work,[77] whereas idleness was considered the source of all vices. Accordingly, those found unwilling to work would have to be forced into it for their own good. Therefore all rehabilitation measures had to be "supplemented – or rather, controlled – by social-psychological treatment".[78]

According to Verwoerd, the future of the vast majority of poor whites could only lie in the cities.[79] However, this meant that he went beyond social reforms, to argue in expressly political terms: "Now the future is in our hands. In the past, the Afrikaner won because he was rooted in the countryside. Changed circumstances call for adaptation. The key position is shifting to the big cities. It is there, in the cities, that the struggle for the continued existence of our people will be won or lost."[80] He himself coined the term of the "Second Great Trek" to the cities that was popular among nationalists in the late 1930s.[81]

Like his teacher Wilcocks, Verwoerd was convinced that the cause of white poverty was not to be found in the inferior mental capacities of those who were impoverished. Within the framework of the Carnegie Inquiry, Wilcocks had, to-

---

76 *Die Burger*, 21.9.1932; see also the statements in his lecture 231/2/4/2, 'Armoede en sy bestryding', pp. 34–35.
77 231/2/3, 'Socio–psigologie van misdaad', p. 32.
78 *Die Burger*, 30.12.1932. In addition, he submitted his own memorandum with concrete plans, which largely corresponded to what he had proposed to the Senate in Stellenbosch, and what had been recommended by the Commission, in turn, as important proposal toward a solution (*Die Burger*, 22.9.1932). On the implementation in the form of forced rehabilitation of the countryside since the 1920s, see Clynick 2007: 266–267; see also Department of Labour and Social Welfare 1937: 42; and Higginson 2014: 276–280. On the apartheid period and the role of Cronjé, see Roos 2015: 1180–1187.
79 See for instance his article on Grosskopf's volume on economic aspects of the poor white problem (*Die Burger*, 28.12.1932), and even more clearly at the end of Wilcocks's investigation (*Die Burger*, 30.12.1932). Later, he even bemoaned the fact that urbanisation had set in at such a late stage (E. Theron 1970: 31; see also G. D. Scholtz 1979: 27). Others, like J. R. Albertyn (one of the authors of the Carnegie Report), in contrast, stressed the need for a substantial rural population as base and resource for the cultural survival of the Afrikaners (Clynick 1994: 2ff). Initially, D. F. Malan, too, expressed his dismay at the rural exodus of the Afrikaners (D.F. Malan 1923: 6ff, 11).
80 Notes toward Verwoerd's lecture 'Betekenis van ons stede vir die politieke toekoms van die Afrikaner', which he presented to the NP (FAV 4.4.6, presumably 1937). Here he states, "Back to the countryside – futile call".
81 "Years ago – I think it was in Malmesbury or in that area – when I was still professor in Stellenbosch, I had termed the move to the cities the Second Great Trek of our people. This phrase has since taken root, and is being cited frequently." (PV 93/4/1/9, Speech at the ATKV Congress, 1963, ff. 172–187, 176).

gether with Malherbe, subjected more than 15 000 school pupils to the South African Group Intelligence Test co-developed by him; by no means did he consider only environmental factors to be relevant.[82] Wilcocks was not partial to the theory of heredity; he also attached importance to the social environment, as his differentiated and theoretical discussion of the concept of intelligence shows.[83] Despite an unmistakable tendency towards cultural essentialism, he pointed out that the Afrikaner conservatism was not static; if only they came out of their isolation, Afrikaners would readily embrace new perspectives.[84] Precisely for this reason, however, he considered racial segregation in the workplace necessary to overcome poor whites' psychological barrier to physical labour; moreover, he advocated privileges for them, particularly through higher wages.[85] But administrators of psychological intelligence tests were more reticent about hereditary factors in the 1920s than in the 1930s and 1940s, when psychologists J. A. J. van Rensburg and M. L. Fick highlighted such factors.[86] Verwoerd explicitly defined "social work" as "service to the underprivileged".[87] Poor whites were primarily victims of circumstances and not themselves to blame for their fate – this was the consensus among members of the Carnegie Commission.[88] The cause of white poverty did not lie in a lower level of intelligence, but primarily in the social environment, which to Verwoerd meant

---

[82] Wilcocks 1931a; Wilcocks 1931b: 7. The test consisted of seven parts. A reviewer (Bolton 1934: 679) highlighted the fact that Wilcocks sought the causes of poverty in environmental and cultural influences, rather than in innate deficits, but criticised the research method applied. Verwoerd rejected Spencer's theses (231/2/4/1, 'Armoede en sy bestryding', ch. 'Algemene oorsake vir die ontwikkeling van armoede', p. 2a). But he adopted social Darwinist forms of argument in maintaining that "a measure of overpopulation is not a bad thing: in the struggle for existence, there has to be a possibility for the weak to go under, otherwise we will end up with a degeneration of the human race." (231/2/1/1, 'Inleiding tot die Sociologie', p. 85) On the tests of the Commission, see Malherbe 1973: 84; see also Wilcocks 1929; Louw 1986: 77–78; Steensland 2013: 96–100; and Bottomley 2012: 45. But other scholars saw the causality in a reverse direction: the poor were poor because they had mentally degenerated (Eybers n.d.: 12).
[83] This point, once again, shows the significance of Selz's Psychology of Thought for the differentiation of Wilcocks's concept of intelligence (Wilcocks 1924: 672–673).
[84] Wilcocks 1945: 297.
[85] Wilcocks 1930:3. With this, he drew conclusions contrary to those of Macmillan's, who had advocated wage increases for black workers. Selope Thema made proposals similar to those of Macmillan's (Cobley 2016: 187–189).
[86] In Fick's biography, a transition can be observed, from a cautious application of the criterion of inheritance to its decided affirmation (Louw/Foster 1991: 62; also Louw 1997: 249–250).
[87] FAV 4.4.6, Notes on a lecture, 'Beginsels en Metodes van Maatskaplike Sorg' presented to the ANS in Bloemfontein (undated).
[88] Malherbe 1973: 83.

competition from low-waged black workers on the labour market.[89] What is apparent here is a striking similarity in the methodological approach to the subject of his dissertation; there, too, external factors influencing the individual were at stake. There, too, the aim was to intervene in the situation in which individuals found themselves, and steer it in such a way that a desired result could be achieved. Just as they appeared in his psychological experiments, individuals were considered recipients of and respondents to stimuli, not actors in their own right.

For all Verwoerd's harping on integrated rehabilitation, his thinking was primarily political. Curbing the spread of poverty was more important to him than rehabilitating those who had already fallen into poverty.[90] To the extent that poverty also affected whites, eugenics never met with wider interest in South Africa; white political rule and access to state resources facilitated the implementation of social rehabilitation measures.[91] Even during the later stages of apartheid, policies were not primarily aimed at biologically conceived outcomes for the various population groups, but at reshaping their social environment align them with particular understandings of biological conditions.[92] Nevertheless, these policies were essentially biopolitical, because they started from biologically defined communities, namely so-called 'races'. There are notable analogies with policy frameworks developed for industrial psychology, which presented two possibilities: either adapt people to the environment or change the environment in such a way that human potential can optimally unfold. Verwoerd and Wilcocks always opted for the latter approach, which explains the general absence of biologistic argumentation.

Verwoerd publicly propagated the new measures he had developed for a programme of social rehabilitation, which were readily taken up in the columns of *Die Burger*. One of the most important activists, M. E. Rothmann, with whom Verwoerd worked together intensively, was co-editor of *Die Burger* at the time; she

---

89 231/2/1/1. 'Inleiding tot die Sociologie', pp. 126–136. Social work, for Verwoerd, does not mean job creation, but "a new social-psychological organisational process" (p. 136).
90 *Die Burger*, 30.12.1932, 'Armblanke-vraagstuk in Suid–Afrika, deel 2'; see also his discussion of the sociological part, in which he posed the question as to whether it is alcoholism that is the cause of impoverishment, rather than its effect (*Die Burger*, 11.1.1933).
91 Verwoerd defined poverty as "deplorable state for an individual or a family, or as societal failure" (231/2/4/1, 'Armoede en sy bestryding', p. 3). The possibility of changing the social environment in order to combat degeneration was in contrast to eugenics and racial hygiene in Europe, where far more emphasis was placed on biological concepts (see Weingart/Kroll/Bayertz 2017: 122).
92 Different approaches designed to tailor the working environment to the needs of workers had already found entry into German psychotechnics (Hinrichs 1981: 231; see also C. Boshoff 1996: 9).

was also a co-author of the Carnegie Report.⁹³ This contributed significantly to the positive reception of his plans. Verwoerd's first public announcements attracted attention and praise also from the English-language press.⁹⁴

The plans and proposals put forward by Verwoerd as sociologist reveal some of the basic features of his later political thinking:

1. He was not concerned with gaining personal power as an end in itself; rather, he was convinced that he had developed a panacea to which there was no alternative. Indeed, he believed that his research had shown previous modes of social work to be completely inadequate. This is indicative of Verwoerd's sense of mission even at this early stage – a mission to which he was to give effect in the political fields in which he was to become active in later years.
2. Every action must be preceded by an analysis of the relevant factors in order to be able to develop appropriate measures. Here, as in his PhD thesis, Verwoerd followed a systematic approach from which he derived an integrated concept of remedial action.⁹⁵
3. Effective action in the field of social policy requires scientific expertise and, building on this, comprehensive planning, for which he received the required backing from nationalist circles.⁹⁶ Science leads to objective results. A scientifically based policy is directed towards the truth and does not allow for alternatives.
4. His politics was profoundly undemocratic, since it ruled out alternatives and discussions on the way forward.

The next step was to extend the work beyond Cape Town, for which the National Congress on the Poor White Problem in Kimberley in 1934 offered a prime opportunity. Verwoerd successfully intervened in the planning and was able to significantly influence the agenda and the proceedings of the event. Such a congress was to facilitate not only an exchange of experiences, but more importantly, "it could thereby build momentum to secure the means for co-operation, and for the application of the best methods of combatting [poverty]". It was to provide an im-

---

93 Throughout his life time, Verwoerd held Rothmann's judgement in high esteem and knew how to appreciate her confidence in his political work (55.K.V.16 [8], Letter by Betsie Verwoerd to M. E. Rothmann, 3.2.1963; also 55.K.V.16 (12), Letter by Betsie Verwoerd to M. E. Rothmann, 23.5.1965).
94 *Cape Times*, 23.9.1932.
95 See also 231/2/1/1, 'Inleiding tot die Sociologie', pp. 78–79; also 231/2/3, 'Socio-psigologie van misdaad', p. 58; 231/2/4/1 and 2, 'Armoede en sy bestryding'.
96 Editorial, "'n Ekonomiese Beleid' (*Die Burger*, 20. 6. 1934).

petus for socio-political action involving the "people as a whole".[97] At the end of 1932, *Die Burger* once again gave Verwoerd the opportunity to publish a whole series of articles, this time in the form of detailed reviews recapitulating and commenting on the most important aspects of the Carnegie Report. The newspaper mandated the study of these articles as national duty.[98] Verwoerd pointed out that the division of the Report into studies from perspectives of different scientific disciplines should not obscure the fact that only an integrated approach could provide a remedy, in other words, that this division was an entirely "mechanistic" one. In these articles, Verwoerd acted as critical reviewer[99] and at the same time as extraordinarily skillful populariser of scientific research findings.[100] To the extent that he also addressed the shortcomings of the Report, especially the sociological part, Verwoerd could signal that this was not yet the last word on the problem of white poverty; his review also raised the putatively authoritative voice of 'science'.

In the process of preparing for the Congress that took place in Kimberley between 2 and 5 October 1934 with 500 participants,[101] it was "above all Dr Verwoerd who set the direction throughout, in terms of agenda items, discussions and resolutions".[102] That is why he was given the honour of delivering the 'keynote speech' opening the Congress. The Congress was not a '*volkskongres*' of the kind that the Broederbond and the FAK regularly held in order to extend cultural nationalist mobilisation to new fields.[103] Rather, it was a congress of all welfare associations at the initiative and under the auspices of the churches, involving English-speaking as well as Afrikaans-speaking groupings. The Speaker of Parliament, E. G. Jansen, and the President of Senate, C. A. van Niekerk, chaired the sessions of the Congress, and thus elevated the Congress to an event of national

---

97 Verwoerd, 'Liefdadigheit in die Weegskaal' (*Vrouewêreld, Die Huisgenoot*, 25.8.1933).
98 *Die Burger*, 28.12.1932, 'Armblanke-Vraagstuk in Suid–Afrika', deel I. On the role of the newspaper before and during the Kimberley Congress, see J. J. Joubert 1990: 138–140.
99 Thus, in a critical review of the medical part of the Report (vol. 3), Verwoerd tore it apart (*Die Burger*, 3.1.1933); while he expressed himself critically on the sociological part, he praised individual sections of it (*Die Burger*, 11.1.1933). With respect to the sociological investigation authored by clergyman Albertyn and two of his colleagues, he bemoaned the lack of an objective, scientific approach; instead, he found only "an accumulation of general impressions and personal opinions".
100 'Armblanke-Vraagstuk in Suid–Afrika, deel 1', *Die Burger*, 28.12.1932.
101 The Congress was followed by a conference on Poverty Relief, organised by the churches, in Kimberley on 6–7 October. Many of those who had participated in the Poor White Congress attended this conference as well (PV93/1/6/75, f. 145).
102 55.K.T. (81), Notes of M. E. Rothmann, March 1967.
103 T.D. Moodie 1975: 105; see also Tayler 1992: 49–50.

significance.[104] Since white poverty was perceived as a 'problem' of potential degeneration and civilisational decay affecting the entire white population, and was thus directly associated with a threat to the racial order, Afrikaner nationalists did not initially separate themselves off from the effort.[105]

That is why circular letters were sent to all those of rank and standing in the field of welfare, inviting them to participate in the Congress.[106] Preparations for the Congress were delegated to three committees – a psychological-educational one chaired by Wilcocks, a socio-ecclesiastical one headed by Albertyn, and a socio-economic one chaired by Verwoerd.[107]

In August, the chairmen of the three committees compiled a list of 99 resolutions, which were submitted to the Congress in October for adoption. The demands of the Congress were indeed comprehensive, addressing marketing opportunities, insurance schemes for the rural population, labour rights and health care, education, and social work in the narrower sense.[108] Verwoerd succeeded in pushing his own objectives to the fore, spelling out the responsibility of the state and highlighting the importance of strategic planning.[109] Writing on welfare state-building during this time period, historian and political scientist Jeremy Seekings speaks of a power struggle between Verwoerd and church representatives: while Verwoerd's proposed solutions were focused entirely on state and administrative interventions, representatives of the church fell in line with the Carnegie Report in considering

---

[104] PV 94/1/5/1/1, Letter by P. du Toit to Jansen, 23.7.34 and the latter's letter of acceptance of 24.7.

[105] See for instance the eugenic considerations of Dunston (1923: 151–152). The Afrikaner nationalists considered the Congress mainly as an effort to "safeguard and consolidate the continued existence of white Afrikanerdom"; in this context, they endorsed comprehensive segregationist measures – as, for instance W.J. Scholtz from Paarl did in his remarks 'Die aanstaande volkskongres in sake die armblankevraagstuk' (PV 93/1/67/3, f. 89.) R. B. Miller (1993: 654) maintains that before 1937, Verwoerd had made the case for a nation in conjunction with the English-speaking section of the population. She bases this on his advocacy of social work; however, she does not consider the fact that this engagement of Verwoerd's stemmed from the inclusive organisational form of the People's Congress, rather than from Verwoerd's own convictions.

[106] PV 93/1/67/2, Circular Letter 28.12.1933; also Circular Letter 13.1.1934.

[107] FAV 4.4.4, 'Die Sociologies–Ekonomiese Komitee', authored by Verwoerd, with proposals for combatting unemployment in urban and rural areas. The Committee "tried to find out how well the State was equipped to combat impoverishment and dependence".

[108] On the way in which the list of demands came to be formulated, see Albertyn 1934: 3–4; see also Verwoerd 1934: 33–39; and E. Theron 1970: 32.

[109] PV 93/1/29/2, f. 100: "Prof Verwoerdt [sic] agrees with the following recommendations of the People's Congress"; it pertained to the resolutions with the numbers 1, 2, 7, 8, 23, 24, 26–30, 35–41.

poverty primarily as a moral problem taking on rehabilitation measures as their domain.[110]

In order to get the draft resolutions passed, discussion time was shortened by design. Each presentation was directly linked to the adoption of a number of thematically related demands of the Congress, so that these 'motions' would appear to be derived as conclusions from the respective presentation. As Verwoerd presented the first and most important speech, he dealt with the central demands of the Congress, which primarily concerned the role of the state.[111]

The professor from Stellenbosch made it clear that it was concrete measures and not academic reflections that were on the agenda. Nor was it supposed to be about a specific group of people, namely poor whites, but about the social problem of white poverty in general; he thus highlighted the need to combat the causes of poverty and to prevent social declassification on a larger scale.[112] Verwoerd was thus no longer moving within the framework of social work; rather, he was engaging in political argumentation. He pointed out that much more radical demands could have been made, "which would have meant a complete overturn of our entire state system [*landsorganisasie*]"; from a pragmatic point of view, however, it was a matter of concentrating on what could be achieved with the existing means. The list of demands was a minimal programme, but it was "the least we can be satisfied with".[113]

This was a cunning preparation for what he then proposed as a plan that he had already formulated in his lectures as a set of state tasks.[114] In his history of "General Welfare Policy" ["*Volkswelsynbeleid*"], A. T. Winckler stated thirty-five years later that "no other body had placed such far-reaching expectations on the State as the People's Congress".[115] It was Hendrik Verwoerd who had formulated these demands. The state was to transform society and establish the envisaged order within the framework of a modernisation of the economy, which for Verwoerd meant rapid industrialisation – which he advocated for South Africa.[116] In his conception, the state was by its very nature a welfare state, in the sense that it was an instrument of the 'community'. This idea reflected his fundamental con-

---

110 Seekings 2008: 527–529.
111 Brochure 'Proposals To Be Laid Before the National Conference on The Poor White Problem'.
112 Verwoerd 1934: 30.
113 Ibid., 31.
114 231/2/1/1, 'Inleiding tot die Sociologie', pp. 35–44; see also D. Prinsloo (1979: 521): "For Dr. Verwoerd, state power was the weapon of the Afrikaner people in their economic struggle."
115 Winckler 1969: 41.
116 Verwoerd 1934: 33.

viction that the welfare of the 'community' enjoys priority over the welfare of the individual. With industrialisation would come the "increased intervention of the community in the actions of individuals and enterprises. . . . more and more the state becomes the medium for social service."[117]

In his outline of the problem, white poverty could be understood only in the context of a multi-ethnic society with a huge black low-wage sector. He noted that it was impossible to "develop proposals for improving the economic situation of poor whites without in one way or another touching on these groups". However, he avoided being more specific about the ways in which the rest of the population should be included in the conceptualisations; instead, he maintained that one would be sure to take appropriate measures. Here Verwoerd can be seen to configure the form of argumentation that was to become typical for his rhetoric throughout his later career: "If, therefore, certain economic proposals are found to be biased towards the interests of white workers, it must be clear that consideration was given not only to what is advantageous not only for our problem group – the poor whites – but for the whole country!" The subtext was clear: support for poor whites was important for the country because it would maintain the racial order, with a clear dividing line between privileged and non-privileged along the lines of skin colour. The welfare of the black population was to be subordinated to this general interest. Verwoerd declared the resulting adversities for the majority of the population as a "negligible [verwyderbare] difficulty".[118] He opined that it was "more economical" for South Africa if a black worker became unemployed than if a white worker became unemployed, which justified "the preference for civilised labour". No reason was given as to why this should be more economical. The displacement of expensive labour by cheap labour could be halted only by allocating jobs to whites. Blacks would have to make do with less attractive employment, for example by displacing migrant workers from abroad or by "improving the economic development of the [native] reserves".[119] In these and related statements, the apartheid politician-to-be announced himself. His pronouncements included the nebulous rhetoric that presented the brutal measures as "temporary discrimination" borne of sympathy: "This is, if you like, a policy statement [beleidsverklaring] on how to sympathetically take account of the rights and interests of whites as well as non-whites, in order then to arrive at a clear decision on what serves the interest of the community as a whole, even if it appears at first sight that this amounts to preferential treatment." Only if one

---

[117] 231/2/1/1, 'Inleiding to die Sociologie', p. 44.
[118] Verwoerd 1934: 31.
[119] Ibid., 32.

shared his view that a clear racial hierarchy was best for the "community as a whole" would his description of the disadvantaged position of the black majority as an "appearance of preference" for whites not seem hypocritical.

Having outlined the serious and extensive nature of the problem affecting South African society as a whole, Verwoerd proceeded to substantiate the first eight demands, all of which dealt with the role of the state – pertaining to which he formulated his own aims. He admonished his audience that with regard to the demand for a "definite state responsibility for the provision of social welfare", Congress must take a definitive stand. The problem of poverty and decline, "and the coloured problem", had been known for ten years and had never been addressed "in a planned way". He attributed this to the fact that welfare measures were distributed among the various ministries, rather than being centrally coordinated. He was convinced "that the state will undoubtedly only really fulfil its duty to solve public welfare problems once an independent department mandated with this task has been established".[120] Responsibility for welfare should be clearly regulated, because only an independent department had the necessary authority and could set its own priorities, whereas the division of welfare measures between different ministries would always lead to the postponement of decisions. "Charity used to be the business of a few self-appointed philanthropists; today, social work is the business of democracy. The changes that we see in recent times throw up new problems and require new mechanisms."[121] Verwoerd always relied on central control units with clearly defined competencies because efficiency, in his understanding, could be achieved only through control and supervision from above. He upheld this view also in his capacity as politician at a later stage.

In keeping with the integral character of his nationalism, his understanding of the state was decidedly authoritarian, always moving from the whole to the parts: as the individual was defined via the nation, so the institutions were conceived from the commanding heights of the state. This fits in with the systematic and comprehensive approach that preceded the large-scale planning and transformation during apartheid. While increasing state intervention in the private lives of citizens became a global phenomenon after the Great Depression, the crucial difference in Verwoerd's case lies in the fact that he developed his idea of the state from an integral nationalism, conceiving of its interventions not as temporary measures but as "essential" ones. The interventionist state of the 1930s was followed by the welfare state. In South Africa, it took the form of social provision

---

[120] Ibid., 36. In the discussion that followed, this proposal was supported by his colleague Geoffrey Cronjé, Professor of Sociology at the University of Pretoria: Ibid., 39.
[121] Ibid., 37. The call for concentrating welfare functions in one state department had been raised ten years before by D. F. Malan (D. F. Malan 1923: 7).

for whites with simultaneous exclusion and marginalisation of the black majority, and of minorities designated as "foreign".

The second call for a state service employing trained social workers was, as Verwoerd himself emphasised, a demand he had already addressed to the Commission of Inquiry of the Cape Province one and a half years earlier.[122] One social worker was to be permanently employed in each constituency[123] in order to co-ordinate welfare work there, and at the same time to gather the necessary information; in this context, Verwoerd spoke of a "nerve system across the whole country ... in order to comprehensively compile the required information".[124] For this specific purpose, a journal was to be established, not with the aim of publishing research, but of informing social workers about the latest developments, and of propagandistically disseminating the findings and proposals presented at the Kimberley Congress.[125] Verwoerd advocated the centralisation and professionalisation of social work through the recruitment of academically trained social workers.[126] The image of the nervous system was not chosen without reason; Verwoerd also envisaged a brain: "In the provincial capitals there can be head offices with a few officials who can process the data of the whole province; from these sites, the service department can controlled. From there, further centralisation through, for example, a Department of Social Welfare, could be accomplished without difficulty."[127] He suggested that co-ordination of existing welfare associations could not be achieved without some degree of coercion.[128] All of Verwoerd's demands were adopted by Congress, albeit with a few minor changes. As his student and collaborator Erika Theron pointed out, his speech became the working basis for the Continuation Committee.[129]

Verwoerd's comprehensive approach that proceeded from the "Poor White Problem" to the restructuring of the whole of South African society, should be

---

[122] Ibid., 37; see also FAV 4.4.4, 'Die Opleiding van Sociale Werkers (en Matrones)', with numerous annotations handwritten by Verwoerd; see also 'Die opleiding en gebruik van geskoolde sosiale werkers en werksters' (ibid.).

[123] It is interesting to note that he based his proposals on constituencies and not magisterial districts or other administrative units; this is what underlined the political character of his plans.

[124] Verwoerd 1934: 37; see also Verwoerd, 'Die Volkskongres van 1934', Part 2, *Die Burger*, 19.2.1935.

[125] FAV 4.4.4, 'Memorandum on the Need and Possibilities of Commencing a Journal of Social Service', esp. pp. 2–3, 5; Verwoerd envisaged himself as editor of the journal (ibid., p. 7).

[126] Verwoerd 1934: 38.

[127] Ibid., 37.

[128] Ibid., 39. See also his survey of the numerous welfare organisations in South Africa (FAV 4.4.4, Manuscript, 'The Organisation of Social Work in South Africa').

[129] E. Theron 1970: 36.

considered within the framework of social engineering. Thomas Etzemüller noted for Swedish social engineers what was also true of Verwoerd's positivist approach: "Alva and Gunnar Myrdal did not impose a world view; as far as they were concerned, they started from reality."[130] The planned reorganisation of society, based on positivist social science, did involve the state, but it essentially relied on the self-empowerment of 'experts'. Justifying their interventions as measures to repair a society that had come apart at the seams,[131] they were determined to extend this social engineering to people's private lives. In the US, the Carnegie Foundation was among the sponsors of social science projects claiming to engage in social engineering.[132]

Verwoerd took over as deputy chair of the congressionally appointed Continuation Committee; in October 1935, he took over the leadership.[133] He made sure that power was effectively vested in a smaller executive committee, with himself as managing director wielding far-reaching and largely unchecked decision-making powers.[134] The Continuation Committee was to push the state and other agencies to implement the resolutions of the Congress. As Verwoerd was the only one with a clear concept and with the required assertiveness, he dominated the Continuation Committee from the start, and brought other members over to his ideas.[135] In his report for 1936, he admitted that it was only during that year that he was able to "consult with management in advance on every important matter; in the previous year he had had no choice but to act according to his own judgement throughout".[136] Sometimes others signed the letters which had been preformulated by Verwoerd, judging by the diction and the form of argumentation. One such example can be found in a submission of the Committee to the Minister

---

130 Etzemüller 2006: 465.
131 Etzemüller 2015b: 20–22; on the claims on positivism which remained largely unfulfilled, however, due to lack of empirical data, see Etzemüller 2015b: 26–31. On the disregard, entailed by social engineering, for the individual and her/his self-determination, see Doering–Manteuffel 2008: 48, 53; see also Marklund 2015. The affinity with psychotechnics becomes evident in Luks 2015.
132 Hochgeschwender 2015: 189.
133 It would appear that Verwoerd was initially elected chair, but announced his resignation on 5.10., because, as he said, "I believe that this would serve the best interests of the matter and of the Congress" (PV 93/1/67/5, f. 143, Letter by Verwoerd to P. du Toit, 5.10.1943).
134 Verwoerd 1936: 3.
135 55.K.T. (81) Note of M.E. Rothmann, March 1967. Rothmann was a member of the Continuation Committee and held the same concepts as Verwoerd. On the Committee's work, she wrote the following: "I could observe and wholeheartedly admire some of the leadership qualities of our chair." Verwoerd appeared at the first session with a fully elaborated concept (E. Theron 1970: 38).
136 PV 93/1/67/7, f. 71, Voorsitterverslag, 5.10.1936, p. 2.

of Health on 16 August 1935, explaining that there was a clear correlation between "healthy housing and the implementation of measures preventing whites and coloureds living together".[137] The Committee's sole task was to implement the resolutions of Congress, which is why it listed and evaluated the responses of the authorities to every single one of the 99 resolutions.[138] Verwoerd unfolded an extraordinary dynamic – he was the driving force behind this multitude of activities.[139] At the beginning of October 1936, he appeared in Johannesburg as a speaker at a conference on social work, and presented lectures throughout the country.[140] He insistently pleaded for the establishment of a state social service whose social workers should be university-educated.[141]

The Committee achieved its greatest successes in its co-operation with the railways which, since the beginning of the Hertzog government, had been systematically developed into the domain of white labour; that is the reason why poor whites were mostly likely to find employment there. That also explains why most of the social care facilities were to be found with the railways. Verwoerd's former student and collaborator Erika Theron established a social work service backed by the Committee and based at the railways. The Committee took advantage of the authority structures within the state-led railway sector to subject poor whites to the control of social workers.[142] The frequent use of the term "weak" in describing poor whites suggests the extent to which Theron, too, perceived work, strength of character and prevention of degeneration to be interrelated concerns. This service was one of the committee's "experiments"; the hope was that, if successful, it would

---

137 Ibid., ff. 26–27, Correspondence with the Minister van Volksgesondheid.
138 Ibid., ff. 10–23, Overview of Congress resolutions and responses of individual ministries (presumably from the second half of 1935).
139 PV93/1/67/6, f. 97, Letter by Albertyn to the Secretary of the Committee, 10.6.35. It would appear that decisions were taken in the Uitvorende Komitee, and that the full Continuation Committee was presented with *faits accompli*. In the case of Albertyn, many of the meetings were scheduled in such a way that he could not participate in them.
140 Verwoerd, List of his lectures (1936: 15), and of his articles (1936: 18).
141 For the manuscript of the lecture, see FAV 4.4.4, Verwoerd 1937b: 90. Verwoerd thought of social work as a woman's profession; even in the academic training, he differentiated between men and women (ibid., 91). The proposals of M.J. Adams (1936: 3–4) on the rehabilitation of poor whites showed a similar tendency.
142 PV93/1/67/1, 'Verslag van die Spooorwegwelsynswerk', Mei 1935 tot Maart 1938. See also PV 93/1/5/1, 17–18 on tasks of social workers, with an emphasis on control of residents, along with advice and support, but also with a strong dose of paternalistic interventionism. See also PV 93/1/67/7, f. 55, 'Report on the welfare work at the railways for the time period January – August 1936'. PV 93/1/67/6, f. 81, Letter by Ministry of Railways and Harbours to Committee, 27.5.35. The Committee was not supposed to interfere with the processes of the Ministry. See also E. Theron 1970: 56–57.

inspire the authorities to take action from their side.¹⁴³ However, the frequently displayed authoritarian demeanour and the nationalistic orientation of the social workers made the railway authorities decide to take over the project and place it under their own management.¹⁴⁴ By no means was the rehabilitation of poor whites motivated by emancipatory aims; rather, it was designed as authoritarian integration into the national community, which a Finnish ethnologist was able to observe in the behaviour of descendants of poor whites right up to the 1990s.¹⁴⁵

At Verwoerd's instigation, the Committee made several approaches to the government to expedite the establishment of a separate authority for welfare.¹⁴⁶ In a letter to the Chairman of his Finance Committee, M. J. Adams, Verwoerd stated his aim bluntly: "to get the government to follow the Conference's advice and to do certain concrete things".¹⁴⁷ Verwoerd did not waste any time: as early as the beginning of February 1935, he requested appointments with Prime Minister Hertzog and Labour Minister A. P. J. Fourie.¹⁴⁸ In a detailed letter, he informed Fourie of the main demands and aims of the Committee, making it clear – in a style typical of him – that the Committee was not interested in "vague theoretical aims". In particular, he rejected the widely held view, shared by the Minister, that white poverty was only a temporary result of the global economic crisis. "Some people believe that poverty and degeneration are mainly an unemployment problem. They do not realise the fundamental importance for employability and efficiency of bad housing, insufficient education, incomplete occupational training, discouragement, indifference, family strife and severed family relationships, low vitality, undernourishment and illness."¹⁴⁹ Therefore it was of no concern to him that the government had allocated 15.9% of the 1932 national budget

---

143 Annual Report of the Work of the Continuation Committee of the National Conference on the Poor White Problem, Stellenbosch 1935, p. 26. See also Verwoerd, 'Armoede en sy bestryding, Algemene oorsake', p. 12, 231/2/4/1.
144 Tayler 2004: 115–116.
145 Teppo 2004: 16, 49.
146 PV 93/1/29/3, Letter by Union Dept of Education to Verwoerd, 26.1.1935, in which it was announced that the Dept had established its own Office for Opvoedkunde en Maatskaplike Navorsing.
147 PV 93/1/67/6, f. 1, Letter by Verwoerd to Adams, 6.12.1934.
148 Ibid., f. 13, Letter to Hertzog with the request to receive a delegation, 5.2.1935.
149 Verwoerd, 'Poverty and the State', *Cape Argus*, 4.10.1935. In this article, he underlines the role that should fall to the state, and the need for a dedicated Department of Social Welfare; see also Verwoerd, 'Die Volkskongres van 1934 – Tydelike Werkloosheid', *Die Burger*, 26.2.1935, in which he criticised unemployment insurance as misleading panacea; the following article (*Die Burger*, 4.3.1935, 11; and 20.3.1933) deals with job creation and motivation for work. On the tendency of the government to deal with white poverty primarily as a problem of unemployment, see also M. C. Potgieter 1970: 22 and Necker 1998: 59.

to combatting white poverty.[150] He also made it clear to the Minister that the Committee was exercising a political mandate, going as far as claiming some kind of control function in relation to government.[151]

On 25 February 1935, a delegation consisting of Verwoerd, ds. Pieter du Toit, M. E. Rothmann, Z. Steyn, J. Pellissier and M. J. Adams met with Prime Minister Hertzog, who in turn was accompanied by Education Minister J. H. Hofmeyr.[152] The delegation was led by Verwoerd; the conversation turned into a direct exchange of blows between him and the Prime Minister. The topic of discussion was the establishment of a separate Department of Welfare, about the need for which Hertzog remained unconvinced until the end. He responded by saying, "I have the impression that you attach too much importance to the concentration [of welfare functions] in one head office. The division as we have it today is based on years of experience and there are good reasons for it."[153] Two different organisational concepts can be discerned here: Hertzog, politically socialised in the rather weak colonial state, rejected the authoritarian, tightly hierarchical administration envisaged by Verwoerd.

Verwoerd insisted that the Department should exercise overall supervision and authority over all welfare organisations, insofar as they received state subsidies. In response to questions from the Prime Minister, Verwoerd justified the necessity of an independent department by pointing to the urgency of the problem, and the advantages to be derived from the co-ordination of authority and competencies: "We recognise that welfare matters are linked to all kinds of other interests, but we insist that, wherever practically possible, they should first be considered in relation to each other rather than to wider interests."[154] The professor proved to be extraordinarily well informed about the distribution of competencies across the various branches of the state administration; he was also able to parry hints about how such matters were organised abroad.[155] He demonstrated his political talents, as he immediately took Hertzog's considerations as firm commitments: "I think that this delegation should gratefully accept the Minister's proposal to re-organise the present Ministry of Labour into a Ministry of Labour and Public Welfare." A proposal to ap-

---

150 Giliomee 1986: 15. On the specific measures, see J. de Villiers 2004: 173.
151 PV 93/1/67/6, ff. 15–17, Letter of the Secretariate of the People's Congress to the Minister of Labour, 5.2.1935.
152 See also PV 93/1/67/6, f. 70, Letter of the Secretary for Education, 7.5.1935, with the request for support for an academically trained South African social worker to venture to the Netherlands for 18 months, in order to investigate the Octavia Hill–System there.
153 Ibid., ff. 20–25, Delegation to the Prime Minister, 25.2.1935, Minutes, p. 3.
154 Ibid., Minutes, p. 2.
155 On this, see PV 93/1/29/3, Verwoerd on the status of welfare departments in different countries.

point an independent commission to delineate the powers of this division of the Department of Welfare was rejected by Hertzog, who referred to the existing Civil Service Commission, saying: "When we see how the first steps pan out, we can possibly establish such a commission at a later stage." But Verwoerd was not willing to let up, insisting "we are now at the first step".[156] It was not acceptable to consider everything from a purely bureaucratic point of view, which is what could be expected if state authorities alone were entrusted with the re-organisation. Again, he turned a vague statement by Hertzog into a firm promise that the activists among the committee members would be allowed to submit their further proposals "on the extension of functions and the establishment of a commission to deal with this matter" at a later date, that is, after the restructuring. Hertzog confirmed this, but asked suspiciously, "would you like to have the power to decide on who is appointed to do this work?" Verwoerd shrewdly contented himself with a say in matters of principle, and assured the delegation that he had no intention of interfering in personnel matters.

One day later, the delegation went to see the Minister of Labour. An open controversy erupted when the Minister disputed the Committee's right to control the government. Initially, Verwoerd tried to appease those present, but then outlined his understanding of nationhood and democracy: "The government controls the property of the people and representatives of those very people gave the Continuation Committee a mandate. You will see that we have no intention to be a kind of government above the government, which would be ridiculous. We are only appealing to the government to ask what the people have decided."[157] This presumptuous behaviour led the Minister to temporarily suspend all co-operation with the Committee.[158]

---

156 PV 93/1/67/6, ff. 20–25, Delegation to the Prime Minister, 25.2.1935, Minutes, p. 5.
157 Ibid., f. 36, Delegation to the Minister of Labour, 26.2.1935, among others Verwoerd. See also PV 93/1/67/6, f. 90. Letter by P. du Toit to Verwoerd, 6.6.1935, in which the former admonished the latter to deal with the Ministry in a more conciliatory way. It is significant that Verwoerd showed a complete lack of awareness of the effects of his communicational style (f. 108, Letter by Verwoerd to P. du Toit, 14.6.1935); see also PV 93/1/67/6, f. 102, Letter by the Committee to the Minister, 12.6.1935, stressing the fact that this would not detract from the tasks to be carried out by the government. In a series of articles published at the same time, Verwoerd emphasised the fact that it is "a labour programme for the entire people [*Volk*]" (*Die Burger*, 18.12.1935).
158 PV 93/1/67/6, 110. Letter by the Minister of Labour (A. P. J. Fourie) to the Committee, 25.6.1935, and reply of the Committee (ibid., f. 118, 9.7.1935), in which they explain their function. See PV 93/1/67/7, f. 24, Minister of Labour to the Committee, 2.8.1935, in which the Minister expresses his satisfaction with the declaration of the Committee, and his preparedness to resume the co-operation. On the tensions, see also E. Theron 1970: 48–54; also Tayler 2010: 143. Having oscillated between Hertzog and Malan for some time at the beginning of the 1930s, Fourie was a

In March 1936, a delegation of the Continuation Committee consisting of M. E. Rothmann, A. Geyer, Z. Steyn, M. J. Adams and Verwoerd met with Fourie again. *Die Burger* reported on this meeting and printed a full-length memorandum issued by the Committee, which reiterated and specified the demands of the Congress with the aim of bringing heightened public pressure to bear on Fourie.[159] Interestingly, Verwoerd extended the vague notion of 'people', otherwise always proclaimed in an exclusive manner by Afrikaans-speaking cultural nationalists, to include a wide range of welfare institutions from both sections of the white population represented at the Kimberley Congress. However, to infer from this a mandate and legitimacy for the Continuation Committee equal to that of the elected Government, was somewhat presumptuous. What it also reveals is Verwoerd's self-image: he passed off the resolutions and the fundamental conceptions of the Congress that were largely of his own design, as decisions of the people.

The Prime Minister nevertheless agreed to the creation of a Department within the Ministry of Labour, placed under its own Under-Secretary; he even acceded to rename the Ministry the *Department van Arbeid en Volkswelsyn*. At a later stage, Verwoerd remarked critically: "Unfortunately, this had been watered down by the responsible Minister to a division under a commissioner";[160] at the same time, he took credit for the fact that the Committee "forced the Government to establish a Department of Public Welfare".[161] Although it was a first step, this was not enough for him; he insisted that this Department should be further expanded to eventually become completely independent and devote itself entirely to work for poor whites. He trusted that it would be possible to let this department "develop naturally afterwards", meaning that it would unfold its own dynamic in expanding bureaucratic competencies.[162] It was especially the disappointment with Minister Fourie that led Verwoerd to devote himself to political work.[163]

---

highly controversial politician; still, as one of the few Cape nationalists, he joined the General in 1934, and tried to bring Malan into the United Party (Koorts 2014: 264–265, 274–275, 281–283, 300).
159 *Die Burger*, 17.3.1936, in a total of six columns. The article was also distributed as an offprint. The memorandum appeared in English in the *Child Welfare Magazine*, July 1936.
160 Verwoerd, 'Poverty and the State' (*Cape Argus*, 4.10.1935).
161 W.J. Verwoerd 1990: 4. See also Department of Labour and Social Welfare 1937: 35.
162 PV 202/6/4/1/1/1, FAK Collection, Memorandum of the Executive Committee [*Uitvoerende Komitee*] (c. 1936). On the further development of the Department, see Winckler 1969: 75–85. See also *Die Transvaler*, 5.10.1937; in an editorial, Verwoerd welcomed the establishment of the Department, but also used the platform to once again criticise Fourie (see *Die Transvaler*. 6.12.1937).
163 PV 72/3, Beukes, 'Ons staan in Drosdystraat . . .'. Report on a walk through Stellenbosch with Len Verwoerd, p. 12.

Verwoerd as Intellectual

Verwoerd was undoubtedly an intelligent man, but was he also an intellectual? Despite his academic career, this label is not suitable.[164] This is attested to by his own statements on the role of the university and of academics in society.

There are different and conflicting definitions of what an intellectual is. This has been the subject of intense debate, particularly within Marxism, as Marxists grappled with the problem of linking the 'bourgeois' intellectuals, as professional revolutionaries to whom Lenin had attributed a leadership role, with a class base different from their own. Nevertheless, they had to confirm Marx's idea that social life shapes consciousness – which applied to intellectuals, too. Antonio Gramsci tried to address this conundrum through his concept of the "organic" intellectual. Verwoerd was an "organic" intellectual in this sense, even though class affiliation was irrelevant in his case, since he was a protagonist of a cross-class, indeed class-negating nationalist movement. Karl Mannheim, on the other hand, introduced the concept of the "free-floating" intelligentsia,[165] to emphasise precisely the social independence of intellectuals. He attributed to intellectuals the capacity to situate themselves outside of their own class affiliation. Thus, for Mannheim, intellectuals were characterised by the capacity to break with their class base by virtue of engaging in a higher level of reflection. It was precisely this higher level of reflection on his own position and activity that Verwoerd lacked.

The graduate of Stellenbosch University, like its long-standing rector H. B. Thom, was a staunch promoter of the idea of the university as a "people's university" ["*volksuniversiteit*"].[166] This entailed the mandate of absolute devotion to serving the nation, in the name of which cosmopolitan intellectual currents were to be warded off: "In the midst of all that is happening, we have in the first instance to remain members of our own people, our own nation. The university is the body that has to see to that. . . . The youth who becomes denationalised by the world-wide stirrings, who only feels at

---

164 Even an author like Max du Preez, who is beyond suspicion of venerating Verwoerd, counts him among the "great white intellectuals" (du Preez 2004: 2004: 19; see also 60).
165 Mannheim 2015: 15.
166 Thom 1965: 14–18; Thom 1969; see also van Zijl 1969: 48–49. For Verwoerd, this meant a close connection of the University with the "life of the people"; young academics would have to be made to understand that they were to acquire their knowledge for "the people" in the first instance: "They have a duty to themselves and a duty to their nation to make sure of gaining that knowledge which forever increases, which makes life more useful and supplements the practical life, and of making it their own, also for the sake of others." (Verwoerd, Opening of the Extra–mural Building of the University of Pretoria, 25.3.1960 – in Pelzer 1966: 370–373, 371) See also D. Prinsloo 1979: 398–406. For a critical perspective on the concept of a "*volksuniversiteit*", see Degenaar 1978b: 152–153, 156–157.

home in the outside world but not in his own country, will surely be lost just as such persons have always been lost."[167] Universities, along with the business world, were the domains of "the life of the people [*volkslewe*]" most exposed to the temptations of cosmopolitanism: "For me this means that we should keep our identity as a people, that we should not become international, that we should not consider ourselves wise or learned or big when we abandon our people."[168] Unlike some of his erstwhile colleagues, who valued intellectual freedom and individualism, Verwoerd understood the university as a "community institution".[169] As early as 1929, in his speech at the opening of the academic year, he had proclaimed this as his credo: "A university must not only be a preparation for egoism, but a preparation for sacrifice."[170] That is why young people should bear in mind that their role is primarily one of being part of the nation and of engaging wholeheartedly in "serving the people [*volksdiens*]".[171] That is why the Afrikaanse Nationale Studentebond was permanently kept under the control of the National Party and the Broederbond.[172] In the process of their education, students should bear in mind that "we prepare ourselves at the university for our own and for our share in our nation's future".[173] In an exhortation to his oldest son who had started studying in Stellenbosch in 1947, Verwoerd maintained that the foundation for later life was built during the time of study. "If one does not heed this, one

---

[167] Verwoerd, Opening of the Academic Year at the University of Stellenbosch, 25.2.1959 (in Pelzer 1966: 248–257, 256). Temporary chair of the AB and Rector of the Randse Afrikaanse Universiteit, Gerrit Viljoen, claimed that the initially bilingual universities of South Africa became monolingual because of the arrogance of the English–speaking section of the population. Much as there is no doubt that there was some truth to this claim, it ignores the nationalist impulses and the concept of a *"volksuniversiteit"* (G. Viljoen 1978: 173–176). That is why Viljoen's claim lacks credibility.
[168] Verwoerd, Centenary Celebrations of the Reformed Church at Rustenburg, 28.3.1959 (in Pelzer 1966: 258–270, 269).
[169] Examples can be found in Du Raan 1998: 11. However Verwoerd's argument proceeded along the lines of what T. J. Hugo had outlined (Hugo, 1941, ch. 5). See also Prinsloo 1979: 2; and Welsh/Savage 1978: 136–137.
[170] E. Theron 1983: 22. Theron cited this from memory, but assigned it the date of 1919 – which was erroneous.
[171] On this, see Verwoerd's relation to the Jeugbond (Prinsloo 1979: 113–120).
[172] Heymans 1981: ch. 7.
[173] Verwoerd, Opening of the Extra-mural Building of the University of Pretoria, 25.3.1960 (Pelzer 1966: 370–373, 370). "As insignificant as our institutions are by comparison with those of the great nations, there is sufficient mental capacity in our country, as well as a form of freedom, also a freedom in the sense of not being too restrained by hard and fast theories and schools of thought, which is what allows us to contribute to the formation of new knowledge, and thereby serve our Republic." (PV93/4/1/9 Address to the ATKV Congress 1963, ff. 172–187, 185).

neglects not only one's own later development and happiness, but also that of all those who depend on one."[174]

Young people who studied abroad and then did not return to put their knowledge at the disposal of their own people, were simply traitors: "How could a nation whose potential leaders deserted it so, itself climb the ladder of civilisation and knowledge?"[175] In a keynote address at the University of Potchefstroom, Verwoerd also demanded that young academics submit to the imperatives of "serving the people": "The people as a whole can only grow culturally if this is done collectively and in following the thinkers and scholars who were born and raised in its midst and who can be the accepted leaders in all fields."[176] He judged as a betrayal not only the exodus of intellectuals, but also their openness to "liberalism", which he regarded as a form levelling posing a great danger to South Africa with its heterogeneous population.[177]

In 1960, when students at Stellenbosch University wrote exams on the day of the Referendum on the Republic, Verwoerd responded angrily:

> For me it is not only the fact that certain students are writing exams on that day and that they therefore cannot pay attention to a special national event, but that something is thereby lost to their young minds, namely that Stellenbosch fully witnessed something which will occupy a special place in history. . . . I know that nothing can be done about it now, and I understand the problems you mention, but to me they seem minor compared to the psychological loss that both the university and the young people could suffer.[178]

Verwoerd's academic interest remained within the narrow confines of an applied knowledge, as is attested to by his pronounced and lifelong hostility to theory. He considered theory as a set of unworldly, abstract fantasies – not as explanatory models that could facilitate structuring and interpreting empirical material. He was too much of a positivist to concede that; for him, explanations and conclusions arose more or less self-evidently from the accumulated material, the data and facts, which is why he deemed theories superfluous.

As a politician, Verwoerd repeatedly rebuked his critics by telling them that they did not have the "facts" straight, and that their argumentation was therefore

---

[174] FAV 4.5.1.1, Letter by Verwoerd to his son Wilhelm, 4.9.1947.
[175] Verwoerd, Opening of the Academic Year at the University of Stellenbosch, 25.2.1959 (in Pelzer 1966: 248–257, 252).
[176] Verwoerd 1957a: 230.
[177] Ibid., 234.
[178] PV 93/1/47/2/6, ff. 180–182, Letter by Thom to Verwoerd, 21.9.1960; f. 183, Verwoerd's reply to Thom, 28.9.1960.

based on false premises.[179] On the one hand, he claimed to have derived his policies from basic principles; on the other hand, he repeatedly emphasised his positivist conviction that the right policies could be inductively inferred from knowledge of the facts. Thus, when M. C. Botha was appointed Junior Minister in November 1960, Verwoerd gave him the following advice: "Remember that it is always best for you to rely on facts: you should not theorise; approach everything realistically and always refute your critics with facts!"[180] The deduction of political concepts from principles, and the factual basis of policies and their justification, did not require a "theoretical" orientation.

In later years, Verwoerd sought to subordinate research at the universities entirely to the economic goals formulated by the state, rejecting the pursuit of knowledge as unnecessary luxury:

> Science in our country is not properly organised and planned as is desirable. Much more central consideration has to be given to, on the one hand, the protection of our scientists and our scientific enterprises and, on the other hand, the utilisation in our practical projects of abilities, knowledge and talents in the scientific field. Eventually we shall have to get away from purely idealistic research, and science can be made useful in terms of what is profitable for South Africa. Thus part of the government's central planning and co-ordinating tasks will also be bringing science into our country under strict, honest and purposeful examination.[181]

Individual glory paled in comparison to national duty. A science like geology could be important "for the building of the fatherland", even though the research was done "by persons who often remain unknown, but [who did] everything for the benefit of us all."[182]

The obsession with dates and facts, which characterised the work of the Department of Native Affairs, but also the apartheid masterminds in the South African Bureau of Racial Affairs (SABRA) and the apartheid government as a whole, stemmed from the naïve belief in a set of science–based policies that could be logically derived and thus be directed towards truth. The more complete the data and facts, the closer any kind of research would come to the truth. Verwoerd can-

---

[179] To adduce only one example: "It is their [the government's] firm conviction that this was the divine purpose in bringing the White man to South Africa, namely to civilize and Christianise the black man and then to preserve this by ensuring the continued co–existence of both. The necessary steps to achieve this can be understood wrongly through lack of full knowledge of the facts as is clear in your case." (PV 93/3/1/23, letter by Verwoerd to Olive Warner, Verulam, 26.6.1959).
[180] M.C. Botha 1977: 9.
[181] Verwoerd, Annual Congress of the Afrikaans Trade Institute, Pretoria, 19.9.1961 (in Pelzer 1966: 611–628, 618–619).
[182] PV 93/3/4/13, Toespraak by geleentheid van die opening van die Museum van die Geologiese Opname op 17 Mei 1966, ff. 124–132, 128.

not be considered an intellectual because he did not have an inkling of freedom of research, and of the intrinsic value of scientific knowledge.

He was not, as Giliomee thinks, a professor in politics, but a politician who had taken a detour through science.[183] Looking back, an old companion had this to say about him: "I could not understand why a man with special talent for popular order [*volkaankantmaak*] wanted to become a journalist. I told him so. I will never forget his response. The older I get, and the more remarkably his career soared, the more clearly his answer tells me about his predisposition: 'If you want to bring improvements to your people, you must also know its politics.'"[184] What he gained from his academic career was not so much reflected in theoretically informed politics, but in his conviction that scientifically based politics was *the* modern form of politics; with this conviction, he pursued its implementation by all available means.

---

[183] That is how his wife saw it, too: "Politics was ultimately his life." (Letter by Betsie Verwoerd to M. E. Rothmann, 12.1. 1973, 55.K.V.16 (27)).
[184] 55.K.T. (81), Note of March 1967.

Propaganda

The Journalist

Verwoerd's role in the People's Congress and especially in the Continuation Committee had brought him to the attention of the National Party. It was witnessed by party leader D. F. Malan himself, who attended the People's Congress in Kimberley and gave the welcoming address.[1] For some time, the NP had been planning to establish its own daily newspaper in the Transvaal; at the suggestion of Paul Sauer,[2] Verwoerd was to become the editor-in-chief. The establishment of a daily newspaper was partly motivated by the fact that the cultural nationalists had been marginalised in party politics in this province since the split of the old NP in 1934. They had one remaining MP, J. G. Strijdom, who rose from backbencher to party leader in the Transvaal. But the Party lacked the organisational underpinnings, the financial basis, and above all a publication channel, which it was now preparing to establish. Since it was also notoriously underrepresented in the urban centres of the Witwatersrand, the planned newspaper was to have its editorial headquarters in Johannesburg. Afrikaner nationalists mobilised the capital, which came partly from the Nasionale Pers group in Cape Town, and partly from established businesses and wealthy private individuals.[3] On 3 March 1936, a separate press concern, Voortrekkerpers, could be officially established for Johannesburg and for the Transvaal province,[4] with a Board of Directors that "consisted

---

[1] Malan 1934. The D. F. Malan Collection contains the official report of the Continuation Committee on its first year of activities (1141/19 (20)), as well as an article in the *Cape Times* of 20.8.1935. Verwoerd's top–down approach was opportune to Malan's idea of how to remediate social ills (Koorts 2014: 68); on Verwoerd's appearance in Kimberley, see Koorts 2014: 307–308.

[2] According to Meiring (1990: 49), Sauer was his neighbour in Stellenbosch (see also Meiring 1973c: 132).

[3] The idea was supposed to have come up during a train trip (Meiring 1987:1; also Meiring 1987: 74–78; and *Die Transvaler* 13.10.1977). On the establishment and the further development of Nasionale Pers, see C. F. J. Muller 1990, chs. 5–12. An impassioned appeal of D. F. Malan's appeared under the title of 'Oproep aan alle Afrikaners' in the brochure *Nasionale Dagblad vir Transvaal* (1935). Shortly afterwards, a new version appeared, with an appeal by Malan and an updated listing of all received share subscriptions (Nasionale Party 1935; see also Le Roux 1953: 81–82).

[4] PV 93/1/39/2/1, Voortrekkerpers Beperk, Declaration by the Directorate of 10.2.1937, which for the first time announces the appointment of Verwoerd as editor-in-chief: "Prof Verwoerd has already become renowned, especially for his engagement with the poor white problem, and for acting as a mouthpiece for popular sentiment against the influx of undesirable elements from overseas into our country." Within the NP at the time, antisemitism was held to be a passport for access to higher office (D. Prinsloo 1979: 32; also C. F. J. Muller 1990: 492, 758–759; also Coetzer/Le Roux 1986: 29).

predominantly of people from the Cape".⁵ This concern was to publish the new newspaper, *Die Transvaler*, for which a separate building was erected near the railway station at De Villiers, Hoek and Noord Street in Johannesburg.⁶

In early 1936, Verwoerd was invited to dinner by Malan and influential nationalist businessman Willy Hofmeyr. On this occasion, they disclosed their plans to him, insisting that he should not only run the newspaper, "but [also] support Adv. J. G. Strijdom in the political arena and take a leading role especially on the Rand."⁷ At first, he was only to become deputy editor-in-chief because of his lack of experience in journalism.⁸ Verwoerd indicated his interest, but demanded an immediate appointment as editor-in-chief, so that he could assert his authority unchallenged, not least as a politician.

Although student representatives tried to persuade him to stay in Stellenbosch,⁹ Verwoerd decided to give up the secure and comparatively well-paid position of professor at Stellenbosch University because he wanted to "make a contribution to solving the problem of the white poor" through stepping into the political arena.¹⁰ It was not until August 1936 that he notified the university management of the job offer he had received and he informed Willy Hofmeyr, Chairman of the Voortrekkerpers, of his acceptance of the offer.¹¹ Although Verwoerd left the university in

---

5 C. F. J. Muller 1990: 610. Meiring (1987: 75) maintains that there is not a single journalist who ever made it onto the Board of the Voortrekkerpers; and even the financial expertise among Afrikaner professionals on the Witwatersrand remained untapped, because the Board was dominated by politicians (ibid., 78).
6 PV 93/1/39/2/1, Letter by Verwoerd to A. J. R. Rhyn, 12.3.1937, in which he requested the support of the editor-in-chief of *Die Volksblad*. The latter responded immediately, and sent out an appeal for funding camouflaged as editorial (20.3.1937). *Die Burger* had done so a few days earlier, on 15.3.1937.
7 FAV 4.6.2.3, (Huldeblyk) to Adv. J. G. Strijdom (1958), typed manuscript.
8 FAV 4.4.1.2, Letter by Verwoerd to Sauer (with whom he was on friendly terms even then), 23.2.1936. Present at the interview for the post of editor-in-chief was pedagogue and writer S. P. E. Boshoff (D. Prinsloo 1979: 37).
9 PV 117, f. 5, Dr Verwoerd (4) reported that the chair of the Junior National Party and Haak himself had been asked by the Board to persuade Verwoerd to stay (FAV 4.5.1.4, Letter by Ben Strauss (Boshof) to Verwoerd, 7.10.1937).
10 PV 117, Notes on Verwoerd, p. 6. To Erika Theron, he said, "I have to get into politics, in order to sort out these matters" (qtd. in G.D. Scholtz 1974, vol. 1: 40). He himself fondly remembered his time in Stellenbosch, "where we spent the happiest years of our lives, both as students and as lecturers" (PV 276/2/1/1/3, Letter by Verwoerd to C. G. W. Schumann, 26.9.1958). On the financial difficulties of the family in Johannesburg, see A. Boshoff 1974: 40, 57.
11 UA Stellenbosch, Personnel File Verwoerd, Letter by Verwoerd to the Rector, 8.8.1936, with the request to shorten the duration of the contract running until the end of March 1937, by one month. Reply of the Registrar on 24.8.1936, giving the University's permission. His official notice was submitted to the Registrar in writing on 1.9.1936 (FAV 4.4.1.2, Letter by Verwoerd to Hofmeyr,

1936 and later hardly ever commented on technical issues in psychology, he retained an affiliation with the discipline. As Prime Minister, he apparently prevented the publication of a disagreeable dissertation[12] and he was still directly involved in the formation of a separate Afrikaans-language professional association in the early 1960s.[13]

In his new position, he first had to become familiar with the work; after his appointment at the university had come to an end, he completed a crash course of several months at *Die Burger* from January 1937, during which he became acquainted with all the stages of newspaper production.[14] At the same time, preparations for the establishment of *Die Transvaler* were in full swing, as the editorial board had to be put in place. Verwoerd was able to poach a few journalists, such as Piet Meiring from *Die Burger*[15] or G. D. Scholtz from *Die Volksblad*.[16] Over some time, he hired other junior employees, some of whom made political careers in his slipstream; Marais Viljoen, for example, made it to minister and state president.[17] At the same time, Verwoerd had to arrange his move to Johannesburg, sell his house and parts of his household effects in Stellenbosch, and find accommodation on the Witwatersrand.[18] Still, he wasted no time getting to know prominent persons, so that he could use his position as editor of the newspaper to political effect.[19] Verwoerd lived frugally during these years, even during his first two

---

28.8. 1936, in which he reported the outcome of his negotiations with the University on the payment of his professorial salary until end–February 1937).

12 Louw/Foster 1991: 79.
13 Bell/Ntsebeza 2003: 38.
14 According to Meiring (1987: 5), the course only lasted for one month.
15 PV 72/3, Piet Meiring's memories of Verwoerd, p. 1.
16 C. F. J. Muller 1990: 438.
17 The rotation printing machine was purchased from Germany (D. Prinsloo 1979: 33); on Viljoen, see ibid., 47; on the members of the editorial committee, see especially Meiring 1987: 4ff; on their further career development, see Meiring 1987: 7; for the individuals involved, see Meiring 1987: 84–93. Shortly before Anton Rupert (who later was to become the most successful Afrikaans–speaking entrepreneur) completed his university degree, Verwoerd even made an offer to him to become a member of the editorial committee (Domisse 2005: 41); on the establishment of the editorial committee, see also G. D. Scholtz 1974, vol. 1: 68.
18 On this, see FAV 4.4.1.2, Outline of a letter by Verwoerd to the Board of Voortrekkerpers, 10.8.1936, with suggestions regarding the cost of the move, and his salary. On the sale of his house in Stellenbosch, see correspondence in FAV 4.5.1.3 of 1940, indicating that Verwoerd could sell his house only three years after the move. The buyer was former judge C. L. Botha (ibid.). Telegram by de Villiers to Verwoerd, 10.6.1940.
19 Meiring (1987: 6) dates the move to May 1937. Some embarked on initiatives of their own, like Senator Stoffberg and his partner who subsequently became close friends and supporters of Verwoerd's (FAV 4.4.1.2, Letter by Cinie Stoffberg to Verwoerd, 27.10.1936. A. Boshoff 1993: 37–43).

years as senator;[20] he faced considerable financial pressures, as his family was continuously growing.

The manager of the directorate, A. J. van Zyl, wanted to start as small as possible, to limit operational costs, and to expand the editorial office only gradually over the years. But Verwoerd vehemently opposed him, stressing the importance of the immediate appearance of a high-profile newspaper "not only in terms of size, but also in terms of in-depth reporting and variety of content". To him, the task was "to win readers and political supporters in that province where we are politically weakest".[21] Verwoerd clearly perceived the challenge primarily as a political one, while the journalistic one was only a means to an end.[22] The first issue of *Die Transvaler* appeared on 1 October 1937, but the newspaper was teetering on the brink for years.[23]

Before Verwoerd, D. F. Malan had followed a similar path, having given up his previous position of pastor (in 1915) to take up the dual role of editor-in-chief of *Die Burger* and party leader of the NP in the Cape Province. In both cases, the move to journalism was motivated by nationalist convictions. Verwoerd, however, took it one step further: possibly inspired by Malan's example, he speculated from the outset that journalistic activity would give him the necessary public attention that would facilitate his political career.[24] *Die Transvaler* was the mouthpiece of the Party's dominant line in the Transvaal, as represented by Strijdom and Verwoerd – consisting of a radical cultural nationalism, an near-fanatical republicanism and a decided hostility to Empire that was more pointed and pronounced than it was in the South. This soon resulted in an estrangement between Verwoerd and the nationalists in the Cape Province.

During the fierce power struggles in the nationalist camp in the war years, Verwoerd set aside journalistic standards; his editorials were one-sided and often little more than party declarations.[25] Thus Verwoerd consistently referred to political opponents, or even those who disagreed, as "enemies".[26] In doing so, he engaged in sometimes petty and sophistic argumentation that would have made

---

20 Van Schoor 1979: 109.
21 FAV 4.4.1.2, Two undated letters (presumably 13. and 15.12.) by A. J. van Zyl to Verwoerd, and Verwoerd's reply of 20.12.1936.
22 Spies/Theron/Scholtz 1981: 77; see also D. Prinsloo 1979: 45; and Meiring 1990: 50f.
23 J. L. Basson 1980: 200–201.
24 Stultz (1975: 74) suggested such a connection for the NP after 1948.
25 D. Prinsloo (1979: 86.) insisted that, relative to party propaganda, news reporting was rather a sideline business – which is what many members of the editorial committee were not used to (ibid. 28).
26 *Die Transvaler*, 16.8.1941 (editorial).

sense only to readers directly involved in the confrontation themselves.[27] In his comments, he sometimes referred to statements and documents that would have been unintelligible to newspaper readers not in the know.[28] He tended to use sentences with embedded clauses; instead of concise commentaries, he wrote long-winded, convoluted editorials.[29]

Soon the first problems arose in his relations with colleagues in Nasionale Pers. The Chairman of the Directorate of Voortrekkerpers, Willy Hofmeyr, resigned after a relatively short time because he could not get along with Verwoerd.[30] Hofmeyr's vacated post went to Strijdom, which meant that the Transvaal branch of the NP controlled the Party's most important press outlet. After a few years, moreover, the editor-in-chief came into conflict with the managing director, A. J. van Zyl. The persistent conflict was carried out in the form of office intrigues and rumour-mongering.[31] Verwoerd complained to Strijdom about Van Zyl, whom he described as having a "hysterical personality" and an "inferiority complex". According to Verwoerd, van Zyl could not stand the fact that he, Verwoerd, was better known and more prominent because of his political activities. For his part, he claimed that his actions stemmed solely from his sense of duty and that he was involved in conflicts only to enforce cultural nationalism in all its purity. According to Verwoerd, his opponents, in this case van Zyl, in contrast, were guided by uncontrolled impulses and frustrated ambition, systematically undermining his authority as editor-in-chief. His interpretation of the dispute corresponded to a pattern typical of Verwoerd: he himself conducted himself rationally, thoughtfully and adhered to legally appropriate procedures and administratively prescribed processes; disputes on his side were about the correct line to take, not about personal power. But Verwoerd caused polarisation in working relations; his relationships with the editors-in-chief of *Die Burger*, A. L. Geyer, and *Die Volksblad* (Bloemfontein) A. J. R. van Rhyn, turned out to be equally uncongenial.[32]

Die Transvaler found itself in precarious states several times during Verwoerd's tenure as editor-in-chief, as circulation figures remained unsatisfactorily low, and sales figures for the newspaper were lower in the city than in the country-

---

27 For instance the editorials in *Die Transvaler*, 11.8.1941.
28 *Die Transvaler*, 8.9.1941.
29 Meiring 1987: 6, 143; see also Prinsloo 1979: 55–56.
30 J. Muller 1989: 125; see also Meiring 1987: 183.
31 FAV 4.5.1.5, Letter by Verwoerd to Chair of Voortrekkerpers (J. G. Strijdom), 5.5.1941.
32 D. Prinsloo 1979; 59, 70–83; see also Meiring 1990: 128. On Geyer, see A. van Wyk 1983: 14.

side;[33] in 1939, the state of the paper was so dire that salaries had to be cut by ten percent.[34] During the War, the newspaper had to deal with paper shortages and was continuously understaffed. It also could not pay its journalists at the same rate as its competitor the United Party-supporting *Vaderland*, which is why staff kept leaving to find better-paid positions with that paper.[35] With its distinct ideological line and its pronounced support for the NP, *Die Transvaler* could establish a base of subscribers who, for political reasons, remained loyal to the paper.[36] In the late phase of the War, the newspaper was met with a declining interest in frontline news sourced from news agencies, which is why it had to fall back on its own reporting, thin on the ground as it was. In 1944, in terms of personnel, the editor-in-chief was back where he had started in 1937: he hardly had any experienced staff. In later years, only editors and political stalwarts like Meiring and Scholtz remained loyal to him; Meiring became information director during his reign, while Scholtz stayed with *Die Transvaler* and became Verwoerd's hagiographer.[37]

Not only *Die Transvaler*, but also the press concern Voortrekker-Pers got into serious turmoil after World War II, partly due to mismanagement[38] leading to heavy losses, especially in revenues from advertising. It even became necessary to sell the building; in 1948, the group had a debt of 84 000 pounds,[39] which meant that the continued existence of Voortrekker-Pers was dependent on a bail-out.[40]

---

[33] Meiring 1973b: 121f.
[34] *Die Transvaler*, 13.10.1977.
[35] D. Prinsloo (1979: 41) describes how Verwoerd also painted *Die Vaderland* as ideological opponent.
[36] See for instance the congratulatory note upon the appearance of the first edition, penned by a former fellow student from Stellenbosch, who remembered having discussed 'The Essence of Intelligence' with Verwoerd in 1923, and who now wished him every success in his endeavours (FAV 4.5.1.4, Letter by J. S. Loubser (Heilbron) to Verwoerd, 6.10.1937). See also Letter by Prof P. J. Schoeman to Verwoerd, 7.10.1937 (ibid.), in which Schoeman complained that eleven subscribers, most of them professors based in Stellenbosch, had not yet received any edition of the paper.
[37] Scholtz complained to Verwoerd, when the paper once published photos of scantily dressed women, which Scholtz found to be improper. This complaint went too far even for Verwoerd, who was arch-conservative in this respect. He admonished Scholtz "not to hold the reins too tightly and to draw the lines too narrowly. Doing so, one would end up in perpetual disagreements." (FAV 4.5.1.5, handwritten note for a letter by Verwoerd to Scholtz, undated) On this, see also Meiring 1987: 113, 151. On Scholtz personally, see Meiring 1987: 145–149.
[38] It was especially the managing director A.J. van Zyl, who elicited criticism (PV 18/3/1/53, Letter by Strijdom to Swart, 19.4.1948). Piet Meiring was entrusted with soliciting advertisements.
[39] PV 18/2/1/51, Letter by Strijdom to Swart, 15.11.1947. See also Meiring 1987: 184–185.
[40] *Die Transvaler*, 13.10. 1977. Even in the early 1960s, the majority of Afrikaners regularly read English-language newspapers (G. D. Scholtz 1963a: 364).

Verwoerd's aggressive journalism, which was more like propaganda than reporting,[41] solicited fierce criticism. The *Rand Daily Mail* was not prepared to recognise *Die Transvaler* as a 'newspaper', contemptuously calling it a "nationalist progaganda sheet": "In Dr Verwoerd's day this publication performed some of the most extraordinary antics in the history of journalism."[42] In an article dated 27 October 1941, *Die Transvaler* had used material from an NS propaganda broadcast from the short-wave transmitter at Zeesen south of Berlin, which it had received from the Information Bureau of the Ministry of the Interior, omitting the additional information provided by South African agencies. On 31 October 1941, *The Star* responded by publishing an article entitled 'Speaking Up for Hitler', in which Verwoerd was accused of engaging in propaganda for National Socialist Germany, and which Verwoerd quite rightly understood as an "accusation of high treason against the responsible person, the editor-in-chief".[43] He used his newspaper to defend himself against the accusation[44] and acted against the explicit advice from Malan and other NP grandees in instituting legal proceedings against *The Star*, which he promptly lost.[45] He had obviously misjudged the situation; as a result, "what was intended as a small matter of self-defence . . . did not succeed, but on the contrary drew ripple effects that affected wider interests, among others those

---

41 Meiring 1973b: 120.

42 *Rand Daily Mail*, 4.6.1954. However, the Voortrekkerpers Board opposed the placement of adverts for a "Komitee vir Navorsing oor Imperialistiese metodes" in the paper, in order to protect the Party from further adverse effects (PV 18/2/1/3, 'Notule van die Direksievergadering van die Voortrekkerpers Beperk', 22.5.1946, p. 5). See also Prinsloo 1987.

43 PV 93/1/65/1, Letter by Verwoerd to Otto du Plessis, 28.4.1943. Ironically, the contrary was the case, as a letter from a certain Denis J. G. Fitz-Patrick to attorney H. de Villiers of 21.6.1943 indicates (copy in PV 93/1/65/1) – namely that the broadcasting station near Zeesen was making propagandistic use of articles published in *Die Transvaler* that had been taken across the border to Lorenço Marques and from there to Germany. It is interesting to note that Verwoerd was so closely acquainted with Erik Holm – the South African who worked for Zeesen -, that he inserted a relief sculpted by his wife, into a wall of his holiday home in Betty's Bay (A. Boshoff 1974: illustration p. 153). The sculpture was the model for the emblem of Orania, the place where right–wing radical Afrikaners attempted to found their own state after the end of apartheid. On Holm, see Marx 2008: 517-518 also D. Prinsloo 1979: 415–421. On the court case brought against *The Star* D. Prinsloo 1979: 422–441; and Meiring 1987: 41–45. One of the attorneys of *The Star* was J. G. N. Strauss, who later became the Chairperson of the United Party and leader of the opposition.

44 *Die Transvaler*, 22.2.1940.

45 PV 93/1/65/8, Judgement of the Supreme Court with detailed justification for dismissal of the application. The extensive materials are located in PV 93/1/65, including the reports on the case published in *Die Transvaler* (P. W. Coetzer 1994: 376–378).

of the company itself".[46] The defeat got him into considerable financial difficulties, because he had to pay the legal costs of £6 192.17.5; and since the case was dismissed with costs, he was slapped with the fees of *The Star*'s legal team.[47] Despite his obvious miscalculation, Verwoerd interpreted the Judge's ruling to effectively mean that "the whole of Afrikanerdom had been wronged in the matter".[48] The lost case also brought Verwoerd criticism from the directorates of Voortrekkerpers and Nasionale Pers.[49] It was only through the help and support of like-minded persons, and of Nasionale Pers that he was saved from bankruptcy.[50]

Verwoerd's peculiar understanding of journalism, and the stance taken by his newspaper, caused a stir again during the British monarch's visit to South Africa. In 1947, Prime Minister Jan Smuts had invited the royal family to a tour of South Africa, not least with the aim of increasing his chances of re-election, which was by no means lost on his political opponents. As dyed in the wool republican, Verwoerd decided to simply hush up the visit and not report on it at all.[51] Even Strijdom, who could not be said to have been exactly sympathetic to the monarchy, registered his objection. He considered Verwoerd's decision and demeanour unprofessional for a journalist. He pointed out to him that there was no Party decision to boycott the visit, but beyond that, he reminded him that *Die Transvaler* was a newspaper whose role it was to publish news: "The arrival and the presence of the King in South Africa are quite important 'news', and I therefore fail to understand why you want to keep this, in so far as it is *news*, out of *Die Transvaler*."[52] Strijdom had no sympathy for Verwoerd's attitude; he did not

---

46 FAV 4.5.1.7, Letter by Verwoerd to A. J van Zyl, managing director of Voortrekkerpers, 14.8.1943.
47 PV 93/1/65/1, f. 84, Letter from Hoofbestuurder Voortrekkerpers to Hoofbestuurder Nasionale Pers, 22.10.1943. In the end, Nasionale Pers and the NP helped him out, but Verwoerd remained in financial dire straits for years after.
48 FAV 4.5.1.7, Letter by Verwoerd to A. Hertzog, 29.7.1943, in a similar vein (ibid., Letter by Verwoerd to M. Nolte (Groot Marico), 29.7.1943 and to N. Diederichs, 30.7.1943).
49 D. Prinsloo 1979: 434.
50 FAV 4.5.1.7, Letter by Verwoerd to A. J. van Zyl, Voortrekkerpers, 6.1.1943, in which he offers to privately contribute 100 pounds to the collection; ibid. 14.8.1943, with thanks to the Voortrekkerpers Board for their support; nevertheless, financial constraints made themselves felt when the attorneys' accounts fell due (ibid., Letter by Verwoerd to A. J. van Zyl, 18.9.1943).
51 The visit was greeted with great enthusiasm by English-speaking whites (see Lambert 2017: 104). After South Africa's exit from the Commonwealth, Verwoerd said to Queen Elizabeth that this did not mean cutting all ties: "The entire country will appreciate it if you were to decide to come to South Africa for a holiday" (qtd. in E. Theron 1983: 27).
52 PV 93/1/56/1, f. 48, Letter by Strijdom to Verwoerd, 28.2.1947. Emphasis in the original.

turn this into a matter of principle, but was mindful of the journalistic obligation to provide the readers with news.[53] Verwoerd's astonishment at Strijdom's disapproval of his attitude[54] is a clear indication that he considered journalistic standards to be subordinate to the propaganda mission of the Party; indeed, it shows that even after ten years of professional practice as editor-in-chief, he had not even imbibed them.[55] Through his radicalism, he manoeuvred himself into a trap without realising it. His distinctly political form of reporting gave rise to all kinds of misunderstandings and a general mistrust, creating the impression that even editorial errors stemmed from his political radicalism. It did not take long for him to feel himself placed under general suspicion, to such an extent that he constantly defended himself against what he saw as unjustified attacks.[56]

Propaganda Techniques

Even in his engagement for the poor whites, Verwoerd attached great importance to propaganda, for he was alert to the possibility that the Congress in Kimberley in 1934 could end up being a mere flash in the pan. That is why he turned to propaganda to keep the issue alive in the public arena.[57] He immediately took steps himself, writing a series of articles on the Congress and the Continuation Committee; in these articles, written in English and in Afrikaans, he candidly addressed the need for propaganda. By now, he had gained considerable reputation as expert in the field – to such an extent that the *Cape Times* and the *Cape Argus* placed their columns at his disposal.[58] In some of the February 1935 editions of

---

53 Ibid., f. 50, Letter by Strijdom to Verwoerd, 10.3.1947. According to Ben Schoeman (1978: 123), Verwoerd's attitude was the reason why the HNP hardly garnered any votes from English-speaking whites.
54 PV 93/1/56/1, f. 49, Letter by Verwoerd to Strijdom, 4.3.1947.
55 The news boycott against political opponents was a strategy that Verwoerd had used before, namely against the Ossewabrandwag during the War; he had recommended it to other newspapers as an example to follow (PV 93/1/1/1, 52ff, Telegram by Verwoerd to Malan, who stayed in Aliwal North at the time).
56 PV 93/1/56/1, f. 55, Letter by Verwoerd to Strijdom, 3.3.1947.
57 Verwoerd gave a lot of thought to propaganda for the reforms he envisaged; to some extent, he presented them in his lectures (231/2/2, 'Metodes van sosiologiese navorsing', pp. 47, 57).
58 Three articles appeared in the *Cape Argus*, on 2., 3., and 4.10.1935, respectively. One article appeared in the *Cape Times*, along with commentary in support of Verwoerd. Unfortunately the articles are not carefully dated; they can be found in FAV 4.4.5.1, with the corresponding manuscripts in FAV 4.4.4. See also the letter dated 22.8.1935 and sent by the *Cape Argus* to Verwoerd, notifying him of the acceptance of the offer of three articles.

Die Burger, he also published a series of articles on the work of the Continuation Committee, which he described as a "propaganda institution" not tasked with social projects in its own right.[59] Propaganda was not limited to newspaper articles; Verwoerd also presented numerous lectures, including at the Rotary Club and other institutions, especially in the Western Cape.[60] He also appeared as a keynote speaker at a three-day course of Oranje Vrouevereniging in Bloemfontein, where he took the opportunity to reiterate his demands.[61]

As was common in South Africa at the time, Verwoerd held a very broad idea of propaganda that included advertising. In acting on this, his preoccupation with the psychology of advertising stood him in good stead. Although he never published on the subject, his notes indicate an intense interest in it.[62] The ruses of the journalist and politician-to-be showed a remarkable consistency, which will be traced here, right up to the stage at which he took office as Prime Minister. The following maxims can be identified:

1. Always keep the initiative. Verwoerd successfully avoided having to react to others' proposals – he was intent on always keeping the initiative. Even if, as in the 1959 case of the High Commission Territories, he temporarily lost the initiative, he still managed to create an impression that the initiative of others was only a reaction to his own. This way he assuaged his fear of losing control.

2. Immediately go on the counter-attack. This was a variant of 1, but it differed in one crucial respect. When Verwoerd launched a counter-attack, it was to convince the public of the correctness of his own position. Thus, as Prime Minister, he collected examples of social and ethnic discrimination in numerous countries, in order to be able to strike back propagandistically – especially against states like India or Sweden.[63] His propagandistic tactic of immediately launching a

---

59 *Die Burger*, 18.2.1935. He gave a clear idea of the aim of his propaganda: "Whenever the Continuation Committee is met with unjustifiable opposition, it will have to be prepared to pull public opinion to its side through propaganda and information. In this way, it will be able to enforce the Congress resolutions and exert pressure on defiant organisations and persons." The propagandistic character is clearly evident also in the *Cape Times* of 20.8.1935.
60 *Cape Argus*, 15.8.1935 and *Cape Times*, 16.8.1935, as well as on a speech presented in Franschhoek (*Die Burger*, 31.8.1935). A full list of his lectures is provided by E. Theron 1970: 43.
61 *Volksblad*, 16.4.1935.
62 PV 93/1/33/2.
63 PV 93/1/53/2/5, f. 45, Letter by Verwoerd to Sekr. Buitelandse Sake, 7.11.1960; see also PV 93/10/1/3, various files, Inligting vir Eerste Minister, with quotes on, and references to, discrimination in India; on 'Voorbeelde van Wetgewing wat aanhouding sonder verhoor moontlik te maak'. Red stamp: 'Dringend/Urgent'; Press Censorship; Northern Ireland, arbitrary detentions and human rights situation; 'vorms van diskriminasie tussen rasse en groupe in ander state',- among others

counter-offensive can be seen in his attacks on the United Party: in this instance, he spelled out the consequences of the opposition's political stance in an argument bristling with relentless logic, thus pushing members of the opposition into a defensive position from which they could no longer escape. Reading Verwoerd's speeches in Parliament, one notices that he often behaved more like an opposition leader and less like a head of government; he picked apart the opposition's policies in pages of diatribes, while presenting his own concepts rather casually. The negative tinge of Verwoerd's propaganda, which often exhausted itself in criticism of the political opponent, was decried by some observers.

3. Personalising conflicts. Verwoerd handled this tactic with great propagandistic virtuosity in the 1948 election campaign, when he targeted Jan Hendrik Hofmeyr with his attacks, styling him as a typical representative of the "liberalist" policy of the United Party. This was not only disingenuous, it was completely misleading, for Hofmeyr took a position that was not shared in the least by the majority of the members of his party.[64]

4. Sense of mission, hard-and-fast stance, inflexibility, uncompromising attitude. These traits characterised Verwoerd in any case; they did not necessarily entail intentional propagandistic calculation. Nevertheless, these traits proved effective, earning Verwoerd the reputation (among his followers) of being a "man of granite"; they gave him the air of someone who could be relied upon and to whom the fate of the Afrikaner people could be entrusted.

5. Repetition. The propagandistic importance of repetition, the constant harping on one and the same central message, was upheld by Verwoerd himself; he distinguished between news and propaganda, the latter being based on "constant repetition".[65] His own manner of repeating the same statements and chains of arguments also displayed obsessive features;[66] it was related to his sense of mission and the

---

the Chinese in Indonesia and Malaysia; Israel, Sweden, Cashmere, Zanzibar, Liberia and others. Louw used this information in the UN-General Assembly (*Rand Daily Mail*, 15.10.1960); see also *Die Transvaler*, 17.10.1960. In 1961, Louw reported that the offensives against South Africa were gaining in strength (PV 4/86. F. 74, Letter by Louw to Verwoerd, 29.9.1921).

64 Brits 1994: 114. A similarly person-centred propaganda strategy was used by Goebbels in his 'Isidor'-invectives (Longerich 2012: 102–103).

65 FAV 4.5.2.4, Verklaring Dr H. F. Verwoerd, typewritten, 13.2.1941, p. 5. It is quite possible that he was influenced by Le Bon (2002: 89) in this regard.

66 Verwoerd himself defended his predecessor Strijdom, who had similarly been reproached for "forever talking about the same things": "He said the same thing, but every time with a different nuance and an emphasis on a different aspect." But this indicated "that it is especially these themes that dominated all his deliberations and actions" (FAV 4.6.2.3, Letter by Huldeblyk to Adv. J. G. Strijdom (1958), p. 4).

conviction that he had found the only viable solution to South Africa's problems.[67] After a lengthy conversation with Verwoerd, former US Ambassador Lewis Douglas concluded "that Verwoerd is a psychopath" and that modifications to apartheid policies were not possible "as long as he remains Prime Minister".[68] Reading his speeches and letters, one is struck by the prayer-like repetitions, which Verwoerd apparently never tired of. Rather, he enjoyed presenting his political principles to others in hours and hours of monologues, without adding any noteworthy new arguments. Verwoerd's later speeches were designed to intimidate his audiences with dazzling mental powers. His speeches, like those of Fidel Castro, lasted up to four hours; even his private secretary, Fred Barnard, who was full of admiration for him, voiced his opinion saying that many things could have been stated more briefly: "He simply talked his opponents down."[69]

Numerous visitors from home and abroad reported the tiring, hours-long impromptu lectures on apartheid that they had to endure, with even interviews being reduced to monologues.[70] As early as 1952, Phil Weber wryly remarked: "I talked with Verwoerd for an hour and a half, or rather, he talked with me";[71] and a German journalist noted: "He takes great pleasure in lecturing."[72] Piet Meiring reported that Verwoerd enjoyed nothing more than refuting others. Whereupon he developed the strategy "to ask for the opposite of what I really wanted!"[73] When A. J. van der Merwe, the DRC's facilitator in the Cape Province and one of

---

67 UP Archive, Report of preliminary UR meeting of Die Afrikaner Broederbond, Johannesburg, 11.12.1944, p. 12: „Much of this oration by Verwoerd was exactly the same as that contained in the report of the morning's proceedings." See Report of a meeting of the Dagbestuur of the UR of the A.B. 13.12.1944, p. 6.
68 DNSA, Telegram by Statterthwaite to Department of State, 12.6.1964, p. 3.
69 Barnard 1967: 23.
70 Flather 1977: 172–173, similarly to Marion Dönhoff in her news report, 'A silver lining for South Africa' in *Die Zeit*, 2.11.1960; see also *Sunday Tribune*, 21.12.1958. Dönhoff's report roused Verwoerd's ire – it was too critical for his liking. He had trusted her credentials on the basis of the reports he had received about her much more conservative brother Christoph (on this, see PV 35/2/1/1/2, Dr Graf Dönhoff, Letter by the German-South African Association to Mr Op't Hof, Department of Education, Arts and Science, 4.2.1966, on a tour of the Choir of Rhodes University that had been considered helpful "for our pro–South African propaganda work"). A similar account was given by Prof. Jan Rabie (Lazar 1987: 69, n. 105).
71 296.K.Ge 112 (2a), Letter by Weber to Geyer, 26.11.1952.
72 Dönhoff 1965: 158.
73 Meiring 1987: 143. Meiring (as well as Scholtz) belonged to the small group of journalists who followed Verwoerd from his days as chief editor of *Die Transvaler*; Meiring was appointed as Director of Information under Verwoerd's premiership.

South Africa's most influential church leaders, led a delegation to see Verwoerd, he could not even get a word in edgewise during the entire 'conversation'.[74]

Repetitions also served to reinforce bogeyman images and to apportion blame. Just as bogeyman images were based on simplifications, the solution was also clear: if one looks at the topics Verwoerd preferred to cover as a journalist, it is easy to see that he always attributed the most diverse events and occasions to the same root cause. Thus, during the war years, "British-Jewish capitalism" was mainly to blame for the poverty of Afrikaners. Verwoerd always offered a solution to most political problems, all of which he attributed to deliberate discrimination (against Afrikaners). The solution was the Republic and the severing of all ties to the British Empire or Commonwealth. This is what he inculcated into his readers in hundreds of articles; he was so successful that he had to dampen expectations of the imminent establishment of a republic when he assumed office as Prime Minister.

Many, especially his supporters, were impressed and often thanked him afterwards for the insights they had now gained: Journalist A. M. van Schoor, who temporarily worked for the South Africa Foundation, arranged a meeting for American finance magnate C. V. Engelhardt,[75] whom Verwoerd treated to his usual barrage of speeches. Engelhardt came out of Verwoerd's office in a daze and suddenly exclaimed in the street, "[t]his man Verwoerd is right. His is the only policy for a multi-racial South Africa".[76] Verwoerd prepared carefully for such visits and laid out his argumentation, which shows how much he tried to impress with the seemingly "spontaneous" implementation.[77] Some found listening to his endless monologues rather "exacting";[78] others remarked admiringly that he hypnotised his listeners "for hours at a stretch".[79]

Repetition, however, pertained not only to the chains of his arguments, but also to reiterations of affirmative responses. These can be identified with remarkable frequency in Verwoerd's speeches and letters; he would restate an argument starting with the formula, "in other words". Through such reformulations, he would generalise his points, and create the impression that it was principles that were at stake. For example, he rebuked opposition proposals to have white repre-

---

74 Meiring 1990: 81.
75 Van Schoor 1979: 123. On Engelhardt, see also DNSA, Memorandum of conversation betw. Governor Harriman and Lawrence Gandar (*Rand Daily Mail*), State Department, 27.11.1964, p. 1.
76 Van Schoor 1979: 126. Engelhardt subsequently wrote Verwoerd once again, showing himself impressed with the idea of border industries (PV 93/1/34/1, ff. 12–13. Engelhardt, 8.9.58).
77 Barnard 1967: 27–28.
78 *Natal Mercury*, 29.8.1959.
79 Barnard 1967: 23.

sentatives for Africans elected to Parliament, saying that this had not worked in Rhodesia. His conclusion followed: "In other words, there is no hope for peace or the continued existence of whites once we have embarked on the slippery road of a diverse people in a diverse fatherland."[80]

6. Simplifications. As part of his style of argumentation, Verwoerd tended to break up complicated issues into separate strands, to bring them together again at a later stage, so that the complexity was revealed in its entirety only at the end; he managed to present this in an intelligible way.

In his Psychology MA dissertation, Verwoerd developed an argument on the double task. In contrast to Westphal's study of the main and secondary task, he saw the special feature of the double task in the fact that it did not lead to partial answers, but that both tasks resolved themselves into one answer. This is precisely the form that characterised much of the argumentation employed by the politician Verwoerd. In one of his frequently used rhetorical strategies, he presented a solution that addressed various problems simultaneously and in one fell swoop. He constructed the problem from a solution previously conceived, and was thus able to present it as manageable from the outset.

This is consistent with the observation that his logical argumentation was always constructed from the result. This is what enabled him to demonstrate his superior ability to come up with solutions that would cut the Gordian knot of complicated political problems. By providing unambiguous solutions to double tasks, he sought to shore up the legitimacy of his position of power. Thus, he criticised the volume of the Carnegie Report written by his doctoral supervisor because it did not distinguish sufficiently neatly between various topics, and did not present them separately, as a result of which it largely failed to reach a general readership.[81]

7. Distortions. Verwoerd often distorted facts to make it appear as if the victims and losers of his policies were the actual beneficiaries. As far as he was concerned, the proclamation of the Republic was actually beneficial above all for English-speaking whites, while apartheid policies served the welfare of the blacks: "The scope of the policy which I have reviewed today is to clear up inconsistencies in our guidance of the Bantu and to place our plans of development for him on a sound footing, as I have just said. It is in the best interest of the Bantu that

---

80 Qtd. in G. D. Scholtz 1974, vol. 2: 183.
81 *Die Burger*, 30.12.1932.

this should happen and it is the wish of white South Africa that we should act accordingly."[82]

Influx control, he said, actually benefitted blacks first and foremost: "In the long run it is perhaps the native who will be the biggest victim of the selfishness of the European if he allows uncontrolled influx, because when excessive numbers of natives are present then the consequences are low wages, inferior housing and vagrancy."[83]

Minister Verwoerd believed that the Johannesburg City Council was spending too much money on its black residents.[84] Passing funding cuts off as benefits was an argumentative turn typical of the psychologist Verwoerd; in his political career, he often succeeded with his logical-sounding rhetoric, presenting certain measures as being in the interest of those adversely affected. Thus, some laws, such as the 'Abolition of Passes and Coordination of Documents Act', promised in their title the opposite of what they actually effected.

Hardly any of his tricks was as successful as this one. Verwoerd achieved mastery in the argumentative contortions by which he presented victims as winners.[85] The propagandistic effect resonated for a long time – in some respects even to the present day. If some South Africans still believe that the intentions of apartheid politicians were honourable, if only these could have been implemented properly, this reflects the long-term success of Verwoerd's propaganda, which sought to legitimate apartheid by making black people out to be the beneficiaries of this policy. In this way, his politics, designed to preserve white power and privilege, was made to appear as an altruistic enterprise, even as sacrifice for the benefit of others.[86]

Verwoerd as Orator

In taking up the position as editor of *Die Transvaler*, Verwoerd entered active politics. This step, combining the twin capacities as editor and politician, merits con-

---

[82] Verwoerd, Policy of the Minister of Native Affairs, 30.5.1952 (in Pelzer 1966: 31–52, 52).
[83] Verwoerd, Speech delivered at the Congress of the Institute of Administrators of Non–European Affairs, held at Bloemfontein, on 17.9.1956 (in Pelzer 1966: 124–148, 130).
[84] PV 276/I/9/5/6/2/10, f. 13, Letter by Verwoerd to Heckroodt, 20.2.1956.
[85] This is what Hepple (1967: 30ff) had already observed.
[86] A discussion of prominent apartheid theologians with a colleague from the Netherlands showed that the South Africans kept referring only to Verwoerd's statements of intent, whereas the colleague from the Netherlands addressed the realities in South Africa (Verkuyl/Gericke/Corster/Snyman 1970).

sideration of Verwoerd's appearances as public speaker. In his public speaking engagements, Verwoerd adopted an intensely committed stance as a means of persuasion. Consonant with the findings of his dissertation on the unreliability of feelings, Verwoerd relied on the persuasiveness of his argumentation and refrained from inflaming the (short-lived) emotions of his audiences. At no stage did Verwoerd act as demagogue or populist agitator. On the contrary, he appealed to logical reasoning. "The power of his argumentation lay in the hypnotising logic with which he built up his points step by step, into a unity that provided the basis for his conclusion."[87] The adjective "hypnotic" is telling, referring, as it does, to a rhetorical instrumentalisation of logic. In this respect, he differed from many other speakers, indeed his logical argumentation was even highlighted as a special feature by A. M. Van Schoor: "That was his technique – Dr Verwoerd never addressed a private or public meeting in the orthodox sense of the word. He always reasoned with his audience, taking them personally along with him in his argument, so complete in its logical content that no one ever left him with any unanswered questions or reservations."[88]

US Ambassador Crowe observed: "The Prime Minister has a great deal of confidence in his powers as a persuader."[89] Verwoerd trusted in the penetrating power of his logical argumentation; from early on, he sought to establish a cult of genius of a certain kind. As a professor, Verwoerd became famous for delivering his lectures extemporaneously displaying what to many members of his audiences seemed like a photographic memory.[90] Thus, on Mondays, he would never have to ask where he had left off the previous Friday. "When he stepped up to the lectern, he immediately started lecturing. It amazed me how he managed to get all the points written up on the blackboard, and to dictate without having to rely on notes." At the time, professors dictated the texts to their students, which is why students worked with books only in exceptional cases.[91] Verwoerd's lectures, for example those on logic or character studies, consisted largely of citations of

---

87 D. Prinsloo 1979: 8.
88 Van Schoor 1979: 121, also 130: "Dr Verwoerd was our psychologist–statesman par excellence, whose speeches were always made at his audience in long masterly exercises in reasoning *with* them"; similarly G. D. Scholtz 1974, vol. 2: 22. See also A. Boshoff 1974: 29.
89 Telegram from the Embassy in South Africa to the Department of State, 30.10.1959 (in LaFantasie 1992: 738).
90 E. Theron 1970: "What also impressed young students was the phenomenal memory of their professor. Never did he have notes in front of him." (see also E. Theron 1970: 25; also J. Basson 2004: 68–69).
91 Du Raan 1998: 60–61. The small University Library was housed in the C.I. Marais Library Building, which also was the seat of the administration, and the venue for Council and Senate meetings (Booyens 1995: 2–3).

textbook knowledge. In fact, he wrote out his lectures beforehand, and then apparently learnt them off by heart; some of the archived manuscripts contain handwritten marks in the margins indicating how far he had gotten in each lecture. The dates indicated in the notes explain why he was always able to continue the lecture at the exact point where he had left off, in the next lesson. Apart from vanity, what certainly played a role was the calculated attempt to gain power and influence through demonstrating his intellectual superiority. The impression he left on his students was that they had come into the presence of an "original thinker" with a "great intellect and photographic memory",[92] but one who did not allow any discussion or questions.[93] "To us, Dr. Verwoerd was the ideal lecturer. . . . He was convincing, one had the feeling that the man stood heart and soul behind what he said."[94] Decades later, politicians would still boast about the fact that they "sat in Professor Verwoerd's class as first-year students".[95] The myth that was being elaborated here endured over a long period of time, and to some extent still lingers today: "his brilliant mind and thinking power, his leadership qualities and his statesmanlike vision."[96] Verwoerd was styled as the towering intellectual who invented and enforced apartheid and who, if only he had been left alive, would have brought things to a good end. Verwoerd, as editor of *Die Transvaler*, "would not have taken long to show himself as a man of extraordinary talent and skill. That was why many people from various quarters urged him to become a member of the legislature."[97] The causal link drawn between his extraordinary talent and his political career is significant; however, to the extent that the real reason, namely that Verwoerd purposefully pursued a career in the Party and in the Broederbond parallel to his editorial activity and with the endorsement of the NP leadership, remained unspoken, his apparent genius could stand out as the real reason. The conclusion could only be that a genius like Verwoerd was bound to land up in the highest government office.

In 1959, H. B. Thom, Broederbond Chairman and Rector of Stellenbosch University, invited Verwoerd to present the keynote address at the opening of the

---

92 PV 117, f. 6, Notes 'Dr. Verwoerd, my professor tree tot die politiek toe', p. 3.
93 Ryan 1990: 20; Meiring 1973b: 119.
94 Tinie Vorster, qtd. in Jones 1986: 57.
95 PV 132/3/6/1, Speech by Vorster in Stellenbosch, 14.9.1966. Former students in different professions congratulated him on the various steps in his career and expressed their satisfaction with the appointment of their former professor. On the Minister, see FAV 4.6.1.1, Letter by ds C. J. J. Brand (Morgenster Mission in South Rhodesia) to Verwoerd, 4.1.1950 and Verwoerd's (Private Secretary) reply, 10.11.1950): "Dr Verwoerd is always pleased to hear from his former students."
96 PV 873/5/2/1/1, Dr. Hendrik Verwoerd †, handwritten, 14.9.1966, p. 3.
97 PV 377/4/1/1, J. W. Rall: 'Hulde ann wyle dr. H.F. Verwoerd (1966), p. 1.

academic year on 25 February.[98] Verwoerd surprised those present when he directly took up a speech he had presented thirty years earlier on the same occasion. Apparently no one thought that he had researched and prepared well in advance, but the speech was generally taken as a display of the good memory and brilliant intellect that he had become renowned for.[99] In actual fact, not even as a politician did he present all his speeches off the cuff, as legend would have it; too many manuscripts have been preserved to disprove that legend.[100] Moreover, this ability was not exceptional, as other politicians were also able to muster it. Jan Hofmeyr also memorised his speeches – he, too, had a photographic memory. But Verwoerd tried to conceal the fact that he learnt his speeches off by heart, thus giving off the impression of being a genius. Hardly any other politician has used the capacity of memory, and the talent for structuring an argument and presenting policies within a systematic overall context as purposefully as he did.

Yet he was not even an outstanding speaker, for he spoke far too rapidly[101] and to many members of his audiences his style was too academic. "Verwoerd spoke last night and his presentation was weak – like that of a junior lecturer who has to cover all his entire syllabus in a short time, and who therefore speaks so fast that he swallows most of the words."[102] As early as 1924, the *Cape Times* reported on his appearance at the University of Stellenbosch Debating Society: "Like a machine gun he rattled off a variety of facts and figures."[103] Moreover, he had "a somewhat high voice that tended to hoarseness."[104] He was not a gifted

---

[98] PV 93/1/60/2/1, f. 36, Letter by Thom to Verwoerd, 27.10.1958 and f. 37; acceptance of the invitation, 4.11.1958.
[99] A. Boshoff 1993: 33. That same year, Verwoerd also received an honorary doctorate from his Alma mater. The award of honorary doctorates by the University of Stellenbosch to its own professors was common practice. In this case, the honorary doctorate was conferred by AB chairman and Verwoerd-confidant H.B. Thom personally (PV 93/3/1/19, Letter by H. B. Thom to Verwoerd, 23.6.1959; also UA Stellenbosch Eregrade, Verwoerd 1959, Correspondence).
[100] See for instance the detailed manuscript of an address to Senate, which had been composed by officials close to him and signed by Eiselen on 15.5.1956 (PV 93/1/31/1/27, Konsept-Beleidstoespraak 1956). Scholtz frankly concedes that he prepared carefully, and noted down the major points (G. D. Scholtz 1974, vol. 1: 75). Barnard (1967: 24) reports that Verwoerd spent hours preparing for major speeches, and destroyed the scripts afterwards, "as if he were somewhat ashamed at something for which he could be ridiculed!".
[101] At the beginning of his career, Verwoerd counted, along with J. E. Potgieter who was to become Chief Whip of the NP at a later stage, as the fastest-speaking orator in Parliament (Haigh 1951: 204). A. Boshoff (1993: 33) notes, "he spoke so inhumanly fast!".
[102] 296.K.GE 127a, Letter by Phil Weber to A. L. Geyer, 27.3.1953; see also I. L. de Villiers 2009: 130; and Meiring 1973a: 76.
[103] *Cape Times*, 15.8.1924.
[104] E. Theron 1983: 25; see also J. Botha 1967: 44.

debater who could charm and fascinate his audiences with his wit like Harry Lawrence or Walter Madeley managed to do. Van Schoor reported that Verwoerd was an excellent conversationalist with whom one could talk about any subject because he had interesting things to say about everything.[105] However, the admiration often expressed in such observations and reminiscences by those close to his political positions cannot obscure the fact that Verwoerd was incapable of dialogue in politics. The media and the opposition often complained that the Minister did not respond to questions.[106]

Stories that began to circulate around 1990 were meant to highlight his genius and intellectual independence. According to these conjectures, he had planned to announce a political U-turn on the very day he was assassinated.[107] Because he presented his speeches extemporaneously, this claim can neither be proven nor disproven. But the whole story is quite transparent; it occurred to the former chief whip of the NP, J. E. Potgieter, of all people, in 1990, when the end of apartheid was becoming foreseeable and the NP had lost all moral credibility because of what had happened at Vlakplaas and elsewhere, that even Verwoerd, with his dogmatic stance, was in fact quite a flexible, adaptive politician.[108] Any Afrikaner nationalist could have asked, if him, then why not all of us? There is, however, evidence that Potgieter was making up a story, for after Verwoerd's death, his son Daniel found notes in his briefcase that were clearly written down to prepare the speech he was then unable to deliver. From these notes, it became clear that Verwoerd did not want to announce a political sea change; on the contrary, he set out, once again, to deduce his political programme from the basic principles of apartheid, as he had done hundreds of times before.[109]

---

[105] Van Schoor 1979: 130.
[106] Graaff 1993: 159. Andries Treurnicht, a great admirer of Verwoerd's and of his politics, maintained that he conducted debates "answering every argument or point in full", with quick wit (PV 873/5/2/1/1, f. 4, 'Dr. Hendrik Verwoerd'). As in other instances, what Treurnicht said was not confirmed by reality. On the contrary, Verwoerd was well-known not to engage with his adversaries' arguments. He was not a quick–witted debater, but preferred to lecture.
[107] Dommisse 2005 (169). See also the apologetic statements of Potgieter's in *Die Burger*, 13.11.1990. On Potgieter, see also J. Basson 2008: 2–3.
[108] Meiring showed himself highly sceptical (1990: 9). Potgieter was a former student of Verwoerd's, and obviously a personal friend (Grobbelaar 1966: 157).
[109] FAV 4.7.2.4.7.5, folios with undated notes, but in their opening sentences clearly referring to the no–confidence debate.

Logic as Rhetorical Device

To deal with Verwoerd's logic in a chapter on propaganda may seem somewhat strange at first glance, considering that a clear distinction has been made between rhetoric and logic ever since antiquity. Rhetoric, the art of persuasion, was the gift of the great orator, who would use arguments in such a way as to produce the greatest possible effect and to bring his listeners around to his own point of view. Logic, in contrast, was the art of arriving at the right conclusion and thus served as a tool essential for finding the truth. Truth-finding and the art of persuasion pursued different aims and often stood in opposition to each other. What was remarkable about Verwoerd's propaganda was the fact that he knew how to reconcile the two, turning logic into a means of rhetoric.[110] His son Daniel put it in a nutshell in recalling how his father listened to the children's arguments in family discussions, in order to "then use logical persuasion, rather than counter-arguments, to argue his point of view".[111] As has been shown, Verwoerd espoused a fact-based concept of science; in his view of it, the collection of comprehensive data sets was the only correct way to establish the truth. Because he wanted his policy to be understood as scientifically based, he presented it as truth-based. It was supposed to convince through truth and logical conclusiveness.

In communication with his older brother, the young Psychology professor emphasised the importance of logic, which the former gratefully accepted as an important lesson for life: "One important thing that Hendrik taught me is to think logically. . . . Once you grasp the logical approach to life, you never forget it. Thinking objectively makes you consistent."[112] The last sentence also indicates the extent to which Verwoerd became and remained a prisoner of his deterministic thinking and its inherent consistency. Erika Theron spoke of his "relentlessly logical talent for persuasion".[113] The deduction of all his actions from fundamental principles imbued his political concepts with a persuasive power that made them appear to be without alternatives; it solicited boundless admiration from his followers, while others were quick to criticise his tendency towards dogmatism.[114] Piet Meyer nailed it in stating that Verwoerd "never stopped until he had gotten to the core, to the essence of a matter. And when something was found to be

---

110 Barnard 1967: 24.
111 W. et al. Verwoerd 2001: 76.
112 PV 72/3, Beukes: Brandfort, Stellenbosch, Arme Blanke vraagstuk, p. 3 (based on an interview with Len Verwoerd).
113 E. Theron 1983: 25.
114 J. Basson 2006: 102. Basson had attended Verwoerd's Sociology lectures in Stellenbosch over the period of one year.

right, it was carried out to the letter, whatever that might be."[115] Meyer's daughter, historian Dioné Prinsloo describes his logical reasoning: "Because he was trained in logic, Dr. Verwoerd thought through a problem step by step until he reached the conclusion, and then explained how to proceed in order to reach that particular solution to that particular problem."[116] Thus he claimed that if coloureds were granted a concession in the form of several parliamentary seats, they would inevitably immediately follow it up with further demands, after which blacks would also demand seats in Parliament. This would lead to black majority rule, which would end in biological assimilation and the demise of the Whites. The causal chain is clearly constructed backwards from the end result, to present the worst horror scenario imaginable to white supremacists, and to convince the audience that only Verwoerd's tough stance could save them from it.

Through its submission to rhetoric, truth and truth-telling came to serve as instrument of persuasion. In fact, the art of finding the truth became a mechanism for the concealment of truth; being bent to suit his arguments to attain a particular goal, it was degraded to sophistry. How did Verwoerd accomplish this artful trickery? How did he manage to use logical argumentation to create the appearance, and precisely just the appearance, of a truth-oriented politics and present it as the only viable one?

In construing premisses from desired or dreaded results,[117] Verwoerd reversed the temporal sequence of logic. Verwoerd's policies concerning coloureds reveal the extent to which he was getting increasingly caught up in his own logic.

> Experience shows that giving a little is the beginning of going further and further down the road to integration. A small measure of political partnership is followed by more demands and more concessions; social and economic integration is next; and then biological assimilation. It may start with the Coloureds, to be followed by the Indians and the Bantu. I can foresee only disaster for all in the course of this first deviation from apartheid, consistently implemented.[118]

He extended the logical chains of a dynamic that would be triggered by the smallest concessions and always end in the horror scenario of black rule. He lectured the ethnologist Johannes Bruwer, saying that "once you start making concessions for the sake of a short-term goal, the pressure does not decrease, but rather increases, and satisfaction tends to decrease. Because one has abandoned one's

---

115 P. J. Meyer 1978: 10.
116 D. Prinsloo 1979: 11.
117 According to my knowledge, attorney David de Villiers was the only one who saw through this procedure (D. de Villiers 2001: 144).
118 PV 93/1/24/11, Reply by Verwoerd to C. H. Badenhorst, Wellington, responding to the latter's comprehensive memorandum on the race question, 12.11.1960, ff. 5–6. Similarly in his reply (29.11.1960) to a telegram of support by E. Theron (PV 93/1/30/1/10, f. 19).

principles, the further process becomes almost irreversible."[119] To prevent such a breach in the dyke, "care will have to be taken to ensure that concessions which may appear superficially fair, are thought out to their logical consequences and that consideration is given to the eventual injustice to others which may arise from apparent friendliness towards one person."[120] In an interview with the daily newspaper *Die Burger* in November 1960, he argued against small concessions to coloureds. Mittner summarised his argument as follows:

> This would be the first deviation from principles, and that is why he emphatically declares that the NP and the government are not prepared to take the first steps on the 'path toward integration'. In the interview, Dr. Verwoerd also outlined the 'consequences' of the 'small concessions' (direct representation): extending the suffrage to the Northern provinces on separate lists; introducing the suffrage for Coloured women; quantitative expansion of Coloured MPs on separate lists in both houses of Parliament; and the return to a common list of eligible voters with full political equality, finally also with a view to the election of political representatives in all constituencies. According to Dr Verwoerd, direct representation and the concessions that go with it will ultimately amount to full integration, in other words, 'biological assimilation'.[121]

From an abominable final stage, he construed an inevitability starting with the "small concession". It had to be made clear to the audience that there was only one correct way, which could be scientifically determined by the most important instrument, namely logic. In this way, they were to be persuaded that there were no alternatives to Verwoerd's policy.[122] He repeatedly reproached the opposition for their policy of small concessions to the black majority, which he thought produced a series of consequences where one consequence triggers the next, with black majority rule as the final outcome of the process. By working from wrong premises, he thought opposition politicians would, if given free rein, set in motion a determinism by which they would relinquish all other possible courses of action with the first incorrect decision. Conversely, with the policy of radical racial segregation, Verwoerd claimed to have set the premise that would lead to "good neighbourliness" and the happiness of all, each in her/his separate life world. The

---

119 PV 93/1/24/10, 110, Reply to Prof. J. Bruwer, Stellenbosch, 30.7.60.
120 Verwoerd, Congress of the Institute of Administrators of Non–European Affairs, Bloemfontein, 7.9.1956 (in Pelzer 1966: 124–148, 141).
121 Mittner 1986: 287.
122 In 1947, Albert Hertzog remarked on another strategy: "[In his speech,] he extracts one or other argument, emphasises it and exaggerates it. That way he appears as a frightfully clever person, but in reality it is all just a logical abstraction from one factor that has been exaggerated." (PV 451/4/1/173, Diary entry, 5.8.1947, p. 358).

ploy worked – one follower attested to the "absolutely masterful logic" he displayed in this line of argument.[123]

However, this does not account for Verwoerd's strategically calculated use of logic as a rhetorical device. He knew the solution beforehand and constructed his syllogisms in such a way that they could only lead to that one conclusion. Politics thus turned from an art of decision-making amidst contingent situations into a sequence of determined causal chains. In making out that there could be only one possible solution, contingency was suppressed and what was actually a decision was made to appear as a necessity. Thus, Verwoerd could visualise the future through unambiguous causal reasoning, and present it as inevitable, depending on the set premises.[124] He was concerned with the future, but he argued like a bad historian who spoke about the past as if it consisted of determinate developments devoid of contingencies. By unfolding his logical argumentation from an imagined goal, he could arrange the premises as he needed them. With this anticipation of future outcomes, Verwoerd succeeded in conveying certainty. Taking the intermediate steps he developed logically backwards from a future goal, a utopia, nothing could go wrong.

The British Ambassador, Sir John Maud, who knew Verwoerd well, described his understanding of politics:

> When I suggested to Dr Verwoerd, before the present parliamentary session, that he must be much preoccupied with the difficult problems ahead, his obviously sincere answer was that this was not so. He said in effect that once the major premise had been clearly established (as of course it had) it was only necessary to apply it to problems and situations as they arose and the conclusions were inescapable. Day-to- day problems therefore presented no serious difficulty. The fact that he was evidently not speaking for effect but expressing his real conviction made his words all the more frightening.[125]

By surrendering to this logic which transformed an uncertain, contingent future into a certain imagination and an imaginary certainty, he ultimately forfeited all political flexibility – for which he paid a high price in foreign policy terms. The

---

[123] Treurnicht 1988: 10.

[124] In quite a similar vein, G. Cronjé viewed society as being shaped by constants and continuities; contingencies did not come into the picture at all (Cronjé 1937: 15–18).

[125] FAV 4.7.1.2 'South Africa's Future', Addendum, inscribed by Eric Louw (in handwriting) with the note, 'top secret'. A note from W. J. Verwoerd at the bottom of the page, dated 2015, reads: "According to what I remember, this secret report had been withheld by an Afrikaans–speaking secretary in the British Embassy, and handed to the Prime Minister." Maud added an equally astute remark on the character of Verwoerd: "Facts which, when the major premise is applied, cannot be fitted into his syllogism, are unfacts." These remarks by Maud are cited also in Hyam/Louis 2000: 455. G. D. Scholtz reported that Verwoerd's reactions were always predictable, on account of his recourse to principles established in advance.

lack of alternatives in a policy based on logic and truth led him into the very trap he always thought his political opponents were caught in. A policy based entirely on inflexibility, no longer allowing any possibilities for negotiation, lost its *raison d'être*; he became a prisoner of his own argumentative logic. Giliomee places great emphasis on the distinction between ends and means in Verwoerd's politics. The end of his action, according to Giliomee, was the preservation, the "survival" of the Afrikaner people, and apartheid was a means to that end.[126] But if it were the only means available, means and ends would converge, which would render Giliomee's distinction invalid. If the means are not available, the claim that apartheid was a pragmatic policy does not make sense. In reality, it was a principled policy that followed its own logic and operated within an extremely narrow scope of action. By focusing on principles, Verwoerd gave up the flexibility that a politician would need to be able to act effectively. The absence of alternatives resulted in the refusal to consider even the slightest 'concessions'.[127]

Through apparently logical anticipation, Verwoerd lent certainty to the achievement of the envisaged goal; it created the idea that his policies were built on truth, based on logical consistency. Evading the persuasive power of such reasoning was not easy, as many contemporaries testified. One admirer spoke of his capacity to "illuminate the future",[128] without seeing through the ruses deployed to create this impression; others considered him a prophetically gifted politician.[129]

With his dramatic presentation of conflicting scenarios, he could appeal to voters' immediate interests, putting them on the defensive against the opposition's 'dangerous' positions. But beyond that, he made the smallest incidental 'concessions' into matters of life and death, sketching out the horror vision of the complete downfall of the whites. The opposition, in its turn, made it very easy for him, because the different wings of the extremely heterogeneous United Party took different positions on apartheid, so the Party as a whole could not settle on a clear line, and not even an alternative.[130] It was easy for Verwoerd to present the

---

126 Giliomee 2003a: 144, 621; see also Giliomee 1980: 18–19; and O'Meara 1996: 52. In a critical comment on Giliomee's position, A. du Toit (2008: 573–574) claims that the former has not left the context of Afrikaner nationalism.
127 As for instance in the case of attorney Duma Nokwe, whom Verwoerd prohibited from establishing his office in the same building as his white colleagues (Maisels 1999: 72–74).
128 PV 425/2/1/1/, Radio broadcast series 'Verkiesings en Premiers 1910–1974', p. 55.
129 M. C. Botha 1977: 10.
130 Thus, there were some members of his constituency who advocated the franchise for university graduates (*Pretoria News*, 7.8.1957); but "for tactical reasons", the Party was intent on hardening its stance on apartheid for the 1958 election campaign (*Cape Times* and *Rand Daily Mail*, 7.11.1958); see also Commentary in *Die Vaderland*, 19.2.1959.

opposition as 'conceptless'[131] or to adduce his logical-sounding projections to 'prove' that every step proposed by the opposition that differed from his own conception had to lead to black majority rule.[132]

By outlining the long-term consequences, he sought to demonstrate how dangerous well-intentioned, tolerant and liberal positions towards the black majority were. They would inevitably lead to the loss of power for whites, and to their cultural and even physical demise. Verwoerd demonstrated this not only with regard to one particular position of the United Party, but with regard to every position other than his own. He thus eliminated all shades of grey and ultimately reduced politics to two contrary forces: Chaos and Order. The trick was that the argument focused on consequences and not on current positions. Thus, any political position envisaging 'concessions' of any kind, even the minutest, was doomed to failure, because it was from these small 'concessions' that Verwoerd developed his causal chains, at the end of which a "Bantu dictatorship" was looming.

For Verwoerd, the need for a slow pace of action was a conclusion drawn from the observation that "the Bantu" and Africans in general were not ready for democracy. "It inevitably leads to dictatorship by a small group of politically interested persons."[133] The example he repeatedly cited in this context was that of Ghana under Kwame Nkrumah.[134] He adduced the Mau-Mau in Kenya, but especially the Congo, as examples for his assumption that whites had no future under black rule. In his Sociology lectures, he had drawn a connection between the use of violence and a lack of civilisation: "In countries with the lowest level of culture, we find the most murders and attacks."[135] What applied to the Congo also applied to South Africa, as he noted in disparaging remarks about black politicians in the Transkei in 1959 – at a time when he was already envisaging the independence of the homelands: "They just concentrated on talking and all their actions were

---

131 So he posed eight questions to the leader of the opposition (see *Die Burger*, 6.2.1954). From the article in the *Sunday Times* (21.11.1954), it becomes clear that, in many respects, the goals of the UP hardly differed from those of the NP (see also the commentary in *Die Vaderland*, 18.11.1954). The heterogeneity of the UP meant that the NP had an easy game in continuously identifying diverging positions in the UP, and in harping on the lack of consensus on its political programme (*Die Burger*, 6.9.1956 – editorial; *Die Transvaler*, 22.12.1954 – editorial). See also the editorial in the *Sunday Express*, 9.12.1956, which contained only vague commonplaces.
132 *Die Burger*, 31.1.1953.
133 Verwoerd, Union Council for Matters concerning Coloureds, Cape Town, 12.12.1961 (in Pelzer 1966: 642–653, 646).
134 *Die Vaderland*, 24.4.1959. The newspaper published an entire series of articles on Ghana, showing the dismantling of democracy. Verwoerd's scanty knowledge of ethnology and history is obvious, because Nkrumah and the population of Ghana on the whole were not 'Bantu'.
135 231/2/3, 'Socio-psigologie van misdaad', p. 89; also p. 91.

aimed at being popular so as to be re-elected. We must guide these people and teach them to govern properly and to assume responsibility."[136]

But Verwoerd was deceiving himself. He thought he could derive rules from basic principles that would guide his thoughts and actions. This gave rise to the illusion of logical consistency in his thinking and argumentation that almost all his listeners bought into – not least himself. Actually, his argumentation was not logical, but analogical. As positivist, Verwoerd believed that through collecting facts, data and individual experiences, hidden rules could be discovered. Once these were found, all further action could be derived from these rules. However, the inductive inference of rules is not logical, since the number of examples is always limited, more limited in number than the range of application of the presumed rule they obey. An example will illustrate this: Verwoerd always cited the events in the Congo, where Independence was followed by fierce internal power struggles fought out in bloody battles; this conflict finally led to the assassination of elected Prime Minister Patrice Lumumba and, a few years later, to the establishment of Mobutu's dictatorship. Verwoerd liked to cite this 'example' to warn his audiences of the developments that were bound to ensue if even the slightest 'concessions' were made to Africans or Coloureds in South Africa. In holding up this 'example', he referred to "the Bantu psychology" from which he derived his analogy to the Congo: "Naturally the psychology of our Bantu is an obstacle to speed, since South Africa cannot allow chaos as in the Congo to develop in the Bantu homelands it creates by similar rapid withdrawal of the Guardian's authority."[137]

Verwoerd thus pointed out how the development had proceeded in what he considered an analogous case, and claimed that it would happen in the same way in South Africa. The semblance of logic arose from the fact that the analogy invoked a regularity which appealed to a basic assumption, namely that Africans could not be granted political power without creating chaos. This basic assumption was treated by Verwoerd as if it was based on a law of history, when in fact he was making a racist claim. This is the reason why he did not draw an analogy between a future South Africa without apartheid and the democratisation of France or Japan, but only with the Congo, Ghana, or other African countries. But this analogy held as little plausibility as all the other analogies. The rule itself did not amount to anything but racism, for it presupposed that it did not matter to which Africans in which country under what circumstances it pertained – the

---

[136] Verwoerd, Bill Promoting Bantu Self–Government, Senate, 20.4.1959 (in Pelzer 1966: 271–195, 277).
[137] PV 93/1/30/1/26, Letter by Verwoerd to O. W. Grinaker, 9.7.1964, f. 70.

road to dictatorship was inevitable. Humanity was not a category for Verwoerd; his analogy exhausted itself in the immanence of racialised behaviour.

Liberal opposition politician Helen Suzman was one of the few who saw through the problematic nature of Verwoerd's logic: "Here was a man who could stand up in Parliament and talk for more than two hours without a note, building up an argument so convincingly that one sat there nodding one's head like a zombie, until one realised that his entire argument was built on a false premise."[138] What she called premises were the apparent rules from which Verwoerd derived instructions for action in deductive conclusions; but his 'rules' were nothing more than mere analogies.[139] Yet it was precisely from this flawed logic that he drew his power of persuasion, for analogies can be so overwhelming "that the conclusion becomes inescapable. So, in short, it is easier to distance oneself from a logical argument than from an argument based on analogy."[140] Verwoerd's persuasive power thus resulted precisely from the fact that he did not argue logically, but presented his audiences with inescapable analogies that disarmed them.

Obviously, Verwoerd pursued a propaganda method different from that of the National Socialists. Goebbels's idea was that propaganda must incite hatred and aggression, whereas Verwoerd relied on the intellectual technique of pseudo-logical reasoning. Kracauer's analysis of totalitarian propaganda does not apply to Verwoerd's propaganda. However, the question remains as to whether Verwoerd's propaganda can nevertheless be considered totalitarian albeit relying on a different technique. (Kracauer examined fascist and Nazi propaganda techniques exclusively.[141]) While totalitarian propaganda was thriving on rhetorical war-mongering, and was aimed at establishing a new form of society through a state of emergency in permanence, Verwoerd aimed at establishing a technicist bureaucratism. In relying on the capacity of audiences to follow logical reasoning, an orator like Verwoerd would open himself to his audiences and establish a kind of trusting relationship with them.

At first glance, this seems to be the opposite of totalitarian thought patterns, but Verwoerd's pseudo-logical argumentation functioned as persuasive rhetoric to the extent that it twisted causal chains. Added to this was his self-stylisation as towering and superior intellect. He displayed the hallmarks of totalitarian thinking: an uncompromising stance not allowing for any shades of grey; conjuring up of enemy images and defamation of dissenters as naïve fools or cunning commu-

---

[138] Suzman 1994: 65–66.
[139] Hofstadter/Sander 2014: 412, 416–423.
[140] Ibid., 417.
[141] Kracauer 2013: 40–52.

nists; the opposition of chaos or order; the breathlessness with which he repeatedly pointed out that there was hardly any time left to prevent the integration of society, necessitating the state of emergency which justified extraordinary measures; and the claim to pursue a scientifically based policy pertaining to the whole of society in all its spheres.

Organised Unity of the "Volk"

When Verwoerd left the University in 1936, the old National Party had already broken up and the radical cultural nationalist wing of the NP had re-constituted itself as the "Purified National Party" ("*Gesuiwerde Nasionale Party*") under the leadership of D. F. Malan. In 1933, the more moderate nationalists had followed General Hertzog into the grand coalition with the South African Party under Jan Smuts, which resulted in a party merger in the shape of the United Party.[1] Under the UP government between 1933 and 1938, the country recovered from the impact of the Great Depression, and experienced a rapid economic upswing; the National Party of Malan seemed to be condemned to take up the opposition benches for a good long period of time.[2] However, the NP could expect to get the majority behind it, as Afrikaners made up three-fifths of the white population, which moreover was socially still relatively homogeneous at the time.[3] It was not until 1948 that the Party managed to unite Afrikaners under the umbrella of nationalism. That is why the 1930s remained turbulent years, as all kinds of extreme right-wing, partly fascist, partly anti-parliamentary, but in any case anti-democratic groups had formed, which saw themselves as alternatives and competitors to Malan's party. The latter responded partly with defensiveness and confrontationalism, and partly with adaptation and adjustment. The latter found expression in the antisemitism represented by the so-called Greyshirts.[4]

Verwoerd's journalistic activity coincided with a period of fierce internal battles and disputes that re-shaped the political landscapes and resulted in a new formation of Afrikaner cultural nationalism. In his role as politician, Verwoerd himself was still playing second fiddle, but in his role as journalist, he was one of the most authoritative and influential players. He had allied himself with J. G. Strijdom, leader of the NP in the Transvaal, whose authority Verwoerd recognised unreservedly; this meant that Strijdom could be assured that Verwoerd would not emerge as his competitor.[5] Aside from his work as editor-in-chief of *Die Transvaler*, Verwoerd

---

1 These processes have been amply documented. A new study clarifies aspects of these processes (see Koorts 2014: ch. 8).
2 United Party 1938.
3 Trapido 1963: 78–79.
4 Marx 2008: ch. 14.
5 Despite their political collaboration, Verwoerd and Strijdom were rather distant in their personal relation (see e.g. Meiring 1987: 5). But in letters penned in 1944, they are on personal terms, that is, they adduced the informal "*jy*" instead of the formal "*u*" (e.g. PV 93/1/56/1, f. 19, letter by Verwoerd to Strijdom, 6.1.1945). On the relation between Verwoerd and Strijdom, see D. Prinsloo 1979: 121–146.

took on particular Party posts: in 1938, he became the Chairman of the National Party on the Witwatersrand, as well as member of the executive committee of the Party in the Transvaal; from 1946, he served as Deputy Chairman. But when Verwoerd wanted to stand for Parliament in 1943, Strijdom instructed him to concentrate on his work as editor-in-chief.[6]

With his withdrawal from academic life, Verwoerd had handed over the work of the Kimberley Congress's Continuation Committee to prominent Broederbond-activists.[7] However, he continued to be preoccupied with the theme of white poverty, albeit within the broader frame of the 'Economic Movement' that was being formed at the end of the 1930s. He recognised that "economic conditions actually dominate our whole lives".[8] He participated in the organisation of a congress on the economic situation of Afrikaners, which sought to harness the enthusiasm following the 1938 Symbolic Ox Wagon Trek.[9] Even during the Trek celebrations, attention was skilfully drawn to the problem of the "poor whites"; "Father" Kestell, the universally revered former field chaplain of the Orange Free State army, was encouraged to give emotionally stirring speeches. Other long-term organisations were to emerge from the People's Congress; one of them was the popular mass organisation Reddingsdaadbond, which was tasked primarily with mobilising Afrikaner capital.[10]

---

[6] D. Prinsloo 1979: 103. On the official positions in the Party, see J. L. Basson 1980: 198.

[7] PV 93/1/67/7, f. 36, Minutes of a meeting of the Committee in Cape Town, 20./21.12.1935. In a circular dated 1.2.1937, Cronjé referred to Resolution 88 of the Congress and announced the establishment of an Institute (PV 93/1/6/1). The minutes of the meeting on 5.4.1939 mentioned J. C. van Rooy as chairman of the Institute (PV 93/1/67/7, f. 5). In his historical retrospective on the Broederbond, Iwan Lombard mentioned that the organisation changed the Continuation Committee into an Institute for *volks*-welfare (FAV 4.5.2.4, Brochure on the occasion of 25 year anniversary of the AB 1943, p. 21): "In the meantime, the A.B. has also turned to the problem of the poor whites and seen to it that the Continuation Committee of the *Volks*-Congress is transformed into the Institute for Public [*Volks*-]Welfare under the auspices of the F.A.K." Chairman of the newly elected UK was William Nicol, his deputy was ds. Albertyn; among other members were Albert Hertzog, Diederichs, and Cronjé, as well as other high-ranking AB-members who initially had very little to do with the Congress in Kimberley (PV 93/1/67/7, f. 77, Minutes of the meeting of the Committee in Johannesburg, 5.10.1936; see also Stals 1998: 121).

[8] 231/2/1/1, 'Inleiding tot die Sociologie', p. 48. He continued to show an interest in the theme, as evinced by a collection with student assignment and excerpts, which date back to the year 1950 (at the earliest) (PV 93/1/29/5–7). Even as senator, Verwoerd was still active in the arenas of welfare and charity (PV 93/1/4/1 and /2; see also various writings on the Armsoorgraad of 1948–1950).

[9] PV 202/1/4/3/2/1, ANS, Minutes of a meeting on 10.2.1939; Verwoerd was singly tasked with the work of the sub-committee for consumer associations; this subcommittee was to prepare the resolutions – as subcommittees did in the run-up to the Kimberley Congress.

[10] Ibid., FAK, Minutes of the 5th Congress, 5.7.1939, p. 2, TOP 8, with a resolution; it became a general rule within the FAK, "in order to follow up on the proposal by the *Volks*-Congresses to deal with unresolved issues of the people through the establishment of various permanent sub-

'Unity of the People': Organised Nationalism

Whoever succeeded in uniting the Afrikaners into a single party, would come into the position of holding state power. But the formation of nationalism was not solely due to such calculations of votes; rather, nationalism was as much a matter of belief and worldview as it was a politically strategic concept. The goal of the National Party, founded in 1914, was national unity, although the Party's founder, General Hertzog, did not specify what exactly he meant by this. His Two-Stream Policy was aimed at uniting both white population groups.

According to the nationalists, equality of opportunity, which would have been a necessary condition for national unity, did not as yet exist for the Afrikaners – not by far –, which is why the unification of English and Afrikaans-speaking South Africans remained a distant goal, and why priority was accorded to cultural and political equality of Afrikaners. Thus, popular unity initially meant the unity of Afrikaners within the National Party, which was entirely consistent with its self-presentation and its constituency. The heterogeneous character of Hertzog's NP resulted from the ambiguity of what the 'unity of the people' was actually supposed to be, although he was wise enough not to resolve this ambiguity, so as not to jeopardise his chances of winning a majority. However, this changed under the impact of the world economic crisis and a massive loss of confidence in his government, which made him decide, at the end of 1932, to enter into a grand coalition with Jan Smuts, his long-time opponent and rival for the office of Prime Minister.[11] The momentum triggered by this, especially at the level of the local branches of both parties, led to a merger – the United Party – in 1934. With this move, Hertzog merged the "two streams" and thereby gave sudden effect to the project of popular unity, which until then had been tentatively envisaged for some unspecified future date. The Prime Minister obviously realised that the demand for equality of the Afrikaners had now been established sufficiently for him to take the next step. There inevitably were supporters of the NP who saw things differently, and for whom the time had not yet come to make common cause with English-speaking South Africans to form a united nation. That is why unification also spelt division: in 1934, the NP in the Cape Province, and minority factions in the two northern provinces broke away from Hertzog and founded the NP anew, but now with a decidedly cultural-nationalist orientation, that is, as an exclusively Afrikaner party.

---

departments of the F.A.K", which were to keep this issue on the agenda in the long term (O'Meara 1983: ch. 10).

11 Ironically, Smuts came to Malan's assistance during the 1933 election campaign, when the latter had to reckon with an electoral defeat in his Calvinia constituency (Korf 2010: 312).

The National Party newly founded in 1934 was characterised and shaped by a particularly intense nationalism which completely seized the individual in its grip. It saw itself as the spearhead of a nationalist movement that included its own party organisation, as well as the secret society named the Afrikaner Broederbond, with its network of subsidiary organisations, the Afrikaner nationalist trade unions, the reformed churches, the Afrikaans-language universities,[12] the Afrikaner professional associations, and numerous individuals professing nationalist tenets in politics, journalism, culture, and other social arenas. While the Party had a conventional organisational structure, it differed from other parties in its self-perception. As late as 1964, on the occasion of its 50th anniversary, Verwoerd emphatically made the point that it was not just a party, "but actually the creative element in the life of this people".[13] The NP formed a kind of a "family", offering mutual help and care, but also exerting control and conformity – in an interesting parallel with the self-image of the ANC in exile and even after 1994.[14]

Verwoerd put it in a nutshell in a Christmas message of 1962: "The National Party is an enlarged family, connected through bonds of love and trust and common ideals and interests."[15] The nationalist understanding of history was one of salvation: South Africa was providentially steered towards a republic, but the achievement of this goal was constantly threatened by conflicts and wrong decisions.

Integrally tied up with Afrikaner nationalism was the Calvinist denomination, and especially the Afrikaans language, which was central to the canon of values. Verwoerd was a particularly fanatical defender of Afrikaans language rights. In October 1948, he complained that only English was used in some circulars issued by the ministries, and by the Johannesburg municipality.[16] This went so far that he started making quite a fuss in his ministry when he found out that the leases in Sophiatown were issued in English instead of Afrikaans, despite the fact that the majority of tenants were Afrikaans speaking and had a right to receive their contracts in the Afrikaans language. The entire administrative apparatus was then set in motion to change this.[17] He likewise complained to his ministerial colleague Swart about the fact that a "Bantu" law firm, namely that of Mandela and Tambo,

---

12 Even the Suid–Afrikaanse Akademie vir Wetenskap en Kuns was closely linked, via the FAK, to the Broederbond for at least some time (Kapp 2009: 63–65).
13 Verwoerd 1964a: 7. On this self–perception, see an early account given by Coetzee 1942: 221.
14 Gevisser 2015: 263.
15 PV 93/4/1/7, 187 Christmas message to newspapers (*Die Burger, Die Transvaler*) 1962.
16 PV 93/1/56/1, f. 96, Letter by Verwoerd to Strijdom, 19.10.1948. Ibid., f. 68, Letter by Verwoerd to Strijdom, 5.5.1947.
17 NA, NTS 5941, f. 488–493, Letter by Verwoerd to Eiselen, 4.5.1953, and subsequent internal correspondence.

had written to him in English. The prosecutor in Pretoria had drafted a response for him, also in English. "Against such a position, which implies that even (!) a native plaintiff or a native law firm . . . can compel me to issue a statement in English, [only] because they initiated the correspondence in English, I raise the strongest objection."[18]

To Verwoerd, the UP was a party without principle. By "principle", he ostensibly understood a cultural nationalism animated by historical and ethnicist myths. But the actual maxim that guided his actions was that of an uncompromising intransigence. His commitment to cultural nationalism, and the ideological meaning that he attached to the settlement of Europeans in South Africa as historical civilising mission, had political implications, including the rejection of British imperialism. The revanchism that had gripped large sections of the Afrikaner population after the South African War influenced the constitutional objectives and gave it the emotional charge that made it possible to mobilise the white Afrikaans population for the goals of cultural nationalism in the first place. Revanchism and anti-imperialism were mobilised to justify the establishment of the Republic, "the greatest among the ideals of the Afrikaans people".[19] The basic feature that characterised Verwoerd's political thinking right up to the end of his life, namely his uncompromising stance, indeed his inability to compromise, was closely linked with this republicanism. During the eleven years of his journalistic activity, Verwoerd used every available opportunity to engage in republican propaganda.[20] The vehemence with which he intervened in the internal disputes of the 1930s and 1940s, can only be explained by this conflation – and confusion – of his professed political stance (cultural nationalism) and his principle of action (uncompromising intransigence).[21] This went beyond political disagreement; it extended to fundamentals, as can be seen from the aggressive tone in which ailing Prime Minister Strijdom encouraged his deputy Swart in a telegraphic message ahead of a parliamentary session: "Hit the enemy where you can [*"heup en skenkel"*] and wipe him out completely."[22] In the spirit of this understanding of principle, the NP now set a competing design alongside Hertzog's goal of unification [*"Vereeniging"*], namely the reunification [*"Hereniging"*] of the Afrikaners in one party.

---

18 PV 276/1/27/8/1, Letter by Verwoerd to Swart, 5.3.1955.
19 *Die Transvaler*, 1.6.1943, qtd. in Geyser 1972: 85.
20 On this, see also D. Prinsloo 1979: ch. 5.
21 On the other hand, he applied different yardsticks, when in 1937, he expected the UP government to accept the Italian invasion of Ethiopia and the imperialist encroachment of Mussolini (*Die Transvaler*, 18.12.1937).
22 PV 18/3/1/63, Telegram by Strijdom to Swart, 20.1.1958.

During Verwoerd's editorship, he was himself involved in three conflicts and power struggles within the nationalist camp:
1. in the attempt to reunite the nationalists [*"Hereniging"*] after the end of Hertzog's government;
2. in the conflict with the far-right paramilitary Ossewabrandwag from 1941; and
3. in the internal party conflict over the electoral alliance between the National Party and the Afrikaner Party under Nicolaas Havenga, which was mooted in 1946.

These three conflicts were about the attainment of ideological hegemony within cultural nationalism; and the Afrikaner Broederbond was drawn into all of them.

The Outbreak of the War and the Failure of "Hereniging"

It was just during the week in which the situation in Europe came to a head and the Second World War broke out, that the South African Parliament coincidentally convened out of session, to decide on a mere formality. Prior to this, the Cabinet had met to discuss the question of South Africa's stance in the event of the outbreak of war. It emerged that the consensus on the adoption of a neutral stance, which Hertzog had assumed, no longer existed. Instead, a majority of ministers led by Smuts were in favour of entering the war on Britain's side. Hertzog put this grave question to the parliamentary vote. When he lost the vote despite the support of the opposition NP, he resigned and expected Governor General Duncan to dissolve Parliament. The latter used one of the few decision-making powers he had in this ceremonial office, and refused on the grounds that there was a majority capable of forming a government. In fact, Smuts succeeded in forming a new government in coalition with the Dominion Party and the Labour Party, and to lead the country into the Second World War alongside Britain.[23]

With the break-up of the government in September 1939, the previous state of affairs seemed to be restored for the nationalists; but the National Party had become much more radical since 1934. It was no coincidence that it adopted the originally derisive epithet of *"Gesuiwerde"* National Party. *"Hereniging"* implied a restoration of unity in the sense that all Afrikaners were to be brought together in one party; this unity now clearly stood under the sign of Afrikaans cultural nationalism.

---

23 D. J. Joubert 1973; see also A. van Wyk 1985.

Leading NP politicians elevated the creed of exclusive Afrikaner nationalism to a principle, which is why they rejected the merger as a non-principled move, and regarded its protagonists with suspicion. Verwoerd in particular suspected many nationalists who had previously supported Hertzog or political positions other than those of the NP, of this attitude. He insinuated that the "Smelters" (that is, the supporters of fusion) were prepared to make expedient compromises with the English, particularly when it came to accepting the Empire or the Commonwealth and maintaining the status of the Union, instead of striving for a Republic. In the final analysis, he saw this amounting to a willing submission to imperial goals and to support for interests other than South African ones, among which he always counted the financial and economic interests of big capital.

Immediately after Hertzog's resignation, talks with Malan were initiated. At issue was the *"Hereniging"*, which had stalled over the question of the Republic, as Hertzog had been vehemently opposed to it.[24] As feisty editor-in-chief of *Die Transvaler*, and rising star in the Transvaal NP, Verwoerd was disparaged by many, including members of his own party, as stickler for principles and rabble-rouser, as splitter rather than unifier.[25] In fact, Verwoerd was most concerned to maintain the clear line of cultural nationalism in the Party, and to push back against all attempts at diluting it through a Two-Stream-Policy. He would rather bide his time and wait for the NP to win a majority than to make compromises. He sought a "people's unity", but on his own terms, that is, according to the principle he stood for. Popular unity was not worth pursuing at any price. He expressed himself, albeit internal to the Party, in a manner that prompted an extremely vehement reaction from Malan: "– (a) Dr Verwoerd does not want reunification [*Hereniging*]. (b) Dr Verwoerd utterly distrusts these people (the Hertzog supporters), (c) if I were to follow Dr. Verwoerd's suggestion, this would be the most foolish step in my entire political career up to this point."[26] Verwoerd rebuked the reproaches in a twelve-page sworn statement submitted to the governing body of the Broederbond.[27] But he was indisputably considered one of the major polarisers; he was variously blamed for the failure of the *"Hereniging"* in 1940.[28]

---

24 PV 18/2/1/2, Aantekening oor konferensie te Pretoria, 23 November 1939.
25 See the clear-sighted portrait of René de Villiers, 1945.
26 PV 93/1/1/3, 36–37. Declaration by P. A. Wilken. See also Meiring 1987: 48 and J. L. Basson 1980: 294–295.
27 FAV 4.5.2.4, Verklaring Dr. H. F. Verwoerd, typescript, 13.2.1941.
28 See e.g. *Die Transvaler*, 17.1.1940: Stryd uitgelok. He similarly trivialised a joint declaration of Malan's and Hertzog's as mere "recommendation" and tried to get Hertzog and his followers to commit themselves to a republican programme (*Die Transvaler*, 29. And 30.1.1940). Possibly the remark of his mother pertains to the controversy over Wilken's claims, and to the dispute with the OB, which made big waves even in Brandfort (FAV 2.2.7, Letter by Anje Verwoerd to Lucie

At the centre of Verwoerd's wariness was General Hertzog himself, whose sudden change of heart after the break-up of the United Party he distrusted. In addition, all of those who belonged to the old general's personal entourage, or adhered to his Two Stream Policy, were also among the suspects, especially Oswald Pirow and Hans van Rensburg. Both of them drifted into the extreme right-wing camp after Hertzog retired from politics, not least because of what they saw as undignified treatment of the general they revered. In maintaining that party politics and professional politicians in the NP – small-minded manipulators and ambitious careerists – were responsible for Hertzog's defeat, they were generalising from their own experience. When Hertzog tried to push through his own draft statutes for the united party of the Orange Free State, his opponents grouped around C. R. Swart, pre-empting and outvoting him. Enraged, the old general withdrew from politics; his disaffected political followers gathered around N. Havenga and founded the Afrikaner Party.[29] Verwoerd contributed significantly to Hertzog's elimination, which was charged with personal animosities. He fought Hertzog's supporters, whether democrats or not, with the same dislike he held for the general himself. In addition to Pirow and van Rensburg and the organisation they led, his suspicion was directed against staunch republicans such as L. J. du Plessis, whom he likewise accused of harbouring an affinity with the "Smelters", even though the ambitious professor from Potchefstroom with his political Calvinist commitments was at least as principled in his arguments as Verwoerd himself.[30]

The Afrikaner Broederbond

Public debates on the Broederbond (AB) in South Africa were long shaped by investigative journalism which, given the nature of the organisation as a secret society, is not surprising. The pronouncements of some publications were bordering on conspiracy theories; reliable information on the Broederbond was surrounded by far-reaching speculation. Above all, assumptions about power and influence were projected into the history of the organisation before 1948, making of it a sin-

---

Cloete, 7.8.1940: "I ask myself how the matter surrounding Hendrik will proceed, people here are all worked up about it."). Even Piet Meiring thought, in retrospect, that *Die Transvaler* was too negative in criticising others, without itself offering an attractive political alternative apart from republicanism (Meiring 1987: 55). See also Grobler 1988: 334; P.W. Coetzer 1994: 202; and B. Schoeman 1978: 42, 46–49, 57–70.
29 Marx 2008: 373–374.
30 Paton (1971: 276) incorrectly claims that du Plessis was a personal friend of Malan's and Verwoerd's.

ister, omniscient and omnipotent force that manipulated social and political conditions in South Africa from behind the scenes. The Broederbond itself responded to the rumours circulating about it on numerous occasions. It launched articles in the NP press; and on the occasion of its fifty-year anniversary, it published an authorised history written by A. N. Pelzer, one of its members and professional historian; however, Pelzer revealed only what the Broederbond wanted to see published.[31] In addition, there are some critical studies published in academic journals not given to speculation, which have attempted to analyse the historical significance of this organisation.[32] They have highlighted especially the systemic character of organised Afrikaner nationalism, showing how interlocking and mutually reinforcing organisations and sub-organisations facilitated the Broederbond's efficiency, and its penetration of ever new fields of social existence.

The founding of the Broederbond was a response to Afrikaner urbanisation in a predominantly English-language environment. New Afrikaans-speaking arrivals in the cities had to adapt to English-language institutions, to English-cultural ways of doing things, and to the English language if they wanted to get a foothold there.[33] It is therefore hardly surprising that the Broederbond was founded by railway employees in the mining capital of Johannesburg. The railways were one of the few state-led enterprises where comparatively large numbers of Afrikaners found employment, and where they could build group cohesion and solidarity networks. After 1924, Prime Minster Hertzog turned the railways into a safety net for work-seeking Afrikaans-speaking whites.[34]

After its establishment in 1918, the Broederbond pursued cultural goals, namely to improve the opportunities for Afrikaans-speaking whites. With this aim in mind, it sought to open up the English-dominated urban cultural environ-

---

[31] Pelzer 1979, and Mouton 2007: 108 on Pelzer as member of the UR of the AB between 1965 and 1970. Even for the occasion of the 25th anniversary, then General Secretary of the Broederbond, Iwan Lombard, reconstructed the history of the Broederbond, which was printed in a brochure for perusal by members, but was not intended for public consumption (FAV 4.5.2.4, Brochure compiled for the 25th anniversary of the AB 1943). Toward the end of its existence, which coincided with the dismantling of the apartheid state and the loss of power of the NP, a much more comprehensive and detailed historical work had been commissioned, which until now has remained unpublished (Stals 1998).
[32] O'Meara 1977; T. D. Moodie 1975.
[33] Stals 1986: 50–51; also Albertyn/du Toit/Theron 1947: 49.
[34] AB Archive, 2/3/19, Bylae by die UR-agenda 17.11.1950, Rapport van die Komitee vir aktuele vraagstukke oor die bestaan, doel, en strekking van die Afrikaner-Broederbond, p. 1. See also the speech by I. Lombard on the history of the Broederbond, delivered to the Bondsraad 1943 (FAV 4.5.2.4, Brochure compiled for the 25th anniversary of the AB 1943, with lengthy excerpts from the diary of co-founder H.W. van der Merwe).

ment to Afrikaans speakers. However, this cultural project was not crowned with success – which is what led to the decision, taken in 1921, to operate as a clandestine organisation in future. In the expectation that this decision would enhance the influence of the Broederbond, it was noted that "this is only a question of expediency".[35] This calculation did work out, not least because of an energetically pursued policy of expansion beyond the Witwatersrand, and beyond the milieu of small employees. The Broederbond established itself in the urban centres and in the small towns in the rural areas of the Transvaal, and soon also in the Orange Free State and in the few Northern districts of Natal, where Afrikaners lived in significant numbers. It was late to gain a foothold in the Cape Province, because of the presence of a combative and culturally nationalist National Party in that Province, which largely obviated the need for such a cultural organisation.[36] Moreover, influential representatives of the NP, like the former editor-in-chief of *Die Burger*, A. L. Geyer, harboured a pronounced aversion to secret organisations.[37] The AB aimed for an ideal size of local sections pegged at 15 to 20 active members of an average age of below forty. But in fact, the AB constantly complained about its ageing membership; the desire to form its own youth organisation became something of a perennial issue.[38]

Soon to lead the way in the Broederbond was the small intellectual elite who flocked to the liberal professions, to teaching positions at schools and universities,[39] especially the small university college of Potchefstroom, which assumed leadership roles in the late 1920s. The College in Potchefstroom, which only attained the status of an independent university in 1952, was a decidedly Calvinist institution, strongly influenced by the Gereformeerde Kerk which predominated in the Western Transvaal. It was the smallest and most conservative of the three Afrikaans churches, whose adherents were also known as "Doppers". Verwoerd established close contact with some of the intellectuals of this university; but he was not motivated to do so by any recognisable religious-churchy affinity. The co-operation was primarily

---

35 AB Archive, 2.3.19, Rapport oor die bestaan, doel en strekking van die Afrikaner–Broederbond, p. 2. See also the list of members for 1921, almost all of them from Johannesburg and the West Rand (FAV 4.5.2.4, Brochure compiled for the 25th anniversary of the AB 1943, pp. f and g; the Brochure also contains the names of all delegates who attended the 22nd Bondsraad in 1943).
36 Marx 2008: 154–156.
37 296.K.Ge.207, Letter by Geyer to Phil Weber, 3.7.1959: "You know what I think of secret organisations!".
38 AB Archive, 2/3/18, UR meeting 12–13.5.1950, Aanhangsel A: Die toekomstaak en reorganisasie van die A.B., pp. 1–2.
39 At the end of the 1970s, teaching professions were still disproportionately represented (Pirie/Rogerson/Beavon 1980: 100).

politically and strategically motivated.⁴⁰ With the entry of these intellectuals, the work of the Broederbond became more professional. It seemed to make sense not to limit its operation to the role of a secret society; for that reason, a "visible arm" in the form of the Federasie van Afrikaanse Kultuurvereniginge (FAK) was established. The FAK, whose leadership largely overlapped with that of the Broederbond, in turn, formed an umbrella organisation with ambitions to exercise centralist control. It combined numerous Afrikaans cultural organisations, an entire *"galaxie métapolitique"*,⁴¹ which thereby attained heightened visibility and clout, and were ideologically set on a cultural-nationalist course. Three approaches can be discerned in the work of the FAK – and thus also of the Broederbond:

1. Bundling and co-ordination of already existing organisations;
2. infiltration of previously independent organisations; and
3. founding of new cultural-nationalist organisations in those fields in which Afrikaners had hitherto been underrepresented or not represented at all, or in which they had hitherto belonged to English-speaking or bilingual organisations.

In this way, an Afrikaans-cultural society emerged parallel to the dominant English-language one, albeit differentiated from the latter by its substantially more tight level of organisation and co-ordination. The Broederbond was and remained an elitist organisation, which carefully selected and co-opted new members (as not everyone could join of their own free will). Each member had to be male, white, and Calvinist, with impeccable convictions and lifestyle. To ensure the fulfilment of these criteria, each prospective member was first carefully investigated, and then approached, interviewed, and admitted by Broederbond members. The Broederbond recruited primarily functionaries of associations, top personnel as well as seasoned propagandists and socially influential men. "The A.B is not looking for superhuman beings, but nevertheless for a select group of men with the capacity to work together in a team."⁴² Although the organisation was highly structured, it resembled informal conservative networks: it was considered more important to build personal connections, to exchange political information and to garner ideological affirmation, than to influence decisions directly.⁴³ But the Broederbond differed from informal networks in the sense that it came closer to what Coser called "greedy institutions", which take over a significant part of the life world of their

---

40 As delegate to Senate, Verwoerd made a strong case for establishing Potchefstroom as a fully-fledged, independent university in 1952, which is what earned him eternal gratitude from the professors of that institution (van der Schyff 2003: 590, 598–599, 620–621).
41 Sabalot 2009: 43.
42 AB Archive, 2/3/12, Report of the UR Secretary to the Bondsraad, Oct. 1946, p. 7.
43 Grossmann 2014: 3–5.

members. Afrikaner nationalism, which saw the family as the nucleus of the nation, discounted the private sphere, including family ties, which could have provided a counter-balance to the total allegiance to the nation, and even reinforced the latter.[44] It was not until the 1930s that the organisation managed to overcome its elitist encapsulation, when it took advantage of the centenary celebrations of the Great Trek to generate a mass cultural-nationalist movement that the AB was to keep under its control. Yet the mobilisation of this mass movement did not change the elitist character of the Broederbond, in which workers, self-employed entrepreneurs of small businesses, and small-scale farmers remained underrepresented. In terms of turnover of personnel, the leadership remained remarkably stable; for the Uitvoerende Raad, which was the organisation's actual centre of power, recruited its members from a comparatively small group of persons.[45] These could attain a reputation among their confreres, of being "prominent Afrikaners".[46]

Verwoerd was recruited in 1936 during his work on the Kimberley-Congress's Continuation Committee.[47] In light of his previous activities, he appeared not only as "good Afrikaner", but also as a promising intellectual, impressively dynamic, with the right kind of mindset. He soon moved up the ladder into the Uitvoerende Raad, of which he was a member between 1940 and 1950. His propensity for hierarchically structured forms of organisation was evident even in his student days; but it was the Broederbond that taught him a lot about efficiency, and ways of defending oneself against external influences and criticisms.

He closely followed Joon van Rooy, professor in Theory of Education based in Potchefstroom, who served as Chairperson between 1932 and 1938, and then again between 1942 and 1952. In 1954, Verwoerd paid tribute to him in an obituary, commending him for having promoted the National Party from behind the scenes.[48] Irving Hexham's claim that Verwoerd broke the power of the *"doppers"* in the Broederbond in the mid-1950s cannot be substantiated and is not very credible, given his good relations with various intellectuals in Potchefst-

---

44 Coser 2015: 40.
45 AB Archive, 2/3/15, Bondsraad, 10.-12.11.1948, p. 12, TOP 19, Komiteeverslag i.s. samestelling van die U.R.
46 PV 93/3/1/4, Letter by J. N. Marais (East London) to Verwoerd, 27.8.1949.
47 Stals 1998: 121. Verwoerd was Broeder no. 1596, see the dedication in his personal copy of the Brochure issued on the 25th anniversary of the AB 1943 (FAV 4.5.2.4). According to P. J. Meyer (1984: 30), Verwoerd's name was put forward for membership of the AB after it became known that he would accept the post of editor-in-chief of *Die Transvaler*. Kenney (1980: 46) indicates the date of his admission to the AB – February 1937 –, but does not substantiate this.
48 Verwoerd 1954: 93.

room.[49] A report of the South African Secret Service attributed to Verwoerd, "who dominated the proceedings as usual",[50] a key position in the leadership of the Broederbond: "Verwoerd held the floor for the major part of the discussions, & his opinion definitely appears to carry more weight than that of any other member of the U.R."[51] He concentrated on expanding the power of the UR and on fighting "enemies".

The activities in the Broederbond suited Verwoerd very well; even in the report that he wrote in his capacity as Chairperson of the Students' Council in Stellenbosch, he insisted on the need for good organisation, clear hierarchies and responsibilities, as well as the discipline that an active central leadership could bring about in an organisation. Formally, the highest organ of the Broederbond was the so-called Bondsraad, an annual meeting of delegates from the local cells who passed important resolutions, and elected the Uitvoerende Raad. In fact, the real power fell to this Council; an inner nucleus of a smaller management committee (*Dagbestuur*) assumed the main decision-making powers. The Uitvoerende Raad, or rather, its managing committee, controlled all communications; despite the apparent democratic character of the organisation, this management committee could direct and manipulate the communications to serve its own purposes.

It was Verwoerd's aim at all times to prevent any overlap in fields of work that could potentially lead to competition and unnecessary friction. He supported the decision of the Broederbond to step back from its initial plan to establish an institute for "*Volkskultuur*", even though a "*Volkskongress*" had already been planned to lay the groundwork.[52] He also issued an explicit warning against teaching Blacks "what organisation means" – for instance, through promoting anti-Communist trade unions: "The history of trade unions shows that the establishment of trade unions for natives is a Frankenstein-Monster that will destroy us."[53]

The situation was different, however, in the case of white trade unions. Immediately after his arrival in Johannesburg, he began to campaign for white mine workers.[54] Through his newspaper, he advanced the cause of the Blanke Werkers Beskermingsbond, of which he remained a board member until shortly before

---

49 Hexham (1981: 190) assumes this, apparently because of the long drawn-out dispute with L. J. du Plessis.
50 UP, Report of a meeting of the Dagbestuur of the U.R. of the A.B, Johannesburg, 13.12.1944, p. 3.
51 UP, Report of preliminary U.R. meeting of Die Afrikaner Broederbond, Johannesburg, 11.12.1944, p. 1.
52 AB Archive, 2/3/11, UR meeting, 14.2.1946, p. 6, TOP 25, Kultuuruitbouing.
53 AB Archive, 2/3/24, UR meeting, 27.–28.10.1947, TOP 9, Naturelle–vakbonde.
54 D. Prinsloo 1979: 370–383.

the 1948 election.[55] In the struggle to take over the previously English-dominated unions, he supported Albert Hertzog's intervention.[56]

But when the white mine workers went on strike in 1947 and Albert Hertzog, one of the masterminds of the nationalist takeover of the white mineworkers' union, asked the Uitvoerende Raad (UR) for financial support for the striking workers, it was Verwoerd who spoke out against it, pointing out that "personal sympathy" was not sufficient reason for providing support. Shortly afterwards, when Hertzog once again asked for 10 000 pounds from the AB for the miners, Verwoerd re-iterated his warning against "not weighing up the matter soberly and objectively in times of such incidents", saying that the AB could not afford such an expenditure "as a friendly gesture".[57] This attitude once more revealed his distrust of spontaneous, emotionally driven actions.

As he set great store on the efficient running of the Broederbond, he repeatedly urged its members to treat the discussions of the UR confidentially.[58] In 1943, he advocated the infiltration of existing organisations and mutual support of Afrikaans enterprises.[59] On the same occasion, Chairman J. C. van Rooy quite openly stated as goal of the AB "that men must be included in the AB who hold leadership positions in various areas of the life of our people [ons volkslewe], or that men from within the AB take over this leadership. Gradually, over time, it turned out that Brothers [Broeders] were able to set the tone in nearly all arenas."[60]

In the election year of 1943, Verwoerd expressed support for the idea of recruiting war veterans,[61] and pointed to the important role of those Afrikaners in the constituency who had turned their backs on the Reformed churches and joined various sects, especially the Apostolic Mission Church. Because of the negative and hostile attitude of the established churches, members of the splinter churches did not make use of their voting rights during elections. Verwoerd was intent on meeting with church representatives to get them to adopt a "better attitude toward the splinter churches".[62]

---

55 FAV 4.5.1.6, Letter by B. W. B. to Verwoerd, 10.3.1948.
56 L. Naudé 1969.
57 AB Archive, 2/3/13, U.R.-Dagbestuurvergadering, Johannesburg, 17.2.1947, p. 1, TOP 3, Staking onder Mynwerkers.
58 AB Archive, 2/3/10/1, UR meeting 24.10.1941, p. 8, TOP 13, Vertroulike aard van U.R.-Vergaderings.
59 AB Archive, 2/3/10/2, Bondsraad, 13.–14.12.1943, pp. 7–8, TOP 12, Ondersteuning van Afrikaneronderneminge. See also A. Boshoff 1974: 57.
60 FAV 4.5.2.4, Brochure compiled for the 25th anniversary of the AB 1943, Speech by Chairman van Rooy, p. 38.
61 AB Archive, 2/3/10/2, UR Assembly, 5.–6.5.1944, p. 9, TOP 38, Terugkerende soldate.
62 AB Archive, 2/3/13, UR meeting, 8.–9.5.1947, pp. 6–7, TOP 25, Sektewese en die Uitoefening van Stemreg.

Although Verwoerd saw the Broederbond as the central institution of Afrikaner nationalism, this did not imply that he granted it a leading role or even the authority to issue directives to the Party. Instead, the two organisations were to complement each other: the Party was to be in charge of policy, in which the Broederbond was not to interfere; but neither was it the role of the Broederbond to merely aid and support the Party. The Broederbond was to use its network of subsidiary organisations to pursue a broadly-based cultural-nationalist mobilisation on a continuous basis. Verwoerd underlined this role, making it clear that "[t]he people must be made to understand and realise that the A.B. was the important factor in the life of the Afrikaner community. It was the duty of the A.B. to advise the people on the cultural aspect & other aspects of their national life through the medium of the F.A.K. and kindred bodies."[63] The Bond itself called its members "the trustees of the highest interests of the Afrikaner people".[64] It avowedly pursued "primarily spiritual values"; its self-declared aim was to act "as planning council and power house of Afrikanerdom",[65] thus underlining its elitist character. The AB was purportedly "not a movement for the masses"; its self-declared aim was to organise "only the few real leaders in particular important spheres of local communal life, or young men with unmistakable marks of future leadership qualities".[66]

Verwoerd defended the elitist orientation because the cells could work efficiently only if they were "small enough" "to effectively deliberate on and discuss what is in the best interest of the country".[67] In defence of the "confidential" nature of the organisation, he deliberately twisted the relation of cause and effect in implying that the "imperialists" would persecute AB members should the names of the latter become known. So it was made out to be the government that was

---

[63] UP, Action Committee of the UR, Johannesburg 12.12.1944, p. 4. Report of preliminary U.R. meeting of Die Afrikaner Broederbond, Johannesburg 11.12.1944, p. 8: "Verwoerd pointed out that what the Afrikaners were today was through the work of the A.B., which had consistently fought against the attempts to oppress the Afrikaner nation, and this must be known to the nation."
[64] AB Archive, 2/3/12, Report by the Secretary of the UR, submitted to the Bondsraad, Oct. 1946, p. 10.
[65] AB Archive, 2/3/15, Report by the Secretary of the UR over the time period July 1946 – June 1948, pp. 1–2, Point 5: Werksaamhede van die U.R.
[66] AB Archive, 2.3.19, Verslag van werksaamhede, 1950, p. 36.
[67] AB Archive, 1/1/142/2, Letter by Verwoerd to Basson, 26.3.1964. In his address to the Bondsraad 1958, Verwoerd stressed that AB members were no better than any others, and that the selection process was based only on the requirements of an efficiently functioning organisation (AB Archive, 1/1/142/1, Verwoerd se boodskap. Bondsraad 1958, pp. 2–3).

urging the AB to observe secrecy – which was a somewhat scurrilous claim, given the history of the infiltration of numerous institutions by the AB.[68]

Organisational efficiency could only succeed if it was linked to a clearly delineated ideology; the "principles" of the Broederbond were non-negotiable. The positions of Afrikaner nationalism were claimed to be derived from history, culture, and religion; they had to be enforced unequivocally, without allowing for compromises and dilutions. The preservation of Afrikaans culture was held to be central, and that is why cooperation with the British was to be rejected if it meant that Afrikaners had to relinquish essential positions assigned to them.

When the government launched its first attacks on the Broederbond in August 1944, the issue was discussed during the Bondsraad. In his opening speech, AB Chairman J. C. van Rooy encouraged the delegates: "But we will not despair, we will not be discouraged, for our cause is just, our cause is holy, and our path is the correct one."[69] Verwoerd moved to embark on a counter-attack directed especially against the Freemasons and so-called patriotic societies.[70] In addition, the Uitvoerende Raad demanded that the NP should respond to Smuts's ban with a motion to ban state officials from membership of the Sons of England, of the Freemasons, of the British Empire Service League, and of the South African Jewish Board of Deputies.[71] Verwoerd's virulent antisemitism was unleashed at the mention of the latter organisation. Yet this body did not in any way operate as a secret society; on the contrary, it was a public organisation openly representing the interests of South African Jews.[72]

On 15 December 1944, Prime Minister Jan Smuts accused the AB of being a secret organisation with political objectives, and the government therefore prohibited state officials from membership.[73] This measure caused indignation in the AB; and,

---

68 UP, Report of preliminary U.R. meeting of Die Afrikaner Broederbond, Johannesburg, 11.12.1944, p. 5.
69 AB Archive, 2/3/10/2, Bondsraad, 2.–3.10.1944, p. 1.
70 Ibid., 8, TOP 24, Vyandige propaganda teen die A.B.
71 UP, Action Committee of the UR, Johannesburg, 12.12.1944, p. 4. Verwoerd warned that after a change of government, the new government could proceed in a manner similar to Smuts now, to ban the Sons of England and the Freemasons (UP, Report of preliminary U.R. meeting of Die Afrikaner Broederbond, Johannesburg, 11.12.1944, p. 6).
72 See also ibid., 14: "A speaker mentioned something about a secret letter regarding the machinations of Jewry, implying that the Jews had their secret organisation as well as the Afrikaners having their A.B., & Verwoerd said if such a letter could be obtained, it would assist their cause greatly if it were made public."
73 AB Archive, 2/3/10/2, Dagbestuur, 21.10.1944, TOP 4, Posisie van staatsamptenare. Initially, the AB submitted a reserved response, but did not encourage the officials concerned to resign. Even

significantly, it was once again Verwoerd who pushed for a counter-offensive.[74] It was his view that the AB should take up the fight, and in the process also come out with information on its own structures and operations. Verwoerd was placing his bets on the element of surprise: "This would come as a great shock to the Government, as they would not expect that the A.B. would be so bold as to disclose the percentages of Government employees in their ranks."[75] Verwoerd himself did not mind if his membership was to become known; but the names of other members would have to remain strictly secret, "as herein lay the strength of the A.B."[76] In 1949, the newspaper *Suiderstem*, which was close to the UP, spread the news that Verwoerd had been elected as new Vice Chairman of the AB – which was not true; but the UR advised him not to refute the news.[77] Apparently, it was seen as an advantage if the structures of the AB remained unclear. Verwoerd firmly rejected Smuts's characterisation of the Broederbond as fascist.[78]

The statement that was adopted by the UR and forwarded to the press by Verwoerd reveals the authoritarian mindset that prevailed in the Broederbond. Thus it states, among other things: "The Uitvoerende Raad will shortly move to take the Afrikaner *volk* into its confidence and to publicly instruct them in its history, its aims, aspirations, and activities."[79] A publicity campaign in the form of newspaper articles was to publicise the general aims of the AB, for which Verwoerd wanted to use the

---

the UR meeting of 3.–4.11. (ibid., 8–9, TOP 45) formulated recommendations for ways in which officials should conduct themselves, but it did not as yet develop an aggressive counter-strategy.

74 See also the discussion about Christian National Education, which had sparked serious criticism. Verwoerd advised launching a counter-offensive (AB Archive, 2/3/16, UR meeting, 20.–21.5.1949, p. 7, TOP 34, Aanvalle op C.N.O.-beleid).

75 UP, Action Committee of the UR, Johannesburg, 12.12.1944, p. 1.

76 UP, Report of preliminary U.R. meeting of Die Afrikaner Broederbond, Johannesburg, 11.12.1944, p. 2.

77 AB Archive, 2/3/16, UR meeting, 20.–21.5.1949, pp. 9–10, TOP 41, Perspropaganda teen die A.B. Even Piet Meyer, who was to become AB-Chairman at a later stage, claimed (as late as 1978) that Verwoerd had been Deputy Chairman of the UR (P. J. Meyer 1978: 3).

78 UP, Report of a meeting of the Dagbestuur of the U.R., Johannesburg, 13.12.1944, pp. 2, 5: "Verwoerd actually seemed hurt on this score." See also *Die Transvaler*, 4.10.1937, in which he articulates the difference saying that the NP was a democratic party, whereas the Nazis and the fascists had established dictatorships. "Under no circumstances would a nationalist want to see such an alien state system introduced in South Africa." See also *Die Transvaler*, 3.11.1937, on a failed agreement between the NP and the Greyshirts. While antisemitism broadly provided some kind of common ground, the different ideas about the form of the state made it impossible for the NP and the Greyshirts to come to an agreement. This did not prevent *Die Transvaler* from printing an image showing Hitler surrounded by swooning women (*Die Transvaler*, 10.12.1937). On Smuts's reproaches, see Wilkins/Strydom 1980: 84.

79 AB Archive, 2/3/10/2, Buitengewone UR-Vergadering, 11.12.1944, p. 1, TOP 5 (e) Besluite.

influence he had gained as newspaper editor.[80] These articles were also meant to showcase the history of the AB "in serial form", "so as to maintain the interest of the public in the affairs of the A.B., & thus enlist their sympathy".[81] The prolonged media coverage of the organisation was an important propaganda tool,[82] which is something that Verwoerd had picked up from his experience with advertising psychology. He sensed that the propagandistic value could be enhanced through the combination of the secrecy to which members were sworn, and the public self-presentation of the AB in a series of articles that "would fire the imagination of Afrikaners".[83]

In his zeal to show the power of the AB, however, Verwoerd lost touch with reality when he suggested that the 900 teacher members of the AB should refuse to leave the Broederbond: "Would the Government have the courage to dismiss such a large number?"[84] He wanted to appoint every civil servant who had been dismissed, as an "official organiser of the H.N. Party". The civil servants were to be confronted with a situation in which no alternative was open to them: "The A.B. must tell these dismissed Government employees that they have no alternative but to work for the H.N. Party in their own personal interests, because their only hope of eventually being reinstated in their former places of employment would be for a Nationalist Government to take power."[85] Verwoerd categorically rejected the possibility of an "honourable discharge" of the civil servants concerned, from the Broederbond.[86] But on 15 December 1944, when the government issued the proclamation to all civil servants, prohibiting membership of the Broederbond, the AB refrained from taking legal action. The UR had gotten cold feet and recommended that civil servants leave the AB, so as not to incur economic harm.[87] This led to a wave of more than 800 resignations.[88]

---

80 UP, Report of preliminary U.R. meeting of Die Afrikaner Broederbond, Johannesburg, 11.12.1944, p. 1. The article appeared in *Die Burger* (among other publication outlets), 14., 21, and 18.12. 1944, 3.1.1945; see the reports in the government–friendly paper *Die Suiderstem*, 14., 28., and 30.12.1944, as well as 3.1.1945 (See also Bloomberg 1989: 195–200).
81 UP, Action Committee of the UR, Johannesburg, 12.12.1944, p. 1.
82 See also UP, Report of preliminary U.R. meeting of Die Afrikaner Broederbond, Johannesburg, 11.12.1944, p. 13.
83 Ibid., p. 2.
84 Ibid., p. 7.
85 UP, Action Committee of the UR, Johannesburg, 12.12.1944, p. 2.
86 UP, Report of preliminary U.R. meeting of Die Afrikaner Broederbond, Johannesburg, 11.12.1944, p. 1. One of the reasons was that the AB would thereby follow the example of the OB, which is what Verwoerd wanted to avoid at all costs.
87 AB Archive, 2/3/10/2, UR Meeting, 21.12.1944, p. 2.
88 Ibid., UR meeting 1.–2.2.1945, p. 9, TOP 42 (d). In September 1945, there were more than 1 000; that means that Smuts's decree cost the Broederbond more than a third of its members (AB Archive 2/3/11, UR meeting, 25.9.1945, Aanhangsel A, Ledetal; the number of resignations stood at

The Struggle against the *Ossewabrandwag*

The extreme right-wing *Ossewabrandwag* (OB) had been established in January 1939. After the outbreak of the War, it had rapidly developed into a broad extra-parliamentary mass movement.[89] In January 1941, the former administrator of the Orange Free State, J. F. J. Van Rensburg, took over the leadership of this paramilitary movement as new Commandant-General (KG). Under his leadership, the movement fast gained a clearer political profile; as admirer of the Third Reich, Van Rensburg openly advocated fascist models of order, and made no secret of his ideologically motivated rejection of party politics and parliamentarism. Initially, the relationship was harmonious, and Verwoerd's newspaper in particular supported the OB through intensive reporting and favourable commentary.[90] On 1 February 1942, soldiers went out of control and, enraged by the newspaper's reporting, began to attack the Voortrekkerpers building, which also housed the editorial offices and the printing press. That is when Van Rensburg unleashed his hit squads in defence.[91]

Van Rensburg turned the movement into a tightly run paramilitary organisation. In the spring of 1941, with its new charismatic leader, and through the skilful adaptation of cultural nationalist symbolism, the Ossewabrandwag changed from an ally into a competitor. Its authoritarian anti-parliamentarism could easily be roped into a fundamental de-legitimation of the National Party.[92]

The Party leadership tried to commit the OB to the so-called Cradock Agreement with the clear intention of reining the OB in and tying it to the Party. The Agreement had been concluded before Van Rensburg took office as KG. He dilly-dallied for a while, repeatedly welcoming and signing off on hollow compromises without really

---

1 095, the number of active members was down to 1 691. At the end of 1946, the AB leadership conceded that the government's interventions had inflicted grave harm on their organisation (AB Archive, 2/3/12, Report of the UR Secretary submitted to the Bondsraad, October 1946, p. 6). Some local sections had been weakened to such an extent that they could no longer operate, and had to be temporarily disbanded.
89 Marx 1994.
90 D. Prinsloo 1985: 77. Even Verwoerd's wife was a member of the OB for some time (D. Prinsloo 1979: 236). As late as April 1941, Verwoerd took a stand against a group of professors from Stellenbosch, who spoke out against the influence of new ideologies, ostensibly meaning the various fascist groupings (ibid., 254). Meiring (1987: 55) writes: "Right at the beginning, Dr. Verwoerd was still quite receptive to the statements of the OB, while it had not [yet] entered the field of politics."
91 For an eyewitness account of the events, see Meiring 1987: 152–157.
92 See FAV 4.5.1.6, Letter by Verwoerd to D.F. Malan, 15.7.1941, on a looming confrontation with the OB, and appended article on a speech by van Rensburg, in which he distanced himself from Kruger's republic (*Die Vaderland*, 14.7.1941).

giving a damn. This double game made the Party leadership around D. F. Malan realise that he was an unreliable partner at best, but far more likely a devious opponent and rival who had to be decisively confronted. Malan received the unqualified support of the radical wing of the Party around Strijdom, Swart, and Louw.

The OB caused outrage in the Party when it published the draft constitution for a future republic, which had been developed by a Broederbond Commission in co-operation with Verwoerd as foremost spokesperson. The draft constitution initially appeared in the form of a circular letter (no. 1/41), issued under the auspices of the OB – which, in the NP's understanding, meant that the OB had overstepped its powers and its domain as cultural organisation, and interfered in politics and hence also in the affairs of the Party.[93] The Party only distanced itself from the authoritarian draft constitution when the OB adopted it as its own, and interpreted it in terms of an "authoritarian state" ("*gesagstaat*"). For the rest, Verwoerd did not explicitly resolve to distance himself from fascist ideas; instead, he emphasised the parallels. In *Die Transvaler*, he stated that it was "the present *volks*-leader, Dr. Malan who, like Hitler for Germany, has for years been pursuing the vision of South Africa as an Afrikaner republic with a happy and prosperous people".[94] On another occasion, he stressed that the Herenigde Nasionale Party "has always shown its high regard for what National Socialism achieved for Germany", but that the ideology was not transferable.[95]

In July 1941, the NP held one of its rather rare nationwide "*unial*" (that is, encompassing all four provincial parties), party congresses in Bloemfontein. "*Volks*-leader" Malan used the opportunity to rally the entire Party to his line. A short while later, van Rensburg publicly took a stand for fascist dissenter Oswald Pirow, thus interfering with the Party's affairs. That was when Malan called on NP members to resign from the OB. Soon afterwards it became apparent that the authority of Malan trumped that of van Rensburg: a mass exodus from the OB ensued, which continued over the next few years. The defeat of the German Army at Stalingrad, and the dwindling prospects of the Third Reich to win the War contributed to the delegitimation of the OB and its leadership, as a result of which it fast lost political clout from August 1941 onwards. Nevertheless, it remained a formidable force. Van Rensburg did not refrain from making radical statements, keeping the conflict simmering until the end of the 1940s.

---

[93] Yet the minutes of the Komitee in sake Algemene Beleid of 28.–29.11.1940 indicate that "the basic ideas of the paper should be publicised in the meantime. The decision is that the paper should not be published in its entirety" (PV 93/1/1/1, f. 118, Minutes. Verwoerd was present.).
[94] *Die Transvaler* 26.8.1941 (editorial). In fact the NP published the draft constitution under its own name: Nasionale Party n.d.
[95] *Die Transvaler*, 16.9.1941 (editorial).

Verwoerd played a crucial role in this conflict; as editor of the Transvaal's most important nationalist daily newspaper, he was at the centre of the action. His editorials expressed his unwillingness to compromise, insisting on the Party's leadership role. Moreover, he clearly recognised that van Rensburg – and within the Party, Oswald Pirow – were long-standing supporters of Hertzog, which meant that the conflict between cultural nationalists and the fusionists ("*smelters*") was being re-ignited in a new constellation. From August onward, Verwoerd proceeded to write editorials launching massive attacks against Oswald Pirow,[96] and then increasingly also against the OB.[97] Van Rensburg, for his part, poured fuel on the flames in stating (according to a witness) "that the O.B. does not recognise any political party. There is now an oath that the H.N.P. members have to take when joining [the Party]; he advises O.B. members to think twice before taking this oath. He also said that one cannot serve two masters."[98]

Because the OB's paramilitary form of organisation proved to be popular, the NP followed suit in organising its local structures in militaristic style. The organisational rearmament of the HNP also included the formation of the Nasionale Jeugbond, in which C. R. Swart, shunned *Grootraad*-representative and hard-nosed opponent of van Rensburg's, played a leading role.[99] Verwoerd was encouraged in his intransigent stance when Swart sent him the manuscript by N. G. S. van der Walt, entitled 'A party stumbling along' ('*kronkelgang*'). This was an internal OB pamphlet penned by the editor of OB's own journal, consisting essentially of a string of quotes from leading NP politicians, especially from Malan, which were designed to show up his opportunism.[100] When attempts at mediation and reconcilia-

---

[96] *Die Tranvaler*, 28.8.1941 (editorial).
[97] *Die Tranvaler*, 11., 16., 18.8.1941. While Verwoerd still advocated a settlement and a path of reconciliation in his editorial of 18.8.1941, he effectively poured fuel onto the flames with his refusal to print letters to the editor and his continued attacks. Similarly on 25.8.1941 and 26.8.1941.
[98] PV 93/1/1/1, f. 1, Letter by Joh. Barry to Verwoerd, 19.8.1941.
[99] Swart played a leading role also in drafting the statutes – on paper, and with the OB letterhead (PV 18/1/10/1, Konstitusie, Nasionale Jeugbond, 1941). Care was taken – without making this explicit – to prevent OB members from becoming members of the youth organisation. The statutes also included the aim of solving "the Jewish question". Jews were explicitly excluded from membership.
[100] PV 93/1/1/1, f. 7, Letter by Swart to Verwoerd, signalling agreement with Verwoerd's attitude. Appended to the letter is the manuscript on the '*kronkelgang van 'n party*', as well as a declaration by J.E.T. Gildenhuys (Hulpsekretaris of the OFS–*Beheerraad*), attesting to the fact that the manuscript originated from the OB office (see also *Die Tranvaler*, 18.9.1941 (several reports) (PV 93/1/1/3, ff. 124–126 'Die Kronkelgang van 'n Party').

tion between the warring factions were mounting, Malan urged party functionaries not to yield to compromises.[101]

For his part, Verwoerd did not fail to use any opportunity to attack the organisation propagandistically, as he did for instance on the occasion of the withdrawal of the chairperson of the *Grootraad* on 4.9.1941, or the resignation of NP politician M. D. C. de Wet Nel from the "Control Council", that is, the governing body of the OB in the Transvaal.[102] On these occasions, he claimed that van Rensburg's ideas did not coincide with those of OB members.[103] *Die Transvaler* began to systematically publish or report on resignations.[104] Verwoerd was devious enough to attach the names of editors of his newspaper who harboured OB sympathies, to articles that were sharply critical of the OB.[105] Verwoerd succeeded with this journalistic strategy, to the extent that the OB soon declared him its number one enemy.[106]

At the height of the dispute, L. J. du Plessis intervened as self-appointed mediator. The professor was one of the leading intellectuals of Afrikaner nationalism. He owed this reputation primarily to his status as a *"dopper"*, that is, a member of the particularly conservative Gereformeerde Kerk with the University of Potchefstroom as its intellectual centre; in this capacity, he derived his politics from Calvinist principles. He was one of the first representatives of the University of Potchefstroom to join the Broederbond, and acted as its Chairman for two years (1930–1932). In addition, he had also been active for some time in a leading position in the NP of the Transvaal. However, in contrast to long-standing Broederbond-Chairman J. C. "Joon" van Rooy, he was an extremely controversial figure. His reputation of combining political moves with selfish ambitions earned him widespread distrust. Through his personal friendship with van Rooy, he was able to secure his influence and to attain a role as arbiter of a certain kind in the incipient dispute between the National Party and the OB. Initially he was chairman of an AB commission "for general policy" (*"algemene beleid"*), which was re-

---

101 PV 93/1/1/1, f. 10, Telegram to Verwoerd: "Cite Dr Malan's position as follows. Struggle cannot be discontinued half way through. Van Rensburg would take full advantage of this, and that is what would leave a bad impression with the people. Van Rensburg wants to see the struggle interrupted by all means, in order to gather his forces. The expectation that keeping quiet about this will neutralise him, is mistaken. The mood in the Cape Province and in the Free State is overwhelmingly in favour of the Party. People are awaiting correct explanations and leadership; if we shy away from these tasks, it will surely be to the disadvantage [of our cause]. Potgieter."
102 *Die Transvaler*, 6.9.1941 (report); on de Wet Nel, see *Die Transvaler*, 9.9.1941 (editorial) and 17.9.1941 (report).
103 *Die Transvaler*, 12. and 18.9.1941 (editorial).
104 *Die Transvaler*, 19.9.1941 (various reports).
105 D. Prinsloo 1981: 15.
106 *Die Transvaler*, 18.9.1941 (report), 19.9.1941 (editorial).

sponsible for the draft constitution of 1940, notorious for its fascist orientation. In the intensifying conflict, du Plessis sought to assume the leadership of a cultural-nationalist camp that he himself had tried to convene.[107]

As late as May 1941, du Plessis advocated Party policy and a leading role for the Party,[108] but, driven by the momentum of his antiliberal thinking, he soon turned away from it. Without further ado, he transformed the *"Kommissie in sake Algemene Beleid"* into the so-called *Afrikaner Eenheidskomitee (AEK)*.[109] In addition to the two contending organisations, the Committee also included the *Reddingsdaadbond*, whose chairman Diederichs was also the head of the Broederbond. The meetings of the Committee were very heated, because the representatives of the Party and the OB brought reproaches and accusations against each other.[110] Verwoerd did not trust du Plessis one bit, as he suspected him of making common cause with van Rensburg. The positions of the Party and the OB proved irreconcilable – even the last meetings of the AEK did not yield any results.[111] In early October 1941, the Chairman of the AEK, du Plessis, urged its members to wait "with [implementing] irrevocable steps" until he had presented his report, which promised to shed a very different light on the matter "than is now being suggested by our leaders".[112]

At the Bondsraad of 1941, du Plessis presented the Chairman's report of the Afrikaner Eenheidskomitee. In doing so, he managed to add his written report to the official Bondsraad files by a trick. This was clearly in violation of the rules – only what had previously been dealt with by the UR could be included in the files. Therefore he was not spared the humiliation whereby all present had to remove the report from those files and hand it in to the convenors. At the request of

---

107 Verwoerd was initially well inclined toward him, and deplored his rash moves (PV 93/1/1/1, ff. 50–51, Undated telegram – possibly 1939 – by Verwoerd to A. J. R. van Rhyn).
108 L. J. du Plessis 1941.
109 PV 93/1/1/1, ff. 121–125, Kommissie in sake Algemene Beleid, 2.6.1941, TOP 8, L. J. du Plessis submitted an application to establish a "Strategy Council" ["*Beleidsraad*"], that was to comprise the Party, the OB, and the FAK. This motion was unanimously accepted (Verwoerd was present, but ostensibly as delegate of FAK and RDB – see D. Prinsloo 1979: 262).
110 Ibid., f. 66, undated handwritten notes of Verwoerd's, with numerous other reproaches, especially against *Die Transvaler*; see also ibid., ff. 89–92, with statements by J.A. Smith and van Rensburg, which Verwoerd had jotted down.
111 Ibid., f. 56, Telegram by Verwoerd to Malan, undated: "Meeting was discontinued at a deadlock, because the other side is not willing to fulfil your demand. No statement will be issued. No proposals have been accepted, except for a proposal submitted by the church ministers, asking that the Chairperson, the Secretary, and van Rensburg meet with them for a personal discussion. The Party representatives abstained from voting. In the meantime, the publication and the developments are continuing like last week, for the Committee realises that a truce is no longer attainable. Verwoerd."
112 Ibid., f. 11, News report of the South African Press Agency (SAPA), 3.10.1941. Ibid., ff. 93–114, Undated notes, handwritten by Verwoerd, ostensibly refer to the same meeting.

T. E. Dönges, a discussion of du Plessis' report was prevented with reference to the "threat of dividing the people"; instead, it was referred to the UR.[113]

At the next UR meeting two and a half weeks later, Dönges recurred to his intervention, which he justified by pointing out that it was now important to preserve the unity of the AB. Van Rooy reported on an initiative that entrusted J. D. du Toit, the "*volks*-poet" Totius, who also held a professorship in Theology in Potchefstroom, with the role of mediator. This initiative had already been approved by van Rensburg. But then Malan scuppered the plans by publicly presenting his own proposal to establish a "National Committee". In his capacity as Party leader, he simultaneously positioned himself as leader of the proposed "National Committee", to whom the various organisations would be subordinate.[114] In invoking a nebulous commitment to the fascist "Italian corporative system" that was now being developed, Malan wanted to turn the affiliated organisations, such as the OB, into mere executive organs of the National Committee.[115] In addition, Verwoerd made it clear "that Dr Malan's proposal should not be interpreted as aiming at a co-ordination of the organisations".[116] Referring to the draft constitution, he insisted on the subordination of the various organisations to the Committee, and thus to Malan's leadership.

Du Plessis immediately countered this decree, claiming that confidence in the Party had declined. An important leadership task was to fall to the UR, especially since the Bondsraad had referred the discussion of its report to that body. His long-winded interventions indicated that he rejected the political leadership role of the Party, while aiming to delegate major powers to the UR, which is why he recapitulated the history of the Broederbond precisely in this sense. In differentiating 'politics' from 'party politics', and designating only the latter as the domain of the NP, he assigned a political mandate to the Broederbond and the OB.[117] The UR appointed a committee consisting of Chairman Diederichs, his Deputy van Rooy, the OB leader van Rensburg, and Verwoerd, tasked with discussing the two proposals, that of Totius and that of Malan himself, with Malan. It did not take long for the envisaged co-operation to break down, however. Subsequently, the UR discontinued any further mediation role; it thanked Verwoerd and du Plessis as the main

---

113 AB Archive, 2/3/10/1, Bondsraad, 6.10.1941, pp. 1–2 TOP 6, Verslag van Beleidskommissie. On du Plessis's approach, see the personal portrait put together by Albert Hertzog (PV451/4/1/169, Diary 1942–1944, p. 110–7, esp. pp. 110–112). See also Bekker 1988: 187.
114 That is what Verwoerd advocated in *Die Transvaler* at an early stage, 26.8.1941 (editorial, paragraph on the OB).
115 PV 93/1/1/1, f. 25, Letter by D. F. Malan to van Rensburg, 24.11.41: Proposal of the Nasionale Komitee.
116 AB Archive, 2/3/10/1, UR meeting, 24.10.1941, TOP 10, p. 3.
117 Marx 2008: 417.

authors of the draft constitution, and returned to its usual tasks.[118] In the meantime, the OB had lost much of its influence, due to a mass exodus of NP supporters; and the NP, in its turn, was busy establishing its hegemony in the nationalist camp. In March 1943, du Plessis threw in the towel and vacated his seat in the UR.[119]

The disciplining of the Trekmaats, the youth organisation of the OB, to which Verwoerd attributed great significance,[120] forms part of the context of the struggle against the OB. The most important OB sympathisers in the Broederbond, N. Diederichs and P. J. Meyer, were in charge of the Trekmaats, which raised concerns that the youth wing of the AB could fall under the influence of the OB.

In 1942, Verwoerd complained that the AB had lost contact with the Trekmaats, "and that the Trekmaats could move into opposition to the AB".[121] He was primarily concerned with the AB's control over the youth organisation, with the prevention of possible rivalries or divergent views and attitudes, and with the establishment of "*volks*-unity". Six months later, on 30 October 1942, Verwoerd submitted a report on this to the UR, on the basis of which the UR took the decision that the AB should "hold the reins of the Trekmaats, the F.A.K. and the Reddingsdaadbond in its own hands", and that the offices of the AB, FAK and Trekmaats should be merged, to be placed under the control of the AB leadership, along with their daily operations.[122] With the dismissal of OB activist Piet Meyer as Assistant Secretary of the AB, the Trekmaats were to be removed from his control and placed under the supervision of the UR. A decision by the AB's Nylstroom chapter advocating the dissolution of the Trekmaats because of a risk of conflict with the

---

118 AB Archive, 2/3/10/1, UR meeting, 23.1.1942, pp. 2–3, TOP 8, Konsolidering van die Afrikanerdom. At the beginning of October, the issue of *volks*-unity was once again raised in the Bondsraad, but this time, a resolution was adopted that was kept so general that it could no longer prompt the UR to take a position (AB Archive, 2/3/10/1, Bondsraad, 6.10.1941 in Bloemfontein, p. 7, TOP 26, Volkseenheid).
119 AB Archive, 2/3/10/1, Dagbestuur, 5.3.1943, p. 3, TOP 12, Bedanking as U.R.-lid: Br. L. J. du Plessis; see also ibid. UR meeting, 3.–4.5.1943, TOP 38; here du Plessis stated health reasons. This was not a pretext – he was not well and the Rector of the University of Potchefstroom urged him to reduce his extramural activities (PV 451/4/1/169, Diary 1942–1944, p. 114).
120 Stals 1998: 245–246. Years later, Verwoerd remained suspicious of new movements and organisations, alleging that they often seek reconciliation "which leads to a dilution of principles" (PV 54/2, Minutes of the Federale Raad of the NP, 18.8.1955, TOP 9b, p. 3).
121 AB Archive, 2/3/10/1, Dagbestuur, 5.3.1942, pp. 2–3., TOP 14, Trekmaats. See also ibid. UR, 24.–25.4.1942, pt 12(d), Resolution of the UR to obtain the statutes of the Trekmaats and to discuss them at a later stage.
122 Ibid., UR, 30.10.1942, p. 4, TOP 21, Koördinering van Organisasies.

AB, came in handy to the NP representatives, who warned that "persons who are not fit to be Brothers [*broeders*] are dangerous as Trekmaats".[123]

In December 1943, the UR discussed the issue again. In the meantime, the Hoofsekretaris of the Trekmaats, Professor J. H. Coetzee from Potchefstroom, had informed the AB in writing that the organisation was ready to join the AB network; Verwoerd was asked to present the issue at the Bondsraad.[124] On 22 February 1944, direct negotiations took place with the board of the Trekmaats. On this occasion, Verwoerd presented the stance of the AB: "The Trekmaats are a creation of the A.B., and should serve as a testing ground for A.B. membership." If this organisation were to continue to expand as it had done hitherto, he said, it would risk getting into competition with the AB. The UR demanded to see the membership lists and undertook to give reasons for their decisions in cases where Trekmaats would not be admitted to the AB.[125] In May of the same year, Verwoerd reported on the negotiations, stressing the urgency of "local handling of the youth".[126] Shortly afterwards, numerous AB departments started admitting Trekmaats to their ranks, issuing them with a questionnaire.[127] A UR commission, set up in August 1944 and chaired by Verwoerd, was to supervise the admission of Trekmaats members to the AB at local level, in direct contact with the AB departments and the Trekmaats. In this way, they sought to prevent undesirables from becoming members of the Broederbond; the number of members taken over by the AB amounted to about 130 at the final count.[128]

While the NP representatives had an easy time with Du Plessis, the purge of the AB leadership itself was a much more complicated affair that took several years to

---

123 Ibid., Agenda en Mededelings, UR, 29–30.1.1943, p. 3. J. G. Strijdom, leader of the NP in the Transvaal, lived in Nylstroom and was a member of the AB, albeit not a very active on. It is possible that he was involved in this decision, in order to assist his ally Verwoerd in the UR. Although Strijdom occasionally participated in the deliberations of the Bondsraad, he kept at a distance, and always insisted that the AB should not interfere in politics (B. M. Schoeman 1982: 11; see also Schoeman 1973: 20).
124 AB Archive, 2/3/10/2, Buitengewone U.R.-Vergadering, Bloemfontein 13.12.1943, p. 1, TOP 5, Trekmaats.
125 Ibid. U.R.–Dagbestuursvergadering, Johannesburg 22.2.1944, pp. 1–2, TOP 4, Trekmaats.
126 Ibid., UR Assembly, 5.–5.5.1944, p. 7, TOP 22, Trekmaats.
127 Ibid., Agenda for UR–Assembly on 18. and 19.8.1944, p. 4, TOP 20, Trekmaats. On individual cases, see also ibid. UR, 30.9.1944, pp. 2–3, TOP 7. Members of the Board of the Trekmaats attended the meeting.
128 Ibid., UR, 30.9.1944, Appendix A Die Trekmaats. Yet the selected Trekmaats had to submit to the usual admission procedures of the AB, which meant that they could still be rejected (ibid., Dagbestuur, 21.10.1944, p. 5, TOP 18, Trekmaats).

enact. Verwoerd led the attack against Trekmaats leaders Diederichs and Meyer, who held leadership positions in the UR (Chairman and Assistant Secretary).

Even during the Bondsraad in 1941, Meyer protested the rumours about office bearers of the Broederbond, which had been purposefully spread.[129] Diederichs stressed that the UR had in no way interfered in politics in favour of any party.[130] He also complained about an article of Verwoerd's on his resignation as a paid officer of the Reddingsdaadbond (RDB).[131] At the next Bondsraad, he failed to get elected; in his place, J. C. van Rooy, a compromise candidate acceptable to all concerned, was elected to the leadership post of the AB, which he would then hold for ten years.[132]

Meyer was dismissed from his position as Assistant Secretary of the UR, because he was not prepared to resign his leadership post in the OB.[133] From the end of 1942, he lost nearly all of his numerous posts in the Broederbond network, which he had systematically 'accumulated' since the late 1930s.[134] The ostracisation was effective: Meyer remained largely without influence until the mid-1950s, before he managed to stage a comeback in the Broederbond. Along with the disempowerment of Diederichs and Meyer, a more wide-ranging purge of the AB took place at the same time; it was noticeable how many members were issued with warnings and expulsions.[135]

---

[129] AB Archive, 2/3/10/1, Bondsraad, 6.10.1941 in Bloemfontein, p. 2, TOP 8, Praatjes teen amptenaaare.
[130] Ibid., TOP 13, A.B. en Partypolitiek.
[131] Ibid., Dagbestuur meeting, 1.12.1941, p. 2, TOP 11, Verklaring in sake Uittrede van Dr. N. Diederichs.
[132] Ibid., Bondsraad, 2.–3.10.1942, p. 4, TOP 16, Prosedure in sake U.R.-verkiesing. For the first time, direct proposals from individual sections were tabled, demanding that certain persons should no longer stand as candidates; see also p. 6, TOP 19 and 20 on the candidates and the result of the election of the Chairman. Diederichs was voted in as Deputy; the other UR-members were re-elected, but du Plessis did not have any allies. One year later, it was not Diederichs who was elected as Deputy, but NP-politician Dönges (ibid., Bondsraad, 13.–14.12.1943, p. 7, TOP 20, Verkiesing van Ondervoorsitter). The 1943 election was obviously rigged, for van Rooy presented a speech as Chairman, which he could only have prepared with the prior knowledge that he would step into this position.
[133] Ibid., Dagbestuur, 3.12.1942, p. 1, TOP 5, Skrywe br. Hulpsekretaris; see also UR, 29.–30.1.1943, pp. 2–3, TOP 12, Koördinering van Organisasies, discussing Meyer's resignation; see also ibid., Agenda en Mededelings, UR 29.–30.1.1943, pp. 2–3, TOP 10, Koördinering van Organisasies, where the correspondence with Meyer is being cited at length. Verwoerd had initiated the confrontation with an editorial in Die Transvaler of 30.3.1942, in which he personally targeted Meyer. P. J. Meyer (1984: 21) dates his resignation as Hoofsekretaris of the FAK to 1943; but the files of the AB clearly give the date of his resignation as end of 1942.
[134] PV 451/4/1/169, Diary 1942–1944, pp. 113–114. Thus, Meyer was, among other things, Secretary of the Afrikaanse Nasionale Kultuurraad and of the Instituut vir Volkswelsyn (PV 202/2/1/1/1, Letter by Cronjé to Meyer with an offer, 23.7.1939, and its acceptance). See also Marx 2008: 426.
[135] AB Archive, 2/3/10/1, UR meeting, 3.–4.9.1943, p. 3.

Once the Party line had been pushed through, the victors preached unity. UR member Dönges even went as far as advocating the opening of the Party to English-speaking whites. Albert Hertzog could not refrain from a caustic comment, in consideration of the fact that Dönges and Verwoerd were regarded as staunch sticklers for principles and hence as prime splitters:

> It was strange to hear these views after he and his friends had chased away and scolded tens of thousands of Afrikaners in recent years, and with so much spite. And it was especially funny to see Verwoerd take the attitude at the meeting, making out as if he approved of everything Dönges said – the very same Verwoerd who caused the great rupture in Afrikanerdom, when it was actually he who was the main force driving Father [General Hertzog] out of the National Party, and when it was he who once again ran up a hate-filled storm against the OB. It struck me all the more that when Verwoerd came to the Transvaal and I saw him again a short while afterwards, he was the old Verwoerd again, the centrifugal force that drives out all Afrikaners.[136]

At the Bondsraad in 1943, the UR held back on statements concerning "*volks*-unity", and instead left it at general comments. However, this did not stop the need for discussion; even a year later, a commission was still busy trying to draft a resolution on "*volks*-unity".[137] Its proposals on how the UR should conduct itself in concrete terms did not go beyond general appeals to the warring factions.[138] The leadership succeeded in preventing the adoption of any resolution by the Bondsraad, and any renewed mediation effort.[139] It refrained from launching a unitary movement again,[140] especially since the 1943 elections had, in the meantime, firmly installed the HNP as the only political representation of Afrikaner nationalism, while the other groups and parties had weakened considerably. The issue came up again and again, right up to the immediate post-war period; but the Party representatives pre-empted any move to rope the AB in again.

The Post-War Period

While Verwoerd showed little commitment to an emergency aid collection for the Netherlands, he was all the more eager to pursue such action for Germany after

---

[136] PV 451/4/1/169, Diary 1942–1944, p. 36.
[137] AB Archive, 2/3/10/2, Bondsraad, 2.–3.10.1944, TOP 9, Volkseenheid en Eenheid binne die A.B.
[138] Ibid., pp. 11–13, TOP 30, Volkseenheid en Eenheid binne die A.B.
[139] Ibid., p. 13, TOP 32, Volkseenheid.
[140] Ibid., UR meeting, 1.–2.2.1945, p. 11, TOP 43, Volkseenheid.

the end of World War II.[141] In August, he even tabled an urgent motion that the UR should deal with the threat of forced repatriation of German families from South Africa.[142] Because of the precarious demographic ratio of English- and Afrikaans-speaking whites, white immigration was a perennial issue for Afrikaner nationalists.[143] But Verwoerd dismissed the idea of setting targets on immigration that would change the demographic situation of whites vis-à-vis the black majority. The issue was discussed in the Broederbond during the immediate post-war period, when a wave of emigration from Britain reached the white dominions and the US. The proposal to support increased immigration from Europe was parried by Verwoerd with the remark "that the absorptive capacity of the Afrikaners is not sufficiently capacious under present conditions, which is why most immigrants become anglicised."[144]

After the War, the Danie Theron branch of the Broederbond in Pretoria, which was close to the far-right OB, instigated a discussion about the future aims of the secret society; for its part, it advocated a more "socialist" orientation along the lines of the OB Labour Front. In the course of the discussion, Verwoerd did not address the socialist orientation, but re-framed the problem of social divergences raised by P. J. Meyer as an ethnic-cultural conflict, referring to "British-Jewish capitalism" and of the perils of materialism as culturally subversive force.[145]

---

[141] Ibid., UR meeting, 11.–12.5.1945, p. 1, TOP 3, Dringende voorstelle (a); see also p. 2, TOP 7: "Br. Verwoerd demands that there should not only be a call to provide emergency aid to Holland, but that assistance should also be given by the Afrikaner *volk* to Germany." AB Archive 2/3/11, The UR took up the theme again in its meeting on 10.-11.8.1945, issuing circular letters calling for donations for Germany, and suggesting this also to the churches (p. 2 TOP 11, Noodlening aan stamverwante lande). Some members of the Bondsraad also advocated plans to bring German orphans to South Africa (ibid., Bondsraad, 26.–27.9.1945, p. 4, TOP 8, 'Noodlening aan stamverwante lande'; see also UR Meeting 14.2.1946, pp. 6–7, TOP 30, 'Duitsers in Suid-Afrika', dealing especially with propaganda for the relase of German internees). However, Verwoerd's sympathies were with Germany rather than with the country of his birth. That would explain why "republican" that he was, he refused to send a message to Wilhelmina, Queen of the Netherlands – a "foreign royal house" – on her abdication of the throne (AB Archive, 2/3/15, UR meeting, 11.–12.6.1948, p. 5, TOP 25, Adres aan Konigin Wilhelmina). On Verwoerd's attitude towards Germany and the Netherlands, see D. Prinsloo 1979: 510–514. During the War years, his children said prayers before going to sleep, "for the poor little children in Germany" (A. Boshoff 1974: 42). See also Dommisse 2005: 168; but also Terblanche 2001: 229 on the condemnation of the German invasion of the Netherlands.
[142] AB Archive, 2/3/11, UR meeting, 10.–11.8.1945, p. 1, TOP 3, Dringende voorstelle.
[143] PV 202/1/7/8/4/1, Immigrasie-Komitee of the Ekonomiese Instituut. Diederichs was the Director, and L. J. du Plessis Chairman, 7.6.1952; 4.3.1955, Maatskappy vir europese immigrasie, which included Mönnig, P. J. Meyer and others. Meyer was elected Chairman.
[144] AB Archive, 2.3.11, UR meeting, 14.2.1946, p. 8, TOP 37, Immigrasie.
[145] Ibid., UR meeting, 16.–17.8.1946, p. 4, TOP 16, Die Toekomstaak en Reorganisasie van die A.B. See also Stals 1998: 181–182.

The UR instructed a commission to delineate the future task of the Broederbond. In the face of the decolonisation process that was getting underway, the commission demanded that the Broederbond concentrate on the racial problems in their own country.[146] Verwoerd, too, saw the future task of the AB as "fighting firstly against a cultural crisis [*"kultuurnood"*], and secondly, against economic hardship. Now it is confronted with the fear of white people in South Africa being ploughed under. This problem, of course, includes the Indian question and the question of immigration." This, he said, is where the AB's main tasks lay, namely in the effective realisation of cultural nationalism, the elimination of the "Poor White Problem", and in the implementation of apartheid policies. Even if white civilisation could be saved, another danger was lurking – the possibility that Afrikaners could come entirely under the influence of "British-Jewish capitalism", which could lead to the destruction of the *"volks*-life".[147]

"Hereniging"

After the War, van Rensburg tried to gain a stronger foothold for the OB in the cities, in forming a "Labour Front" and announcing his own "Parliamentary Front".[148] Both of these initiatives remained largely unsuccessful. Strijdom observed that in 1944, the OB was losing ground in the countryside as well.[149] Malan thought the time had come to issue a circular calling on Party officials to convince all Party members who simultaneously held OB membership, to break with the OB because of its continued hostile activities.[150] Verwoerd was more sceptical about the decline of the OB; many OB-members were lying low, but this did not

---

146 Ibid., UR, 9./10.5.1946, Aanhangsel, Re–Organisasie van AB, Deel II, pp. 1–3. The Bondsraad, which met 3–5 October in Bloemfontein, rejected the division proposed by the UR, especially the creation of a category of Assessor-Broeder (ibid., UR, Johannesburg 16.–17.8.1946, p. 5, resolutions (a); AB 2/3/12, Bondsraad, 3.-5. October 1946, Bloemfonein, p. 4, TOP 12, Reorganisasie van die A.B).
147 AB Archive, 2/3/11, UR, Johannesburg 16.–17.8.1946, p. 4.
148 Malan–Collection 1/1/2130, Notes of a speech presented by van Rensburg in Pretoria, beginning of 1944, see covering letter by Verwoerd to Malan, 8.8.1944. See also Marx 2008: 468–473.
149 PV 93/1/56/1, f. 13, Letter by Strijdom to Verwoerd, 22.8.1944.
150 PV 93/1/1/1, f. 34, circular letter by Malan, 10.11.1944. But Verwoerd's former colleague Erika Theron did, for some time, serve as general in the women's division of the OB in the Cape Province (E. Theron 1983: 41ff); M.E. Rothmann and her daughter Anna also were members of the OB, as late as 1944 (55 K.T. (3), Letter by M.E. Rothmann to Ida Theron, 27.6.1944). Nevertheless, as early as 1930, before their trip to Europe, Rothmann cautioned Erika Theron against the Germans: "They are also snobs and imperialists, and look down on the Afrikaners." (55. K.T (1), Letter by M. E. Rothmann to E. Theron, 7.4.1930).

mean that they had switched their allegiance to the NP.[151] When he got hold of an internal report by van Rensburg's deputy, which revealed the desolate state of the OB, he suggested to Strijdom to publish it immediately, in order to put an end to any reconciliation efforts.[152] Similarly, he rejected peace offers by individual OB officials because he thought they left the OB too much leeway.[153]

Since the NP's prospects of winning the election on its own did not look all too good, it went in search of possible alliance partners with whom it could reach election deals and thus improve the chances of its candidates. Thus, there were secret negotiations between the HNP and a group of politicians from the "communist-infiltrated Labour Party"[154] around Walter Madeley; but the negotiations failed due to the Madeley group's demands for funding.[155]

At the beginning of the 1940s, the dispute between the NP and the OB, as well as small right-wing extremist groups such as the Nuwe Orde (NO) had foiled the project of *"volks-unity"*. Before the 1948 elections, however, the conflict shifted; now the Broederbond made efforts to bring the NP and the Afrikaner Party together, to form an electoral alliance. Albert Hertzog, who entertained good contact with his father's erstwhile follower and successor Havenga, was the first one to raise the issue – and the UR found that the time was right. It proposed a meeting between Malan and Havenga to explore the possibility of talks.[156] In fact, these consultations took place at Dönges's home in Cape Town; the outcome was an electoral arrangement that was to facilitate the 1948 electoral victory. But even these proposals met with misgivings, opposition, and fierce resistance from Strijdom and Verwoerd, for they rightly suspected the OB behind the resurrection of the AP, which was clearly in decline at that stage. They sensed van Rensburg's political ambitions; but the latter showed only resignation.[157]

---

151 PV 93/1/56/1, f. 14, Letter by Verwoerd to Strijdom, 29.8.1944.
152 PV 93/1/56/1, f. 47, Letter by Verwoerd to Strijdom, 28.11.1946. See also Malan-Collection 1/1/2246, Letter by Verwoerd to Malan, 28.11.1946, with appended report by Smith.
153 See Verwoerd's handwritten notes, written from memory, on a meeting with OB-General Louis Bootha, which had been convened at his request (PV93/1/1/3, undated notes).
154 PV 18/4/1/1, Verkiesings Manifes 1948, p. 3.
155 PV2.1.56, f. 90, Letter by Jan de Klerk to F. C. Erasmus, 16.4.1948: "We did negotiate again with the Madeley Group. Concerning the mandates, we managed to reach agreement, but they also want money from us." See also PV 2/1/76, f. 31, Telegram 1.4.1948 and f. 32, Letter by De Klerk to F. C. Erasmus, 2.4.1948; the Labour Party demanded a number of seats which the NP thought it had good chances to win; so they could not reach agreement. Verwoerd had become aware of this; the whole affair was suspect to him, as he presumed that Pirow and others were behind it (PV 93/1/56/1, Letter by Verwoerd to Strijdom, 15.4.1946).
156 AB Archive, 2/3/13, UR, 22.–23.1.1947, p. 4, TOP 20, Gees van toenadering.
157 See Marx 2008: 542–545.

While the Cape NP and its sister parties in the OFS[158] and in Natal supported the agreement with the Afrikaner Party, Strijdom opposed it. What he articulated as "principle" was in reality a power struggle between the Party and the OB that had been going on since 1941. Havenga, in collusion with van Rensburg, had only been able to reactivate his defunct party by letting OB members join his party in droves. Neither Havenga nor Malan had concluded any clear agreements with the OB regarding their political stance. Malan did not negotiate with van Rensburg, but had so much confidence in Havenga that he believed his assurances – and was proven right. Strijdom, on the other hand, was filled with deep mistrust; until shortly before the election, he feared that the OB could make a kind of parliamentary comeback.[159] This apprehension was fuelled not least by the fact that local OB leaders, in order to save face, tried to force the NP candidates into agreements in which they officially recognised the OB as partner-organisation; failing which they threatened the NP candidates with an election boycott. In the Brakpan constituency, the OB almost succeeded in getting its own candidate, John Vorster, elected, and in obtaining the support of the local NP.

Despite the staunch resistance of Strijdom and Verwoerd, Malan received approval from the Party's Federal Council for the way in which he conducted the negotiations, and for the outcome of the negotiations. Strijdom tried to make the best of the situation by introducing a resolution calling on the AP to unite with the HNP as soon as possible, to get the OB to dissolve, to withdraw from politics, and to abandon its anti-democratic aims.[160]

It was probably not only for tactical and journalistic reasons that Verwoerd refused to print articles of the NP's Information Bureau; he more likely wanted to include them in the news sections as he saw fit.[161] Similarly, he rejected the request to report on the OB's rapprochement with the AP in *Die Transvaler*. He stressed that it was his decision to consistently ignore the OB that had contributed

---

158 In September 1960, Swart wrote a letter to the publisher of Malan's autobiography and to historian and journalist G. D. Scholtz, defending himself against accusations by Malan, who alleged that Swart had spoken up against the agreement with Havenga (PV 18/3/1/65, Letter by Swart to Nasionale Boekhandel, 1.12.1960 and with similar wording to Scholtz, 5.12.1960). PV 18/3/1/66, Letter by Nasionale Boekhandel to Swart, 9.2.1961 on the agreement that Malan's autobiography would state the facts correctly, and Swart's reply of 15.2.1961.
159 PV 18/3/1/53, Letter by Strijdom to Swart, 19.4.1948. Strijdom blamed the "demoralisation" in their own ranks – as he called the preparedness to make concessions to the OB – on Malan and the latter's agreement with Havenga. D. Prinsloo (1979: 150–151) outlines the differences between pragmatic and compromising Malan and principled, consistent Verwoerd, regarding their understanding of politics. On the general picture, see J. L. Basson 1980: 520–547.
160 PV 18/2//1/3, Minutes of the Federal Council of the NP, 21.5.1947, p. 2.
161 PV 93/1/1/1, f. 47, Letter by Verwoerd to P. W. Botha, 10.7.1947.

to its downfall.¹⁶² Moreover, he said, reporting positively on the OB would only provide ammunition to political opponents who might imply that the NP had an affinity with National Socialism. It was Havenga's task to publicly demand the dissolution of the OB, "because it is completely illogical for people to join a democratic party, when they are at the same time members of a political organisation with completely opposite aims".¹⁶³

According to Verwoerd and others, the future of Afrikaners lay in the cities, and thus primarily on the Witwatersrand. Therefore, if the NP wanted to win a national election, it had to focus on the cities. Although this idea had already spread far and wide, and had been elevated to a strategic priority after 1943, its practical implementation was limited. By 1946, hardly any parliamentarians felt the need to become active in supporting a by-election in the West Rand constituency.[164] Instead, they joined OB representatives and the leader of the fascist Greyshirts in their appearances at certain events, even though this was against the orders of the Party leadership.[165] One year later, the situation had not improved, as the Party had obviously failed to organise and target Afrikaans-speaking mine workers as future voters.[166] Meanwhile Verwoerd had attained such a prominent position within the NP that the various constituencies of the Party had approached him with the request to stand for elections.[167] However, disagreement arose over his candidacy and that of other Party leaders; Party leader on the Witwatersrand, Ben Schoeman, stood accused of "dictatorial behaviour" in pushing through individual candidacies.[168] In fact, Schoeman was an avowed opponent of Verwoerd; Schoeman deeply distrusted Verwoerd on account of his lust for power. The tension between them only eased

---

162 FAV, 4.5.1.7, Letter by Verwoerd to E. Louw, 29.7.1943. "This tactic of silencing was possible only because we had previously worked so hard to enlighten our people. As far as I am concerned, we can continue with this silencing, because they don't have any energy left. I just hope that we will not have to deal with charitable attempts at rapprochement and kind offerings again." See also P. W. Coetzer 1994: 576–577.
163 PV 93/1/1/1, f. 39, Letter by Verwoerd to P. W. Botha, 22.4.1947. M. E. Rothmann was unhappy about van Rensburg's rapprochement with the AP and the NP, because she saw it as a deviation from the correct line (55.K.T. (14), Letter by Verwoerd to E. Theron, 13.6.1952).
164 PV 2/1/55, Letter by Ben Schoeman to J. G. Strijdom, 12.4.1946.
165 Ibid., f. 64, Letter by P. J. Steyl, Assistant Secretary to Dr. S. J. Swanepoel, Pretoria, 6.9.1946, and f. 87, Letter by Steyl to Sekr. HNP–Hoofkantoor, 11.11.1946 on Dr. N. J. van Nierop, who had also appeared together with the Greyshirts.
166 Ibid., J. A. Louw to L. J. Rautenbach, Secretary of the Transvaal NP, 23.3.1947.
167 PV 2/1/56, f. 54, Letter by Jan de Klerk to Adv. A. J. van Zyl, Chief Executive of Voortrekker Pers, 27.11.1947. Apparently there were still some obstacles concerning Verwoerd's work contract that had to be cleared.
168 PV 2/1/56, Memorandum to the Chairman of the HNP Witwatersrand (without mentioning any names), 11.10.1946.

when Verwoerd became Prime Minister and decided to keep Schoeman in the government, as he was influential in the Party, and very efficient as cabinet minister.[169]

Because of Verwoerd's hostility to the OB, its members boycotted the election in Verwoerd's constituency of Alberton, making sure that the UP candidate won with a small majority and Verwoerd lost out.[170] However, the two allied parties of Malan and Havenga won a narrow majority of five seats over the previous governing parties, with seventy and nine mandates, respectively. The result of the 1948 parliamentary elections surprised all sides, not least the alliance partners NP and AP. Although the UP garnered the most votes nationwide, it received only a minority of the mandates, due to the constituency-based system of direct elections. In the election campaign, Verwoerd had presented himself as a representative of ordinary people, referring to his expertise as former professor of Sociology and co-organiser of the Kimberley Congress.[171] However, his allies in the Party were powerful and Verwoerd was, after all, a member of the Federal Council, the highest structure within the Party. After a futile attempt to sideline Verwoerd by appointing him to the post of ambassador in the Netherlands,[172] Malan relented and supported the feisty editor's candidacy for election to the Senate.[173]

---

[169] Ben Schoeman 1978: 62–63, and 67ff, 76, 81. For Schoeman, Verwoerd's election to Senate had "the advantage that he had to step down from his position as editor of *Die Transvaler*" (ibid, p. 160).

[170] See FAV 4.5.1.6, Letter by Ben Schoeman to Verwoerd, 4.6.1948, on the election results. See also Prinsloo 1979: 105–106.

[171] FAV 4.5.2.2, Parliamentary Election 1948. Alberton Constituency.

[172] FAV 4.5.1.6, Letter by Verwoerd to Malan, 14.7.1948, rejecting the offer.

[173] D. Prinsloo 1979: 109–110; Government Gazette of 30.7.1948 with the list of elected and appointed senators. On Verwoerd's membership of the Federale Raad, see PV 54/2/2, Minutes of the Federale Raad, list of members present, 2.11.1948, and all subsequent meetings. In the minutes of the meetings from 5.6.1954 Verwoerd appears under the list of delegates from the Transvaal. Verwoerd was furious about the fact that Malan did not include him in the Cabinet (Ben Schoeman 1978: 148).

Chaos and Order

While the Transvaal Afrikaner nationalists in particular invoked a more strongly articulated dichotomy of chaos and order that found its justification in Calvinist fundamentalism,[1] Verwoerd's idea of order was accompanied by an intolerance of ambiguity: the idea that order could dissolve was unbearable to him.[2] The significance of his intolerance of ambiguity manifested itself even physically, as his wife's secretary, Anna Boshoff, recalls: "His meticulousness was well known. We often saw him adjust a picture that was skew, or a chair that was out of place, or an ornament that was not in the right place."[3] Obviously, this was of existential significance to him, since the opposition of chaos and order, the horror of dissolution, fundamentally shaped Verwoerd's thoughts and actions. His daughter Anna reported: "In his view, the systematic execution of work or the orderliness of a person, of a room, or of behaviour all resulted from a well-ordered world of thought."[4]

Verwoerd's obsession with order is clearly noticeable even at the beginning of his academic career. The example of his lecture on character studies shows how incisively his need for clarity and his intolerance of ambiguity marked his academic work. In his lecture, he went to great lengths in expounding differential psychology along with the study of character, and to present its methods and the basic positions. Victorian notions of character with positive and masculine connotations set a continuum between 'strength of character' and 'weakness of character', for the latter of which poverty, and a tendency to alcoholism and criminality were taken as indications. With the professionalisation of psychology, a new interest in 'objective' standards for character assessments emerged. Various psychologists designed typologies that went beyond the simple dichotomies of strong vs. weak.

During his stay in Germany, Verwoerd had been able to observe this heightened interest in character psychology. It was a central theme among the Leipzig Holistic Psychologists, especially Klemm.[5] William Stern's differential psychology in particular left a lasting impression on Verwoerd. The proximity of differential psychology to developmental psychology was related to the idea that differences between people were set in early childhood. Significantly, Stern himself did not follow the move from differential psychology to characterology; on the contrary,

---

[1] The opposition of chaos and order, however, was also found in self–proclaimed fascists such as Le Grange, who published a book about it (Le Grange 1944).
[2] Like many Afrikaners at the time, Verwoerd was an authoritarian personality with an obsessive character (van der Spuy 1978: 6).
[3] A. Boshoff 1974: 39.
[4] W. Verwoerd 2001: 70.
[5] Krueger 1939:62. On Spranger see also the research overview by Selz 1924b: 8f.

he even warned against it, stressing that personality, which was his central concept, did not merge completely with type.[6] Even if his stance on characterology remained ambivalent, the heuristic value of an intermediate stage between general psychological laws and individual manifestations was obvious to him. A major factor that allowed for classification as we find it for example in applied psychology, was the ascription of certain manifestations to groups of individuals. An element was singled out as the central basic trait of a person, which was thought to decisively determine the person; this is what gave rise to talk of 'character'. On the one hand, this resulted in a variety of possibilities for characterological classification; on the other hand, it also was cause for caution for most authors who highlighted the fact that their classifications could not really do justice to the person in each individual case.

Even before his stay in Europe, as a young lecturer, Verwoerd had been interested in the subject; but in 1924, he was still strongly inclined to develop the early modern temperament theory with a tendency toward characterology, as it had been formulated by Dutch philosopher and psychologist Gerard Heymans (1857–1930) and his student Henri J. F. W. Brugmans (1884–1961) in Groningen.[7] In his lectures, Verwoerd examined the various explanatory approaches and methods, which resulted in the publication of two essays presenting his own new approach.

First, he dealt with the value of tests.[8] Tests are not examinations of individuals; they address the same questions to numerous individuals whose responses are compared with each other. Similarly to laboratory studies, they have to isolate a few variables, that is, undertake a massive reduction in complexity, in order to arrive at valid results. It is precisely this factor that explains why a scientist like Stern, who moved from differential psychology to personality psychology, viewed such tests with considerable and, over time, with increasing scepticism. Verwoerd was similarly critical of the value of tests, but for reasons different from those of Stern. Tests investigated behaviour in a specific situation, and they were also to explore basic inclinations and motives; but the test methods used so far were not ade-

---

6 Stern 1911: 4–5, 169. Significantly, Stern then tried to free psychology from its all too "nomothetic", i.e. scientific, orientation and to give it an additional idiographic direction: "Psychography must step alongside psychology proper: Representation of individualities according to their psychological side." (ibid., 5, 136–139, and 3rd main part, ch. 21).
7 PV 93/1/33/3, p. 108ff, dated 1.9.1924. Two years later, he visited Brugmans in Groningen (FAV 4.3.2, Verwoerd's diary, 15/16.4.1926).
8 While Wilcocks and some of his colleagues were already working out job aptitude tests in the 1920s, Verwoerd does not seem to have been involved in them (see M. Scholtz 2002: 30. 198).

quate to the latter task. Looking at various tests, Verwoerd came to the conclusion that "nothing useful has as yet been achieved in this difficult field".[9] In none of them had it yet been proven that it was really stable character traits that were being tested in this way; the possibility remained that the tests produced snapshots of a certain condition of the test person.[10] Even though Verwoerd remained fundamentally sceptical, he adhered to the testing protocols and procedures, especially in their practical application, when it came to selecting persons for certain activities. This approach was shared by numerous other social scientists.[11]

Psychophysical theories sought to explain the emergence of a psychological personality in terms of instincts. Citing an example, Verwoerd referred to American physician and psychologist Morton Prince (1854–1929), who was primarily concerned with neurological questions and with so-called "abnormal psychology". According to Verwoerd, instincts were "innate psycho-physiological structures on the basis of which a person pays attention to particular subjects or contents", that is, the associations are innate.[12] It is only as modifying elements that experiences find their way into the knowledge of man, defined as an instinct-driven being.[13] Some biologists, on the other hand, looked for an organic basis, which was supposed to be found in various bodily glands, for instance in the thyroid gland.[14] Verwoerd's evaluation of instincts as glandular functions clearly revealed his scepticism towards biological explanations.[15]

He then turned to the human science of psychology, especially the character typology of Eduard Spranger. Spranger's fields of specialisation, psychology of adolescence and characterology, were close to his own interests, which is why he attended two of Spranger's seminars at Berlin University in 1926. Spranger was not concerned with the aggregation of certain character traits, but with personality as a self-contained unit, which brought him close to Stern's personality psychology, despite all methodological and ideological differences. In his own lectures in Stellenbosch, Verwoerd expounded on Spranger's division into different character types.

For Spranger, the tried and tested way was to differentiate the cultural products, and to draw inferences from them about their producers. His culturalist method was analogous to that of Wundt's ethnopsychology. Spranger identified six cultural arenas, and correlated them with six character types: Science, art, re-

---

9 PV 93/1/33/3, f. 55, Persoonlikheidstoetse, p. 7.
10 Ibid., pp. 7–8.
11 Fleisch 1995: 357–360.
12 PV 93/1/33/3, B. 77, Die Grondslag waarop die psigiese persoonlikheid berus, p. 1.
13 Ibid, pp. 2–3.
14 For instance also Kretschmer 1922: 188.
15 PV 93/1/33/3, B. 75, Die Grondslag waarop die psigiese persoonlikheid berus, pp. 3–8.

ligion, economy, society, and state.[16] In his view, there were people whose values manifested themselves in dedicated pursuits of any one of these arenas. But they always coexisted with pursuits to realise other values. "For Spranger, these aspirations to power, and to values like the theoretical, the religious, and the aesthetic, among other things, are orders of value that form persons with a certain personality. This is what gives the personality unity and structure."[17] The types developed by Spranger were admittedly constructs – "six basic types of the whole personality", namely the theoretical, the aesthetic, the religious, the economic, the social, and the political type. "Now these may well be ideals or pure types, constructed and not found in reality. To [Spranger], their value lies in the fact that they can serve as standards by which we can decipher the meaning of what individuals try to do in daily life, namely the pursuit of whatever value or words or goals are expressed in them, perhaps even unbeknown to themselves."[18]

Verwoerd found Spranger's division convincing; he adopted the construction of characters to elaborate certain basic features. In a public lecture, he spoke about the "theoretical personality": "theoretical type of person perceives book otherwise than economic".[19] While the theoretical person is entirely committed to the search for truth, and to abstract, coherent intellectual constructs, the economic person is motivated by considerations of utility.[20] The other character types are just as one-sided; thus, in Verwoerd's reading of Spranger, the "social man" is certified as being primarily driven by love for other people, and the "political man" is equated with the man of power. Verwoerd adduced these examples in his lectures, without being critical of such one-sidedness in Spranger, presumably because Spranger's typology addressed his own need for clear-cut categories and unambiguous classifications, and thus met with his approval.

At the end of his lectures, Verwoerd summed up the range of different character-typological approaches. "In describing a type, usually [only] certain basic traits are taken into account, which are called typical because they occur in a number of people."[21] A typology would not be possible at all if one tried to include

---

16 See also the account in Hoffmann 1926: 3–7.
17 PV 93/1/33/3, f. 105, Indeling volgens Spranger, pp. 1–2.
18 Ibid, p. 2. Here it also becomes clear that Verwoerd had not read Max Weber; these are obviously ideal types in Weber's sense of the term.
19 FAV 4.4.6, Notes in English on 'Personality' (n.d.), in which he also referred to Kretschmer's theses without critical commentary.
20 Interestingly, for Spranger the pragmatic philosophy of, say, William James or Charles Sanders Peirce would not be a genuine theory or philosophy. This indicates that Spranger himself was strongly rooted in the German intellectual tradition. Similarly, liberalism could not be a genuine form of politics for him (see PV 93/1/33/3, f. 100, Indeling volgens Spranger, p. 6).
21 PV 93/1/33/3, f. 84, 'Persoonlikheidstiepes volgens Jung en Kretschmer', p. 8.

all the traits of a personality, but here only certain basic traits would be emphasised. Nevertheless, they would have a value in that they helped to understand people better, because one got "an indication of a normal personality if one can say to which type, in the various classifications, the respective person corresponds. This would possibly allow one to direct attention to the central personality schemes and motives."[22]

The problem with the various typologies lay in their diversity, even if all of them could be justified.[23] Verwoerd developed his thoughts on a unification of character typologies in two essays published shortly afterwards, in 1930, in the *South African Journal of Science*. In these articles, he systematised his findings and indicated procedures for measuring personality traits objectively. He aimed at nothing less than extracting a universally binding typology from the various typologies he found in the psychological literature.

First of all, he found that all procedures, including those of hereditary biology, as well as tests, were ultimately based purely on assumptions, i.e. they were not at all as objective as they purported to be. Ultimately, they relied on the experience of the psychologist adducing them – that is, the procedures remained subjective to a certain extent.

In a short article entitled 'Oor die persoonlikheid van die mens en die beskrywing daarvan' ['On the human personality and its description'] (1930) Verwoerd critically noted that the psychological terminology was blurred, leaving each scientist to either use his own or to apply an extant one in highly idiosyncratic ways, so that there could hardly be two researchers who would understand the same terms in the same way. This gave rise not so much to misunderstandings as to a general lack of clarity on the part of the reader, as to what he was dealing with. Verwoerd set out to systematise personality psychology and thus to establish the necessary clarity. He sought to capture regularities in people's conscious life and behaviour through the concept of "personality".[24] This, in turn, could be characterised only on the basis of regularities for which Verwoerd proposed the concept of "personality traits". Accordingly, the human personality could be broken down into the following personality traits: Everything to do with the will was subsumed under the concept of "character", while emotional life was assigned to "temperament", and thought processes to the concept of "intelligence". "The intelligence of a person is thus a descriptive term indicating a certain regularity in intellectual processes. The means by which intelligence is described, in turn, are

---

22 Ibid, p. 8.
23 Ibid, p. 9.
24 Verwoerd 1930a: 578.

characteristics or traits, such as stupidity or cleverness or profundity, etc."[25] Verwoerd's definition of intelligence differed markedly from its common understanding as a measurable faculty; his version was more comprehensive, since the perceptive faculty manifests itself in intellectual processes exceeding the testable faculties.[26] As a fourth term, Verwoerd introduced 'behaviour' into the series of the four categories that he believed constituted the human personality – temperament, character, intelligence and behaviour. The various personality traits could be assigned to these categories; such a grid, he thought, would bring greater clarity to psychological terminology. He therefore demanded that the terms be clearly defined in every instance, so that in the long run, a "uniformity in the use" by each individual psychologist would become entrenched.[27] Nevertheless, each time terms such as "dishonesty" were used, it was necessary to clarify what it was specifically about, for instance theft or plagiarism, so that these traits could then be assigned to one of the four categories.[28] A further step was that of examining the relationships of these personality traits to each other, starting with individual cases, in order to be able to work out certain patterns.

In the second essay, 'Oor die opstel van objektiewe persoonlikheidsbepalingskemas' ['On the development of objective personality assessment schemes'], he went a step further in an attempt to render the procedures objective. The two short essays were related to each other in terms of content; it was not coincidental that they were published directly following one another in the same edition of the *South African Journal of Science*. Adducing the conclusion from the first essay, Verwoerd suggested constructing experimental situations for the assessment of persons in such a way that they allowed comparability, for instance of different applicants for the same job. Here his own experience with laboratory experiments came into play; variables were reduced in order to ensure comparability. This was not possible for selection procedures, yet a basis for the comparability of test subjects had to be created. In such a set-up, Verwoerd wanted to have a certain number of psychologist-assessors (10) assess a certain number (100) of applicants. The situation was deemed comparable if a significantly high number of assessors, say nine assessors, assessed a significantly high number of applicants, say 99 applicants, in the same way.[29] He thus assumed that comparability had to reach a very high level of statistical probability if it was to be considered objective. In this way, the decisive step was taken: the assessor could be largely eliminated as a subjective

---

25 Ibid., 579.
26 Stern 1920: 145.
27 Verwoerd 1930a: 579.
28 Ibid., 580.
29 Verwoerd 1930b: 584. See also 231/2/2, 'Metodes van sociologiese navorsing', p. 78.

person. Thus, a test procedure could be developed that was transferable and could achieve objective results. The procedure developed by the ten psychologists could then be adopted and applied by others. In this way, the four categories identified in the first paper, along with their respective terms designating individual characteristics, were to form a coherent system and become generally binding. During his stay in Germany, Verwoerd had repeatedly criticised the testing procedures applied there as not being sufficiently objective. He sought to address this perceived inadequacy by developing his character-psychological classification grid.[30]

Despite individual differences between people, which Verwoerd by no means denied but understood as a methodological challenge for psychologists, the human personality could, in his view, be subdivided by the grid developed in the first essay, into a number of personality traits that could then be compared with each other. It was not people as individuals but as aggregates of personality traits that became comparable. Nevertheless, by breaking them down into personality traits, he wanted to achieve a decontextualisation that alone would make it possible to compare them.[31]

Verwoerd had committed himself to a science that claimed to be objective. Despite the fact that psychology borrowed its methods from the natural sciences, it considered itself in close proximity to the humanities. In their interpretations, psychologists based in the natural sciences vied with those based in the humanities. Thus, there was a constant tension between a claim to objectivity and its fulfilment, which proved to be near-impossible. Interestingly, Verwoerd did not take up the approaches of *Gestalt-* and Holistic Psychology. Instead, he turned to the approach that, in his view, had developed the most comprehensive explanatory models, namely Stern's personality psychology. It was this approach that he sought to develop so as to make it applicable to psychotechnics.

In his own scientific work, he had come to adopt a positivist approach, with putatively objective results. This indicated a basic trait in Verwoerd's thinking – namely an absolute confidence in the possibilities of science. If only the right method could be found, science would be able to dissect even the most complex

---

30 See also FAV 4.4.6, Psych. Tests as an Aid to Personnel Selection in Industry, handwritten notes for a lecture to an unnamed Econ. Soc. In these notes, he cited the testing procedures in various industrial companies in Europe, with an exclusive focus on the practical applicability of test procedures. See also ibid., 'Die Waarde en Gebruik van Beroepstoetse', setting out to systematically typify the various test procedures. See also Ehrenstein 1934: 147, albeit with uncritical reference to Kretschmer, p. 156. Others were much more sceptical as to whether typologies could be so clearly determined on the basis of empirical research results (Schmidt–Durban 1939: 81–83).
31 This kind of psychology was contradicted at the height of apartheid by C. K. Oberholzer, Heideggerising professor of Philosophy at the University of Pretoria (Oberholzer 1970:70), admittedly without knowing Verwoerd's essay.

interconnections, such as those constituting the human personality, and thus arrive at objective findings. Verwoerd was convinced that he could work with the basic units of the human personality that he had identified, namely the personality traits, in a completely logical and rational way. Of course, this also implied that one could manipulate people as soon as one had correctly, that is, objectively, seen through them. Only the desubjectification of science, behind whose reliable methods the scientist as a person was effaced, would allow the personality of the test subject to become recognisable as an aggregate of personality traits; then applied psychology would also be able to use these traits for specific ends. Behind the teeming visible world was the clear order of categories that the scientist only had to recognise in order to see through the world of phenomena. Of course, Verwoerd was deluded to seriously believe that binding categorisations could be imposed on all psychologists – and ultimately on all persons.[32] But the fact that he was convinced of this was characteristic of his thinking; he postulated an objective and universally valid truth.

In his essays, he went further than Stern, on whose work he otherwise based his personality psychology. He even took on board Stern's cautions against the apparent uniqueness of statistical data such as test results. Stern had placed personality at the centre of his psychology and thus demonstrated the limits of psychology as science. With all the ambitions of psychology, which he fulfilled and promoted in his own works, there always remained an unresolvable remainder – the "magic" of personality. Stern noted this without regret about the limits of his science; in fact, he affirmatively welcomed it from a humanistic and a conservative position. Verwoerd, in contrast, saw it as more of a challenge, namely as a task to be taken on, in order to overcome tenets of personality psychology as it stood at the time.

However, Verwoerd's psychodiagnostic schematism could hardly be applied in everyday life. Thus it is not surprising that his contemporaries considered him not a good judge of character. His metrically oriented psychology failed precisely in its applicability to everyday life, which is how he sought to justify it. His propensity for rendering human personalities 'readable' by isolating and measuring different aspects of their personality, such as emotions and intellect, made him a bad psychologist in social reality, as Diederichs attested: "His assessment of individuals was often wrong. He tended not to forget certain individuals who, in his opinion, violated principles he believed in. On the other hand, there were also cases in which he did the opposite – when, for example, he promoted former political opponents to cabinet members. All this can be understood only if one as-

---

[32] Hofstadter/Sander 2014:325–328.

sumes that it was not the individual, but the nation, to which he gave priority."[33] Piet Meiring was even more explicit: "Subtlety was never a prominent feature of Dr Verwoerd's behaviour, nor was knowledge of human nature."[34]

More significant than these biographical details, however, is the harping on orderliness evident in his theses and in his academic career, which found expression in the idea that people could be classified according to a number of characteristics. In his dissertation, Verwoerd sought to distinguish thoughts and feelings. In a similar way, he proposed to analyse human personalities through clear-cut categories of will, feeling, thought and behaviour, without taking sufficient account of the interdependencies and ambiguities of the concepts themselves.[35] Verwoerd knew no shades of grey; instead, he postulated unambiguous classifications relying on binary opposites, such as 'white' and 'non-white'.

Publicly speaking as a politician, Verwoerd frequently invoked the stark dichotomy between his own politics of order and the chaos that would ensue if one were to follow other political concepts. This juxtaposition was clearly propagandistic – an expression of a profoundly undemocratic consciousness that did not admit of any alternatives to its self-proclaimed politics. All possible political options were being reduced to two, thus presenting voters with another possibility that did not actually amount to an alternative. The contrasting possibilities were more than a matter of pure propaganda, however. Verwoerd and other apartheid politicians who argued in a similar vein were expressing their own fears of ambiguity.

In his role as a politician, Verwoerd tended to equate everything transgressing clear delimitations and certainties with chaos; the slightest inkling of a dissolution of order was intolerable to him. To him, communism fell into that category: it was the epitome of the dissolution of any order, of the transgression of all boundaries, of the destruction of all norms and values: "The communist states see their interests in creating chaos wherever they can."[36] Verwoerd did not tire of highlighting the worldwide danger of communism: "It is unfortunately true that, as a result of the diabolical machinations of agitators, there have been attacks on the lives of whites from time to time. . . . This is unfortunately a worldwide phenomenon. World communism is everywhere creating problems through various subversive activities."[37] It was not coincidental, he opined, that communism was atheistic;

---

33 Diederichs 1975: 5–6. Similarly, C. Bakkes, Piet Meiring and J. H. Abraham (D. Prinsloo 1979:10; also Meiring 1973b: 131).
34 Meiring 1990: 156. See also the survey of people who knew him well (*Rapport* 21.9.1975).
35 On the related fallacy pertaining to the notion that categories reflected reality, see Hofstadter/Sander 2014: 576.
36 FAV 4.7.2.4.5, Speech at the Natal NP Party Congress in Durban, 27.8.1963, p. 3.
37 PV 93/1/30/1/18, Letter by Verwoerd to Mrs G. Nothnagel, 25.2.1963, f. 38.

South African communists were decided opponents of racial segregation; the Eastern Bloc and especially the Soviet Union were pursuing the goal of overcoming the nation state, and thus represented the epitome of chaos. The Sharpeville massacre stood as a sign of the chaos to come. Since Verwoerd did not hold the police responsible for the massacre, but the organisers of the "insurrection"; it was easy for him to identify those whom he considered the real insurgents, namely communists,[38] the anti-communist orientation of the PAC notwithstanding. He pronounced his trust in the insight of the "mass of the Bantu" that it was better for them to work with white South Africans than with "foreign countries, which would result in conflict and chaos".[39] Here we are back at Verwoerd's principle of the national community, according to which humanity is divided into nations as a matter of a divinely ordained order.[40] He held this also to pertain to the post-colonial order in Africa. There were no real nation states on the African continent, he thought, only "immature" ones: "I think there will rather be chaos between competing states in Africa, born out of conflicting ambitions."[41] Only South Africa stood "unshaken" by the "chaos, poverty and internal strife which is overwhelming Africa".[42] In post-colonial Africa, only a few enjoyed privileges; "[f]or the masses socalled freedom has meant impoverishment, chaos and often death through famine and disorder."[43] Therefore, one of the greatest challenges for the person tasked with "maintaining the civilisational order" was to find his way amidst the "spiritual and moral chaos which daily threatens to over-

---

[38] "It is very clear that a communist-inspired mastermind is behind the riots, working according to a pre-prepared plan. Furthermore, it is also clear that the vast majority of the Bantu population is order-loving and not intent on any form of insurrection. However, this vast majority is not organised like the gangs of agitators and intimidators. [. . .] We will continue our defence of white civilisation in our interest and that of our descendants." (PV 93/1/36/1/2, Letter by Verwoerd to J. E. Pieterse (Denver), 7.4.1960). PV 93/1/36/1/7, Letter by Verwoerd (Private Secretary) to Rev. A. W. Blaxall (Roodepoort), 7.4.1960: "Through the action of agitators and intimidators a situation was created which did great harm to peace–loving and orderly Bantu people, as well as others. Through their actions they disrupted the lives and home life of men in the Police and Defence Force, and this disruption and discomfort and their separation from loved ones will continue till the situation so created has been satisfactorily ended and order restored." Even in the early 1950s, Phil Weber could only explain the resistance of the Coloureds to their political disenfranchisement with the work of communist agitators among them (296.K.GE 54, Letter by Weber to A. L. Geyer, 15.4.1951).
[39] Verwoerd, House of Assembly, 23.1.1962 (in Pelzer 1966: 660–689, 685–686).
[40] The belief of Afrikaner nationalists in a divine and perpetually given division of mankind into peoples displays striking parallels to the early psychology of peoples by Steinthal and Lazarus (Graevenitz 1999: 23–24, 34, 39–40).
[41] Verwoerd, House of Assembly, 9.3.1960 (in Pelzer 1966: 340–369, 363).
[42] PV 93/4/1/11, New Year's Message by the Prime Minister, 31.12.1964, ff. 279–283, 279.
[43] PV 93/1/30/1/30, Letter by Verwoerd to John Salmon (New York), 9.7.1965, f. 48.

whelm him".[44] There was a pseudo-morality that was only used as a cover by Christian and other critics of apartheid to pursue quite different goals. Here logic could help destroy the false pretence: "But we must try by logical thinking to tear away all the cloaks that hide the true facts."[45]

In the discourses of Afrikaner nationalists, the opposition of chaos and order is a recurring theme in widely differing contexts. While the statements of Verwoerd quoted here refer to the political independence of the former colonies, we find numerous oppositions of chaos and order in contemporary descriptions of the situation of newly urbanised Afrikaners and in diagnoses of cultural decay. As far as can be discerned, this opposition appeared from around the 1920s and probably has to do with the simultaneous rise of Calvinist fundamentalism. The opposite of order is 'chaos', which crops up with striking frequency in the contemporary literature, and in speeches and correspondence of Afrikaner nationalists. Chaos is defined negatively as the dissolution of order, as decadence and degeneration, as sin and violation of the divine order. Verwoerd himself participated intensively in this discourse; the distinction between chaos and order became fundamental to his view of the world, but above all to his perspective on society as he found it and as he wanted to shape it. The religious references were less important to him, though, apart from their propagandistic value.

Nationalist ideology drew its justification from the opposition of chaos and order, which was ultimately theologically based. This is illustrated by the notion that chaos does not have a negative connotation per se, for chaos releases creative forces that lead to the spontaneous formation of institutions.[46] However, the spontaneity of human creative processes is not a reflection of a divine or divinely inspired order, but something else. Creative chaos would have been a typical humanistic figure of thought for the religious Afrikaner nationalists which placed man instead of God at the centre.

In adducing the contrast between chaos and order, the biblical references are unmistakable; it is especially the first book of Genesis with the creation of the world order by God out of the pre-existing chaos that is invoked. God created the world by introducing distinctions and creating contrasts: between light and dark, earth and water, between unstructured and divided time, between an amorphous world and the form taking shape in living beings. The narrative counterpart to the story of creation was that of the Flood, where sinful humans were unable to maintain order, and God punished them by temporarily bringing back chaos in

---

44 PV 93/4/1/15, Verwoerd, Notes or Speech Manuscript, n.d.: ff. 13–15, 13.
45 FAV 4.7.2.4.5, Speech at the Natal NP Party Congress in Durban, 27.8.1963, p. 5.
46 Cf. Seyfert 2011: 46.

the form of a return of the water masses from which he had once created the world. In addition to the order-creating God, chaos-creating humans are accorded an inverted demiurgic function: through their misconduct, they shake the world in its foundations; through their sinfulness, they can destroy the world. Whereas the world was created and consolidated by God in an inherently orderly fashion, man was the one being who did not take his place in that order; despite his gift of reason, he was fallible and weak and therefore always in need of divine guidance. It was hardly surprising that Calvinist fundamentalism re-evaluated this opposition between divine order and human disruption, since Calvinism accorded great significance to human fallibility and sinfulness, as well as to the need for submission to God's guidance. The divine order could be grasped in the form of God's law. God's rules were recognisable to man, who had to abide by them in order to live his life pleasing God. Neo-Calvinist philosophy in Kuyper's wake endeavoured to make this thinking, based on an order of laws, the foundation of its view of the world and of society.[47] One of its proponents was Hermann Dooyeweerd, who spent some time in South Africa and made deeper inroads, to more lasting effect, in Potchefstroom and Stellenbosch, than in the Netherlands.[48] Besides Hendrik Stoker, numerous Calvinist intellectuals referred to God's law as the supreme guide for human everyday action, but their 'Calvinist nationalism' never attained a hegemonic position within Afrikaans cultural nationalism.[49] However, the influence clearly went beyond the Doppers, since professors of theology of the NGK had also obtained doctorates at the Vrije Universiteit in Amsterdam.[50]

But there is a crucial difference between what can be called Calvinist fundamentalism cultivated by some prominent representatives at the University of Potchefstroom, and the orientation towards a divinely ordained order, for which Verwoerd stood.[51]

The attempt to structure society according to the law of God is definitive of fundamentalism. In this framework, there is no place for freedom of the human will; if man does not submit to God's will and carry out His laws, he simply perishes, he sinks into self-induced chaos. There is only a limited role for man's creative freedom; due to man's fallibility, human laws are only a weak reflection of divine law. It is important for human beings to align their own laws as closely as

---

[47] Kuyper 2007: 52–53.
[48] Dooyeweerd 1931: 93–95; see also N. Smith 2009: 170–171, 203–207.
[49] Norval 1996: 67–76 puts store in this Calvinist trait. For the foundation of a Calvinist philosophy, see the text by Stoker 1935: 18, 22.
[50] N. Smith 2009: 97.
[51] Furlong 2015: 9–12 underlines the essential differences between Kuyper's socio–political concepts and apartheid. See also Marx 2008: 194–205.

possible with the divine order. Fundamentalism refers to the revealed Word of God in the Bible, which is to be taken as a direct guide for action in the world. The Word of God is understood as a literal instruction; in it, and only in it, God Himself and His legal order are directly expressed. In the nascent discourse of apartheid, a normative order was asserted, with the biblical justification of racial segregation being given high priority. For if racial segregation could be interpreted as the will of God, apartheid could be justified theologically and thus also morally.

Verwoerd, on the other hand, interpreted the world as God's willed order in a more general and abstract sense, for which he did not need a direct revelation of the divine will in Scripture; in his understanding, the divinely willed order could be read directly from the order of the world itself. Although the theological efforts to legitimise the policy of racial segregation by reference to the Bible were opportune in securing the acceptance of his policy in pious churchy circles, he did not need them for himself. The divine order was recognisable to man because man, as a rational being, participated in the divine despite his fallibility. The divine order was the truth, since it had been established by an infallible omniscient spirit. It was through the "divine spark" in man, his reason, that the truth could be discovered. Reason had a method of searching for the truth – namely, the logical faculty of thought –, which opened the way to the knowledge of the divine order. The combined findings of the Würzburg School, of the Psychology of Thought, and especially the writings of Otto Selz, seemed to suggest that logic was located in man's thinking capacity.

The intolerance of ambiguity also affected other aspects of Verwoerd's politics. It played itself out in relation to coloured South Africans. Verwoerd understood the coloureds as the descendants of mixed couples and this posed a problem to him; in his view, their presence was a sign of the dissolution of the God-given order. For Verwoerd, apartheid policy was part of the nationalist creed; in an essay for a student newspaper in 1950,[52] he established a solid, inextricable connection between nationalism and apartheid. Conversely, he linked the dissolution of racial barriers to imperialism or communism. Those who disregarded and violated ethnic divisions violated racial segregation, just as those who disregarded racial segregation violated the criteria of nationhood; for Verwoerd, the underlying sentiment was the same.

In 1960, he complained to the Broederbond's General Secretary, J. P. van der Spuy, that the internal opposition, above all SABRA, was ready to mitigate its attitude to the coloureds, and thus to soften apartheid and move towards equality. He claimed to have previously succeeded in highlighting the contrast between apartheid as a policy of hardline segregation and other policy designs that were

---

52 Verwoerd 1950: 13.

bound to result in equality and integration. "Now these people are coming along to blur the clear distinctions by starting to go the same way with regard to Coloureds and maybe also the Indians." He appealed to van der Spuy to support him, seeing that these tendencies were also present within the ranks of the AB.[53] The choice of words is significant: the notion of a "clear difference" [*"helder verskil"*] reveals Verwoerd's deep-seated rejection of all nuances and ambiguities, which can only be psychologically explained. His intolerance of ambiguity found expression in a putative danger of 'confusion', which he projected onto black people: "If we allow the Native Representatives to remain in Parliament . . . it will only result in confusion amongst the Natives and in the implementation of this policy."[54] In reality, it was Verwoerd himself who did not tolerate ambiguity and who was always searching for clarity. Douglass Mitchell, the UP leader in Natal, observed: "When he was taken up, point by point, on a stand he had adopted and shown what its inevitable [!] consequences would be he would accept them no matter how deplorable they might have seemed."[55]

Death was chaos, the dissolution of all order, just as the decay of the body was tantamount to formlessness. The fear of falling into bottomless depths would call for a symbolic counter-strategy. According to psychoanalyst Robert Jay Lifton, the desire to live beyond death invokes symbolisation.[56] Man knows about his mortality, and can only imagine survival. In order to 'put in order' the chaos with which this knowledge confronts him, and which deprives him of the foundations of a normal continuation of life at the most basic level, he moves to the level of symbolic survival. For Verwoerd, it is about the survival of the nation, which must have power over itself. The individual has to subordinate himself to this ultimate goal, because the national community, that segmentary cell that makes up humanity, is the epitome of order. The community survives the death of the individual, which is why apartheid policy itself can be seen as a strategy for overcoming death: it was supposed to prevent and eliminate chaos once and for all, and to create a final order corresponding to the perfect order of eternal life.

The pre-existing world was seen as the degeneration of an original God-created order, the restoration of which was a providential mission. Afrikaner nationalists' descriptions of the pre-existing world were coloured by a strong sense of crisis, corresponding to the idea that this world continued to degenerate, moving from order to chaos. Thus, even the urbanisation of the black population that ac-

---

53 PV 93/1/47/2/7, Letter by Verwoerd to van der Spuy, 31.10.1960.
54 Verwoerd, Reply to the Motion of No Confidence, 27.1.1959 (in Pelzer 1966: 216–247, 245).
55 Wilks 1980: 152.
56 Lifton 1970: 27.

companied industrialisation, the dissolution of their ethnic affiliations and their "traditional order", was considered an alarming symptom of a general decline.

Verwoerd and Afrikaner nationalists saw disintegration all around them: the dissolution of their own ordered rural world, the disintegration of African "tribes" and the chaos of uncontrolled urbanisation. The Ministry regarded migrants coming to the cities as parasitic and incapable of independent development; for Secretary of Native Affairs Werner Eiselen, unregulated new forms of coexistence were an abomination, "which often amounts to degeneracy due to lack of planning."[57] In 1947, Eiselen's colleague, ethnologist P. J. Coertze, one of the most important pioneers of apartheid, sounded the alarm in a detailed memorandum: "The social life of natives in towns and villages, especially in large cities, is chaotic in every respect; in commerce, change and thought, the urban native spontaneously turns into a revolutionary and recalcitrant individual. It only takes being organised by communists – which is already happening on a large scale today."[58]

Verwoerd's idea of the immaturity of Africans was expressed particularly intensely in statements on the rural exodus that underlined irrational motives: "The Bantu are pressing blindly into the towns whether or not there is work for them there, and those not employed are taking to vagrancy and crime in alarming proportions."[59] The adverb "blindly" indicates his idea that "the Bantu" were not able to take control of their own lives, and that therefore, the state had to do it for them. He could see no social progress: "The Bantu who works in the European cities, searches and finds, is allowed and even encouraged to break away from his tribal connections with their sound communal rules, and then to lead an uncontrolled and disorderly life, seeing that the vast majority are not in the least ready for community life on the Western levels, with its generally acknowledged although unwritten laws."[60] Here the mix of contradictory racist and ethnopsychological figures of argumentation comes to the fore: on the one hand, blacks were supposedly not "yet" ready for forms of life such as those developed by whites, and on the other hand, they were unsuitable for big city life in general and required constant control. He therefore found it scandalous that in the past

---

57 FAV, 4.6.2.2, Memo Eiselen to Verwoerd., 7.9.1951.
58 PV 94/1/53/2/1, doc. 34, P. J. Coertze, Memorandum insake rasseverhoudingsprobleme en 'n beleid van segregasie (c. 1944), p. 3.
59 PV 276/3/1/1, Bantu in the Urban Areas (undated and no author named, but official Ministry account), pp. 3, 1.
60 Verwoerd, Policy of the Minister of Native Affairs, 20.6.1955 (in Pelzer 1966: 86–101, 87). Verwoerd himself considered the speech so important that it was printed as a separate pamphlet and even reprinted in 1958 (Verwoerd 1955).

"these persons were practically left to find their own housing".[61] Concerning the eviction of the residents of Pageview, a Johannesburg suburb, he emphasised the fact that "whites, Indians, Coloureds and natives" had lived there "side by side and in confusion", which had only produced "hotbeds of mischief and crime".[62] This description of contemporary social life probably came from Eiselen: "The present day scene in South Africa is a queer patchwork of the European and Bantu ways of life."[63] The contrast with the European way of life was perceived to be stark: "Bantu life in the reserves takes one right back to pre-history."[64] What was crucial to Afrikaner nationalists, however, was the orderliness of a life steeped in tradition, where everyone knew their place. For Afrikaner nationalists, as Hermann Giliomee points out, racial segregation was not merely an order based on skin colour, on racial and ethnic criteria, but it was so emotionally charged because it was also a social order. The dissolution of racial barriers meant "equality" and thus the destruction of the God-given order, that is, chaos. In the 1940s, it had become apparent that the type of consciousness traditionally rooted in the order of estates had come close to fascist-corporatist ideas of order.[65]

If nationalism was the basic political principle for Verwoerd, what stood behind it was the idea of the segmentation of humanity into collectives. For him, these collectives were defined as cultural communities; all the others, such as social classes, were categories dependent on and derived from them, so there could only be an Afrikaans, an English, a Sotho labour force, but no working class as such. He could understand class conflicts only as symptoms of crisis – as forms of degeneration and deficits when, for instance, "a weakening of spiritual ties occurred, such as patriotism, the memory of common descent, pride in a common religion or history, etc."[66] The nation, the community was the given order, and only when it got out of kilter did class struggle become possible, which therefore appeared as a kind of pathological symptom. Social classes, interest groups, etc. could only be temporary and transient social units, while the nation was eternal.

The horror vision of 'mixing' was directed not only to "races", but also to institutions and procedures. Thus, for Verwoerd, problems arose as soon as the tribal

---

61 Verwoerd, Institute of Administrators of Non-European Affairs, Bloemfontein, 17.9.1956 (in Pelzer 1966: 124–148, 132).
62 Even during his time as sociologist, Verwoerd had dealt with the topic and with various empirical recording methods, such as maps on which the different "races" in a city district were to be entered (231/2/2, Metodes van sociologiese navorsing, pp. 88–90).
63 FAV, 4.6.2.2, The Bantu in South Africa (ca. 1953, author presumably Eiselen), p. 6.
64 ibid. p. 7.
65 Marx 2008: 492-493.
66 231/2/1/1, 'Inleiding tot die Sociologie', p. 75.

structure was mixed with a Western administrative structure. In his view, the establishment of councils whose tasks remained unclear was only bound to provoke the demands of the Native Representative Council for equality.[67] This could only be countered by a clear decision for one or the other. The insistence on clarity of basic principles informed clarity of policy, with unambiguous results.

By presenting politics as a restoration of order as it was established and willed by God, the utopian character could be disguised; the revolutionary order of apartheid masked itself as a return to a lost order. Verwoerd sold apartheid as feasible political system; through his logical deductions, he transformed it from an abstract into a concrete, that is, realisable utopia. "His policies were executed almost as mathematical deductions from the few basic tenets which he inherited."[68] In this way he succeeded in presenting his monstrous and subversive modernisation policy as oriented towards tradition and directed towards a theological concept of order: Homo Faber presented himself as the executor of the divine will.

If logic was the faculty available to man to recognise God's laws in the world, then it also served to shape human laws in order to produce a world of (human) order that, as far as man was able to do so, approximated, modelled and reproduced the divine order.[69] If logic helped to open up God's order, then laws were the means to maintain it. Verwoerd's existential need for order gave rise to the legalism that characterised the apartheid state as a whole. The reference to the community, whose "general will" it expressed – with an unmistakable reference to Rousseau – was fundamental to a legal order; the laws expressed the general will, were therefore absolute and above individual wishes. Even at the age of 21, young Verwoerd had recognised this:

> Law comprises the commands which render the general will of the members of a community in their dealings with one another essential, and enforce it. This command, guarantee and security of the essentialised general will is the only absolute valid value of the law. If a community is to persist, then only those acts must be permitted by it which are deemed right and just. It shall be without meaning, aim or value if their deeds are not in accordance with their will. Thus the acts expressing their will, and captured in the legal command, remain eternally valuable, while individual demands can be destroyed at any time.[70]

For Verwoerd, human freedom was extremely constrained by virtue of being imprinted by the natural order; ethnicity, in particular, did not merely reflect the

---

67 Verwoerd, Policy of the Minister of Native Affairs, 30.5.1952 (in Pelzer 1966: 31–52, 39–41).
68 J. J. Venter 1999: 440.
69 This meaning of logic was conveyed by philosophy (Thomas 2005, vol. 1: 8–16).
70 Verwoerd 1922b: 38.

natural order, but was the natural order itself. Thus, in his view, apartheid ethnicity restored the natural order, while cosmopolitanism, intercultural contact and internationalism stood for chaos.

The fear of chaos resulting from unregulated social dynamics was matched by an obsessive need for order and control. Thus, influx control was upheld as the prerequisite for "better control over the people who stay there, for better order, and for better way of combatting frustrations, because the work-shy, the criminals and the redundant are out of the picture". In this context, the following list of goals was indicative of Verwoerd's thinking. Building townships "is a form of neighbourhood segregation, a form of elimination of undesirable housing conditions; it introduces better health conditions and better control".[71] The key words were "neighbourhood segregation", "elimination" ["*opruiming*"] and "control", all antithetical to chaos. They stood for visibility, cleanliness and controllability. Order was the goal and the prerequisite for conducive coexistence. It was necessary to ensure "that the native also understands the import of the laws and learns to see how all this fits into a scheme of order and planning, which ultimately contributes to economic self-reliance, prosperity and happiness of the native, and to help those who are orderly to free themselves from the pressures now exerted on them by disorderly elements." Criminals were primarily "disorderly elements", representing chaos, while planning and order went together.

Apartheid thus derived its legitimacy not only from its moral justification as a supposedly just solution; logic itself was an intrinsic source of legitimation, since it had to coincide with morality as a means of seeking truth. Order was thought to manifest its moral character by being logically coherent and free of contradiction. Verwoerd thus moved within the thought structures of the Age of Extremes; realising the truth of the world order, they sought to adapt the real life world to this realisation.

If one compares Verwoerd's utopianism with future-oriented Marxism, the function of his logic can be described more precisely. Orthodox Marxism gains its certainty of the future from an interpretation of history that affords it the self-confidence of being a "scientific socialism". History as the dialectical dynamic of class struggles is extended into the future by radicalising the process of capitalist accumulation producing extreme polarisation, which would then lead to revolution. Verwoerd lacked such certainty about the future premised on a historical-philosophical interpretation of the world. His historical view was limited to a professed commitment to his own national history in mythical form, which held no

---

71 NA NTS 4562, 1049/313, Conference between Officers of the Native Affairs Department and Managers of Departments of Non-European Affairs, p. 8 (Verwoerd's opening address).

concrete guidelines for actions in future. Instead, he drew from it a legitimation of an open field of actions for the future, which broke with that same national history at a decisive point – since those action-orientations were radically modernist and anti-traditional. This is how Verwoerd's logically derived, reverse-engineered action-orientations become explicable. He created a pseudo-determinism along a one-way street towards the land of Utopia. Verwoerd's utopianism was not historically based; it lacked the philosophical underpinning of history that Marxism had. Instead, he construed the future from the present, but justified it historically as a kind of repair measure returning man to the path towards the divinely ordained order.

Difference and Purity

Purity is a concept of difference; purity establishes order, whereas chaos is associated with impurity and mingling. This dichotomy of order and chaos, difference and diversity, is consonant with Verwoerd's racism. A notion of 'community' is predicated on the identification of differences between people. Ethnic difference in the context of the coexistence of different communities was a principle of Verwoerd's thought and action. To him, differences between individuals, the range of which he did not deny in his lectures on Personality, were less significant than differences between groups of people. Thus, a black economically savvy person of sanguine temperament was more remote from an equally endowed white than he was from a black sociable phlegmatic. Where entire groups of people were differentiated from and pitted against each other, those who foiled such differentiation and created a situation of ambiguity were being singled out and categorised, so as to eliminate ambiguity. The notion of purity can capture such thought and action, since it ties difference to a scheme of valuation, thus transforming a symmetrical relationship into an asymmetrical one. The concept of purity is related to asymmetrical antonymic concepts, as Reinhart Koselleck explains. Thus, difference does not signify interchangeability or affinity of its constituent terms.[1] Rather, the notion of purity as self-attribution creates a gradient. It is the other that is the impure.[2]

In her ground-breaking study *Purity and Danger*, Mary Douglas associates purity with orderliness; on the basis of various examples, she demonstrates how purity is being invoked to ward off and eliminate ambiguity.[3] Ambiguity is the state of impurity; as the antithesis of purity, ambiguity acquires a label of its own, on another level. In racist discourses, so-called "half-breeds" are described as impure. In fact, biological racism in South Africa always came to the fore in statements and policies concerning the coloured population, whose mere existence – deemed to have resulted from miscegenation – was denounced as impure.[4] While for whites, differentiation from the black population would be determined culturally, differentiation from the culturally closely related coloureds would be stated

---

[1] Koselleck 1985: 213.
[2] For a certain Judge Snyman, the ANC was among the "defiled organisations" (qtd. in G. D. Scholtz 1974, vol. 2: 187).
[3] Douglas 2010: ch. 5; see also Burschel/Marx 2011: 12–13.
[4] Abercrombie 1938: 6–14, 87, which in his case is coupled with open fascist sympathies (ibid., 28–29). See also Smit 1989:239 on similar considerations in Cronjé and Willemse, two leading Afrikaans criminologists of the interwar period. See also Kuyper; but he identified miscegenation as a movens of history (Kuyper 2007: 34–38). Giliomee (1975: 42) sees racial purity as functionally related to the preservation of white privileges.

in biological terms. This is what renders Verwoerd's attitude towards this population group and his ideas of purity the most reliable criteria for deciding the question as to whether he was a racist. It must be noted, however, that Verwoerd was by no means an exception in this respect; the rejection of "miscegenation" was widespread among the white population, even in liberal circles, while the discourse of racial segregation in South Africa was generally based more on cultural essentialism than on biological doctrines of race.[5]

What does it mean to be a racist? The undeniable fact that Verwoerd projected his extreme cultural nationalism onto black people and imputed cultural-nationalist action-orientations to them, does not in and of itself refute the accusation of racism. Rather, racism and nationalism lie on a continuum, with overlaps and transitions.[6] This is especially true of the cultural nationalism advocated by Verwoerd, for whom membership of a nation was decided by seemingly objective criteria such as language, history and culture, despite the fact that this was somewhat problematic in his own case. In contrast to civic nationalism, which entails voluntarism in the sense that it relies on the individual's professed commitment to his or her nation, what cultural nationalism and racism have in common is the fact that the ascription is being made by a third party.[7]

I would like to present two working definitions, which serve as a guide for the following considerations. Firstly, I see racism as a special case of ethnocentrism. Secondly, Ethnocentrism entails the elevation of one's own culture to the measure of all others. Thus, the others are defined in terms of what they are not (yet), i.e. in terms of developmental deficits. This attitude was widely held in European colonialism; it was also advocated by numerous missionaries, but this did not necessarily make racists of the missionaries, even if they believed themselves to be culturally superior to Africans. So what is racism? It is important to clarify this, as there is some confusion on this issue in the literature.

The confusion arises because Afrikaner nationalists did not adduce a biological notion of race. Is biological racism some kind of normal form of racism and cultural racism a special case, a deviation? This is not so – they are different manifestations of the same phenomenon. Racism establishes a causal link between

---

[5] J. J. Venter 1999: 427; see also Dubow 1992: 209; and Giliomee 2008: 84. On the reference to culture rather than biology, see Rich 1983: 5.
[6] This is evident in the cultural nationalist writing of J. A. Coetzee 1931:19–22. On the close connection between racism and nationalism, see Geulen 2007: 78–86.
[7] Detlev Peukert has developed a plausible explanation for the popularity of racism (see 1989: 110). I owe the reference to Bajohr 2015: 152.

culture and biology, which is applied to entire groups of people.[8] Like ethnocentrism, racism elevates one's own culture to the standard for all others. But more than that, it establishes a causal link between cultural achievements or abilities of people and certain biological characteristics, be they visible ones such as skin colour or invisible/ presumed ones such as genetic make-up. Racists can therefore argue from both sides – biologistically, as did the National Socialists in particular, or culturalistically, in foregrounding culture while always implicitly relating it to biological characteristics. In much the same way, Afrikaner nationalists and other white racists do not regard mission-educated blacks primarily as educated, but as blacks. Thus it is a question of concrete argumentation, but not of basic assumptions: When people like Eiselen or Verwoerd foregrounded culture, they simply approached the causal nexus from the cultural rather than the biological angle; but what remained was the basic racist assumption that skin colour and culture were directly related to each other and that cultural developments or abilities were directly related to "race".[9] Racism is a special case of ethnocentrism, because it considers other cultures as inferior and justifies this putative deficit in biological terms, whereas ethnocentrism does not necessarily deny the perfectibility of those it considers less developed. Most missionaries were ethnocentric, but only few among them were racists, since they considered Africans to be convertible and civilisable.

That is why biological and cultural racism are different sides of the same coin. When biological racism places 'blood', the biological foundation, at the centre of its argumentation, it is primarily concerned with explaining cultural differences as natural. Cultural racism, in contrast, argues from culture, but always presupposes that cultural differences can be explained biologically; groups that are identified via cultural differences are simultaneously 'racially' defined, that is, they are distinguished by a certain characteristic, such as skin colour.[10]

---

8 An explicit example can be found in Gerdener 1950: 85. In their anthropological explanations, ethnologist P.J. Coertze and sociologist G. Cronjé linked culture and biology (inherited characteristics) in such a way that culture could no longer be an independent variable, but had to become the substance of a racially determined "people" or "ethnos" (P. J. Coertze 1980: 71–73, 91–92; 1963: 169–170; see also Cronjé 1937: 6). Coertze often referred to German ethnologist Wilhelm Mühlmann, whose publications from the Nazi period he liked to quote (P. J. Coertze n.d.: 2–4).
9 This also dissolves Eiselen's opposition of cultural versus biological–racist argumentation: he simply shifted the focus of his argument (Bank 2015c: 191). Similarly Bruwer (PV 123/4/5/1, Manuscript 'Towards a New Deal for Those Between', p. 2).
10 Rhoodie (1965: 118) even declares race to be the "primary determinant and norm" in South Africa. This does not come as a surprise because this dissertation, which is completely uncritical of its subject, reads like government propaganda over long stretches.

In one of the short stories that Verwoerd wrote during his time as professor of Psychology, he made the following statements about black people:

> Even if one does not get much out of the native, there is a reserved joyfulness in him – or should he rather call it *joie de vivre* – which he had noticed on several occasions with the cattle herders. And that was no wonder: for these creatures [*skepsels*] it must be a kind of release, to be able to enjoy their lives so freely, in a way that only they can, by virtue of their heredity and disposition.[11]

If Verwoerd's assumption was that cultural traits such as *"joie de vivre"* and a way of enjoying life were hereditary and thus biologically determined, such remarks provide evidence of his racism. Verwoerd assumed that Africans could not be free to choose, but remained prisoners of 'their' respective cultures. Even when he stressed "that the government's policy is not based on people being inferior but being different",[12] this distinction, and with it apartheid as a whole, remained biologically based. Contemporaries emphasised that it was precisely Verwoerd who made skin colour a criterion and that this is what led him to make short-sighted decisions.[13]

Apartheid highlighted cultural differences; it was based on a differential valuation of cultural patterns and their linkages to biological characteristics such as skin colour. It was therefore no less racist than the biological variant, and was even ahead of its time, since apartheid discourses were developed at the height of biologistic explanations, which then occupied a hegemonic position. The time of cultural racism came later.[14] In fact, biological racism was propounded in the interwar period mainly by English–speaking authors such as Harold B. Fantham

---

11 VEE [Verwoerd], 'Die Skok'. *Die Huisgenoot*, August 1931, p. 75. In another detective story, however, the black murderer is described as extremely clever and able to determine developments in advance. (Ockert Witte [Verwoerd]: 'Die vermiste egpaar'. *Die Huisgenoot*, 23.10.1931, pp. 19, 36; 30.10.1931, pp. 35, 39; 6.11.1931, pp. 41, 49).
12 Verwoerd, South Africa Club, London 17.3.1961 (in Pelzer 1966: 502–512, 506). In an interview with the British Independent Television Network on 17 March 1961, Verwoerd emphatically stated: "It's not a matter of inferiority. It's a matter of difference." (FAV 4.7.1.3.1, transcript of interview with Richard Goold–Adams).
13 Ben Schoeman 1978:308. However, it remains unclear what he meant when he said in relation to Malaysia, "there are no colour differences but racial differences" (Verwoerd 1964a: 23).
14 McCarthy 2015: 141–151. This reciprocal relationship between culture and race was also observed by T. D. Moodie (2017: 158).

(1876–1937), a zoologist at the University of the Witwatersrand;[15] from the 1930s onwards, it was replaced by discourses of cultural difference.

Deborah Posel has described the everyday racism shared by Verwoerd, which was unscientific and vague in its derivations, but could rely on widespread agreement and consent based on experience, aptly termed "common sense". This racism, which was based more on general social impressions rather than 'scientific' biological characteristics or ancestry, also underlay the Population Registration Act.[16] It was not until after the Second World War, and after the Holocaust, when racism was increasingly questioned and when its overt expression declined worldwide, that I. D. MacCrone, professor of Psychology at the University of the Witwatersrand, no longer problematised race, but racism.[17]

Verwoerd was undoubtedly an ethnocentrist, though in this respect he was also a representative of Afrikaner nationalism, that is, he shared the opinions that were widespread within the Broederbond, the NP, and intellectual circles. There are some clear indications from his everyday life that he was racist: apart from black gardeners, for example, he had mostly white domestic servants in his employ.[18] Ethnocentrism determined his nationalism, and the criteria of difference that came into play there offered the basis for racial categorisations.

Although Verwoerd was certainly aware of biological racial theories, and was interested in and had read the relevant literature, statements in which he openly admitted to holding such theories himself are extremely sparse. However, in his first publication as a student, he articulated his abhorrence of mixed residential arrangements in Cape Town's slums. In 1938, he authored a racist pamphlet for an NP election campaign, in which he blew up the consequences of intermarriage be-

---

15 Fantham linked human culture and morality to human genetic material; he minimised the importance of environmental influences in favour of genetic disposition (Fantham 1924: 499–508) and thereby advocated eugenic measures (Fantham (1918: 304). He considered miscegenation to be highly problematic, and considered the coloureds a hybrid, culturally infertile population group (Fantham 1927: 12–13), on account of which he did not want to exclude the implementation of forced sterilisation (Fantham 1926: 628; Fantham 1925; see also Abercrombie 1938). For a critical assessment of Fantham, see Duerden 1925: 68–69; see also Louw 1986: 111–117; Louw 1997: 238–245. On Fantham, see also Brits 1994: 51; Appel 1989: 553–554; and Rich 1990: 667–670.
16 Posel 2001: 100–103.
17 MacCrone 1947: 7–10, 15.
18 *Natal Daily News* 21.1.1959. H. Macmillan 1972: 152; A. Boshoff 1974: 40; A. Boshoff 1993: 38; J. Botha 1967: 33. This, however, is explained as not so much as a matter of a racist attitude than as a duty of care to "poor whites" (B. Verwoerd 2001: 44). Fred Barnard, Verwoerd's private secretary, maintained that he also had a black domestic servant (*Die Transvaler*, 7.6.1972).

tween whites and coloureds to conjure up a sense of great danger.[19] He also published a poster for the NP in *Die Transvaler*, in which a black and white couple appeared in front of a run-down house, with their 'mixed' offspring being presented as the future of South Africa under a UP government.[20] His party held ideas similar to those of Verwoerd himself: as early as 6 June 1940, C. R. Swart addressed the Afrikaanse Nasionale Studentebond of the University of the Orange Free State in Bloemfontein on the dangers of and defences against mixed marriages.[21] Ever since the beginning of his journalistic career, Verwoerd himself had been discussing the theme of miscegenation in his editorials, accusing the UP of being too lax.[22]

Even during his time as a scientist, Verwoerd put out numerous disparaging statements about racial mixing – mostly in connection with the "poor whites" and their physical proximity to coloured neighbourhoods; they run like a thread from his first publication in 1919 to his time as Prime Minister. The distinction drawn by Johannes Degenaar between a "hard" and a "soft" racism becomes pertinent here; Verwoerd never expressed a "hard" racism in the sense of casting Africans as inferior, but time and again, his "soft" racism, with its rejection of miscegenation, came to the fore.[23] Verwoerd was representative of Afrikaner nationalists in whose thinking Degenaar sees "race hav[ing] played an important role".[24]

The biological basis of apartheid is most clearly evident in the key eugenic laws, namely the various bans on mixed marriages and sexual relations.[25] The Mixed Marriages and Immorality Acts of 1949 and 1950, respectively, were the

---

[19] Verwoerd 1938, NP election campaign leaflet, 1938, written by Verwoerd. In his Sociology lectures, Verwoerd claimed that white youths' contact with coloureds made them lose their self-respect and made them susceptible to criminal behaviour (US 231/2/3, Socio–psigologie van misdaad, pp. 15, 51).

[20] Spies/Theron/Scholtz 1981: 771. On the right hand side at the bottom of the flyer, the four masterminds stand together in unison, with their identities printed on their trousers, namely Jew, imperialist, communist and capitalist. The poster can be found in the Verwoerd Family Archive under FAV 4.5.2.2. It caused indignation in the UP and in certain circles of the white population, possibly contributing to the poor performance of the NP (see *Suiderstem*, 3.5.1938, *Volkstem*, 3.5.1958). On this and on Verwoerd's attitude to 'mixed marriages' and miscegenation, see also D. Prinsloo 1979: 475–488. In retrospect, even a nationalist historian writing for the press described Verwoerd's journalistic activities during the election campaign as "often too clumsy" (C. J. H. Muller 1990: 666). According to Basson (2006: 182–183), the poster can be traced to Verwoerd, but see also Steyn 1987: 134–135. For a further example of Verwoerd's rejection of miscegenation see Serfontein 1979: 72.

[21] See notes on this in PV 18/4/1/1, Gemengde huwelike, handwritten notes 6.6.1940.

[22] *Die Transvaler* 3.12.1937.

[23] Degenaar 1980: 19.

[24] Degenaar 1978a: 55.

[25] Furlong 1983: 7–10. Interestingly, in 1958 Prime Minister Strijdom expressed his dismay to his Minister of Justice: he was shocked by the behaviour of the police, who had lured a white man

measures that were most clearly racist; but despite parallels variously drawn with the Nuremberg Laws, it can be shown that it was the American injunctions that were taken as the models.²⁶ Not surprisingly, it was Verwoerd the politician who took the most unequivocal racial-biologistic stance. Thus any form of miscegenation was "in spite of the well-known pride of both the Bantu and the European in their respective purity of descent".²⁷ The Great Trek, whose exemplary character he never ceased to praise, "was a struggle of the whole family – man, woman and child – side by side to safeguard the future of their posterity and to preserve the purity of the blood of the nation".²⁸ The importance of the biological side for Verwoerd is evident from this remark of his: "I shall not go down in history as the man who led the Afrikaner people to bastardisation [*verbastering*]. Should the majority be in favour of it, I will resign."²⁹

Whenever it came to the nation and its racial purity, Verwoerd tended to drop his usual sober demeanour to trump up some pathos: "And if with admiration we look back at the way the forefathers by the purity of their lives left us a White nation, then we have to realise that it is our task also by a pure, decorous life to maintain a White nation here. Great is the pain and suffering of any family and any friend when this highest law has been infringed. But greater still is the pain and the damage to a nation when some of its children have sinned against its blood."³⁰

Although it must have been clear to Verwoerd and other apartheid ideologues that cultural innovation and development was based on cross-cultural influences, they insisted on an abstract and unrealistic principle of purity that precluded such cultural enrichment.³¹ As soon as demands for concessions to the black majority were voiced, Verwoerd visualised an dynamic that would irrevocably lead to ma-

---

into a trap with the help of a black sex worker, to then charge him under the Immorality Act (PV 18/3/1/63, Letter by Strijdom to Swart, 30.1.1958. See also Bunting 1986: ch. 9).
26 Heese 1989a: 70–76.
27 Verwoerd, Policy of Apartheid, 5.12.1960 (in Pelzer 1966: 20–30, 24).
28 Verwoerd, Address at Blood River, 16.12.1958 (in Pelzer 1966: 206–211, 208).
29 Statement to his wife (qtd. in G. D. Scholtz 1974, vol. 2: 171).
30 Verwoerd, Kruger Day, Pretoria, 10.10.1959 (in Pelzer 1966: 313–318, 317). As Prime Minister he also saw this as a global problem: "How right you are that some evil spirit seems to be passing through the world making people believe that White civilization has spent itself and that the new vision of the future depends upon the bastardisation of all nations. Yet I believe that this will not come about, and that the creative power and greater initiative of the White man will make him survive – here and elsewhere." (PV 93/1/30/1/19, Letter by Verwoerd to H. G. Kibler (Johannesburg), 10.6.1963, f. 123). In his lectures, he also repeatedly highlighted the dangers that could arise from whites and coloureds living too closely together (US, 231/2/4/1, Armoede en sy bestryding, p. 43).
31 See also J. J. Venter 1999: 424–425.

jority rule and, beyond political equality, to a horror scenario of miscegenation and the biological demise of the *"volk"*: "if we begin to have Coloureds represented in Parliament by Coloureds, this will not elicit much gratitude, but will rather be the springboard for ever more concessions to Coloureds, Indians and urbanised Bantu. ... This will eventually lead to the mixing of the races."[32]

One of his first speeches as a senator in 1948, commenting on the Fagan Report commissioned by the previous UP government, was among the few occasions on which Verwoerd explicitly invoked racial biology. Since the Report rejected insinuations of racial biology, its recommendations, in Verwoerd's understanding, could only lead to integration: "It virtually boils down to this, that the distinctions are of a social and educational nature and then necessarily administration and trusteeship must some day fall away. Thus, though you dare not draw the distinctions on racial and biological lines, yet you will eventually find yourself on the course which leads to equality."[33]

One can only speculate about the reason for his reticence with regard to biological-racial doctrines. It is possible that they did not fully convince him, but it is more likely that it was political considerations that reined him in; he could not afford to be seen abroad as a proponent of biological racism of the kind practiced in National Socialism. Apartheid was officially based on the notion of different stages of civilisation, but if it was touted as "separate development", it had to affirm the capacity of the black population to develop. In one of his statements at least, Verwoerd indicates that this is what he assumed: the different population groups, he said, "are at different stages of development and therefore [*dus*] have different capacities to fulfil the duties currently incumbent on them, to the com-

---

[32] PV 93/1/24/10, ff. 134–9, Letter by Verwoerd to S. Pretorius, 26. 10. 1960: "Notwithstanding the fact that the coloureds increased during the last few years, becoming more and more black, as far as these people are concerned, the whites should not only integrate them politically, economically and then socially, but also legislate changes that will make biological integration possible." Verwoerd collected newspaper articles reporting on actual or alleged violations of South Africa's racial laws (PV 93/1/24/6; PV 93/1/24/3), which opened the door to snitches and peeping toms, some of them installed even in the press (*Die Vaderland*, 14.1.1957). Social and moral decline, as it was expressed in such reports and rumours planted by spies, apparently did not worry Verwoerd. He had always supported and defended racial segregation in everyday life down to its most pettifogging details (see also his collection of newspaper reports on beaches, churches and other segregated institutions, in PV 93/1/24/2).

[33] Verwoerd, Policy of Apartheid, 3.9.1948 (in Pelzer 1966: 1–19, 13). I cannot agree with T. D. Moodie's observation (1975: 276–277) that Verwoerd became more racist in his statements after 1958 than he had been before. Moreover, it must be borne in mind that it was only after 1958 that he was involved in political measures targeting the coloureds, for whose case references to cultural differences were moot, leaving only skin colour as criterion of differentiation.

munities of their own people".³⁴ The word "therefore" ["*dus*"] is the crucial one here, as it establishes a direct causal link between civilisational development and capabilities – that is, it argues developmentally, not biologically. But this is an isolated statement that is not further substantiated by others. Nevertheless, he did not by any means rule out a biological rationale; the question as to whether he considered the black population capable of ever fully reaching a level of civilisation equal to that of the whites or not, was left open. What he did emphasise again and again is his idea that Native Affairs was not a "mere administrative procedure", but "a process of development which can only gradually gain momentum".³⁵ Ethnologist Johannes Petrus van Schalkwyk Bruwer even went as far as denying any connection of apartheid with racism, describing it as a "technical method of control" instead.³⁶

Racist stage theories are closely related to developmental-psychological ones; they radicalise the latter in the sense that they do not justify the differences between societies on the basis of climate, space or cultural history, but on biological grounds. In this view, today's societies represent earlier stages of development that they have not overcome. This is explained by the fact that they could not have developed any further, at least they would never reach the level of Europeans. Racist stage theories question the perfectibility of the 'others', taking the supposedly lower level of development of culture as proof of a restricted developmental *capacity*, which is then again supposed to explain – in a process of circular reasoning – the low level of culture.³⁷

Africans and other "primitives" were therefore considered civilisationally retarded and not in a position to catch up with Europeans; they were thought to be stuck in a certain phase observable in the individual psyche, and therefore unable to reach adult maturity. A popular assumption was the notion of "arrested development": African children developed like European children until puberty. This is where the developmental paths diverged: while European children experienced a significant surge in intellectual development, Africans would be so overwhelmed by their sexual drives that they would never get past puberty.³⁸ Dudley

---

34 PV 93/1/24/11, f. 43, statement by Verwoerd, apparently for the press, 22.11.1960, p. 5.
35 Hansard, 25.5.1956, col. 3997.
36 Bruwer 1956a: 96.
37 In this line of argument, intelligence and general cultural aptitude, which Volkelt had separated from one another, are brought together again. In this way, ethnopsychology became compatible with popular racism, which became widespread at the end of the 19th century, especially in settler colonies such as South Africa.
38 Duerden (1921: 15) strongly disagreed with this theory.

Kidd, who wrote a racist book on the psychology of African children, also drew conclusions from the thesis of "arrested development" for education:

> When puberty is drawing to a close, a degenerative process seems to set in, and the previous efflorescence of the faculties leads to no adequate fruitage in later life. . . . Our main aim in the education of backward races should be to draw out, discipline, and strengthen the various faculties . . . of the children so that, when the age of puberty arrives, these faculties may be able to resist the degenerative and blighting tendencies that must soon arise.[39]

Europeans are considered capable of controlling their drives, and to direct them towards intellectual maturity and cultural progress. Africans, on the other hand, are not able to do this and remain children forever. This assumption, in turn, would justify paternalism, racial segregation and corporal punishment.[40]

Verwoerd rejected neo-Lamarckianism because its central tenet of the inheritance of acquired characteristics would have cast the rehabilitation of poor whites as an unpromising and unconvincing scientific project. However, this does not exclude the possibility that Verwoerd saw the differences between blacks and whites biologically founded, and that he assumed superior intelligence for whites. In one of his Sociology lectures, he posed the question "whether the general intelligence of the [black] child is equal to that of the white".[41]

To explore this further, it is worth looking back into Verwoerd's academic career. In his lectures on character studies, he accorded significant scope to hereditary psychological theories. He paid particularly close attention to the books by two German psychiatrists, Ernst Kretschmer and Hermann Hoffmann. "It is a fact that in some psychoses (mental illnesses), one is quite clearly dealing with a disintegration of the personality, so that the unity which characterises the mental life of the normal person is lost."[42] This interpretation was based on his own view that the human personality was composed of certain "personality traits" into which it disintegrated again in the case of mental illness. Verwoerd showed an ardent interest in the book *Körperbau und Charakter* [*Physique and Character*] by Marburg psychiatrist Ernst Kretschmer (1888–1964), whose "insights" were advocated also by psychologist Paul Skawran, who came from Germany and taught in Pretoria.[43]

---

39 Kidd 1906: viii–ix. Volkelt had evidently taken note of Kidd's book (see also Abercrombie 1938: 55). On this thesis, see also Loram 1917: 206–218. On the notion in historical context, see Dubow 1995: 197–203.
40 Marx 2000: 274–279.
41 US, 231/2/1/1, 'Inleiding tot die Sociologie', p. 107.
42 PV 93/1/33/3, f. 91, Persoonlikheidstiepes volgens Jung en Kretschmer, p. 1.
43 It is possible that Verwoerd was made aware of Kretschmer and Spranger in Leipzig (UA Leipzig, Krueger papers, notes apparently from a colloquium, 1930s, in which the two names are frequently mentioned). In addition to Verwoerd, W. A. Willemse, one of the leading criminolo-

The assumption of a connection between a person's external appearance and his or her character was by no means a new idea. Racial anthropologists had already been busy for decades correlating skull shapes, brain sizes, etc., with certain abilities; they ascribed such characteristics to large groups of people whom they categorised biologically. Racial anthropology was a distinct form of research that had originally been concerned with individual differences within a population group. That is the reason why character studies were not tantamount to racial anthropology; character studies examined the differentiation of characters within a given population, whereas racial anthropology tended to neglect these differentiations in order to compare large groups with each other. Common to both, however, was the search for a connection between cultural and biological characteristics.

Thus Physiognomics, which claimed a connection between facial features and character, can be traced back to the work of Johann Caspar Lavater in the 18th century. Kretschmer did not by any means rest content with assessing facial features as an expression of character; rather, he claimed to be able to deduce a person's character from the overall appearance. Spranger's and Kretschmer's typologies of character were repeatedly discussed in Leipzig;[44] aspects of their work found a striking echo in Verwoerd's lectures.[45] Kretschmer believed that there was a connection between the patients' psychiatric profile and their physique; he then proceeded to apply these observations to healthy persons. From these investigations, he developed a kind of basic grid that enabled him to identify certain characteristics that appeared in extreme forms in cases of illness, and in the form of disposition, and therefore as character trait, in healthy persons. Thus he claimed that persons with manic-depressive (bipolar) disorders, whom he called circular, were more rotund than schizophrenics, who tended to be more slender – either lean or athletic.[46] On the basis of these observations, he found that healthy persons with similar physical features had similar psychic features, which appeared intensified to the extent of pathological extremes in psychiatric cases. Healthy persons whose physique and character showed similarities with schizophrenics he called schizothyms; "circular persons" he called cyclothyms. His argument got caught up in circular reasoning:

---

gists in South Africa in the 1930s was interested in Kretschmer, on whose theories he wrote his doctorate (Smit 1989: 230). On Skawran, see Louw 1986: 79–80. This was taken up by other criminologists in turn (H. J. Venter 1952: 124–130).
44 UA Leipzig, Krueger papers, 7, Minutes of the Colloquium, probably 1936.
45 PV 93/1/33/3, Persoonlikheidstiepes volgens Jung en Kretschmer (see also Kretschmer 1922: 87).
46 Kretschmer 1922: 14–28; on asserting a critical distance from the physiognomy of Lavater and his successors, see 11–12.

observations on the physique and certain character traits confirmed each other. Common notions about biological heredity associated healthy people with schizothymal traits and schizophrenics.[47] Verwoerd adopted Kretschmer's argument, stating, "[w]hat is important is his insistence that one need not study all the manifestations of mental illness in detail; whenever one encounters something of the sort, it suffices to be able to immediately judge a person to be partially abnormal. It is rather the other way round: in the semi-normal and the mentally ill one is getting a caricature of the normal personality, as it were, with some traits being proportionately enlarged."[48]

Kretschmer undertook a characterological classification which regarded the pathological as normal, arriving at a determination of health on the basis of pathology and illness. He pursued his arguments on hereditary biology with extreme one-sidedness – for him, experience was largely irrelevant. He was not interested in psychological questions, because he judged people exclusively from a medical point of view.[49] The strange mixture of medical jargon expressing the medical gaze and medical expertise,[50] lyrical descriptions of people, and far-fetched cultural descriptions of everyday life – colourful milieu descriptions and tales of oddballs and loners – whose vagueness and indeterminacy contrasted with apparently precise scientific language, allowed him to reduce the whole of humanity to two types.[51] Reading Kretschmer's descriptions of people, it becomes clear that these are purely subjective impressions and assumptions. Kretschmer pathologised these character types and subjected them to the interpretative sovereignty and authoritarian grip of the psychiatrist;[52] he epitomised the self-empowerment of psychiatric experts.

In its focus on pathology and its monocausal hereditological diagnostics this conception of man took on delusional features; what is really perturbing is the fact that this book, first published in 1922, became a veritable bestseller, reprinted

---

[47] Kretschmer 1922: 154; also 29. Etzemüller (2015a: 119) sees this as a basic feature of hereditary biology.
[48] PV 93/1/33/3, f. 89, Persoonlikheidstiepes volgens Jung en Kretschmer, p. 5.
[49] Kretschmer 1922: 79–87, 90–98, with blatantly racist references 81, 9.
[50] Foucault 1985: ch. 7.
[51] Kretschmer 1922: 113–114. This is also evident in his description of types in the singular, so that the description of an individual appears at the same time as that of a character type (ibid., 103–104). This does not differ in the form of representation from the description of actual case studies (108–113). On Kretschmer's artistic inclinations, see Priwitzer 2004: 90–94.
[52] See also his pathologisation of homosexuality (Kretschmer 1922: 77; see also Mildenberger 2002).

in numerous editions right up to the 1960s – and that it was cited and recommended by psychologists as a standard work.[53]

In one his psychology lectures, Verwoerd did raise critical objections against individual authors and their positions, yet what he accepted without comment was Kretschmer's insistence on a connection between physical appearance and character traits. The amount of time that he devoted to presenting Kretschmer's typology is noteworthy. Similarly to Kretschmer himself, Verwoerd was virtually indulging in describing human types, as if they did not concern types, but real live persons.

In a study entitled 'The Problem of Character Structure' ['*Das Problem des Charakteraufbaus*'] and published in 1926, Hermann Hoffmann, Kretschmer's colleague from Tübingen, developed another typology based on biological heredity. In this study, he elaborated the heredity of character traits, especially in criminals. In contrast to Kretschmer, he sought to identify not only "certain peculiarities of an individual", but also "the peculiarity of the respective individuality in its entirety".[54] In his lecture, Verwoerd referred to a case study involving a hereditary-biological reconstruction – namely Hoffmann's investigation of the character traits of various members of the Bonaparte family.[55] Hoffmann identified a number of character traits in the Bonaparte family, such as ambition, vanity and constancy. He thought it necessary to find out how these characteristics inherited from the parents come together in the respective individual, to enter into a new fusion and create a new structure. Hoffmann started from individual character traits, stating that central traits of the parents could be peripheral in their children and vice versa, thus indirectly conceding that there are no diagnostic criteria for his assertion. According to Hoffmann, the contribution to hereditary biology was the insight that individual traits were independently heritable, so that the respective individual could be adequately classified as a composite of

---

53 Kretschmer was not a member of the NSDAP, but he supported the SS. In 1934, he advocated the sterilisation of the so-called "feeble–minded" and was sympathetic (to say the least) to the Nazis' euthanasia campaigns; even if he was not actively involved in them himself, he legitimised them with his professional authority (Klee 2003: 339). Priwitzer (2004: 286–287) provides a differentiated account. Kretschmer had a South African admirer in German-born psychologist Paul Skawran at the University of Pretoria, who considered the "sterilisation of the feeble-minded and mentally ill, as well as the detention of habitual criminals in concentration camps" in Nazi Germany as steps towards the practical application of scientific knowledge (Skawran 1936: 5, n. 7); he also expressed his admiration for Hitler, whom he considered well–versed in psychology (ibid., 6).
54 Hoffmann 1926: 27.
55 See ibid., 97–111. On the importance of hereditary biology for the "bioscientific objectification" of racial theories, see Potthast 2003: 276; on the connection with psychological aptitude tests, see Schmuhl 2003: 26–30.

such traits. All the while he was intent on retaining the overall framework of biological heredity; the factor of experience was relevant only to the extent that it could have a modifying or reinforcing effect.[56] In his adaptation of Hoffmann's tenets, Verwoerd failed to realise that the characteristics themselves were abstractions and constructions, which is why the determination of a mixing ratio would be extremely problematic from a methodological point of view.[57] The theses of the Tübingen psychiatrist convinced him to such an extent that he explicitly referred to his book in a lecture that presented a general overview of developmental psychology of puberty and adolescence.[58] In his capacity as sociologist, Verwoerd had also addressed the factor of heredity, as he saw it pertaining to so-called "imbeciles" and their possible reproduction:

> The imbecile needs institutional care, maybe even protection, when he has reached adulthood. The big problem, however, is that feeble-mindedness is hereditary and the danger that currently threatens society lies in the rapid increase of the feeble-minded if they remain at large. Moreover, we find that the percentage [of imbecility] among the very poor and among criminals is very high. Probably between 30 and 50% of those who may be called permanently poor, and about the same percentage among criminals are those whom some psychologists and sociologists judge to be intellectually deficient.[59]

Indeed, Verwoerd considered character traits to be heritable. In one of his short stories, which he published in *Die Huisgenoot* while he was working as a professor of Psychology, he described a small child. The insights which he drew from child psychology, and which he applied with considerable sensitivity in other stories,[60] contrasted with the cynical tone of this particular narrative. The child's father is portrayed as stubborn. This character trait, and the subsequent development of little Jannie, is explained by reference to the ancestry of Jannie's father: "The first ancestors he heard of were tramps and layabouts, nothing more than that. They were

---

56 Hoffmann 1926: 62–63 89; p. 70 on puberty, with emphasis on racial differences between Jews and "Teutons" (ibid., 71). He makes reference to Eugen Fischer's Rehoboth study on p. 77, n. 1. In his Introduction to Sociology, Verwoerd, too, viewed certain character traits, which he attributed to "instincts", as being inherited (US, 231/2/1/2, Eerstejaar Sociologie: Algemene kursus, p. 30).
57 PV 93/1/33/3, f. 49f. See also Studie v.d. Voorgeslag (Erbbiologiese Ondersoek).
58 PV 93/1/33/3, f. 22, Onderlinge verskille, p. 16.
59 231/2/1/1, 'Inleiding tot die Sociologie', p. 147, although it is not clear whether the figures refer to South Africa; presumably they are taken from the general literature, as he also refers to doctrinal opinions here, as can be seen from the last sentence.
60 FAV, 4.4.7, Elsa op die Plaas, handwritten manuscript, which breaks off in mid-sentence on p. 9. In the fragment of another story, the narrator ironically refers to the family background: the hero says of himself that he has a hereditary disposition owed to his forefathers, who had always fallen in love, which is what now happened to him as well (ibid., Grille en Giere (van famielie–lewe), typescript, 2 pp.).

succeeded by a few good-for-nothings. . . . They lived merrily – just as a child merrily plays with dirt – and then died, leaving no legacy other than their descendants. But this legacy was significant because it did not lack the characteristic qualities of weeds." The poor qualities came out in later generations; they manifested themselves in their questionable ways of making money, which Jannie's father adopted, leaving his farm "pretty much to natural development, which was due to the fact that he, like his forebears, had farmed with money". Because he was inept at it, he still did not strike it rich. Jannie's mother, on the other hand, came from a "good family" of honest craftsmen. She did not grow up on a farm, but in the village, where she was exposed to all manner of bad influences. "And this mixture of innate inclinations and habits of his parents was to form the basis of Jannie's character."[61]

Verwoerd also dealt with the character studies of Adolf Ehrhardt, head of Vocational Counselling at the Leipzig Employment Office [Arbeitsamt], who published on the subject and also occasionally worked as an assistant in the Department of Applied Psychology at the Institute,[62] albeit not during Verwoerd's stay there. However, Verwoerd presumably got to know him during his visits to the Arbeitsamt. Like Kretschmer, Ehrhardt established a connection between his psychological character studies, physique and racial doctrines.[63] Verwoerd knew Ehrhardt's publications and drew from them in his own courses.

For decades after the end of his academic career, Verwoerd remained interested in racial-biological research, and was friendly with some of its proponents, while actively promoting others. This was especially true for those who were considered protagonists of biological racism within the nationalist camp. These included Geoffrey Cronjé, sociologist at the University of Pretoria. With his biologistic arguments, Cronjé was much closer to Eugen Fischer's theories than most Afrikaner nationalists;[64] but he did not necessarily represent the majority of nationalists, for whom culturalist derivations of the differences between blacks and whites were paramount. In 1946, during an internal discussion of the Broederbond, a "committee" of the Danie Theron Cell approached the Uitvoerende Raad (UR) to make proposals to address the "future task" of the Bond after the end of the Second World War. Among other things, it referred to the importance of eugenics as a subject of study at universities,[65] and urged the establishment of an "active office to

---

61 FAV 4.4.7, 'n Mense lewe, handwritten manuscript that breaks off after five pages.
62 UA Leipzig, Psych. Inst., Letter by Krueger to Sächs. Ministerium f. Volksbildung, 29.3.34.
63 Ehrhardt 1954: 153 with reference to Kretschmer; see also Krueger 1939: 13–14.
64 E.g. Cronjé 1945: ch. 2; J. M. Coetzee 1991: 13. On the limited impact of Cronjé's and Eloff's biologistic theses see Dubow 2014: 26. On similarities in Fischer, see Etzemüller 2015a: 108–109.
65 AB Archive, 2/3/11, UR, 9/10 May 1946, Aanhangsel, Die Taak van die Bond. Verslag van 'n Komitee van die Afd. Danie Theron, 4 May 1946, pp. 7–8. Eugenics was accorded an important role

work out the position and policy of the Afrikaners with regard to race relations".[66] It was certainly no coincidence that among the committee members were well-known right-wing extremists such as H. J. Piek, P. J. Meyer, and future minister M. C. Botha, as well as eugenicist Gerhard Eloff, who, like the first two, was a member of the extreme right-wing Ossewabrandwag (OB).[67] In a book series which was published in the 1940s, and which was programmatic for Afrikaner nationalism during those years, Eloff had pronounced himself on miscegenation along the lines of biological racism; referring to Eugen Fischer, he had issued a strong warning against it.[68] Verwoerd spoke up for former internees, even if they had belonged to the OB; over a lengthy period of time, he was particularly concerned about Eloff, whom he assisted in finding employment,[69] and whose appointment as professor of Genetics at the University of the Orange Free State in Bloemfontein he vigorously promoted. It is not clear from the documents whether this was a matter of a personal attachment, or whether he considered Eloff's activities particularly valuable contributions.[70]

Saul Dubow examined the reception and adaptation of racist theories by South African intellectuals in detail, focusing in particular on aptitude and intelligence tests.[71] After Verwoerd left the Institute of Psychology in Stellenbosch, one of his successors there was J. A. J. van Rensburg. Driven by his own interest in "racial differences"[72] (as he notes at the outset), and encouraged by R. W. Wilcocks, van

---

not only in terms of the policy of racial segregation, and the distinction of whites from coloureds in particular, but also in terms of practical measures with a view to an envisaged selection among the white population itself. Among the measures to be introduced were those related to an increase in the number of children of Afrikaans-speaking upper class families. Universities were to contribute to selective breeding among Afrikaners in order to eliminate congenital disorders.

66 Ibid, p. 7. Whether this proposal was the first impetus for the founding of SABRA remains uncertain; it can only really be determined after much more systematic evaluation of the AB files.

67 The topic of racial biology appears mostly in connection with the name of Eloff (AB Archive, 2/3/37, UR meeting, 1.8.1958, p. 14, TOP 34, Biologiese verskille blank en nie–blank).

68 G. Eloff 1942: 65, ch. 5.

69 AB Archive, 2/3/11, UR meeting, 24.2.1946, p. 2, TOP 6(c).

70 Ibid., UR meeting, 9–10.5.1946, TOP 5: "Br. G. Eloff. Br. H. F. Verwoerd informs [the meeting] that Br. Eloff has applied for the position as psychologist in the Department of Education under Dr. Cook. He [Verwoerd] and Adv. Strydom have tried to use their influence and have received assurances that the internment of Br. Eloff at the State Service Commission should not be counted against him." When Eloff asked for an appointment to see Verwoerd, he received it immediately (PV 93/1/34/8, 107 note. See also Furlong 1991: 229).

71 Dubow 1991; see also Dubow 1995: ch. 6.

72 J. A. J. van Rensburg 1938: 1; the reference to Wilcocks is in the preface.

Rensburg conducted such tests in the late 1930s. He reflected at length on the procedures of other tests that disregarded cultural differences and testing situations, claiming that he had incorporated these differences into the design of his own tests. Van Rensburg applied a test method developed by Moede, with whom Verwoerd had attended some courses at the Technical University Berlin in 1926, and whose procedures were considered exemplary by applied psychologists at Stellenbosch University for quite some time to come. Van Rensburg came to the conclusion that blacks did much worse in the tests than whites, and that learning effects were weaker and delayed. However, he did not recognise his fundamental methodological flaw, namely that he uncritically took the test unit, that is in this case the racial group, as a given, and attributed differences in the test results not to individual, but to collective differences, which cannot actually be measured.

Verwoerd was in discussion with race theorist J. D. J. Hofmeyr[73] from the Institute of Genetics at the University of Pretoria, whom he knew from his student days in the 'Dagbreek' dormitory in Stellenbosch, and had met again during his stay in the US. Hofmeyr described apartheid as something natural: "Apartheid is the process that nature uses successfully to form a balanced, harmonious whole. Ecological and other environmental factors give rise to apartheid in nature, inevitably resulting in the formation of races." On his assumption that both the formation of races and their separation were given by nature, Hofmeyr believed that he could develop a kind of scientific justification for Verwoerd's policy. In March 1956, he founded the South African Genetic Association at the University of Pretoria, with himself as president. In this capacity he initiated the establishment of an Anthropogenetic Institute, which was to deal with human genetics and to bring together research in this field at all South African universities.[74] Hofmeyr sent Verwoerd a copy of the book *Race and Reason* by Carleton Putnam, indicating that he would provide an Afrikaans translation. Verwoerd found it so interesting that he vowed to circulate it among colleagues and friends.[75] Writing in the 1960s under the impact of the American civil rights movement, Putnam presented himself as a somewhat short-sleeved common-sense American intent on demonstrating the self-evidence of racial superiority and inferiority to his countrymen. The originator of what he called "self-delusion" and "trance" was Franz Boas, "a foreign-born Columbia University professor", in whose circle of students Putnam identified dangerous members of the

---

73 On Hofmeyr, see Billig 1981: 100.
74 FAV 4.7.2.1, Letter by Hofmeyr to Verwoerd, 23.9.1958. Verwoerd replied on 3.10., without going into the substantive aspects but expressed great interest and offered to talk to him about the subject. On Hofmeyr, see Dubow 2015: 238–242.
75 PV 93/1/30/1/12, University of Pretoria, Letter by J. D. J. Hofmeyr to Verwoerd., 26.5.1951, and his reply of 16.6.1961 (f. 109).

political left.[76] Initiated by Boas, defeatism has supposedly spread in American society, which has obscured the view of the truth as Putnam would have it, namely that blacks were less gifted than whites. It is hardly surprising that this crude pamphlet appealed to Verwoerd's anti-intellectualism.

Given his professions to, and his self-image as, a democrat, it is astonishing and telling that Verwoerd was not more wary of contact with racist and extreme right-wing milieus both in South Africa and abroad.[77] Thus he did not miss the opportunity to allow the central organ of the European neo-fascists, *Nation Europa*, to reprint a speech in which he castigated the hypocrisy of the West.[78] He cultivated the best of relations with former Greyshirts and their former leader, and now NP MP, Louis Weichardt and Johannes Strauß von Moltke, both ardent supporters of National Socialism and, like Verwoerd himself, avowed antisemites.[79] In the apartheid state, neo-Nazis and right-wing extremists of various kinds, such as Oswald Mosley, Manfred Roeder or David Irving, were welcome guests.[80]

In particular, Verwoerd maintained close contact with Scottish racist Robert Gayre of Gayre, who frequently visited him in South Africa and for whom he al-

---

76 Putnam 1961:10. The attribution of "self-delusion" is to be found on p. 8. The complimentary preface to Putnam's book is signed by Gayre of Gayre, among others. The implicitly antisemitic denunciations of Boas and his disciples, who were accused of having communist leanings, were further disseminated in circles of Afrikaans–speaking racial scientists (Hitzeroth 1966: 20–21).
77 PV 93/3/2/9, 1 Letter of solidarity from Otto Strasser, 12.5.60. On 12.10.1949, the Greyshirts thanked him for a donation of 5 pounds (PV 93/3/1/5, Letter by Greyshirts to Verwoerd, 12.10.1949: f. 27). Before that, they had already sought a rapprochement with the NP (PV 93/3/1/5, Letter by R. A. Swieger (Aksie Committee) to Verwoerd, 5.9.1949, f.1). In 1951, the Party expressed concern about an illness of L. T. Weichardt, former leader of the fascist Greyshirts, who was promised financial support (PV 54/2/2, Federale Raad, session of 15.8.1951, TOP 8, p. 2). Right–wing extremist Strauss von Moltke was a member of Parliament for the NP in the 1960s. He threatened the South African Jewish Board of Deputies, claiming that he had been prevented by a court from publishing a book because he wanted to quote from minutes of meetings of the Board of Deputies. He would now do it in Parliament if the Board did not abandon its opposition to the Bill to abolish the conscience clause (PV 93/1/51/6/1, N. Philips (President South African Jewish Board of Deputies), Correspondence with J. von Moltke (MP for the NP) to Prime Minister (copy), 30.3.1961, ff.130–132). An overview of right-wing extremist movements in post–war South Africa is provided by M. M. Visser 1999: ch.3.
78 Verwoerd 1964b. After his assassination, the journal published a commemorative leaflet which it sent to his widow (4.7.8.1, Arthur Ehrhardt (Nation Europa) to E. Verwoerd, 17.10.1966; her letter of thanks, 24.10.1966).
79 Therefore D. Prinsloo (1979: 256) is not quite correct in claiming that Verwoerd rejected the Greyshirts on account of his democratic principles. On the contrary, Verwoerd did not hold democratic principles, only nationalist ones. On Moltke, ibid. p. 373. J. H. Hofmeyr (1945: 18–21) had already pronounced antisemitism an import from Nazi Germany.
80 Shain 1998: 10–11.

ways found time in his densely dotted appointment schedule.[81] The ethnologist and future chairman of Verwoerd's Scientific Advisory Council, H. O. Mönnig, had met Gayre in Edinburgh. The latter wanted to establish an institute there and come to Pretoria for a conference organised by Hofmeyr. For Mönnig, Gayre was "one of the few scientists in his field who has the courage, contrary to liberal world opinion, to clearly state the facts of the situation and for that reason, he is one of our few anthropologist friends".[82] In his reply, Verwoerd confirmed that Gayre was "doing a good job" and that he himself was "a subscriber of the journal *Mankind Quarterly*".[83] This journal, edited by Gayre, is still in existence today, as a forum for the most extreme views on racial biology; it is the pseudo-scientific flagship of international racism.

Gayre was not only a zealous propagandist and defender of apartheid; beyond that, he assigned the country a world-historical task: if South Africa persevered and successfully implemented the policy of territorial racial segregation "with a conservative point of view, and standards of conduct", "then in due course, from Southern Africa there would flow back to the U.S.A., the U.K., Holland, and the northern European countries, concepts which we once had and have now lost, and from this European greatness could arise again". In that sense, apartheid was by no means a defensive policy, but the harbinger of a new world order to be aspired to.[84] On the recommendation of the South African ambassador in London, A. J. R. van Rhyn, former editor-in chief of the *Volksblad* in Bloem-

---

81 PV 93/1/34/9, Letter by H. O. Mönnig to Verwoerd., 6.7.1962, with attached memorandum and his reply dated 10.7.1962, pp. 123–132. See also PV 93/3/1/33, Letter by R. Gayre of Gayre to Verwoerd, 28.7.1960, p.1: Verwoerd arranged to meet Gayre in the afternoon of 6.9.1966, the day he was murdered. PV 93/1/34/16, Verwoerd also followed Gayre's recommendations, for instance the recommendation to receive Sir John Greig Dunbar, who was "very active" in the Conservative Club in Edinburgh (PV 93/1/34/15, f. 128, Letter by Gayre of Gayre to Verwoerd, 24.11.65). Under Verwoerd's successor, the cooperation continued: Vorster agreed to receive Gayre shortly after Verwoerd's death; interestingly, the meeting was arranged by the South Africa Foundation (PV 132/2/6/2/1/1, Letter by G. L. Dickerson to Vorster, 14.9.1966). On Gayre, see Billig 1981: 96–101.
82 PV 93/1/34/9, Letter by H. O. Mönnig to Verwoerd, 6.7.1962. Enclosed with the letter is a memorandum by Gayre, in which he explains why he considers an International Research Institute for Racial Studies important: The Nazis had advocated Lamarckism and therefore denied innate racial characteristics; however, this was the wrong doctrine (ibid., ff. 124–131).
83 PV 93/1/34/9, Letter by Verwoerd to H.O. Mönnig, 10.7.1962, ff. 123–132.
84 PV 93/1/34/16, Letter by R. Gayre of Gayre to Verwoerd, 13.5.1966; the latter's reply, 14.5.1966 as well as Gayre's letter of 16.6.66 (ff. 69–74). In addition, he advised him to take repressive measures against the English-speaking universities in South Africa. In a chatty vein, he recalled his time as a member of the British occupation in Italy, when he targeted political left-wingers specifically. S. le Roux, a former minister, spoke of the important role South Africa played in the world (PV 18/3/1/72, Letter by S. le Roux to C. R. Swart, 13.3.1966: ". . . that we should play a path-

fontein, the Scottish nobleman turned to Piet Cillié of *Die Burger* with a proposal to publish one of his book manuscripts. It was a two-volume 'Foundation of Ethnology', which was supposed to prove the "inheritance of mental and temperamental characters, both in individuals and racial groups".[85]

Hofmeyr's Anthropogenetic Institute was the result of an initiative by Gayre, who wanted to establish a counterpart to his racial genetics Institute in Scotland. The Department of Home Affairs attested to the fact that Gayre's proposal had met with great interest in South Africa. However, the researchers involved were hand-picked and the whole thing was kept secret, presumably because of the international reputation of Gayre and his journal.[86]

Among Verwoerd's international racist contacts were also numerous old Nazi and racist Germans who, in their letters and other writings, expressed sympathy for South Africa, often accompanied by practical suggestions for more effective enforcement of racial segregation.[87] Support also came from American racists, including Scientology founder Ron Hubbard, who offered his services as apartheid propagandist, along with practical suggestions.[88] Among the German correspondents were the Tübingen geographer and former NSDAP activist Warhold Drascher, who boasted of his friendship with controversial missionary Heinrich Vedder,[89] and sent Verwoerd

---

breaking role for a new approach to the world's problems"). On South Africa taking a leading role in the face of a resurgence of racism in future, see also Nixon 1993: 127.

85 220.K 59 (42), Letter by Gayre of Gayre to Cillié, 26.5.1959; no reply from Cillié has been found.

86 Eloff later withdrew from the Africa Institute because, contrary to earlier announcements, this had become a general institute for anthropology instead of one specialised in anthropogenetics and eugenics (PV 93/3/1/65, Letter by Gerhard Eloff to Secretary of the Africa Institute with copy to Verwoerd, further letters and memorandum for Minister of the Interior, 1.4.1964, f. 33). Incidentally, the Director of the Institute was leading SABRA intellectual and extreme right–winger P. F. D. Weiss.

87 See for instance PV 93/3/1/45, Letter by Hermann Gauch to Verwoerd, 31.5.196, f. 21; also PV 93/3/1/27, Letter by Fritz Winter (Freiburg) to Verwoerd, 7.2.1960, f. 130. The most repugnant case is that of former navy paymaster Fritz Huhn, who covertly suggested genocide to Verwoerd (PV 93/1/30/1/19, Letter by Marine Oberzahlm. a.D. F. Huhn (Osnabrück) to Verwoerd., 3.5.1963). Albr. C. Matingen from Rotenburg o.d.T., a former Wehrmacht officer, in turn, offered his experience in combatting partisans: "I would gladly make myself available for this task, which requires a clear position." (PV 93/1/36/1/2, Letter by A. C. Matingen (Rothenburg o.d.T.) to Verwoerd, 31.3.1960).

88 PV 93/1/30/1/9, Letter by Ron Hubbard to Verwoerd, 9.11.1960, f. 95. See also PV 93/1/53/2/5, ff. 40–42, Letter by S. J. Parkhouse (Hubbard Association of Scientologists International) to Verwoerd., 7.11.1960 with attached proposal for a lawsuit by South Africa against Liberia and Ethiopia.

89 Vedder later gave him a copy, with dedication, of the autobiography of the Commandant-Generaal of the Ossewabrandwag, J. F. J. van Rensburg; the book can be found in the Tübingen University Library. Hans U. Granow, German ambassador at the time, also conveyed greetings to Verwoerd from Vedder, who assured him of the high esteem in which he held him (PV 93/3/1/19, Letter by Granow to Verwoerd, 7.11.1959).

a copy of his defence of colonialism, published under the title, *Schuld der Weißen?* ('White Man's Guilt?').⁹⁰ Right-wing extremist writer Peter Kleist announced a fact-finding trip to South Africa, with the intention to write a book glorifying apartheid.⁹¹

The kinds of fruit borne by such cooperation are displayed by Verwoerd's correspondence with Austrian Nazi Theodor Soucek, who sent him samples of his journalistic defence of South Africa, which was favourably received by the Prime Minister – until the correspondence was interrupted by a notice from the South African Police, informing the latter that his corresponding interlocutor was an internationally wanted Nazi sentenced to death in Austria. Soucek was promptly deported from South Africa.⁹²

Verwoerd's Antisemitism

Casting Verwoerd as antisemite is what his son Wilhelm views tantamount to making "hackneyed accusations" against his father.⁹³ Nevertheless, his antisemitism becomes clearly evident even before the start of his political career. This attitude of his was not a matter of political opportunism; on the contrary, antisemitism was part of his basic convictions. In one of his Sociology lectures, he spoke about the problem of immigration, without naming the Jews directly, but insinuating that "the new immigrants do not help in opening up new resources, drawing instead

---

90 PV 93/3/1/29, Letter by Warhold Drascher to Verwoerd, 23.3.1960: f. 74. Drascher joined the NSDAP in 1937. His articles appeared in the *Völkischer Beobachter*, among other publications; he also published colonial apologetic literature with strong racist overtones, which did not make a dent in his academic career in the Federal Republic of Germany (Bundesarchiv (formerly Berlin Document Center), Personalakte Drascher, No. 5455042).

91 PV 93/1/34/10, Letter by Peter Kleist to Verwoerd with attached *curriculum vitae*, 7.9.1962, f. 74. On Kleist, see also 220.K 64 (94b), Report of the S.A. Jewish Board of Deputies on antisemitic visitors in South Africa, in which Kleist is the first to be named, and 94d, Some Notes on right-wing movements throughout the world, p. 3. Among the anti-Semites was A. K. Chesterton, who two years later founded the National Front in Britain and attended the International Symposium on Anti-Communism, which was also attended by Koot Vorster and Hendrik van den Bergh (ibid., 94–95, S.A. Jewish Board of Deputies (L. Hodes) on Chesterton's visit, 11.6.1964).

92 PV 93/1/30/1/20, Theodor Soucek, correspondence with Verwoerd of various dates, 27.6.1963, p. 46. Soucek spent 1963/4 in South Africa, where he was involved in dubious business deals in connection with arms and armaments, a detailed list of which was provided by the South African authorities. He was then deported by the South Africans to Switzerland, from where he fled to Spain to avoid extradition to Austria. See also 220.K 64(94b), S.A. Jewish Board of Deputies, Report on right-wing extremist visitors in South Africa, p. 3 on Soucek.

93 W. J. Verwoerd 2001: 8.

from the existing productive capacities of the country, by engaging in trade, among other things".[94] In the early 1930s, he wrote a series of short stories, some of which were published in *Die Huisgenoot*. One of these stories was not published, but is still available in manuscript form. Hardly any antisemitic cliché is left out in the story entitled 'The Return of Moses Levinsohn'. Moses Levinsohn is a small shopkeeper who envies the success of his Indian competitor, laughing gleefully when children play tricks on the latter. He himself is not a good businessman and not a particularly clever dealer, which is why his business goes from bad to worse after getting married. His dire circumstances lead him to set fire to his shop in order to defraud the insurance company, but he was so clumsy that the insurance company exposes the fraud and refuses to pay out. A settlement is reached, and he continues to run his shop. After some time, he lands in bad financial shape again; he believes that he is bringing his wife nothing but bad luck, so he decides to take his own life. He hangs himself in the synagogue, of all places, to which he has a key. Soon after, rumours start circulating that the dead man would return and that the synagogue was haunted.[95] When his wife finally decides to get to the bottom of the matter, she finds her husband, who was believed dead, alive. By an unfortunate coincidence, his brother had hanged himself and the body was mistaken for that of Moses Levinsohn. Since his wife is now living off the life insurance of her husband, who was declared dead, he assumes his brother's identity and they start a new life elsewhere.

The Jewish shopkeeper Levinsohn is portrayed as being inept, insinuating the first antisemitic stereotype in this story – namely the lack of creativity attributed to Jews. Levinsohn cheats the insurance company twice over, and has no problem changing his identity – which corresponds to Verwoerd's idea that a person of Jewish background does not really have an identity; Levinsohn can start a new life anywhere because he is not really rooted anywhere. Even the description of Levinsohn's appearance indicates that Verwoerd was an antisemite through and through, even at this stage: "Actually Moses was just a troubled little fellow [*besukkelde ventjie*]. His height of five feet three inches did not endow him with dignity. His lips were too thick for that, his back too crooked, his head too big and

---

94 US, 231/2/1/1, 'Inleiding tot die Sociologie', p. 87; on the following page, however, he explicitly states that Jews are not a South African, but a worldwide problem, and defends the Quota Act of 1930. In complete ignorance of the facts, he claimed that today (1933!) religious or political persecution was no longer the main reason for the emigration of Jews, but rather economic pressure, such as too little land for agriculture – when in fact, in most European countries, Jews had been forbidden to own land for centuries (ibid.)

95 Verwoerd was apparently processing a childhood experience here, since the Verwoerds lived in Wynberg in proximity to the synagogue, which was said to be haunted (L. Cloete 2001: 32).

his eyes too watery. But he was not old – at least not noticeably so." As a Jew, he is assigned to the realm of darkness: after his presumed death, he reappears hauntingly, at night. The haunting, meanwhile, is debunked because Levinsohn turns out not to be dead, so the haunting does not pose a threat. Jews are not powerful, is the implicit message; they only become powerful because there are enough people who believe in their power. Verwoerd was intent on presenting Levinsohn the Jew as a farcical figure who could be successful in life only through fraud and lucky coincidences.[96]

During his time as professor at Stellenbosch University, Verwoerd organised protests against the entry of Jewish refugees from Germany.[97] He was joined in this campaign by a colleague, German-born Christian Gustav Waldemar Schumann, professor of Economics at Stellenbosch University. Together with Schumann and his colleagues Johannes Basson and future ministerial colleague T. E. Dönges, the right-wing extremist student organisation ANS staged a protest when the refugee ship 'Stuttgart' arrived in Cape Town;[98] theologian J. S. Gericke, who later was to hold the position of Vice Chancellor of the University for a long time, and who was a close confidant of Verwoerd, was the student representative agitating against Jewish immigration to South Africa. Professor Verwoerd publicly displayed his antisemitic stance, saying, "the cardinal problem of this Jewish colonisation lies in the fact that the hope of the Afrikaners lies in occupying the influential positions in commerce and industry commensurate with their proportion of the population". He used the next occasion of a public speech – this time in Malmesbury – to respond to Minister Hofmeyr's admonition of tolerance: "The tolerance which Minister Hofmeyr asks of us is the tolerance of weakness, betrayal and suicide."[99] Hofmeyr's criticism of their intolerance was interpreted as a restriction on freedom

---

96 FAV 4.4.7, O. Nieuwenhuys [Verwoerd], 'Die Terugkeer van Moses Levinsohn', typescript.
97 Schumann, for his part, was apparently influenced by the writings of the antisemitic social scientist John Atkinson Hobson (PV 118 Haak–Sammlung, notes on Prof. C. G. W. Schumann (unpaginated), first page). Schumann's argument was clearly racist, as can be seen from his reference to "Jewish genius": "The Jew occupies a special position in the economic structure. His genius succeeded in turning the capitalist system to his advantage. He becomes not a worker but a master." (Ibid., second page).
98 Bekker 1988: 107–109 and G. D. Scholtz 1979: 485–486; also Sichel 1966: 17, 24, without mentioning Verwoerd by name. For those involved, see Shain 2015: 131–134. On antisemitism in the NP as well as in the Reformed Churches, see Saron/Hotz 1955: 384–385.
99 PV 118 Haak Collection, Notes '1937. Die Jode', p. 2 with quotations from the speeches of the three as well as those of Verwoerd, citing as sources *Die Burger* of 5.11 and 29.11. (Speech in Malmesbury). Even decades later, Haak does not indicate an admission that the antisemitic actions might have been wrong; instead, he quotes extensively from Malan's relevant remarks in Parliament and Verwoerd's in *Die Transvaler*, p. 194.

of speech, and rejected for that; the statement signed by the six professors did not display a trace of an awareness of injustice; on the contrary, they considered their antisemitic tirades as perfectly legitimate. Those who had refused to appear on behalf of the right-wing extremist student association ANS at an antisemitic event, were assumed "not to be free from Jewish influence". The professors, in turn, considered themselves unprejudiced. Even at this stage, Verwoerd showed one of his characteristic traits, namely the incapability of self-criticism; when confronted with criticism, he immediately responded with counter-accusations. This was also the case this time round, when he once again made a public appearance in Worcester, and used the opportunity to cast the professors in the role of victims: "And may we ask ourselves how the highly vaunted tolerance which Minister Hofmeyr expects from the professors towards the Jews in Germany, is being practiced by him towards the professors in South Africa who, with the deepest seriousness and sense of responsibility, have taken the unaccustomed path to go directly to their people, when they noticed how the existence of the people was threatened?"[100] He was ostensibly not targeting any group of immigrants in particular; but his motive was clearly antisemitic; in another speech at an NP event he railed against Jews, arguing for a stop to their immigration – not only to South Africa, but "also not to Palestine", which is noteworthy, since Verwoerd had always maintained that he was interested only in South Africa and the Afrikaner people.[101] The assertion of the professors that they did not belong to any party and had nothing to do with party politics, was refuted by Verwoerd himself in a speech at a National Party event held a week earlier during the provincial elections in Worcester.[102] Looking back on Verwoerd's stay in Germany, where he studied with Jewish scholars such as William Stern, to whose writings he frequently referred in his lectures, the question arises whether he gave a single thought to the possibility that among the refugees to whom he offered his very special welcome could have been one of his teachers.

According to Verwoerd, "foreign elements who do not assimilate to Christianity" (by which he meant Jews), were among the factors responsible for the situation of the "Poor Whites".[103] This antisemitic interpretation of the "Poor White

---

[100] *Die Burger*, 29.11.1936. Signatories were Professors J. Basson, A. C. Cilliers, C. G. S. de Villiers, C. G. W. Schumann, H. F. Verwoerd and J. A. Wiid, all of Stellenbosch. In the official history of the University of Stellenbosch, the event is not mentioned anywhere (Thom et al. 1966). On Verwoerd's involvement in the protests against the 'Stuttgart', see Mendelsohn/Shain 2008: 110.
[101] Notes on his lecture 'Betekenis van ons stede vir die politieke toekoms van die Afrikaner', which he presented to the NP (in FAV 4.4.6) (probably in 1937). Hepple (1967: 219–227) also makes it clear that these were not one-off opportunistic lapses. See also Sabalot 2009: 63.
[102] *Die Burger*, 23.11.1936. See also Paton 1971: 193–194.
[103] PV 93/1/67/3, Bylae op toeligting van beskrywingspunte, ff. 88; also 86.

Problem" did not find expression in Verwoerd's public statements during the Kimberley Conference in 1934, nor in the corresponding official papers; on this occasion, he was very careful not to offend English-speaking participants, since he himself had agreed to admit Morris Alexander, a Jewish member of parliament, to the Congress because of the influential position that he held. Verwoerd openly expressed his antisemitism in other activities which he simultaneously pursued and which were much more closely aligned to a sectional Afrikaans cultural nationalism – such as the public actions against Jewish refugees mentioned above, and the antisemitic article which he deliberately placed in the first edition of *Die Transvaler*, and which was still strongly influenced by his work with the "Poor Whites".[104]

In the pilot edition of *Die Transvaler*, which featured prominent nationalists as authors, editor-in-chief Verwoerd published a lengthy article which was distinctly programmatic.[105] Entitled 'The Jewish Question Seen from the National Point of View', it was a clear manifestation of Verwoerd's antisemitism. In the opening sentences, he shielded himself from the accusation of racism. Afrikaners, he said, were always accused of racism when they simply defended their rights; but when Englishmen defended themselves, this was considered perfectly natural. In the case of the Jews, he said, one can assume that "some of the accusers wrongly, but nevertheless in all honesty, think that the nationalists' point of view stems solely from hatred of that racial group". What followed upon this self-immunisation against accusations of racism was the circulation of an antisemitic pamphlet highlighting the domination of the South African economy by Jews. This was a well-rehearsed antisemitic tactic. Verwoerd adduced a typically antisemitic argument, correlating the proportion of Jews as a percentage of the total population with the incidence of antisemitism, thus blaming antisemitism on Jews. He claimed that his argument was motivated by a positive attitude, namely the love for his people; being the cultural nationalist that he was, this meant that he radically distinguished himself from others who, after all, were citizens of the same country. The Jews, too, would be committed first and foremost to their own

---

104 Verwoerd himself saw his journalistic work as a continuation of his previous activity (University Archives, Stellenbosch, Senate Minutes, vol. XI, 9.12.1935–19.3.1937 undated [1937] Letter from Verwoerd to Rector Wilcocks: "Only the conviction that in my new field of work I can continue the activities with which I was involved with during my time as a lecturer, has prompted me to take on the new task.") I do not agree with the suggestion of T. D. Moodie (1975: 167) that Verwoerd's antisemitic statements were made under pressure from the Party base; his antisemitism was too consistent and was clearly borne by deeply held convictions (see also P. Beinart 1996: 69).
105 This article led to a break between Verwoerd and Willy Hofmeyr (O'Meara 1983: 105).

people, as the resistance to the crackdown on Jewish immigration had shown. This is what led Verwoerd to insinuate that Jews, as a tightly knit community, were planning actions to improve their position at the expense of others. He consistently spoke of an "influx" of Jews, whom he called "foreigners" having "burrowed their way into the urban professions". Afrikaners at first did not really take notice of Jews and of their conflict with the English. Jews were "so hospitably received" but then it turned out that they aspired to political domination "in the country of their hosts". Verwoerd was insistent in his claim that South Africa belonged only to the Afrikaners; he ignored the conquest by Great Britain and instead classified immigrants as "foreigners", regardless of how long they had resided in the country. The urbanisation of Afrikaners had started too late – all the lucrative positions in the economy were already occupied by others. "In the case of some Jewish businesses, the business ethics and methods were different from those of Christians – at least to some extent." He was wise enough not to specify these shortcomings.

As prominent activist in the patronage network of the Broederbond, Verwoerd then complained that Jews helped each other. Even if individual Afrikaners managed to get into leading positions in "Jewish" companies, Verwoerd could only recognise base motives at work, such as calculated moves to attract Afrikaans-speaking customers. Jews were now also pushing into professions, including the medical or legal ones, in which Afrikaners had until then been well established. Politically, the Jews were pursuing individual self-interests, which did not quite fit with Verwoerd's previous assertion of strong bonds of solidarity within the Jewish community. In explaining why Afrikaners came to realise the state of affairs only now, he explicitly mentioned the "events in Germany" and the organisations that "received their inspiration" from there. He cited his own activities as an example of this new realisation, counting himself among the "young Afrikaners of the professional classes" "who, in their analysis of the social conditions of their people, clearly saw the circumstances as described above". In fact, the article was illustrated with photos of the far-right professors from Stellenbosch, including Verwoerd himself. Verwoerd reproached South African Jewish citizens for having brought it all upon themselves because they had not followed a call from the Stellenbosch professors to participate in the protests against immigration of Jewish refugees from Germany. Instead, they had been "excessively emotional in taking a stand against the express wishes of the majority of the country's inhabitants". Verwoerd's claims to represent the majority are part of a consistent pattern. He had been working with this assumption way back in his work in the Continuation Committee. Towards the end of the article, he openly threatened repression in the event of a National Party takeover; at the same time, he wooed the English-speaking population to join forces with the Afrikaners in forming an alliance against the Jews.[106]

By no means can this article be seen as a slip-up. Verwoerd frequently peppered his articles with antisemitic references; in one instance, he called the Afrikaner Party "semi-imperialists" who would accept a republic only on condition that "three quarters of the Jews and English also voted for it".[107] The sequence was not coincidental, since capitalism and imperialism were denounced by Verwoerd and other nationalists as distinctly Jewish phenomena. The Broederbond shared this view of a Jewish hegemony, since it supported the quota regulation for professionals; it denounced what it saw as a scandal – that there were too many Jewish doctors with "base methods": "For the 7½% of Jews in the white population, 7½% of doctors should suffice."[108] In its 1938 election programme, the NP explicitly called for an immigration stop for Jews.[109] As late as 1950, an internal paper of the Broederbond warned against a "general danger posed by Jews" and issued the following recommendation: "The appointment of professors and lecturers must be more strictly controlled. The two largest Universities are teeming with liberalists, in whose ranks communist driftwood from the War [*oorlogsopdrifsels*], even from Eastern Europe, feels perfectly at home and eagerly participates in destroying the Afrikaner way of life and, above all, in deliberately blurring the dividing line based on skin colour."[110] At the centre of Verwoerd's attacks remained Jewish immigration, which he rigorously opposed and actively

---

106 *Die Transvaler*, 1.10.1937, Die Joodse Vraagstuk Besien vanuit Die Nasionale Standpunt. See Meiring 1987: 9–10 on the advertising boycott of *Die Transvaler* by Jewish businesses that followed the article. Subsequently, the NP chairman in the OFS, N. J. van der Merwe, responded with another antisemitic outburst, see *Die Transvaler*, 27.11.1937; the Jewish Board of Deputies then issued a statement saying that there were no advertisement boycotts, which Verwoerd denounced in the same issue as false. See also *Die Transvaler*, 30.11.1937, wherein he issued threats in an attempt to persuade Jewish companies to place advertisements in his newspaper. According to Meiring (1990: 52–53), Verwoerd wrote his article – despite the foreseeable consequences – without consulting with the publishing Directorate. Meiring (1973a: 73–75; see also Shain 1994:147; also Uys 1959: 1) maintains that numerous antisemitic articles appeared in *Die Transvaler*.
107 *Die Transvaler*, 20.9.1941 (editorial). See further examples in Shain 2015: 194–195, 258.
108 FAV, 4.5.2.4, Aanhangsel G, Tekort aan Afrikaner-Verpleegsters en Geneeshere (opgestel deur Mediese Kommissie, Afd. Kaapstad) [1936]. The Broederbond cultivated its antisemitism at the highest level, see AB Archives. 2/3/8/2, UR meeting on 12.8.1938, Bylae B 'Die Christen-Afrikaner en die Joodse Vraagstuk', which abounds with anti–Semitic clichés, and insinuates that Jews are the enemies of the Afrikaners.
109 Erasmus 1938: 5.
110 AB Archive, 2/3/19, Report van die Mediese Komitee van Afdeling Kaapstad: Toename van Joodse dokters.

fought against – even after the end of the War, when news of the Holocaust reached South Africa.[111]

This form of racism, which blamed the Jews for antisemitism, was shared by the NP, and elevated to its official party line.[112] The NP propagated this notion right into the post-war period, even endowing it with the attribute of inevitability: "When the proportion of Jews in any country exceeds a certain percentage, antisemitism is the inevitable consequence."[113] Verwoerd also supported the decision that the NP in the Transvaal would not accept Jews as members.[114] In numerous articles, he railed against Jewish-British capitalism and in particular against Jews whom he generally considered unassimilable, even though there was a large number of Jewish English-speaking South Africans who showed greater willingness to learn Afrikaans than did their Christian compatriots.

During his time as editor of *Die Transvaler*, Verwoerd tried to use his connections with the Rector of the University Stellenbosch, his doctoral supervisor Raymond Wilcocks, to arrange for the award of an honorary doctorate to English-speaking Canadian mining engineer Carleton Jones, who, in his eyes, was not only held in high esteem, but also had the special virtue of being "anti-Jewish". But Verwoerd did not succeed with this bid.[115]

After 1945, when news of the Holocaust had become a matter of public knowledge in South Africa and could no longer be dismissed as Allied propaganda, public expressions of antisemitism subsided noticeably. Instead, the xenophobic animus and some of the same stereotypes were redirected towards persons of In-

---

[111] Further examples are to be found in D. Prinsloo 1979: 407–414. P. J. Meyer (1984: 30) maintains that the main themes expounded by Verwoerd in the 1930s and 1940s were the Jewish domination of the business world and black population growth.
[112] In January 1937, Malan blatantly advocated a ban on Jewish immigration to South Africa in Parliament, even putting the word refugees in inverted commas to cast doubt on their motives (PV 18/2/1/2, Voorstel in Volksraad, 12.1.1937).
[113] PV 93/1/30/1/2, f. 95 Circular of the Inligtingskantoor, Oct. 1947, p. 99. See also the antisemitic anti-immigration propaganda in 1946 (NP, 'n Roekelose Regeringsplan. Onbeheerde Immigrasie bedreig Suid–Afrika, Cape Town [1946], p. 4). Malherbe (1946: 6–8) reports that during World War II, the anti–Black racism among soldiers declined, but not antisemitism.
[114] HNP 1940: 11. According to J. Basson (2006: 75), the decision can be traced back to Verwoerd (see also ibid., 102).
[115] UA Stellenbosch UA, Eregrade afgewesen, Letter by Verwoerd to Wilcocks, 15 April 1939. The attachment does give an indication of political calculation, even if it is not entirely clear what it was; the University of the Witwatersrand had presumably considered an honorary doctorate for the same man. Verwoerd himself admitted that it would be difficult to justify the award on the basis of scientific activity via publications, but it would be possible if more practical, applied science were to be the criterion. The whole letter is not worded in such a way as to suggest that Verwoerd's proposal would have had any chance of success. On Jones, see also J. Davenport 2013: 320.

dian background. The campaigns against Indians, which included business boycotts, were organised and propagated by some of the same people who had previously participated in antisemitic activities.[116]

Verwoerd's concern for post-war Germany, which went as far as appealing for donations for the German "victims" of the War, was in stark contrast to his insensitivity to the fate of the Jews. He never said a word about it, there is not a single statement of his about the Holocaust and the lessons to be learnt from the conditions and processes that facilitated it. On the contrary, even after the War, he persisted in his stance on undesirable immigrants. During the Bondsraad in October 1946, Verwoerd emphatically pointed to the dangers of a new wave of immigration, with the Allies seeking above all to get rid of the so-called "uprooted". Persons from the Scandinavian countries, Great Britain, Germany or the Netherlands were not willing to come, or were being barred entry, "and thus, all those who are available will be Italians, Balts, Slavs, Poles and Jews".[117]

It is interesting to see Verwoerd in agreement with J. G. Strijdom on this. Like Verwoerd, Strijdom made no secret of his antisemitism; it was Strijdom who saw to it that a clause barring Jews from membership of the Party was included in the statutes of the Transvaal National Party. As late as 1947, Strijdom wrote to F. C. Erasmus expressing outrage at the contention of the NP of the Cape Province, that the policy did not apply to long-standing Jewish residents, only to those who had newly immigrated from Europe in the 1930s; Strijdom never referred to them as refugees – who in fact they were –, but as "superfluous" people. He cautioned the Party against risking the loss of votes of "thousands of Greyshirts, German and English speakers", weighed up against "the doubtful prospect of a small group of Jewish voters".[118] Strijdom attempted to commit the NP of the Cape to an antisemitic consensus, arguing that discrimination was directed not only against refugees, but against all Jews, regardless of how long they had lived in South Africa.[119] While antisemitism was a matter of conviction for Louw, Verwoerd and others, it turned out to be an opportunistic stance in the case of Malan and the Cape NP.[120] Eric Louw was outraged when

---

[116] On the geographical spread, see Millar 1988: 10–16; Marx 2008: 248–249; Shain 1994: 53–54, 152.
[117] AB Archive, 2/3/12, Bondsraad, 3–5.10.1946, p. 12, TOP 21, Immigrasiebeleid. See also Peberdy 2009: 110, 125–126.
[118] PV 97/1, Letter by Strijdom to Erasmus, 10.11.1947, the term "these superfluous people" is to be found on p. 3 of the letter.
[119] PV 97/2, Letter by Erasmus to Strijdom, 29.11.1947, in which he points out that it is only the Transvaal NP that denies membership to Jews in their Party statutes.
[120] Koorts 2014: 310–314.

Malan abandoned the antisemitic consensus, seeking to end discrimination against Jews after the War.[121]

The three leading politicians of the radical right within the NP, Strijdom, Swart and Louw, felt marginalised by Malan, sensing a Cape NP agenda against them, which they saw confirmed by the Cape NP's abandonment of antisemitism.[122] Since the wrath of these three radical right-wing politicians was directed against the alliance of the Herenigde Nasionale Party and the Afrikaner Party, and hence against the ever-improving personal relationship between Malan and Havenga, it is clear that neither Strijdom nor the other two could be considered upright democrats in opposition to the OB. What was at issue, rather, was Havenga's rise to power and the fear of a new 'fusion' ['*smeltery*'], i.e. a dilution of the cultural nationalist principles, of which antisemitism was an integral part.[123]

---

121 PV 18/3/1/1, Letter by Louw to Erasmus, 17.11.1947.
122 Especially clear in PV 18/3/1/51, Letter by Louw to Strijdom, 24.11.1947; ibid., Letter by Swart to Louw and Strijdom, 29.11.1947; ibid., Letter to B. Sachs with transcript and antisemitic note to Malan, 28.11.1947. See also ibid., Letter by Malan to Swart, 2.12.1947; also J. L. Basson 1980: 551–554.
123 PV 18/3//51, Letter by Strijdom to Swart, 3.12.1947.

Apartheid

This chapter deals with political concepts, planning and scenarios for the implementation of apartheid – the system of legally determined segregation that prevailed between 1948 and 1994. It was an attempt to re-organise the state and society on the basis of race. This chapter takes account of the implementation of these plans only to the extent that they indicate particular conceptions. Hendrik Verwoerd as political agent is as little the subject of this chapter as it is of the book as a whole.

Despite the fact that differences could be discerned between British colonies and Boer Republics in South Africa in the 19th century, as far as forms of racial discrimination are concerned, a discourse of racial segregation took hold in the early 20th century. Preceding policies and practices, such as the territorial segregation introduced in colonial Natal by long-serving Secretary for Native Affairs, Theophilus Shepstone, can hardly be considered a model, as apartheid policy-makers seldom referred to them.[1] There are other influences from the 1920s that proved more decisive.[2] American models played a role, as did the need felt by the white administration to control the black population and, as far as possible, to prevent the rural exodus and urbanisation. Since the 1930s, biological-racial doctrines, which had been particularly popular among English-speaking intellectuals and civil servants, were gradually replaced by an emphasis on cultural differences. Segregationism was compatible with, and eagerly embraced and adapted by, Afrikaner cultural nationalism.[3]

In the 1930s, and then with gathering momentum in the 1940s, the fault lines in Afrikaner nationalism shifted. While the British Empire remained a major adversary, the accelerated urbanisation of the black population during the Second World War moved the rapidly changing demographics of the black population centre stage. Afrikaner nationalists were alarmed at the demographic expansion of the "non-whites", but even more so at their accelerated urbanisation; the proportion of "de-tribalised" Africans was estimated to amount to 50%.[4] The number

---

1 Welsh 1971: 29.
2 Rich 1980: 171, who points to SABRA's reception of E. T. Stubb's ideas. See for example Stubbs's advocacy of territorial segregation (1953). Jan Smuts was one of the early protagonists of segregation (Smuts 1940: 11–21).
3 Rich 1990: 685–686.
4 AB Archive, 2/3/14, Die Verhouding van die blankes tot die nie–blankes, listing of 28.10.1947. Apparently it was the speech of the Chairman at the Bondsraad that is not reproduced in the minutes, but was announced as a separate document, see ibid. p. 3, reference to the Bondsraad. See also Mostert 1985.

of black employees in the manufacturing industry doubled between 1937/8 and 1947/8.[5] Many whites had been enlisted as soldiers to fight at the war fronts, so racial segregation had been temporarily relaxed in order to keep industrial production going. Blacks were thus able to take over the jobs of whites and embark on strike action for wage increases.[6] For the first time, blacks formed the majority of the urban population in Johannesburg. In the 1940s, a so-called "apartheid discourse" unfolded in the various discussion circles of Afrikaner nationalism, in which theologians and ethnologists, constitutional lawyers, educators and, in the end, also politicians participated.[7] The so-called "apartheid discourse" indicated a reorientation of the policy of racial segregation towards a systematised and integrated overall concept.[8] As early as 1939, Badenhorst delivered a Kuyperian variant of ethical Calvinist theology justifying racial segregation.[9]

Whereas Aletta Norval speaks of an *apartheid discourse* and Hermann Giliomee of an *apartheid plan*, we are talking here about the *apartheid concept*. The terms designate quite different things: apartheid discourse encompasses the discussions in different circles within Afrikaner nationalism in the 1930s and 1940s, whereas the apartheid plan is the direct translation of a – supposedly elaborated – concept into a workable policy. The transition from discourse through concept to plan implies at a gradual narrowing of the persons and groupings involved. While the discourse involved wide circles of the Afrikaans-speaking intelligentsia, the concept became a matter for 'experts'; the plan, on the other hand, was the work of leading politicians of the National Party.

It is commonly held that apartheid played a secondary role in the election campaign.[10] This is contradicted by statements in an election brochure of the NP, which described apartheid as "supreme task".[11] However, the NP did not really have a clear plan, which was reflected in the fact that the basic formula for the envisaged racial segregation was already contained in the Party's 1914 founding programme.[12] Apartheid, as distinct from segregation, announced something

---

5 Van Eck 1951: 13–14.
6 Hirson 1990: 86–87.
7 Ds. J. C. du Plessis of Pretoria claimed to have first coined the term at a lecture in Kroonstad on on 28.6.1929 (Cillié 1965: 49).
8 Rhoodie 1960: 178–181.
9 Badenhorst 1939: 113, 161–163, 192–196.
10 Giliomee 2003a: 480–486.
11 NP 1948. The pamphlet consists essentially of a reproduction of a speech by Malan. See also, with special reference to the coloureds, 'Rassevrede langs die weg van Apartheid. Spesiale opleidingskanse vir kleurlinge' (FAV 4.5.2.2). Dubow (2014: 28) sees the purpose of apartheid primarily in its function as an "election- winning force".
12 Nationale Partij in Transvaal 1914: 3.

new; yet it was not clear what that was supposed to entail. Strijdom concluded from the election result that voters had voted for the preservation of white civilisation.[13] In a leaflet addressing his Alberton constituency, Verwoerd himself stated: "The Colour problem dominates everything."[14] In an interview with the NP's Inligtings Committee, D. F. Malan emphatically stated "that the colour issue [*"kleurvraagstuk"*] will play an important role in the coming elections".[15] An HNP election manifesto of 1948 explicitly stated, with reference to apartheid: "There is, however, a greater problem which overshadows all others. *The volk* who now, perhaps forever, determines its own destiny, must therefore also keep it in mind above all else."[16] Historian Jaap Brits sees apartheid as the all-pervasive theme that is pushed into the background only temporarily by the symbolic ox-wagon trek and the Second World War.[17]

Dunbar Moodie and Patrick Furlong suspected the influence of German nationalism and National Socialism, respectively; but the proponents of this thesis never provided clear evidence for their claims. It is much more plausible that apartheid emerged from the context of colonial racism typical of settler colonies.[18] Racial segregation was introduced in almost all settler colonies, but in the African settler colonies, in which whites always remained in the minority vis-à-vis the indigenous population, it was pursued with a particular sense of urgency and aggressiveness, since the white population felt its existence threatened.[19] Thus, white South Africans derived the model for racial legislation, as far as the prohibition of intermarriage was concerned, from American precepts, and not from the Nuremberg Laws.[20]

While acknowledging widespread vulgar racism in the white population, it turns out that apartheid was a project of intellectuals in church circles, universities, the media and politics. For a long time, historical research on apartheid was dominated by the idea that the influence of the Transvaal, especially that exerted by the University of Potchefstroom, was decisive because of its significant role in

---

13 J. L. Basson 1980: 568.
14 FAV 4.5.2.2, NP pamphlet: Parliamentary Election 1948. Alberton Constituency, followed by the 'bread-and-butter-issues'.
15 PV 17/2/1/3, Notule. Spesiale Vergadering van die HNP–Inligtingskomitee, 5.11.1947, p. 2.
16 PV 18/4/1/1, Verkiesings Manifes 1948, p. 1 and after criticising the UP as the first point of its own programme, ibid., p. 7. See also the NP's campaign leaflets, each four pages long, with Malan's exposition of the Apartheid policy (NP 1948), in which the abolition of the NRC was unequivocally announced as one of the first steps.
17 Brits 1994: 100; see also ibid., 118–126.
18 Thus already De Kiewiet 1956: 32.
19 Marx 2015b; see also Giliomee 2003: 495.
20 Heese 1989a: 79, but see Furlong 1983: 4, 45.

the Broederbond.²¹ Giliomee, in turn, points to a politically salient regional dichotomy between the Transvaal and the Western Cape, which may, however, be exaggerated. This is borne out by the fact that original contributions by successive editors-in-chief of the Nasionale Pers A. L. Geyer, Phil Weber and Piet Cillié, to whom Giliomee attributes major importance,²² are not discernible. Arguably, Geyer was an influential member, later even chairman of SABRA. Weber and Cillié repeatedly expressed their views on apartheid, but rarely in a conceptually innovative way; instead, they made propagandistic statements, spreading and popularising their views on apartheid through their newspapers.

In September 1948, Prime Minister Malan presented a detailed explanation of his government's apartheid policy in a speech to Parliament. He denied that "comprehensive territorial segregation" was planned; instead, racial segregation was planned "in the social and political fields, and in housing policy". However, a form of self-government for the "non-whites" in their own areas was envisaged. To him, racial segregation in urban residential areas, in industry, but above all in politics, took precedence.²³

In actual fact, Malan played a rather subordinate role in the elaboration and implementation of apartheid, even though he advocated racial segregation and pushed for it in the election campaign.²⁴ For him, the defensive character of apartheid in the sense of 'saving' the Afrikaner people was more important than the development of a 'positive' policy aimed at transforming society; it is significant that the term 'apartheid' does not even appear in his autobiography.²⁵ It is not without reason that, as late as 1952, an influential man from Malan's circle, Phil Weber of the Nasionale Pers, expressed doubts "as to whether the old doctor really understands our colour question".²⁶ Malan's advisers were sometimes appalled by his limited knowledge of current affairs. As Weber notes, "[h]e was prepared to draft a statement, but when he dictated the wording, it made my skin crawl".²⁷ As late as

---

21 Giliomee 2003c: 230 with direct reference to Verwoerd and Gerdener; see also Giliomee 2003a: 454–457.
22 Giliomee 2003b: 375, but see Giliomee 2004: 3, indicating that while no conceptual impulses emanated from Cillié, propagandistic ones did.
23 *Die Burger*, 3.9.1948.
24 Rhoodie 1958: 197, a disciple of Cronjé, also maintains that "[t]he National Party did not create anything new, it only interpreted the prevailing influences, sentiments and aspirations among Afrikaners in terms of a clear–cut formula".
25 Korf 2010: 459 also points out that Malan was not quite consistent in his views on race and republicanism, but cleverly hid this behind a façade of steadfastness.
26 296.K.GE 106a, Letter by Weber to A. L. Geyer, 29.9.1952.
27 296.K.GE 172a, Letter by Phil Weber to A. L. Geyer, 27.3.1953. See also a report on a speech by Malan in Standerton on the foundations of apartheid – *Die Transvaler* 29.8.1949. Giliomee (2004:

1948, the NP's own supporters were still so incognisant of its positions on apartheid that P.W. Botha felt moved to publicly deny that Malan was in favour of voting rights for Coloureds and Indians.[28] While Giliomee assumes a preponderance of the Cape NP in the formulation of apartheid policies, it must also be borne in mind that de Wet Nel from the Transvaal was one of the most important protagonists in the National Party and an "expert" on apartheid.[29]

The influence exerted by sociologist Geoff Cronjé on the conceptualisation of apartheid may have been overestimated, yet it cannot be neglected, even if the reception of his ideas on racial hygiene was only patchy.[30] There are some claims that Cronjé was "a great friend of Dr. Verwoerd's", and that his book *Regverdige Rasse-apartheid* was very influential for the formulation of apartheid policies.[31] The Broederbond contributed to the dissemination of ideas on apartheid; it was a significant institution not only in the Transvaal, but meanwhile also in the Cape. Numerous representatives of Stellenbosch University with affiliations to SABRA were members of the Broederbond. Verwoerd's confidant H. B. Thom, longstanding rector of the University of Stellenbosch, was chairman of the secret society from 1952 to 1960. For many years, prominent NP politician Eben Dönges was the most important representative of the Cape NP in the Broederbond.[32]

Apartheid was the specifically South African response to the internal social dynamics triggered by the Second World War. It ran counter to development policies in other regions of the continent because it further marginalised the black educated elite, which was comparatively well established and organised; eventually it even criminalised and imprisoned them, while integrating the chiefs into the administrative apparatus to a much larger extent than before.[33] This was

---

8), on the other hand, attributes to Malan and his circle a central role in the formulation of apartheid. This claim is not sufficiently substantiated; it seems essentially to be based on the observation that at the time, the NP of the Cape Province was the most powerful wing of the Party.
28 P. W. Botha 1948.
29 Brits 1994: 102–103.
30 E.g. FAV 4.5.2.4, Die Verhouding van die Blankes tot die Nie–Blankes met inagneming van die jongste sensussyfers, Memorandum of the Broederbond, p. 4. See the chapter on racial differences by J. D. J. Hofmeyr in Schumann (1962: 115–135), according to which blacks were not suited to life in cities (125). On Cronjé see also Smit 1989: 232–236.
31 Meiring 1990: 103; see also Smit 1989: 230, 236.
32 On the influence of the Broederbond on the conceptualisation of apartheid, see, in contrast to Giliomee, Brits 1994: 79–86 and on Cronjé: 81–82, 96. Stals (1998: 188, 196, 204) denies a decisive role of the AB, see also ibid., 301–305.
33 In other countries, the influence of the chiefs was systematically repressed after the Second World War; instead, the educated elite took part in the administration, for example in Ghana (Rathbone 2000: 18–22).

combined with the retraditionalisation and retribalisation of the rural areas, and tendentially also the urban areas.[34] According to Verwoerd, this task proved difficult due to the "activities of agitators", which is why time and goodwill were needed more than anything else, to achieve a "psychological readjustment"[35] – namely a reorientation of "the Bantu" towards the homelands and away from integration with whites.[36]

From Concept to Plan: The Sauer Report

For all the rhetoric of the nationalists, who contemptuously dismissed the previous policy as a patchwork, the apartheid concept was initially aimed at little more than a radicalised form of this same segregation policy. However, in the course of the 1940s, it gradually took on a systematic character, as can be seen from the convergence of the content of the various memoranda, which were moving towards a jointly held concept.[37] The innovative thing about the policy of apartheid was the new function accorded to the reserves which were now regarded as "homelands", that is, as places where identities were supposed to be cultivated; the term *"Tuisland"* ["Homeland"] was an invention of Verwoerd himself.[38] Now for the first time, the reserves were brought into a functional context with urban segregation, which was quite different from the earlier policy; moreover, both urban and rural apartheid were fundamentally territorial.[39] After a few years of NP rule, apartheid became recognisable as something new. It no longer differed from the previous policy of segregation only in degree, but fundamentally: it was a comprehensive, total and tendentiously totalitarian policy of an authoritarian transformation and modernisation of state and society. This was

---

34 Retribalisation served above all to extend central government control (I. Evans 1997: 168, Ch. 6). It even went as far as experimenting with 'traditional' forms of dwelling in the townships of Pretoria, on the assumption that the "bonding effect of traditional Bantu housing" was the best way of combating the negative consequences of urbanisation, such as crime (C. W. Prinsloo 1950: 13, 16). The contention that the "spiritual fathers" of apartheid "pretended" to be convinced that Africans still lived in tribal conditions was one of the few accurate assessments in an article otherwise characterised by half-truths and misjudgements (anon. 1959: 37; see also Tabata 1980: 18).
35 FAV, 4.6.1.1, Letter by Verwoerd to Isaac Frank, Milnerton, 22.4.1953. Quite similar in his speech at the Party conference of the Transvaal NP 1957 (FAV 4.6.5, p. 11).
36 D. F. Botha 1951: 18, 22: The tribal order was thought to be conducive to the proper socialisation of young blacks, whereas city life threw them completely off track.
37 See the numerous memoranda in PV 94/1/22/3/1&2.
38 M. C. Botha 1977: 3.
39 Territorial segregation was the main difference with the US, where it did not exist.

disguised to the extent that representatives of the NP and the government persistently tried to pass off apartheid as a "traditional" policy, emphasising its conservative character.[40]

The overall concept took shape in the so-called 'Sauer Report', named after the chairman of an inner-party commission set up by Paul Sauer, one of Malan's closest collaborators and, ironically, son of one of the leading Cape liberals, J. W. Sauer.[41] The Commission included leading National Party politicians such as M. D. C. de Wet Nel (Transvaal) and J. J. Serfontein (OFS), who were considered experts on racial issues. They came from all over South Africa, so one cannot really say that it was NP politicians of the Cape Province in the ambit of Malan who had developed apartheid.[42] E. G. Jansen was appointed Minister for Native Affairs only a few months after the presentation of the Sauer Report, and G. B. A. Gerdener, theologian and expert on missionary issues, was a professor at Stellenbosch University. Thus was established a link with Reformed mission theologians in South Africa, who had already developed their own discourse on racial segregation in 1935, and translated it into social practice.[43] A church congress on 'The Native Question' organised by Gerdener in 1950 anticipated essential concepts of Verwoerd's policy and came out firmly in support of apartheid.[44] Gerdener was also a leading member of SABRA, and thus of the intellectual circles involved in the Commission that prominently shaped the Apartheid discourse of the 1930s and 40s.[45]

The Sauer Report was not a 'blueprint' in the sense of only waiting to be cast into legal form and passed by Parliament after the election victory in 1948. The text was too vague, it was a collection of numerous demands from the nationalist camp

---

[40] Particularly pronounced in van Biljon (1956: 4), who also imputes an anti-imperialist impulse to territorial segregation (see PV 93/4/1/1, p. 42ff, Toespraak deur Sy Edele M. D. C. de Wet Nel, Minister van Bantoe-Administrasie en –Ontwikkeling, voor die Calvinistiese Beweging, Potchefstroom, 17.9.1960, pp. 3, 15; at the same time, he insisted that the policy would be pursued "on a scientific basis" (ibid., p. 13)).
[41] Sauer himself is said to have admitted that he only supported 60% of the NP policy (J. Basson 2004: 123).
[42] Giliomee 2003b: 388.
[43] Rhoodie (1958: 190) traces the preoccupation with "racial problems" in the Reformed Church back to the 1920s.
[44] Gerdener 1950; see also Kinghorn 1997: 145. On Gerdener, see van der Watt 1981: 186.
[45] Gerdener 1964: 28, 44–47; on a commitment to planning, see 68–70; a reference to Warneck's concept is not detectable in this text. Giliomee (2003b: 382–383) refers to a few church representatives; but in actual fact, there was, at this time, a diversity of opinions, in which dissenting voices could also be heard, until the end of the 1950s. It was only after Cottesloe that a biblical derivation of apartheid became hegemonic; but this predominance of racial segregation discourses should not be projected back to previous decades. On Gerdener's biographical details, see also Bruwer 1956b.

and consisted largely of general declarations of intent. Although the document was called the 'Report' of a commission that was to investigate the 'race problem', there was no analysis of the situation, only a formulation of goals. Numerous demands from the electorate were included, and at times the text seems more like a condensation of populist demands, combined with economic interests.[46]

For the National Party, apartheid became a question of the constitutional order.[47] If the goal was to be a white nation-state, all forms of political participation by the black majority had to be ruled out; black South Africans were to be given their say in the reserves. In fact, the NP politically disenfranchised the black population after 1948. Towards the end of the 1950s, it also abolished the white Native Representatives in the House of Assembly, "thus safeguarding the white character of this supreme institution for times to come".[48] Instead, it sought to institute ethnic segmentation into 'homelands'.

Minister Verwoerd's Concept of Apartheid

E. G. Jansen was a conservative who, during his two-year term as Minister for Native Affairs, did not embark on new initiatives; instead, he perpetuated the well-rehearsed paternalism of his ministry, which soon led to unrest among the radicals in the National Party. They feared that the party was failing to deliver on its electoral promises and demanded that Jansen be replaced with a more dynamic person; soon, the name of Verwoerd came up. When Jansen planned to give urban blacks property rights,[49] he was moved sideways to the post of Governor-General. At the suggestion of Paul Sauer, of all people, Verwoerd was appointed his successor on 19 October 1950; in liberal circles, this was understood as a "concession to extremism".[50] Verwoerd succeeded in ideologically homogenising the Ministry which, like most state institutions, was dominated by English-speaking civil servants. Within a short period of time, he transformed it into a bastion of Afrikaner nationalism through a targeted appointments policy.[51] This is what

---

46 PV 18/4/1/1, Verkiesings Manifes 1948, pp. 7–11 on how apartheid was to be implemented step by step. On the genesis of the Sauer Report, involving a survey of his own constituency, see Brits 2000: 66.
47 *Dagbreek en Sondagnuus*, 16.10.1949.
48 PV 93/1/30/1/3, 'n permanente aparte blanke Suid–Afrika (undated [1960]), p. 3.
49 B.M. Schoeman 1973: 35, 42–47.
50 Kentridge 1959: 376.
51 Malan/Mulder 1966: 3; Posel 1997: 64, 117; I. Evans 1997: 57, 69–78. This alignment with Verwoerd's approach to the appointment of personnel also affected the otherwise rather independent Native Affairs Commission (73).

gave it a great deal of clout; the new Minister was able to turn what had hitherto been a rather subordinate department into a key ministry. This Ministry attained all the more prominence during the years that followed, as he withdrew competencies from other ministries and assumed overarching powers in the administration of the affairs of the black majority.[52] As Ivan Evans summed it up in his pathbreaking study, it changed "from a vacillating liberal outpost into an arrogant apartheid fortress".[53]

In 1950, Verwoerd convened the Natives Representative Council (NRC), in order to create clear institutional structures. This Council had not met since 1946. With the reorientation of policy towards the homelands, and the government's denial of a black nation, the NRC became superfluous for the NP, indeed its very existence was considered counterproductive. Verwoerd himself blamed it for turning away from its role as a purely advisory body and dealing with general political issues instead, thereby exceeding its powers; as the Ministry stated on another occasion, "[t]he time has passed when native leaders could make irresponsible demands with impunity."[54]

In his introductory speech, Verwoerd responded to the request from members to explain the main features of the new apartheid policy. If they had agreed to cooperating with the government on the government's terms, the abolition of the NRC may have been prevented, he said. However, it depended on whether the Minister, for his part, was willing to compromise; however, in Verwoerd's case – that is, in view of his plans for ethnic policies – this could not realistically be expected. As early as 1944, he had already advocated the abolition of the NRC in *Die Transvaler*.[55] Giliomee's claim that Verwoerd had presented the option of a new politics of representation and self-government in the cities, different from apartheid, one that implied the inclusion of the black majority in decision-making processes, is not confirmed by the sources.[56] Instead, he insisted that the Council should not discuss political issues;[57] he only agreed to talk to individual members

---

52 For an insight into the inner workings of the Ministry in the early years, see Mills 2001: 155–156. After only a few years, Verwoerd was regarded as the authoritative voice of his government and party on apartheid issues (Rheinallt Jones 1953: 16).
53 I. Evans 1997: iv, 2–3.
54 FAV 4.6.2.2, Punte vir die Ministers vir die opening van die 1ste Kongres van die O.V.S. en Noord-Kaaplandse Vereniging van Bestuurders van Nie–Blanke Sake, point 10.
55 G. D. Scholtz 1974, vol. 1: 114.
56 Giliomee 2012a: 54–55. On the fact that such a thing could hardly be expected from Verwoerd, either, see Roth 1987: 560.
57 Verwoerd, Policy of the Minister of Native Affairs, 30.5.1952, in Pelzer 1966: 31–52, 39: "With this a body disappeared from the scene which by the very nature of its composition and its lack

privately afterwards, that is, outside of the meeting.[58] The attempt to turn the Council into a purely consultative body, which would only discuss the implementation details, but not the political content of draft laws, proved decisive. In the ensuing debate, members insisted on their right to negotiate policy issues, as they saw the NRC as one of the legislative institutions of the state. This is what led to a disagreement between the members of the Council and the Chairman Werner Eiselen, and ultimately to an indefinite adjournment. Through the provisions of the Bantu Authorities Act of July 1951, the Council was finally disbanded.[59]

Until then, Hendrik Verwoerd had hardly appeared in a prominent role in the conceptualisation of apartheid.[60] After taking office as Minister, he arranged apartheid into a cohesive system, co-ordinated all the individual measures and gave it the appearance of a coherent ideological concept. Even before he became Minister, Verwoerd caused a sensation with a speech that he presented to the Senate on 3 September 1948. It was the first time that he presented apartheid as a coherent overall concept, which made a great impression on his own party. It is possible that this speech contributed to his appointment as Minister of Native Affairs soon afterwards; at least, it was the first time that an NP politician turned apartheid from an election slogan into a programme, and transformed the various position papers within the nationalist camp into a coherent concept. He was not an original thinker and certainly not the "chief theorist" that the first black president Nelson Mandela believed he was,[61] for hardly any of the apartheid ideas actually came from him;[62] nevertheless, as editor-in-chief of a newspaper, he was at the cutting edge of then current discussions.[63] The qualitative leap from segregation to apartheid lay in the systematisation undertaken by Verwoerd, not in the transition from the apartheid discourse of the 1940s to the Sauer Report. It went hand in hand with the transformation of a series of rather defensive and conservative racial segregation measures into a cohesive project of the future.

---

of a positive task devoted itself exclusively to the fighting of the traditional native organization of South Africa."
58 PV 93/1/31/1/5, Verwoerd's speech to the NRC, 5.12.1950; the speech is not included in the minutes of the NRC (see following note). On the events of 5 December, see also Roth 1987: 542–547.
59 Ibid., 545–547; Report on the Proceedings of the NRC 1951: 6–8.
60 Ally/Mooney/Stewart (2003: 82) claim this, but without providing the evidence.
61 Mandela 1995: 513; Mbeki (1992: 65) is also of the opinion that Verwoerd developed the apartheid ideology together with Eiselen.
62 Thus a central demand of apartheid in general, and of Bantu Education in particular, already appears in an FAK document in 1931: "The development of natives and coloureds must take place in accordance with their own ways and traditions, using their own language as a medium." (PV 202/1/2/3/2/1, 1931, FAK Congress Resolutions, Cape Town, 21–23 Dec. 1931, item 10).
63 D. Prinsloo 1979: ch. 8; see also G. D. Scholtz 1974, vol. 1: 109.

Having made a name for himself as "the ablest and most energetic man any South African Government had placed in charge of Native Affairs" in no time flat,[64] Verwoerd went beyond the Report by linking the various demands and presenting them in the form of an argument; he thus became the leading 'glossator' of apartheid.[65] This is what gave apartheid a dogmatic character – an impression reinforced by Verwoerd's intolerance of anything that he perceived as deviation from his line.

Comparing the Report with Verwoerd's later policies, the following points stand out:

1. According to his own statement, Verwoerd worked through the catalogue of demands in the Sauer Report, adding some modifications.[66] He was thus not the "architect" of apartheid as he is so often called.
2. Even in its Introduction, the Sauer Report made it clear that there were only two paths, namely apartheid on the one hand, and 'equality' that is, integration into an egalitarian society, on the other. All alternatives to apartheid were thus levelled and reduced to the same denominator: "Any middle way or compromise is temporary at best, and remains a mere patchwork."[67] The Sauer Report mapped out contrasting political possibilities, which provided Verwoerd with a hinge for his argumentation at a later stage.
3. Even in the Sauer Report, the reserves were functionally linked to urbanisation, and shifted to take political centre stage: "The native reserves must become the fatherland of the native. They must be the cradle of his nationhood and the soil on which his love of country and national pride can grow and expand. For every native they must be the spiritual home. They must be the seat of his system of government. They must be the centre of his churches. They must be the place where his most important educational institutions are located. In short, they must be the home of his personal and national ideals and aspirations."[68] Even before coming to power, the NP territorialised racial segregation and linked it to ethnic identities.
4. For the authors of the Report, apartheid was only conceivable as a morally based policy: "Every form of oppression is therefore rejected as wrong, harmful to the people, whites and non-whites alike, and contrary to the policy of

---

64 US diplomat Joseph Sweeney, qtd. in Brits 2002: 191.
65 T. R. H. Davenport 2000: 392.
66 FAV, 4.6.5, Speech by Verwoerd, Transvaal NP Congress 1957 in Johannesburg, which at the same time took stock of his tenure as minister (Dubow 2014: 65–68).
67 PV 93/1/25/2, Verslag van die Kleurvraagstuk-Kommissie van die Herenigde Nasionale Party (Sauer Report), p. 2.
68 Ibid, p. 9.

apartheid."⁶⁹ In all his subsequent speeches and actions, Verwoerd was at pains to present his politics as being morally justified and in the interests of the black majority. He understood it to be a "double task", as indicated by a note referring to a conversation with his spiritual adviser and political ally J. S. Gericke. "An ethics of basic principles. Choice between one ethical duty + another. Duty is to care for the people and the descendants, another duty is to care for the less developed and the less capable. Is there any way out of this moral dilemma in S.A. other than apartheid?"⁷⁰ Verwoerd answered his question elsewhere: "It is not permitted to sacrifice one nation to another, whether greater in number or not, and less permissible still to destroy an existing nation for the sake of one or more just in an embryonic stage. Separate development, justice to each."⁷¹ Without going into the different conditions, he repeatedly underlined that territorial racial segregation would give black people control in "their territories", implying that this would bring an end to white "domination [*baaskap*]" over black people.⁷² In reality, the NP's 1958 electoral programme clearly indicated where the priorities lay, namely in the "preservation and protection of the white population of South Africa as a pure white race, and the safeguarding of its rule".⁷³ Because the preservation of white privilege could not be reconciled with a just order for all, Verwoerd resorted to rhetorically skilful propaganda, seeking to secure the success of his policies by logical rhetoric.

Verwoerd cleverly tapped into the need of many Afrikaners for moral justification, for it was precisely the post-1959 homeland policy that responded to the wish, widely held among Afrikaners, to make apartheid a 'positive' policy. Although he preferred the formula of "separate development" to designate apartheid, especially in its early stages, this was not a propagandistic magic formula; rather it indicated the way in which he wanted apartheid to be understood. For the Prime Minister in office since 1958, apartheid was "in line with the perspective that has always determined the thinking of nationalists. It means that he saw all the inhabitants of the country as valued human beings, with rights, and with

---

69 Ibid, p. 1. Similar arguments were also put forward by English–speaking segregationists (Heaton Nicholls 1937: 6).
70 PV 93/6/1/1, note of Verwoerd's. The whole mendacity of Verwoerd's homeland policy has been exposed by Tatz (1962: 19–23).
71 PV 93/6/1/1, note of Verwoerd's; see also Giliomee 1994: 535.
72 Verwoerd 1959a.
73 Nasionale Party 1958: 2.

justified ambitions of their own."[74] Was Verwoerd a cynic, who could win over his followers as well as the public by pretending to be truthful, and of noble intentions? Or was he a well-meaning politician who could not foresee the consequences of his actions, or turned a blind eye to them?

In 1990, Deborah Posel pointed out that apartheid was not based on a master plan in the sense of a 'blueprint' that only had to be signed into law after the electoral victory in 1948.[75] She is undoubtedly right in this, especially since she and numerous other authors have repeatedly pointed to the internal diversity and contradictions in the Afrikaner nationalist camp.[76] But she construed the argument in such a way that one can only agree with her, for when in history has there ever been a 'blueprint' for a policy that would subsequently have been implemented to the letter? If there is no such thing as a 'blueprint' in this sense, there may nevertheless have been a master plan in the sense of a strategy, which did not by any means exclude tactical flexibility in the process of implementing this policy. Moreover, as early as 1952, Verwoerd admitted that the NP government would not be able to immediately shake off everything initiated by the previous government. "Real life is not like that. Where one's progress along the path of apartheid is not impeded by such influences from the past, one must, even if it means going against one's intuition, take a diversion to get where one wants to get to."[77] He reproached SABRA and the churches for presenting the distant goal as if it could immediately be part of practical politics at the time.[78] Even if Verwoerd's actions and the authorities' approaches were characterised by trial and error, at times also by opportunistic manoeuvring, there was a clearly recognisable plan. Koorts aptly describes the difference: "It was a principle – not a set of measures."[79] Still, on the whole, we can agree with Posel's finding that "the construction of Apartheid has not been a wholly linear, systematic or monolithic project".[80]

---

74 PV 93/1/24/11, f. 43, Statement by Verwoerd, apparently for the press, but without indication for which newspaper, 22.11.1960, p. 5.
75 Lazar (1987: 27) agrees, claiming that "vital aspects of apartheid policy had not yet been clearly defined when the nationalist alliance won power". This is doubtful, as far as basic conceptualisations are concerned; the implementation in practical policy proved to be the main problem, especially as far as the 'positive' aspects – that is, the envisaged development of the Bantustans – were concerned.
76 Korf (2010: 459) calls the self-representation as political monolith "one of the greatest public relations successes in the history of South Africa". Important contributions to deconstruction came from Posel (1987) and Giliomee (1980).
77 PV 276/I/14/5/1, transcript, confidential letter by Verwoerd to G.B.A. Gerdener, 5.12.1952, p. 6; this letter is also reproduced in Barnard 1967: 32–44.
78 Ibid., p. 7.
79 Koorts 2014: 366.
80 Posel 1988: 1.

A master plan to enforce apartheid in all arenas of society could not be implemented by any other than a flexible approach; it involved necessary but – as Verwoerd emphasised – temporary compromises, among others with industry. In a speech in 1948, he asserted that "apartheid as we understand it" was "not total segregation".[81] He derived his objectives from fundamental principles, while the means to achieve them were chosen from those that were available.[82] As Prime Minister, Verwoerd sought to eliminate contingency in economic affairs through comprehensive planning. Posel maintains that the distinction between short-term flexibility and the single-minded pursuit of long-term objectives was an attempt by the Native Affairs Department to mask the internal conflicts "and present a united Afrikaner nationalist front"; however, she does not provide empirical evidence for such deliberate action on the part of the NAD.[83] She contends that the Homeland Policy after 1959 should be seen as a fundamental change of tack in apartheid policy, which should be understood as a reaction to the failure of the previous policy. This interpretation was contradicted with good reason;[84] in fact, the radicalisation of apartheid coincides with Verwoerd's assumption of office as Prime Minister and the concomitant expansion of his powers. It can therefore be seen in connection with gaining direct access to the levers of power, and with the attempt to make racial segregation the basis of state and society.

On numerous occasions, Verwoerd found – to his great dismay – that his own supporters failed to distinguish between short-term and long-term objectives. "This plays into the hands of opponents, who are only too happy to frighten our own people by suggesting that subsequent steps (which can only be taken after [appropriate] development and preparation are in place) are plans for the immediate future, which is sure to result in their disruption."[85] Even in terms of urban apartheid, one would have to distinguish between short-term and interim decisions on the one hand, and long-term policies and solutions, on the other. Thus, at first glance, the construction of townships and the resettlement of the black population from slum areas to permanent settlements would seem as if Verwoerd had given up on a fundamental principle. In reality, it was due to economic requirements that the country would "retain its current character until some time in the

---

81 FAV 4.5.2.7, Speech to the Afrikaanse Sakekamer Cape Town, 27.9.1948, Notes.
82 This is evident, for example, in a memorandum in which Verwoerd, starting from basic principles, explored the scope for practical political action; in many cases, he was not yet sure what the best solution should be, but knew what it should look like in the final analysis (FAV 4.7.1.5 Memorandum, Wat vorentoe gedoen moet word, 27.4.1960).
83 Posel 1997: 262.
84 Eidelberg 1997: 100–101. N. J. J. Olivier (1973: 2) already spoke of a "gradual process".
85 296.KV.32 (5), Letter by Verwoerd to P. A. Weber, 9.1.1956.

future". Certainly a number of blacks would continue to live in the cities "performing the economic activities that exist for them"; but the influx would have to be slowed down. Through a long-term economic redirection, and especially through the development of industrial centres close to the 'homeland' borders, the number of blacks in the cities would be reduced.[86] The nature of long-term development required that the "uncontrolled influx" had to be stemmed. "For as long as we do not keep them in ethnic areas [*groepsgebiede*], they will be swarming around everywhere among the whites, uncounted and uncontrolled."[87]

As impressive as the system of apartheid may have appeared in Verwoerd's eloquent remarks, it could not escape the notice of critical contemporaries that it was practically unworkable.

> The truth is that apartheid is not a calculated policy expressed through a known programme of action. It is an attitude of mind expressing itself in a series of random, ad hoc responses to situations as they arise. Apartheid is reflexive rather than determinative in character, and as such it is negative rather than positive. The result is that the apparatus of apartheid, which is now grown cumbrous, works in fitful jerks without consistent purpose. It prods and pricks and jostles the non-White population at a hundred points, but it does not induce any broad movement in a predetermined direction.[88]

What is more, behind the paper system, there was no clear political direction and no clear objective. This was of course due to the fact that Verwoerd sought to force together what was incompatible: a system of white privilege and an equitable solution for all.

Convinced of the correctness of his system, Verwoerd was distrustful of anyone who criticised even minor aspects of his policy; for such criticism threatened the systematic consistency of his policy. He feared that unworldly theorists would interfere in 'his' affairs, of which they knew nothing anyway:

> For quite some time now, we have been observing a tendency on the part of some members of our intelligentsia, and a few church leaders, with regard to the colour question. I want to give you the assurance from the outset that the government will not shrink away from those who wish to exert pressure on us in this regard. We will not be dictated to by theorists who have no idea about realities on the ground; . . . we will . . . single-mindedly proceed on the path we have taken since 1948.[89]

---

[86] NA NTS 4562, 1049/313, Conference between Officers of the Native Affairs Department and Managers of Departments of Non-European Affairs and other Officers concerned of Urban Local Authorities, p. 8 (Verwoerd's opening address).
[87] Ibid., p. 9.
[88] Owen Vine, in *Rand Daily Mail*, 26.3.1958.
[89] PV 93/1/24/10, 146, Letter by Verwoerd to Senator S. F. Malan, 3.11.1960.

In his speech in Kimberley in 1934, and in his testimony before the Wilcocks Commission, Verwoerd had assigned a key function to the reserves. The early timing of the Bantu Authorities legislation in 1951, shortly after he took office as Minister, indicates that he was intent on upholding the reserves.[90] Until then, the reserves established by the Natives Land Act in 1913 had functioned as a kind of agricultural supplement to migrant labour.[91] Although the 1959 announcement of the prospect of political independence for the homelands added something new, territorial segregation itself showed a remarkable continuity. That is why Posel's thesis that a second, new phase of apartheid had begun in 1959, which should be understood as a learning experience from the 'failure' of the first, lacks plausibility.

In many areas, African farmers had acquired land in 'white' territory and established productive farms there, which was not compatible with the plans for complete racial segregation. These areas, some of them comprising individual farms, some entire villages or larger areas, were now declared "black spots", the results of an undesirable development to be addressed by a programme of comprehensive unbundling. The Minister wanted to exclude the possibility that land acquisition would lead to an expansion of the black settlement areas generally; instead, newly acquired areas were to be reserved for those who had been resettled.[92] Land purchases for purposes of the expansion of the reserves were undertaken only to facilitate the removal of "black spots", not to facilitate a more fair distribution of land.

In addition to the "black spots", however, there was white land ownership within the reserves, which was not covered by the 1913 Land Act. Verwoerd made it clear that he would adhere to the principle "that the indigenous person has the same right to enter white spots and consolidate the native territory, as the white man has the right to make the white territory perfectly white, at least as far as property rights are concerned". While the government bought up "black spots" and 'compensated' the previous owners, the blacks in their areas were to do so themselves, if they wanted to take over property from whites. Not with one word did Verwoerd mention the differential price structure and negotiating power of those concerned, nor did he take into account the fact that the black population paid taxes to the 'white' state which would then buy the land from them.[93]

---

90 For Heale (1981: 381), it was the Bantu Authorities Act that kicked off apartheid.
91 Verwoerd and the Afrikaner nationalists, contrary to what Marxists like Wolpe conjectured, were primarily concerned with securing the future for the white population and less with industrial interests, which Verwoerd did take into account, but they were by no means the top priority. Economic policy remained subordinate to securing national identity and continuity.
92 PV 276/I/7/1/1, f. 16, Memo by Verwoerd to Secretary for Native Affairs, 29.7.1957.
93 PV 276/2/1/1/1, Letter by Verwoerd to J. J. Nepgen, Fort Beaufort, 9.5.1955. Verwoerd saw himself as a guardian of black people "who do not understand their own interests properly". He re-

The functional reorientation of the homelands took a different turn, though. If apartheid was to link urban and rural segregation, the homelands could not remain purely agricultural areas in the long run.[94] It was the declared aim of the NP government to establish a parallel economy in the homelands: they were to be industrialised and provided with a service sector, in which the black educated elite would find a role in future.[95] African nationalism was to be de-legitimised through tribalism, and replaced by newly created ethnically based educated elites relying on the Bantustan structures for social advancement and the leadership positions to which they aspired. This is how the rural exodus was to be reversed in the long term, and the economy unbundled: "As far as the towns are concerned, the reserves play quite a big part apart from the development there; one would try gradually to induce more and more of those who are seeking opportunities to move there, out of the towns."[96] At a later stage, Verwoerd elevated himself to the position of a prophet in predicting the turning point for the return of blacks to the homelands for 1978.[97]

That is why Verwoerd's politics was aimed at spatial diversification of 'white' South Africa, where he wanted to create conditions and incentives for companies to no longer invest in the industrial centres of the Witwatersrand or in the port cities of Durban, Cape Town or Port Elizabeth, but in the immediate vicinity of the homelands.[98] The rapid industrial expansion of the 1950s worried him because it attracted more and more black migrants to the cities, which is what made his work much more difficult.[99] To establish border industries, he had to rely on co-operation from industry, as he could not achieve anything if he were to apply coercive measures; that is why he emphasised the need for co-operation

---

fused to issue mining permits if it turned out that they could be economically detrimental to a reserve population (ibid., p. 63, Letter by Verwoerd to Jacob Wilkens (NP MP), 26.10.1952).
94 Verwoerd 1952: 3.
95 FAV 4.5.2.7, Notes for speech to the Afrikaanse Sakekamer in Cape Town on 27.9.1948. The connection between the industrialisation of the homelands and cultural–anthropological claims was first noted by P. A. Theron (1952). It is quite possible that Verwoerd, as SABRA member, was aware of the essay.
96 Verwoerd, The Policy of Apartheid, 3.9.1948 (in Pelzer 1966: 1–19, 17).
97 Verwoerd 1964a: 15.
98 As early as 1937, Verwoerd advocated greater industrialisation of the 'white' rural areas (*Die Transvaler* 20.12.1937 and 22.12.1937). This picked up on trends from the USA towards a wider distribution of industrial centres, away from the conurbations (van Nierkerk 1950: 26).
99 "Above all, I am experiencing set–backs caused by the tremendous industrial development which is bringing more and more natives together around our cities. If we cannot divert the flow to the native areas or to their neighbouring regions, we will fail." (PV 93/1/13/1/2, Verwoerd to J. de Beer, 9.8.1951: f.116).

between state and economy.¹⁰⁰ The state was to provide the infrastructure; by means of tax breaks and other benefits, he sought to encourage white companies to set up businesses in these regions. "The object of border development is of course to hasten the process of withdrawing the Bantu from the White areas."¹⁰¹ Employers were not to be forced to relocate their businesses to the border regions, only new businesses should be established there. These plans met with only limited interest among entrepreneurs; by the mid-1960s, only 38 of the 168 applications for state support for such new businesses had been approved.¹⁰² Workers were to be housed in new urban settlements within the homelands, and commute to the new industrial zones of 'white' South Africa on a daily basis. This point was at the centre of the controversies surrounding the Tomlinson Report.

The 'Commission for the Socio-Economic Development of Bantu Areas within the Union of South Africa' was chaired by agricultural economist Professor Frederick Tomlinson of the University of Pretoria. The work of the Commission extended over several years; when it eventually presented its report in the mid-1950s, Verwoerd regarded the very existence of this Commission as interference with his prerogative. Fearing a possible loss of control over the basic conception of apartheid, Verwoerd did not hold back on his misgivings.¹⁰³ The Commission had been set up by his predecessor in the Ministry for Native Affairs, E. G. Jansen, and was supposed to promote ethnically divided structures "based on purposeful socio-economic planning".¹⁰⁴ The mandate thus went beyond a purely economic analysis; it was to investigate the feasibility of separate development, taking into account social differentiation in general, and ensuring that cultural specificities

---

100 Verwoerd, Federated Chambers of Industry, Cape Town, 26.5.1954 (in Pelzer 1966: 53–63, 58). After all, van Eck (1951: 8) had pointed to the possibility opened up with electrification, of decentralising industry. It was precisely the unresolved relationship between politics and the economy, as well as the half-baked conception, that was criticised loudly and clearly – even mentioning Verwoerd by name – by one of South Africa's leading economists in 1964 (Lombard 1964: 170).
101 Verwoerd, Budgetary Committee, 14.4.1961 (in Pelzer 1966: 576–600, 593).
102 Andrews/Berrill/Guingand/Holloway/Meyer/van Eck 1965: 221; see also Rautenbach 1965: 109. Thus, the border industries were not a new policy that was initiated only in the 1960s; it can be traced back to Verwoerd's concepts directed against the Tomlinson Report in the mid–1950s (Posel 1997: 230; see also Lipton 2007: 54–55).
103 "The present Commission had largely been appointed [before my time], and was essentially inherited by me." (PV 276/I/18/2/1, f. 6, Letter by Verwoerd to T. B. Floyd, Johannesburg, 2.11.1950; see also *Die Burger* 28.3.1956). Verwoerd and Tomlinson had not seen eye to eye since their student days together (B. M. Schoeman 1973: 231; on his personal attacks on Tomlinson, see Welsh 2010: 59; see also Steyn 2002: 107; and A. H. van Wyk 2005: 9–12).
104 Tomlinson Report 1955: xviii.

were kept intact.[105] For decisions concerning fundamental issues (rather than technical details), Verwoerd did not need experts: "The Government and my Department did not have to wait for this report in order to have a policy and objectives. This forward movement has been in progress for a long time. Long ago we adopted positive directions."[106] To play down the significance of the Tomlinson Report, he made sure that it was never published in its considerable length of 17 volumes; thus, it did not become official. He justified his decision by pointing to the exorbitant printing costs;[107] only later did he agree to release at least a summary of the Report as a government publication.[108] The poet N. P. van Wyk Louw criticised Verwoerd's attitude in a radio broadcast on Dutch radio, which may have been one reason for his conflict with Verwoerd at a later stage.[109] Like many other Afrikaner nationalist intellectuals, he looked to Tomlinson's proposals as the economic solution to the basic moral problem of apartheid,[110] without considering that such a solution could only be found in dialogue with the sections of the population directly affected by it.

When the Tomlinson Report was debated in Parliament in May 1956, therefore, no one could have been surprised by Verwoerd's negative reaction, even though it was expressed in a somewhat cryptic manner: "[N]o report, not even this one, speaks the final word or suggests the only possible methods. There is a certain object, and in order to attain that object, all kinds of possible methods can be evolved."[111]

He had already told his Party friends and supporters beforehand that he would not make the Report the basis for his future policy. In a conciliatory tone

---

[105] PV 276/I/18/2/1, Letter by Eiselen to Private Secretary Minister of Justice, 3.10.1950, with attached memorandum. For an instructive overview of the Commission's work and the public debate, see Horrell 1956: 139–152.

[106] Verwoerd, Commission for the Development of Bantu Areas, 14.5.1956 (in Pelzer 1966: 102–123, 110).

[107] FAV, 4.7.8.3, Uittreksel uit gesprek tussen Erika Theron en Rykie van Reenen, Hermanus, Junie 1981. SABRA supported the recommendations of the Tomlinson Commission including investment in the "homelands" (E. Theron 1983: 47–48). For a restrained critique of Verwoerd, see Sadie 1960: 62–63.

[108] The debate took place in the House of Assembly on 14 May 1956. In a keynote speech on apartheid delivered only a few days later in the Senate, Verwoerd deleted the passages from the manuscript prepared by his officials, which highlighted the findings of the Tomlinson Commission, mentioning them only in passing (PV 93/1/31/1/27, Konsep-Beleidstoespraak 1956, p. 7). Tomlinson was, however, able to present his central theses in a "*volkskongress*" organised by the AB (Tomlinson 1956).

[109] Steyn 1998: 787–788.

[110] M. Sanders 1999: 629.

[111] Verwoerd, Commission for the Development of Bantu Areas, 14.5.1956 (in Pelzer 1966: 102–123, 103).

he initially tried to cover up the wide discrepancy between the Report and his own views: "I now find to my surprise and pleasure that the Commission, with its more detailed analysis of the figures, comes to approximately the same conclusions and gives approximately the same answer."[112] He even spoke of the fact that the Report "is accepted in principle notwithstanding the obvious provisos concerning the methods and measures proposed. It is obvious that there should be freedom to judge the merits of every proposed method and every detail."[113] The appraisal of the Report served the purpose of damage control in view of the fact that it had met with effusive praise from the white public who greeted it as the beginning of a new era, with the expectation that, for the first time, realistic policies would be set in motion.[114] The Minister resorted to relativising its merits, pointing to some wide-ranging historical horizons: "It is nothing but the continuation of the continual search by the population of the country for a solution of an old and historic problem, a problem which was not always seen very clearly and one which, as it develops, now becomes clearer to us."[115]

Looking at Verwoerd's justifications, the differences that substantially separate his conception of apartheid policies from those of the Tomlinson Commission become clear. Verwoerd was convinced that, in the long run, the homeland policy would be less costly than urbanisation – it was less expensive than building more and more settlements in the urban areas. Moreover, the homeland policy entailed costs below those calculated by the Tomlinson Commission, which is why he rejected the Commission's estimate of £104 million in necessary investments as being far too high.[116] Verwoerd did not want to ask his voters to make the sacrifi-

---

112 Ibid., 104.
113 Ibid., 105.
114 PV 442/2/2/1, Letter by Thomas Boydell to Tomlinson, pp. 1, 2, 24.12 and 26.12.1954.
115 Verwoerd, Commission for the Development of Bantu Areas, 14.5.1956 (in Pelzer 1966: 102–123, 103).
116 Tomlinson Report 1955: 194; Verwoerd, Toespraak in die Volksraad, 14.5.1956 (in Pelzer 1963: 95–114, 101). An economist close to the government put the investment needed to set up 100 border-related businesses at 200 million pounds (*Rand Daily Mail* 28.3.1955); on the special conditions for entrepreneurs, see Horrell 1973: 102–107. Interestingly, in a propagandistic book on the history of South Africa written for German readers, this rejection was not mentioned; the author claimed that even Prime Minister Verwoerd had used the Tomlinson Report to formulate his policies (De Kock 1970: 52). Up to that point, Tomlinson had worked mainly on the white farming economy. In his 1939 inaugural lecture, he mentions the workers only in passing and as a factor of production, he does not mention exploitation etc. with a single word (Tomlinson 1939: 11). Van Eck (1951: 27) had already proposed the establishment of a separate investment company along the lines of the Industrial Development Corporation.

ces that some regarded as inevitable if apartheid was to succeed – for instance in having to let go of domestic servants.[117]

The solution he offered was to solve all problems in one fell swoop, for a self-reliant inclusion of "the Bantu" was much cheaper.[118] It would supposedly educate blacks to act responsibly while at the same time bringing them economic prosperity in the longer term, and promoting a civilisational mission. "That means that instead of extensive soil conservation works and the improvement of small areas, less intensive and more extensive work is done in a large area by stabilizing against deterioration."[119] Thus, he himself admitted that the ecological measures that would have been necessary to keep the overgrazed areas habitable were too expensive; only the decline could be halted. "I feel that the new direction must be that the Native himself be trained in the conserving of his own land so that each work of improvement is his, not only that we say it is his, but that he believes and he feels that it is his, and that he must maintain it."[120]

Taking the example of building a dam, he calculated the effects of this form of education for self-help. A dam would cost £6,000 to £8,000 under the old system; the residents would then leave the maintenance of the dam to the government. "Under the new system, by having the dam built by the Bantu authority with our assistance, it cost between £650 and £750, and the dam is accepted by the tribe as its own."[121] One of the points at which his view diverged from that of the Commission was the inclusion of "the Bantu" in "helping to help themselves". But the crucial difference turned on the question of investment by whites in 'homeland' areas.

For Verwoerd, the investments in the homelands recommended by the Commission amounted to a policy of integration; industrial settlements counteracted the central goal of territorial racial segregation.[122] These disputes over the Tomlinson Report do not by any means contradict the idea that Verwoerd was a "possessed ideological visionary" – quite the contrary.[123] While historian John Lazar and other authors see Verwoerd as a pragmatist, this incident at least shows that

---

117 Barker 1953: 24–25; the fear of decadence through idleness always resonated in this context.
118 Verwoerd, Begrotingskomitee, 14.4.1961 (in Pelzer 1963: 537–559, 549).
119 Verwoerd, Commission for the Development of Bantu Areas, 14.5.1956 (in Pelzer 1966: 102–123, 109).
120 Verwoerd, Policy of the Minister of Native Affairs, 20.6.1955 (in Pelzer 1966: 86–101, 93).
121 Verwoerd, Commission for the Development of Bantu Areas, 14.5.1956 (in Pelzer 1966: 102–123, 109).
122 Strydom 1967: 61–67.
123 Lazar 1987: 209–210.

he was more dogmatic than Tomlinson and Verwoerd's critics in SABRA.[124] Verwoerd's concept of radical territorial segregation, which did not allow any investment by whites in the 'homelands' was clearly more rigid than Tomlinson's proposals, based as they were, on criteria of economic feasibility. He insisted on principles of total apartheid, whereas the SABRA intellectuals, with their demand for direct investment in the Bantustans, were aiming for something more pragmatically attenuated.

Indeed, Lazar's juxtaposition of apartheid "utopians" in SABRA, and a "pragmatic" Verwoerd is highly problematic. It creates the impression that, unlike well-meaning but unworldly academics, Verwoerd had realistic goals in mind. But this was not at all the case. In fact, Verwoerd pursued goals that were just as distant and unrealistic as those envisaged by SABRA intellectuals; they differed only in method, as Verwoerd himself put it. In fact, Verwoerd was the dogmatist among them; in pursuing his distant goals, he gave himself ample time, prompting Secretary of Native Affairs Werner Eiselen to speak of a process that could take generations.[125] In fact, contemporary authors saw the main difference in the time frames set: while the Tomlinson Commission pushed more for a faster pace of policy implementation,[126] Verwoerd thought in terms of a longer haul. The rejection of the Tomlinson Report was not an indication of a more realistic plan on Verwoerd's part, but of his adherence to rigid principles, which was also reflected in his use of the term "exploitation".

In the discussion of the Report, Verwoerd used the term "exploitation" in a peculiar way – not primarily in an economic sense, but in an ethnic sense. A white businessman who made money from selling to white customers was conducting legitimate business; but if he conducted himself in the same way in his business dealings with black customers, he would be labelled an "exploiter".[127] With this designation, Verwoerd was referring specifically to Jewish entrepreneurs who were willing to invest in the homelands. It is quite possible that his rejection of the Tomlinson Report was influenced by antisemitism.[128] If whites were allowed to invest in the homelands, which is what influential Afrikaans en-

---

124 See also A. H. van Wyk 2005:18; Gordon (1988: 546) on the correspondence between the ideas of SABRA and those of the Tomlinson Commission.
125 Eiselen 1953: 23; Eiselen 1959: 7.
126 J. F. Eloff 1959: 58, 61.
127 PV 276/I/9/5/6/2/9, Interview with London *Sunday Times*, 15.2.1955; see also Verwoerd 1964a: 28.
128 Meiring 1990: 97.

trepreneur Anton Rupert had demanded as early as 1950 and repeatedly in the 1960s,[129] a new colonialism would be unleashed, with economic exploitation and low wages.[130] In this way, industry in 'white' South Africa would be put under unfair competitive pressure: "A low wage policy in the Bantu areas would, therefore, be opposed and it would not necessarily attract a White firm."[131]

The argument was ultimately a moral one and touched on the actual problem of legitimising apartheid: "that is that if the White guardian foists a private undertaking on it or allows it into those areas, it will be viewed as economic colonialism. It will be regarded as an attempt by the Whites to rid themselves of the responsibilities of government in the political sphere, but to carry on with economic exploitation."[132] If whites were allowed to invest in the homelands, they would have to be allowed to settle there permanently and develop their own interests as a settler population. In that case, no argument could be made for prohibiting "the Bantu" from doing the same in the white towns: "[I]f in the Bantu areas you are going to give the White industrialist such rights as the ownership of property, the same rights would have to be given to the Bantu in the White areas and that would put an end to the possibility of Separation, which is what the Commission wants and what we want."[133] In contrast to 'white' investment which he viewed as a form of "exploitation", the development of border industries appeared to him to be unproblematic,[134] but he did not give any plausible and convincing argument as to why investment in the areas bordering on the homelands would not give rise to the same problems as the investments in the homelands themselves, namely the stifling of independent black initiative, and cheap labour creating competition for white businesses in the urban centres. Verwoerd's economic rationale was flimsy, since the actual consequences of white investment inside and outside of the homelands would have had to be quite similar – as was confirmed by further developments.

The controversy surrounding the Tomlinson Report, and Verwoerd's dismissive attitude, should not create the impression that an important opportunity had

---

[129] PV 206/3/2/1, Anton Rupert: Die Afrikaner in die Nywerheid (1950), p. 107, see also Lazar 1987: 155–156. On unedifying discussions with Verwoerd about Rupert's planned investments in the homelands, see Dommisse 2005: 128–129 and 154–159; also Welsh 2010: 194.
[130] Verwoerd, Wetsontwerp ter bevordering van Bantoe–self bestuur, 20.5.1959 (in Pelzer 1963: 254–275, 266).
[131] Verwoerd, House of Assembly, 23.1.1962 (in Pelzer 1966: 660–689, 677).
[132] Ibid., 678.
[133] Verwoerd, Commission for the Development of Bantu Areas, 14.5.1956 (in Pelzer 1966: 102–123, 115).
[134] Verwoerd, Naturelle–verteenwoordigende Raad, 5.12.1950 (in Pelzer 1963: 17–26, 23). Observers such as German journalist Werner Holzer considered this venture futile (Holzer 1961: 194).

been missed here. In fact, Tomlinson and his colleagues, too, disregarded the fact that the majority of blacks rejected the homeland policy. Whether white entrepreneurs would have invested in the homelands on a large scale, is doubtful.[135]

Similarly counterfactual was Verwoerd's argument that the homelands were large enough to sustain the black population. He was convinced that any doubt about this was based on a common miscalculation. The assumption that the homelands are too small was based on the wrong-headed idea that all Africans must be engaged in agriculture. About Pondoland, he claimed "that if a European nation which is accustomed to making great use of small and difficult land had lived there – if the Italians or the Danes, the Dutch or the English had lived here – those areas alone could perhaps have carried 19,000,000".[136] Of course, this could not happen, he admitted, if the Bantustans were used purely for agriculture; people would have to find jobs in other areas, because "it is in addition clear that other sources of earning incomes will have to be created for the large numbers who will live there. It is self-evident, as in all countries which have developed in that way, that one must look to secondary industries."[137]

Verwoerd therefore rejected the demands of parts of the opposition to increase the size of the reserves, pointing to these possibilities for the development of the 'homelands'. Instead of providing more land, the quality of agriculture should be improved and a first step towards this goal would be to reduce the number of farmers:

> That does not necessarily mean a decrease in the population of the native areas, but a regrouping of them according to occupation. We must get away from that idea of the past that the salvation of the native in his own areas should be done only by way of agriculture. Other sources of income and other occupations must be created for him as well. To contribute effectively to the building up of a Bantu community the separation between the rural native on the one hand and the townsman or city man on the other must take place actually within those areas.[138]

The present backwardness of the Bantustans was the fault of the whites –

> for neglecting them, for expecting so little from them, for leaving them to their beer pots. As Europeans we colonized those areas by simply taking over control. We did not teach the

---

[135] Sadie 1989: 153–154. According to Saayman, the Tomlinson Report led to an intensification of racial segregation in the Reformed Church (Saayman 2008: 7, 14).
[136] Verwoerd, Commission for the Development of Bantu Areas, 14.5.1956 (in Pelzer 1966: 102–123, 119).
[137] Verwoerd, Policy of the Minister of Native Affairs, 20.5.1952 (in Pelzer 1966: 31–52, 37).
[138] Ibid., 34.

Bantu to control himself. We did not allow him to develop. We tried to put ourselves in his place in his own area.[139]

Verwoerd also rejected the accusation "that Bantu authorities are established to return the Natives to their primitive conditions".[140] He explained that a process was to be set in motion and supported by the whites as 'guardians', which would give blacks full scope to follow their own cultural logic of development. He did caution, though, that one should not expect immediate results from the new authorities, "as though they were westerners with centuries of civilisation behind them. Their leadership is a progressive leadership starting with their people and thereafter rising in steps to which the capacity of the Bantu can adapt itself".[141]

According to Verwoerd's calculations, the establishment of border industries on 'white' territory would not only provide jobs for those directly employed there, but would have an impact on services and trade:

> [I]f 100,000 persons are employed as wage-earners in secondary industry, or in primary industry, it means that provision has to be made for roughly 500,000 persons (at 5 persons per family). But on a basis of that kind the scope of the superstructure, that is to say, the number of people who fulfil all sorts of tertiary duties, is so great that the total number earning a livelihood on this basis is roughly 2,500,000 (husband, wife and child).[142]

In 1956, Verwoerd triumphantly pointed out that the number of black traders in the homelands had increased considerably.[143] With regard to the role of the Natives Representative Council, he pointed to the possibilities that the emergence of a parallel society in the reserves would create for the educated elite: "According as a flourishing community arises in such territories, ... the need will develop for teachers, dealers, clerks, artisans, agricultural experts, leaders of local and general governing bodies of their own. In other words, the whole superstructure of administrative and professional people arising in every prosperous community will then become necessary."[144] Through social differentiation, the "learned Bantu", who were currently still seeking a livelihood in the white areas, would be able find a future in the reserves.[145]

---

[139] Verwoerd, Policy of the Minister of Native Affairs, 20.6.1955 (in Pelzer 1966: 86–101, 95).
[140] Ibid., 94.
[141] Ibid., 94.
[142] Verwoerd, Commission for the Development of Bantu Areas, 14.5.1956 (in Pelzer 1966: 102–123, 117).
[143] Verwoerd, Volksraad, 14.5.1956 (in Pelzer 1963: 95–114, 105).
[144] Verwoerd, Government's Policy of Apartheid, 5.12.1960 (in Pelzer 1966: 20–30, 26).
[145] PV 93/1/31/1/31, Memo Dorpsontwikkeling in Naturellegebied, p. 2.

In order not to have to give additional land to "the Bantu", Verwoerd stuck to the 'betterment' schemes of the past decades, even though these had met with staunch resistance from the black rural population, and could hardly be called a success story. For Verwoerd, this resistance was not due to the practical application of the concepts concerned; to rationalise the failures of his schemes, he invoked the need "to protect the natives from themselves",[146] instead. To this end, the Minister set up projects on which Africans were forced to labour without being consulted: "Dams are being built with free labour, fences are being erected without payment, and for fire wood, trees are being planted by the natives themselves."[147]

Verwoerd moved within a closed interpretive framework that had successfully immunised itself against any real life experience: "The betterment proclamations ... demand of the native population considerable immediate sacrifices for the sake of long-term benefits which appear to it to be very doubtful. Hence the resistance of the natives who, incited by irresponsible elements from outside, in certain cases have gone over from passive resistance to active sabotage and rebellion."[148] They had to be forced to develop, the comprehension – slow as it was in any case – would eventually come. This is what provided the legitimation for adopting coercive behaviour or repressive measures.[149]

In the homelands, only black entrepreneurs were to be allowed to set up businesses, which Verwoerd touted as a just solution,[150] always, of course, accompanied by expressions of doubt as to whether black people would be able to do so at all – which is what pandered to white voters: "We all realise ... that the Bantu, due to his financial position and the limits of his knowledge and experience, and to a very important extent, his character, will not make the development of industry on a large scale by himself in Bantu areas possible within a short enough time to absorb all those workseekers who must seek an outlet for their energies."[151] While black-owned industrial enterprises would take a long time to develop due to a shortage of capital and the supposed immaturity and incapacity of blacks, the border industries should be established as quickly as possible. In 1955, he ex-

---

[146] Verwoerd, Policy of the Minister of Native Affairs, 30.5.1952 (in Pelzer 1966: 31–52, 36; see also Delius/Schirmer 2000: 729–730).
[147] PV 93/1/31/1/31, Dorpsontwikkeling in Naturellegebied, p. 3.
[148] Verwoerd, Policy of the Minister of Native Affairs, 30.5.1952 (in Pelzer 1966: 31–52, 33).
[149] "By doing missionary work and sometimes by exercising a little pressure, much has been done in that regard." (Verwoerd, Commission for the Development of Bantu Areas, 14.5.1956 – in Pelzer 1966: 102–123, 110).
[150] Verwoerd, Volksraad, 23.1.1962 (in Pelzer 1963: 615–641, 631).
[151] Verwoerd, Federated Chambers of Industry, Cape Town 26.5.1954 (in Pelzer 1966: 53–63, 56).

plained to concerned businessmen who had long been doing business in the Transkei, that "it will be the need of the native for his white overlord that will keep [the latter] in the Transkei, and secure his livelihood there for many years to come".[152] He did not expect a rapid pace of development, which was due not only to a lack of knowledge but also to "certain character traits" of "the Bantu", which he did not specify.[153] He had such great confidence in the slow development of "the Bantu", he said, that he saw no reason for uncertainty in the longer term: "Similarly, native traders, once they have enough business sense and morals as well as money – which will take a long time yet – will be competition to white traders and [eventually] replace them."[154] These relativisations of his otherwise consistent policy of segregation, presented as a just solution, revealed his true intentions. For him, the preservation of white privilege always had priority over development opportunities for the black population. Despite all his evocations of the development of the Bantustans, he did not actually expect any independent industrialisation there. Because of the low wages, border industries could operate on the basis of extreme exploitation. That is why Verwoerd's announcements of increasing wages for black workers was wishful thinking at best, and – what was more likely – cheap propaganda at worst.[155]

Apartheid was to appear as a policy of modernisation embedded in tradition, which is why Verwoerd preferred to call it "separate development". However, the homelands had to be "psychologically built up" first. Whites could not do the building, because that would be tantamount to colonialism. "So the black man has to develop and he has to do it faster than in the past if he wants to have his own industrial development." Since, according to Verwoerd, blacks did not have a sense of their own needs, it was unnecessary to try and negotiate with "the Bantu" in the same way as with whites.

In the case of blacks, political leadership, in Verwoerd's opinion, had to be "traditionally based, within their tribe and ethnic group", which is why there should be no "parties in the Western sense".[156] Instead, the "traditional" chiefs were promoted to the centre of the new administrative structures as "the real

---

152 PV 276/2/1/1, Letter by Verwoerd to J. J. Nepgen (Fort Beaufort), 9.5.1955; see also Verwoerd, Volksraad, 14.5.1956 (in Pelzer 1963: 95–114, 105).
153 1373 PV 276/I/6/1/8, pp. 146–147, Letter by Verwoerd to T. W. N. Hitge (Pretoria), 15.3.1957, p. 2; see also Verwoerd 1964a: 17.
154 PV 276/2/1/1, Letter by Verwoerd to J. J. Nepgen, Fort Beaufort, 9.5.1955; see also Dönhoff 1965: 160.
155 It may also have been his response to critical reports in the South African and British press on the insufficient purchasing power of blacks as an obstacle to further economic growth (*The Star*, 6.4.1955 & 26.2.1958 (commentary); see also *Rand Daily Mail*, 19.3.1958 (commentary).
156 FAV, 4.6.1.3, Letter by Verwoerd to W. L. Marais (Germiston), 31.8.1956.

Bantu leaders".[157] They were thought to implement the innovations more readily, "for there are still strong superstitions opposing the adoption of new practices into tribal life, unless introduced by the chief in person". That is why the councils had not succeeded in awakening the "sense of proprietorship and responsibility which is the essence of true democracy".[158] This meant that the chiefs now became part of the administration. Not having been consulted, they had to take orders from elsewhere; only two options were left to them – either to play along or to subvert the instructions.[159] They were to form the transmission belt between the Native Commissioners as the lowest administrative level of the Native Affairs Department and the black population in the medium term, not only in the countryside but also in the urban settlements. When it came to judging African politicians such as the Prime Minister of Basutoland, Leabua Jonathan, Verwoerd claimed that he was always "aware that the perspective and morality of the natives in political as well as in other matters are different from ours".[160] In keeping with the spirit of integral nationalism, the most urgent task was to teach blacks the need for 'community building'. Relying on their own traditions, an 'organic' community should reconstitute itself, develop appropriate institutions and structures, and thus follow a predetermined path of development.

For Verwoerd, the Bantu Authorities Act of 1951 had an inherently ethnopsychological-pedagogical function:

> The Government with its Bantu Authorities Act created the framework for the logical and natural development of the Bantu community in the administrative field. Nobody will deny that it is educationally sound to give rights of self-government to a backward people not suddenly, but gradually. That is why the [Bantu] Authorities Act makes provision for the creation in native areas in succession to tribal authorities, regional authorities and territorial authorities, and it makes provision further for the expansion of their powers and authority as they earn the moral right to that through their initiative and sense of responsibility.[161]

The Bantu Authorities were to form a multi-pronged hierarchy, with the chiefs at the lowest level, and above them "district authorities [*streeksowerheide*]" and "territorial authorities [*gebiedsowerhede*]", with higher-order and supreme chiefs, who were not elected. That means that the whole system of Bantu Authorities was undemocratic, which contradicted Verwoerd's repeated announcements stat-

---

157 PV 276/I/7/1/1, f. 11, Letter by Verwoerd to G.G. Mabunda (Letaba, Tvl.), 6. 12. 1956.
158 PV 276/3/1/1, Bantu Self Government (undated and anon., possibly by Verwoerd himself, but in any case an official account by the Ministry), pp. 2, 1.
159 PV 276/I/8/1/4, f. 292, Letter by Verwoerd to L. W. Yates (Pietermaritzburg), 17.10.1953. For the ambiguity in the chiefs' responses, see the instructive account by Kelly 2015: 274.
160 FAV, 4.7.2.1, Letter by Verwoerd to Minister of Justice Vorster, 24.2.1966 (secret).
161 Verwoerd, Policy of the Minister of Native Affairs, 30.5.1952 (in Pelzer 1966: 31–52, 39–40).

ing that the system would gradually be built up democratically from below.[162] Instead, traditional customs concerning the rules of succession of a hereditary nobility were to be followed in selecting office-bearers from families entitled to those offices; but the final decision was to rest with the Minister of Native Affairs. This was, in effect, a renewal of colonial practices under the banner of self-reliant development; the manipulation started right at the outset, that is, with the selection of personnel.[163]

Until the second half of the 1950s, Verwoerd showed no intention of holding out the prospect of state independence to the homelands. His reservations and doubts about the capacity of Africans to develop made him project his calculations over a long time frame: "Progressive farming is impossible unless you make the farmer progressive."[164] The development of territorially based tribal authorities would, in Verwoerd's estimation, "still take a considerable time". Everything else the future would tell, but the present government had initiated the "development of rights within the Bantu areas".[165]

The introduction of the Bantu Authorities included the promotion of traditional culture, or what the officials believed it to be. In contrast to the earlier policy in the colony and province of Natal, which was designed to destroy the Zulu kingdom, Verwoerd wanted to preserve the dignity of the kingship, but not its power. This was a clever move, since the royal family continued to be held in high esteem by its subjects. Thus he prompted the Historical Monuments Commission to visit the royal tombs, and to erect memorial stones; he also wanted the state to buy up the land on which the royal tombs were located, in order to link them up with the Zulu settlement areas.[166] However, in the case of Zulu king Paramount Chief Cyprian, he remained suspicious of the latter's efforts to "bring about the establishment of Bantu authorities from above" and insisted that the new authorities had to be built "from below". Verwoerd's reluctance was by no means due to his democratic sentiments, but to the attempt to prevent Cyprian

---

162 Thompson 1966: 79–81. See also Hammond-Tooke 1975: ch. 12.
163 In areas such as the Ciskei, there was not even a traditional elite; the power structures only emerged with the establishment of the Bantu Authorities and the massive forced relocations to the Ciskei, see L. Evans 2014: 27–33.
164 Verwoerd, Policy of the Minister of Native Affairs, 30.5.1952 (in Pelzer 1966: 31–52, 35).
165 Verwoerd, Commission for the Development of Bantu Areas, 14.5.1956 (in Pelzer 1966: 102–123, 120).
166 PV 276/I/8/1/1, f. 245, press statement, n.d.; see also PV 276/I/27/11/4/1, 54 Letter by Verwoerd to Henning Klopper, 18.11.1952: "A few weeks ago, three members of the Native Affairs Commission were in North Zululand to investigate problems in connection with the royal tombs."

from gaining too much power and influence: "Cyprian's advisers want to take over the reins and we must not allow that."[167] Instead of being able to rely on an independent power base, Cyprian, too, was to be given the status of public official and incorporated into the state administrative structure.

The government's intention to support 'traditional' institutions such as the Office of the Chief achieved exactly the opposite, because it ensured that the basis of his legitimacy was undermined by financial dependencies and administrative command structures.[168] In fact, Verwoerd's main interest was the tightening of control and the strengthening of authoritarian structures, while economic development and ecological sustainability remained of secondary importance,[169] as they were envisaged as the outcomes of a learning process yet to be set in motion by the whites. Moreover, the talk of cultivating a democratic culture through institution-building "from below" contradicted the constitutional reality that was created along with the Bantu Authorities – namely top-down lines of command, within the constraints of the ruling apparatus of the Native Affairs Department. The newly introduced self-governing structures, forming a compromise between the originally envisaged tradition-oriented system and Western models, were intended "as a complement and extension of the existing system of territorial authorities rather than a wholesale break with the past".[170]

In public, Verwoerd emphasised the autonomy of retribalised self-government; in his private correspondence, on the other hand, he underlined its authoritarian features: "The further we entrench the Bantu system of authority in the Transkei as well, the more will chiefs not only be able to control their people with greater authority and be better equipped to deal with no-goods and rebels, but we will also be able to act more forcefully against them if they do not meet their responsibilities."[171] Verwoerd believed that this reform was the only way that the political ambitions of blacks in their own territories could be safeguarded, and that it would not lead to power conflicts with whites. "[T]he tribal System ... [was] the springboard from which the Bantu in a natural way, by enlisting the help of dynamic elements in it, can increasingly rise to a higher level of culture and self-government on a foundation suitable to his own inherent character."[172]

---

167 PV 276/I/7/1/1, Memo by Verwoerd to Secretary for Native Affairs, 30.4.1956.
168 *Rand Daily Mail*, 13.11.1952, see also Keppel-Jones 1968: 186.
169 See Hendricks 1989.
170 PV 93/1/20/4/1, f. 100, Verduidelikende Bylae to the Memorandum on Self–Governing Units, p. 3.
171 PV 276/I/19/11/3, f. 226, Letter by Verwoerd to Daan de Wet, NP, (Transkei), 17.11.1954.
172 Verwoerd, Policy of the Minister of Native Affairs, 30.5.1952 (in Pelzer 1966: 31–52, 40).

Urban Apartheid

One of the first projects of the Minister for Native Affairs was the eviction of the so-called "Western Areas" in Johannesburg, which included Sophiatown, where some black residents were property owners. Since the residents were from diverse backgrounds, from all population groups, and since Sophiatown was the place of a vibrant urban culture where South African jazz and a new metropolitan black literature were emerging, there were several reasons for Verwoerd to set an example: he spent years intensively engaged with the demolition of Sophiatown and the forced removal of its residents to the new Meadowlands settlement southwest of Johannesburg.

In this context, a fundamentally different view of the legal situation emerged: while the Johannesburg City Council was of the opinion that the forcibly relocated residents should be granted similar 'freehold titles', that is, property ownership, in Meadowlands, Verwoerd insisted on the principles of apartheid in implementing strict territorial segregation.[173] In doing so, he referred to the provisions of the first Urban Areas Act of 1923 stipulating that the cities were to be places for whites, and that blacks were therefore not entitled to property rights. In the case of the forced resettlements, he advocated residential tenancy for those resettled, adding, "I do not ... like leases as long as 30 years". It would have to be borne in mind, he said, that local authorities should be able "to move Natives in case of need".[174] He did not want anything to stand in the way of realising his long-term goals. He impressed on the officials that the municipalities were by no means autonomous, and had no power to make their own policies; and that the only source of political decisions was the central government.[175] The resettlement and the refusal to sell land and houses to black people was part of Verwoerd's comprehensive concept of apartheid, as it was gradually emerging. Another factor was that of cost-cutting, aimed at relieving the public budget.

The Report commissioned by Verwoerd and compiled by his Party colleague Frans Mentz developed a programme for the urban areas of the Witwatersrand,

---

[173] PV 93/1/24/10, ff. 77–87, Letter by H. W. van der Merwe (Kroonstad) to Verwoerd, 20.6.1960, Verwoerd's reply of 30.6.1960, van der Merwe's reply of 16.7.1960, and Verwoerd's reply of 26.7.1960. For Verwoerd, it was a basic principle "that the native cannot acquire any right to own land in the European areas, or in the location or native residential quarter". Verwoerd, Congress of the Institute of Administrators of Non–European Affairs, Bloemfontein 17.9.1956 (in Pelzer 1966: 124–148, 129).
[174] PV 276/I/9/5/6/2/2, Conversation on 24.9.1951 between City Council and Minister Verwoerd, p. 3 (f. 110).
[175] Verwoerd 1957b: 6–9.

which was implemented in the course of the 1950s.[176] In the densely populated industrial area, there was a shortage of space to build new settlements, and to plan for their expansion; and for permanent territorial segregation in future. The planning also had to take into account industrial sites still to be developed, as well as the existing facilities, while at the same time keeping in mind the longer-term goal of relocating industry to the areas close to the homelands.[177] In a complex settlement area like the Witwatersrand, the growth of individual suburbs had to be projected into the future and included in the planning so as to exclude the possibility of a renewed territorial 'mixing' in decades to come. Verwoerd was set on final solutions:

> The demand for one adequate site per town or urban area is necessary to avoid a series of smaller locations around every town, which would within a foreseeable time lead to the fusion of white and non-white residential areas, as experience has taught us in the past. The latter development must further be avoided by arranging the hinterlands for the town and the location that their development will be away from one another.[178]

The Mentz Report was the first example of large-scale planning that changed the lives of millions of people in multiple ways. During the 1950s, a settlement pattern had been established in mining towns, whereby the towns defined as 'white' were surrounded by black townships, which were constituted according to military criteria rather than the needs of the inhabitants.[179] Verwoerd was by no means alone in his staunch position; conservative municipal governments like that of Potchefstroom even surpassed him in callousness, and in the sophistry with which they tried to play it down.[180]

A township was "preferably separated from the European area by an area of industrial sites where industries exist or are being planned; ... the provision of suitable open buffer spaces around the proclaimed location area, the breadth of which should depend on whether the border touches on a densely or a sparsely occupied white area, and a considerable distance from main, and more particularly national roads, the use of which as local transport routes should be dis-

---

176 Bonner/Nieftagodien 2008: 171.
177 Verwoerd, Gefedereerde Kamers van Nywerheid, Kaapstad 26.5.1954 (in Pelzer 1963: 48–58, 54).
178 Verwoerd, Policy of the Minister of Native Affairs, 30.5.1952 (in Pelzer 1966: 31–52, 42). S. H. Frankel 1952: 2–3 showed how nonsensical the search for "final solutions" in questions of human coexistence is.
179 Thus, even planned cities around industrial plants were designed along the lines of racial segregation (Brockett 1996: 168, 172–175). In the process, actual population growth was always set far too low (Sadie 1950: 7).
180 F. J. van Rensburg 2006: 134–137.

couraged."[181] In 1957 Verwoerd drew up an interim balance sheet and reported that since 1948 his ministry had established 59 new townships and had expanded 64.[182]

The cities were places of the white man, "citadels of his culture" and "strongholds of white civilisation",[183] and should remain so or become so again. "There is the home of the European's rights and there the native is the temporary resident and the guest, for whatever purpose he may be there."[184] The aim of urban racial segregation was to reduce the black urban population, even if this initially meant compromises and concessions to the interests of white employers.[185] In a manner typical for his deductive style of argumentation, Verwoerd derived political measures, such as preventing the influx of black families, from abstract principles.[186] In the long run, black families were to be offered opportunities to live in the cities temporarily, but permanent settlement had to be prevented. Urban blacks, even and especially families, remained disposable, which was one of the main reasons for Verwoerd's refusal to grant them longer-term leases. The assumption that "the same persons will always be domiciled [in the townships] permanently" was unfounded.[187] The idea was to have a permanent fluctuation of a population which was only temporarily urbanised, and which was not to become accustomed to city life in the first place; it was therefore treated by the state as a disposable mass. Verwoerd wanted to maintain the system of migrant labour not only for mining; he even sought to extend it to industry.[188] At the same time, it was to be consolidated by recruiting workers through labour bureaux, by tightening the reins of urban influx control, and by standardising the pass laws.[189]

---

[181] Verwoerd, Policy of the Minister of Native Affairs, 30.5.1952 (in Pelzer 1966: 31–52, 42–43). In some areas, this led to protests by the white inhabitants in whose neighbourhood townships were being built (*Star*, 2.4.1952). PV 2/1/33, Protest letter by P. G. T. Geyser to Town Clerk, Randfontein, 25. 9. 1953. On the implementation, see Christopher 1994: 106–107.
[182] PV 93/1/31/1/31, Draft speech by Verwoerd on housing, p. 18. On the decades-long neglect of housing for the black population by overstretched city administrations, see Sevenhuysen 2012: 110–111.
[183] PV 276/3/1/1, Bantu in the Urban Areas (anon., n.d.; official account of the Ministry), pp. 2, 1.
[184] Verwoerd, Congress of the Institute of Administrators of Non-European Affairs, Bloemfontein 17.9.1956 (Pelzer 1966: 124–148, 128).
[185] Posel 1997: 132–135.
[186] Verwoerd, Instituut van Administrateurs van Nie-blanke Aangeleenthede, Bloemfontein 17.9.1956 (in Pelzer 1963: 115–137, 120).
[187] Verwoerd, Commission for the Development of Bantu Areas, 14.5.1956 (in Pelzer 1966: 102–123, 120).
[188] Lipton 1989: 25; see also Terreblanche 2012: 404.
[189] Platzky 1985: 107–108; see also Unterhalter 1987: 31–32.

With the systematic establishment of black townships, the Minister also wanted to change the previous administrative structures: ". . . in one way or another we will have to assist to promote the administration of native residential areas by the establishment on a sound basis of a form of Bantu authority in the urban areas."[190] The ethnic segregation in the cities, which was linked to the forced removals and the construction of the townships, was to facilitate a seamless migration back to the countryside, just as the establishment of traditional "Bantu authorities" in the cities was to facilitate cultural reintegration into the rural areas: urban dwellers were to "exercise their rights as part of those ethnic entities. That is why (unlike the present position) they will be able to go back later on and will not become weaned in the meantime of any rights which they may have there."[191] To the extent that Verwoerd considered black people immature and unable to cope in an urban environment without becoming morally degenerate, the influence of city life on the black population appeared harmful to him.[192] In his view, Africans were oriented towards community life, whose wholesome influence – replete with communal controls and the patriarchal authority of chiefs – was missing in the urban areas.[193]

He therefore sought to extend the system of Bantu Authorities from the countryside to the towns. The urban authorities should "derive their authority directly from the tribal authorities anchored in the homelands, from where the various groups originated".[194] These measures revealed the pedagogical principle that Verwoerd wanted to see applied in the rural areas as well: the inhabitants were to learn to take responsibility.

---

[190] Verwoerd, Congress of the Institute of Administrators of Non–European Affairs, Bloemfontein 17.9.1956 (Pelzer 1966: 124–148, 140).
[191] Verwoerd, Bill Promoting Bantu Self–Government, Senate, 20.5.1959 (in Pelzer 1966: 271–295, 276). He turned the argument the other way round, saying that ethnic segregation should be the precondition for limited self- government (Verwoerd, Gemeenskapsontwikkeling deur die Bantoe, 20.6.1955, in Pelzer 1963: 80–94, 91).
[192] A remarkably similar position was taken by P. J. Coertze (1963: 172–173).
[193] PV 276/3/1/1/1, The Bantu in South Africa, pp. 3–8. It is not clear whether this document was written by Verwoerd; but in any case, he shared the opinions expressed there, as is evident from other texts. Hardly anywhere does one find the bizarre assumptions about African culture expressed in as condensed a form as in this memorandum.
[194] NA NTS 4562 1049/313, Memorandum (initialled by Verwoerd) to the Secretary for Native Affairs on 'Konferensie tussen plaaslike besture en die Department van Naturellesake', 9.7.1953. Verwoerd's obsession with detail went so far that he even issued clear regulations as to where the offices of the Native Commissioners should be located in the cities (PV 276/I/27/11/2/1, ff. 40–41, Memorandum by Verwoerd to Eiselen, 7.6.1955).

He did not share the concern that large-scale restructuring along ethnic lines would break up established social ties in the cities, with serious consequences for social cohesion, and an increase in problems such as crime.[195] In his understanding of ethnic units as organic 'communities', the newly formed social ties in the cities could not be viable by definition, as they disregarded ethnicity and hence were "inorganic". In his view, rather than being socially disruptive, ethnic segregation would lead to a reduction in violence and crime.[196]

The former professor of Social Work applied his findings, imbued with nationalist convictions, to the black population. Addressing the Senate he stated: "Social and welfare services take place within the perspective and policy of this side of the House and best by providing for the Native through the Native himself. The hand that gives must be drawn from the people to whom the services are given. That is the first principle of all welfare services."[197] For him, the traditional order of "the Bantu" was characterised by "strict discipline" and "great respect". With urbanisation, these virtues would disappear, as "the Bantu" would sever "his bonds with the tribal usages". "It is necessary that there should be a restoration in this sphere for the sake of order and peace, and especially for the sake of the welfare and prosperity of the Bantu themselves."[198] Peace and welfare were thus based primarily on discipline and subordination, not on civic participation, dialogue and joint decision-making in the process of finding solutions.[199] The white government knew best, certainly better than the people concerned, what was good for the black majority: "The masses of the Bantu population are not concerned with political matters. . . . If there is anything they prefer in that respect it is, as far as one can ascertain [!], that they want to be left alone, i.e. to develop separately. That is also the tendency in Africa. . . . If the masses desire anything, it certainly is not a mixed form of government."[200]

In a conversation with Verwoerd, journalist Margaret Lessing noted with astonishment "that he was in all seriousness bent on doing the thinking for the

---

[195] Opposition leader De Villiers Graaff took a contrary position: he blamed the high crime rate on legislative over-regulation, arguing that black people saw the laws primarily as instruments of oppression (*Star*, 16.11.1957). In typical fashion, ethnologist Bruwer, who clearly recognised poverty as the social cause of black and Indian population growth, twisted his arguments to attribute the latter to cultural practices of '*lobola*' (Bruwer 1955: 21).
[196] Verwoerd, Senaat, 30.5.1952 (in Pelzer 1963: 27–47, 42).
[197] Verwoerd, The Policy of Apartheid, 3.9.1948 (in Pelzer 1966: 1–19, 11).
[198] Verwoerd, Congress of the Institute of Administrators of Non–European Affairs, Bloemfontein 17.9.1956 (in Pelzer 1966: 124–148, 130).
[199] Verwoerd, Kongres van die Instituut van Administrateurs van Nie–Blanke Aangeleenthede, Bloemfontein 17.9.1956 (in Pelzer 1963: 115–137, 134). See also Thompson 1966: 10.
[200] Verwoerd, Motion of No Confidence, 27.1.1959 (in Pelzer 1966: 216–247, 229).

blacks".[201] This was also true of his Secretary of Native Affairs Werner Eiselen, who maintained that the decision for integration or development lay with the blacks themselves, while at the same time categorically ruling out a decision in favour of the former and attributing such a decision to false consciousness on the part of the educated elite.[202] Similarly, there were claims by 'experts' that Africans would, as a matter of 'habit', opt for migrant labour rather than being prepared to stay with one employer for any length of time.[203]

The establishment of a limited form of self-government was not a concession to demands by the majority; instead, Verwoerd made it clear "that the native residential areas, the locations, in the European cities and towns are not native territory. They are parts of the European area."[204] This meant that black self-government in those areas was to remain strictly limited. Under no circumstances should an independent black community come into being, "with its own governing body standing on its own feet as an independent co-ordinate, urban authority over and against the European urban governing body".[205]

Verwoerd consistently rejected a merger of the local administrative units of the urban Bantu Authorities at a higher level, "in a sort of general country-wide congress of advisory boards", because "ordinary members have been made vulnerable to the influence of agitators, both Black and White. . . . They will have to be municipal bodies, local organisations, and local they must remain."[206] Anything else would have meant allowing truly independent self-government in "white" areas of South Africa. Such independent self-government was foiled especially by the pass laws, designed as they were, to limit the influx into the cities and to control the movement of the black population.[207] Influx control was introduced in 1952

---

201 Qtd. in Meiring 1990: 172.
202 This becomes particularly clear in the highly contradictory argumentation in Eiselen 1965: 6, 8,12–15; and Eiselen 1959: 14.
203 P. A. Theron 1950: 23.
204 Verwoerd, Congress of the Institute of Administrators of Non–European Affairs, Bloemfontein 17.9.1956 (in Pelzer 1966: 124–148, 128).
205 Ibid., 138; see also also NA NTS 4562, 1049/313, Conference between Officers of the Native Affairs Department and Managers of Departments of Non-European Affairs, p. 10 (Verwoerd's opening address): ". . . what we are achieving with the Act concerning urban Bantu authorities is not the transfer of the black residential areas [lokasies] to the Native for as long as the Native is not yet sufficiently experienced to be ready for it. The aim is to transfer to the person certain powers that are limited by the local guardian and builder of his dwelling, of the owner of the property on which [that dwelling] is situated."
206 Verwoerd, Congress of the Institute of Administrators of Non-European Affairs, Bloemfontein 17.9.1956 (in Pelzer 1966: 124–148, 140).
207 A good overview of the legal situation regarding urban apartheid is provided by N. J. J. Olivier (1984).

with the help of standardised "reference books" and rigorously enforced by means of arbitrary inspections and raids. Despite its declared intentions to modernise the economy, the government continued to rely on cheap migrant labour; thus, employers did not receive any incentives to upskill the workforce and mechanise the factories. Instead, they were encouraged by government policy, right into the early 1960s, to stick with labour-intensive methods of production, for which cheap, low-skilled new migrants from the countryside were suited just as well as long-standing city dwellers. The government saw only one effective way of solving this problem: even more extensive bureaucratic intervention. Through an extremely restrictive application of Influx Control, and through "the closing of the urban labour market", it sought to reduce the number of job seekers, "until the young urban seekers for work have been absorbed".[208] These measures were centrally co-ordinated by the Minister, with the aim of reducing the "wasteful employment of labour power" through "the expansion of the labour bureaux system".[209] However, Verwoerd was able to reassure employers that he had not the least intention to impose "juvenile offenders and hardened vagrants" on them. These should rather be accommodated "in work colonies and as labour groups in Native areas for the benefit of the Native communities", "to rehabilitate them there".[210] What clearly lay behind the tightening of the laws was the fear of riots that would become uncontrollable with further urbanisation.[211] Verwoerd did not perceive any risk in the increased number of farm labourers living in widely dispersed areas; it was the influx of job-seekers into the cities[212] that he saw posing a danger, since the cities provided many more possibilities for organising.

The internal correspondence between Verwoerd, the state officials, and the Party functionaries addressed the political conundrums which were outwardly masked by ostentatious optimism. The fact that Verwoerd did not shy away from brutal action, is evident from a 1954 statement warning that those who were to be expelled from the cities and were not clearly assignable to any group "should be brought together temporarily into evacuation camps of some kind".[213] He boasted to his confreres in the AB that he wanted to introduce more strict legislation

---

208 Verwoerd, Policy of the Minister of Native Affairs, 30.5.1952 (in Pelzer 1966: 31–52, 49).
209 Verwoerd, Congress of the Institute of Administrators of Non-European Affairs, Bloemfontein 17.9.1956 (in Pelzer 1966: 124–148, 135). In reality, the system did not work because both employers and employees did not use the labour bureaus (Sambureni 1996: 79–80).
210 Verwoerd, Policy of the Minister of Native Affairs, 30.5.1952 (in Pelzer 1966:31–52, 49).
211 Verwoerd asked Justice Minister Swart to put the Watchtower movement, which in his eyes was potentially dangerous, under surveillance (PV 276/I/19/11/3, f. 219, Letter by Verwoerd to Swart, 4.11.54).
212 PV 93/1/24/8, Letter by Verwoerd to L. L. S. J. Kruger (Potgietersrus), 1.3.1955, p. 3.
213 Verwoerd, Federated Chambers of Industry, Cape Town, 26.5.1954 (in Pelzer 1966: 53–63, 62).

against "idlers and undesirable natives, such as had never existed before".[214] He was quite confident: "In time we will get hold of the natives who disappear to Johannesburg, for example. But even at this stage, those who elude our labour machinery are much fewer than ever before."[215]

Since the founding of the Union, there had already been several attempts to extend the pass laws to African women; but they could not be implemented. For Verwoerd, registering women and issuing them with passes in 1956 was an essential move, as he believed it was the only way to stop the influx of families into the cities.

In addition to Influx Control, emigration control was to be established in the countryside, to prevent young men from moving to the city and, in the event of not finding work, possibly turning to criminal activity and thus exacerbating the social problems. "That is why the labour bureaux to which I have repeatedly referred have been established on a national scale to canalize manpower in the interests of both employee and employer. Emigration control must be established to prevent manpower leaving the platteland to become or to create loafers in the cities."[216] What Verwoerd had in mind in announcing these measures, were the rural voters who demanded cheap black labour.

Bantu Education

An important influence on Bantu Education came from Verwoerd's Secretary for Native Affairs, Werner Eiselen. Even before he was instated in this office, Eiselen was appointed on 19 January 1949 to chair the Commission of Inquiry into Native Education, which submitted its Report in 1951. He was chosen because he had long experience working in education, was a prominent member of the Broederbond, and came from a missionary family. He started from essentialist concepts of ethnicity, which shaped his findings and recommendations for Bantu Education; but in important respects, he articulated a pre-existing consensus among Afrikaner nationalists.[217] Bantu Education was an integral part of apartheid policy; in a 1954 resolution on the Report of the Eiselen Commission, SABRA commended the Report for paying heed to the "organic connection [with the 'community'] in

---

214 PV 276/2/3/1/2/1, Letter by Verwoerd to J. P. van der Spuy (AB), 14.12.1951.
215 PV 276/I/25/1/1, f. 23, Letter by Verwoerd to W. G. v. d. Merwe (Louis Trichardt), 12.5.1955.
216 Verwoerd, Policy of the Minister of Native Affairs, 30.5.1952 (in Pelzer 1966: 31–52, 50).
217 Many of the findings and recommendations of the Eiselen Commission are to be found in the two–volume work of B. F. Nel, published as early as 1942. Similar findings, such as those of the former De Villiers Commission of 1947, are noted by Rakometsi 2008: 50. For African responses to the Eiselen Commission see ibid, 54–56.

which the education of the Bantu" must be conducted.[218] The apartheid education system aimed at "community building" among blacks, to strengthen ethnic identities through mother-tongue instruction, which was enforced with a nationalised and standardised curriculum. In the 1940s, Verwoerd had rigorously rejected bilingual schools for whites, because in them "there could no longer be proper character formation or cultivation of a sense of ethnic [volks-] belonging".[219] History, for example, could only be conveyed "if it is done in the right light, in one's own language and by an instructor from one's own ethnic group".[220] While there is something to be said for the pedagogical principle of mother-tongue instruction, as it was advocated as early as 1917 by education expert C. T. Loram,[221] it has to be seen, in this particular case, in the context of nationalist indoctrination. The schools were not in the least prepared for the changeover and there were no textbooks in African languages.[222]

Eiselen's advocacy of ethnicised Bantu Education was inspired and supported by the Broederbond. It was to be made clear to educated blacks that an education other than the "academic" education as it had been on the books until now, was required for the black man to serve his own people. "The aim must not be to make of him an imitation of the European, but his own good native.... He must receive the education that suits him and his people, and he must receive it in his mother tongue."[223] At the beginning of the 1950s, calls could be heard from within the NP for the transfer of black education to the jurisdiction of the Native Affairs Department, and for the black population to pay for their own schooling.[224] Even before the establishment of the Eiselen Commission, essential arguments of what later was to become the system of Bantu Education were being articulated in this discussion. Verwoerd did not invent these arguments, but only systematised them. In December 1952, the Federale Sendingraad of the Gefedereerde Nederduitse Gereformeerde Kerke adapted the recommendations of the Eiselen Commission, including the transfer of education to the state, while insisting that the Christian character of education be preserved, and that its alignment with precepts of African culture be taken only as far as it could be reconciled with Chris-

---

218 PV 276/I/14/5/1, f. 73 Resolutions of the 4th SABRA Annual Meeting, p. 4.
219 Verwoerd 1948: 4. See also Fleisch 1995: 365–368 and Verwoerd's criticism expressed in *Die Transvaler*, ibid., 368–369.
220 Verwoerd 1948: 12.
221 Loram 1917: 227–232; see also Maphalala 1996: 110.
222 Chisholm 2017: 81–85; see also Johnson 1982:221. After 12 years, psychologist Bloom (1965: 90–93) came up with a decidedly negative assessment.
223 AB Archives, 2/3/14, Bondsraad, 1–3.10. 1947, pp. 7f. TOP 15 D.
224 PV 276/5/1/1/1, '*Beskrywingspunte*' and responses from an NP Congress (1953) with recommendations following extreme restrictions.

tian principles.[225] The ideological objectives were obvious: it was a matter of promoting the principle of ethnic identity through the education system. The poor condition of the mission schools was a welcome excuse, but not, as Giliomee makes out, the cause of Bantu Education.[226]

Verwoerd succeeded in placing the authority over education for Africans with his Ministry. In June 1954, he justified the Bantu Education Act passed the previous year in a long speech addressed to the Senate. This speech is most notorious for a few frequently quoted sentences which contain his programmatic ideas in a nutshell:

> The Bantu must be guided to serve his own community in all respects. There is no place for him in the European community above the level of certain forms of labour. Within his own community, however, all doors are open. For that reason it is of no avail for him to receive a training which has as its aim absorption in the European community while he cannot and will not be absorbed there. Up till now he has been subjected to a school system which drew him away from his own community and particularly misled him by showing him the green pastures of the European but still did not allow him to graze there. . . . It is abundantly clear that unplanned education creates many problems, disrupts the communal life of the Bantu and endangers the communal life of the European.[227]

Giliomee is correct in pointing out[228] that apartheid ideologues sought a vertical (territorial) and not a horizontal (social) division. Thus, Verwoerd said that all opportunities and career opportunities were open to Africans in their own population group and territory, while denying that this was meant to keep them down. The curriculum was designed to be culturally specific; this meant that it was geared not only to African culture per se, but that it was imagined along the lines of a primitive and evolutionarily backward culture. That meant that the education planned for black students was less demanding than that for white students. Even though the curriculum was aimed at vertical segregation, it focused on the expansion of primary education, so as to meet the economy's need for unskilled labour.[229]

Education was no longer to be an end in itself, but to serve the community. Instead of allowing the mission churches free rein to continue to nurture false hopes in black pupils, to instil in them educational ideals that had nothing to do with their own culture, and to thus make them receptive to "liberalist" and egalitarian ideas, Bantu Education was to redirect them entirely towards "community

---

225 PV 276/I/6/1/1, Letter to Verwoerd with comments from the Federale Sendingraad, n.d. (1952).
226 Giliomee 2009: 191–192; see also Giliomee 2012b: 68.
227 Verwoerd, Policy of the Minister of Native Affairs, 7.6.1954 (in Pelzer 1966: 64–85, 83–84).
228 Giliomee 2003b: 384.
229 Giliomee 2008: 95; see also Posel 2011: 340.

building", that is, towards 'their own' ethnic culture.²³⁰ In other words, the aim of this education system was what Zungu calls "the production of 'Bantus'".²³¹

For Verwoerd, the purpose of the Bantu Education Act was to transform "a service which only benefits a section of the Bantu population and consequently results in alienation and division in the community, into a general service which will help in the building up of the Bantu community".²³² He sought to provide primary school education for the entire black population.²³³ Indeed, Bantu Education introduced broad school enrolment, generalised educational standards, and a state-enforced uniform curriculum for the first time. As a matter of policy, Verwoerd stated, "[s]uitable educational matter and an effective curriculum for the schools which keeps track of the psychological factors are required."²³⁴ Resistance campaigns organised by the ANC were largely unsuccessful because many parents were content with getting their children off the streets and receiving at least a minimal education.²³⁵ In fact, the standard of education in mission schools varied widely and was usually not very good. With Bantu Education, there was a quantitative expansion of schooling, focussing particularly on primary schools, but it came at the cost of severe limitations at the intellectual level. Nevertheless, as Glaser has convincingly demonstrated, it did offer committed teachers some loopholes and opportunities for subversive adaptations.²³⁶ With the new school system came lowered educational standards, among other things through a reduction in the number of teaching hours,²³⁷ along with tightened discipline im-

---

230 See PV 276/I/6/1/3, memorandum by Verwoerd to Eiselen, 8.12.1954, on the extent to which the teaching of "the laws and customs of [the] tribe" was planned.
231 Zungu 1977: 211.
232 Verwoerd, Policy of the Minister of Native Affairs, 7.6.1954 (in Pelzer 1966: 64–85, 67).
233 Verwoerd himself emphasised that this was the same envisaged broad impact as with the 'betterment schemes' in agriculture (Verwoerd, Gemeenskapsontwikkeling deur die Bantoe, 20.6.1955, in Pelzer 1963: 80–94, 87).
234 Verwoerd, Policy of the Minister of Native Affairs, 7.6.1954 (in Pelzer 1966: 64–85, 77). However, compulsory education was by no means the aim, as Verwoerd specifically pointed out (PV 276/I/6/1/6, 9 Letter by Verwoerd to W. C. du Preez, Senekal, 28.4.56:" . . . there was never any idea of introducing compulsory schooling for natives.") Apparently he had to defend himself against accusations that he was doing too much for blacks (PV 93/3/1/22, f.139, Verwoerd to Anne M. Bromfield (Fishhoek), 14.4.1959).
235 Hyslop 1999: 78–80; see also Hyslop 1991: 95–96; and Hyslop 2001: 394. On the ANC's failed campaigns, see Mandela 1995: 197; also Gerhart/Karis 1991: 30–34 and Lodge 1990. For a Marxist assessment of Bantu Education, see Christie/Collins 1990: 181. Ross (1967: 9) describes it uncritically as a great success.
236 Glaser 2015: 163–167.
237 Verwoerd, Bantoe-onderwysbeleid, 7.6.1954 (in Pelzer 1963: 59–79, 69). The reduction of the number of school lessons served the purpose of enabling teachers to teach twice as many classes

posed on learners and teachers.[238] Verwoerd explained: "Besides the usual acquirements already mentioned, religious instruction, handicraft, singing and rhythm will come into their own. That is self-evident. The economic structure of our country, of course, results in the Natives in large numbers having to earn their living in the service of Europeans."[239]

The introduction of Bantu Education was directed against the black educated elite, the bearers of African nationalism. Most of the leading members of the ANC and other organisations had come from mission schools. Verwoerd wanted to cut off the next generation of mission school students. This is what explains his plan to move secondary schools from the cities to the reserves in future, since that was where the field of activity of school leavers would lie in future; they would not even be allowed to come into contact with city life.[240] Until now, Verwoerd opined, the black population had only ever been faced with the contrast between assimilation to Western culture or remaining in a primitive state; with Bantu Education, new possibilities would open up: "[t]hat you may remain a Bantu, that

---

as before. In this way 180,000 more pupils could be admitted without major investments (PV 93/1/31/1/31, Positiewe stappe sedert 1948 om verhoudings tussen blanke en nie-blanke te bevorder – Bantoe-Onderwys, p. 1).

238 "The daily cleaning of the school building and grounds, will obviously be the job of the pupils under the supervision of the teaching staff." Verwoerd, Policy of the Minister of Native Affairs, 7.6.1954 (in Pelzer 1966: 64– 85, 73). On the dismissal of disagreeable teachers, see Hyslop 1989: 208.

239 Verwoerd, Policy of the Minister of Native Affairs, 7.6.1954 (in Pelzer 1966: 64–85, 77). See also the following statement: "The curricula, in the fundamental stage cannot go further than teach them to read, write and do arithmetic through the mother tongue medium, and give them the beginnings of Afrikaans and English along with religious education and singing. There was a great deal of difference between theory and practice in the past when this was considered." (ibid., 76) Verwoerd had already announced the aim to step up Afrikaans–medium instruction (Verwoerd, Bantoeonderwysbeleid, 7.6.1954, in Pelzer 1963: 59–79, 63) which, however, was not implemented until 1976 by late-Verwoerdian Treurnicht, and resulted in the well-known Soweto student uprising.

240 Ibid., 77. Therefore only primary schools were to be "transferred to local Bantu controlling bodies under the supervision of the Department", while all secondary schools remained under the direct control of the Ministry for the time being (Verwoerd, Policy of the Minister of Native Affairs, 7.6.1954, in Pelzer 1966: 64–85, 71). However, he was opposed to the expansion of secondary schools, in this case vocational training facilities, for reasons of cost (PV 93/1/24/12, f. 22, Letter by Verwoerd to C. A. Haupt (Durban), 27.5.1961). But it was also for political reasons, because he feared that it could undermine apartheid: "I am also afraid that certain less useful subjects will be taught and that certain kinds of vocational training will be abused at the expense of the whites, for instance, if native textile workers do not make clothes for the natives, but apparently work secretly for white textile manufacturers, as the Malays in the Cape do." (PV 276/I/6/1/9, Memorandum by Verwoerd to Secretary for Native Affairs, 11.6.58).

your Bantu language can become a medium to civilization, and that you and your whole community together with you in this manner can achieve far quicker a higher spiritual, social and economic level of living, is for them a brand new and almost unbelievable thought."[241]

With the envisaged intellectual reorientation of the black elite towards the homelands arose an insoluble contradiction internal to Bantu Education. On the one hand, Verwoerd proclaimed that the future of the educated elite lay in the 'homelands', where all possibilities would be open to them, up to the highest level of offices and professions;[242] on the other hand, he deprived them of the standard of education that could make this possible in the first place. How could there be doctors, lawyers, university lecturers, journalists and priests in the 'homelands' if the only curriculum open to them was that of Bantu Education, which denied them precisely this 'Western' knowledge?[243]

Bantu Education ironically pursued an aim similar to the policy that Milner implemented at the beginning of the century – namely that of anglicising children from Afrikaans-speaking families through the school system, with the aim of securing control, stability, and rule in the long term. But the means used by Milner to achieve this were diametrically opposed to those used by Bantu Education: in the latter case, it was not a matter of alienating children from their cultural background, but instructing them exclusively within the parameters of that cultural background, as it was construed by Bantu Educationists. Both experiments failed; unfolding their own internal dialectics, they produced exactly the opposite of what they were aiming at. Milner's policy fuelled Afrikaner nationalism, and Verwoerd's policy fuelled African nationalism.

At the end of the 1950s, when Verwoerd had already ascended to the position of Prime Minister, the universities were being segregated.[244] This measure met

---

241 Verwoerd, Policy of the Minister of Native Affairs, 20.6.1955 (in Pelzer 1966: 86–101, 88; see also Verwoerd 1959b: 6).
242 This is contradicted by the way in which he openly appealed to the social resentment of "the Bantu", whom he purported to protect from exploitation by small elites, such as those which had come to power in other African states, and which, in Verwoerd's perception, would automatically lead to parasitic dictatorships. But when he sought to promote exactly this elite to power in the Bantustans, this did not fit with his reasoning. (PV 93/1/31/1/42, ff. 224–226. Nuwejaarsboodskap aan Bantoe deur Eerste Minister [n.d. early 1960s]).
243 Despite his overall support for apartheid, this was criticised, albeit rather indirectly, by ethnologist J. P. Bruwer 1967: 71.
244 Thompson 1978: 289. Verwoerd conceded that there still had to be exceptions, because black universities could not yet offer all subjects such as medicine, but this was only temporary (PV 34/1, Letter by Verwoerd to J. L. Lombard (Vereeniging), 26.2.1966). Nationalists in the Cape Province such as M. E. Rothmann wanted to make a distinction between coloureds and the black popula-

with limited resistance, which in retrospect tends to be rated more highly than it actually was at the time.[245] The indignation was ignited to a greater extent by the encroachments on university autonomy, than by the racist character of the laws.[246] For the majority of Afrikaans-speaking coloureds, the lower level of tuition fees, as well as accommodation facilities and mother-tongue instruction also brought some advantages.[247] The Ministry justified the Extension of University Education Act not only by reference to cultural essentialism, but also by reference to psychological factors: a black student at a white university would live for some years "in a state of unreality", "for his social coexistence with the whites cannot continue outside, after his university career".[248] This assumption simply entailed a transfer of the Afrikaner cultural nationalists' concept of the *"volksuniversiteit"* to the black population. The establishment of separate universities for the black population afforded the Bantu Education Ministry extraordinary powers of intervention in academic affairs, which was justified by the supposed immaturity of blacks; but more than anything else, it spoke to Verwoerd's mania for control.[249] The University of the Western Cape in Bellville was established as a separate university for coloureds; and the University of Durban-Westville as a separate university for Indians. Blacks received ethnically differentiated universities – the University of Zululand, and the University of the North near Pietersburg (today Polokwane). Despite numerous student protests, the University of Fort Hare,

---

tion with regard to university education (55.K.T. (47), Letter by Rothmann to Erika Theron, 30.3.1959). Despite all her admiration, she also kept a certain critical distance to Verwoerd and placed more trust in his wife's judgement: "The short conversations with Hendrik during dinner did not bring any clarification, only that he seemed to me to be like I knew him in the Stellenbosch period. But I am still looking for confirmation of this. But I am yet more disposed to trust his policy; and I cannot think that Betsie would not know if he were wrong; nor can I imagine that she would go along with anything wrong."

245 Murray (1997: ch. 9) on Wits's own discriminatory practices that compromised the credibility of the resistance (314–315). See also G. Moodie 1994: 9.

246 This is already apparent in T. B. Davie (1955: 5–9). To some degree, the English universities themselves practiced racial segregation on their campuses (McKay 2015: 183). On the other hand, what is often neglected is the fact that at Afrikaans–language universities, there were indeed some deviations from the official government line (ibid., 236; and especially A. du Toit 2005: 44–47).

247 Van der Ross 1978: 239.

248 Verwoerd's Ministry provided propaganda support for advocates among white students, such as R. Gernholtz, who wanted to take action against the resistance at the University of the Witwatersrand (FAV 4.6.1.3, Letter by Verwoerd to Gernholtz, 5.9.1956, Note by Piet Koornhof, 12.9.1956, and Report by Piet Koornhof of 7.9.1956, with a detailed explanation of university apartheid, from which the above quote is taken); see also Koornhof 1957: 80.

249 Beale 1992: 88, 95.

which up to that point had been open to all, was converted into a university for Xhosa speakers only, and lost the autonomy which it had previously enjoyed.[250]

Even if Verwoerd, with his insistence on the importance of mother-tongue instruction, implemented a pedagogic insight that is widely recognised even today, Bantu Education was devoid of any emancipatory intent; as a strategy of 'social engineering',[251] it formed part of a structure of domination and control. It was not aimed at producing critically-minded young people, but ethnic conformists. In characterising it as "a key factor in community development", Verwoerd demonstrated its instrumental role in the "organically interconnected system" of apartheid.[252]

---

[250] Williams 2001: 27, 88, 111, 125–128, 193–194, 376–381, ch. 9; see also Kgware 1978: 226.
[251] Johnson 1982: 214.
[252] PV 93/1/31/1/27, Konsep-Beleidstoespraak 1956, pp. 8, 9, 3.

Knowledge and Epistemologies of Ignorance – Justifications of Apartheid from the Human Sciences

Running through Verwoerd's speeches is a form of internally consistent political thinking built on unalterable principles. It creates the impression of apartheid as a comprehensive solution to a unique constellation of problems that would establish justice for all. This is how he himself described it. He frequently invoked this idea to legitimate it; at the same time his statements on apartheid represented the position of the Afrikaner nationalist power elite that ruled the country since 1948.[1]

But abstract principles alone are not sufficient to judge a set of policies such as those that have become known as 'apartheid'. Apartheid failed not because of its inadequate implementation; it was not a matter of an essentially 'correct' fundamental idea, as Verwoerd's last white successor as head of government, F. W. de Klerk, still believed as late as 2012.[2] Another representative of the state apparatus stated his conviction, in retrospect, that a "highly intelligent person like Verwoerd must have been well aware of the intolerability of such a situation" of injustice in land distribution. In his assessment, he causally correlates intelligence and morality, in order to retrospectively conjecture about Verwoerd's imminent policy adjustments shortly before his assassination.[3] In the 1960s, apartheid propagandists of the likes of sociologist N. Rhoodie emphasised Verwoerd's good intentions.[4] NP dissident and long-standing parliamentarian Japie Basson and other observers found that Verwoerd's political thinking was convincing only if one accepted the premise that the coexistence of different ethnic groups in one state was bound to lead to conflict. On this assumption, Verwoerd built a completely consistent and logical programme.[5] The problem lay in the basic assumptions, the methodology, and the theoretical approaches underpinning this political thinking. If they were based on presuppositions which could not be fulfilled, and which either defied empirical verification or were blocked by dogmatic intransigence, their logically consistent rea-

---

[1] O'Meara 1996: 64–74; see also Norval 1996.
[2] *The Telegraph* online 11.5.2012, quoting from CNN interview with de Klerk: http://www.telegraph.co.uk/news/worldnews/africaandindianocean/southafrica/9260637/FW- de-Klerk-not-allaspects-of-apartheid-morally–repugnant.html (6.12.2015). Giliomee (2003b: 375–376) reports on poll results, which show that De Klerk was by no means alone in his opinion.
[3] J. P.Coetzer 2000: 44.
[4] Rhoodie 1966: 71–75.
[5] J.Basson 2004: 146–147; see also Heard 1991: 107.

soning could only amount to an immanent rationality built on irrational foundations. What Herbert Marcuse attested to industrial civilisation is particularly true of apartheid, which was borne by the "rational character of its irrationality".[6]

In the following, the ideologically significant basic knowledge that served as the legitimation of apartheid will be examined more closely. How could the segregation of population groups, extending to the territorial segmentation in the context of the so-called homeland policy introduced in 1959, be scientifically justified? Giliomee identified three ways in which apartheid was legitimated: racial, ethnic and historical.[7]

Thus, in the following, three sciences – ethnopsychology, ethnology, and history – will come under the spotlight, in order to examine the extent to which Verwoerd actually relied on evidence-based knowledge as basis for his policies. Even if apartheid and its implementation had a lot to do with technocratic knowledge, bureaucratic expertise, and a positivist obsession with data, it was the humanities that provided the concept of apartheid with the basis for its legitimation. The question arises as to whether the knowledge gained from these human sciences could, in fact, justify the kind of social reconstruction envisaged by apartheid.

Ethnopsychology (*Völkerpsychologie*)

Ethnopsychology has already been described in more detail in Chapter 3; it will be dealt with here only in terms of the basis of knowledge that it afforded in the conceptualisation of apartheid. Verwoerd's legitimation of apartheid relied partly on the ethnopsychological distinction between different stages of civilisational development, from barbarism to civilisation. Moreover, in his utilisation of ethnopsychological props, there were some peculiarities related to the application-orientation and the propagandistic utilisation of culturalist tenets in the context of South Africa's policy of racial segregation. Although all of humanity was thought to pass through the same stages of development, this did not exclude civilisational diversity; in other words, cultural differences were possible within the various stages. The task of the ethnopsychologist was to discover the stages behind this diversity in the first place, and to determine for each culture in which stage it found itself. Because this development was based on an individual-psychological sequence, and the unity of humanity was not necessarily called into question, diversity moved within a comparatively narrow range of variation.

---

6 Marcuse 1976: 29.
7 Giliomee 2003b: 385.

However, unrelated and even logically contradictory to these stage theories were cultural-relativist arguments, possibly borrowed from German ethnology.[8] According to these arguments, the culture of "the Bantu" is fundamentally different from that of Europe, and therefore European culture is neither directly comparable, nor is it compatible with "Bantu culture" when considered from the perspective of acculturation. The conclusion apartheid politicians such as Verwoerd drew from this cultural-relativist argumentation was that "Bantu culture" could not follow the course of European culture in its further development; indeed, emulating European civilisation would be fatal for "the Bantu". The latter should reconnect with the development of their own culture, and avoid the misguided developmental path. The envisaged cultural line of development was thought of as quasi-biological, that is, akin to a genetic programme determining cultural development. While insisting that this should be a clearly and distinctly recognisable course, Verwoerd never spelled out the distinguishing criteria of this developmental path.

The inclusion of cultural relativism in the ethnopsychological sequence of stages greatly expanded the possibilities of the cultural-evolutionist imaginary. Yet the sequence of stages became less and less recognisable, since the putatively fundamental alterity of "the Bantu culture" precluded a comparison with European development, and thus also the measurement of the difference between barbarism and civilisation, which formed part of the basis of Verwoerd's argumentation. If "the Bantu" followed completely different laws of development, they could no longer be placed on a certain stage of a generally valid civilisational development; by the same token, they could not be assigned to the stage of "barbarism". Verwoerd never reflected on the incompatibility of stage theories and cultural relativism; it is even doubtful that he noticed it at all. In any case, his pronouncements tended to become blurred when he adduced ethnopsychological statements in conjunction with cultural-relativist ones; they were often interchangeable or conflated with one another in his argumentation. Even the frequently adduced euphemistic formula for apartheid, "to develop along their own lines", contains the contradiction: "to develop" refers to the ethnopsychological idea of civilisational deficits, whereas "along their own lines" invokes cultural relativism.

Verwoerd's assessment of "Bantu culture" was reflected in the peculiar way in which he spoke to persons he thought of as representatives of that culture. Ap-

---

8 Rich (1983: 56) sees one of the roots of cultural essentialism in the functionalist school of English social anthropology, which he incorrectly associates with A. R. Ratcliffe-Brown, who worked for a time in Cape Town, whereas functionalism is in fact associated with Bronislaw Malinowski. In this context, it is instructive to note that Malinowski had studied with Wilhelm Wundt for some time.

parently, he was convinced that the primitiveness of Africans was reflected in their syntax, which is why he thought that, in order to make himself understood, he had to lower himself to their level. In contrast to his other speeches, his speeches addressed to Africans were characterised by an extremely simple sentence structure using mostly main clauses. Moreover, he attempted to imitate – to unintentionally comical effect – what he believed to be "the Bantu way of thinking" when presenting facts, spliced with proverbs or imagery from rural settings – in the way he imagined it, that is, without ethnographic knowledge. In Witzieshoek, in what was to become the 'homeland' Qwaqwa on the border of Lesotho, Natal and the Orange Free State, where he ventured after the violent crushing of the resistance in 1952, he explained his delayed arrival saying that "there had been thorn branches and boulders in the way".[9]

In his ministerial farewell message to "the Bantu", he pontificated in the manner of storyteller:

> [Development] means growing. A man should never go backwards, he must always tackle new things. Through the work of the human hands or the mind, something new must constantly come into being. That is what it means to create. That is why separate development means the growth of that which man creates for himself and his people through his own efforts. Separate development . . . is a tree, a fruit tree, which the government has given to the Bantu of South Africa. The government has planted the tree, but the tree needs care, so that it can grow.[10]

In a speech presented at Thaba N'Chu, he likened communism to a snake;[11] and he warned recalcitrant Zulu chiefs never to "throw back honey at the honeybird".[12] In parts, it sounds like an adult's effort to explain things to uncomprehending little children, knowing that they do not really understand. Verwoerd's stipulation that "the Bantu" should speak to him "like a child to its father" must be interpreted in this context. As a father, he said, he could judge "what is good for my children and what is not good".[13]

---

9 *Pretoria News*, 8.11.1952. For other examples, see G. D. Scholtz 1974, vol. 1: 214.
10 PV 93/1/31/1/32, Boodskap van sy Edele die Eerste Minister van Suid-Afrika, dr. H. F. Verwoerd, aan die Bantoe van Suid–Afrika, p. 1.
11 FAV, 4.6.2.2, Speech at Thaba Nchu and accompanying letter from Eiselen, who was not yet satisfied with the manuscript. Verwoerd had Twana proverbs compiled (FAV 4.6.5, Tswana Spreuke).
12 Kelly 2015: 284.
13 G. D. Scholtz 1974, vol. 1: 213, in Scholtz's words. Other examples include his New Year's message to "the Bantu" in 1961, where he tried to explain the decolonisation of other African states as simply as possible: "It is like a diamond that a man picks up in the desert but that still cannot buy him the food and water he needs." (PV 93/1/31/1/42, Nuwejaarsboodskap vir Radio Bantu, 14. 12. 1961 or W. et al. Verwoerd 2001: 61; see also Uys 1959: 10; Mills 2001: 162 as well as Dyason

Only occasionally did he resort to milieu theories: "This nation will never grow big if it continues to enjoy the easy times of the Africa of the past. This ease resulted in no civilization being built in Africa. We have built up something because life for us, and for those before us, was not as easy as life in the tropics where people merely gathered their food and vegetated."[14] Statements like this about a supposed land of milk and honey in a region hit by drought on average every third year, where stockpiling was therefore essential for survival, revealed Verwoerd's limited knowledge of the ways of life and of the differentiated agriculture practiced by Africans, but this in no way prevented him from repeatedly criticising them as deficient.

How little he really knew about the African population, about the causes of the rural exodus, about the hopes and goals of those who moved to the cities, becomes clear from the following statements, which also clearly show how prone he was to purely wishful thinking. The spread of the "tribal system" into the cities, he said, was "in the interest of the Bantu". Equally distant from reality was his assertion "that the Bantu prefers, because of the social consideration, the migratory labour system to removal to the European areas. . . . It is clear that the Bantu who have not yet become city-acclimatized in general prefer this system, provided commerce and industries grant fair leave arrangements."[15] There was no empirical basis for these statements about the wishes of "the Bantu" – he did not engage in any dialogue with them. The self-referentiality of his assumptions in developmental psychology prevented him from gaining insight: having set individual and ethnological development on parallel tracks, "the Bantu" appeared to him as little children who could not judge for themselves what was good for them, thus obviating an open discussion with them.

How seldom Verwoerd entered into dialogue with members of the educated elite and with black people in general, is evident from the astonishment with which he noted Basutoland (Lesotho) Prime Minister Leabua Jonathan's high-level proficiency in English when he met him a few days before his assassination.[16]

While there was potential for development among "the Bantu", it was to be a development on the basis "of what historically speaking is his own: but that does

---

2001: 229–230). This too had a tradition (see Wiederroth 2016: 215–216). Very similar was his tone at the opening of the Bunga in the Transkei (Verwoerd 1951a).
14 Verwoerd, Opening of the Hendrik Verwoerd Tunnels, 18.11.1961 (in Pelzer 1966: 636–641, 640).
15 Verwoerd, Policy of the Minister of Native Affairs, 20.6.1955 (in Pelzer 1966: 86–101, 92).
16 PV 72, Note 'Die laaste dag in dr. Verwoerd se lewe . . .', p. 1.

not mean a reversion to the primitive. It means the only sound and the only psychological manner in which a future can be given to a people."[17]

In this way, he was able to present apartheid as a psychologically, and thus scientifically, well-founded and reflected form of decolonisation: "It is true that their political rights are limited – limits imposed by history and their own psychological deficiencies. Notwithstanding this programme the Government has set for their political development will gradually lead to full political control of their own peoples and destinies . . . [The white man] is even to cut off portions of his own land to increase their chances of development."[18]

But this could only be achieved through recourse to traditional African forms of democracy:

> What is happening elsewhere in Africa can't happen here. . . . The Bantu Authorities in the South African reserves, which receive progressively more administrative powers as they show themselves capable of exercising this in the interest of their own people, are being developed along the lines of their home-grown democracy. The traditional tribal leadership-in-council, based on the family unit is in fact only another form of democracy than that to which the West is accustomed, and it can progress and change gradually in accordance with modern needs.[19]

Here, an ethnologically based neo-traditionalism came together with an ethnopsychological derivation of practical development policy.

The fundamental methodological problem of ethnopsychology lay in the fact that ethnopsychologists did not do any fieldwork themselves, but relied on secondary sources. This shortcoming was exacerbated in the case of Verwoerd, as he himself was not an ethnopsychologist, but was acquainted with ethnopsychology only through what he had read and heard. In addition, the sequence of civilisational stages was a construct devoid of an evidential base – because of the mere fact that the source material was spatially and temporally far too disparate; and because peoples as a whole were being assigned to a certain developmental stage without taking account of internal social differentiation. Verwoerd's knowledge remained highly derivative. On the whole, there was a paucity of empirical social-psychological research on the condition of blacks in South Africa.[20] Similarly to Verwoerd's statements on History and Ethnology, his statements on Ethnopsychology were based on subjective assumptions.

---

17 Verwoerd, Policy of the Minister of Native Affairs, 20.6.1955 (in Pelzer 1966: 86–101, 95).
18 PV 93/1/30/1/26, Letter by Verwoerd to Irene Lees (Manchester), 19.6.1964.
19 PV 93/1/34/1, pp.166–170, George H. Pipal, interview with Verwoerd for United Press, 13.12.1958.
20 Louw/Foster 1991: 61.

Ethnology

Afrikaans ethnology was laced with cultural nationalism. Preeminent representatives of the discipline were prominent members of the Broederbond – which indicates the importance of ethnology for the legitimation of apartheid. Integral nationalism and cultural-essentialist ethnology considered individual developmental possibilities only within a communal framework, which was thought to determine everything and to which the individual was supposed to be subordinate. Considering that nationalism and cultural essentialism were working hand-in-glove, the question as to whether the picture of African ethnicities was a projection of Afrikaner nationalists, is a moot one. What is significant is that their basic concepts reveal the same structure, which is what accounts for the matter-of-fact manner in which Afrikaner nationalists assumed that "the Bantu" were to be defined primarily on the basis of ethnicity. Verwoerd's successor in the Ministry, de Wet Nel, maintained that "blood relations are the basic reality underlying the unity of the Bantu tribe". That is why such a tribe formed "a firm psychological and cultural unity".[21] He understood ethnicity as a biological unit, and spoke even of "natural ethnic groups". This view was shared widely by Afrikaner nationalists.[22]

Even Verwoerd's hagiographer Scholtz had to (indirectly) admit that Verwoerd's knowledge of African cultures was quite limited. But, according to Scholtz, Verwoerd relied on the expertise he found in his own circles: "It speaks for itself that Dr. Eiselen, with his vast knowledge and experience, could be of great help and support to Verwoerd. The man who was to succeed Verwoerd as Minister of Native Affairs, Mr M. D. C. de W. Nel, was a member of the Commission for Native Affairs at the time and he, too, was very knowledgeable about the natives. Verwoerd was always able to draw on this [knowledge]."[23] One employee in the Ministry even believed that Eiselen devised the policy and Verwoerd implemented it.[24] There is no indication as to whether or how closely Verwoerd ever studied the eth-

---

[21] PV 93/4/1/1, ff. 42, Toespraak deur M. D. C. de Wet Nel voor die Calvinistiese Beweging, Potchefstroom. 17.9.1960, p. 11.
[22] Verwoerd 1952: 13. On the adoption of the term "ethnic" by apartheid ideologues, see Dubow 1994: 358–359. Even a psychologist who was not a direct supporter of apartheid claimed that "the differences between African cultures far outweigh the similarities" (Biesheuvel 1959: 10).
[23] G. D. Scholtz 1974, vol. 1: 208, vol. 2: 196. In fact, de Wet Nel was regarded as a kind of ethnological expert: "Throughout his life, he studied Bantu customs and now this work has become his life's work." (55.K.V.16 (10), Letter by Betsie Verwoerd to M. E. Rothmann, 18.8.1963). Eiselen himself acknowledged that Verwoerd had only limited knowledge (Kenney 1980: 88).
[24] Mills 2001: 159. On Eiselen's 'crash course' in ethnology for his new minister, see also Bank 2015c: 190.

nological literature, or whether his statements about African culture were based on his own experience. Even if he boasted about having visited all the "Bantu" communities, he lectured them in monologue, only rarely engaging in dialogue with his audiences on those occasions. Historian William Beinart describes such scenarios: "Bowler-hatted, dark-suited ministers were helicoptered in to wax eloquent in deliberately archaic language about the virtues of progress through tradition."[25] Precisely because there are no experiential accounts by Verwoerd himself, we would need to look beyond his person to the history of Afrikaans-language ethnology.

In its evaluations of African cultures, the conservative and essentialist ethnology of Afrikaner nationalists was not very far removed from ethnopsychology and its stagist models; in fact, many of the interpretive ingredients of ethnopsychology can be found in the constructions of African societies by Afrikaans-language "*volkekunde*".

The debate on Afrikaans *volkekunde* is strongly inflected by an approach tracing concrete influences via teacher-student relations. As important as this is – and these influences will be traced in the following sections –, it is important to bear in mind what role ethnology played in the politics of racial segregation. Since the main problem of racial segregation was seen to consist in the African educated elite and the urbanised blacks, the discipline was bound to base its arguments on cultural essentialism and cultural determinism; any relativisation would have undermined the argument for segregation. In this respect, the significance of teacher-student relationships should be attenuated; in the adaptation of certain ideas, a functionalist principle of selection was at work, which was steered by political objectives.

At the same time, the closeness of expert testimony to popular assumptions should caution one against one-sided historical reconstructions that focus too much on the transmission of certain basic conceptualisations from teacher to students; what gets neglected in the process is the prior learning that students acquire in interaction with their social environment and its stores of 'knowledge' about "the Bantu".

Afrikaans ethnology, or "*volkekunde*" was initially dominated by a few individuals, among them Werner Eiselen (1899–1977) and P. J. Coertze. As a student of Carl Meinhof, Eiselen was influenced by the linguistic strand of ethnology in Germany.[26] He advocated the idea of ethnic groups as self-contained, objectively determinable cultural communities, which was also espoused in Germany by Diedrich Wester-

---

25 Beinart 2001: 163.
26 In addition, there was a cultural–historical ethnology that was hardly taken up in South Africa. On Eiselen's relationship to Meinhof, see Eiselen 1946: 78–79.

mann and Bruno Gutmann. Gutmann, a missionary working in East Africa, collaborated with the Leipzig Holistic Psychologists and published in their book series.[27] That is why Werner van der Merwe's thesis is plausible – that it was the cultural-essentialist attitude of the Berlin Mission Society that brought many mission representatives into close ideological proximity to apartheid. Eiselen's father, the missionary Gustav Eiselen, was one of the most outspoken proponents of these tenets;[28] in that sense, the parental imprint on ethnologist Werner Eiselen may have been more decisive than that of his teachers; one may even venture to speculate that it was the influence of his parents that led him to ensconce himself with these teachers. Throughout his life, Eiselen upheld the idea of the sequence of civilisational stages which is why he viewed African societies as particularly "backward" compared to Asian societies, for example.[29] Ultimately, the idea of the "people's spirit" ["*Volksgeist*"] that can be traced back to Herder, was just as influential for Eiselen's thought on ethnicity as Afrikaner cultural nationalism.[30]

About other Afrikaans ethnologists, such as J. A. Engelbrecht[31] or B. I. C. van Eeden, not much more is known than the fact that they studied with Meinhof. All in all, the whole debate about the origins of Afrikaans cultural essentialism suffers from the fact that it assumes nationally uniform intellectual cultures. In contrasting a 'German' ethnological tradition with an 'English' one, this debate reproduces precisely what it sets out to criticise, namely the coherence and homogeneity of cultures.[32] After all, Meinhof was controversial in Germany; it was the link he sought to establish between ethnic and linguistic units that met with criti-

---

27 Eiselen 1957: 117–118; see also Wellek 1954: 15; Krueger 1926b: 747 with a culturally relativistic position; and Krueger 1948: 93. Eiselen's estate cannot be found at present. Kros (2010) provides hardly any new insights and does not reveal any archival material, for instance on his activities as Secretary for Native Affairs. On Eiselen see also Kallaway 2015: 158–159 and K. Ward 2015: 236–237.
28 W. van der Merwe 1987: 11; see also Bank 2015c: 173. However, the influence also went the other way round, from an essentialist ethnology to a younger generation of missionaries such as Carel Boshoff (C. Boshoff 2012: 96).
29 Eiselen 1961: 105.
30 In English-language literature, Herder is often portrayed as being a right–wing nationalist conservative, when in fact he was a subversive writer opposed to the prevailing order of absolutism (Israel 2013: 298, 301; see also Danziger 1983: 304).
31 Stoecker 2008: 113.
32 In my opinion, Pugach 2004: 841 attaches too much importance to the fact that F. S. Malan thanked Meinhof; the context is not explained and it is not clear to what extent Malan did this in his capacity as government representative and out of pure politeness, or whether he was expressing personal convictions.

cism.³³ In fact, Meinhof was not an ethnologist; confining himself to desk research, he himself never conducted research on the African continent.³⁴ As a linguist, he was searching for affinities between African languages; his theses met with critical reception even at the time. He linked linguistic elements to ethnological assumptions which were not empirically supported, ultimately reflecting his own prejudices about 'the savages'. But because he enjoyed a reputation as an authority in linguistics, he could give his speculations on ethnicity the appearance of scientificity. This pseudo-scientificity was perpetuated by his students, as Andrew Bank has convincingly shown for the case of Werner Eiselen.³⁵ Afrikaans ethnologists tended to hold onto precisely those theories in which Meinhof conflated biological traits, such as skin colour, with observations on linguistic particularities. Meinhof believed that certain invading "master races" had subjugated the "primitive original inhabitants". He understood linguistic units as anthropological-cultural communities, that were clearly delimited externally and remained homogeneous internally. Moreover, he was influenced by Wilhelm Wundt's ethnopsychology.³⁶ Thus the Bantu were classified as a racial group in its own right, resulting from a mixture of Central African "Negroes" and Hamites. This assumption became an article of faith in South Africa for decades.³⁷

The most thorough study of Meinhof is that conducted by Sara Pugach, who also examines the connection with South Africa. But with regard to Meinhof's influence on Van Warmelo and Eiselen, she mostly identifies parallelisms and similar affinities, rather than drawing causal connections. Her assertion that the theory of cultural circles, and diffusionism in general, would have been taken up in South African conceptions of ethnicity and apartheid is not empirically supported. And this assertion contradicts the cultural essentialism of those concep-

---

33 Pugach 2012: 84–91 and ch. 4. R. D. Coertze (1998: 11, 13, 23), in contrast, denies a one-sided orientation towards German concepts.
34 This is part of what influenced his student Eiselen (Bank 2015c: 179).
35 Bank (2015c: 170, 176ff). In contrast, van Dyk/Coertze (1987: 247–248) play down the German influence to such an extent that they do not even mention Meinhof.
36 Pugach 2012: 74, 83, 92. This is why Meinhof called for the introduction of lectures on ethnopsychology in Hamburg (Ruppenthal 2007: 171; on Meinhof's appointment to the position in Hamburg, see 176–181).
37 Stoecker 2008: 32–33.; examples from South African literature are Schumann (1962: 195) as well as Bruwer (1957: 54–55) who, along with Meinhof, associated the Hamites as a superior population group with "conquest". Schüler (1956: 168) maintained that the divisions into major groups were purely linguistic, but then proceeded to a detailed description of anthropological phenotypes, similar to Meinhof's student B. I. C. van Eeden (1956: 179). On the implications see *Springbok Atlas* (1978: 11, Map: Races and Languages).

tions, which start from the assumption of an immutable core substance, and therefore tend to minimise, if not exclude, cultural influences.[38]

Another element of German ethnology was cultural relativism, which remained linked to cultural nationalism and opened itself up to racial theories in the 20th century. In addition to the strands of the history of ideas stemming from Herder, the racist scholars active in Göttingen in the late 18th century, such as Christoph Meiners and Johann David Michaelis, may have contributed to this tradition. This went as far as the revival of polygenetic assumptions about human origins in several places, which implied deeper biological differences than descent from common ancestors.[39] The impact of Diedrich Westermann may not have been too profound either. He was a specialist in Ewe, a language spoken in Togo; and he tended to direct the focus of his work to West Africa. From 8 July to 22 November 1933 he spent time at the University of Stellenbosch,[40] where he probably came into contact with Verwoerd, considering that he presented a total of five lectures at the University.[41]

As a lecturer (since 1926) and professor (since 1933) of ethnology at Stellenbosch, Eiselen exerted a strong influence on the development of Afrikaans-language *volkekunde*.[42] As Secretary for Native Affairs (1950–60), he was Minister Verwoerd's most

---

[38] Nor does Pugach mention anything about the reception of the *Kulturkreis* theory by Meinhof himself (Pugach 2002: 19–20; see also Pugach 2012: 16). Hammond–Tooke (2001: 61) mentions that Frobenius's theses were taught in Stellenbosch during Eiselen's time, but this says nothing about the impact on the apartheid conception. In 1927/28, Meinhof spent time in South Africa, lecturing at the University of Cape Town (176–177); on Eiselen, see Pugach 2012: 179–181. In the case of Van Warmelo, however, it is still unclear how much influence he actually exerted on apartheid policy. This also applies to his predecessor, government ethnologist Gerard Lestrade (Dubow 1985: 63).
[39] On early racial anthropology, see Etzemüller 2015a: 78. Despite sharing the same roots, cultural relativism developed in a completely different direction under the influence of the German emigrant Franz Boas in the US, which is why one should be cautious about construing path dependencies.
[40] HU Archive Berlin, W252, Personalakte Westermann, f. 10, Ministerium to Westermann, 31.1.1933; see also Stoecker 2008: 45–49, 66–69, 134; and Meier 1994: 51.
[41] Racist remarks by Westermann are quoted approvingly by J. D. J. Hofmeyr (in Schumann 1962: 131). The lectures dealt with 'Group and Individual in African Society', 'Secret Societies in West Africa', 'Some Features of Negro Mentality', 'Language and Education' and 'Growth and Effects of the Islam in Africa' (see *Die Stellenbossche Oudstudent*, 2. 1, 1932, p. 38). Eiselen resigned from the University exactly one month after Verwoerd (De Bruyn 1989: 10). According to Kros (2010: 32), he did not really feel he was in the right place there, but the author offers no evidence for this.
[42] Gordon (1988: 539). As an academic teacher, he attracted many more students than his English-speaking colleagues.

important collaborator.⁴³ "For hours on end and late into the night, they would ponder problems, debate and argue until they found a solution. A better cooperation than the one that took place over the years between these two workhorses is hardly imaginable," Verwoerd's private secretary recalled.⁴⁴ Eiselen's early writings were still full of racist presuppositions about Africans whom he considered culturally backward, less talented, and characterised by excessive libido.⁴⁵ But in the 1930s, as Andrew Bank has shown, he tempered these overtly racist explanations with cultural-relativist ones, which nevertheless remained racist by virtue of their continued reference to skin colour. In later years, Eiselen showed greater scepticism towards biological theories of race. Asked by M. L. Fick to write a foreword to the results he compiled of intelligence tests conducted on black children, Eiselen even went so far as to distance himself from the content of the study and to call its methodology into doubt (and rightly so).⁴⁶ In 1948, Eiselen still presented a lecture at the South African Institute of Race Relations and at the Johannesburg Bantu Men's Social Centre.⁴⁷

Eiselen used the term "Bantu" as early as 1929; the fact that it was not 'Natives' but "Bantu" that featured in official documents and in the political language of the Ministry, was probably due to his terminology, which was supposed to lend scientific respectability to apartheid policy.⁴⁸ According to Verwoerd's own testimony, it was upon Eiselen's advice that his staff were instructed to initiate contact with African correspondents with 'greetings' as a form of address. "This was introduced after ethnologists and Bantu leaders had been consulted; they considered it a polite form of address used in letters. . . . The practice is therefore not aimed at humiliating the Bantu; rather, a manner of address was sought that was considered proper [according to his own culture]."⁴⁹ Verwoerd's successor, de Wet Nel, ordered that his officials should no longer shake hands with Africans because this was supposedly contrary to their culture.⁵⁰

---

43 Zöllner/Heese (1984: 75–76); see also Gordon (1991: 80–81). On his influence in missionary circles, see Stals 1998: 236.
44 Barnard 1967: 49.
45 Bank 2015c: 183–184. This obsession with African sexuality was inspired by Meinhof's amateurish ethnology, and continued among Eiselen's students (Bank 2015a:187–189; see also Bank 2015b: 165–167).
46 Fick 1939, Preface by W. Eiselen, p. iv; see also Eiselen 1929a: 5. Bank (2015b: 168–169) interprets this differently.
47 Kathrada 2012: 36; see also Gillespie 2011: 505–507.
48 Eiselen 1929a: 3.
49 PV 93/1/24/12, 1961–1963, 25 Letter by Verwoerd to N. M. Smit, NGK missionary in the Transkei, 20.6.1961.
50 Holzer 1961: 197, 231–232.

For Afrikaans ethnologists, cultural relativism and essentialism were by no means mutually exclusive, on the contrary: monadic cultures were thought to carry their value within themselves. They were not supposed to influence each other, but to follow their own laws of development; every cross-cultural influences could become fatal. "Their habit of mind is to think in terms of the group"; the individual had not yet been set free.[51] Cultural relativism could be applied in the context of apartheid; Eiselen and Verwoerd were fully convinced that cultural relativism was part of an anti-colonial project. Their views coincided to a large extent; they differed only in minor nuances.

Preserving African cultures and preventing them from disintegrating in a modern industrial society was a goal that Eiselen ardently pursued.[52] Like most Afrikaans–speaking ethnologists, he had hardly conducted any ethnological fieldwork himself; whatever little he did in that respect, was limited to interviewing black chiefs and persons affiliated to the mission society. He himself remained primarily a linguist.[53] Like Verwoerd, he elevated basic assumptions of cultural nationalism to the level of integral nationalism and transferred them to African societies. Eiselen remained a cultural essentialist *par excellence*. His membership of the Broederbond was not coincidental: he drew his inspiration mainly from Afrikaans cultural nationalism. He derived his ethnological ideas from projecting his own cultural nationalism onto Africans.[54] It is doubtful whether this move could be said to have been influenced by Meinhof. The notion of one's own, organic culture, which was believed to be found also among black people, was too widespread in Afrikaner nationalism to require any specific elaboration from ethnology.[55] Even if some people attest to Eiselen's benevolently paternalistic attitude towards the black population, it must be noted that he did support the authoritarian and inhumane measures of his Minister during his entire term in

---

[51] FAV, 4.6.2.2, The Bantu in South Africa, p. 3. J. Bruwer enthusiastically collaborated on documentaries in which African cultures are represented as self–contained entities (PV 123/2/1/3, Letter by E. G. Tabor, Ethnofilms, to Bruwer, 14.2.1966; Bruwer's reply, 23.2.1966; Letter by Bruwer to Tabor, 17.3.1966 with promise and further proposals on South West Africa; Letter by Tabor to Bruwer, 20.3.1966).

[52] See Eiselen 1929a: 11; also Dubow 2014: 60–61.

[53] Bank 2015b: 170; see also Hammond–Tooke 2001: 57–64. As late as 1962, J. Bruwer justified a research proposal, stating that Stellenbosch University had never before undertaken "such a fundamental ethnological project" (PV 123/4/19/5, Letter by Bruwer to H. B. Thom, 10.3.1962, with attached project proposal, p. 4).

[54] Gordon (1988: 549) also notes that it was not so much ethnological concepts such as the ethnos theory, but the nationalist demand for "service to the people" that motivated many Afrikaans ethnologists (on this, see P. J. Coertze 1977: 65–66; also van der Waal 2003: 5).

[55] On van Wyk Louw, see M. Sanders (1999: 618).

office; in fact, he defended them, and in many cases even took the initiative himself. Because of his prominent activity in politics and administration, Eiselen's impact persisted even after his retirement from academic life.

Pieter Johannes Coertze (1907–1998), like Eiselen's successor in Stellenbosch, P. J. Schoeman, was leaning even further to the right than his teacher. He affirmed racial theories and, in his roles as an academic teacher and author of influential textbooks, he was one of the most important representatives of apartheid ethnology.[56] In his publications, he invoked organic metaphors to describe societies and cultures; yet, despite the organicist castings of cultures and societies, he construed them in a decidedly mechanistic way, working from abstract ideas, and only rarely providing examples drawn from fieldwork.[57] He often went into pages and pages of anthropological platitudes, mostly without references and without differentiations based on empirical evidence.[58] What is more, no intellectual development can be detected in his writings. His 'knowledge' about Africans consisted to a considerable extent of erudite-sounding popular imaginings. Two examples may suffice to demonstrate this: He wrote of Africans' tendency to imitate; and, relying on the authority of his position, he declared black nationalism an impossibility – something that has no place in the cultural development of "the Bantu". Their acculturation to the Western way of life would only create "inner chaos". Coertze did not deign to back these claims up with interviews, which he obviously considered to be superfluous, since he knew better anyway.[59] His book on *The Afrikaner People and the Coloureds* was not based on ethnological field research; it does not contain much more than a history of the coloureds, which, moreover, relies on completely outdated literature. For Coertze, this had the advantage that he did not even have to begin to engage with new research findings that would have contradicted his assumptions and convictions.[60]

---

56 P. J. Coertze (1977: 6–56) introduces racial science. In another book, Coertze stated one of the criteria in his definition of 'a people': "the biological growth and the spiritual growth of a people are equally important for its continued existence and cannot really be separated from each other." (P. J. Coertze 1983: 4).

57 E. F. Potgieter (1956: 54–55) can serve as an example of the extent to which deductions were being made from abstract presuppositions. This applies especially to his attempts at conceptualising long–term contact in terms of "logical processes" (ibid: 64).

58 For example, P. J. Coertze 1966a and b; in these two articles he does not mention South Africa at all.

59 P. J. Coertze 1952: 18–21. His terminology was remarkably unscholarly, over decades, as for instance when he referred to African healers as "magic doctors [*toordokters*]" and first nation North Americans as "redskins".

60 Only in the case of Hans Heese could he not avoid referring to it because of the public recognition of Heese's research. Still, he mentioned it only cursorily, without engaging with it (P. J. Co-

As co-ordinator of scholarship across the humanities and social sciences, he was a powerful figure in the Afrikaner Broederbond and in SABRA, where he chaired a research commission.[61] As founder of ethnological institutes in Bloemfontein and at the University of South Africa, and as successor of Eiselen, he was immensely influential at the University of Pretoria from 1950 onwards. Almost all professorships in ethnology at Afrikaans-language universities were filled by his students.[62] As Sharp points out, numerous writings of Coertze's referred to German ethnologist Wilhelm Mühlmann's concept of 'ethnos'. Within German ethnology, Mühlmann followed the strand of German ethnology that sought to connect ethnology with theories of race.[63] A textbook by his colleague Hennie Coetzee of the University of Potchefstroom, who in turn referred to Coertze, also described "primitive peoples" in abstract terms and without empirical evidence, which only came into the assignments set for students.[64]

Most of Coertze's students later worked as government ethnologists, in the Native Affairs Department or in the South African army.[65] Thus, in 1955, the number of ethnology students at UNISA stood at 240; within four years this number tripled.[66] However, they hardly did any serious field research, which, apart from their own reluctance to live together with Africans, apartheid laws would not have allowed them to do.[67] One of the focus areas of Afrikaans ethnologists lay in the field of legal ethnology, which they used to construct an African legal tradition that could serve as a basis for apartheid as politics of cultural difference.[68]

---

ertze 1983: 74–75). The final chapter had already appeared as a separate SABRA publication some years earlier (P. J. Coertze 1975).

61 PV 123/2/14/1, Letter by Hoofsekretaris SABRA to J. Bruwer, 25.1.1966.
62 R.D. Coertze 1991: 25; see also Bank 2015a: 186. The exception was Stellenbosch.
63 Sharp 1981:19, 32; see also Sharp 1980: 5. Mühlmann played a highly ambivalent role in the context of National Socialism: on the one hand, he was convinced of the importance of race, and often made explicitly racist remarks; nevertheless, he kept a certain distance from the particular form of racism that characterised the Nazi movement (Fischer 1990: 39–41, 160–161, 170–172, 220–223). Mühlmann had no influence on Eiselen (see Bank 2015c: 177).
64 For examples of the questions, see Coetzee/Booysens/van Rensburg (1980: 41).
65 Gordon 1988: 536; on Coertze's influence, see ibid., 540; see also Hammond–Tooke 2001: ch. 6. Carel Boshoff studied for an M.A. with Cronjé and Coertze (C. Boshoff 2012: 153–154; see also R. D. Coertze 1998: 15).
66 Boucher 1973: 311.
67 Gordon 1988: 544; see also Bank 2015a: 191. This is contradicted by R. D. Coertze (1991: 28). However, ethnologist E. F. Potgieter (University of South Africa) emphasised the need for field research and language skills; also expressed himself in a somewhat differentiated way about Anglophone ethnology (E. F. Potgieter 1956: 17).
68 Gordon 1989: 291, 294. On the imaginary character of legal constructions, which are hardly substantiated by actual field studies, see ibid., 292, 295, 301–302, 308.

By the 1950s, at the latest, Afrikaans-language ethnology had lost its academic connection to the methodologically and theoretically innovative English-language social anthropology of South Africa, and had largely cut itself off from the latter.[69] Instead, it continued to orient itself towards German ethnology. It did not produce methodologically innovative research; there was hardly any ethnologist who had ever published a monograph.[70] In spite of the significant institutional influence of Afrikaans ethnologists in the administration and in the Department of Native Affairs, it must be kept in mind that their intellectual impact was rather modest. When it came to reviewing manuscripts of Afrikaans ethnologists for publication, their counterparts at English-language universities were usually very critical in their comments, and in some cases, even cast aspersion on the scholarly character of the manuscripts submitted.[71] Apart from a few dogmatic cultural-tenets, proficiency in African languages, and claims to "knowing the Bantu", they usually did not have much to offer. Thus, as African journalist Selope Thema speculated, changes to the orthography of African languages were occasionally undertaken, in order to make them easier for whites to learn.[72] A contemporary American observer noted: "Assertions are rife, data are few."[73] Even Erika Theron had to admit in 1950 that the Afrikaners did not know the coloureds whose fate was decided by their politicians.[74]

They acted as "experts" who followed their own imagination and unquestioned beliefs rather than consulting scholarly research. This pertained especially to the claim that "the Bantu" were determined by their culture from the outset, and hence unable to adapt to Western culture.[75] In 1952, A.W. van Schalkwyk, professor of Bantu Studies at the University of the Orange Free State in Bloemfontein and an active SABRA member, suggested that a separate press be set up for "the Bantu" in order to bring "the point of view of the Afrikaners to the attention of our Bantu population in a clear and sympathetic manner". From his deep knowledge of Africans, he claimed he knew that the written word had "much greater authority" for them than the spoken word. "The Bantu child grows up ... with the understanding that the spoken word has very little meaning. It can be twisted,

---

69 Gordon (1990: 30–34) provides a more differentiated account, however, by pointing to the reception of Malinowski by Afrikaans ethnologists, while Radcliffe–Brown found no or only negative resonance. On the latter's stay at the University of Cape Town, see Phillips 1993: 22–25.
70 Hammond–Tooke 2001: 137–138.
71 For examples, see Bank 2015a: 189–192.
72 Cobley 2016: 130–132.
73 Allport 1956: 11.
74 E. Theron 1950: 21, 23.
75 P. A. Theron 1952: 15.

disputed and forgotten. On the other hand, it has learned that what can be read in black and white is indisputable. It has learned the authority of the written document."[76] A younger representative of the discipline, who had studied Psychology with Verwoerd for some time, was F. J. Language. Together with Coertze he co-authored one of the programmatic writings on apartheid; at the time, he worked as administrative official in Brakpan, where he implemented apartheid in a particularly harsh and ruthless manner.[77]

The striking congruence of scientific "findings" put forward by Afrikaans ethnologists with popular prejudices among the white population can be explained by the fact that their expertise was unfounded, to put it mildly. This is what would account for the attraction that 'Bantu Studies' and Ethnology held for many Afrikaans students.[78] In fact, a tradition of pseudo-scientificity as far as ethnological knowledge was concerned stretched from Meinhof through his South African students to the ethnologists in the service of the state administration. This tradition came under the vehement criticism of the few ethnologists who held themselves to higher standards.[79]

One of these few field researchers among Afrikaans ethnologists, for some even the "*voorste Afrikaner-antropoloog*"[80] was Johannes Bruwer, who expressed scepticism about racial theories. About an encounter with a representative of this group, he wrote: "Their views begin with Gobineau and end up being bogged down in a whole series of nonsensical publications on inherent racial differences. . . . There are in fact no objective methods of measuring racial differences in an inherent sense."[81] In various publications, he maintained that race only pertained to physical characteristics such as skin colour, but not to cultural level or intelligence.[82] Nevertheless, like Eiselen, he distinguished South African population groups primarily on the basis of skin colour, without clarifying what this criterion was actually supposed to mean.[83] In contrast to many other ethnologists, Bruwer still maintained contact with intellectuals such as Z. K. Matthews, a leading ANC

---

76 PV 276/I/27/11/4/1, 44f. Prof. A. W. van Schalkwyk, 31.10.1952.
77 PV93/1/13/1/1, Letter by H. F. Language, Brakpan, to Verwoerd, 19.10.1950. Unfortunately, he does not state whether he studied psychology or sociology. His inflexible attitude is expressed in Language 1950: 33; see also Sapire 1987: 358–361, 383–387. Language later became a professor in Bloemfontein (Language 1961; see also Coertze/Language/van Eeden 1943).
78 R. D. Coertze 1991:30; esp. Coertze 1998: 3, 14.
79 On the social background of many Afrikaans ethnologists, see Bank 2015a: 181–182.
80 De Jongh 1987: 107.
81 PV 123/2/1/4, Letter by Bruwer to Valentyn Büchner, 18.5.1966.
82 Bruwer 1958: 124; see also Bruwer 1953: 72.
83 Bruwer 1956a: 104; see also Eiselen 1950: 11.

member,[84] even in the late 1950s. Ethnologists like Bruwer who did actually know better were, according to Gordon, driven to conformity against the convictions that they held as scholars; they were seduced by ritualised sessions and the sense of belonging to an exclusive circle of the elect, which membership of the Broederbond conveyed to them.[85]

Thus, despite all the outward displays of expertise, the actual knowledge about the African population remained rudimentary in the Ministry responsible for it. A manuscript probably penned by E. Wyatt Sampson,[86] an employee of the Ministry, provides insight into the views on black people prevalent within the Ministry. Sampson wrote this article in 1951, at a time when Verwoerd was already Minister and Eiselen had been Secretary for two years. Given the control both of them exercised over the Ministry, one can be sure that the views expressed in this article could by no means have been Sampson's private opinion; and his was certainly not a dissenting voice. In an introductory passage, facts and figures about the reserves were presented in great detail; and the legend was repeated that the reserves had been the original homelands of the blacks, "when the Europeans took over the government of the country" (p. 2). In what follows, the article presents a justification of the land distribution by which Africans allegedly received the best parts. It was true that there is poverty, the article admitted, but this was not due to the poor quality of the land, but to the "human element" (p. 3). This then became the main theme of further explanations referring to the supposed mental deficiencies and the reason "why it is so difficult for the Bantu to orientate themselves to western agricultural ideas" (p. 4). The 'proof' is delivered in the second part, in which the author provides a detailed description of 'Life in a typical Kraal', without the differentiation of ethnic groups that was otherwise so important for the Department. Cultural differences among black social groups were ignored in favour of an emphasis on the generally primitive state of all Africans. Through the anecdotal interweaving of personal experiences, the reader was informed that the author was speaking with the authority of long experience.

---

84 PV 123/2/19/5, Correspondence with Matthews about a publication in 1958. He also co-operated with English–speaking colleagues such as Monica Wilson (ibid., various letters 1960).
85 Gordon 2018: 98, 107–112, esp. 112; see also Gordon 2004: 5–9. On Bruwer, see also Kapp 2009: 401.
86 NA BAO 733/400, vol. 6, f. 331, Letter by Syndicate Publishing Company to E. Wyatt Sampson, 6.7.1951, with request to read through the enclosed galley proofs and to return them. As the article itself does not contain a name and it is not clear whether the above–mentioned letter was the accompanying letter, I believe that a certain caution should be heeded in attributing it to the author mentioned. In what follows, the numbers given in round brackets refer to the page numbers of this manuscript.

In this presentation of everyday life, the author emphasised how much of the main work in agriculture was done by women, who were more or less explicitly presented as oppressed. When men successfully engaged in farming, the poor relatives would immediately come and hold out their hands, leading the author to conclude that "[i]t is thus best not to be exceptional in any way in Bantu society" (p. 5). The social structures supposedly prevent individualisation and progress. This picture of general indolence was painted with relish; the daily routine of the men in particular was said to consist essentially of "the serious business of sitting either in the sun or in the shade for the rest of the day" (7). In addition, the belief that all adversities were caused by spirits further encouraged indolence, as problems could not be solved but had to be accepted (9). Sampson identified the belief in the power of spirits as the main obstacle on the way to improving the situation (10).

Like Verwoerd himself, Sampson had nothing but contempt for 'theorists' who lacked empirical knowledge and who argued in an unworldly manner: "Those who believe that the Bantu have only to be shown better methods to have them generally adopted have little conception of the true position." (10). He then repeatedly hammered home the idea that progress was hardly possible in such a society. In what he presents under the heading 'Love of repetition' he maintains that "the Bantu" are generally hostile to innovation: "Tribal life . . . is an unthinking rhythmical thing that goes drowsily on without mental effort. . . . These customs are so ingrained in a mature tribal Native that they appear verily part of his basic nature." (10) Africans supposedly enjoy performing repetitive activities in the industrial world, because this was very much in line with their basic mental constitution. This also included the "avoidance of harsh and impalpable facts, in both of which traits [the Bantu] is thoroughly schooled as a child". (11) The text guides the reader to gradually realise what heroic efforts the government has undertaken to make improvements to this world, which are being listed in detail (11–14). Accordingly, Sampson admonishes officials to, "use great tact and patience to better the people's lot in spite of themselves and their age-old prejudices." (13).

A Native Commissioner added his own insights into "the Natives" to this wisdom: "For them, authority is the ability to enforce an order by punishment."[87] Another employee justified the de facto ban on trade unions by saying that they "have not yet reached the stage at which they can assume so responsible a role". In any case, the most suitable work for them was the Tayloristic production process, that

---

[87] PV 276/I/9/4/3/3, f. 78, Letter by T. F. Coertze (Native Commissioner Witzieshoek) to Chief Native Commissioner Western Areas (Potchefstroom), 6.8.1952.

is, "repetitive work at which the Bantu excel".[88] Similar insights came from another official: "As we know, the native is not made for responsible work."[89] The curiosity to learn something new was allegedly also very limited. Another official, for example, ascribed African peasants' resistance to "ecological" measures to their indolence, rather than soliciting their views.[90] J. L. Sadie, professor of Economics at the University of Stellenbosch claimed that "thousands of migrant workers who regularly return to the Bantu Areas after spells of work outside, do not return [to the cities] because they are prevented from settling permanently in the existing urban areas by influx control, but because they much prefer to have their domicile in their tribal area".[91] How did he know this? Instead of discussing the issues with the people concerned, it was easier to perpetuate the familiar commonplaces about tribal identities.

This, then, was the state of expert ethnological knowledge that Verwoerd had secured in his Ministry.[92] It was a kind of experiential knowledge that served to reinforce prejudices, impervious as it was to scholarly findings or ethnological knowledge; instead, it reproduced the opinions widespread among white South Africans claiming to know "the blacks", laced with the arrogance of expertise.[93] Even patent misjudgements could not change this. In the case of the unrest in Witzieshoek, for instance, officials had not the slightest inkling of the importance of cattle for local residents; instead, the measures for ecological 'betterment' were developed through desk-research, and imposed on the local population.[94] The idea that Africans were not only trapped in their traditions by their living conditions and religion, but that they were psychologically unable to free themselves from these because, like children, they avoided the real problems, and preferred to accept them rather than solving them, coincided with Verwoerd's ethnopsychological ideas. Commenting on a black teacher who, remorseful about a transgression, asked for forgiveness and reinstatement, the Minister noted condescendingly: "These people are often like children in their follies."[95]

---

88 PV 276/3/1/1, Native Labour Conditions (anon., n.d., probably 1953), pp. 6, 3.
89 PV 276/I/8/2/1, 1 Letter by Research Officer (anon., carbon copy) to Secretary of Native Affairs, 30.7.52.
90 T. F. Coertze 1950: 25.
91 Sadie 1960: 58.
92 A text presumably penned by Eiselen did not differ in its assessment of the indigenous way of life, but in the more objective tone in which it was written (FAV 4.6.2.2, The Bantu in South Africa).
93 During World War II, the Smuts government's radio propagandists also preferred to follow their preconceived opinions, unclouded by knowledge (see Wiederroth 2016: 293–300).
94 Beerstecher 1994: 31–37, 52–53, 105–106, 109–113, 122, 185–188.
95 PV 276/I/6/1/5, f. 127, Letter by Verwoerd to Stanton Thomas Ntuka, 3.11.1955.

The Department had provided for the post of a dedicated ethnologist since 1926, and allocated prizes to encourage staff to acquire additional training in ethnology or a related science.[96] Yet the ethnological knowledge of Ministry officials remained extremely limited, although the department had its own ethnologist and the universities which taught social anthropology had been offering their services to the state since the early 1920s.[97] Between 1930 and 1969, Meinhof's student N. J. van Warmelo held the post of government ethnologist.[98] His impact was apparently very limited; ethnologists external to the Department, such as Bruwer, were more influential.[99] Van Warmelo even refused to cooperate with the Sauer Commission, because he believed that apartheid should be kept out of party politics.[100] Therefore, he influenced apartheid policies only indirectly, not conceptually,[101] by providing the descriptions of ethnic groups to which the state could then refer.[102]

Ethnological research results were hardly taken up in political decision-making and administration. The accumulation of knowledge progressed very slowly, if at all. In fact, there were numerous complaints from various quarters about inadequate knowledge. In response, a demand was voiced that all those directly involved in the administration of "the Bantu" should be taught at least the basics of ethnology.[103] Even 15 years later, in 1965, ethnologist Johannes Bruwer gave as reasons for his resignation as Commissioner General for "the Bantu" of Southwest Africa "[t]he complete lack of knowledge and empathy with the people on the part of the administration, where knowledge and power are only derived from laws and rules, whereas a Commissioner General is actually powerless and [good] advice has no meaning". This, he said, made it impossible for him to "win over" the Ovambo as well as the Herero, Dama and Nama "to us". He was missing leadership "from the

---

96 Herbst 1930: 484.
97 Dubow 1985: 57–61. From the less than enthusiastic response of NAD officials despite the career incentives associated with it, it is clear that many saw no need to learn about African societies and cultures, presumably assuming that they already knew what they needed to know.
98 Pugach 2012: 180–184 and Pugach 2002: 10, on Van Warmelo's uptake of the link between linguistic and racial criteria.
99 Gordon (2004: 8) expresses serious doubts about Van Warmelo's ethnological competence. On Bruwer's influence in the Broederbond, see Stals 1998: 317–319, 423–424.
100 Brits 2000: 80.
101 Gordon (1990: 41, n. 6) also doubts whether Van Warmelo really influenced the direction of the Native Affairs Department. See also Hammond–Tooke 2001: 111–116; Kuper (1987: 2) seems to judge him in a similar way when he rates him, together with Isaac Schapera, as outstanding scholar.
102 Lekgoathi 2009: 71, 73.
103 C. W. Prinsloo 1951: 14, 19–21.

top", maintaining that a purely technocratic administration could not create trust "without deeper empathy for other people". Even a knowledgeable civil servant in the upper echelons of the hierarchy like himself could not do much to counter the cold bureaucratism prevalent in the NAD, especially since he had found that "civil servants there have no idea of human development beyond a little technical knowledge". He had not expected, he said, "that civil servants would be so ill-prepared for the task ahead, as I discovered there". The same mistakes that had been made in Northern Rhodesia in the 1940s, were repeated in South West Africa and, as he explicitly pointed out, in South Africa as well.[104] Thus he indirectly addressed core problems of Verwoerd's approach, namely authoritarianism and the refusal to engage in dialogue, which were exacerbated by the widespread incompetence and poor training of civil servants in the state administration,[105] as he had noted years earlier on his first trip through the territory.[106] Even at a later stage he persisted with his criticism of the ethnological incompetence in the Department of Native Affairs, which is why the cultural differences between "the Bantu" had not hitherto been taken into account.[107]

In replying to Bruwer, Verwoerd did not address the latter's criticism; he only took up Bruwer's suggestion, that instead of addressing "the Bantu" as a whole, more of an account should be taken of the differences between the "peoples", which coincided with the general view among Afrikaans ethnologists anyway.[108] Bruwer held the differences between "the Bantu" to be more important than their commonalities;[109] in that respect, he shared the basic assumptions of cultural relativism. To him, there was no question that every one of the South

---

[104] PV 123/2/11/6, Letter by Bruwer to Verwoerd, 29.7.1965. On his resignation, see also ibid., Letter by Bruwer to Verwoerd, 15.1.1965. See also PV 123/2/1/2, Letter by Bruwer to G. J. Jordaan, 10.11.1965 in reply to his letter of 5.10. See also I. Evans 1997: 194–195. On the errors in Northern Rhodesia, see Bruwer 1967: 69. Stellenbosch ethnologist Nic Olivier took a similar view of the state of knowledge in the administration (Gordon 2018: 106–107; see also Gordon 1991: 88).
[105] Posel 1999: 103.
[106] Gordon 2004: 6.
[107] Bruwer 1966: 72f. In Bruwer 1962: 87–90, he emphasised the need to teach basic knowledge about black societies in schools. Eiselen (1953: 24–25, 1955a and 1965: 21) also vehemently advocated the introduction of 'population studies' in schools – with which other SABRA activists agreed (e.g. Gerdener 1952: 9 and with regard to universities, N. J. J. Olivier 1956a: 36–37).
[108] PV 123/2/11/6, Letter by Verwoerd to Bruwer, 4.8.1965.
[109] PV 123/2/14/1, Letter by Bruwer to Hoofsekretaris SABRA, 17.1.1966: "I would be very sorry if S.A.B.R.A. were to continue to confirm the global Bantu policy!".

African population groups had "its own kind of specific ways that can no longer be recognised from a global perspective".[110]

Interestingly, Bruwer picked up on the trend towards large-scale planning. In a memorandum penned in 1963, he called on ethnology to provide a scientific foundation for segregated development. Noting a gap in this respect, he stated, "[f]undamental planning based on expert knowledge is as important in this context as in any other field". In much the same way as Verwoerd had called for a pooling of knowledge in a Department of Social Welfare in the early 1930s, Bruwer called for systematic scientific research on the various ethnic groups in South Africa and, based on this, further planning of apartheid policy: "It can undoubtedly be said that applied ethnological knowledge must underlie South Africa's population policy and development".[111] Eiselen himself had acknowledged the limited knowledge of many officials, but ultimately did nothing to change it. In his book *Liberale Nasionalisme*, the writer N. P. van Wyk Louw, another outsider, noted that, generally speaking, the various population groups knew very little about each other:

> Practically, in our own country, what do we know of one another? – white of black, black of white, white of brown, brown of white, brown of black, black of brown? Knowledge, yes, in some respects; and 'speaking with competence in certain specialised fields' we can easily do; but that remains an external way of knowing, always from our own point of view, never from inside, just as we think we know 'our people'; we read something into others which our perspective compels us to see in them.[112]

As early as 1955, yet another outsider, the apartheid-critical theologian B.B. Keet, posed the question as to "what the people's own non-white culture that is to be preserved actually is". The answer to this, he said, was "extremely vague. Usually it goes no further than [a supposed] understanding of community, [a] reverence for authority (of parents or the authorities) and . . . strict mores."[113]

Thus, ethnological research confirmed the largely sterile preconceived opinions of Afrikaans *volkekunde* typical of European and settler societies.[114] This resulted in a self-referential system of a conceited non-knowledge. Confirming colonial self-understandings, it provided the basis of legitimacy for the apartheid system as a whole. Thus Afrikaans ethnology, like the knowledge of other 'ex-

---

110 PV 123/2/19/5, Die Volkekunde en Bevolkingsbeleid, manuscript (*Afr. Inst. Bulletin*, Junie 1963), p. 3.
111 Ibid., p. 1.
112 N. P. van Wyk Louw 1958: 85.
113 Keet 1955: 82.
114 Eiselen (1955a: 28) admitted the widespread ignorance about "Bantu" cultures, but did not problematise the fact that these ignoramuses all had the right to vote.

perts', did not go beyond popular assumptions widespread among whites, which attained the fixity of certainties, and immunised themselves against any criticism from outside.[115] Despite the involvement of numerous ethnologists in government and administration, there is no evidence of any better understanding of "the Bantu". It remained at the level of what French journalist Alfred Fabre-Luce observed in 1961: "In truth, although one rubs shoulders with him ["the Black"] every day, one does not know him."[116] Ignorance was not a deficit, but an integral part of the system; one could even say that it was indispensable for the functioning of the apartheid state.

History

When we speak of Verwoerd's understanding of history in this context, it is not the historical self-image of Afrikaner nationalists that is meant. Since it is the justification of apartheid policies that is at issue, we will turn our lens on his knowledge of pre-colonial African history. Verwoerd did not derive the historical legitimacy of apartheid from colonial history; rather, the decisive factor for him was the level of civilisational development that Africans had achieved of their own accord, that is, before the beginning of colonisation. An explication of his sources and his statements on this subject should be preceded by a brief historiographical overview to show what he could and could not have known at the time, based on the state of historical research of the late 1950s.

Since its beginnings as a historiography with scientific pretensions in the late 19th century, South African historiography told a triumphant colonial story of white settlers. It was the archivist and historian George McCall Theal, in particular, who laid the foundation for a history from the settlers' perspectives, and with European settlement as its most important subject matter. When, from the 1920s onwards, a group of young researchers around historian and social scientist William Macmillan, questioned this view and, above all, its legitimating implications for a policy of discrimination and exclusion, they, like Theal, thought that pre-colonial African societies were largely barbaric. Unlike Theal and other authors, however, they were confident about the development potential of Africans. With regard to pre-colonial history, they remained within the interpretive framework set by Theal and others, centred on the figure of Shaka Zulu who occupied a

---

115 See for instance the investigation by Hudson/Jacobs/Biesheuvel 1966: ch. 9.
116 Fabre-Luce 1961: 427. That also applied to criminology (Smit 1989: 244).

prominent place in colonial historiography.[117] Shaka (c. 1787–1828) who, through military innovations in the early nineteenth century, had formed the Zulu Kingdom as the most powerful political entity outside of the Cape Colony, was stylised into the epitome of an African despot.[118] African despotism formed the basis of the historical image held by Afrikaner nationalists, for whom the history of Africa was defined by chaos and permanent ethnic conflict. "For it is true that South Africa was never a country of blacks, as many uninformed people claim. It was precisely the whites ... who saved the Bantu from himself."[119] This motif of the pacifying and civilising power of white rule[120] came up numerous times in the context of unfolding apartheid ideology from the 1930s onwards.[121] In 1956, Daniel de Wet Nel, the minister who succeeded Verwoerd and who was likewise renowned for his expertise on "the Bantu", claimed in all seriousness that "in the Basutoland area alone, more than half a million Bantu were devoured by man-eating tribes during this period [that is, the Mfecane period]".[122] It was common 'knowledge' in the Ministry that "the Bantu" needed an authoritarian form of rule, otherwise they would "still [be] prone to acts of senseless violence when stirred up by agitators".[123] The adjective "senseless" refers to the assumption that black people were stuck in a kind of prelogical mentality. This idea was adduced to justify the repressive action against "agitators" and demonstrators, such as that taken in Sharpeville in 1960.

It was not until the late 1960s that critical historical scholarship began investigating pre-colonial African societies intensively and with politically inspired verve. Their history was now being discovered and reconstructed in all its facets.[124] Verwoerd was thus still moving in a field that had hardly been empirically researched

---

117 Saunders 1988: ch. 4 on Theal, Macmillan, and the latter's students ch. 5 (see also H. Macmillan 1989).
118 On the revision of this image, and the relativisation of the importance of Shaka, see Hamilton 1996. A comparable case is that of Ndebele–king Mzilikazi (c. 1790–1868), on whom South African ethnologist Peter Becker wrote a book entitled *Path of Blood*, which he recommended to Verwoerd as "a true and unbiased history of South Africa" (PV 93/1/34/9, f. 39, Letters by Peter Becker to Verwoerd's private secretary Barnard, 13.3.1962 and f. 20, 27.3.1962).
119 PV 93/3/1/38, Letter by Verwoerd to W. J. N. Badenhorst (Klerksdorp), 17.1.1961. In a very similar vein, N. J. J. Olivier 1956b: 22–23.
120 PV 93/1/30/1/26, Letter by Verwoerd to A. Graham (Bournemouth, England), 24.8.1964, f. 144.
121 University of the North-West, Ossewabrandwag Archives, van der Westhuysen–Collection. 11/79, H. N. Theunissen (in Commemorative Book of the Johannesburg Committee, pp. 21–22). Quite clearly, for example, in Holloway 1964: 40, 45.
122 M. D. C. Nel 1956: 5.
123 FAV, 4.6.2.2, The Bantu of South Africa (c. 1953, presumably by Eiselen), p. 4.
124 This intense interest in pre-colonial history, which also encompassed archaeology, was itself a reaction to apartheid policies. On the rise of 'radical', often Marxist-oriented, historiography

by the time he assumed office as Prime Minister. All the more striking, then, is the self-assurance with which he presented his historical ignorance as objectively established knowledge. This indicates that he could rely on a broad consensus among whites. No Afrikaans historian at the time even felt the need to study African history at all, since it was understood as a cycle of despotic rule, tribal feuds, campaigns of extermination and expulsions, which ruled out the very possibility of cumulative cultural development. In 1962, T. S. van Rooyen, who summarily equated history with change, assigned Africans to prehistory, so as to make it appear that they had only been brought into the light of historical development by industrious white colonists.[125] Afrikaans-language historiography – an emphatic nationalist historiography centered on the history of the Afrikaners – was introverted; moreover, the personnel policy and the influence of the Broederbond tied it to a certain view of history, which is why it persisted in a sterile positivism right into the 1980s.[126]

The central myth, which Verwoerd repeated on numerous occasions, was that South Africa was a deserted country, with the exception of the Khoisan population whose historical presence in the territory was indisputable.[127] This notion was not difficult to convey because South African whites were given to the homegrown myth that the coloureds were "half-breeds", thus ignoring the fact that most of them were descendants of the Khoisan or of slaves.[128] The "indigenous people" were part of present-day living inhabitants, but now as so-called coloureds; their history was explained in terms of a causal relation between white settlement and "miscegenation", thus obliterating the older history of the Khoisan. According to Verwoerd, the whites had therefore had every right to settle here

---

since the early 1970s, see Wright 1978; for more general overviews see Saunders 1988 and K. Smith 1988.

125 T. B. van Rooyen 1962: 108.

126 In particular, H. B. Thom, historian and long-time rector at Stellenbosch University, and from 1952 to 1960 chairman of the Broederbond, ensured that the chairs at the Afrikaans universities were filled with historians loyal to the line, several of them his own students (D. J. Kotzé 1969: 19); Kotze provides further details of his patronage, which he accrued through multiple memberships and chairmanships of commissions, and by virtue of the fact that he supervised 16 doctorates – more than any other historian of his time –, ensuring that he had a base of loyal supporters among his staff (Kapp 2004: 46–48; see also Kapp 2005: 45–51). G. D. Scholtz (1970: 18) emphasises the 'vocation' of the historian, who would have to serve his people. On the isolation and methodological sterility of Afrikaans nationalist historiography, see Grundlingh 1987: 42–43. Even at the "Bantu" universities such as Fort Hare, one of the criteria for appointments in the Department of History was that of the 'right' political views (Williams 2001: 528).

127 N. J. J. Olivier 1954: 23. The Khoisan were game-hunting and cattle-herding societies that were not counted among Bantu–speaking Africans (see Marx 2022: 12–14).

128 Adhikari 2006: 19–32.

and to claim the land for themselves, right up to the present day, because "the Bantu", that is, Bantu-speaking Africans, had migrated from Central Africa at the same time:

> In South Africa, a white state came into being through the seizure of an empty land. Over three centuries, they have developed the whole country into a highly modern state and created a white nation. At the same time, various black nations arrived from Central Africa and settled in different places. In fact, they did not develop anything, but when they were defeated in an attack on the whites and then protected by the whites in all sorts of areas, they found their subsistence through the work which enterprising [*inisiatiefvolle*] whites gave them.[129]

From this account of their time of arrival, whites claimed a privilege, in view of the alleged primitive state of the blacks.[130]

Verwoerd catered to popular attitudes and views when he propagated such views;[131] the Christian Afrikaner nationalists took some credit for the fact that the black population was not wiped out as in other settler colonies, but actually increased under their rule. In 1950, A. W. van Schalkwyk from Stellenbosch, who at a later stage became professor for Bantu Studies at the University of Bloemfontein, thus reported to the Bondsraad of the Broederbond: "While the non-white part of the population in other parts of the world was reduced to an insignificant remnant, our ancestors brought protection and peace to the non-whites of South Africa."[132] The demand for black labour and the extreme exploitation and slavery-like conditions were carefully concealed while the Afrikaners presented themselves as selfless, humane conveyors of civilisation.

In a speech on 23 January 1962, in which he called for the establishment of autonomous self-governing structures in the Transkei, the first 'homeland', Verwoerd emphasised the importance of this historical derivation for the legitima-

---

129 PV 93/1/30/1/24, Letter by Verwoerd to A. E. Breytenbach, 31.1.1964, p. 94.

130 PV 93/1/30/1/29, Letter by Verwoerd to John McKenzie (Auckland, New Zealand), 10.11.1964, p. 5; see also another letter, in which he is even more explicit about the supposed barbarism of Africans: "In fact, if it were not for the initiative of the white man and his care of the black people very few of the latter would still have existed due to internecine strife, famine and lack of own health services." (PV 93/1/30/1/24, Letter by Verwoerd to C. Sutherland (Madison, Wisconsin), 10.2.1964). Louw gave a similar account in an interview (in *U.S. News & World Report*, 22.7.1964, pp. 58–60); see also the propagandistic use of this idea (in *South African Embassy* 1981: 4–5). The myth of the late immigration of "the Bantu" had already been advocated by Westermann (Pugach 2012: 174).

131 F. Tomlinson held very similar views on the history of South Africa (*Die Vaderland* 17.9.1952). But see also the massive criticism of the Voortrekker myths that Verwoerd repeatedly adduced (*Cape Times* 14.4.1959 (commentary)).

132 AB Archives, 2/3/19, Bondsraad, 2–3.10.1950, p. 2, TOP 7, Die Afrikaner en sy toekoms.

tion of his entire policy. He referred to racial segregation as a practice that dated back to the time of the alleged simultaneous arrival of Africans and Europeans in Southern Africa: "These two groups established themselves in specific areas and generally speaking these specific areas did not encroach upon each other."[133] Crucial to his argument was the assertion that the areas did not overlap, but were clearly distinguishable from each other. The early settlers had already recognised these areas, the later homelands, as territories belonging to the blacks,[134] thus giving rise to the idea that mixed habitats were a relatively recent phenomenon that only became apparent with British colonial rule, industrialisation and urbanisation from the end of the 19th century.

The historical picture of the late arrival of Bantu-speaking Africans in Southern Africa was partly supported by research findings at the time, especially from Bantu Studies. Not only German, but also English historical linguistics assumed a rapid spread of the Bantu-speaking population from their original location in what is now Cameroon.[135] The settlement of Central, Eastern and Southern Africa was supposed to have taken the form of migration of Bantu-speaking peoples. Verwoerd's assertion that they were distinct nations that spread across the continent in this way, seemed plausible in light of the research at the time. On the other hand, there were a number of discoveries that challenged this view of history. The southernmost Bantu-speaking peoples were found to have adopted clicks from the languages of the local Khoisan, which was a clear indication of much older and continuous contacts.[136] In addition, an archaeological site had been discovered in the 1930s in the far north of the country – Mapungubwe –, which not only confirmed the presence of Bantu-speaking Africans at a much earlier period, but also testified to a highly developed culture. It was a centre of power that had its heyday between c.1000 and 1200 AD.[137] This gold-producing empire was integrated into the long-distance trade networks of the Indian Ocean, as finds made in Mapungubwe prove. Burial objects made of gold indicate the high level of cultural development and advanced state of political centralisation. But such facts did nothing to unsettle the image of the late immigration of the 'barbarians'. For this reason, the site was declared a restricted military area and

---

133 Verwoerd, House of Assembly, 23.1.1962 (in Pelzer 1966: 660–689, 660–661); a similar, but more differentiated account is provided by the historian Pelzer (1963: 147–148). Sociologist Rhoodie (1958: 208) also claimed that blacks were "not the original inhabitants of South Africa."
134 PV 93/1/30/1/17, Letter by Verwoerd to H. J. Bekker, 5.11.1962.
135 On this, see Flight 1988; also Duerden 1921: 6.
136 Parkington/Hall 2010: 96–97.
137 M. Hall 1987: 74–90; see also Huffman 2005: 32–51.

closed to the public and to non-governmental scientists. Steeped in racial anthropology, the hand-picked, party-loyal archaeologists of the University of Pretoria were intent on proving that the human skeletons found at Mapungubwe were not those of "Bantu" but of 'proto-Hottentots', so as not to have to admit that they had been in the country before the whites, and had established urban settlements and centralised rule.[138]

In view of the scarcity of research on African history at his time, Verwoerd's statements, which had an important legitimating function, did not reach beyond mere assumptions. They could not draw on evidence-based knowledge; in the case of Mapungubwe, such knowledge was deliberately suppressed. Verwoerd's knowledge of the society and culture of "the Bantu" was anything but scientifically sound. His statements clearly demonstrate that his knowledge hardly went beyond the popular views prevalent among whites, and beyond what was taught at school in his youth. However, his familiarity with ethnopsychology coaxed him into believing that it had a scientific basis. Taking a wide view on these issues, prominent palaeoanthropologist and medical-biological scientist Philip Tobias concluded: "Science provides no evidence that any single one of the assumptions underlying South Africa's racial legislation is justified."[139]

The legitimation of apartheid did not proceed from biologistically couched racial theories, but from the humanities disciplines, since it explained differences between groups of people as cultural differences. But from the three sciences, which were repeatedly invoked as key disciplines, it created a knowledge base that was neither empirically sound nor methodologically reflected. At the time of Verwoerd, the history of Southern Africa had not been established on a firm basis, empirically and methodologically speaking. Thus, all Verwoerd could do was make and repeat assertions, which he presented with the greatest self-confidence as sound knowledge, certain that he was tapping into a basic colonialist consensus among South African whites.

This chapter dealt with non-knowledge at the basis of apartheid not in order to expose fundamental knowledge deficits. More importantly, this non-knowledge was constitutive of apartheid. Without this non-knowledge, racial segregation would not have been feasible, because well-founded knowledge based on credible research could have contributed to seriously questioning the notion of cultural dif-

---

138 On the research context, see A. Meyer 1998: P. J. Coertze was entrusted with the excavations in the 1950s; during this period, the focus began to shift to physical-anthropological research, not least with the aim of proving that the inhabitants of Mapungubwe were not "Bantu" but 'Proto–Hottentot', i.e. Khoisan (see also Voigt 1983: 4–7, 130–135). Such claims were spread by H. W. Hitzeroth in the Anthropology Department of the Africa Institute in Pretoria (1966: 17–18).
139 Qtd. in Thompson 1966: 172.

ference conceived of as civilisational-developmental gap between whites and blacks. Moreover, it would have exposed uncomfortable truths unsuitable for legitimating the racial division of the South African population. Apartheid politicians claimed a knowledge for themselves that they did not have; they pretended to know African cultures in which they had no interest. They responded to any criticism of apartheid coming from European scholars, activists, and political spokespersons, alleging that the latter did not know the realities on the ground. Thus, Verwoerd criticised the Scientific Research Council's department dealing with housing, because there was, among others, "a scholar of Dutch origin", who obviously lacked the necessary knowledge of "the background and way of life of the natives", and conducted his research in a way "strongly theoretical and European in orientation".[140] Bringing in the knowledge and experience of Africans themselves was out of the question for apartheid ideologues, because it would have implied admitting knowledge gaps in a field that was crucial for the legitimation of apartheid. White rule was partly based on the claim to superior civilisation and knowledge in all fields.[141] The persons who took on the role of interlocutors were precisely the black intellectuals to whom apartheid politicians ascribed "false consciousness" for not only refuting the civilisational gap between white and blacks, but for disproving it through their very existence. White politicians, for their part, clung to their notion, born of ignorance, that black intellectuals were members of a 'barbaric' population incapable of producing knowledge about themselves, seeing that they had so thoroughly misunderstood their own social station and had been striving for equality – which was disallowed.

Ignorance and non-knowledge was reproduced within the Native Affairs Department in the guise of expert knowledge; in its intellectual poverty, it was hardly different from the popular assumptions of other white people.[142] Non-knowledge creates social facts – as the example of apartheid amply demonstrates. Thus, it is not simply the negative of knowledge in the sense of a deficit or, even more precisely, of a *desideratum*, that is bound to disappear with the advancement of knowledge.[143] Non-knowledge is not simply the absence of knowledge; it tends to become a guiding principle for action in its own right. A regime of ignorance is "a constellation of discursive practices and power relations giving rise to epistemological gaps and forms of unknowing that have generative social effects

---

140 PV 276/I/4/1/1, f. 18, Letter by Verwoerd to Eiselen, 24.8.1951.
141 Eiselen 1955a: 25.
142 See also Marx 2015 on the subject of this chapter.
143 Dilley and Kirsch, Introduction (in Dilley/Kirsch 2015: 20–23); see also Graeber 2012: 86–87, also on violence as basis for state structures based on non–knowledge.

and consequences".[144] This opens up a new perspective on the function of ignorance: ignorance becomes a factor in its own right, drawing effects in history, "as though it had a social life".[145] As the example of South Africa shows, ignorance can generate certainties. Apartheid was based on convictions that would not have been possible without ignorance. It could only take effect to the extent that ignorance was carefully nurtured and immunised against a different knowledge of African cultures and social structures.[146] Among apartheid ideologues, beliefs thus regularly took precedence over knowledge; ethnologists consistently adopted ahistorical forms of argumentation, assuming abstract regularities in the interaction of ethnic groups.[147] If Bruwer's approach would have been followed, and the differences between the various ethnic groups would have been taken account of, a perspective on social differences within these groups would have opened up, which would have recognised intellectual capacities and rapid cultural change among black population groups. A different kind of knowledge would have put paid to a bureaucratic and inevitably sweeping implementation of racial segregation policies. Non-knowledge, closely related to the myth of the empty country, became a political resource. One could even say that apartheid would not have been possible without the prevailing ignorance of African social and cultural structures, because it would not have been possible to maintain the image of a radically different other.

---

[144] Dilley/Kirsch 2015: 2.
[145] Ibid., 2.
[146] On this, see also Gordon 2018: 113.
[147] For example, E. F. Potgieter 1956b: 56–59.

'Homelands'

Prime Minister Verwoerd

J. G. Strijdom had been ill for some time, in fact he had not been in good health ever since he became Prime Minister in 1954. Yet his death on 24 August 1958 was sudden and unexpected.[1] As often happens, disputes over succession began during the period of mourning. The Cape NP, which entered into these disputes hoping to regain its influential position in the Party as a whole, supported the candidacy of T. E. Dönges. By now, the Minister of the Interior was pulling rank on the basis of seniority; moreover, he was well connected in the Broederbond.[2] The other candidate was Justice Minister C. R. Swart, one of the hardliners who, during his term of office, had pushed the draconian security laws through Parliament and supervised their application. Strijdom is said to have recommended him as his successor shortly before his death.[3] In the Transvaal, the choice quickly fell on Verwoerd; during his eight years as Minister for Native Affairs, he had made a name for himself as an exceptionally dynamic and assertive politician.[4]

The ensuing vote was the first one of its kind in the history of the NP; up to then, rival candidates had always backed down at the prospect of losing the election. Two ballots were necessary; in the first one, Verwoerd received the most votes, namely 80, but not an absolute majority, as Dönges received 52 and Swart 41. After the first ballot, Swart withdrew his candidacy and his supporters realigned themselves: 18 voted for Verwoerd, who received a total of 98 votes, while 23 voted for Dönges, who received 75 votes.[5] Verwoerd was thus elected Party

---

1 The obituaries in the English–language and international press were rather critical (e.g. South Africa (London), 30.8.1958, pp. 179–180, 193–194). Swart had held the office of Prime Minister since 21 August 1958. (*Die Burger*, 22.8.1958). On Strijdom's long illness, see Munger 1967: 45.
2 However, there were reservations even in the Cape NP, since Dönges was regarded as an egotist and had repeatedly drawn attention to himself for his lack of solidarity (296.K.GE 54, Letter by Phil Weber to A. L. Geyer, 15.4.1951). During the constitutional crisis over the abolition of coloured suffrage, he advocated compromise, which was rejected by others in the Party, such as P. W. Botha and Phil Weber, as "cowardice [*papbroekigheid*]" (296.K.GE 103a, Letter by Weber to A. L. Geyer, 2.9.1952).
3 This is what Marquard maintained – but without evidence (Marquard 1962: 165).
4 Ben Schoeman (1978: 239–240) reported, however, that he pulled out all the stops to prevent Verwoerd's election. Albert Hertzog had observed for some time that Verwoerd always made sure he was in the picture when Strijdom was photographed (PV 451/4/1/176, Diary 22.7.1948, p. 1481; see also B. M. Schoeman 1973: ch. 8).
5 For details of the events, see M. C. Botha 1979: 102–118; also Uys 1959: 6–7; and M. P. A. Malan 1964: 279.

leader and, with the majority in Parliament, he was also de facto Prime Minister-elect. Verwoerd's position was by no means secure at first; he was controversial within his own party and had yet to secure an unchallenged position of power.

In this quest, the opportunities for patronage afforded to him by his new office served him well; in 1963, only six members of his government had been appointed by one of his predecessors; all of the others owed their ministerial posts to him,[6] which would partly explain Verwoerd's powerful authority over Cabinet. The power of the new Prime Minister, tenuous as it still was at the time, was also reflected in the expansion of the political-ideological spectrum to the right, since it was only from those quarters that he could be threatened.[7] Verwoerd quite deliberately brought politicians into the government who had been active in the war years, either as members of the OB (Vorster), or as its ideological supporters (Diederichs, Hertzog).[8] In this way, the new Prime Minister, who had previously been the most bitter opponent of the Ossewabrandwag, sought to ingratiate himself to the most important representatives of the movement in the NP, thus expanding his power in his home base. This sheds a telling light on his supposedly principled opposition to OB. He managed to tie Albert Hertzog into cabinet discipline. As one of the leaders of the NP-affiliated 'labour movement' and secretive networker in the Pretoria area, Hertzog was one of the NP's potentially most dangerous figures. He had his own power base, yet was appointed to a more subordinate cabinet post – that of Postmaster General.[9] The NP of the Cape Province, in contrast, was further weakened. While Dönges was made Minister of Finance, Sauer was marginalised.[10] P. W. Botha was only appointed at Dönges's insistence.[11] Finally, the Prime Minister also rehabilitated one of his fiercest opponents

---

6 Thompson 1966: 118–119, 158.
7 This was criticised above all by the opposition UP (*Rand Daily Mail* and *Cape Times*, 22.10.1958). The writer D. F. Malherbe, an opponent of Afrikaans right–wing extremism during the War, also warned against the inclusion of "Nazis" in the cabinet (PV 18/3/1/63, Letter by D. F. Malherbe to Swart, 20.10.1958). On the danger from the right wing, see Kenney 1980: 164. On his approach to forming the new government as a whole, making extensive use of Albert Hertzog's diaries, see B. M. Schoeman 1973: 147–154; B. M. Schoeman 1977: 367–368.; also van den Berghe 1967: 174; and Troup 1975: 318.
8 B. M. Schoeman 1982: 53.
9 Du Pisani 1988: 7–9. These motives were also recalled by E. Verwoerd, since the astonishment at Hertzog's appointment to Cabinet was widespread (FAV, 4.7.8.6, Letter by O. Geyser to E. Verwoerd, 25.3.1988, and her reply of 1.4.1988) See also O'Meara 1996: 118–119; and Ben Schoeman 1978: 244. On Hertzog's intrigues, see S. P. Botha 2001: 114.
10 On the persistently tense relationship between Sauer and Verwoerd, see D. and J. de Villiers 1977: 122, 125. See also Meiring 1990: 48.
11 J. J. van Rooyen 1976: 77; see also Daan Prinsloo 1997: 31.

of the past, P. J. Meyer, who became head of the South African Broadcasting Corporation in 1958, and Chairman of the Broederbond soon afterwards. Verwoerd invited him to co-operate, saying, "[t]he differences of the past do not matter to me – we must all look forward and work together in the interest of our country and our *volk*".[12] Under Meyer's leadership, the Broederbond took on activities such as the manipulation of election results in the homelands and High Commission Territories, which the government itself could not carry out.[13] With his aim of combating 'liberalism', Meyer also introduced a more authoritarian leadership in the Broederbond, which in turn gave rise to the growing concerns among members who later emerged as dissidents, such as Beyers Naudé.[14] In 1960, Verwoerd arranged for Henning Klopper, a founder of the Broederbond and a loyal supporter, to be elected Speaker of Parliament.[15]

Superficially, the South African cabinet system resembled that of Britain, but in reality, the South African Prime Minister's position was much more powerful than that of his British counterpart.[16] Verwoerd wielded these powers like none other, and dominated his cabinet to such an extent that there was talk of autocratic tendencies, or even comparisons with dictatorships. "Verwoerd was more than a prime minister. He was de facto minister of almost everything else as well."[17]

While Prime Minister Verwoerd clearly set new accents, he wanted to build on the foundations of apartheid he had laid in the previous eight years. His term of office can be divided into two overlapping phases that followed one another – that is, the second phase would not have been possible without the first one. With the more wide-ranging powers accorded to him as the head of government, Verwoerd pushed the transformation of state and society to another level – from the sectorally limited, albeit ever-expanding, 'native policy' to more general and fundamental changes that also pertained to Coloureds and Indians; from the transformation of certain sub-sectors of society limited to the black majority to the state as a whole.

---

12 PV 93/1/34/2, Letter by Verwoerd to P. J. Meyer, 14.1.1959, f. 52. See also Verwoerd's letter to J. G. van der Merwe on this matter (PV 93/3/1/24, Letter by Verwoerd to J. G. van der Merwe, 15.6.1959: f. 15; see also D. Prinsloo 1987: 51). However, Meyer's rehabilitation was due to A. Hertzog, to which Verwoerd initially reacted with great displeasure (B. M. Schoeman 1982: 46–47).)
13 Marx 2011; see also Stals 1998: 322–324; on Meyer's authoritarian leadership of the SABC, see Hayman/Tomaselli 1989: 62–63.
14 Stals 1998: 253–255, 269, 402, 527.
15 J. Basson 2008: 62.
16 Thompson 1966: 60–61; see also van der Walt 1968: 229.
17 Thus stated by diplomat Marc Burger (in Wolvaardt/Wheeler/Scholtz 2010, vol. 1: 101; see also, similarly, his colleague Don Sole in vol. 2: 11).

The first step after 1958 was the transformation of the South African constitutional order, the second the expansion of the state's capacity to intervene, especially in the economy. The transformation of the constitutional order involved three central aspects, namely the homeland policy, the establishment of a Republic, and the withdrawal from the Commonwealth. These are usually treated separately in South African historiography: they are not seen as part of the integrated programme of transformation that in fact they were. The homeland policy was not simply a continuation of the previous apartheid policy nor, as will be shown, was it a defensive reaction to the decolonisation of Africa; rather it was the flipside of the establishment of the Republic. As the fulfilment of the central promise of Afrikaner nationalism, the Republic was to be a white republic. And the homeland policy was the precondition for the Republic to be declared as a new state form: "We must ensure that the Republic will be a white republic. That is why the resolution of the colour question is a priority. But it cannot be a general priority – how long would we then still have to wait for the Republic?"[18] Once the constitutional transformation was complete, i.e. from the second half of 1961, Verwoerd started to devote his efforts to building a strong, interventionist, forceful state focused on policy planning.

The Homeland Policy

Shortly after taking office, in November 1958, the new Prime Minister announced his intention to get rid of the Native Representatives – white MPs chosen by black voters on a separate electoral roll –, at the next opportunity.[19] This was a consequence of territorial segregation, which Verwoerd had been pursuing with great zeal ever since he took office as Minister.[20] In his first speech as Prime Minister, he surprised not only Parliament, but also his own party with the announcement that the 'native reserves' were to be constitutionally developed into self-governing units

---

[18] Verwoerd quoted in *Die Burger* 20.10.1958; the connection between the establishment of the Republic and territorial apartheid was also remarked upon by *Die Transvaler*, 24.2.1960. The extent to which the Promotion of Bantu Self-Government Act was linked to the project of the white nation-state was highlighted by the NP itself, maintaining that this law gave "us whites political security of our own for the first time in our history" (PV 93/1/30/1/3, Text "'n permanente aparte blanke Suid-Afrika' (n.d. [1960]), p. 5).
[19] *Cape Times*, 6.11.1958; *Rand Daily Mail*, 7.11.1958 (editorial), *Cape Times*, 15.1.1959 (report and comment).
[20] *Die Burger*, 19.1.1959.

with the prospect of becoming independent states.[21] Verwoerd himself had rejected this shortly before, always citing the low level of civilisation of Africans. A 1957 propaganda brochure disdainfully referred to such rumours as "Bantustan spookery".[22] The enthusiastic reactions in the NP-aligned press stemmed from the conviction that, for the first time, the homeland policy provided apartheid with a moral basis: Verwoerd had not only sought the 'solution' in "a series of negative steps", but had shown "that it was a matter of taking a positive stand".[23]

In his speech, Verwoerd presented some twisted arguments replete with comparisons wide of the mark:

> Moreover, what is happening in this country is similar to the development which is taking place in the relations between Britain and her Protectorates. Has the Basutoland Protectorate any representatives in the British Parliament? It has not. But what is Britain doing? She is considering granting Basutoland a system of government whereby they will be given a controlling body which will consider and decide upon their own affairs to an ever-increasing extent.[24]

With this comparison, Verwoerd gave the impression as if South Africa was already a white nation-state, now ready to grant independence to those population groups considered not to belong to the country. The Bantustans were to become independent states, linked to South Africa through intergovernmental structures and economic cooperation. The nine Bantustans were upgraded to "nation states", which were falsely claimed to be ethnically homogeneous entities. A subtle distinction between "tribe" as a political unit and "ethnic group" as a biological com-

---

21 F. W. de Klerk 1999: 30. On the other hand, as early as 1957, apartheid–critical theologian B. B. Keet spoke of the aim of apartheid as "the creation of an independent state or states" (Keet 1957: 10). In the early 1960s, van den Berghe (1967: 146) still considered independence highly improbable, speculating that it was rather a kind of modernised indirect rule that was meant. In an article that appeared at about the same time (Eiselen 1959: 8), even Verwoerd's closest collaborator Eiselen had ruled out independence.
22 M. P. A. Malan 1957: 3.
23 PV 377/4/1/1, J. W. Rall: Hulde aan wyle dr. H. F. Verwoerd, p. 1. See e.g. *Die Transvaler*, 28.1.1959 (commentary 'Die groot visie'); *Die Burger* 29.1.1959 (commentary). See even, though otherwise rather dismissive, *Cape Argus*, 28.1.1959 (commentary). See also O'Meara 1996: 72–73; and J. Botha 1967: 46. Individual MPs, such as Japie Basson, however, found Verwoerd's actions deeply undemocratic (J. Basson 2006: 106). The hope that apartheid would offer a morally justifiable solution to South Africa's 'problem' was present in Barker (1949), for example. The US administration, in contrast, found territorial partition to be a less morally than politically possible solution, but was by no means convinced of the sincerity of the South African government, because it was not willing to invest in the homelands (DNSA, William Duggan, Memo on Background of the South African Problem, 10.7.1963, pp. 1, 4–5).
24 Verwoerd, First Speech as Prime Minister, 18.9.1958 (in Pelzer 1966: 164–190, 173).

munity of descent was adduced: "a tribe is not necessarily an ethnic group, but the Natives domiciled in a certain area."[25] Since the kinship groups of the Southern Bantu did not correspond to residence groups, and because "clans" were larger units comprising several lineages scattered over large areas, the NAD defined "ethnic groups" as such kinship units. The notion of "tribe" as a distinct unit, in contrast, took into account the fact that the decisive units were politically linked, that is, through loyalties to a chief and thus through common residence. Therefore, the jurisdiction of a chief was that of the "tribe", not of the ethnic group. Despite this distinction, "tribal" and "ethnic" groups were treated equally as nations, just as linguistic and political units were not precisely distinguished. This can be seen in the equation of the linguistic distribution of isiXhosa with an ethnic settlement area, even though completely different groups lived there, and the Transkei was not culturally but linguistically homogeneous.[26]

Verwoerd's abrupt change of direction in the homeland policy has been the subject of intensive discussions. There is a broad consensus that the new direction of apartheid can only be understood in the context of the independence movements on the African continent.[27] Ghana was the first sub-Saharan country to become independent in 1957 and the decolonisation of Nigeria was in full swing at the time of Verwoerd's speech. As far as the French colonial empire was concerned, it became apparent that de Gaulle's plans for a Communauté were not sustainable, especially after the independence of Guinea in 1958. Even the Belgians made a rapid U-turn in preparing for the independence of the Congo in 1959. Verwoerd's policies seemed to be a reaction to these developments, which he knew to instrumentalise for his propaganda in the most cunning way.[28] Again and again, he pointed out that white South Africans, in their generosity, had done of their own accord what Europeans had to be forced to do by the pressure of nationalist movements: "If our policies were rightly understood, we believe . . .

---

25 PV 276/I/27/11/1/4, Letter by M. Smuts, Native Affairs Department, to Chief Native Commissioner, Pietermaritzburg, 19.9.1951.
26 Actually, there was no ethnological or linguistic reason not to combine the Transkei and Ciskei into one territory, but the government refused to agree to the Transkei government's entreaties to expand the territory (Benson 1966: 247–248).
27 However, this also applied to the Republic, which Vorster justified in a resolution at the 1960 NP Party Congress, referring to "the events in Africa and world affairs, with the threats to all sections of the population and to peace and order in our fatherland". (PV 54/2, Minutes of the Unial Party Congress of the NP, 29/30.8.1960 in Bloemfontein, p. 2) The reactive character of Verwoerd's homeland policy was also emphasised by his collaborator and admirer G. D. Scholtz (1960: 21).
28 Terreblanche 2012: 348.

that it would be seen that what we are attempting to do is not at variance with a new direction in Africa but is in the fullest accord with it."²⁹

It seems quite plausible to interpret the political turnaround as a reaction to decolonisation.³⁰ After some initial irritation at the rapidly proceeding decolonisation, the South African government welcomed the independence of colonies like Nigeria, at least in principle; but it considered the pace way too fast. With regard to settler colonies, on the other hand, the attitude was completely different – in that case, decolonisation was equated with betrayal of the whites. The British government allegedly did not fulfil its duty to the white settlers, and recklessly left their fate in the hands of "immature" Africans, as it happened in Kenya. Verwoerd and his government closely observed and documented developments in Ghana in particular, in order to propagandistically exploit misguided decisions and increasingly clear dictatorial tendencies of the first Prime Minister, Kwame Nkrumah. Why would the South African government emulate the misguided developments that were already clearly recognisable as such? Verwoerd thought that dictatorial rule in the homelands was inevitable, due to the barbaric state of development of Africans. To prevent this from happening, he proposed to gradually build up democratic structures starting at the local level. But considered from further developments, establishing and practicing democracy proved to be mere rhetoric. There was actually nothing to be said for initiating such a radical change in policy, which is what cost Verwoerd sympathy among his own supporters, and put him under considerable pressure to justify himself to his voters, even within the NP. The 1959 announcement was followed by swift action; the government began to institute self-governing structures in all reserves. This meant that parliamentary bodies were juxtaposed to previous chiefs acting as Bantu Authorities. However, only some of these parliamentary bodies could be elected by the population.³¹

Rather than Ghana's independence, it was in fact the developments at home that prompted Verwoerd to reconfigure apartheid. From the early 20th century onwards, South African governments had been fairly blatant about expansionist intentions. Since 1915, they had sought a stronger connection – one recognised by international law – with South West Africa, which they had taken over. The aim was to annex the territory as a fifth province, but this they never achieved. In 1923, the government of Jan Smuts failed in his attempt to annex the territory of

---

29 Verwoerd, Speech of Thanks to Harold Macmillan, 3.2.1960 (in Pelzer 1966: 336–339, 337); Begrotingspos van die Eerste Minister, 10.4.1961 (in Pelzer 1963: 512–527, 514).
30 This is the opinion commonly expressed in the literature (see e.g. Barratt 1979: 220–223); Lazar (1988: 104) interprets Verwoerd's change of tack as an attempt to channel black resistance.
31 G. D. Scholtz 1974, vol. 2: 134. In 1962, Verwoerd admitted that he could not have foreseen the developments in Africa that now make these steps towards self-government necessary.

the northern neighbour, Southern Rhodesia, as an additional province. But more than anything else, successive South African governments never came to terms with the fact that Britain had kept the three High Commission Territories of Basutoland, Swaziland and Bechuanaland under their own administration, rather than annexing them to the newly formed Union of South Africa in 1910.[32]

In the decades that followed, every succeeding South African government had persistently sought a revision of this decision, and had fought for the integration of the three territories into the South African state, albeit without making the slightest concessions regarding voting and civil rights for the black population.[33] As early as September 1951, Verwoerd had announced that the same policy that had been implemented in the reserves, should also be applied in the territories.[34] The integration of the three colonies into the South African national territory would have given the South African government more opportunities for control, supervision, and repression. The Homeland policy is usually perceived as an intra-South African problem, but in reality, it was conceived as a programme of regional territorial restructuring beyond the Union of South Africa, with the aim of making South Africa a white core surrounded by a ring of small black "nation states" with tribal structures of governance.[35] As ethnically homogeneous entities, the High Commission Territories were already constituted governance units that had yet to be created within the Union Territory. They were also territorially consolidated and did not represent a patchwork of small enclaves like KwaZulu or Bophuthatswana. "One must also consider that the Bantu South of the Limpopo already possess 50% of the country for one must take Bechuanaland, Basutoland and Swaziland into consideration as well as the territories in the Republic."[36] This looked quantitatively much better than the 13% share of South African territory that fell to the homelands. But one also has to consider the fact that the largest area, Bechuanaland, was situated almost entirely in the Kalahari Desert. The South African population groups that were ethnically related to those in the High Commission Territories were to be territorially combined with them – specifi-

---

32 Thompson 1960: 271–274.
33 On the advances of Botha and Smuts, see T. R. H. Davenport 2000: 290–291; also Hertzog, ibid., 305; and Halpern 1965: 52–58.
34 Thom 1980: 233; see also Maylam 1995: 196.
35 PV 93/1/30/1/13, f. 31, Letter by Verwoerd to Rev. Pholo Mokhozi (Lesotho), 26.9.1961.
36 PV 93/1/30/1/33, f. 141, Letter by Verwoerd to Nassey Simaan, Johannesburg, 4.8.1966: "In fact, the heartlands (in situation, not in numbers) of that horseshoe are Basutoland, Bechuanaland and Swaziland. Just look at the map; those are the heartlands of that horseshoe, apart from the Transkei and Zululand." Verwoerd, Bill Promoting Bantu Self-Government, 20.5.1959 (in Pelzer 1966: 271–295, 282); see also *Business News*, Nov. 1954, 'Is this the 'Master Apartheid Plan?'; also Stultz 1979: 140.

cally: Qwaqwa with Basutoland, Kangwane with Swaziland and Bophuthatswana with Bechuanaland.[37] This would have meant that the number of homelands would not increase with incorporation, but actually decrease, as three ethnic groups were to be absorbed by the Protectorates, so that the number of homelands to be excised from South Africa could be reduced to seven: Transkei, Ciskei, Kwa-Zulu, Venda, Lebowa, Gazankulu and (from 1975) KwaNdebele. The consolidation of the Protectorates could define their character, but also the 'national' character of the 'homelands', even more sharply and feasibly: "Were it possible for them to be joined to those High Commission Territories to which their people are ethnically linked, then the present difficulty of establishing one big Tswana area, or one large Sotho or Swazi area in Southern Africa would fall away."[38] In his geo-political account published in 1962, T. E. W. Schumann, the physicist close to Verwoerd, stated: "A well thought-out and co-ordinated plan for the development of the Bantu territories will be very difficult as long as the Protectorates are not part of the Republic; their incorporation must be considered necessary."[39]

The Protectorates were to serve as a model for the other homelands; there was only a sprinkling of whites residing there, especially in Basutoland and Bechuanaland.[40] The prohibition preventing whites from investing capital there was intended to bring about a kind of economic unbundling – that is, to maintain a state of affairs in the Protectorates that was only mooted for territories in South Africa at that stage; in the meantime, the presence of a black urban industrial proletariat in 'white South Africa' would continue for the foreseeable future.

In the course of the 1950s, apartheid was intensifying, as Verwoerd pursued his policies vigorously and ruthlessly. By the end of the decade, Britain felt compelled to establish self-governing structures in the three Protectorates.[41] In 1956, the British High Commissioner informed the South African government that a "Tribal Council" would be established, which was to be vested with consultative powers for the Bamangwato in Bechuanaland (Botswana). For the South African govern-

---

37 PV 93/1/42/1/4, Letter by Verwoerd to Hermann E. Martins, (NP MP 1952–72), 21.9.1962. Martins was also a member of the Broederbond (Wilkins/Strydom 1980: A156). See also *Cape Argus*, 6.9.1958; also PV 93/1/34/1, George H. Pipal, Interview with Verwoerd for United Press, 13.12.195, ff. 166–170. Verwoerd, Opening of the Transvaal Congress of the National Party, Pretoria 12.11.1958 (in Pelzer 1966: 191–205, 197).
38 Verwoerd 1963: 15. This was the argument put forward by Bruwer (1966: 67) at the same time.
39 Schumann 1962: 215.
40 Research has often focused on similarities and differences between the decolonisation of the High Commission Territories and homeland politics, but the focus was on independence and power–building processes rather than the chronological sequence (see L. Evans 2012: 119–123).
41 Halpern 1965: 126–130. It was no coincidence that South Africa's claims were clearly highlighted again in 1956 (Barker 1956).

ment, this meant nothing less than a system change, that is, a departure from the "traditional Bantu system of tribal rule, which has always been maintained in the Native areas of South Africa".[42] In 1951, South Africa had just installed such a system in the form of the Native Authorities Act, intent on harmonising the systems of rule in South Africa and the Protectorates. But now Pretoria was forced to realise that Great Britain was steering the Protectorates in a different direction, namely towards the establishment of self-governance according to the European model of states. The intention on the part of the British government to prepare the three territories for independence under international law was clearly recognisable, prompting submissions and enquiries from the South African government.[43]

Immediately after taking office, Verwoerd attempted to prevent the moves to grant full independence to the Protectorates.[44] He called on Britain to transfer the territories to South Africa, which would be better able to develop them economically.[45] He paid close attention to the political developments in the Protectorates, and intently studied the new constitutional systems that Great Britain was establishing in the three territories. But he had to realise that the British retained the initiative in the whole affair and that all he could do was to react. Only a few weeks after he had taken office as Prime Minister, representatives of the Basuto had entered into negotiations with the British government on a new constitution for the Protectorate situated in the middle of South Africa. The plan was to establish a Parliament, called the Basutoland National Council, indirectly elected by the District Councils, and partially appointed[46]; a partially appointed Executive Council was to run the affairs of government, with the High Commissioner still having an important function.[47] It was a case of limited autonomy, "representative government", which usually was the first step on the way to "responsible government", meaning actual political self-determination. In Basutoland, this paved the way that other African colonies had followed a few years earlier. The development towards independence was foreseeable.

---

42 PV 93/1/42/2/2, pp. 47–49, Aide Memoire, October 1956.
43 PV 93/1/42/1/1, Letter by Foreign Minister Eric Louw to Lord Home, 20.8.1957. See also the report on a speech by Scrivenor in the *Cape Argus*, 29.6.1956.
44 See the coverage in *Die Vaderland* as well as in the *Rand Daily Mail*, 14.11.1958.
45 "I therefore appeal to Britain to approach the problem differently in future: they should understand and trust us when we say that we want the Protectorates under our tutelage – not because we intend to extend our territory, but because it gives us the chance to have peaceful and progressive Bantu populations at our borders instead of hostile, impoverished groups." (Verwoerd, Opening of the Transvaal Congress of the National Party, Pretoria 12.11.1958, in Pelzer 1966: 191–205, 197; see also *Pretoria News* and *The Star*, 13.11.1958.
46 *Die Burger*, 19.12.1958.
47 *Cape Times*, 19.12.1958.

Verwoerd had barely regained the political initiative with the Promotion of Bantu Self-Government Act a few months later, when he endeavoured to present this development to the public as if this had been the case all along. On 3 September 1963, Verwoerd gave a political speech in Pretoria, in which he emphasised the similarities of the constitutional developments, but presented them as if Britain was following the South African example, when in actual fact it was the other way round: "Great Britain is aiming at exactly what we are achieving in the Transkei this year, namely the granting of self- government."[48]

Verwoerd's Bantustan policy was a reaction to the incremental self-rule of the High Commission Territories, in the hope to incorporate these territories into his future model for the region, namely a 'constellation' of states comprising South Africa, the Bantustans, and the three territories.[49] Verwoerd never really put his further plans for the 'homelands' on the table. Behind the propagandistic smokescreen of benevolent decolonisation by 'white' South Africa, the manipulation of elections in the Transkei shows that what he was actually aiming for was permanent economic and political hegemony, which would at the very least include the three High Commission Territories.[50] The 'homelands' were to be developed into independent economic systems, but Verwoerd did not want to provide the required funding. The homeland policy, like apartheid as a whole, remained caught in an irresolvable contradiction: It was supposed to bring about a morally justifiable segregation of population groups, but at the same time maintain the high living standards and the privileges of the whites.

When the populations of the Protectorates now faced the prospect of state independence, the incorporation as it had previously been envisaged could no longer be sustained: "Mere incorporation therefore no longer offers any possibility of establishing a sound relationship with the Protectorates. However, the pol-

---

48 Verwoerd 1963:12; the coincidence was also emphasised by Eiselen (1965: 12). Indeed, in the early 1960s, Verwoerd had to point out to his own supporters that no territorial integration of the three territories was planned, but that they were very much part of the overall concept of apartheid (PV 93/1/42/1/4, Letter by Verwoerd to D. H. W. Wessels, 19.6.1962). Shortly after his speech in Pretoria did he feel compelled to issue a press statement making it clear once again that he had not demanded the incorporation of the territories (PV 93/4/1/9, press release of 5.9.1963).
49 "Dr. Verwoerd said he foresaw that there would be in time a number of friendly states in Southern Africa, black and white, who would not interfere with each other's policies but have common interests. This could lead to a Southern African Common Market. The Congo would also perhaps belong to this group." (PV 93/4/1/10, Speech at NP Congress in Port Elizabeth, August 1964, f. 141) Kondlo (2010: 89) is correct in pointing out that the idea of a constellation of states, which is usually associated with the tenure of P. W. Botha, originated with Verwoerd.
50 Marx 2011b.

icy of separate development which we advocate does in fact offer a possibility of establishing a sound relationship."[51] In view of the prospect of independence, they could hardly be persuaded to unite with South Africa. A federation, as had been suggested on various occasions,[52] was rejected by Verwoerd because it would lead to black supremacy. Instead, he proposed "to follow the example of the Commonwealth. In a Commonwealth of Southern Africa which we are contemplating for a time when our Bantu territories achieved more independence, any neighbours who would wish to do so, could join. This would mean that really independent States with quite different forms of Government and independent of colour, could co-operate in one or more common causes."[53] If the three territories, together with the ten Bantustans and the remaining parts of South Africa would form a closer community, South Africa's influence could be maintained and stabilised by virtue of her economic power.[54] In order to keep the Protectorates in the direct sphere of influence of the Union, he had no choice but to hold out the prospect of independence to the South African Bantustans as well, in order then to capture all territories, 'homelands' and former Protectorates, in his hegemonic 'constellation of states'.[55] In the following years, he repeatedly tried to include the High Commission Territories in his policy of a 'constellation' in Southern Africa; his meeting with Lesotho's Prime Minister Leabua Jonathan shortly before his assassination served the same purpose.[56]

The Republican on the Path to Victory

Transforming South Africa into a republic was one of the most urgent goals of the new Prime Minister. At the Cape NP Party conference shortly after his election, in October 1958, Verwoerd announced a new political beginning and predicted a reorientation of the party landscape.[57] What he had in mind was constituting a republic in the near future. In the Party's new programme of principles, the goal

---

51 Verwoerd, Speeches in Connection with the Republican Constitution, 9.2.1961 (in Pelzer 1966: 434–488, 461). See also Verwoerd, House of Assembly, 23.1.1962 (in Pelzer 1966: 660–689, 684).
52 Even a liberal like Arthur Keppel-Jones proposed a radical territorial separation and the establishment of a federation based on it (Keppel-Jones 1949: ch. 13).
53 PV 93/1/24/10, Reply to W. C. Brown, Bulawayo, 30.7.1960.
54 PV 93/4/1/9, Prime Minister's Press Statement, 5.9.1963, ff. 1–3; Verwoerd, First Speech as Prime Minister, 18.9.1958 (in Pelzer 1966: 164–190, 175).
55 PV 93/1/30/1/32, ff. 100–102, Letter by Verwoerd to J. S. Maritz, Ohrigstad, 2.5.1966.
56 FAV, 4.7.1.5, Joint press statement by the two Prime Ministers, 2.9.1966.
57 He had already announced this in his radio address after the election. How important this was to him can be deduced from the fact, that in the speech manuscript, this one sentence is

was explicitly stated as "the republican form of government, detached from the British Crown", which meant nothing other than leaving the Commonwealth (since the Queen was head of the Commonwealth still called "British").[58] By his own admission, it was concerns expressed in Cabinet that made him wait another six months before announcing (on 20 January 1960) that he would leave this for the white population to decide in a referendum. In doing so, he was following the resolution of the National Party, which was committed to such a referendum; his predecessors Malan and Strijdom had repeatedly stated that they would not leave the decision to Parliament alone.[59]

Given the importance of republicanism for Verwoerd, this move was hardly surprising. What was more astonishing was the fact that it took the National Party twelve years after coming to power to act on this intent. After all, the goal of a republic was stated in the NP's election manifesto as early as 1943.[60] Admittedly, D. F. Malan had always been a rather lukewarm republican, which was not least due to the fact that he came from the former Cape Colony.[61] The latter was only absorbed into the Union of South Africa when Malan was 36 years old; he had spent his formative years in a self-governing colony within the framework of the British Empire. His pro-republican pronouncements during the Second World War were essentially opportunistic, aimed at integrating the republican wing of the Party under his leadership. After attending the Commonwealth Conference in 1949, Malan was even less inclined to swing into action than he had been before,

---

highlighted in capital letters (PV 93/1/11/2, ff. 14–20, Radio address on 3.9.1958, p. 6; see also *Die Burger*, 29.10.1958).
58 PV 54/2, Dagbestuur of the NP's Federale Raad, 15.9.1958.
59 PV 93/1/47/2/4, f. 128, Letter by Verwoerd to Col. W. A. Booysen, Bellville, 23.2.1960. Verwoerd himself had taken this position in 1937 (*Die Transvaler*, 11.10.1937). On the history of the referendum, see Sussman 2006: 271–275.
60 Nasionale Party 1943.
61 However, this did not apply to all NP representatives in this province. Eben Dönges, for example who, significantly, was one of the politicians from the Cape Province most involved in the Broederbond, strongly supported the withdrawal of South Africa from the Commonwealth during the war years, which Malan wanted even less than the Republic (AB Archive, 2/3/10/2, UR, 1.–2.2.44, p. 8, TOP 32, Toekomstaak van A.B.: "Breaking off ties with Great Britain is an indispensable demand.") As late as 1966, Eben Dönges complained to Verwoerd because the latter had published an article in which he described D. F. Malan as "cold" on the question of the Republic. In fact, in 1918, the NP of the Cape had distinguished between Independence as a political principle and the Republic as a form of state, which goal was not accorded the highest priority (Koorts 2014: 164–169). Dönges felt very offended by this (FAV, 4.7.2.1, Letter by Dönges to Verwoerd, 20.5.1966; reply by Verwoerd, 21.5.; and Dönges's reply, 23.5). The rapid succession of letters underlines the extent to which the question strained the relationship between the wings of the Party.

as he realised the benefits of international consultation, and was assured that the Commonwealth did not pose limitations to South Africa's sovereignty.[62]

In 1954, Verwoerd's political friend J. G. Strijdom became Prime Minister. Strijdom was of one of the most vehement proponents of a republic; he owed his great prestige not least to his unwavering republicanism. He had also never left any doubt about his view that the constitution of a Republic was inseparably linked to South Africa's withdrawal from the Commonwealth. Verwoerd defended this view even more vehemently.[63] But for tactical and increasingly also for health reasons, Strijdom was unable to pursue his goal with the necessary energy. He also wanted to wait until the number of English-speaking whites sympathetic to a republic had grown sufficiently to turn the change toward a republic into the expression of a national consensus among whites. As legal practitioner, Strijdom also had reservations about procedural issues, because he could only imagine a successful vote in the sense of a clear majority, as a "broad basis of the popular will".[64] Moreover, unlike Verwoerd, he feared that failure would preclude repetition.

For Verwoerd, on the other hand, the Republic was not to be the end of the nation-building process, but the precondition for it to get under way in the first place. Verwoerd reversed the logic, as he so often did. He anticipated the desired outcome as if the creation of the Republic would bring about national integration by default. The main obstacle to bringing the white population into a common nation was the emotional attachment of many English-speaking whites to Britain.[65] Therefore, he argued, only a republic could provide the basis for the emergence of a South African national consciousness among English-speaking whites as well. That is why a simple majority was sufficient for him to derive a mandate for the constitution of a Republic: "Majority will mean a bare majority, even if it is one vote."[66]

Even before presenting his plans to the public, Verwoerd had already had the chances of winning a majority checked by the state bureaucracy on the basis of the available data.[67] The officials came to the conclusion that a majority was not

---

62 Korf 2010: 461; see also Koorts 2014: 384.
63 G. D. Scholtz 1974, vol. 1: 105, 182, in which he maintains that Verwoerd's political actions to push through the Republic could be understood only if one included his activities as a journalist.
64 Nasionale Party, Oranje Vrystaat 1930: 12. PV 18/4/1/1, Verkiesings Manifes 1948, p. 6. See also *Nasionale Partynuus*, no. 9, Oct. 1954, esp. p. 1 and Strijdom's statement in Naboomspruit on 10 Nov 1956 (in FAV 4.7.1.4.1), asserting that continued membership of the Commonwealth was not linked to this, but was to be decided "when the time comes" (Nasionale Party, 1958, pp. 6–7).
65 *Die Transvaler*, 15.10.1958.
66 Verwoerd, Motion of No Confidence, 20.1.1960 (in Pelzer 1966: 323–335, 325).
67 See e.g. PV 93/1/45/1/1, Memorandum by J. I. Raats of April 1958, 'Politike orientasie van die Suid–Afrikaanse (blanke) kieserkorps', Algemene Verkiesing 1958.

to be expected, but Verwoerd was not deterred by this.[68] Many contemporaries considered Verwoerd's approach to be blatantly risky; the opposition was hoping that, for the first time, they would be able to deal a serious blow to the government.[69] But Verwoerd was confident of winning a majority, if he kept the Referendum entirely free of party-political wheeling and dealing:

> I want to say unequivocally that I do not believe that the decision should be obtained by means of an election. . . . We do not want the casting of a vote to be determined on party lines. I do not want to bind members of my party who do not wish to vote for a republic to do so. . . . I do not even want the question of confidence or no-confidence in a government to be linked up with it.[70]

He expressed his conviction that many English-speaking whites were in favour of a Republic, but were reluctant to declare it.[71] Nevertheless, he emphasised that he would by no means give up in the event of defeat, but would continue to pursue the goal of a Republic.[72] To the Broederbond, at whose 1958 Bondsraad meeting he was the first Prime Minister to appear, he calmly urged prudence. One should not follow one's feelings, but proceed thoughtfully and deliberatively: "every now and then, the head must rule the heart if the *volk* is ultimately to win."[73]

Verwoerd's speech of 20 January 1960 in the South African Parliament was a successful surprise coup.[74] When he announced a referendum on the Republic, he ruled out white participation in South West Africa because the area was not, by international law, part of the South African state, even though the white inhabitants of the territory had the South African right to vote.[75] However, he soon found a pretext to revise his position, because he could count on the fact that the overwhelming majority of whites in South West Africa were in favour of the Republic. Even though they were relatively small in number, their votes could be decisive in case of a close Referendum, which is why the Prime Minister an-

---

68 See also PV 873/5/2/1/1, 'Dr Hendrik Verwoerd', p. 3. M. P. A. Malan 1964: 303.
69 *Pretoria News*, 20.2.1960.
70 Verwoerd, Motion of No Confidence, 20.1.1960 (in Pelzer 1966: 323–335, 324). In the preceding year, he had still announced, nonchalantly, "[b]y what method they will vote, whether by a referendum, an election or some other method, is of no importance" (Verwoerd, Motion of No Confidence, 27.1.1959, in Pelzer 1966: 216–247, 238).
71 PV 93/1/47/2/1, f. 5, Letter by Verwoerd to S. Kichenside (Durban), 13.5.1959; similarly PV 93/1/47/2/2, Letter by Verwoerd to S. B. H. Estcourt (Salisbury, Rhod.), 15.9.1959.
72 *Die Burger*, 16.3.1960; *Die Transvaler*, 17.3.1960.
73 AB Archive, 1/1/142/1, Verwoerd se boodskap, Bondsraad 1958, p. 4. The old ideas of a presidential system were still circulating in the Broederbond (Stals 1998: 397).
74 Kenney 1980: 173.
75 Verwoerd, Motion of No Confidence, 20.1.1960 (in Pelzer 1966: 323–335, 326; see also Verwoerd, Statement of Policy, 9.3.1960, in Pelzer 340–369, 356).

nounced in Parliament on 9 March that South West Africans would be allowed to vote after all.[76] The extent to which this attitude was determined by election-tactical opportunism, can be gleaned from the simultaneous refusal to allow the coloureds who were entitled to vote, to participate in the Referendum on the flimsy pretext that the Republic was a matter for whites only.[77] In the absence of any plan to grant the coloureds their own territory, and with their continued affiliation to the South African state, this sounded unconvincing. Verwoerd's remarks amounted to pure sophistry; the real reason for the exclusion of the coloureds was that the majority of them voted for the United Party. Because it was a white nation-state that was at issue, Verwoerd also refused to solicit the views of the other population groups on the question as to whether to remain in the Commonwealth.[78]

The announcement of the Referendum must be seen in the context of British Prime Minister Harold Macmillan's trip to Africa.[79] The highlight of this trip was his speech to the South African Parliament on 3 February 1960, in which he described the "wind of change" that was sweeping across the African continent; at the same time, he laced his speech with cautious and restrained, but nevertheless unequivocal criticism of apartheid.[80] In doing so, he pointed out that the principle of non-interference applied in the Commonwealth, but that there could be cases in which a country's internal policies had international repercussions.[81] In an angry reply, Verwoerd rejected Macmillan's criticism, invoking the 'positive' aspects of his policy, instead. This was a theme that Verwoerd would tirelessly repeat in the months that followed, and especially at the meeting of the Prime Ministers a year later.[82] Macmillan deviated from his usual practice in not making the content of his speech available to his hosts before presenting it. Thus, it is pos-

---

76 Ibid., 359.
77 Verwoerd, Speeches in the House of Assembly in Connection with the Republican Constitution, 9.2.1961 (in Pelzer 1966: 434–488, 467). In the same way, he answered a question in the House from MP Lee-Warden, on whether "the Bantu" should be consulted (PV 93/1/51/6/1, f. 65, Question No. 14, Friday 12.2.1960; see also Verwoerd, Speech at Meyerton, Transvaal 26.3.1960, in Pelzer 1966: 374–387, 384; and Mosie van Wantroue, 20.1.1960, in Pelzer 1963: 305–316, 308).
78 PV 93/1/51/6/1, 117 House of Assembly, 27.1.1961, reply in the negative to a question on the matter by MP Henry Tucker.
79 Verwoerd welcomed Macmillan's proposal to visit South Africa as well (Baker 1998: 174–175).
80 The speeches appeared in print in Parliament of the Union of South Africa 1960; see also Ovendale 1995; on the wider impact on the settler colonies, see S. Ward 2011. Dubow (2011: 1100) maintains that Macmillan did not want to support the black opposition in South Africa.
81 Carrington 1960: 123.
82 On the speech and the controversies it provoked, see H. Macmillan 1972: 155–160; see also Hutchinson 1980: 108–113; and Horne 1989: 193–198.

sible that Macmillan's speech, which unpleasantly surprised Verwoerd, would have strengthened Verwoerd's resolve to go for a Republic, and withdraw from the Commonwealth.[83]

In a conversation on the eve of the speech, Verwoerd vehemently complained to Macmillan about Britain's Africa policy, particularly with regard to the High Commission Territories. The issues he complained about were closely linked to the sense of a continued membership of the Commonwealth[84] which, in view of what he made of the British attitude, was becoming increasingly questionable. After Macmillan intimated how much he and the other members valued South Africa's continued membership of the Commonwealth, Verwoerd tried to wring concessions from Macmillan on the British Africa policy, especially regarding the Protectorates, which were so important to him.[85]

Few events of these years contributed as significantly to a turnaround in international public perception, not least among members of the Commonwealth, as the Sharpeville massacre on 21 March 1960.[86] In March 1960, the African National Congress (ANC) called for civil disobedience against the hated pass laws on 31 March. The rival Pan Africanist Congress (PAC) then announced its own campaign to take place a few days before that of the ANC. It was poorly prepared; the call to action was heeded only in some urban areas that were PAC strongholds. In Sharpeville, the African township of Vereeniging south of Johannesburg, a momentous incident occurred when a large crowd gathered in front of the local police station to hand in their passes. The few but heavily armed police officers lost their nerve and fired into the crowd, even as the crowd was dispersing and no longer presented a threat to the police. In the Sharpeville massacre, at least 69 people lost their lives, most of them shot in the back, and more than 100 were injured.[87] Despite some uncertainty even in government circles,[88] Verwoerd

---

83 Makin 1996: 83–88 who, however, limits his considerations to the referendum on the Republic. See also Dubow 2011: 1112.
84 PV 93/1/55/2/2, Private gespreek tussen die heer Macmillan en myself te Groote Schuur op 4 Februarie 1960, 10–11.30 v.m; see also PV 93/1/55/2/2, Notes (p. 15) for talks in which "Use of High Commission territories as an escape area for Union" was mentioned.
85 Ibid., p. 2; Macmillan also accused him of this, but Verwoerd then vehemently denied that he wanted to impose conditions (ibid. p. 9).
86 Horne 1989: 203–204; see also Horrell 1961: 56–68.
87 On the Sharpeville massacre, see P. Frankel 2001:109–156. See also the account by journalist Ruth Weiss, claiming that the crowd had only come together on the basis of mere rumours, and that the 'demonstration' had nothing to do with the PAC campaign ('Witnesses of the Century', ZDF (German Television), 30.11. and 7.12.1994).
88 Proposals to soften the pass laws also came from organisations close to the Broederbond, such as the Afrikaanse Handelsinstituut, and specifically from Verwoerd's confidant J. G. van der

maintained his customary intransigence[89] and shifted the blame entirely onto black organisations, which were immediately banned. He imposed the state of emergency and ordered large-scale arrests.[90]

On 9 April 1960, Verwoerd survived an assassination attempt at the opening of an agricultural exhibition in Johannesburg. He was shot twice in the head by a white farmer, David Pratt, who was later diagnosed as being mentally ill.[91] Verwoerd was seriously injured and had to undergo several operations, which is why he was unable to perform his duties for several weeks.[92] Paul Sauer, as longest-serving minister, took over the reins of government and tentatively announced a change to the policy as it had been implemented up to that point.[93] Verwoerd had hardly recovered from the assassination attempt, when he resolutely set about restoring his authority by ruling out any concessions on apartheid policies. Into the time of his recovery fell a meeting of the Commonwealth Prime Ministers, to which he had intended to travel. Instead he asked his party colleague and Foreign Minister Eric Louw to stand in for him.[94] Louw was infamous for his impulsive character, so it must have been clear to Verwoerd that asking Louw to attend the meeting would in no way contribute to an improvement in the atmosphere.[95]

Merwe (PV 93/1/36/1/8, ff. 19–26, Memorandum from business representatives, including the Afrikaanse Handelsinstituut, 12.5.1960). I. L. de Villiers (2009: 133) reports on a delegation from the DRC of the Cape Province that was calling on Verwoerd to resign. However, he reportedly persuaded them otherwise and permanently converted their leader, J. S. Gericke, to his own position.

89 Demands for reform also came from the Afrikaans business community (Giliomee 2003a: 522).
90 Horrell 1961: 79–89. The South African Institute of Race Relations, on the other hand, confirmed in its report that the crowd had not been aggressive towards the police officers (SAIRR 1961: 6, 12–13).
91 Rusty Bernstein met him in prison and did not have the impression that he was mentally disturbed (Bernstein 1999: 208). Newspaper articles portrayed him as apolitical, but a person grappling with some problems (*Cape Argus*, 11.4.1960; see also *Sunday Times*, 10.4.1960; and *Haarlems Dagblad*, 11.4.1960).
92 Boshoff 2012: 191–192; see also Barnard 1967: 82–87.
93 As late as July 1960, he told Tomlinson that he hoped to be able to implement his proposals now (PV 442/2/2/1, f. 13, Letter by Sauer (Minister van Lande) to Tomlinson, 12.7.60: "The whole line of thought of your Committee runs absolutely parallel with my own . . . .")
94 PV 93/1/53/2/3, Letter by Private Secretary of the Premier to Louw (secret), 15.4.1960 (FAV 4.7.4.7.3, piece of paper with Verwoerd's dictation of 19 April instructing Louw to represent him in London because he could not yet bear the strain).
95 Geyser 1983: 69; see also Meiring 1990: 53, 59. On Louw's notorious aggressiveness, see also Shearar 2007: 255–256, 306–310; Wolvaardt/Wheeler/Scholtz 2010, vol. 2: 13–14; and van der Schyff 1987: 471.

During the Commonwealth Conference in May 1960, Louw informed the Prime Ministers gathered in London that the South African government had asked the country's white population to vote in a referendum on a republic. In this context, he asked the meeting to admit a Republic of South Africa as a member. Since the Balfour Report of 1926, the "British Commonwealth" was defined as a confederation of independent and sovereign states held together by allegiance to the British Crown.[96] India had been the first country to break this principle when it became a republic, while asking to remain in the Commonwealth.[97] In the years that followed, other former colonies had chosen the Republic as their form of state; like India, they had to obtain the agreement of the other Commonwealth states in order to be able to remain members, as a matter of adhering to the stipulations of the Balfour Report, even as these were now obsolete. In order not to unduly influence the Referendum, Macmillan insisted that South Africa should submit its application to remain in the Commonwealth only after the Referendum had been concluded.[98]

Verwoerd, whose recovery was astonishingly rapid,[99] issued a statement of his own after the Conference. He underlined the principle of non-interference in the internal affairs of other countries and stressed that it was only a question of changing the form of the state from a monarchy to a republic.[100] In his republican propaganda, Verwoerd spoke of the transformation of the Kingdom of South Africa into a Republic and ostentatiously called the opponents of the republic monarchists – which, in this context, was wielded as propagandistic rhetoric immediately snapped up by the nationalist press.[101]

---

96 Mansergh 1969: 233–237.
97 Then South African Prime Minister D. F. Malan had explicitly agreed to the Republic of India remaining in the Commonwealth (D. F. Malan 1959: 89–90).
98 Diefenbaker 1978: 175; see also Tennyson 1982: 156. See also the final communiqué of the meeting, reprinted in Mansergh 1963: 362.
99 55.K.V.16 (6), Letter by Betsie Verwoerd to M. E. Rothmann, 26.4.1960. Verwoerd's wife reported that her husband was "almost back to his old self" barely two weeks after the assassination attempt. However, the two bullets still had to be surgically removed. 220.K 60 (24), Letter by A. L. Geyer to Cillié, 2.6.1960, on Verwoerd's speech to the Union Festival in Bloemfontein on 31.5.1960: "He still speaks with some difficulty, but nevertheless clearly."
100 PV 93/1/55/2/2, ff. 5–9, Verwoerd's statement after Commonwealth Conference 1960 (no exact date), p. 4.
101 PV 93/1/45/1/3, ff. 96–103, Radio address on 3.10.1960 (*Die Transvaler* 17.3.1960; see also the derisive commentary in the same newspaper, 15.3.1960). Foreign Minister Louw also referred to opposition leader De Villiers Graaff as "the leader of the monarchists" (PV 4/55, Louw in Paarl, 16.8.1960).

Verwoerd's republican project[102] met with distrust – for good historical reasons, for it was no secret that Verwoerd had been one of the authors of the notorious 1940 draft of the republican constitution.[103] The authoritarian presidential regime envisaged in the draft had borrowed from fascist ideas of order; the anti-British and antisemitic rhetoric that accompanied the draft had caused much dismay and remained a bad memory for many. In several speeches and pronouncements, Verwoerd responded by asserting that the Republic was not intended to bring about a constitutional reorientation, but that the existing constitution would only be modified with regard to the provisions concerning the head of state.[104] To objections from within the Party, he responded by pointing out that it was a matter of an important concession to English-speaking South Africans. As he explained to the latter, it was a compromise in which not only English-speaking South Africans, but also the Afrikaners would have to make important concessions, who should therefore not consider themselves as losers.[105]

---

102 *Rand Daily Mail*, 18.3.1959. Verwoerd vehemently denied a report in the *Cape Argus* of 17.3.1959, which mentioned plans for a mixed federal republic, and which was in fact diametrically opposed to his plans. Explicitly with reference to the 1940 draft constitution, see *Cape Argus*, 29.1.1960. See also *Rand Daily Mail*, 29.1.1960. Similarly, opposition leader De Villiers Graaff referred directly to the draft constitution (*Cape Times*, 18.11.1958 and earlier the *Cape Argus*, 5.11.1958) on the decision of the UP of the Cape Province to oppose the Republic; see also *Pretoria News*, 5.11.1958. However, due to numerous experiences with assurances of the National Party, there was little confidence in the Prime Minister's statements (*Cape Times*, 7.10.1958, editorial). On Verwoerd's ideas of a complete reorganisation of the state, see W. A. Muller 1973: 66–67).
103 Spies/Theron/Scholtz 1981: 772; see also Stals 1998: 116.
104 *Sunday Times*, 18.9.1960; see also PV 93/1/30/1/11, f. 48, Letter by Verwoerd to T. M. Zini, 1.2.1961. On criticism from the right, see Floyd 1975: 115. Verwoerd, however, saw this only as a temporary state of affairs, since he held fast to his long–term goal of introducing a presidential constitution modelled on the old Boer Republics of the 19th century (Verwoerd 1966: 9); on his role in drafting an authoritarian corporatist constitution in 1940, see also Marx 2008: 407–409; and Marx 2010: 54. Piet Meyer reported on his last conversation with Verwoerd on 29.8.1966, in which they discussed the further development towards a form of presidential republic, albeit one deviating from the model of the Boer Republics (P. J. Meyer 1978: 14–15; see also Stals 1998: 491; and Geyser 1983: 49, who wrote that the time was "not yet ripe for this"). Jurist C. A. Coetzee, in contrast, advocated the Republic because the constitution was not to be changed. Through the change in the state form, however, the Prime Minister as the de facto head of state would be limited in his powers by a dual function that included the President; Coetzee did not explicitly direct this against Verwoerd personally (C. A. Coetzee 1960: 68–69).
105 PV 93/1/47/2/5, ff. 74–75, Letter by Verwoerd to D. L. Glenn (Bloemfontein), 31.3.1960; see also PV 93/1/47/2/5, f. 166, Letter by Verwoerd to Mrs S. L. Mackinnon (Germiston), 9.7.1960, in which he emphatically denies that the establishment of the Republic had anything to do with hatred of English-speaking whites.

The government and the National Party did not miss any opportunity to reach out to the electorate. The NP carried out its propaganda in a highly coordinated manner.[106] In doing so, it was quite innovative in its methods: it sent out a letter advocating the Republic, hand-written by Verwoerd and reproduced in facsimile, to all white households.[107] The most important speaker was the Prime Minister himself who attracted audiences on an unprecedented scale after the failed assassination attempt, with the Broederbond helping to mobilise supporters behind the scenes.[108]

In his radio address of 3 October 1960, the Prime Minister insinuated that it was his opponents themselves who wanted a constitutional amendment in the form of a 'partnership' with Indians, Coloureds and blacks; thus, he was suggesting that they wanted to relinquish apartheid while he, on the other hand, saw it attaining constitutional significance.[109] In insinuating this, he did exactly what he accused his opponents of doing, namely to drag the vote on the Republic into party-political disputes, which is precisely what he had said he wanted to avoid.[110] This last appeal to the electorate ahead of the vote was remarkably combative and lacking in statesmanship.

The result was not overwhelmingly in favour of the constitutional amendment, but confirmed Verwoerd's calculation that a majority could be trumped up: it came to 850,458 votes in favour to 775,858 against. The result closely reflected the split of the white population between English-speaking and African-speaking sections, which contradicted Verwoerd's conviction that it would heal the old rift between them.[111] Nevertheless, the National Party celebrated the outcome of the

---

106 PV 93/1/45/5/1, 140-page Handbook of the NP of the Transvaal, with a Foreword by the Hoofsekretaris J. H. Steyl, who urged utmost secrecy. The book described in detail all the steps, the necessary organisation up to the postal vote. Not least in order to reassure the English–speaking whites, the government published Verwoerd's speech of 20.1.1960 in pamphlet form; it contained a series of guarantees for parliamentary democracy (Verwoerd 1960a and b). On the opponents, see Reid 1982: 91–94.
107 PV 276/2/1/5, circular letter of 20.9.1960.
108 AB Archives, 2/3/39, Dagbestuur, 22.4.1960, pp. 4–5, TOP 12, Noodtoestand en sluipmoordaanslag op Premier.
109 PV 93/1/45/1/3, p. 97, Radio address on 3.10.1960.
110 Ibid. See also the NP pamphlet Statebonds-Verhoudinge. Suid-Afrika se lidmaatskap, Bloemfontein 30.8.1960, in Nasionale Party 1960, as well as the pamphlet 'Sal Suid–Afrika as republiek lid van die Statebond bly?', Bloemfontein n.d. [1960]. Both pamphlets quoted numerous statements of Commonwealth politicians saying that South Africa could remain a member of the Commonwealth.
111 For detailed information on the results in each constituency, see FAV 4.7.1.4.1, filled in by hand by Verwoerd's private secretary J. F. Barnard, 5.10.1960.

Referendum as a triumph that ended the crisis of 1960;[112] it mobilised Afrikaners and unified them behind their Prime Minister. In their eyes, Verwoerd had once more demonstrated his assertiveness and his sense of what was possible.

During the time he worked as a journalist, Verwoerd had continuously and vehemently advocated transforming the state into a republic. He had left no doubt that for him, this was conceivable only on condition of a withdrawal from the Commonwealth.[113] There are no indications that he changed his mind on this issue. In fact, he saw no future for South Africa in the Commonwealth. In the historiography dealing with this issue, the prevailing view still is that South Africa was forced out of the Commonwealth by the other member states, but this does not stand up to scrutiny.[114] In a letter written on 24 August 1960 to his Australian colleague Robert Menzies, Verwoerd noted that "an important change in the character of the Commonwealth was taking place". For with decolonisation "the non-white members would gradually dominate by weight of numbers or due to the fact that the others wished to appease them at all costs and for whatever reasons". Verwoerd saw this as a threat to South Africa, quite independently of the question of becoming a republic. The resulting conflicts would be "most embarrassing" to South Africa's long-standing friends in the Commonwealth, "and could easily lead to estrangement from them as well. Under such circumstances a Republic outside the Commonwealth might have a better chance of retaining and cultivating friendship and co-operating wherever possible with those member states who would be willing and could then avoid taking sides in conferences which could no longer be confined to seeking common ends."[115] The date of the letter alone suggests that Verwoerd had intended the withdrawal from the outset or that he had at least calculated it closely.[116]

In fact, as early as March 1959, Verwoerd had bluntly advocated the withdrawal from the Commonwealth. However, an interview with the daily newspaper *Die Burger* conducted shortly after he took office, was never published, following an intervention by its editor-in-chief Piet Cillié.[117] In the interview, Verwoerd discussed how friendship with Britain could be maintained in the face of

---

112 On this crisis, see the following chapter.
113 For examples of Verwoerd's strategy of making the Republic conditional upon withdrawal from the Commonwealth, see Geyser 1972: 44, 50, 64, 74ff, 76–77, 81, 87–88. Ben Schoeman (1978: 255) viewed Verwoerd's proposal of a republic within the Commonwealth as a purely tactical move.
114 Hayes 1980: 476.
115 Menzies 1967: 208.
116 On the process, see also Marx 2014.
117 Weber (1973: 5) on the exact circumstances and with the conjecture that Verwoerd had intended the interview to test the reactions of English–speaking South Africans.

Ghana's recent threats to withdraw from the Commonwealth if Britain did not support majority rule in certain African countries. In his typical style of argumentation, Verwoerd was construing a deeply rooted and irreconcilable conflict of interest with Britain, only to open a way out that would remove all problems in one fell swoop. "In my opinion, it is the different attitudes of Britain and the average white man in Africa as to how best to establish relations with the black man in Africa, that jeopardise the desired friendship." Britain first tried to maintain white rule in the settler colonies, but when that proved no longer possible, she was looking to establish a system of partnership. "Rule by partnership is probably her second choice." However, should pressure continue to mount, "Britain will concede to black rule, rather than lose all of the goodwill of that population altogether, and the advantages accruing to herself".[118] For the white man in Africa, the situation was completely different. "He cannot simply accept a political system in which he will perish as a white man and as a nation, even if it were to happen only with time. He has to sustain himself." This, according to Verwoerd, was precisely the conflict of interests: "In the end, Britain's perspective on the benefits accruing to herself, and thus also the form of good race relations in Africa, fundamentally clash with the benefits and hence the form of good race relations for the white man in Africa."[119] In a style typical of Verwoerd's argumentation, he presented the way forward as if his proposal was primarily in the interests of Britain, offering her the opportunity to pursue her own interests in relation to the new black states. "That means, plainly, that a greater measure of constitutional separation will entail a greater chance of a fruitful friendship in all respects, between Britain and the white man in British-aligned Africa, while the preservation of constitutional and formal ties may become the cause of a growing and injurious enmity." He then let the cat out of the bag and spoke plainly:

> The question I therefore pose for all to ponder is this: would it not be in the best interests of friendship and a good relationship between Britain and the black states of Africa, between Britain and the white man of Africa, between the white man of Africa and the black man of Africa, if not Ghana, but the white man of Africa leaves the Commonwealth and goes his own way in Africa, and in this way ends the embarrassment in which Britain finds herself, freely and purposefully establishing his friendship with her in all other fields, detached from the controversial issue of race relations?[120]

---

118 PV 93/1/9/2/4, ff. 107–111, Interview with Verwoerd by *Die Burger*, 14.3.1959, preceded by the handwritten note, "Never published [Nooit gepubliseer]", p. 108. The contents were first made public by J. J. van Rooyen (1971: 115–122), but never taken up in the literature on the withdrawal from the Commonwealth.
119 Ibid, f. 109.
120 Ibid, f. 110.

Would it not be better for Britain to retain the black states in the Commonwealth and "establish a productive friendship with the white man in Africa outside the Commonwealth, or is it in her interest to maintain constitutional (be it dominant or colonial) ties with the white man in Africa at any cost, and thereby run the risk of losing the friendship of both, as well as the membership of the black states in the Commonwealth?"[121] The irreconcilable antagonism between Britain and South Africa did, indeed, exist; that is why Verwoerd only had to bring about a situation that could result in the withdrawal from the Commonwealth, without making it seem intentional. Macmillan's speech was a welcome opportunity for Verwoerd to point out that Britain would drop white South Africans, regardless of South Africa's membership of the Commonwealth.[122]

The obvious thing for Verwoerd to do, therefore, was to deliberately create and escalate a conflict in order to be able to slip into the role of the victim. With reference to the sovereignty of South Africa, Verwoerd was able to justify the withdrawal of his application on grounds other than his long-held motives. Moreover, the conflict could be made palatable to the audience at home if it could be presented as an antagonism between white and non-white members of the Commonwealth.

In an interview conducted in November, after the successful Referendum, he spoke about the politics of racial segregation, insisting that no one should believe "that the abandonment or dilution of principles is now at hand. Now, more than ever, a principled stand must be taken."[123] In this context, a letter written by J. P. van der Spuy to the Prime Minister on 23 February 1961, that is, shortly before Verwoerd's departure for London, is particularly revealing, as it contains a further indication that Verwoerd was in fact aiming for South Africa's withdrawal from the Commonwealth. The sender was the Secretary General (*Hoofsekretaris*) of the Afrikaner Broederbond and thus, along with its Chairman, historian Hendrik Thom of the University of Stellenbosch, the most important office bearer in the secret society. He wrote:

> Still strongly under the impression of the great responsibility you have assumed, to lead the people to a resolution concerning our becoming a Republic, and deeply grateful for its wonderful outcome, the U.R. wishes to express its interest, support, and deep appreciation for the step you are about to take, and to assure you of its loyalty and support. No one understands the gravity of this task better than you, but the U.R. has full confidence in what you stand for, and trusts that you will find strength and inspiration in the knowledge that you will set out on your journey with the best wishes of the U.R. and our organisation, and that

---

121 Ibid., f. 111.
122 Verwoerd 1960c: 8. Douglas Mitchell expressed a very similar view (Wilks 1980: 124).
123 PV 93/4/1/4, text without heading, in effect a string of quotations, the context of an interview is not discernible (22.11.1960, p. 2).

earnest prayers will accompany you. It is the wish of us all that you will receive the necessary strength in body and mind and that the blessings of the Lord will be with you.[124]

This letter is unusual, for the Broederbond did not usually address the Prime Minister on matters of general policy. When van der Spuy wrote in such an unctuous tone to the Prime Minister, the question arises as to what he actually meant. The suggestion that no one understood the scope of the task better than the UR of the Broederbond, would be meaningless if the aim had been to keep South Africa in the Commonwealth.[125]

For his part, the British Prime Minister tried to prevent South Africa's exclusion, because this would more likely reinforce the intransigent attitude of the South African government and deprive the other states of important, because informal, opportunities to influence the government of the country. On the other hand, the African Commonwealth members were officially "invited" by the African countries represented in the UN "to take all possible steps to secure the exclusion of the Union of South Africa from the British Commonwealth".[126] However, some African and Asian countries signalled their willingness to compromise, thus initially allaying his fears.[127]

But a threat to a possible compromise came from the Canadian Prime Minister John Diefenbaker, who only the previous year had been clearly in favour of South Africa remaining, but was now changing tack. Diefenbaker had distinguished himself as a champion of civil rights and integration in Canada; in his position as Prime Minister, he had for the first time introduced a set of fundamental rights into the constitution. With South Africa's application, he thought the time had come for the Commonwealth to show its colours. Since Sharpeville, apartheid could no longer simply be treated as an internal affair; after all, the policy had international repercussions, not least for the Commonwealth itself, but also for Great Britain's and Canada's voting behaviour in the UN.[128]

---

124 PV 93/3/1/28, Letter by J. P. van der Spuy to Verwoerd, 23.2.1961. On van der Spuy in the AB, see Stals 1998: 199–200.
125 In fact, as late as 1957, the Broederbond had (in an internal paper) clearly opposed the continued membership of South Africa, as Republic, in the Commonwealth. (AB Archive, 2/3/34, UR Agenda, 20.2.1957, Bylae B. Ons republikeinse beleid en taak, p. 6, item 17).
126 Resolution adopted by the Second Conference of Independent African States, Addis Ababa, 24.6.1960, point 5, reprinted as Document 16 (in Boutros–Ghali 1994: 245). For a comprehensive discussion, see Goodwin 1965: 686.
127 See Wilson 1961: 443; also H. Macmillan 1972: 173; and Menzies 1967: 195. See also interview with Nkrumah on his delayed arrival in London (*Times*, 10.3.1961, *Guardian*, 10.3.1961. *Rand Daily Mail*, 13.1.1959, comment).
128 H. Macmillan 1972: 169; see also Henshaw 1994: 99–100. For a critical perspective on the opportunistic stance of the US, see Marcum 1967: 8–10.

In the immediate run-up to the Conference, the British Prime Minister was in close consultation with his conservative Australian colleague Robert Menzies, whom he gratefully praised as "a tower of strength".[129] With the backing of Menzies, Macmillan set out to first decide on the continuation of South Africa's membership in the Commonwealth, and to separate this issue from the discussion on apartheid policy, which now had become inevitable, but was to be deferred to a later stage.[130] However, the chronological sequence was reversed, as Verwoerd himself, with his "readiness to concede" set the course. "When we started on Monday, ... it was clear that the other countries wanted to link up the question of policy with the constitutional issue and to discuss it immediately. So as not to spoil the prospects of harmonious relations, I then made this further concession and permitted this discussion."[131] Such a course of action was completely uncharacteristic of Verwoerd, who would normally have insisted on separating the two issues. In the previous year, Louw had insisted on keeping these discussions private and thus unofficial; but Verwoerd went much further and gave these talks a quasi-official character. Thus he significantly contributed to linking South Africa's continued membership of the Commonwealth with the discussions on apartheid. And what is more: now the outcome of the discussion on apartheid would become the deciding factor in the question of South Africa's continued membership of the Commonwealth. Verwoerd's intransigence with regard to apartheid policies could lead to one outcome only – and that was foreseeable.[132]

If emotions were allowed to come into disputes on apartheid policies, and if these influenced political pronouncements to such an extent that his colleagues were drawing each other into taking anti-South African positions, this was not unintentional.[133] Verwoerd knew how to stir up emotions, through deliberate provocations, for instance. His consistent friendliness and politeness, combined with extreme severity in reaching and implementing political decisions were bound to provoke – and he knew that very well.

About the impressions gleaned from an earlier meeting with Verwoerd, Macmillan noted: "His charming smile, his courtesy, his readiness to expound his views without any concealment and at any length were in a sense impressive. But they

---

[129] H. Macmillan 1972: 174.
[130] Ibid: 288–289.
[131] Verwoerd, House of Assembly, 23.3.1961 (in Mansergh 1963: 380).
[132] Verwoerd, House of Assembly, 23.3.1961. It was the Prime Ministers of India and Nigeria who took offence at Verwoerd's euphemistic characterisation of apartheid as "good neighbourliness" (J. D. B. Miller 1961: 61; see also *Daily Herald*, 6.3.1961: Premiers answer Verwoerd; and *Daily Telegraph*, 6.3.1961; *Cape Argus*, 4.3.1961). See also Hawkes 1968: 74.
[133] After the conference, Diefenbaker made the point that "Dr. Verwoerd . . . himself introduced the discussion which led to his country's withdrawal" (*Daily Sketch*, 18.3.1961).

filled me with gloom."[134] Verwoerd remained intransigent, unwilling to make the slightest concession, even though Macmillan wrote to him during the conference imploring him to do so.[135] He started his address to the meeting of Commonwealth Prime Ministers by lecturing for an hour in frontal teaching-style, explaining his policy to the supposedly ignorant colleagues.[136] In subsequent speeches, he commented on the fact that they continued to criticise him after his elaborations, dismissing their criticisms while referring to their usual obstinacy or incapacity to learn; with the latter comments, he was targeting Asian and African premiers in particular. Verwoerd's remarks contributed significantly to the fact that over the following few days, a compromise was becoming increasingly unlikely. "It was Dr. Verwoerd's attitude and method of arguing his case, as well as the inflexibility of his dogmatic position, which finally turned the balance."[137]

It was an article of Julius Nyerere, published on 12 March 1961 in the London *Observer*, that prompted the delegations of the Asian and especially of the African members, Ghana and Nigeria, to toughen their stance. As head of the government of Tanganyika, which was on its way to independence, Nyerere stated unequivocally that "we cannot join any 'association of friends' which includes a State deliberately and ruthlessly pursuing a racialist policy. . . . We believe that the principles of the Commonwealth would be betrayed by an affirmative answer to South Africa's application for readmission as a Republic." He referred explicitly to Diefenbaker:

> And how can Canada, or any other Commonwealth country which believes in justice and human rights, vote for the inclusion of South Africa . . . as long as South Africa allows herself to be ruled by men whose policies are an outrage to such beliefs? A vote in favour of South Africa . . . could logically be interpreted as a vote against the future membership of countries such as Tanganyika whose political philosophy condemns any form of racial discrimination as evil.[138]

---

134 H. Macmillan 1972: 153. The claim that the discussions on apartheid lasted a total of 15 hours is exaggerated; it was intended primarily to highlight Verwoerd's staunch persistence (S. van der Merwe 1966: 216).
135 "I fully understand that you base your policies upon a theoretical thesis which is very fundamental to you. Nevertheless men are not ruled entirely by logic, but often by sentiment." He then asked him for concessions regarding ambassadors (Letter by Macmillan to Verwoerd, 13.3.1961, in Hyam/Louis 2000, Doc. 456: 424, see also Doc. 457, Minutes of six meetings of Commonwealth prime ministers, 13.–15.3.1961, in ibid., 425–451). The question of diplomatic relations with African and Asian states proved to be a "turning–point" (see Horrell 1962: 5–6).
136 Hyam/Louis 2000, Doc. 457: 425–451, 432–436, Minutes of six meetings of Commonwealth prime ministers, 13–.15.3.1961; see also the detailed exposition of apartheid in the correspondence with Menzies (Menzies 1967: 202–209).
137 H. Macmillan 1972: 298.
138 Julius Nyerere, South Africa or Us (*Observer*, 12.3.1961; see also *Daily Mail* 13.3.1961; *Times*, 13.3.1961; and *Guardian*,7.3.1961 with reference to an oral statement by Nyerere). Nyerere, for his

This statement was followed by the openly announced threat that if South Africa remained, Tanganyika would not join. This is what alarmed Nkrumah, who saw his role as spokesman for decolonisation and Pan-Africanism in jeopardy; he, too, threatened to leave, as did Nigeria's Prime Minister Abubakar Balewa.[139]

Diefenbaker insisted that the Commonwealth proclaimed its basic principles;[140] in particular, he insisted on a declaration stating that the Commonwealth was in favour of general equality. The Canadian articulated the dilemma faced by the Prime Ministers: "[I]f we were to accept South Africa's request unconditionally our action would be taken as approval or at least condonation of racial policies which are repugnant to and unequivocally abhorred and condemned by Canadians as a whole."[141] With his unequivocal advocacy of fundamental principles, Diefenbaker effectively dashed the hopes of South Africans to divide the Commonwealth along the lines of skin colour.[142]

In the end, everything foundered on the final communiqué; Verwoerd was not prepared to accept the proposed wording. He emphatically rejected the kind of declaration of principle on individual rights and principles of equality that Diefenbaker had in mind. India and Ghana threatened that if South Africa remained a member, they would reserve the right to raise the issue of apartheid again and again, and to put South Africa's exclusion on the agenda of future meetings.[143] Macmillan persuaded Verwoerd to withdraw his application under the circumstances, which Verwoerd did after a recess on 13 March.[144]

Speaking after the Conference, Verwoerd said that he had made concessions in agreeing to the communiqués. This soft stance had encouraged the other prime ministers to ratchet up their demands, which then made him decide to withdraw

---

part, claimed to have been influenced and encouraged in his stance by a letter written to him by Luthuli (*Daily Mail*, 13.3.1961).

139 J. D. B. Miller 1961:61; Hyam/Louis 2000, Doc. 457: 425–451, 447: Minutes of six meetings of Commonwealth prime ministers, 13–15.3.1961.

140 Robinson 1989: 184–185; see also Graaff 1993: 182. Verwoerd had previously argued with Diefenbaker about his policies.

141 Diefenbaker in the Canadian House of Commons, 17.3.1961 (qtd. in Mansergh 1963: 367–368).

142 M. P. A. Malan 1960: 2.

143 Hyam/Louis 2000, Doc. 457: 425–451, 448: Minutes of six meetings of Commonwealth prime ministers, 13.–15.3.1961. The statements by some prime ministers vowing to raise the issue again at each meeting were cited by Menzies as the main reason for Verwoerd's decision (PV 4/122, Office of Australian High Commissioner in the Union of South Africa, with remarks by Menzies in the press conference on 19.3.1961, p. 1).

144 The text of Verwoerd's statement is reprinted in Hyam/Louis 2000, Doc. 457: 425–451, 449–450, Minutes of six meetings of Commonwealth prime ministers, 13.-15.3.1961 (see *Daily Express*, *Guardian*, and *Daily Herald*, 16.3.1961; *Die Transvaler*, 14.3.61; *Die Burger*, 14.3.61; *Cape Times*, 14.3.61; *Die Transvaler*, 16.3.61 with the headline, 'S.A. is uit').

the request. Relying on a well-worn tactic, he used this escalation as the reason for his refusal to make concessions. With this explanation, highlighting his seemingly conciliatory attitude, he indirectly admitted to having deliberately provoked the demands of the delegations from other member states.

In the House of Commons, Macmillan lamented "that had Dr Verwoerd shown the smallest move towards an understanding of the views of his Commonwealth colleagues", an amicable solution would not have been out of the question.[145] Diefenbaker met Verwoerd and his wife again that evening at the Queen's reception and banquet in Buckingham Palace; on this occasion, he observed that "there was no suggestion that anything had happened to either surprise or shock them".[146] In a photograph showing Verwoerd and Louw in the back seat of the carriage that drove them back from the meeting, the two appear extremely cheerful and not at all in a depressed mood, which is what one would have expected if Verwoerd had really wanted to stay in the Commonwealth.[147] He was only somewhat less pleased when a visit to France and Germany, previously announced in the media,[148] was cancelled because both governments refused to receive him and were looking for excuses.[149]

An indication of Verwoerd's calculating behaviour can also be found in the way in which he turned what according to the official reading would have been a resounding defeat into a triumph – so much so that there was even talk of a "miracle".[150] He sent his Director of Information, Meiring, ahead with the task of organising cheering crowds for the reception, which was accomplished through the Broederbond channels.[151] On arrival from London, Verwoerd dropped his mask

---

145 Macmillan before the House of Commons, 21.3.1961 (in Mansergh 1963: 374).
146 Diefenbaker 1978: 182.
147 A. Boshoff 1993: 72 reported that Verwoerd was not downhearted – quite the opposite.
148 *Guardian*, 4.3.1961; *Scotsman*, 4.3.1961; *Die Burger*, 4.3.1961. *Cape Times* 7.3.1961; the visits had both been confirmed; the meeting with de Gaulle was scheduled for 20.3., and with Erhardt for 21.3.1961; the return to Johannesburg was planned for 24.3.1961 (FAV 4.7.1.3.1, Plan for the return journey, with the handwritten note 'Wat kon gewees het' above it). Verwoerd's wife also mentioned the forthcoming visit to Bonn (FAV, 4.7.3.1.7, Letter by E. Verwoerd to W. J. Verwoerd, 10.3.1961; see also Wischnewski 1961: 2).
149 PV 4/72, E. H. Louw: 'Dr. H. F. Verwoerd. So Onthou Ek Hom' (n.d.), p. 6; Louw also pointed out that Verwoerd was "very pro–German". In the Afrikaans press, however, this was not the way it was portrayed; *Die Burger* (17.3.61) reported that Verwoerd had cancelled the visit.
150 Meiring 1973b: 142. The government published Verwoerd's address to the South Africa Club in London in the form of a propaganda pamphlet with photographs of his triumphant return to South Africa, among other things (Verwoerd 1961a; 1961b).
151 Meiring 1979: 140, who of course did not mention the Broederbond with a single word. In a prefatory note to Verwoerd's speech presented at the airport, the editor claimed that a "great number of Afrikaans cultural organisations" had prepared the reception. This can be seen as a coded reference to the Broederbond, especially seeing that the editor was also the author of the

and admitted that he had realised his true aim: "It shall remain for us a memory of one of the greatest days of our lives – the arrival on the soil of our fatherland, after what has been not a defeat but a victory for South Africa."[152] The 20,000-strong enthusiastic crowd gathered to welcome him consisted entirely of Afrikaners and supporters of the National Party, who saw a long-held dream realised.[153] Verwoerd saw it similarly; with a few years' hindsight, he wrote:

> No matter how independent the Union was in its internal and external government as a State within the Commonwealth with the British Sovereign as its own hereditary head of State, it was these very ties – however informal – which in the eyes of its own citizens, as well as those of the rest of the world, limited its true sovereign independence. In law and in practice there may have been no limits to our independence, but in the hearts and minds of the people limitations did indeed exist.[154]

In terms of domestic politics, there was no risk for Verwoerd to have himself celebrated for what he had set out to achieve ever since the 1930s. The Republic was a done deal and English-speaking South Africans had no possibility of reversing the withdrawal from the Commonwealth.[155] Since the opposition United Party also did not want to see an integrated society and majority rule, a Prime Minister appointed by them could hardly have brought back a different result – at least that is what Verwoerd suggested in the speeches he presented during his stay in England and after his return to South Africa.[156] In fact, the resistance among white English-speakers collapsed even in Natal, without any attempts to revive it.[157]

On 8 April 1961, immediately after Verwoerd's return from the Prime Ministers' Conference, Colonel Rupert D. Pilkington-Jordan, Senate member for the opposition United Party and co-author of the new republican constitution, published a letter to the editor in which he confessed, against prevailing opinion, "I do not believe that the Prime Minister ever intended to keep South Africa in the Commonwealth". He based this on Verwoerd's unwavering willingness to enter into a discussion on

---

official history of the Broederbond (Verwoerd, Speech on Arrival from London, Johannesburg 20.3.1961, in Pelzer 1966: 513–516, 513). G. D. Scholtz (1974, vol. 2: 116) presents this response as 'spontaneous'. About a quarter of students at the University of Potchefstroom attended the reception (E. S. van Eeden 2006: 509).

152 Verwoerd, Speech on Arrival from London, Johannesburg, 20.3.1961 (in Pelzer 1966: 513–516, 513); see also A. Boshoff 1993: 74.
153 As richly illustrated propaganda over several pages (*Die Transvaler*, 21.3.1961).
154 Preface by Verwoerd to Mulder/Cruywagen 1964: 11.
155 See also G. V. D. 1961: 538.
156 Verwoerd, Speech on Arrival from London, Johannesburg, 20.3.1961 (in Pelzer 1966: 513–516, 514).
157 Wilks 1980: 144–145.

apartheid that was bound to exacerbate the confrontation.[158] Even Jaap Basson, himself a republican,[159] who had been expelled from the NP by Verwoerd, was convinced that Verwoerd had sought the de facto exclusion of South Africa from the outset – a move which he described as "the greatest act of opportunism in the history of South Africa".[160] Verwoerd was sure that the withdrawal from the Commonwealth did him no harm; he set an early date – that of 18 October 1961 – for parliamentary elections, which gave his party an overwhelming electoral victory and a retrospective endorsement of his actions by the electorate.[161]

Although Verwoerd originally thought that the time was too short to stage a celebration truly appropriate to the occasion,[162] 31 May 1961 turned out to be a triumph for his politics: He had achieved the goals he had pursued and advocated for decades, namely to turn South Africa into a republic and to leave the Commonwealth. The withdrawal did not entail any harm for him; on the contrary, through skilful organisation and self-promotion, he succeeded in making himself appear as a victim of anti-South African machinations, and managed to turn the tide to be hailed as hero. The Prime Minister even took the time to write articles for the popular Afrikaner family magazine *Huisgenoot* as well as for *Die Brandwag*, in which he teleologically interpreted past history, with the Republic as the moment of fulfilment: "Preparatory steps have been taken, one after the other, since 1910, some purposefully, others unknowingly." In this way, the development towards the Republic was presented not only as a sequence of steps and stages, but as an inevitability based on a philosophy of history: "In accordance with the tendency of world history, this development is natural, since a nation is being formed."[163] This was followed by the call to jointly turn to the future – as of now.[164] The extent to which the withdrawal from the Commonwealth was part of

---

158 *Natal Mercury*, 8.4.1961. On Pilkington-Jordan and his reputation as a politician who would not allow anything or anyone to shut him up, not even Party discipline, see Scher 1988: 77; also on his contribution to the formulation of the republican constitution.
159 J.Basson 2008: 22.
160 J.Basson 2006: 120. Douglas Mitchell, UP leader in Natal, had already predicted the withdrawal in the run–up to the Republic referendum (Wilks 1980:123).
161 See Stultz/Butler 1963: 87, 103, 107.
162 PV 93/1/47/1/6, ff. 6–7, Press statement by the Prime Minister, 21.11.1960.
163 PV 93/1/47/1/6, ff. 42–43, Manuscript for *Huisgenoot*. Similarly Scholtz 1963b, who saw the Republic as historical fulfilment.
164 On 7 December 1912, in the small town of De Wildt, General Hertzog had presented a rousing speech in which he attacked the English "soldiers of fortune". The speech is regarded as the first step towards the founding of the National Party.

Verwoerd's strategy to constitute a republic is evident from some statements he made in 1962, on the occasion of the 50th anniversary of Hertzog's De Wildt Speech;[165] referring to symbolic dates, he also used this occasion to place the Republic in the larger context of Afrikaner nationalism. Verwoerd maintained that South Africa would have remained dependent on Britain, despite all its constitutional freedoms. "The government could ascertain the new attitude towards the Republic from direct communications received from other governments. These now realise that they are now dealing for the first time with the government of the Republic of South Africa as that of a totally independent state, without always having to simultaneously look to London."[166] These and related statements revealed Verwoerd's aversion to nuance and his intolerance of ambiguity.

From Cultural Nationalism to Nation-Building

After 1961, Verwoerd was confronted with a problem: having 'achieved' the state of the Republic, Afrikaner nationalism lost its most important mission. It had lost the glue that had held the various groupings together. Even before the Republic was founded, Verwoerd appealed to his compatriots: ". . . we must not stand still, we must make an immediate effort to realise the ideals of our Republic. We must look further into the future in order to pass on new ideals to our successors."[167] However, this was not to be – the Bantustan policy was too controversial and did not generally appeal. In the years that followed, Afrikaner nationalism lost its focus,[168] and the various sectional interests came to the fore, as it happened in the fierce internal battles after Verwoerd's death.

Afrikaner nationalism, especially its radical cultural-nationalist variant to which Verwoerd and the NP more generally subscribed since 1934, took it for granted that the nation was fully constituted in the form of the Afrikaner *volk*. Up to the 1950s, Afrikaner nationalists had placed particular emphasis on their cultural autonomy as a people within South Africa; their cultural mobilisation was essentially geared towards capturing state power to ensure their cultural "survival" and the "continued existence of a unique nation through time".[169] But the growing momentum of decolonisation to the north of the South African borders impelled them

---

165 PV 93/1/47/1/6, f. 181, Die Betekenis van Republiekwording vir Suid-Afrika. Boodskap van E. M.: De Wildt 50 jaar.
166 Cillié 1965: 200 (3.12.1960); see also van der Walt 1968: 246; and Stals 1998: 250, 400.
167 PV 93/1/47/1/6, f. 26, manuscript for Brandwag.
168 Van Jaarsveld 1978: 47.
169 220.T.8 (10), handwritten notes of Verwoerd's speech in 1960 (n.d.).

to seek an expanded power base. For Verwoerd, the only way to do this was to open up to English-speaking whites. The reorientation of apartheid was by no means a reaction to the changing international order alone; it was part of an overall concept of nation-building – on the terms of the cultural nationalists.

However, this was possible only at the expense of the previously held exclusive understanding of the nation. In this understanding, the Afrikaner nation was viewed as a historically evolved, homogeneous cultural entity, defined as an 'organic' or even 'natural', but in any case God-given, community of people. This ideology served to stem centrifugal tendencies, by emphasising egalitarianism within the national community, while denying the consequences of increasing social differentiation. In reality, Afrikaner identity was inconceivable without an accompanying discourse of alterity. It was initially directed against the British who were demonised as foreigners, exploiters, financial powers, etc., and later against the black population, who were considered to be uncivilised, barbaric and culturally completely different. As soon as Verwoerd reached out to English speakers, appealing to them to overcome the historical divisions and unite as a common white nation against the black majority, he effectively gave up on the Afrikaner community, notwithstanding his continued commitment to it. The cultural nationalist turned into a nation-builder; the nationalism based on supposedly objective criteria was replaced by a voluntarist understanding of nationalism.

Verwoerd viewed Afrikaners as the 'normal' people: they were at home in South Africa, with a clearly identifiable culture, as nationalist propaganda had been suggesting for decades. This was in contrast to English-speaking whites, who were living not only in the United Kingdom, but had established themselves as settlers and colonial functionaries in Australia, Canada and New Zealand – throughout Empire. Because the transformation into a republic had deprived them of the possibility of holding on to their British identity, the way was now open to the creation of a common white nation. Verwoerd reiterated time and again how important this step was to him. He extended strong gestures of friendship to English-speaking whites, explaining that it was a matter of cultural equality within a white nation, i.e. that neither Afrikaners nor British should be disadvantaged in any way.[170] After 1961, he repeatedly appeared in front of exclusively English-speaking audiences; he demonstratively supported English South African traditions and emphasised that the English had their place in South African history: the 1820 Settlers, for example, had a historical significance comparable to that of the Voortrekkers, he said.[171] This was a remarkable step for a cultural-nationalist firebrand like Verwoerd, but one

---

170 For example PV 93/1/47/2/6, f. 49, Letter by Verwoerd to T. A. Stewart (Nairobi), 15.8.1960.
171 Verwoerd, 1820–Setlaarstrust, Johannesburg 27.4.1962 (in Pelzer 1963: 642–647, 643).

that was by no means pointing in the direction of liberalism, as Munger speculated at the time.[172]

For Verwoerd, the transformation of South Africa into a republic marked a historical caesura,[173] the conclusion of constitutional revisionism. At the same time, however, he emphasised that it was a new beginning, since the new constitution had finally created the conditions, clearly and explicitly. "Let us immediately begin to look to the future. Throughout I maintained that the change to a republic must be a means and not an end, not revenge for the past but consolidation of our efforts for the future, not so much the end of a period as the beginning of a new era."[174] Verwoerd appealed to goodwill, for nation-building was not a process that could be taken to happen automatically, even though he had repeatedly insinuated exactly that: "The creation of the Republic has not only constructed a bridge, but has closed the gap. The quarrels disappear. The nation becomes united."[175]

After 1961, Verwoerd appeared convinced that the formation of a new nation would be carried along in the slipstream of the newly constituted Republic; yet he was compelled to invoke nation-building over and over again in almost every speech, indicating how far away it was from being realised. The notion of national unity was changing now, too. The new nation was more heterogeneous, which is why he emphasised diversity in unity: "The nation is a unity, although its people belong to various churches, each professing a faith unique in its own way, but all are partly the same and partly different, though bound together."[176]

The policy of separate development in the form of the homeland policy was supposed to support the nation-building process. Verwoerd also opened up the possibility that the Republic would free the English-speaking population from

---

[172] Munger 1967: 67.
[173] FAV 4.7.2.4.5, Speech at the Natal NP Party Conference in Durban, 27.8.1963.
[174] Verwoerd, Message to the People after the Referendum on 7.10.1960 (in Pelzer 1966: 409–414, 411). Even before the Referendum, in an appeal sent to all white households, he emphasised the future-oriented nature of the Referendum, linking it to nation-building: "With the aim of self-preservation and in the interest of our children, we must learn to look to the future rather than to the past." Furthermore, he stressed the need to unite in view of the "struggle between Eastern and Western nations, between communism and Christianity" (PV 276/2/1/5, Circular letter on the referendum).
[175] PV 93/1/47/1/6, f. 181, Die Betekenis van Republiekwording vir Suid-Afrika. Boodskap van E. M. (De Wildt 50 jaar). But even in the Broederbond, nation–building was not considered the route to be followed (Stals 1998: 482).
[176] Verwoerd, Centenary of the Municipal Administration of King William's Town, 8.2.1961 (in Pelzer 1966: 489–495, 490). See also Barber 1999: 172–173. With this vision, Verwoerd supported plans to establish a bilingual university in Port Elizabeth (E. J. Marais 1978: 201).

their political isolation, and to participate in the national government.[177] Behind this was his view that the United Party was a heterogeneous party held together only by anti-republicanism, and that English speakers in favour of apartheid were loyal to the United Party only because of its anti-republican stance. "I place my hope in the fact that when the Republic comes about, all those who agree on the question of colour will come together because then another great point of contention will be removed – and then the politics of colour will be less conflictual than it is now."[178] In order to promote this 'normality', Verwoerd appointed two English-speaking ministers for the first time in 1961; they were NP members fully behind the government line, namely Frank Waring and Alfred Ernest Trollip, the erstwhile administrator of Natal.[179] He predicted that the old camps would disappear. Instead of competing nationalisms, political parties would realign themselves along ideological lines – along the lines of liberal vs. conservative parties, for instance. The prerequisite, however, had to be a consensus on racial policy; in other words, controversies on racial policies had to be 'resolved' and thus removed from party-political disputes. In the early twentieth century, political scientist Paul Reinsch saw the consequences for democracy in no uncertain terms: "It is evident that when the most important concerns of a nation are thus withdrawn from the field of party difference, party government itself must be largely weak, as dealing no longer with vital questions."[180] For Verwoerd, however, it was only in a clearly defined and secure white nation state that South African politics could find the 'normality' that Verwoerd observed in Western states.[181]

The kind of nation-building that Verwoerd had in mind was more complicated than it appeared at first sight, for it was not clear how it was to accommodate minorities, especially Jews. After all, Verwoerd had been an outspoken and rabid antisemite until then. Would he include the Jews in the new nation?

While Verwoerd hardly ever expressed himself openly antisemitic after the Second World War,[182] there is no evidence that he changed his mind. As Prime Minister, he tried to integrate the Jews, especially after the establishment of the Republic, because now every white person counted. "Jews are not looked upon as

---

177 *Die Transvaler*, 31.10.1958.
178 PV 93/1/24/10, 117, Reply to D. J. Wolfaardt, Heilbron, 4.8.1960. On this, see also observations in *Die Burger*, 6.7.1959, on the racism common to both Afrikaans- and English-speaking whites.
179 PV 93/1/20/1/2, p. 1, Press release by Verwoerd, 1.11.1961, in which no department was named for Waring's posting – it was only announced that both Waring and Trollip would join the NP.
180 Reinsch 1900: 300.
181 PV 93/1/47/1/6, f. 182, Die Betekenis van Republiekwording vir Suid–Afrika. Boodskap van E. M. (De Wildt 50 jaar).
182 However, J. Basson (2006: 103) provides an example.

a separate racial community but only form a separate religious group with the White community, just as there are Catholics, Protestants, etc."[183] Nevertheless, he evaded an unequivocal statement, instructing his private secretary to announce that "[t]he Prime Minister believes in fact that such specific references to a population group as if it must be on the defensive and needs separate assurances, is unwise".[184] Like Strijdom, he said, he had issued "a sympathetic statement with reference to the Jewish people of our country" on his assumption of office.[185] He even went out of his way to highlight the activities of Jewish members of the NP of the Transvaal,[186] that is, in the provincial party structure that had denied them membership for years. It was not until 1962 that Verwoerd asserted that the government was against antisemitism "[as] a matter of principle". Nevertheless, in one instance, he was prompted to state that "in view of his associations in the past he wished to state categorically, and to avoid all misunderstanding, that he was wholly opposed to antisemitism".[187] In her propagandistic book, Dutch journalist Mary Pos denies any antisemitic tendencies of Verwoerd's, and tries to present apartheid in the best possible light.[188] Her view seemed credible because there were a few Jews who denied that Verwoerd was an antisemite, which Weisbord attributed to some level of support for apartheid.[189] However, there are a number of incidents that attest to his antisemitism. His son Wilhelm wanted to enlist the communist Sam Kahn, along with his father, as contributors to a student magazine. His father refused, "because he did not want to be seen in that company". But this had nothing to do with the fact that Kahn was a communist. Verwoerd senior suggested Bram Fischer instead, who was also a communist but "an educated person from a good family".[190]

---

183 PV 93/1/30/1/12, Letter by Verwoerd to Constantin Paul Lent (New York), 27.2.1961, f. 41.
184 PV 93/1/30/1/4, f. 20, Letter by Verwoerd to J. Nossel, 13.12.1958.
185 PV 93/1/30/1/7, f. 65, Verwoerd to E. Bernstein, 16.9.1960. PV 93/1/34/1, f. 7, Letter from the S.A. Jewish Board of Deputies (E. J. Horwitz) to Verwoerd, 5.9.1958, requesting an interview and pointing out to him that "it is customary for the leading members of this Board to convey their congratulations to the Prime Minister personally"; f. 8, affirmative reply, 22.9.58. (PV 93/1/30/1/7, f. 84, *S.A. Jewish Times*, Leon Feldberg, 17.10.1958, Request for an interview). Verwoerd refused, referring to his conversation with the Board of Deputies. He pointed out that the interview with Strijdom did not lie that far back, and that he had already made it clear "that there will be no deviation by his Government from the policy towards Jewry in South Africa and the State of Israel".
186 PV 93/1/30/1/5, f. 75, Letter by Verwoerd to J. Nossel, 9.11.1959.
187 PV 93/1/34/9, ff. 135–142, Letter by Verwoerd to Mendel Levin 20.7.1962.
188 Pos 1967: 99–101.
189 Weisbord 1967: 241.
190 W. et al. Verwoerd 2001: 52–53. In the 1940s, Fischer allegedly tried to convert Verwoerd to socialism (Clingman 2000: 135, 376; see also G. Frankel 2000: 84). However, this conjecture is not clearly verifiable and lacks credibility.

At the same time, the NP led by Verwoerd continued to move in close proximity to right-wing extremist circles such as Rudman's Boerenasie; in some instances, it had recruited known antisemites from among the Greyshirts and other organisations to its ranks, and even promoted them by issuing them with parliamentary mandates.[191] There were also voices within the NP pushing for the integration of Jews as potential voters: besides that of Albert Hertzog, this was, for example, the position of Rev. P. W. Venter, whom Verwoerd reassured that there was no longer any "active" antisemitism in the NP.[192] In 1965, when Israel had supported the UN's condemnation of apartheid, Verwoerd was annoyed, giving rather dubious reasons: "We can no longer see Israel as we did before – that we have an obligation to help. It looks more like Israel, having rebelled on numerous occasions in history, followed foreign gods, and was punished for it".[193] As Prime Minister, Verwoerd commissioned a private inquiry into the extent of the Oppenheimers' fortune,[194] which was almost certainly antisemitically motivated. His antisemitism also explains why he rejected Tomlinson's proposals to invest in the reserves: he did not want to give Jews access. Piet Meiring reported that he had approached Verwoerd together with a Jewish businessman friend who wanted to support the development of the homelands; and all Verwoerd said was: "You Jews are always out to make money somewhere new – what is it this time?"[195]

Understandably, many Jews were deeply suspicious, considering Verwoerd's past. When a correspondent published a letter addressed to him by Verwoerd in a newspaper, stating his position on Israel, the Prime Minister, enraged at this "breach of trust", cut off any contact with him.[196] The aggressive tone of his response stirred up anxiety among many South African Jews,[197] whom he had to

---

191 See for instance the letter by Mendel Levin to Verwoerd, urging him to distance himself from statements by Rudman and Schoeman, and demanding that Vorster distance himself from Leibbrandt (PV 93/1/34/9, ff. 135–142, Letter by Mendel Levin to Verwoerd, 11.7.1962, and Verwoerd's reply, 20.7.1962).
192 PV 93/1/30/1/7, f.112, Letter by ds. P. W. Venter to Verwoerd, 21.9.1960, and Verwoerd's reply, 28.9.1960.
193 PV 93/3/1/74, f. 84, Letter by Verwoerd to A. F. C. Swanepoel (Kimberley), 3.12.1965.
194 B. M. Schoeman 1973: 133.
195 Meiring 1990: 98; Meiring confessed that he had never been so ashamed in his life as he had been after Verwoerd's spiteful outburst. Maisels (1999: 288) also attested to the fact that Verwoerd was an antisemite.
196 "You have not respected that privacy but have become, directly or indirectly, responsible for the publication of the contents of a private letter, and should be held responsible by all Jewry for whatever harm they may feel may result from this act." (PV 93/1/30/1/14, Letter by Verwoerd to E. A. East, also letter to Sylvia Resnik (ibid.), as well as identically worded reply letter to A. S. A. East, 2.11.1961. East published the letter [Letter by Verwoerd to East, 20.11.1961]).
197 PV 93/1/30/1/14, f. 97, Letter by Verwoerd to C. Leventhal, Johannesburg, 22.11.1961.

reassure by issuing a public statement. Nevertheless he saw himself in the role of the innocent persecuted victim, alleging that it was only a hostile press that attributed "sinister motives" to his statements.[198] The defensive attitude that many Jews and Jewish organisations displayed towards the NP and to Verwoerd in particular was noticeable; it gave an indication of the extent to which the Party had succeeded in intimidating the Jewish population and put them under pressure to justify themselves; this state of affairs continued after the end of the Second World War, right into the 1960s.[199]

South Africa and the Global Racial Conflict

The only state visit undertaken by Verwoerd during his eight years in office, was his attendance at the 1961 Commonwealth Conference.[200] More than anything else, it was the lack of compromise and perspective in his policies that contributed to this isolation.[201] Another factor was the lack of diplomatic sensitivity, which further strained the already tense relations with the Netherlands.[202] Despite his foreign policy failures, Verwoerd made international relations a top priority, leaving his Foreign Minister little autonomy.[203] The stubbornness with which he stuck to apartheid policies creates the impression he was hardly concerned about South Africa's growing isolation. But in actual fact, it caused him serious concerns: "The main problems will undoubtedly be the external issues."[204] Indeed, at a time when the issue of human rights was coming to the fore in international politics, there was hardly a

---

[198] PV 93/1/30/1/14, f. 108, Letter by Verwoerd to Enid Alexander, 5.12.1961. In reviewing Verwoerd's correspondence, it is nevertheless noticeable that he usually refused requests for talks from Jews. See also Bunting 1986: 68.

[199] This is also the view of Suzman 1997: 431.

[200] See also the extraordinary interest of the South African government in a state visit by the Prime Minister of New Zealand, Walter Nash, who had expressed this intention (PV 4/14, f. 70, Letter by Louw to Nash, 13.6.1960, and his cancellation due to scheduling pressures, f. 75, 24.6.1960).

[201] See the numerous examples in Troup 1975: 366–367. Thus, in 1960, the press service of the German Social Democrats praised the Americans who had, in the case of South Africa, given precedence to democratic principles over the requirements of the Cold War (anon. 1960: 4–5).

[202] Terblanche 1998: 141; see also Terblanche 2001: 238. Puzzlingly, Kenney (1980: 260) credited him with "exceptional abilities" in foreign policy. On the particularly pronounced criticism of apartheid in the Netherlands, see Terblanche 2010: 454–456.

[203] Geldenhuys 1984: 22–25; see also Meiring 1990: 30.

[204] PV 93/3/1/24, f. 11, ASB University of Pretoria (Johan Strauss), telegram to Verwoerd, 15.6.1959.

country that stood as permanently accused and isolated as South Africa.[205] Verwoerd welcomed the visit of UN Secretary-General Dag Hammarskjöld, as he was hoping to maintain international contacts. Through skilful diplomacy, Hammarskjöld was able to win the Prime Minister's trust, without holding back on criticism of his policies.[206] Verwoerd, for his part, was still not inclined to make concessions. In 1961, he turned the Information Department, which had previously been part of the Foreign Department, into an independent ministry;[207] he actually believed that he could address the alleged ignorance of the outside world through propaganda campaigns, and induce a friendly attitude towards his country. As a former journalist, he knew how important it was to assert the prerogative of interpretation even in domestic politics; while he was still a Minister, he had his most important speeches printed in pamphlet form.[208]

International criticism did not cause him to rethink his policy; rather, in his view, the fault lay with Western countries courting the favours of the newly independent states, while avoiding South Africa – they even had the audacity to tune into the UN's condemnations of apartheid. By abstaining instead of taking a clear position, he thought, they were pursuing a half-hearted policy at best.[209] But he did not develop a plan to take his country out of isolation; instead, he tried to reassure his supporters, and simultaneously rally them behind him, accusing the West of weakness.[210] The same, he said, applied to independent African states, some of whom were putting out feelers toward South Africa, but Verwoerd refused to establish relations with them on ideological grounds.[211]

According to Verwoerd, Western countries had to realise that with their attitude towards South Africa, they were shooting themselves in the foot, not realising that it was the interests of Western civilisation that were at stake: "The world

---

205 Eckel 2015 with several examples. On the regime's self-perception, see Eiselen 1953: 22. For the year 1965 alone, see Horrell 1966: 84–87; see also Gurney 2000: 133–144. There were, of course, also exceptions. German Minister of Agriculture at the time, Heinrich Lübke, played down the situation in South Africa, saying: "The racial problems of the country are in good hands." (qtd. in Holzer 1961: 251).
206 Verwoerd got along better with Hammarskjöld than with Macmillan (see Saunders 2011: 71). At the same time, the government largely prevented the Secretary General from contacting black persons in opposition and, indeed, the general population (see Sellström 2011: 44–46).
207 Swanepoel 1982: 85.
208 An example is provided by Verwoerd (1958) in a speech presented in 1957, which served him as a justification for the homeland policy even after his election as Prime Minister.
209 This is also the tenor of his 1963 speech in Florida (FAV 4.7.2.4.5, transcript of the speech).
210 FAV 4.7.2.4.5, Transcript of the speech in Florida.
211 Wolvaardt/Wheeler/Scholtz 2010, vol. 1: 101; he related towards Japan in a similar manner (Wolvaardt/Wheeler/Scholtz 2010, vol. 2: 186).

powers of the West seem to be becoming increasingly aware of the reality that South Africa and South-West Africa are only pawns in the game which is mainly directed against themselves, and that they will weaken their own cause by placing South Africa on the altar of appeasement."[212] He diagnosed the West to be afflicted with "a psychotic preoccupation with the rights, the liberties and the privileges of the non-white peoples".[213] He did not shy away from drawing a parallel to the policy of Neville Chamberlain towards Hitler, without admitting that in this specific case, he had advocated much more than mere appeasement.[214] He was hoping that he could convince Western countries of South Africa's good intentions once the homeland policy was finally realised beyond the previous declarations of intent. As a "normal" nation-state, South Africa should be acceptable, for "the Republic will be a recognisably white state, with a minority of Coloureds and no Bantu. Their national affiliations lie elsewhere. In this sense we will become internationally more secure, as the disparaging arguments will also disappear."[215]

Thus, in numerous letters and other statements, he vowed that international opinion was gradually changing and that the perception of South Africa was about to turn: "For the moment the spirit of the times may seem to be against us but this has happened before and just as in the past the pendulum of world opinion may be expected to swing back."[216] In addressing his Party, he was even more explicit ideologically, predicting that "more and more the right-wing movement in the world is beginning to triumph over the left".[217] Firmness would pay off, which is why he was convinced that "the attitude that we and other Whites are adopting in Africa is causing the wheel of world opinion to turn".[218]

In general, businessmen seemed more reliable to him, as they were interested in the security of their investments and had recognised the stability of South Africa: "The confidence of world finance in the economic security and prog-

---

212 Verwoerd, New Year Message, 31.12.1961 (in Pelzer 1966: 654–659, 657–658).
213 Verwoerd 1960c: 1.
214 Ibid., 3.
215 PV 93/1/30/1/32, ff. 100–102, 102, Letter by Verwoerd to J. S. Maritz, Ohrigstad, 2.5.1966.
216 PV 93/1/47/2/3, V. to Mrs H. D. Bruyn, (Westville, Natal), 22.2.1960. Similarly PV 93/1/30/1/25, f. 93, Letter by Verwoerd to Martha Flinte, 20.5.1964: "The world is also beginning to notice the latest turn of events in Africa, and in the disillusionment begin to wonder if South Africa has not perhaps got something after all. We must not be too impatient and expect a too rapid change"; see also PV 93/1/30/1/22, f. 155, Letter by Verwoerd to B. D. Rosière (Johannesburg), 8.10.1963.
217 Verwoerd 1964a: 13.
218 Verwoerd, Statement of Policy, 9.3.1960 (in Pelzer 1966: 340–369, 367).

ress of South Africa is a natural consequence of this stability."[219] The economic interests of the Western world were a kind of safeguard for him, meaning that they would not abandon South Africa despite all verbal attacks: "This economic relationship will not be torn apart easily. In that lies a major guarantee."[220] Political steadfastness seemed to him the best guarantee for winning the trust of investors: "If they can only have the assurance that we shall be able to retain control, that these threats mean nothing, they will stay here and leave their investments here. It is because they fear that we will have to submit and that in the long run this may lead to difficulties and defeat and incompetent Black rule and disorder, that they fear a depreciation in the value of their assets."[221]

South Africa's isolation was placed in the context of the Cold War in two ways. On the one hand, the isolation was explicable in terms of the Cold War; on the other hand Verwoerd used the East-West confrontation to recommend South Africa as reliable partner of the West – especially on occasions when Western countries were turning against South Africa:

> South Africa is the only reliable friend the Western world has. . . . We are the one area on which the West can rely absolutely, the foremost fort in any possible east-west clash. Our friendship must remain even in spite of misunderstanding created by such attitudes and tactics because our interests are the same. If however we are left in the lurch in the present cold war for the friendship of Africa, and the whites lose out in this country, then even this bastion is lost to the Western World.

The decolonisation of Africa took place at a time of confrontations between blocs. This meant that communist countries attempted to promote decolonisation in their own interest, and to influence the newly independent states politically. As Verwoerd saw it, "[t]he real danger from communism [was] not that the native peoples of Africa would take over the communist ideology . . . but that they would come under the spell of other aspects of communist propaganda. By this I mean accep-

---

[219] Verwoerd, New Year Message, 31.12.1958 (in Pelzer 1966: 212–215, 214): ". . . I may add that in the industrial field the leaders are best informed on the position in South Africa and they help to disseminate the correct information."

[220] Verwoerd, Convention for the Promotion of Export Trade, Johannesburg 16.5.1962 (in Pelzer 1966: 697–712, 702). On the calculated pronouncements in the context of the withdrawal from the Commonwealth, see Makin 1997: 156–157.

[221] Verwoerd, Budgetary Appropriation of the Prime Minister, 10.4.1961 (in Pelzer 1966: 549–566, 556); in a similar vein PV 93/1/30/1/12, f. 84, Letter by Verwoerd to Adv. G. F. van L. Froneman, M.P., 15.5.1961; see also Verwoerd, First Speech as Prime Minister, 18.9.1958 (in Pelzer 1966: 164–190, 182).

tance of the idea that the colonial powers or the white people of South Africa harmed them instead of creating civilised conditions on this continent."[222]

Verwoerd insinuated that the West could not find allies in the Cold War among the former colonies that had just become independent, as they lacked the requisite maturity, but only in South Africa which, as a white state, shared the values of the West: "In the competition between Europe and America on the one hand and Russia and the East on the other, the important question is with whom will Africa side? . . . How can the East or Communist Russia get the great, uncivilized, slow-thinking masses of Africa on their side?" Through their propaganda, they were making Africans forget "what the so-called colonial powers have done for the territories of Africa. They continually place the accent on certain disadvantages such as, for example, that they have not yet received freedom and independence." The communists were busy trying to stir up "the average dweller in Africa". Thus Africans would become enemies of "those who are actually their benefactors."[223]

According to Verwoerd, the West did perceive the risks in the possibility that African states could turn towards the Soviet Union, but it responded by pandering to Africans.[224] With a hasty decolonisation, the West had played right into the hands of communism, "by creating new states, many small and not economically viable, left and right in Asia and Africa, and even by competing in the stimulation of grievances, for example in connection with 'colonialism', and of ambitions, such as the demand for political independence even if it came precipitately and without efficient preparation."[225] The reason for the rejection of South Africa and for their confrontational course was, according to Verwoerd, that these newly formed states tried to divert attention from their own shortcomings and found a scapegoat in South Africa: "Sometimes they behave in this way towards South Africa to gain the reputation of what sound, strong, leading Black states they are which can take ac-

---

[222] PV 93/1/34/1, ff. 166–170, George H. Pipal, interview with Verwoerd for United Press, 13.12.1958. The interview took place on 6.12. A transcript, in the form of a UPI report, can be found in FAV, 4.7.1.2.
[223] Verwoerd, Transvaal Congress of the National Party, Pretoria 12.11.1958 (in Pelzer 1966: 191–205, 200).
[224] Verwoerd, Budgetary Appropriation of the Prime Minister, 10.4.1961 (in Pelzer 1966: 549–566, 551). "South Africa is landed in the position where both sides attack her, not because it is really a country in which injustice is done, because in fact it is a peaceful country, but because in this way the friendship of the Afro–Asian countries can be sought. [. . .] But it is mostly instigated from abroad and sometimes by incitement from within and this while the Government is trying to bring about reforms for their benefit" (ibid., 550).
[225] Verwoerd, New Year Message, 31.12.1961 (1966: 654–659, 655).

tion against a White state or against the White man."[226] In actual fact, it was not about apartheid at all; the reason for the attacks lay in the internal conditions of these newly formed states or, in the case of the West, a policy of appeasement towards Africans.[227] Since communism was contrary to everything that was important and sacred to the nationalist Verwoerd,[228] the ideological conflict was significant; nevertheless, it only touched the surface.

Leading South African politicians, not least Verwoerd himself, placed the Cold War in a larger context. Behind the ideological confrontation, they sensed a global racial conflict, which in South Africa took the form of a conflict between the Indian minority, a "trader race",[229] and whites; but this was only part of a global confrontation. The antagonism between East and West, as one nationalist writer would have it, began in 500 B.C., and persists to this day. In North Africa, specifically, it was being carried out in the form of the advance of Islam, but it was no longer limited to that; "an extremely important phase of it is currently being fought out on South African soil. . . . In South Africa today, there are both Westerners and Easterners."[230]

In their book, *Drawing the Global Colour Line*, Australian historians Marilyn Lake and Henry Reynolds thematise transnational solidarities in the Anglophone world up to the Second World War. They draw attention to the extent to which intellectuals and politicians from various countries influenced and confirmed each other in their racially coloured perceptions of imagined and actual conflicts.[231] The Australians and New Zealanders in particular, but also US-Americans, saw themselves threatened by the rise of Japan, and banded together more closely. The migration of Indian and Chinese contract workers to numerous countries led to collusion between those countries in promulgating xenophobic legislation.[232] The for-

---

226 Verwoerd, Budgetary Appropriation of the Prime Minister, 10.4.1961 (in Pelzer 1966: 549–566, 551).
227 Verwoerd, New Year Message, 31.12.1961 (in Pelzer 1966: 654–659, 657). He also expressed this assessment to American interlocutors, but he did not convince them (DNSA, Telegram Ambassador Rountree to State Department, 24.1.1966, p. 2).
228 Verwoerd had already appeared as an expert on communism during his years as editor, as he did, for instance at a church congress on communism organised by the NHK, where he spoke on communism and the press (PV 202/2/3/1/1, Letter by D. F. B. de Beer (NHK Johannesburg) to the Secretary of the FAK, Aug. 1946). The congress took place on 9.10.1946.
229 PV 93/1/20/2/3, ff. 75–79, Departement van Gemeenskapsbou, Memorandum on Indian Trade, p. 1, item 6.
230 PV 93/1/16/2, Memorandum on the "Indian Question" (anon.); see also Te Water 1953: 9.
231 Lake/Reynolds 2008, Part 3. Although they deal with the Anglophone world, the networks went beyond that (see Kühl 1997).
232 On this, see Huttenback 1976: 154–157.

mula of 'Asia against Europe' could be filled with any conflicts, thus making it appear plausible under the most varied circumstances. The 'yellow peril', the rise of Japan and the foreseeable rise of China to a super power were interpreted as a confrontation between Asia and Europe, similar to the independence movements in India and Southeast Asia. Above all, however, the Soviet Union was seen as an Asian power, and communism, by the same token, as an Asian ideology:[233] Asian faceless collectivism vs. European-Western nation-statehood. Verwoerd embedded the Cold War in an imagined deep structure of European-Asian antagonism. In this scheme, antisemitism also found its place, seeing that Afrikaner nationalists, at least for some time, defined Jews as Asians.[234]

Verwoerd saw the international controversy over apartheid policy entirely in the context of a conflict between European and Asian continents, both of which wanted to win Africa over to their respective sides. "The jumbling of peoples, the formation of new states, the change in human relations, and the clashes between continents are processes already in full swing."[235] Africa could be a counterforce, but for this to come into effect, "the mind of man as it exists in Africa" would have to be transformed to meet the requirements, which in the event could be of "the greatest value" in the search for good relations and peace.[236] However, he was sceptical to say the least, if not pessimistic: "The Western world is losing the psychological battle for the mind of Africa." For him, Western accusations against South Africa were solely due to their ingratiation with the new states. "The Western world would have been much wiser if they had countered the communists' generalised and vague attack by a clear and specific exposition of what the white man and the Union of South Africa has done, is doing and is still prepared to do for Africa, and the black man."[237] He called for solidarity where none was possible anymore; which is why he saw the attitude of "the Western world" as a deviation from the right path, as opportunism and a passing fad.[238]

---

233 Verwoerd in *Die Transvaler* 19.9.1945 (qtd. in D. Prinsloo 1979: 361).
234 See e.g. Cronjé 1946a: 168; also Shain 1994: 53–54, 88, 117. This West–East opposition was systematically developed in Schumann 1962: 10–30, with unambiguous racist connotations (ibid., 47 and ch. 7). On Schumann's right-wing extremism, see W. van der Merwe 1988: 19–22.
235 PV 93/1/47/1/6, f. 23, Verwoerd, article manuscript for *Die Brandwag*.
236 Verwoerd, Speech of Thanks to Harold Macmillan, 3.2.1960 (in Pelzer 1966: 336–339, 337).
237 PV 93/1/34/1, ff. 166–170, George H. Pipal, interview with Verwoerd for United Press, 13.12.1958.
238 See FAV 4.7.2.4.5, Speech at the Natal NP Party Congress in Durban, 27.8.1963, pp. 6–7, in which he reminded his audience that before the Second World War, segregation was practised by all colonial powers and was considered as legitimate. This view was widespread among Afrikaner intellectuals, see e.g. Scholtz/D'Assonville 1966: 3–4.

The accusation of political stupidity that Verwoerd repeatedly levelled against Western countries condemning apartheid[239] was based on the conviction that his own view of the world was the right one. His thinking was still framed by the prewar international consensus, as Lake and Reynolds reconstructed it.[240] He did not understand why South Africa was now the only country that still held this position. The consequences of racism, as they were clearly revealed in the Holocaust, had passed him by; this blind spot in his thinking would explain why he had not registered this change.[241] For many Western countries, South Africa was primarily an unpleasant reminder of their own racist past. Verwoerd remained impervious to this historical insight. Where there would have been an opportunity for co-operation, Verwoerd noted Western states' blindness to imminent dangers. Western civilisation was '*the*' civilisation for Verwoerd, which shows the extent to which he clung to 19th-century notions of civilisational development in a sequence of stages, his cultural-relativist rhetoric notwithstanding. The East stood for 'chaos', that is, the opposite of order and civilisation.

A triumphant advance of communism, that is, 'the East', Verwoerd thought, was equivalent to the inundation of South Africa by Afro-Asian peoples: "If they try to abdicate and to surrender on our behalf, then in the long run the flood of colour will not only overwhelm us but will reach their country in the years to come and eventually overwhelm them as well."[242] Politically-ideologically speaking, South Africa was not only aligned to the West, a natural ally to Europeans and Americans, but it was also a white state: "The blind eye is turned to the fact that this could, nay must, lead to unilateral Nonwhite domination over the whole of Africa and the shrinking of white man's domain to encircled Europe and partly South and North America."[243] The preservation of white civilisation and the de-

---

239 *Cape Times*, 19.10.1958. PV 93/4/1/15, ff. 13–15, 15, Verwoerd, Notes or speech manuscript, n.d.: "The tragic surrender of the West was a clumsy attempt to ingratiate itself to hostile powers, instead of a correct appraisal of the facts, circumstances, and a sober approach resulting therefrom."
240 Lake/Reynolds 2008; see also Heese 1989b: 42–43. On the erosion of the racist consensus since the 1930s, see Barkan 1992: ch.6; and on the role of Franz Boas, see ibid., 281–285.
241 Verwoerd's newspaper, *Die Transvaler*, concealed the Holocaust or, on the few occasions when it could not avoid it, described it as Western propaganda (S. L. Friedman 1982: 22, 25, esp. 28–31, 56); on the difference between *Die Transvaler* and *Die Burger*, see ibid., 31; in the case of the Reichspogromnacht in 1938, Verwoerd even used the opportunity to increase antisemitic propaganda (ibid., 12–13, 40–41). He was not isolated in taking this stance. As late as 1953, M.E. Rothmann expressed shock at the news of the Holocaust, but tended to dismiss it as typical British and American propaganda (55.K.T. (20), M. E. Rothmann to Erika Theron, 26.10.1953).
242 Verwoerd, Statement of Policy, 9.3.1960 (in Pelzer 1966: 340–369, 369).
243 PV 93/4/1/9, ff. 105–112, f. 109, New Year's message for 1964.

fence against communism were thus part and parcel of the same stance: "The stand of this Republic of South Africa is in the interests of white civilisation throughout the world against the rising tide of colour."[244] The Western outpost at the Cape of Good Hope was simultaneously a bulwark against the advance of communism in Africa and a protection of white civilisation: "We shall remain the outpost of western civilization in the possible struggle between East and West; we shall still remain the outpost on the southern tip of Africa, inter alia, for spreading civilization through the rest of Africa."[245]

For Verwoerd, it was the question of the survival of Western civilisation that was at the base of the conflict between political systems:

> Nevertheless the leading white nations are in danger of sacrificing their position and their fundamental duty for the sake of temporary objectives which seem important during the present period of the liberation of nations and the struggle for power between the major states, each of whom attempts to obtain at all costs the support of the smaller and backward ones. Such white nations feel so safe in their own homogeneous countries, that they do not realise the extent of the retrogression of the white man's position in the world and the consequent gradual undoing of his civilizing influence.[246]

To the extent that the Western countries were "related by blood", their attitude was not so much based on principle: "Votes and economic expectations count for far more than truth or even ethical principles."[247] As early as 1957, he saw the population development of Asian countries as an ominous sign; he interpreted the East-West conflict as a confrontation of ideas, as "a struggle for the spirit of man".[248] He was "deeply convinced in [his] soul that we are fighting for the survival of white civilisation."[249]

---

[244] PV 93/1/30/1/32, Letter by Verwoerd to Miss P. J. Greenhalgh (Salisbury), 3.5.1966. On South Africa's futile attempts to enter into a military and colonial alliance with Western states, see Berridge 1992.

[245] Verwoerd, First Speech as Prime Minister, 18.9.1958 (in Pelzer 1966: 164–190, 177). See also Centenary of the Municipal Administration of King William's Town, 8.2.1961 (in Pelzer 1966: 489–495, 494): "We have lessons to teach the civilized world. We have services to render to Africa. We are in a certain way the most advanced post in a possible struggle between the East and the West, which may be waged for the sake of everything in which we believe and which we love. We have been planted here, we believe, with a destiny – a destiny not for the sake of the selfishness of a nation, but for the sake of the service of a nation to the world of which it forms a part, and the service of a nation to the Deity in which it believes." Similarly Eiselen 1961: 107.

[246] Verwoerd, New Year Message, 31.12.1959 (in Pelzer 1966: 319–322, 321f.). See also PV 93/1/30/1/5, f.143, Letter by Verwoerd to Neil Pascoe (Pinetown), 28.1.1960. Even as Minister he had denounced this attitude of Western countries (Verwoerd 1957a: 233).

[247] PV 93/1/30/1/23, f.145, Letter by Verwoerd to Harald Hedenets (Krefeld, Germany), 17.10.1963.

[248] Verwoerd 1957a: 232.

[249] Verwoerd, Day of the Covenant, 16.12.1958 (in Pelzer 1966: 206–211, 210).

Verwoerd's cultural essentialism led him to see South Africa as a quasi-natural outpost of the West. He held on to these ideas when the European governments discarded them, even though there were still many sympathisers of a racist world view in their ranks, who saw decolonisation in the context of a racial conflict posing an existential threat.

Repression and Control

Verwoerd was a politician who could not tolerate ambiguity; he tended to oppose order to chaos, in absolute terms. The question arises how a politician of this description would have dealt with any criticism of his policies? This question attains all the more salience in view of the fact that Verwoerd described himself as a democrat; to him, the democratic character of the South African state stood as a beacon of Western civilisation. In numerous statements issued after 1960, he sketched out the future scenario of a 'normal' democracy in South Africa after the Republic had been constituted and the way had been paved for nation-building. However, the racial polarisation and separation of whites from the black majority posed a problem for the integration of whites into a common nation; and with it, the question of the survival of whites attained a new urgency. The way Verwoerd saw it, the survival of whites was possible only once fundamental discussions about apartheid per se had been laid to rest, and once radical racial segregation formed the basic consensus among whites. Of course, democracy could not emerge if discussion on apartheid policies was to be shut down, with opponents being declared illegitimate critics at best, and potential or real enemies of the state at worst. And so the National Party remained the only officially recognised party in control, because it was the only party affirming apartheid. Consequently, it became the embodiment of the white nation, and the state party. Aiming for a de facto one-party system, Verwoerd's policy was designed to de-legitimise any opposition to it, even if, for cosmetic reasons and for the sake of international prestige, the façade of a multi-party democracy was being upheld.[1] This was confirmed by Verwoerd's continued attacks on the opposition, which always went for the jugular. He denied the opposition its *raison d'être* and used every opportunity to accuse it of hatching policies that would end up in black majority rule. To the extent that the opposition was relegated outside of the basic consensus postulated by Verwoerd, it could no longer be seen to represent the interests of the white nation.

The notion that political alternatives presented a mortal threat to the white nation served to delegitimise the opposition. Thus, the concept of democracy was used in an instrumental way. Even the Republic was not necessarily associated with democracy, as Verwoerd's imprint on the 1940 draft constitution revealed. Rather than standing as fundamental principles of his policies, his professions of democracy can be understood as proclamations of South Africa's affiliation to 'Western civilisation'. At the end of the Second World War, for example, Verwoerd criticised the British for waging the war out of self-interest; in defeating

---

[1] Adam 1977: 57. See for instance the argument by G. D. Scholtz 1950: 21.

Germany, they had destroyed that power that they would now need as ally against communism.² He considered an alliance with a totalitarian dictatorship to be opportune.

If apartheid was morally justified, as Verwoerd repeatedly proclaimed, and was accepted by the majority of the population, the question arises as to how Verwoerd justified the ever-increasing repression exercised by his government.³ Although the National Party government had begun to enact anti-democratic laws shortly after coming to power, this was the responsibility of the Minister of Justice, not of the Minister for Native Affairs. Since Verwoerd had become Prime Minister in 1958, he was politically responsible for the repression. He fought opponents of segregation, but also took harsh measures against critics within his own camp, even if they questioned only individual aspects of his policies. In their case, he used means of discipline within the Party as well as the possibilities of indirect and informal influence. Both his justifications and his actions provide insights into his political thinking and his self-image as a politician. The two aspects will be dealt with one after the other. The year 1960 is central, since it coincides with British Prime Minister Macmillan's visit, Sharpeville, the first assassination attempt on the Prime Minister, the Referendum on the Republic, and the internal party dispute over the coloureds – all of which were to pose challenges to which the then still new Prime Minister had to prove himself equal.

Repression against Political Opponents

Even during his time as sociologist at the University of Stellenbosch, Verwoerd had advocated authoritarian *dirigisme* in the co-ordination of charitable activities for the "Poor Whites". He drafted an ordinance stipulating the compulsory registration of charities with the provincial administration; non-compliance was to be punishable by imprisonment with hard labour for up to three months.⁴ Coercive

---

2 *Die Transvaler*, 8.5.1945.
3 Horrell 1978: 414–418; see also Horrell 1964: 37–57. On detention without trial, see Horrell 1965: 64–73 and Horrell 1966: 46–70. See also J. J. Kruger 1961: 144: Swart would have made "constant use of these measures". PV 276/1/27/11/4/1, f. 8, Letter by Verwoerd to A. L. Geyer (London), 21.11.1950: Even upon taking office Verwoerd made it clear: "Certain negative actions will soon enough be forced upon me by circumstances. I do not seek them out, and will avoid them for as long as is possible." In 1952, ANC President A. B. Xuma, who had been voted out of office, broke his silence and challenged Verwoerd on his repressive policies (Xuma 2012: 362).
4 PV 93/1/29/2, ff. 76–84, Draft ordinance for the co-ordination of social welfare work in municipalities, districts, divisions or other local government areas within the Cape Province. In his lecture Verwoerd justified these penalties: "Members of the Council are volunteers and also have

measures suited his temperament; they stemmed from the conviction that the nation had the right to coerce individuals into their happiness. In a memorandum most likely drafted by Verwoerd himself, he also advocated coercive measures against those "Poor Whites" who supposedly did not want to work.[5] He probably did not even register the fact that his interventions entailed an encroachment on individual rights of citizens, because he saw the problem exclusively from the perspective of 'the community', and of the salvation of "the volk" in particular. In his thesis, he vented about a judge who found it "extremely burdensome" to follow the call of duty in condemning someone to death; but because it was a matter of fulfilling a duty, "he attained a strong sense of satisfaction".[6] As early as the 1930s, Verwoerd defended the police against all criticism; he routinely attributed any violence to the black population.[7] After the National Party came to power, police violence increased significantly. It was systematically enacted and exacerbated by the state, as any resistance against its policies was being criminalised.[8] The bureaucratic relentlessness with which the agricultural 'betterment schemes' were enforced in the reserves, the government's persistent refusal to engage in dialogue, and the promotion of political structures that were anything but democratic resulted in revolts in numerous Bantustans at the end of the 1950s. Some of these were spontaneous and localised; in some cases, such as Pondoland, they were organised by migrant workers and quickly spread to larger regions.[9] Wherever the uprisings occurred, they were met with the usual police brutality. In Sekhukhuneland north of Pretoria, for example, police began arresting people during a protest that the police had declared illegal. When the crowd then threatened the police officers, the latter claimed to have been forced to use armed force against the protestors. As usual, live ammunition was fired, targeting people in the crowd. Four persons were killed. Police reinforcements did not engage in de-escalation, but sought to quell the unrest by arresting over 120 more people.[10]

---

the right to publicly raise funds for their work, which is why the organisation is semi–private in this limited sense; but in practice, it is actually known as a public or a kind of state corporation"; US, 231/2/4/2, Armoede en sy bestryding, p. 66.

5 PV 93/1/29/2, ff. 1–4. Compulsory Labour Colonies. Compulsory labour for so-called "work-shy" coloureds was evidently more common practice at the time (*Die Burger*, 31.7.1935). On juvenile delinquents, see also US, 231/2/3, Socio–psigologie van misdaad, pp. 62, 68–69.

6 Verwoerd 1924a: 246–247.

7 *Die Transvaler*, 22.11.1937.

8 Local councils dominated by the UP, such as the Johannesburg City Council, also contributed to this (*Rand Daily Mail*, 27.1.1950).

9 Mbeki 1984: 117–123; see also Horrell 1961: 39–48 and Horrell 1963:12. See also I. Evans 1997: ch. 8. See Mnaba 2006: ch 3 on the multiple causes of the revolt.

10 *Pretoria News*, 19.5.1958. See also P. Delius 1996: ch 4.

Criticism of the Betterment Schemes was interpreted by the authorities as 'interference' from outside, either by the ANC or by certain individuals, and was met with intensified repression.[11] Verwoerd himself claimed that the current unrest was "a trial of strength fought out between the ANC and the socially uprooted on the one hand, and the mass of law and order-abiding natives on the other".[12] He accused "several of the churches", the Liberal Party, but especially the ANC, of boycotting Bantu Education by inciting the population with the help of the "Tsotsi-hooligan element".[13]

In 1954, he also advocated the establishment of penal camps for black urban youths, sweepingly labelled as tsotsis, in rural areas. A year earlier, Eiselen had noted that "some Bantu youths have been spoilt by idle habits in such a manner that they have become work shy and they should receive treatment in order to impress upon them the value of industry and discipline".[14] Verwoerd, for his part, took up a proposal to instruct the "work shy" in these camps in brickmaking, and to then employ them in construction projects and reintegrate them into society with these skills, as a matter of a "cheap and useful" way of "rehabilitating" them.[15] The youth camps that were passed off as educational institutions,[16] were nothing other than forced labour.[17] Thus there was nothing by way of actual rehabilitation and education in these measures; forced labour was supposed to be educational in and of itself.[18]

When Verwoerd was appointed Minister, he staunchly suppressed the resistance of the black inhabitants of Witzieshoek, which had been triggered by the authoritarian and brutal methods of the white administrators. An allegedly independent Commission of Inquiry was appointed, which was rejected by the people

---

11 PV 276/I/27/11/1/4, ff. 363–364, Inmening van Naturelle in administratiewe aangeleenthede (n.d.).
12 PV 93/1/36/1/1, Notes handwritten by Verwoerd.
13 PV 93/1/31/1/7, Statement to be published by Minister of Native Affairs (n.d.). Verwoerd set a deadline for students (and their parents) by which they had to return to class, failing which they would be permanently excluded. To numerous requests and pleas from expelled pupils, and from teachers who had lost their jobs, he answered with an iron fist without responding to their plight, as he did not want to encourage the ANC to embark on further boycotts (see also *Pretoria News*, 4.12.1954; *Cape Times*, 16.4.1955; *Rand Daily Mail*, 20.4.1955; *The Star* (editorial), 30.8.1955).
14 University of the Witwatersrand, Cullen Library, A 2628, Box 72, W. W. M. Eiselen, Urban Native Administration. A Review of the first Quarter Century and the second in being, p. 9.
15 PV 276/I/6/1/1, Memorandum by Verwoerd to Secretary of Native Affairs, 22.10.1953.
16 PV 276/I/3/1/1, 67, Draft letter (file number at bottom: VRZ/AMN), n.d.
17 PV 276/I/3/1/1, 50, Letter by Verwoerd to J. C. Dobey (Johannesburg), 23.2.1953.
18 In an editorial in *Die Transvaler*, Verwoerd fiercely attacked Alan Paton, who at the time was in Diepkloof, working to rehabilitate black juvenile delinquents (see Alexander 2009: 102).

on whom it was to pronounce its findings. Indeed, it did not fulfil its mandate to investigate the causes of the protests, advising intensified repression instead. The Commission went as far as recommending that the proposed deportation of the leaders should not proceed according to law and order, because this could have made it possible to appeal the decision; instead, the deportation was supposed to be carried out as a purely administrative measure, while dismissing court cases as 'formalities'. The Ministry followed these recommendations.[19] Verwoerd's intention was clearly not to bring the eleven 'wrongdoers' to court, but to keep them in custody without a verdict.[20]

The first repressive law of the apartheid state was the Suppression of Communism Act. Passed in 1950, it was a major break in the rule of law. 'Communists' were banned, with African nationalists simply being presumed to be affiliated to communism.[21] Thus, in 1963, Verwoerd placed the Rivonia Trial in the context of the Cold War:

> Finally, it must be emphasised once again that sabotage in South Africa is communist-inspired and supported by the world communist movement. The sense of connection with the Rivonia trialists is clearly demonstrated by the fact that here, for the first time, direct attempts were made by a number of communist countries which have never had any communication with South Africa, to persuade the South African government to release them.[22]

In its fantasies about the manipulability of supposedly 'childish' Africans, the government assumed that resistance by blacks was inspired and incited by white subversive forces.[23] These were mere assertions; evidence, of course, was lacking.

As Minister, Verwoerd systematically ensured that decisions were shifted from the elected parliament to the bureaucracy;[24] similarly the authorities were divested of any trace of democracy when real decision-making powers were vested in small executive bodies. Behind a democratic façade, an edifice of bureaucratic decision-making powers emerged, which operated by way of authori-

---

19 PV 276/I/9/4/3/1, Vierde tussentydse verslag, 16.1.1951; PV 276/I/9/4/3/2, Copies of proclamations 293 of 1950 and 32 and 33 of 1951, in which the names corresponded exactly to those in the interim reports of the Commission of Inquiry.
20 PV 276/I/9/4/3/2, f. 29, Letter by Verwoerd to Swart, 13.4.1951.
21 PV 276/I/9/11/1, Letter by Verwoerd to Swart, 8.2.1951, inquiring whether Dr O. B. Z. Bikitsha of Butterworth, who had applied for a passport, was a communist, to which Swart replied in the negative, 22.2.1951.
22 PV 93/4/1/10, ff. 97–99, Verwoerd, Press Statement, 28.7.1964.
23 PV 93/1/53/6/7, Letter by Verwoerd to Vorster, 1.11.1961. After white agitators had been quiet for some time, so Verwoerd surmised, there were signs that they were stirring again at the OFS border with Basutoland, and in the Transkei, "with the aim of instigating riots in various places within a short period of time".
24 Maisels 1999: 191.

tarian top-down control structures. Throughout his political career, Verwoerd systematically refused to engage in dialogue with those directly affected by his policies; instead, most decisions were taken internally within the bureaucracy.

Even in his previous work, both as a student representative and as a university lecturer, and even as editor-in-chief, Verwoerd had displayed a penchant for control; he was "a kind of dictator" even then, comparing his position to that of a Minister.[25] Verwoerd always thought practically; yet he did not proceed intuitively, but in a considered manner. Efficiency was of paramount importance to him in achieving his political goals as expeditiously and comprehensively as possible.[26] This included clear delegation of tasks and responsibilities; inefficiencies resulting from competing institutions were to be avoided as far as possible.

These are procedures and organisational principles that he did not develop with his appointment as Minister – he had applied them previously on numerous occasions. There were two imperatives that always stood out: efficiency and control.

To achieve both of these objectives, three measures in particular were crucial:
1. the development of knowledge in the form of a database facilitating the most thorough monitoring possible;
2. a hierarchy of organisations, with a central, powerful control unit bringing together all the information, capacitated to take all the pathbreaking decisions; and
3. the regrouping of organisations according to the criterion of efficiency, so that for any particular problem, a new control unit would be established, sufficiently assertive and powerful to fight for the envisaged goal even in the face of opposition.

While Posel pointed out the grotesque contradiction between the mania for data collection, and the preference for statistics and information on the one hand, and the state's ability to act, on the other, Breckenridge showed that the South African state had been quite innovative in its collecting frenzy by introducing the world's first biometric surveillance system along with the standardised Reference Book;

---

[25] D. Prinsloo 1979: 46, 51.
[26] This was also evident, for example, in his proposals to make the Bondsraad meetings more efficient by limiting the issues to be discussed to one topic, and reducing the Chairman's speech to a short welcome address. (AB Archive 2/3/13, UR-Dagbestuur, 23.5.1947, p. 2, TOP 6, Agenda vir Bondsraad 1947).

yet it failed miserably due to the limited reach of the state.[27] In his book entitled *The Biometric State*, he radicalised the argument by identifying South Africa as a field of experimentation with biometric data collection, whose successfully tried methods were subsequently exported.[28] The claim of complete surveillance, however, was not due only to a centralised police service and to the demands of the mining industry. Contributing to all-round surveillance were also pressures exerted by individuals, especially by Verwoerd, with his mania for control. Even the Institute for Social Research, which Verwoerd had wanted to found in Cape Town as early as the beginning of the 1930s, had similar ambitions, albeit more modest in scope. The Institute was to compile a database on all "Poor Whites" in the greater Cape Town area, differentiated according to the particular social problems with which individual families and individuals were confronted. Such a database was to underpin the work of charitable organisations, with social workers acting as co-ordinators, so as to achieve the greatest possible efficiency.[29] Even earlier, in his position as Chairman of the Student Council in Stellenbosch, Verwoerd had launched a number of new initiatives, each linked up with their own committees and commissions; over and above those initiatives, he had created a powerful central steering unit, namely the Student Council or rather, its Executive Committee.

Piet Cillié aptly described Verwoerd's thinking on the topic of 'order': "Dr. Verwoerd's orientation was predominantly intellectual: orderly thinking, clear doctrines, fixed images of the future. What is responsible and correct in terms of principles must also be executable. Obstacles presented by human nature must make room for order and systematicity. The ideal must be imposed on the community."[30] This is contradicted by the assertion of Lazar, Posel and, from a somewhat different perspective, Giliomee – that Verwoerd was above all a pragmatist.[31]

The pattern was repeated when Verwoerd became Prime Minister. He was vested with central decision-making authority; to exercise this authority, he established new institutions that were to achieve the greatest possible efficiency, and at the same time increase the power of the centre, in this case the Office of

---

27 Breckenridge (2005: 101) posits a connection between the failure of the system and the use of police violence that is, in my opinion, too clear–cut, as the NP regime has always shown a pronounced penchant for violence.
28 See for instance Breckenridge 2014: 88. However, I am not convinced by his idea that this indicates a distinct and new type of state, since in his analysis biometric surveillance is ultimately no more than an instrument, albeit an innovative one.
29 PV 93/1/19/1, Cape Town Charity Commission. Summary of Evidence, Prof. Verwoerd, 3.6.1932, pp. 56–58, esp. p. 55.
30 Cillié 1980: 25.
31 Lazar 1987: 70.

the Prime Minister. These included, for example, the Economic Advisory Council, which was deemed necessary for the establishment of a planning state, and which at the same time allowed Verwoerd to take decisions bypassing the ministries that were actually responsible.

Verwoerd's authoritarian method did not go unchallenged. When he asked for advice on the establishment of the Economic Advisory Council, E. I. Rowland, possibly unaware of the origins of such practices on the part of the addressee of his letter, criticised the way in which the state solicited such advice: The 'consultation [oorlegpleging]' as it is practised by the state, usually means that an institution of the state notifies an organisation of its intentions, demanding "full co-operation or rather, unconditional obedience in carrying out the new regulations". His own view of this process was different: the state institution should "discuss its ideas with the organisations early on, assessing the importance of the proposals submitted, and considering the necessary steps". He resisted the top-down approach practised by Verwoerd in particular, which immunised ministries against all new ideas; instead, he advocated a more cooperative form of consultation.[32]

With the new passport system introduced in 1952, there were three ways of identifying an African: "namely, his identification number, his passport photograph and his fingerprints",[33] the latter being deposited in state offices.[34] Keeping the information gathered on individuals secret from them, the state built a comprehensive knowledge of domination designed to ensure management of the labour market and control over the spatial movements of people.[35] The pass laws were intended to support the implementation of the Masters and Servants Acts: the employer had to certify a dismissal, so that black people unable to show this certification in their passes were immediately suspected of having left their jobs

---

32 1/53/3/1, f. 2, Letter by E. I. Rowland to Premier, 1.10.1958.
33 PV 93/1/24/8, Letter by Verwoerd to L. L. S. J. Kruger, Potgietersrus, 1.3.1955, p. 1.
34 NA, NTS 9792/ 1027/400, Report of an Inter-Departmental Committee to Review the Pass Laws, 22.1.1952. This Committee presented proposals on the reform of the pass laws, which then led to the Abolition of Passes and Coordination of Documents Act. Since this is a transcript, the names of the Commission members are not provided. Duplicates of passports, and fingerprints of all ten fingers were to be collected in a central file under the Native Affairs Department. Directly linked to the surveillance system was the collection of taxes, which was to be implemented end-to-end, without any logjams. Verwoerd was able to confirm that this had been successfully accomplished in 1957 (PV 276/I/5/1, Letter by Verwoerd to W. F. Bezuidenhout, 10.6.1957, in which he established the link between the pass system and the collection of outstanding tax debts). In the 1956/57 financial year, the black population paid taxes of about £3 million (PV276/I/27/11/3/1, Bylae A, Inkomste van Naturelle).
35 PV 276/I/25/1/1, f. 23, Letter by Verwoerd to W. G. van der Merwe (Louis Trichardt), 12.5.1955; see also Breckenridge 2005.

'unlawfully'. "In other words, if the native deserts, he is an offender and if another employer hires a native whose passport is not signed off, he is also guilty of an offence."[36] Thus was forbidden what was not expressly permitted – which is the hallmark of an authoritarian, if not totalitarian, state.

At every possible opportunity, Verwoerd denied that the ANC spoke for the African people. Instead, he claimed, "[t]hey act on behalf of a very small portion of the Native people and reflect the opinion of a very small portion. The large portion of Native opinion is still inarticulate and also not in a position to judge". The 'natural leaders', that is, the chiefs, in contrast, supported his government's apartheid policy.[37] If they did not, they were summarily disempowered, as happened to Zulu chief Albert Luthuli, who was also President of the ANC.[38] It is fairly certain that Verwoerd's assessment of black resistance was influenced by French theorist Gustave le Bon's cultural-pessimistic book on mass psychology entitled (in English translation) *The Crowd. A Study of the Popular Mind* (1895).[39] On the basis of social-psychological assumptions, Le Bon believed that human collectives were fundamentally irrational; without guidance from elites, they would degenerate into an emotionally driven mass.[40] Verwoerd was convinced that he was dealing with people stuck in the stage of development that early anthropology had termed 'barbaric'; with this idea in mind, he found in their history numerous examples indicating that the irrationality of the masses and despotism were two sides of the same coin. The only remedy for this state, he thought, was the stabilising element of 'natural authority' vested in the chiefs, coupled with archaic punishments. South Africa was one of the few countries in which the number of offences sanctioned by corporal punishment increased during the 20th century. In other words, it ran counter to a worldwide trend towards the humanisation of the penal system.[41]

The nationalist press used violent incidents such as those at the end of the 1952 Defiance Campaign to discredit the whole movement and the white 'liberalist' forces advocating dialogue and political *détente*.[42] The Congress of the People of 1955, and the Freedom Charter adopted on this occasion, constituted treason in

---

36 PV 93/1/24/8, Letter by Verwoerd to L. L. S. J. Kruger (Potgietersrus), 1.3.1955, p. 1.
37 FAV, 4.7.1.2, interview by George Pipal (United Press) with Verwoerd, 6.12.1958, p. 10.
38 Luthuli 1965: 109–112; see also Pillay 1993: 47–50.
39 See also the Verwoerd quote in Kenney 1980: 187.
40 Le Bon [1895] 2002: 7–8. Le Bon repeatedly drew comparisons with groups that he deemed primitive, viz. "savages", women, and children (pp.10); in the age of the crowd he saw a relapse into a primitive state (p. 27); moreover, he claimed that "race" "dominates all human feeling and thinking" (pp. 25, 45, 102, 122).
41 Marx 2000: 271–272; see also Hoernlé 1948:15–16.
42 E.g. *Dagbreek en Sondagnuus*, 26.10.1952 (commentary).

the eyes of the government. It was followed by extensive arrests one year later; charges were brought against the entire leadership of the extra-parliamentary opposition. However, the court case prepared by the state, and the prosecution, were so unprofessional that after a five-year trial period, all the accused were acquitted. However, such setbacks did not mitigate the government's repressive stance. During Verwoerd's term of office as Prime Minister, draconian laws were passed that allowed the police to arrest people without a warrant, and detain them for up to three months – with the possibility of immediate re-arrest upon release.[43]

Verwoerd even justified the Sharpeville massacre as an appropriate response:

> The unfortunate events of recent times in the Union were represented by liberalists and leftists, and by a large section of the press, as if a small number of white police officers acting in self-defence, had reacted irresponsibly and unnecessarily severely. The real situation, however, was that the small number of law enforcers was outnumbered by more than 100 to 1; they had to shoot at the terrorist mass [!] in self-defence. Despite the unjustified and wanton campaigning on the part of left-wingers, the government is determined to continue to fight for the survival of Western civilisation and for the preservation of the white man.[44]

For Verwoerd, repressive means were fundamentally necessary, even if their use should be restrictive, but the state had to have them in its arsenal.[45]

Violent repression reached a new dimension when Minister of Justice John Vorster took office on 3 August 1961. The control that Verwoerd exercised over the entire policy domain was tighter than that implemented by his predecessors and successors; and sometimes he interfered with the mandates of ministers. Yet he gave Vorster an astonishingly free hand and largely kept out of his political domain. It is not unlikely that the two of them practiced a division of labour along the lines of a 'good cop – bad cop' pattern, whereby the Prime Minister presented the friendly face of the regime who, with an endearing smile,[46] proclaimed apartheid as a benevolent policy and a way to peaceful co-existence, while Vorster played the tough law-and-order man.[47] This calculation worked, as the mis-

---

43 J. P. J. Coetzer (2000: ch. 14) still considered these measures justified in 2000.
44 PV 93/1/36/1/2, f. 119, Letter by Verwoerd to A. C. Matingen (Rothenburg o.d.T.), 8.4.1960, in German original.
45 Verwoerd, Institute of Administrators of Non–European Affairs, held at Bloemfontein, 17.9.1956 (in Pelzer 1966: 124–148, 147).
46 After having taken office as Prime Minister, official photographs always presented Verwoerd as a friendly man with a magnanimous smile.
47 A. Delius (1970: 372) wrote of a division of labour in which Vorster took charge of repression of political opponents, while Verwoerd saw to discipline within the Party. Danziger (1993: 179) and Stultz (1969: 3) noted a tightening of centralism and repression, and a more pronounced anti-communism (see also Stultz 1969: 8; and Benson 1966: ch. 16).

judgement of German journalist Christoph von Imhoff shows. After Verwoerd's death, he expressed concern about Vorster because of his OB past and his harshly repressive policies. He said that "of all the evils, Verwoerd had always been the lesser one".[48] In contrast to Vorster, he said, Verwoerd was "not a vicious man"; he saw in him an "uninhibited idealist".[49] While he cast Vorster as "a new type", that is, as repressive and racist, he saw Verwoerd in line with his predecessors, as "invariably worthy patriarchs in their own way, convinced and often also convincing politicians in the old Boer style",[50] whatever that was supposed to mean. Unlike Verwoerd, however, Vorster was more accessible to opposition figures such as Helen Suzman,[51] who, despite all differences, was able to establish a good personal relationship with him, whereas she considered Verwoerd completely incorrigible and fanatic.[52]

In fact, Verwoerd always defended his Minister's approach, including the bannings under the Suppression of Communism Act, the tightening of the law that allowed for detention without a court order for 90 days – which was an invitation to torture and abuse of power by the security police.[53] Even back in the days of his term of office as Minister, he insisted on being notified of every detail regarding banning orders, and individual persons concerned. This indicates that he approved of such measures, if he hadn't initiated them in the first place.[54] He had the nerve to maintain that his government, unlike that of Ghana, rejected 'de-

---

48 Institut für Zeitgeschichte, Munich, ED 339, vol. 43, Letter by Imhoff to Ruth Weiss, 17.10.1966. Imhoff worked for various German newspapers as well as radio; he was quite critical of developments in South Africa.
49 Ibid., vol. 44, Broadcast manuscript Deutschlandfunk (DLF), 2.7.1976.
50 Ibid., Broadcast manuscript DLF, 13.9.1966. He emphasised this contrast between hard-line Vorster and more patriarchally inclined Verwoerd in a series of broadcasts shortly after Verwoerd's assassination (ibid., Broadcast manuscripts DLF of 9.9. and 15.9.1966). See also the broadcast on the day of the assassination, 6.9.1966: "The white–haired, calm and composed gentleman was the prototype of those Boers who had lived with the Bantus [sic], as black Africans are called in South Africa, in good patriarchal relationships for generations."
51 Helen Suzman approached Vorster directly when she was planning to visit political prisoners, such as Nelson Mandela or Robert Sobukwe (see PV 132/2/5/1/7, Letter by Suzman to Vorster, 2.8.1966; see also D'Oliveira 1977: 229–230).
52 Suzman 1994: 65.
53 PV 93/1/30/1/25, f. 69, Letter by Verwoerd to Dr Jack Penn (Johannesburg), 4.5.1964; see also PV 93/1/30/1/24, f. 262, Letter by Verwoerd to F. M. Purcell (Hermanus), 31.3.1964; and Foster 1987: 21–29.
54 FAV 4.6.2.2, Various memoranda of Verwoerd's from the ministry, mid-1950s. See also the threat of banning orders publicised in a press release [1956] (FAV 4.6.2.3). Of course, this was passed off as if "representatives of the order–loving Bantu" had urged a reluctant Minister to assert his powers.

tention without trial', and that measures such as the imposition of house arrest were directed only against communists, not against the opposition in general.[55] Shortly after Verwoerd's assumption of office as Prime Minister, the government decided to build a maximum security prison on Robben Island, which was a clear indication that the subsequent repression had long been planned.[56]

Dealing with the Press

With Strijdom assuming the highest office in government, the balance of power within the Party and Government soon shifted towards the Transvaal, whose politicians, primarily Strijdom and Verwoerd, demanded unconditional support from the NP press in the Cape Province. It sheds a telling light on Verwoerd's understanding of journalism when even the cautious distance that *Die Burger* kept from the government went too far for him – to such an extent that he suspected treason. Quite contrary to custom, he used the occasion of a caucus-meeting in 1957 to criticise the press in the south: "In recent years, Nasionale Pers grew distant from the National Party, it does not support the MPs as in the past." Paul Sauer was "shocked" at the allegations, but Verwoerd received support from other MPs and from Strijdom himself.[57]

When Verwoerd assumed office as Prime Minister, the Executive Director of Nasionale Pers, Phil Weber, congratulated him and took the opportunity to urge him to show more tolerance toward the press: "As an old journalist, you would know that newspapers that just parrot don't gain influence in broader circles."[58] Verwoerd replied in a conciliatory manner, but emphasised: "But I hope that if you wanted to write differently from the way the Party seems to think, you will first take the opportunity I offered to inform yourselves about the reasons for our position. It is always regrettable when differences of opinion are based on misunderstandings."[59] Since he believed that his political concepts were based on truth, differences of opinion could only be caused by a lack of understanding. His commitment to toleration of dissenting opinions was mere pretence, for the internal

---

55 PV 93/1/30/1/17, f.180, Verwoerd to W. A. Dugmore (Grahamstown), 1.12.1962.
56 Bassman 1978: 26.
57 SU, 296.D.5, typed note, Koukusvergadering, 9.4.1957. After the meeting, Louw reportedly expressed his view that the shareholders should be approached directly.
58 SU, 296.KV.32, Draft letter by Weber to Verwoerd, 14.9.1958. The numerous deletions and corrections indicate the efforts undertaken by Weber to formulate his criticism in such a way that Verwoerd would actually take cognisance of it.
59 Ibid., Letter by Verwoerd to P. A. Weber, 14.10.1958.

critics had to be proved wrong, or else be taught better, or they were cast out as unteachable.

Under pressure from the Prime Minister, most newspapers underwent self-censorship from 1962 onwards. Nasionale Pers representatives actively helped to convince their English-speaking colleagues of the benefits of the measure.[60] Two years later, however, Verwoerd judged the practice of anticipatory self-censorship as a failure, since no progress had been made "towards our goal of orderliness in the midst of hostility from the press".[61] He therefore contemplated direct censorship measures; during his term in office, the state administration engaged in systematic shadowing and surveillance of foreign media representatives.[62] One of them aptly characterised Verwoerd, saying "Verwoerd had no tolerance for dissent, no tolerance even for tolerance".[63] Assent within his own camp to conformism, and to the suppression of dissenting opinions, was based on the idea that it would be impossible to convince foreign countries of the sincerity of one's own policies if internal dissent prevailed.[64]

Refusal to Engage in Dialogue

Verwoerd consistently refused to engage in dialogue with any organisations he considered illegitimate, i.e. opponents of the segregationist policy. This becomes clear from the frequent handwritten instructions noting "no reply" on the letters.[65] Which form of criticism was acceptable was decided by him alone: "No one has anything against criticism and advice, especially when it comes from within

---

60 Ibid., Letter by P. A. Weber to Verwoerd, 14.3.1962. See also Horrell 1964: 66f.
61 SU 296.KV.32, Letter by Verwoerd to Weber, 14.8.1964.
62 PV 93/1/53/2/3, Buitenlandse persverteenwoordigers en rolprentfotograwe in die Unie, secret, dated 20.10.1959. The document lists the movements of individual reporters down to the minute and reports on meetings apparently intercepted; in the case of the reporters of the German magazine "Der Stern" (p. 3) it was pointed out that they had received their photos from Jürgen Schadeberg. See also B. M. Schoeman 1973: 218–223.
63 Lelyveld 1989: 14. For an overview of the 1960s, see Merrett 1995: ch. 4.
64 Gerdener 1952: 6–7.
65 See the collection of protest telegrams from all over the world, but also from the Congress organisations in South Africa, after Sharpeville, in PV 93/1/36/1/3–5 and PV 93/3/2/2–3. The international press reported extensively on Sharpeville, with devastating consequence for the government's reputation (*Daily Mirror* and *Daily Express*, 22.3.1960). In the Verwoerd papers, there is a substantial collection of unanswered letters including letters from clearly mentally disturbed and malcontents, but also a number of protest letters and telegrams from all over the world, challenging the violent police response in Sharpeville, and the introduction of the pass laws for black women (PV 93/3/2).

one's own ranks, because no one's thoughts are infallible. But it is a different matter when one is asked to effectively adopt the political direction of the enemy, even if this is not called surrender at first."[66] In the 1930s and 40s, in his capacities as a professor and journalist, as well as AB functionary, Verwoerd had claimed the right to formulate political goals and to criticise political agendas; yet once political agenda-setting had become his own prerogative, he refused to grant this right to those disagreeing with him. This throws a telling light on the way in which he understood his own role as Prime Minister.

In 1963, the Vice-Chancellor of Rhodes University in Grahamstown wrote to him, complaining that Albert Hertzog had insulted English-speaking universities; the latter had insinuated a link between these universities and some of their graduates who had joined left-wing groups. Verwoerd dismissed this complaint, and refused to distance himself from Hertzog's statements.[67] When his old adversary E. G. Malherbe, at the time Rector of the University of Natal, publicly criticised his policy, he saw it as "undermining the authority of the state", and called on Minister Maree, NP leader in Natal, to take action against Malherbe:

> The least we could do is to impeach the Rector before his University Council. That may not make much difference, but it will cause him some inconvenience. The most hard-hitting measure would be to freeze the state subsidies to the University, or some of them, until the Council and the Rector change their attitude. But this could cause legal and other difficulties. Therefore, I think, careful consideration should be given to all possible ways of stopping the outrageous behaviour of E. G. Malherbe.[68]

In general, he was quick to dismiss critics as "theorists"; he regarded "theoretical humanitarians" or "theoretical liberals" as unworldly and politically disaffected visionaries pursuing abstract ideas.[69] Thus he said of the Progressive Party: "This kind of liberalist you find among the rich. They can theorise and hold talks with whomever they like – but they themselves do not live in mixed neighourhoods."[70] This was no less true of Verwoerd himself: his alleged experience of living in a 'mixed' neighbourhood could only be based on fantasies. Liberal politician Edgar

---

66 PV 93/1/24/12, 11, Letter by Verwoerd to P. C. Jooste (Parow East), 22.5.1961.
67 PV 451/1/28/1/1, Letter by Verwoerd to Minister of Posts and Telegraphs, with attached correspondence with J. M. Hyslop, Vice–Chancellor of Rhodes University, 2.12.1963.
68 FAV, 4.7.2.1, Letter by Verwoerd to W. A. Maree, 1.3.1961. Maree, like Verwoerd, had attended school in Brandfort.
69 Both terms in PV 93/1/36/1/9, undated press statement after Sharpeville.
70 FAV, 4.7.2.4.2, Notes for a speech in the debate on opposition censure motion 20.1.1960, p. 5.

Brookes was right to turn the accusation of being an unworldly idealist back onto the National Party politicians themselves.[71]

In relation to those parties and organisations that were not openly in favour of societal integration or even black majority rule, Verwoerd formally adhered to democratic rules of the game. He 'only' accused the women's organisation Black Sash, which defended civil rights, of undue interference in politics, and largely steered clear of the silently protesting ladies in public.[72] However, he was always quick to sense communist activity, using insinuations and threats. This was particularly evident in his dealings with the South African Institute of Race Relations, which was a politically conservative and anything but revolutionary organisation. It did not have a clear political line; when Verwoerd became Minister, the Institute offered him its cooperation.[73] Soon things turned sour when the Institute wanted to send a 'mixed' delegation to the Minister; Verwoerd was prepared to receive the envoys only in racially segregated delegations.[74] A few years later, Verwoerd's attitude hardened, turning into vehement rejection. Some of the letters replying to the Institute were rude in tone, indicating a general refusal to engage in dialogue. In response to a letter in which the Institute sent him the results of the last Council meeting,[75] Verwoerd had his private secretary reply: "You will no doubt realise that the Minister has usually found your organisation's findings to be propagandistic and prejudiced, and therefore not worthy of consideration."[76]

The hostility continued into the years during which Verwoerd was head of government. In 1962, he issued a circular to his ministers ahead of an Institute conference on 'Human Relations and Communication Today' announced for January 1963. He expressly forbade all government staff to attend, alleging that it was a propaganda event organised by "intellectuals" against government policy.[77] When a

---

71 Brookes 1950: 11. At the height of the controversy over University apartheid, J. J. Serfontein, the then Minister of Education, apparently under pressure from Verwoerd (McKay 2015: 122), also refused to accept a letter from student representatives (ibid., 106).
72 PV 93/3/1/25, pp.82–114, Black Sash and Verwoerd, correspondence of September 1959, 28.9.1959; also p. 15. On attempts to move more ruthlessly against the Black Sash, see D'Oliveira 1977: 150; and on their implementation, see E. Benjamin 2004: 50.
73 PV 276/I/14/6/1, ff. 1–2, Letter by van Wyk to Verwoerd, 4.11.1950; Verwoerd's reply, 8.11.1950. In his reply, Verwoerd declared his willingness, in principle, to meet. Verwoerd was even a member of the Institute in the 1930s (Brits 1994: 76).
74 PV 276/I/14/6/1, f. 21, Letter by Verwoerd to Whyte (SAIRR), 4.2.1951.
75 PV 276/I/14/6/3, f. 6, Letter by SAIRR to Verwoerd, 1.2.1956.
76 PV 276/I/14/6/3, p. 7, Letter by Verwoerd to SAIRR, 7.2.1956.
77 PV 93/4/1/7, Confidential circular of the Prime Minister's Secretary to "all Heads of Departments, Provincial Secretaries and Private Secretaries", 27.9.1962, with attached press statement by the Prime Minister, 30.4.1962.

group of concerned citizens of Port Elizabeth objected to the 1962 General Law Amendment Bill, he replied curtly, "[y]ou are wrong in every respect",[78] without taking the trouble to justify this verdict.

He did not dignify the Liberal Party with a response when they objected to the imposition of the state of emergency after the Sharpeville massacre.[79] International protests against bannings or prison sentences were always dismissed by reference to the internal affairs of a sovereign state.[80] This was particularly true of protests following the Rivonia trial.[81] In the case of inquiries by private individuals from abroad, he took the opportunity to go on the propaganda offensive: the South African government was showing the same sense of proportion as the British government towards the Irish; there was no threat of revolution in South Africa; and the black "hordes" would be given a future in their own areas, "even politically".[82]

Conflicts with the English Churches

Verwoerd's conflicts with the English churches were the result of his nationalistic rejection and his general distrust of the British. Various prominent dignitaries of the Anglican Church were critical of apartheid, such as the English canon Collins, who travelled the country and sharply denounced apartheid on several occasions.[83] But no one took as decisive a stand as Archbishop (1957–63) Joost de Blank.[84] Other English churches, such as the Methodists, also made no secret of

---

78 PV 93/1/30/1/16, Citizens of Port Elizabeth, Telegram to Verwoerd, and his comment on it, n.d. (1962).
79 PV 93/3/1/33, f. 47, Letter by Liberal Party to Verwoerd, with resolution, 4.8.1960.
80 PV 93/3/1/25, f. 172, Letter by Fédération internationale des droits de l'Homme to Verwoerd, 13.10.1959, and reply, 7.11.1959; see also PV 93/3/1/26, f. 13, Letter by International Press Institute to Verwoerd, 24.10.1959.
81 FAV 4.7.1.5, Verbatim Verslag van die Eerste Minister se verklaring in die Volksraad op 16 Junie 1964 i/s wêreldwye reaksie op uitspraak in Rivonia-saak. Verwoerd saw the protests as a movement controlled by world communism which was directed against the West in general, but had chosen South Africa as a target. As evidence, he cited the protest telegrams and letters sent from communist states for the first time.
82 PV 93/1/30/1/19, f. 91, Letter by Verwoerd to R. O. Hellyer (GB), 3.6.1963.
83 The nationalist press really pounced on him, e.g. *Die Burger* 20.7.1954, but also an UP MP like Piet van der Bijl (*Rand Daily Mail*, 16.7.1954). On the criticism pronounced by churches in Britain, see generally Skinner 2005.
84 *Cape Argus*, 25.1.1958; see also Paine 1978: ch. 4. On the Anglican Church during Verwoerd's reign, see also Elstadt 1988: 36–43.

their opposition to apartheid,[85] while the Baptists supported it.[86] Verwoerd took the same attitude towards critical church representatives as he did towards non-governmental organisations such as the SAIRR or the Black Sash: he dismissed them.[87] When the Anglican Church in Cape Town requested a meeting to discuss the Group Areas Act and its consequences for the people concerned, for instance, he had a brusque response: "The spirit in which the request is made would make such an interview utterly futile."[88] When the government expelled Bishop Ambrose Reeves of the Anglican Church in 1960, and representatives of the Church protested, Verwoerd replied with remarkable sophistry: "Naturally the Government regards your statement as wholly beside the point since action had to be taken against an individual. It is looked upon as mere propaganda to publicise this as an affront to the Church of the Province of South Africa which as such is surely in no way associated with politics or any activities against which the State must protect its people."[89] One of the most senior representatives of the Church became a mere 'individual' whose deportation was supposed to be none of the Church's business.

In the context of nation-building after the establishment of the Republic, the English churches were given a new status: they were to be committed to apartheid policies as the basis of the state. With regard to the churches, the Prime Minister emphasised that English-speaking whites were learning the value of steadfastness because it was the basis of their own security.[90] In claiming that racial segregation had always been practised in the churches, Verwoerd was distorting history. It was only later, he claimed, that some English churches had introduced mixed congregations for political reasons.[91]

---

85 For example, the President of the South African Methodist Conference, Rev. S. B. Sudbury (*The Star* 10.10.1955). Catholic Bishop Denis Hurley of Durban also expressed criticism (Hurley 1964).
86 FAV, 4.6.1.1, Letter by F. W. Schwarz (Wepener), who was trained in theology in the Southern states of the US, to Verwoerd, 18.3. and 29.3., as well as 6.4.1957, clearly expressed the theological criticism of the churches opposing apartheid.
87 As early as 1948, he had given a dressing–down to a delegation of church representatives who wanted to keep segregation out of the election campaign, telling them that they should not interfere in matters of which they did not have sufficient knowledge (D. Prinsloo 1979: 338).
88 PV 93/1/34/3, f. 159, Anglican Church, Diocese of Cape Town, 22.2.1960.
89 PV 93/3/1/20, f. 61, Letter by Verwoerd to Dean and Rector, St Mary's Cathedral (Johannesburg), 26.10.60.
90 PV 93/1/30/1/29, f. 36, Letter by Verwoerd to Mrs C. J. Hamel (Mt. Ayliff, Pondoland), 11.12.1964.
91 PV 93/1/30/1/28, f. 23, Letter by Verwoerd to J. Valentyn (Glencoe, Natal), 20.8.1964; similarly PV 93/1/30/1/17, f. 162, Letter by Verwoerd to Dierk Böger (Vryheid), 6.2.1963.

Verwoerd was also not choosy in dealing with critics from within his own camp – he turned against them with all available means. This was the experience that the South African Bureau of Racial Affairs, the churches, and the newspaper *Die Burger* could attest to. In 1960, the dispute over the policies enacted by the Prime Minister on the coloured section of the population escalated, involving all three of the institutions mentioned above; all three of them were subsequently brought into line by Verwoerd.

Since the mid-1930s, Afrikaner intellectuals, church leaders and missionaries had been concerned with the 'race problem'. An initiative to institutionalise and bring together all interested parties was launched in the 1940s; it was explicitly directed "against the existing Institute of Racial [sic] Relations". Its aim was "to maintain the dividing line between white and non-white in South Africa in the ecclesiastical, social and economic fields".[92] A *Volkskongres* on the subject was held in 1944,[93] but it was not until 1948 that the Broederbond founded the South African Bureau of Racial Affairs (SABRA), in which the Reformed churches, as well as "individual lecturers" from the University of Stellenbosch were involved.[94] Addressing the Board of the AB, Verwoerd advocated the establishment of a committee of "only three most competent members". "Many are thinking of some kind of Afrikaans Institute of Race Relations, but [Verwoerd] is afraid that the creation of such an Institute would mean the establishment of a purposeless organisation."[95] He did not give up this position even at a later stage. Diederichs disagreed with Verwoerd, advocating a comprehensive committee of several hundred members, yet with a decentralised structure, not least because it would have more authority, also vis-à-vis the government.[96] The Uitvoerende Raad (UR) decided to discuss the issue in the Bondsraad,[97] which it did. The Chairman of the Broederbond, J. C. van Rooy, justified the decision of the Bondsraad to focus on "native policy" "in order to gain greater clarity as to the form, nature and

---

92 PV 202/1/1/3/1, Verslag van Samespreking van Verteenwoordigers van F.A.K., die Instituut vir Volkswelstand en the Afrikanerbond vir Rassestudie, 30.4.1940, p. 2 (G. Cronjé on SAIRR and I. Lombard on the Jewish question) and Appendix (second quote). However, the management of the Commission for Race Relations, which emerged from this meeting, decided one year later that the Bond should remain in place until the planned institute had been founded (PV 202/1/1/3/1, Dagbestuur der Kommissie vir Rasseverhoudinge, 7.6.1941).
93 PV 202/1/4/3/2/1, FAK. Minutes of the People's Congress on the 'Rassebeleid van die Afrikaner', 29. and 30.9.1944.
94 Stals 1998: 208–212. On the role of academics at the University of Stellenbosch, see also Broodryk 1991: 204–212; links between SABRA and the Reformed churches were and remained close (Redaksie 1950).
95 AB Archives, 2/3/14, UR–Dagbestuur, 29. 8. 1947, p. 1, TOP 5, Komitee i.s. Kleurvraagstuk.
96 Ibid, pp. 1–2, TOP 5, Komitee i.s. Kleurvraagstuk.
97 Ibid., UR Assembly, 30.8.1947, p. 3, TOP 14, Komitee i.s. Kleurvraagstuk.

consequences of our apartheid policy, and to examine the Afrikaner's attitude towards it".[98]

The Bondsraad appointed a committee to make contact with Prof. B. I. C. van Eeden[99] and other ethnological 'experts' from Stellenbosch University. Shortly afterwards it became foreseeable that Diederichs's idea of a large institute would prevail. At its foundation on 31 January 1948, SABRA, which was also tasked with carrying out propaganda work, was unequivocally identified with apartheid policy.[100] At the next Bondsraad in November 1948, Prof. H. B. Thom, a historian from Stellenbosch University, introduced the newly founded SABRA. It was a research and policy institute, which was to be "an extension, an instrument of the Bondsraad of 1947". It was to be "the visible arm of the A.B. in racial matters"; its task was to "scientifically justify the principle of apartheid", and promote it among all sections of the population, as well as abroad.[101] The Executive Committee of the Broederbond chimed in with the demand for a new composition of the Native Affairs Commission,[102] which indicates SABRA's inclination to leave the conceptualisation of apartheid to scientific experts in future.[103]

Verwoerd shared this initial goodwill and set an example when he presented the opening address at SABRA's annual congress in 1950, shortly after his appointment as Minister.[104] He also regularly received SABRA delegations for talks, and

---

98 Ibid, Bondsraad, 1.-3.10.1947, CT., p.4, TOP 15, Die verhouding van die blankes tot die nieblankes. The issues raised are recorded in the minutes only in key words, but the discussion is summarised.

99 Van Eeden, for his part, was a student of Carl Meinhof's, see Pugach 2012: 1, 177.

100 PV 94/1/66/1/1, f. 18, Minutes of the founding meeting on 31.1.1948 in Cape Town, chaired by AB chairman J. C. van Rooy; PV 94/1/66/1/1, SABRA, f. 6, Letter by B. I. C. van Eeden to Jansen, 2.4.1948; and PV 94/1/66/1/2, Letter by SABRA (van Schalkwyk) to Jansen, 19.10.48: Announcement of the formal establishment of SABRA on 23.9.

101 AB Archive, 2/3/15, Bondsraad, 10.-12.11.1948 in Bloemfontein, p. 1, TOP 5: Die S.A. Buro vir Rasse-Aangeleenthede (SABRA). See also AB Archive, Sekretariele Verslag van die U.R. oor die tydperk Julie 1946 – Junie 1948, p. 8, in which the UR credits itself with bringing together the various initiatives of churches, academics and the AB itself in SABRA, thus avoiding frictional losses.

102 AB Archive, 2/3/18, UR meeting, 6.–8.2.1950, pp. 4–5, TOP 26, Apartheid; it is not clear from the context whether it was the AB's own commission or the state commission.

103 Ibid, p. 6, TOP 20, Die Kleurvraagstuk en SABRA. In February 1950, the FAK as an organisation became a member of SABRA (PV 202/1/2/3/2/4, p. 72–74, UK meeting, 9.2.1950, Item 11: SABRA). One year later, Thom urged the FAK to support SABRA; he pushed for a circular letter to be sent out, encouraging Afrikaners to become members (PV 202/1/2/3/2/4, f. 127, UK meeting on 22.2.1951, Item 26: SABRA).

104 PV 276/I/14/5/1, f. 1, Letter by SABRA (F. S. Language, Chairman of the Tvl. Org. Committee) to Verwoerd, 8.11.50 and the latter's reply, 11.11.50). Ibid., f. 9, Letter by SABRA to Verwoerd, 24.1.51, Secretary P. J. N. Myburgh thanked Verwoerd again for his speech. Ibid., f. 11, Letter by SABRA to Verwoerd, 1.2.51, thanking Verwoerd for referring to SABRA in his parliamentary speech; and the organisation sent him its publications and resolutions.[105] As late as 1953, SABRA was still operating in the hermetic world of apartheid policy, which considered all protest to be illegitimate, and dialogue with the rest of the population as futile (allegedly because of their childlike level of development). The fourth Annual General Meeting condemned the Defiance Campaign in the strongest of terms, denying it any legitimacy and criminalising it.[106] With a strong influence wielded by professors from Stellenbosch University, SABRA supported the government's stance, especially that of Eiselen, to stop the immigration of blacks to the Western Cape.[107] In this context, however, there was, for the first time, more concrete talk of "first-hand knowledge of each other's positions" – knowledge that could be gained only through "joint discussions", that is, dialogue with other sections of the population.[108]

While the AB Board took a positive view on the meetings of SABRA representatives with "Bantu" and coloured delegations,[109] Verwoerd had a completely different opinion. His relationship with SABRA had deteriorated over the years. He perceived it as a platform for the self-empowerment of experts, which was becoming threatening to him; in his view, the monopoly of decision-making would have to lie exclusively with politics.

Leading academics in SABRA were by no means opponents of apartheid; they even considered this set of policies justified on moral grounds if it was aimed at

---

f. 34, Letter by Myburgh to Verwoerd, 25.9.51, thanking Verwoerd for allowing them to print his speech in their journal. See also PV 93/1/13/1/1, Telegram by SABRA to Verwoerd, 1950, f. 20; and PV 93/3/1/7, Letter by H. J. van Eeden to Verwoerd, 12.12.1950.

105 See the correspondence of these early years in PV 276/I/14/5/1. Lazar (1987:169) stresses that Verwoerd translated these SABRA studies into practical policy. For agreement on key points, see Verwoerd 1951b: 3.

106 PV 276/I/14/5/1, f. 76, Resolusies geneem op die vierde Jaarvergadering van SABRA, Resolutions 1–4.

107 PV 276/I/14/5/2, f. 2, Letter by SABRA (N. J. J. Olivier) to Verwoerd, 24.1.1955, with a request for an interview, to which Verwoerd replied immediately, namely on 27.1. (f. 3) with a proposed date. Eiselen (1955b: 6) emphasised community-building among the coloureds, and control over blacks; N. J. J. Olivier (1953: 8, 11) argued similarly. The resolutions of SABRA's 6th Annual Meeting (1955) which was postponed several times, also supported the Coloured Preferential Policy (ibid., p. 10, resolution no. 9 on the "Eiselen–Line") (see Cole 2012: 2–6). After ten years, it had to be conceded that the measures had not been very effective (N. C. de Klerk 1963:120), which is why the border industries at Ciskei and Transkei were to be given top priority. On the racist attitude of many SABRA members and the initially still good relationship with the government, see Lazar 1988: 105.

108 PV 276/I/14/5/2, f. 9 Resolusies van die sesde Jaarvergadering van SABRA, no. 2.

109 AB Archives, 2/3/36, UR meeting, 13.12.1957, pp. 11–12, TOPs 38, Voeling met nie-blanke leiers and 39, SABRA.

reaching a just solution.¹¹⁰ Like Verwoerd himself, they were motivated by Afrikaner cultural nationalism, looking to apartheid primarily to ensure the cultural and physical survival of the white Afrikaans-speaking minority.¹¹¹ Many of them were racists who saw biological miscegenation as a fundamental evil, which they wanted to combat through criminal law. They differed with Verwoerd on his policy to the extent that they did not, by the same token, support a system of racial privilege and territorial apartheid, since the latter, in this combination, amounted to a continuation of colonialism and exploitation. Similarly to the dissidents at Potchefstroom University, they tended to be apolitical intellectuals driven by idealistic notions.¹¹²

When it became clear that Verwoerd's policy was aimed at perpetuating the existing relations of exploitation and that, not least for this reason, he had abandoned any real dialogue with recognised political and intellectual leaders of other population groups, a break-up was bound to happen sooner or later. As a member of the Tomlinson Commission, Professor N. J. J. Olivier, who was also the leading figure in SABRA, had declared "the Bantu" capable of development, and therefore entitled to equal civil rights, as soon as they had reached a certain level of development.¹¹³ Two years later, he spoke out in favour of opening up to the majority of the population, and against the forced implementation of racial segregation, even though he adhered to the principles of apartheid and considered himself a nationalist.¹¹⁴ SABRA called for sacrifices from whites, so as to make their economy less dependent on black labour; domestic work, for example, was to be carried out by whites themselves.¹¹⁵

---

110 SABRA was already criticised in the mid–1950s by Keet (1955: 49–52) as being out of touch with reality and guided by wishful thinking.

111 See e.g. *Cape Times*, 1.4.1954. According to the article, SABRA was prepared to accept lower economic growth and to prioritise the continued existence of the whites over economic development.

112 See the comments of educationalist C. F. Gunter of Stellenbosch University in *Die Burger*, 2.5.1958.

113 N. J. J. Olivier (1956b: 16). For a more positive assessment of urbanisation provided by him, see N. J. J. Olivier 1959a: 41–45. It was institutions, not cultural conditions or even lack of talent that posed obstacles to development, he thought (N. J. J. Olivier 1961: 210). On Olivier's important role, see Schüler 1989: 6–14.

114 N. J. J. Olivier 1959b: 68; see for example his role at the SABRA Congress in 1958 (*Die Burger*, 3.5.1958).

115 SABRA failed to do so even in its own house, as the students of Stellenbosch University refused to make up their own beds and clean up their rooms because this was supposedly the work of black servants (*Cape Times*, 7.11.1958).

Verwoerd, on the other hand, balked at SABRA's willingness to enter into an open discussion with representatives of the black majority; his own policy was rooted precisely in the refusal to engage in such a dialogue.[116] Similarly, he viewed the establishment of the Tomlinson Commission in 1950[117] as interference in politics.[118] This was during the term of office of Verwoerd's predecessor, Ernest Jansen. In early December 1957, tensions erupted into open conflict when Verwoerd sent a letter through his private secretary stating that "he no longer saw the possibility of continuing to be involved with SABRA's work, after the latter had expressed its willingness to set up an office for the dissemination of literature, together with the Institute of Race Relations and others – which was to be a multiracial body like the Institute itself. By entering into an unholy alliance with a liberalist mixed and politically hostile organisation, even if the intention should be good and other Afrikaans church persons or institutions do the same, SABRA has made it impossible for the Minister to remain associated with it through membership or contributions."[119]

The attack was a direct hit, causing dismay in SABRA circles. Cognisant of the fact that he had the upper hand, Verwoerd was not inclined to be conciliatory. He demanded that Olivier be removed from power and that the organisation redirect its course.[120] He became more insistent on ousting Olivier when the 1958 annual meeting of SABRA instructed its executive committee to initiate talks with "non-whites", with only one dissenting vote.[121] Verwoerd told Eiselen that he intended to make SABRA aware of the dangerous deviations of its leading members, meaning Olivier in the first place. "Perhaps the cause can be salvaged if they are confronted with a frontal attack or a warning."[122] Shortly afterwards, he forbade

---

116 SABRA's consultations with representatives of the black majority revealed a widespread rejection of government policy (anon. 1961: 174); it is also significant that for many white intellectuals, who liked to pose as 'experts', this was the first opportunity "to see the Bantu in proper perspective for the first time" (p. 198).
117 Broodryk 1991: 215.
118 Lazar 1987: 186–187 who also noted that the initiative to establish the commission came from de Wet Nel.
119 1987 PV 276/I/14/5/2, f. 18, Letter by Verwoerd to SABRA, 5.12.1957.
120 Olivier did not make himself any more popular when he spoke out against the proposed racial segregation at the universities, calling it an interference in the right to education; he saw it as an encroachment on the freedom of universities (*Cape Times*, 9.1.1958 (editorial)).
121 *Rand Daily Mail*, 3.5.1958; *The Star*, 2.4.1958. See also the critical commentary by Jordan Ngubane in *Cape Argus*, 14.10.1958. Verwoerd and Olivier could not stand each other (Schüler 1989: 10).
122 PV 276/I/14/5/2, Memo by Verwoerd to Eiselen, 26.5.1956. At the same time, he assured himself by deferring to Prime Minister Strijdom, stating, "I do not have the impression that a lenient and conciliatory attitude will bring about the desired result" (ibid, f. 25, Letter by Verwoerd to Strijdom, 26.5.1956).

officials in his ministry to support SABRA's talks with African politicians by providing information to them.[123] To senior SABRA members, he stressed that Olivier should be prevented from making his press statements and demanded that "even before the parliamentary session, a statement be made by a reformed SABRA leadership, clearly setting the record straight on the repudiated views, and on the allegedly mixed-race Congress plan".[124]

Shortly after issuing these instructions, Verwoerd began to prepare the purge of the organisation, silencing critics of his policies, similar to the way in which he had, at the time, dealt with critical voices among students at Stellenbosch University.[125] Thus, he used publication channels favouring his policies, such as the far-right *South Africa Observer* edited by S. E. D. Brown, to stir up animosity against Olivier and his "liberalistic" friends.[126] Nevertheless nothing changed at first; in fact, under the impression left by the Sharpeville massacre, prominent members of SABRA like ds. Brink took part in the theological discussion between various Protestant churches, including English ones, in Cottesloe (Johannesburg) at the end of 1960. It is possible that this visible connection between SABRA, the churches and circles in the Cape NP was a reason for Verwoerd, by then Prime Minister, to finally clarify the situation. The occasion for this attempt was his policy towards the coloureds.

This issue came to a head, which developed into a crisis of authority for Verwoerd. In 1960, his leadership had been challenged several times, even though he had won a major victory with the Referendum on the Republic. With this wind in his sail, the Prime Minister was able to rule out criticism from within his own camp, which was due not least to the fact that he was not picky about the means he used: he managed to intimidate the rest by making an example of some on whom he inflicted severe punishments.

Indians and Coloureds

With his assumption of the highest office in government in 1958, Verwoerd also took over the policies pertaining to Indian and Coloured minorities. Departmental ministers had to execute policies formulated by the Prime Minister himself. The

---

123 PV 276/I/14/5/2, f. 33, Memo by Verwoerd to Eiselen.
124 Ibid., f. 32, Letter by Verwoerd to Eiselen, 5.6.1958.
125 McKay 2015: 137, 163, 174–178.
126 *South African Observer*, 11.3.1959.

expansion of his powers coincided with the ruthless assertion of his authority and the suppression of open discussion within the nationalist camp.[127] With regard to the Indian minority, there was a broad consensus within the white population. Like most NP supporters and beyond that, most of the whites, Verwoerd was fundamentally opposed to the presence of people from Indian background in South Africa because he considered Indians, as Asians, to be unassimilable.[128] Verwoerd's undifferentiated rejection of South Africa's Indians could not be mitigated by personal acquaintances. Deeply rooted as it was in his view that the East-West conflict was primarily a conflict between Europe and Asia, it was ideologically motivated. Until 1961, Verwoerd and his government advocated the repatriation of Indians.[129] Only after 1961 – in one of the few course corrections to apartheid policy – was he prepared to face reality and accept people of Indian background as permanent residents of the country. The attempt to include Indians in consultative structures deliberating on apartheid policy was a matter of minor concessions, including the possibility of continuing to do business outside the "group areas" specified for Indians.[130]

While the government's policy on Indians met with widespread approval of the white population, its approach to the coloureds was controversial. In 1956, the apartheid government had withdrawn the right to vote, which the coloured population had been able to exercise since 1853.[131] The reason for this was not apartheid dogmatism, not an abstract principle, but simply the fact that coloured voters had been decisive in some constituencies.[132] Since the NP traditionally had little to offer to the coloureds, the majority of them supported the United Party, albeit unenthusiastically.[133] Instead of wooing coloured voters and creating an attractive programme for them, the NP decided to punish them for their 'wrong' voting behaviour by disenfranchising them.[134]

---

127 Adam/Giliomee 1979: 202.
128 P. J. Meyer (1984: 188) was still of this opinion in 1984.
129 That is why he rejected the idea that the South African government had a responsibility to develop social policy pertaining to persons of Indian descent (PV 93/1/16/1, Treatment of Indians, handwritten, n.d. [1959]). See also G. D. Scholtz 1974, vol. 2: 177–178.
130 Andrews/Berrill/Guignand/Holloway/Meyer/van Eck 1965: 207.
131 Chronicle of development (in Horrell 1956: 21–31; see also Bekker 2005: 72–85).
132 However, Meiring (1990: 119) doubted this with convincing arguments. It was therefore a matter of ideological dogmatism rather than party-political calculation.
133 Lewis 1987: 178.
134 This was done with the support of the Party-affiliated press, and Piet Cillié specifically (Cillié 1965: 96). Such–like demands came from the NP as early as the 1930s (Abercrombie 1938: 146). On the neglect of the coloureds by the NP, see also J. Basson 2004: 127.

As Professor of Sociology and Social Work, Verwoerd had included the coloureds in his 'social engineering' plans,[135] but expressed reservations about their right to vote as early as the 1920s.[136] At a later stage, he toughened his bureaucratic approach that would see coloureds only in terms of his overall plan for apartheid. This provoked resistance in the Cape Province, where the vast majority of coloureds lived; it was exacerbated by tensions within the Party. Despite their support for the disenfranchisement of the coloureds in the 1950s, many nationalists harboured sympathy for a population group the majority of whom was culturally close to whites,[137] and whom they variously referred to as "the dear brown people".[138] Some may also have felt guilty about the political disempowerment of a population group for whom many whites felt a kind of duty of care.[139] Sociologist S. P. Cilliers of the University of Stellenbosch underlined the demographic dynamics of the coloured population, in which the proportion of young people was particularly high;[140] this can be read as a reference to their potential as allies of whites.

Thus there were people who questioned the extension of the Immorality Act, job reservation etc. to the coloureds and demanded more rights for them, including their direct representation in Parliament.[141] Verwoerd vehemently rejected this, making it out to be the work of "irresponsible and impractical or theoretically nice-sounding political directions".[142] "It is extremely unfortunate when people who have nothing to do with the practical implementation and the consequences of public policy, try to pressurise politicians in government, only for the sake of their own

---

135 In an article of 4.10.1935 in the *Cape Argus*, for example, he named the "Cape Coloured" alongside the "Poor Whites" as the "two groups of people in our community" who had not received the "attention they merit". He made similar statements to the Coloured Commission in 1937 (77.17.3, Coloured Commission, Evidence, vol. 3, pp. 2941–2952).
136 231/2/1/1, 'Inleiding tot die Sociologie', p. 106: "In politics, there are numerous complaints about the abuse of voting rights on the part of the Coloureds; and there are numerous persons who think that they can bring about political irregularities."
137 This emerged clearly from a letter by Phil Weber to A. L. Geyer, 18.2.1951, in which he referred to the dissent within the Party over the coloureds; behind the hard–line stance of Strijdom and others, he sensed a deeper conflict (296.K.GE (42)). Cillié emphasised this as late as 1963 (Cillié 1965: 261 (26.10.1963)).
138 55.K.T. (65), Letter by M. E. Rothmann to Erika Theron, 28.11.1963.
139 See the report of a farmer on the situation in the Northern Cape Province expressing deeply felt sympathy for the coloureds (220.K 61 (54), Letter by F. J. van Zyl to Piet Cillié, 8.9.1961). See also Adam/Giliomee 1979: 124–125.
140 Cilliers 1966: 15, 18.
141 PV 93/1/47/2/4, f. 107, P. A. Weber to Verwoerd, 26.8.1960.
142 PV 93/1/24/11, ff. 5–6, Letter by Verwoerd to C. H. Badenhorst (Wellington), in response to the latter's extensive memorandum on the race question, 12.11.1960.

intellectual gratification."[143] He took offence at two things – the first being that this discussion started just before the Referendum on the Republic, and secondly that it could get into the wider public sphere and could cause "disunity". For him, the unity of the nationalist camp always took precedence over internal diversity of opinion; opinions diverging from his own could only be based on lack of knowledge of the facts.[144] He believed he had observed that such quarrels "arise most easily when everything is quiet and Afrikanerdom is perceived to be particularly strong by the outside world".[145]

The re-admission of the coloureds to a common electoral roll with the whites was out of the question for him, and parliamentary representation of coloureds by coloureds even more so.[146] In his view, apartheid had to be enforced uncompromisingly and consistently also among the coloureds, even though there could be no homeland for them, because they did not even come close to inhabiting a closed settlement area. Their cultural proximity to whites was certainly one of the reasons why Verwoerd saw their future in a common state with whites, but only as segregated junior partners. At the same time, he himself initially had no clear plans, as F.W. de Klerk reported after a conversation with him: "The absence of any principled approach troubled me."[147]

Since the coloureds were dispersed, priority was to be given to "community building";[148] sentimentalities such as "the understandable but selfish desire to stay where one spent one's childhood years", should not stand in the way of establishing the coloureds as a "national group".[149] By this he meant forced relocations because, as he said, "[i]t is easier to achieve good relations when there is a side-by-side existence instead of a mixed-up one",[150] that is, order instead of chaos. Once segregation was completed, there would be "no reason why people who differ from one another cannot live close together".[151] In what respect whites and coloureds differed from each other, he was never able to specify, because

---

143 PV 93/1/24/12, f. 15, Letter by Verwoerd to ds. J. A. J. Steenkamp, Moderator N.G. Sendingkerk (Goodwood), 22.5.1961.
144 296.KV.32, Letter by Verwoerd to P. A. Weber, 6.9.1960. In his reply (PV 93/1/47/2/4, f. 111) of 12. 9. 1960, Weber announced that Verwoerd's letter would be read at the next meeting of the AB Department: "It is necessary that our people know how you think."
145 PV 72/3, Piet Koornhof reports a conversation with Verwoerd on 10.8.1966.
146 PV 93/1/30/1/10, f. 49, Letter by Verwoerd to J. D. A. Crafford, 16.1.1961.
147 F. W. de Klerk 1999: 41.
148 Verwoerd, Uniale Raad vir Kleurlingsake, 12.12.1961 (in Pelzer 1963: 599–609, 604). He argued similarly in PV 93/1/30/1/29, f. 192, Letter by Verwoerd to Mrs. C. Greenland (Fishhoek), 5.4.1965.
149 Verwoerd, Union Council Concerning Coloureds, 12.12.1961 (in Pelzer 1966: 642–653, 647–649).
150 Ibid., 644.
151 Ibid., 642.

apart from skin colour, there was no noticeable difference. His policy was based on the intention of keeping Indians and Coloureds on the side of the whites by giving them limited privileges, and to prevent them from joining forces with the black majority;[152] this was to remain the strategy until the end of apartheid and beyond.

The dissent within the nationalist camp stemmed from the logical inconsistency of Verwoerd's policies. While his policy towards the black majority, who were to be settled in self-governing homelands, was seen by some as morally defensible, at least in theory, his policy towards the coloureds, whose future was to take shape in a common state with whites and Indians, envisaged permanent disenfranchisement. They were to be granted political rights only at the local level, that is, in the neighbourhoods and rural communities that, according to segregationist policies, could be classified as 'coloured' – but not at the level of a common state.[153] In fact, Verwoerd never gave plausible reasons why the black majority was promised state self-government, while the coloureds were not. They were not to become citizens but to remain subjects.[154]

One of the first moves towards political rights for coloureds was made in 1959 by Prof. N. J. J. Olivier, Vice-Chairman of SABRA, who pointed out that, according to international standards, coloureds should be represented by their own MPs, in proportion to the size of the population.[155] Verwoerd remained unmoved and retorted, as he had done on many previous occasions, that a concession would only trigger further demands.[156]

---

152 PV 93/1/30/1/7, f. 5, Letter by Verwoerd to ds. W. J. Wentzel, 22.7.1960. This included the policy of designating the Western Cape as an area where coloureds were to be accorded privileges over blacks, in the labour market, for instance. This policy was as ineffective as apartheid in general (Humphries 1989: 178).

153 Cf. PV 93/1/25/2, Departement van Gemeenskapsbou. Verslag van Ondersoekkomitee na die ontwikkeling van plaaslike bestuur vir Kleurlinge, 11.12.1961. This Committee came to the conclusion that coloureds were not at all capable of self-government. It stipulated that self–government should begin at the provincial level; placing it under the direct control of the Uniale Kleuringraad proved to be unfavourable.

154 Mamdani 1996: 90–96.

155 *Die Burger*, 16.6.1959.

156 PV 93/1/24/10, f. 149, Letter by Verwoerd to J. Crafford (Ceres), 14.11.60. "If Coloureds are allowed to be represented by Coloureds in Parliament, then they will demand representatives in the Provincial Council tomorrow, and what right would we have later on to deny them representation in all other bodies, and even in our schools? Besides, it would be illogical to then give representation only to the Coloureds and to deny representation to the other groups. Persons who advocate such integration do not understand the consequences that necessarily arise from it." Similarly PV 93/1/30/1/9, f. 22, Letter by Verwoerd to P. J. Venter (Upington), 5.11.1960. However, Verwoerd conceded that coloureds in the Cape Province should continue to be able to elect white

In October 1960, he expressed his dismay at the "unpredictable Professor Olivier and his friends", whose "continued control over Sabra" he opposed.[157] This response has to be seen in the context of the fact that, on the theme of the coloureds, he faced much more vigorous internal opposition and criticism than on any other aspect of apartheid policies. A few weeks later, on 22 November 1960, Verwoerd reaffirmed his stance in a lengthy press statement, attributing "liberalistic" inclinations to his critics, "some of whom had previously been nationalists". He insinuated that since their criticism of apartheid, as it was applied to blacks, had lost its appeal, they were now shifting it to apartheid as it was applied to coloureds. In claiming that those NP members who disagreed with the policies pertaining to coloureds were fundamentally opposed to apartheid, he deliberately polarised political camps.[158] But in making them out to be only "a small group of mainly businesspeople and clergy . . . who are now deviating from whatever has always been the policy of the National Party",[159] he was underestimating the opposition to his hard-line policy.

Verwoerd was careful to keep the initiative. As early as 7 December 1960, the Information Division of the Department for Coloured Affairs published a "positive development programme". It contained statements by the Prime Minister emphasising the government's unified stance on the policies pertaining to the coloureds; once again, he rejected all proposals for coloured representation in Parliament. Instead, he focused on the development of the Uniale Raad vir Kleurlinge, which was to be given self-governing powers in a step-by-step process,[160] so that it could develop into a kind of parliament.

MPs to Parliament, albeit on a separate electoral roll (PV 93/1/30/1/30, f. 7, Letter by Verwoerd to Dr M. Vera Bührmann (Cape Town), 10.6.1965).
157 PV 93/1/47/2/7, Letter by Verwoerd to J. P van der Spuy (AB), 31.10.1960.
158 FAV, 4.7.1.5, Press statement by Verwoerd, 22.11.1960.
159 PV 93/1/24/11, p. 27, Letter by Verwoerd to Dr W. Venter, L.V. (Barkly West), 7.12.1960. For an example of such advice, see PV 93/3/1/48, f. 125, Letter by ds. S. Grosskopf to Verwoerd, 20.11.1961.
160 PV 93/1/24/11, ff. 59–62. Positive ontwikkelingsprogram van die Regering ten opsigte van die Kleurlingbevolking aangekondig deur Sy Edele die Eerste Minister, 7.12.1960. To his Party colleague S. P. Botha, he insisted on the need for the Party organs to take a clear stance on the matter (ibid, f. 76, Letter by Verwoerd to S. P. Botha, M.P. (Louis Trichardt), 3.1.1961). See also PV 93/1/25/2, Departement van Gemeenskapsbou. Verslag van Ondersoekkomitee na die ontwikkeling van plaaslike bestuur vir Kleurlinge, 11.12.1961. According to this Report, the Kleurlingraad was not in a position to do so. It was not by chance that this committee was appointed at this time: in the face of staunch opposition to Verwoerd's radical form of apartheid, the government felt the need to take action, in order to create facts. Whether the rather sceptical Report of the Committee worked in his favour cannot be determined, but it is doubtful.

Since this will be a *Uniale* [nationwide] Council, it will be more important than if it were to remain bound to provincial authorities and interests, and this will further satisfy their ambitions. Instead of giving them representation in the Senate, which may also be abused and seen as the beginning of a joint platform with whites, we propose annual consultations between the Coloured leaders and the leadership of the White State, more or less along the lines of the Prime Ministers' Conferences.[161]

Verwoerd claimed to be under no illusion that coloureds would have great sympathy for Afrikaner nationalists and that he would be able to win their sympathy through dispensing favours:

As far as the Coloureds are concerned, we must help them in their own development, just as we did help the Bantu to develop on their own; this is the way to keep them off our backs. However, I agree with you that even if we embark on this path, we are not going to make them positively inclined towards us, which is why we should not go out of our way to create goodwill, but remain level-headed; this is what would be politically and socio-economically healthy within the framework of our apartheid policy.[162]

Many nationalists in the Cape Province saw the coloureds as potential allies against the black majority, which is why they sought to strengthen their ties with them.[163] This period saw a flurry of publications by theologians and other academics who were seeking a path other than that of radical segregation. In his book *Die Opkoms van ons Derde Stand* [*The Emergence of our Third Estate*] (1960), Reformed pastor D. P. Botha made an impassioned plea for the social integration of whites and coloureds, which was to include political participation of "the brown people".[164] N. P. van Wyk Louw, probably the most famous Afrikaans-speaking poet of the time, wrote a foreword to the book; what is more, he openly distanced himself from Verwoerd by participating in protests against university

---

161 PV 93/1/24/11, f. 35f., Letter by Verwoerd to Dr. W. J. B. Pienaar (Rondebosch), 7.12.1960. In mentioning "the Prime Ministers' Conferences", what Verwoerd had in mind was the model of the Commonwealth.
162 Ibid., ff. 72–73, Letter by Verwoerd to N. J. Basson, 3.1.1961.
163 When a "non–white united front" of coloureds was to be launched in early 1961, Minister P.W. Botha immediately tried to play off the coloureds' fear of black majority against this initiative. Rather curious is his justification of discrimination against the coloureds on the grounds of their supposedly lower level of development, evidence for which he found in the establishment of this united front, since "they reject the development programme announced by the Government, and the effective functioning of the Department of Coloured Affairs". Criticism of the government's workings was thus taken as evidence of a lower level of civilisation (PV 93/1/20/2/2, f. 165, Statement by Minister Botha, 24.2.1961).
164 D. P. Botha 1960: 150–152. For him the coloureds were the proletariat of the Afrikaner people.

apartheid.¹⁶⁵ With the emerging conflict over the policies pertaining to coloureds, the old antagonisms between the provincial parties resurfaced, which had repeatedly boiled up in the process of cabinet reshuffles. The nationalists of the Cape Province had found themselves politically marginalised since the resignation of Prime Minister Malan in 1954. Their leading politicians had been relegated to lesser cabinet posts and the Party as a whole was dominated by the Transvaal branch. In addition, there were antagonisms between the various newspapers and press groups of the party-affiliated media, with the Prime Minister and former journalist chairing one of these groups, namely Voortrekkerpers in Johannesburg. Verwoerd's responses tended to be mean and petty; he engaged in fierce competition with Nasionale Pers, because he found it too far out of line with his own approach.¹⁶⁶

Mutual mistrust fuelled a conflict that came to a head in December 1960 and was focused on Piet Cillié, editor-in-chief of *Die Burger*, the journalistic flagship of the NP.¹⁶⁷ As it often happens in cases like these, personal animosities¹⁶⁸ and political disputes could hardly be separated from each other, even though Cillié never questioned apartheid policies; he did not raise an eyebrow over territorial segregation, in fact, he even defended it with full conviction.¹⁶⁹

In his 'Dawie' column at the end of November, Cillié smugly maintained that the idea of representation of coloureds in a central parliament was not being put forward by the UP or the Progressives, but by the ranks of the nationalists. He gleefully quoted Verwoerd's ministerial successor Daan de Wet Nel, who considered the representation of blacks by blacks as the only realistic and ethically defensible policy, adding, "[t]hat was the kind of logic that led supporters of the Government and of separate development to the idea of representation of Coloureds by Coloureds".¹⁷⁰ Cillié wanted to make it clear that nationalists advocating this goal were entirely within the framework of apartheid policy and could not

---

165 Steyn 1998: 897–898, 907–908.
166 See Cillié's detailed report in 296.K.D.11 (9/1), Letter by Cillié to T. E. Dönges, 31.7.1964 and attached copy of a letter from Verwoerd to Dönges, 16.6.1964 (9/2). See also Cillié's article of 6.1.1960, in which he underlined his right not to simply parrot the party line (Cillié 1965: 169).
167 On earlier disagreements, see PV 18/3/1/63, Letter by Cillié to Swart, 20.1.1958 and attached a letter by Cillié to Verwoerd, 20.1.1958. On the conflict, see Steyn 2002: ch. 7; on Cillié's inconsistent attitude toward the coloureds, see ibid, 206. On the press and the events surrounding the coloureds and Cottesloe, see Mouton 2002: 42–47.
168 Cillié himself characterised his relationship with Verwoerd as rather distant: "A certain distance seemed to me to be the golden way and I think he saw it the same way." (Cillié 1980: 17).
169 296.K.C.5 (1), Letter by Cillié to Phil Weber, 26.3.1954; see also Steyn 2002: 125; also Mittner's (1986) chronology of the dispute.
170 Cillié 1965: 196 (26.11.1960).

be labelled "liberalists". It did not stand him in good stead; de Wet Nel and Verwoerd accused him of spreading "liberalist" ideas, which is what Cillié dismissed with indignation. He generally defended himself against such accusations and spoke of a "witch hunt" and the threat of a split in the "unity of the people". This was an accusation directed against the Prime Minister, who was not mentioned by name. Readers knew who was meant when Cillié captured the speech gestures, enunciating, "[n]ow, unfortunately, there are signs that some of us are losing patience with the tiresome process of discussion and persuasion. Those disagreeing with us on this matter will be reined in with power and force."[171]

Cillié's call for tolerance and open discussion was to fall on the deaf ears of a Prime Minister driven by a sense of mission and by the conviction that he alone knew the hard and fast solutions to South Africa's problems. Cillié, meanwhile, immediately received encouragement from his predecessors and superiors in Nasionale Pers. A. L. Geyer thought the article a "masterpiece": "while giving Verwoerd a few of the slaps he deserves, he rightly accords him the responsibility for preserving unity."[172] Phil Weber expressed his admiration: "Since we came to power 12 years ago, no national newspaper has addressed its Prime Minister quite like this."[173] Cillié received support not only from old comrades-in-arms in his own stable, but also from the Transvaal, where Verwoerd had silenced dissenters with similarly authoritarian gestures.[174] Support also came from pastors, as well as citizens of the South Western Cape Province, who deplored the social situation of the coloureds.[175]

---

[171] Ibid, 199 (3.12.1960).
[172] 220.K 60 (55), Letter by A. L. Geyer to Piet Cillié, 4.12.1960.
[173] 220.K 60 (59), Letter by Phil Weber to Piet Cillié, 12.12.1960.
[174] 220.K 60 (57), B. J. Slabber to Cillié, 6.12.1960.
[175] 220.K 60 (58), Letter by T. Bruynzeel (Stellenbosch) to Cillié, 12.12.1960, and the latter's reply of 19.12.1960, stating that he felt encouraged "by the attitude of the N.G. Churches of the Cape and Transvaal on this matter, as it was publicised in the Johannesburg Church Declaration"; on the evaluation of Cottesloe, see Cillié 1965: 202–205 (17.12.1960); see also ibid., Letter by J. S. van der Spuy to Cillié, 14.12.1960 also 220.K 61 (36), Letter by Myra Davis (Benoni) to Cillié, 10.4.1961: although the sender pleads for more rights for the "civilised" among coloureds and blacks, she calls blacks by derogatory terms. Others sided more with Verwoerd and rejected the stance taken by Cillié's and by the Cottesloe Declaration (220.K 60 (58), Letter by Bill Bezuidenhout to Phil Weber, 16.12.1960; see also Letter by H.L. Minnaar (Strand) to 'Dawie', 17.12.1960; and numerous other letters in the same collection). More than anything else, however, Cillié now received anti-intellectually tinged accusations alleging that he was responsible for the destruction of Afrikaner unity (ibid., Letter by J. P. W. Jacobs to Cillié, 26.12.1960). See also 220.K 61 (9), Anonymous letter from Molteno to Cillié, 6.1.1961, heaping the blame for the quarrel solely on him. See also Cillié's perception that Verwoerd always countered the centrifugal forces within the Afrikaner population (Cillié 1980: 56).

Verwoerd struck back and initiated a veritable smear campaign against *Die Burger* and against Cillié in particular. *Die Transvaler* was agitating against Nasionale Pers, which came to be labelled "liberalist" in Johannesburg. This had a negative impact on its book trade.[176] On the eve of Christmas 1960, *Die Burger* received numerous aggressive and insulting letters to the editor, "all of them unjust and unwarranted".[177] Cillié was appalled: "To see the rage of the anti-people – now also against the Church – is frightening. We are receiving letters filled with hatred."[178] The editor-in-chief confessed to his erstwhile hope that the attainment of the Republic would bring greater flexibility. "But what now dominates the life of our people, to an alarming degree, is dull immobility, Afrikaners-only-and-to-the-hell-with-the-others – all the things I admire the least in our people." The aggressiveness was so pronounced, he opined, because it had been deliberately fomented, which is why he himself had lost sympathy "with the whole course and spirit in which we are now being led". In a private letter he vented his anger, confessing that "it was hard to express my indignation and anger at what this man has done to our Afrikaner people, and my fear of what he can still do. In these letters, you can see the hatred for coloureds, dominees, professors and *Die Burger* that he has unleashed. He has evoked the Neanderthal in our people, going against everything intelligent and searching, following the classic recipe of the tyrant who seeks to exert his power by inciting the mob against its recognised leaders in all walks of life."[179]

Verwoerd, to whom British High Commissioner Sir John Maud attested a "bully's mind",[180] once again showed his ruthless side; in such confrontations he took pleasure in targeting the livelihoods of his opponents.[181] The dispute was

---

176 220.K 60 (59), Letter by Phil Weber to Cillié, 18.12.1960.
177 Ibid., Letter by Phil Weber to Cillié, 20.12.1960.
178 296.K.C.5 (3), Letter by Cillié to Phil Weber, 21.12.1960.
179 Ibid., Letter by Cillié to Phil Weber, 21.12.1960; the racist designation "hotnot" has been translated here as "coloureds". He mentioned that Dönges approved of his actions. Dönges was also of the opinion that the assassination attempt had "strengthened the despotic tendency. Apart from official matters, they no longer speak to each other." Weber, for his part, had heard via Verwoerd's pastor, A. M. Meiring, that the latter had "on an earlier occasion politely informed Verwoerd that he was going to burst. Piet [Meiring] diagnosed paranoia: in private conversations, he [Verwoerd] now uses expressions such as, "they will have to kill me dead" and "they will have to cut my throat".".
180 FAV 4.7.1.2., South Africa's Future, additional text, above which appears the handwritten remark by Eric Louw, "Top Secret". At the bottom of the page appears a note by W. J. Verwoerd, handwritten in 2015: "This secret report was, to the best of my recollection, intercepted by an Afrikaans secretary in the British Embassy and passed on to the Prime Minister."
181 Probably the best-known example was the Treason Trial, which was conducted over a period of several years in a deliberate attempt to destroy the livelihoods of the accused. Verwoerd

clearly not so much about policies pertaining to coloureds, but rather about the power to interpret apartheid policies, on which Verwoerd claimed a monopoly and which he implemented ruthlessly and undemocratically.[182]

Towards the end of the year, Weber drew the sobering conclusion: "We realised that the Afrikaner is not ready for open dialogue." Verwoerd's approach clearly revealed a deep-seated anti-intellectualism. He contrasted supposedly unworldly intellectuals with people allegedly having their feet planted on the ground and concerned with 'real life'. That is also the reason why he took offence at certain letters to the editor published in *Die Burger*, such as the letter penned by well-known apartheid critic Prof. Jan Rabie of Stellenbosch University: "For the letter writers, it is an intellectual exercise with intellectual satisfaction when they derive all their designs pretty theoretically. For the people concerned, on the other hand, it is about their way of life, their hopes, and their honour."[183]

Above all, he was embittered by the fact that his critics had launched this dispute shortly after the victory in the Republic Referendum. "Therein lies the tragedy, that these people did not even give us the opportunity to consolidate this victory and to thereby further weaken the opponents. Instead, they themselves threw the bone of contention into the ring, affording our opponents new courage and new fighting chances."[184] He had tried again and again to reach an understanding with the newspaper, he said; and he knew to distinguish "between *Die Burger* as a paper whose editors and some other office bearers express their own opinions, and *Die Burger* as an institution of the National *Volk*".[185]

---

targeted L. J. du Plessis in a similar manner, with the aim of depriving him of his professorship. For more on the Cape press, see O'Meara 1996: 129–131.

182 Mittner 1986: 303–304. In 1972, Cillié even adopted Verwoerd's argumentation (Treurnicht 1988: 10–11).

183 220.K 60 (59), Letter by Weber to Cillié, 29.12.1960; on "open discussion" as a formula for an attitude, see Nash 2009: 14–17,123–127.

184 220.K 65 (8a), Letter by Verwoerd to Cillié, 3.2.1965. In this context, it is interesting to note that a Party official such as P. W. Botha, whose anti-intellectual attitude was well known, argued in a similar way; at the same time, he reproached Cillié for not criticising the letters to the editor in sufficiently robust terms: "But I think you could be less passive and highlight the successes in the government's policy towards the Coloureds while at the same time attacking the wild ideas of these theorists." "Persons like W. A. de Klerk and Jan Rabie", he continued, were only "spout[ing] nonsense from their armchairs, while my Ministry and myself are working hard and mak[ing] great progress" (ibid. 8b, Letter by P. W Botha to Cillié, 4.2.1965).

185 PV 93/1/24/11, ff. 72–73, Letter by Verwoerd to N. J. Basson, 3.1.1961. Similarly PV 93/1/24/11, ff. 5–6, Letter by Verwoerd to C. H. Badenhorst, 12.11.1960: "It is most regrettable that it is precisely in this hour of triumph for our People in one respect, that this Coloured bone of contention is thrown into our midst, which can only lead to disunity and new problems." A year later, he showed himself alert to the risk that the Coloureds might be stirred up "when some of our

A few days after the confrontation with *Die Burger*, the Federal Council of the NP, at Verwoerd's instigation, issued a long statement rejecting a softening of the line on the coloureds hitherto pursued.[186] The supreme Party body gave the Prime Minister's attitude a party-official stamp of approval, resolved "that Coloureds are not to be represented by Coloureds in an institution, where such exists, namely in Parliament and in the Cape Provincial Council. Instead, they must be represented there by whites. It is also the policy of the Party that institutions of governance for Coloureds are to be developed at various levels, where they are to be represented solely by their own people." To this was added the clarification, that this was not a provisional opinion, but "that the Party will adhere to this principle now and in future".[187] In this way, Verwoerd also imposed the discipline of the governing party on his minister responsible for coloured affairs, P.W. Botha, who was actually known to be in favour of political representation for coloureds.[188]

On 17 May 1961, the Prime Minister authorised the management of the Federal Council – a typically Verwoerdian inner circle of power in the NP's most important joint committee –, to issue a statement on improved co-operation between the Party and the press; this statement was an attempt to use the discussion with the management of Nasionale Pers to put its editors on a leash.[189] After the election of 1961, Verwoerd was prudent enough to express his gratitude to the party-affiliated press, singling out Piet Cillié in particular, "because there were some things we did not always agree on".[190] The message was clear: conformism was rewarded, the sun of benevolence once again shone upon an editor who had been pulled into line, and who was now toeing that line.[191] Verwoerd's resolve that representation of the coloureds in the 'white' parliament was out of the question disappointed

---

own friends began to make propaganda for more rights for the Coloureds last year, straight after the Referendum". See also PV 93/1/24/12, f. 15, Letter by Verwoerd to ds. J. A. J. Steenkamp, Moderator N.G. Sendingkerk (Goodwood), 22.5.1961.
186 296.KV.32, Verklaring Federale Raad NP, 23.1.1961; see also PV 93/1/25/2; and Horrell 1962: 10.
187 PV 54/2/2, Minutes of the Federal Council of the NP, 21.1.1961, pp. 2–3. This was so important to him that it was placed on the agenda of the meeting of the Dagbestuur (PV 93/1/30/1/27).
188 Daan Prinsloo 1997: 35–36.
189 PV 54/2/2, Minutes of the Dagbestuur of the Federal Council of the NP, 17.5.1961, TOP 3.
190 296.KV.32, Letter by Verwoerd to Weber, 31.10.1961; and Weber's reply of 6. 11. 1961: "The paper owes a considerable part of its influence to the fact that it displays adult and independent thinking within the framework of the Party's policy."
191 Over the years, Verwoerd increasingly targeted Schalk Pienaar (rather than Cillié), a more independent thinker than Cillié, whose criticism of right-wing activists like Albert Hertzog provoked the full gamut of intolerant responses on the part of the Prime Minister (Mouton 2002: 62–67).

many nationalists in the Cape Province;[192] but in the medium term, it contributed to ending the discussions, especially since Cillié never presented a credible alternative in the sense of making an unequivocal case for the political participation of coloureds.[193]

In a speech presented to the Union Council for Coloured Affairs on 12 December 1961, Verwoerd outlined his plans. To those present, he held up the vision of a bright future, that the coloured population "can participate in the development of a Union Control Board for the Coloureds with actual, even legislative powers, and its own officials (call it a civil service) so that it can attend to the administration of its resolutions in different spheres".[194] Instead of being represented in Parliament themselves, the Councils of Indians and Coloureds "exercise authority over their own affairs, similar to the powers now enjoyed by the provincial authorities".[195] Given the limited powers of the Provincial Councils, this was a clear announcement that the coloureds would be granted only very limited self-government. The tax revenues generated by the coloureds were to be put at the disposal of the Union Council for Coloured Affairs "to be spent on the Services under its control".[196] In plain language, this meant that they would not receive any money from the fiscus, but were to finance all the services themselves. The responsible Ministry did not want to "rule the roost", Verwoerd said, but during the "transition period", it would have to provide "the necessary guidance". It should first take over the responsibility for the education system from the provinces and develop it "with the help of its officials, who as far as possible will be Coloureds". It could then, if well organised, "be placed under Coloured control".[197] The majority of the councillors were ap-

---

[192] 55.K.T. (60), Letter by M. E. Rothmann to E. Theron, 7.2.1961: "It is precisely because I remain loyal to Hendrik and Betsie that I regret this statement so much." However, she judged his behaviour in the discussion about the coloureds as "the only dubious thing in Hendrik's career as Prime Minister so far".

[193] Giliomee 2004: 16.

[194] Verwoerd, Union Council Concerning Coloureds, 12.12.1961 (in Pelzer 1966: 642–653, 650). The speech was also printed in pamphlet form for propaganda purposes (Verwoerd 1962; also Verwoerd, Begrotingspos van die Eerste Minister, 10.4.1961, in Pelzer 1963: 528–536, 531). The manuscript of the speech differs from the published text, but since Verwoerd spoke freely most of the time, this version is probably the more authentic one (FAV, 4.7.2.4.3).

[195] Verwoerd, Budgetary Appropriation of the Prime Minister, 10.4.1961 (in Pelzer 1966: 567–575, 571): "On the lines of separate development and good neighbour treatment, we shall also have to grant increasingly rights and opportunities to Coloureds and Indians on a separate basis and, other than in the case of the Bantu, within the same boundaries." See also PV 93/1/24/10, f. 97, Verwoerd to Col. C. F. Miles–Cadman, 28.7.1960.

[196] Verwoerd, Union Council Concerning Coloureds, 12.12.1961 (in Pelzer 1966: 642–653, 652).

[197] Ibid, 651–652. The reason for this he stated in a private letter, namely "that there is no common ('*gemeenskaplike*') Ministry of Education such that it could be accused of discrimination if it

pointed by the government itself, thus making it clear that it was not at all willing to give up control and allow democratic structures to be set up.[198]

The declaration of the Party's Federal Council intimidated not only *Die Burger*, but also SABRA, most of whose members also belonged to the NP. This is the reason why SABRA decided to indefinitely postpone a Congress on the situation of the coloureds that it had scheduled some time before.[199] Presumably through the channels of the Broederbond, Verwoerd made sure that many of his supporters appeared at the 1961 Annual Conference in Bloemfontein – obviously with the intention of voting Olivier and his friends out of leadership positions.[200] The extreme right-wing theologian P. F. D. Weiss, a former student of Verwoerd's,[201] was elected as the new Vice-President, replacing Olivier. In 1964, the SABRA office was moved to Pretoria.[202] The press was correct in attributing the purge to the intrigues and the "sledgehammer methods" used by Verwoerd.[203] SABRA was thus subjected to party discipline and did not step out of line in the following period. The expulsion of L. J. du Plessis from the Party the previous year may have served as a warning. In the end, the Prime Minister's line was to prevail, moreover since SABRA relinquished its role as a think-tank on apartheid in the years that followed; it lost much of its importance and its influence on the public.[204]

---

proceeds on the basis of different norms" (PV 93/3/1/71, f. 164, Letter by Verwoerd to J. Burger Read, 6.4.1965).
198 When leading representatives of the coloureds then formed a Coloured Convention, the government threatened to impose a ban (van der Ross 2015: 147).
199 *Natal Daily News*, 6.2.1961. On the strategies of intimidation and submission, see also *Rand Daily Mail*, 25.4.1961.
200 P. Hugo 1989: 27–32. On the exact course of the purge, see Holleman 1989: 42, 45; also E. Theron 1983: 49; Stals 1998: 311–316, esp. 315–316; on attempts to force Olivier out of the Broederbond as well, see ibid., 283.
201 UA Stellenbosch, Personnel file of Verwoerd, Letter by Ass. Registrateur to Verwoerd, 22.8.1930.
202 *Sunday Times*, 1.10.1961. A lawsuit filed by Olivier's wife, claiming abandonment by her husband and suing for maintenance payments, may have served to prepare the purge. Her ex-husband appeared as a person who did not care about his family (*Sunday Times*, 8.1.1961; see also Du Pisani 1988: 11). SABRA remained a 'think tank' in the service of the apartheid government. Since Verwoerd's son-in-law, Carel Boshoff, took over as Chairman in 1972, it increasingly concerned itself with concepts for a "white people's state" (C. Boshoff 2012: 257–264). This also led to accusations of corruption because SABRA, a private organisation, received about a quarter of its income from state sources (*The Star*, 9.10.1980).
203 *Sunday Times*, 8.1.1961. It was probably also due to the purge that SABRA spoke of Verwoerd in wholly positive terms after his assassination, not mentioning anything about the conflict (PV 123/2/14/1, circular letter by Hoofsekretaris SABRA, Niekerk, 9.9.1966).
204 C. Boshoff 2012: 251–253.

Another critic whom Verwoerd silenced during this period, albeit by even more ruthless methods, was L. J. du Plessis. Their mutual animosity dated back to the war years, when du Plessis was the chief ideologue of the extreme right-wing Ossewabrandwag. By the 1950s, it had become quiet around him, but after Verwoerd took office as head of government, du Plessis emerged as a vocal critic of his policies. As an arch cultural nationalist, he supported apartheid, because he believed that that was the only way to secure the existence of his own *volk*. But as a radical Calvinist, he could only imagine this if it was implemented in a way justifiable before God. He pleaded for an open discussion with the majority of the population. He even called for negotiations with the ANC and demanded that the Afrikaners, as the longest-standing anti-imperialists on the continent, take the lead in the decolonisation movement.[205] Verwoerd started a campaign against du Plessis in the Afrikaans media and in the cultural nationalist organisations. Du Plessis was ostracised and expelled from the NP; he was largely forgotten and died a bitter, broken man.[206]

For Cillié it must have come almost as a relief when, a few days after Verwoerd launched the letters-to-the-editor campaign against him, a dispute broke out with church representatives over the Cottesloe Declaration. This took *Die Burger* out of the firing line to some extent. Convinced "that it is better to fall out of step with the Party than to fall out of step with the Church",[207] Cillié made common cause with some of the theologians. The joint statement of the English and Afrikaans churches involved in the Cottesloe talks included the demand for parliamentary representation of the coloureds; but Verwoerd asserted his line even in the face of challenges from the churches.[208] The risk to his definitional authority was not least due to the fact that with the Cottesloe Declaration, one of the most important centres of Afrikaner nationalism was giving rise to an alternative to apartheid, thereby discrediting and delegitimising his own policy. "The argument concerning the unacceptable alternative was no longer convincing. Alternatives were becoming conceivable."[209]

---

205 Apart from du Plessis, other professors of the University of Potchefstroom, such as ethnologist J. H. Coetzee, were involved in this 'rebellion' (E. S. van Eeden 2006: 510–511, 516–517).
206 P. J. J. S. Potgieter 1976: 17–18; see also P. J. J. S. Potgieter 1981: 23–26; Marx 2010: 72–73; and Holzer 1961: 237.
207 296.K.C.5 (2/1), Letter by Cillié to Phil Weber, 14.12.1960. On the Cottesloe statements about the coloureds, see Lückhoff 1978: 62, 87; and the reaction of the then editor of the church newspaper *Die Kerkbode*, Andries Treurnicht (ibid., 108–109).
208 See also the description of J. J. van Rooyen (1971: 102–114); he reduces the significance of the Cottesloe Convention to the dispute on the question of the coloureds, though.
209 Kinghorn 1986: 120. Similarly Piet Meiring (2013: 46–47); also Horrell 1962: 63–68.

While the relationship of the NP government, and Verwoerd in particular, with most of the English churches, primarily with the Anglican and the Roman Catholic Church, was tense and conflictual, it was much more complicated with regard to the three Dutch Reformed Churches. In this context, the question of Verwoerd's own relationship to religion needs to be probed.

Verwoerd's attitude towards religion and the church poses some difficulties. In public, he always professed his Christian faith, repeatedly and emphatically stating that for him, civilisation and Christianity belonged together, but he does not seem to have been very religious himself. His modernisation policy was a thoroughly secular one; in its hybrid claims, it did not display a trace of Christian humility. Several contemporaries remarked that Verwoerd was not devoutly religious. He liked to spend time on his farm, particularly over weekends, in order to avoid attending church services – or so the story goes. Piet Meiring, who had known him for a long time, described him as an "agnostic"; he was convinced that Verwoerd "was not really a believer at all".[210] On the other hand, those who were close to him in everyday life reported that he listened to radio broadcasts of church services on his farm.[211] Verwoerd's daughter Anna experienced some social pressure due to the fact that "my father so seldom went to church".[212] But as early as 1942, Verwoerd vigorously defended himself against the accusation of being a "*godloënaar*" ["God denier"], brought against him by AB member J. G. van der Merwe.[213] In 1958, rumours to that effect were still being spread in order to undermine his chances of being elected Prime Minister.[214]

Verwoerd's father was a devout Calvinist and missionary. After successfully completing his Master's degree, the young Verwoerd was set on studying theology to become a pastor. Because of his rude behaviour towards the examiners at the entrance examination, he was expelled, and subsequently turned away from the church.[215] Quite independently of his personal religiosity, he was cognisant of the importance that religion held for contemporaries, and of its significance for cultural nationalism. That is why he maintained good relations with numerous pastors of the various Calvinist churches, and sought advice from some of them, for

---

210 I. L. Villiers 2009: 132; see also Meiring 1973b: 125–126.
211 A. Boshoff 1974: 57.
212 W et al. Verwoerd 2001: 71; see also the statement by Verwoerd's son Hendrik (ibid., 93); also Meiring 1990: 35.
213 Serfontein 1979: 56.
214 G. J. Kruger 1985: 156.
215 NGK Archive Stellenbosch, Admissie–Eksamen Notulen S10 1/3, 6.2.1923, pp. 91–96. One of the examiners was the father of journalist Piet Meiring, who was therefore able to report on several occasions how upset his father was about Verwoerd's demeanour (Meiring 1973a: 29–30; Meiring 1973b:118–119; Meiring 1990: 45).

example from J. Gericke. He also answered letters from pastors, especially from those supporting his policies. The letters always went into detail, and were couched in friendly tones.[216] The task of the church, according to Verwoerd, lay in "character-building", which was especially important for young people:

> Character-building, which is so essential, does not only demand the Inspiration that a people draws from its deeds in the material field and from its national ideals. Such building of character calls for inspiration from the ideals set by the Church and religion, and which are all-embracing, as the Bible itself. Once again a field where Church and State should go hand in hand if we wish to remain a people who can triumph in the difficult times that lie ahead.[217]

Verwoerd had a particularly close and cordial relationship with representatives of the small Gereformeerde Kerk, the so-called Doppers, but this had little to do with their theological orientation. By no means did he support the idea of 'sovereignty of each particular sphere'[218] that was advocated by Dutch theologian and politician Abraham Kuyper, with whose church and University[219] the Doppers maintained particularly close contact after he had unsuccessfully offered his services as mediator in the Boer War.[220] However, it cannot be denied that some attempts to justify apartheid theologically did indeed refer to Kuyper.[221] However, whereas Kuyper and his followers were essentially aiming for a limitation of state power, Verwoerd strove precisely for its expansion.[222] His close connection to Potchefstroom was primarily owed to the Broederbond; numerous professors of this small university college were involved in the secret society. Among them was educationist J. C. "Joon" van Rooy who, with one interruption, was Chairman of the Broederbond for 20 years. With some of the Potchefstroom academics, especially with van Rooy, Verwoerd maintained a close relationship.

---

216 PV 93/1/30/1/11, Letter by J. M. Venter, Kerkraad of GK Naboomspruit, to Verwoerd, 31.1.1961; and Verwoerd's reply through his private secretary, 6.2.1961.
217 Verwoerd, Centenary Celebrations of the Reformed Church at Rustenburg, 28.3.1959 (in Pelzer 1966: 258–270, 263).
218 On 'sovereignty of each particular sphere', see also PV 873/5/2/1/1, Handwritten Records, Hoofstuk 5: Soewereiniteit in eie kring as beperking op staatssoewereiniteit, pp. 66–67.
219 Kuyper 1880: 9, 11. Kuyper emphasised that this sovereignty was part of God's order of creation. See also Schutte 2005:357–364. On Kuyper's founding of the university, see Koch 2006: 221–238.
220 Kuyper's continuing interest in South Africa is also reflected in the fact that he devoted an entire chapter to the country in the first volume of his *Antirevolutionaire Staatskunde* (Kuyper 1916, vol. 1: ch. 11).
221 F. J. M. Potgieter: 1958.
222 On the anti-totalitarian and democratic potential of Kuyper's doctrine of 'sovereignty of each particular sphere', see J. J. Venter 1997:112–113.

For the Prime Minister, the NGK, to which he himself belonged, was the most important ecclesiastical basis of legitimacy, because the Reformed denomination was a central point of reference for national identity: "It would be inconceivable that the Afrikaner people did not stand fast on these two mainstays of Church and State."[223] Any criticism of the policy that came from the church weighed particularly heavily, since it could endanger the basis of his legitimacy.

The NGK was organised autonomously in the four provinces, but only the churches in the Orange Free State and Natal were consistently conservative. The mission branch of the Church, which was strongly developed in the OFS, had contributed significantly to the formulation of apartheid ideology since the 1940s.[224] A wider range of opinions and attitudes existed in both the Transvaal and the Cape Province. Because the question of the moral justification of apartheid policy was a central issue, the government reacted with concern to any criticism from the ranks of the Church. Verwoerd feared that a relaxation of racial segregation in the churches would become the gateway for general egalitarianism. That is why he rose to defend the Reformed Churches. In his view, it was precisely because they were the "mainspring in the life of the Afrikaner" that they were "systematically belittled [by their opponents] as narrow-minded in order to cause dissension and a weakening of the churches' influence. Alternatively, every indication of support for the principle of mixed congregations is encouraged and exaggerated in the hope that multi-racialism may increase in religious activities and then be transplanted to the political scene."[225]

At times, prominent NGK theologians expressed reservations about apartheid and the rigor of its implementation; some theologians, such as B. B. Keet,[226] Ben Marais[227] or, for the NHK, Albert Geyser, even took an unequivocal stand against apartheid.[228] Thus, the prominent Stellenbosch theologian Keet argued that the

---

223 Verwoerd, Centenary Celebrations of the Reformed Church at Rustenburg, 28.3.1959 (in Pelzer 1966: 258–270, 261–262).
224 PV 94/1/3/1/1, Memorandum van die Gefedereerde NGK of SA, Sept. 1947. Ibid., Memorandum of Reformed mission churches.
225 PV 93/3/1/24, f. 113, Letter by Verwoerd to D. G. Steyn, 5.8.1959.
226 On Keet's proposals of a middle way along the lines of the Central African Federation, see *Pretoria News*, 18.6.1956 (commentary). Keet (1955: ch. 2) fundamentally criticised the biblical justification of apartheid and the resulting consequences of racial segregation.
227 Maritz 2003:152–156 on Cottesloe.
228 On the heresy case against Geyser because of his stance on apartheid, see Horrell 1963: 4–5. There were occasions on which theology students changed their minds after experiencing encounters with Africans. Attie van der Colf was impressed by a conference in Umtata where black people "so spontaneously, and with goodwill, took the initiative in meetings to make both whites and non–whites speak and act in a mature way, rather than to be guided by mere feelings of

individual should be placed above the community; he called the racial divisions of apartheid "a caste system of the worst kind"; on the basis of physical appearance, it condemned the individual to become a prisoner in his/her 'own' group.[229]

Under the impact of the Sharpeville massacre, the question of the ethics of apartheid became more urgent than before, as many church members were shaken by the scale of the violence. In this context, and in the face of the increasing frequency of mutual attacks, the World Council of Churches proposed to convene meetings to discuss theological issues between the Dutch Reformed and the English-speaking Protestant churches. The main reason for the disputes was the attitude of the churches towards apartheid. This is what was to be the central topic to be discussed between the representatives of eight different churches who got together for a ten-day retreat at the Cottesloe hostel of the University of the Witwatersrand. This meeting was also attended by black church representatives. From the side of the English churches, lay people such as social anthropologist Monica Wilson, writer Alan Paton and liberal politician and publicist Edgar Brookes, also attended the Convention.[230] Through the skilful moderation conducted by representatives of the World Council of Churches, it was possible to overcome the initial mistrust; after ten days of deliberations, the Convention could issue a declaration that deviated from official apartheid policy on essential points.[231] The church representatives called for representation of the coloureds in Parliament. They saw no biblical justification for bans on mixed marriages. They could conceive of the right to vote for the black urban population if the homeland policies offered them no real alternative. These positions were by no means new, they had been expressed by the churches before.[232] But the joint statement of the churches was prominently featured in the media; through its connection with the World Council of Churches, it could also attain international resonance.

However, the arch-conservative NHK immediately distanced itself from the final statement.[233] This is what put the NGK in a very difficult situation amounting to a conflict of loyalties, seeing that many of the members and pastors of this church were also members of the ruling National Party or its supporters and vot-

---

superiority – or inferiority and grudges –, so that everyone can participate fully in the building of our country" (PV 58, Letter by Attie van der Colf to Japie Basson, 13.11.1957).
229 220.K.56 (44), B. B. Keet to Piet Cillié, 15.8.1956. Cillié treated the letter as a letter to the editor and replied to it in *Die Burger*, for which he received praise from SABRA (220.K.56 (46), Letter by J. W. Germishuys (Secr. of SABRA) to Cillié, 27.8.1956).
230 Lückhoff 1978: 71–72.
231 The document is printed in ibid., 83–92.
232 Ibid: 154–156.
233 Dreyer 2013:134. It was only the NHK and not, as Meli (1989: 188) erroneously claims, all the Reformed churches.

ers. Conservative forces in the churches used this to isolate the theologians involved.[234]

According to Cillié, the aggressive criticism of Cottesloe was owed to the 'shock waves' that the churches had set in motion by daring to contradict Verwoerd; the Prime Minister's response, on the other hand, displayed cold calculation: "The difficulty is this: everything we know about the man indicates that he actually wants conflict and will want to set the congregations against the pastors, just as he is now stirring up the masses against us and against the 'intellectuals'."[235] In fact, the very next day, Cillié intimated that the letters to the editor received could no longer be printed, that it was as if a sewage pipe had been opened: the letters contained "the most appalling and repugnant complaints against the Church, all without a direct connection with the [Cottesloe] Declaration.... The bloodhounds have been let loose in politics and the Church; they are feeling very powerful, knowing that the Prime Minister is backing them."[236]

After Cottesloe, Verwoerd appeared to remain aloof; he tended to play down its significance. However, he used his New Year's address to issue blatant threats against the supporters of Cottesloe:

> I do not intend to discuss recent announcements on colour policy by individual churchmen. It is, however, necessary to correct the wholly wrong impression, which has been created by antagonists to the policy of separate development, that certain Afrikaans churches have thereby declared their standpoint.... I express the hope that the names of our churches will no longer be dragged in unfairly in a debate which can as yet only be conducted by individuals as such.[237]

In the opposition to his coloured policy, in Cottesloe and in the resistance still emanating from some circles in SABRA, Verwoerd perceived "dangerous currents in our own ranks"; but the National Party should not be allowed to become "attuned to liberalist politics".[238] In his understanding of society and politics, churches had

---

234 A. C. Cloete 1981: 44–47. However, Cloete is decidedly apologetic and uncritical of the Broederbond. On the part of the Broederbond, and especially Gericke, in the rejection of the Cottesloe decisions by the synods, see N. Smith (2009: 124ff). On the criticism of Cottesloe and the World Council of Churches mounted by circles of the NGK, see PV 93/1/30/1/11, Letter by Dr D. R. Snyman (East London) to Verwoerd, 7.2.1961 and 9.2.1961; and Verwoerd's (Private Secretary) reply, 16.2.1961. See also Wilkins/Strydom 1980: 296.
235 296.K.C.5 (3), Letter by Piet Cillié to Phil Weber, 21.12 1960.
236 296.K.C.5 (4), Letter by Cillié to Weber, 22.2.1960; Treurnicht in particular was especially aggressive in *Die Kerkbode*.
237 Verwoerd, New Year Message, 31.12.1960 (in Pelzer 1966:429–433, 432); see also Lückhoff 1978: 116; and Ryan 1990: 64.
238 PV 93/1/34/5, f. 131, Letter by Verwoerd to W. Bührmann, Volkskas, Pretoria, 22.12.1960.

no place as civil society organisations; he would denounce the involvement of the World Council of Churches as external interference.[239]

Verwoerd's close ally H. B. Thom, Rector of the University of Stellenbosch, reached an understanding with Verwoerd's confidant and theologian J. S. Gericke on a concerted approach. He was particularly grateful for Verwoerd's "leadership" in the matter, as it meant "a lot, especially for the Cape; unfortunately quite a number of our educational and church leaders there have taken a dangerous path".[240] In the meantime, the Prime Minister had pulled out all the stops, and mobilised his supporters within the Church as well as the Broederbond to do more than simply distance the most important representatives of the Church, and the Synods of the Provinces, from the Cottesloe Convention.[241] The church representatives and the Provincial Synods rejected the final Cottesloe document; what is more, the NGK in the Transvaal as well as in the Cape Province withdrew from the World Council of Churches, and subsequently came under the control of their conservative representatives.[242] Since the most eminent theologians of the NGK involved in the discussions in Cottesloe were now on the defensive, church representatives close to the government took advantage of the personnel vacuum to make a steep climb within the church hierarchy. Interestingly, these were persons such as J. D. "Koot" Vorster, the right-wing brother of the future Prime Minister, as well as J. S. Gericke, a former student of Verwoerd's,[243] who was also a prominent member of the Broederbond; the latter was later appointed as Moderator of the Church, as well as Vice–Chancellor of Stellenbosch University.[244]

In this way, Verwoerd broke up the resistance within the Church.[245] It was the treatment of the theologian Beyers Naudé, ostracised for decades to come, by which Verwoerd set yet another intimidating example. Naudé attracted such intense hatred, because he had facilitated the release of secret Broederbond documents, which were published by the weekly *Sunday Times*.[246] Verwoerd now also wielded interpretive power in church and religious circles: not only did he ask his church friends to provide biblical justifications of apartheid, he himself rose

---

239 Piet Meiring 2015: 220.
240 PV 93/3/1/39, Letter by H. B. Thom to Verwoerd, 25.1.1961.
241 Meiring 1990: 106–113. On the machinations of Meyer in the Broederbond, see Stals 1998: 504–507.
242 Kinghorn 1986: 119; see also Lückhoff 1978: 138–151.
243 PV 72/3, Beukes, Brandfort, Stellenbosch, Arme–blanke vraagstuk, p. 1.
244 On these machinations, see also Lückhoff 1978: 116–120, 130–131.
245 Ibid., 165–166, 170–171.
246 On the campaign against Naudé, obviously co–ordinated, see. N. Smith 2009: 102–107; also Horrell 1965: 12–13. On the AB, see Pelzer 1979: 70–71. Bruwer/Olivier (1964: 71–76), too, participated in the denunciations against Naudé.

to present speeches assuring his audiences of the Christian character of the policy of racial segregation.²⁴⁷ Up to that point, Afrikaner nationalist groupings were ideologically heterogeneous and diverse, united only by a common aim. But in the crisis year of 1960, Verwoerd subjected the Afrikaner nationalist movement to his authority.²⁴⁸ In the long run, it would be impossible to suppress dissenting views, especially those regarding to the policies on coloureds. But Verwoerd and his allies Thom, Gericke, Vorster and others prevented open discussion about his policies during his lifetime.²⁴⁹

With the examples he had made in 1960, of du Plessis, Olivier, Cillié, and Naudé, Verwoerd sought to alert various institutions and groups of people to his power; and he palpably demonstrated that he was lashing out at dissenters *ad personam*.²⁵⁰ The systematic nature of his approach is evident from the fact that the only opposition MP, Helen Suzman, was also subjected to a campaign of intimidation and agitation by the NP in 1963.²⁵¹ Verwoerd's position subsequently remained largely unchallenged. His position was further elevated by the nimbus of the nationalist martyr who had survived the April 1960 assassination attempt only through divine intervention.

---

247 Thus on 12.5.1963, addressing students in Cape Town (FAV 4.7.2.4.5, Handwritten notes 'Is ons Rassebeleid Christelik?', in which he describes the homeland policy as morally just, because one grants others what one claims for oneself (p. 4)). See also F. J. M. Potgieter 1958; and Ngcokovane 1989: 148–155 on developments in the NGK, and especially on the basic theocratic attitude towards the state.
248 Giliomee 2003a: 530.
249 M. J. Olivier (1964), who could hardly hide his understanding for the situation of the coloureds and his criticism behind a general defence of apartheid.
250 O'Meara 1996: 204, note †.
251 Suzman 1991: 36.

Modernisation

Addressing the House of Commons in 1961, British Prime Minister Harold Macmillan, spoke about the Commonwealth Conference and expressed his regret at South Africa's withdrawal. He summed up his impressions as follows: "What shocked the Conference was that the policy of the present South African Government appeared to set up what we would regard as an unhappy practice, inherited from the past, perhaps, as a philosophy of action for the future. [. . .] All this accentuation and systemisation of the policy of apartheid is something very new."[1] Indeed, it was a shock that many external observers felt when they realised that apartheid was by no means a relic of a rapidly fading colonialism that could be overcome. Apartheid did not turn out to be the panic-stricken rigidity of a white minority on the defensive; in fact, Verwoerd presented it as a forward-looking, modern policy. Where the other prime ministers had thought they were meeting a conservative, they now had to recognise that he was a modernising state builder who wanted to make racism the basis of state and society. Apartheid, in his eyes, offered a permanent solution, it was by no means a policy that had to be overcome. At the same time, it became clear that his inflexibility resulted precisely from this conception.[2] Even during his trip to Africa the previous year, in the course of talks with Verwoerd, Macmillan had noted "the full degree of obstinacy, amounting really to fanaticism": "Apartheid to him was more than a political philosophy, it was a religion. . . . He was certainly as convinced as John Knox himself that he alone could be right, and that there was no question of argument but merely a statement of his will."[3] While small concessions, wrung from him by colleagues such as Macmillan or Menzies, would, to them, have been a first step on

---

[1] Macmillan's speech in the House of Commons 22.3.1961 (qtd. in Mansergh 1963: 373; see also Geyser 1983: 90). British Labour MP James Griffiths expressed the widespread view of apartheid as a reactionary policy: "South Africa remains the country which is trying to put the clock back." (*Times*, 26.4.1960) As early as 1944, Verwoerd had described the decision of the Johannesburg City Council to make Joubert Park accessible to blacks as a "step backwards" (qtd. in D. Prinsloo 1979: 336).

[2] Macmillan, House of Commons, 22.3.1961 (in Mansergh 1963: 373); see also H. Macmillan 1972: 303–304.

[3] H. Macmillan 1972: 152. Somewhat later, he writes: "I had the unusual experience of soon noticing that nothing one could say or put forward would have the smallest effect upon the views of this determined man." (ibid, 153) See also the assessment of the American ambassador after his inaugural visit to the new Prime Minister in 1959: "He is a fanatic with a fanatic's absolute faith in his own righteousness." (Doc. 337, Telegram from the Embassy in South Africa to the Department of State, 27.4.1959 – in LaFantasie 1992: 732) Roux (1978: 430) even compared him to Metternich.

South Africa's path to post-colonial normality, for Verwoerd they represented a dangerous soft-pedalling on a political programme that he had devised for the future. During the conference in 1961, when the assembled prime ministers advocated small concessions to plant hope, Verwoerd interpreted their attitude was yet more proof that concessions would only result in new demands and, in the end, in black majority rule.[4]

The instrument for his modernisation policy was an assertive, strong state. The apartheid state differed fundamentally, at least in its ambitions, from the colonial state of the first half of the 20th century with its weak bureaucracy. The first signs of a strong state were manifested in the policy of state-controlled industrialisation, which Prime Minister Hertzog initiated with the founding of an iron and steel industry (ISCOR) in the 1920s. He wanted to free South Africa from its one-sided dependency as a supplier of raw materials for British industry, and to introduce import substitution in order to put South Africa on a path of self-sustaining modernisation. The numerous parastatal industries that emerged over the following decades, as well as the importance of planning in the context of World War II, show that the South African economy depended to a large extent on political initiative.[5] Apartheid, for its part, can be understood as a reaction to the consequences of this modernisation. It countered them with a further push for modernisation, which was even more clearly state-driven.[6]

On 29 July 1944, veterinary surgeon and Broederbonder Hermann Otto Mönnig (1897–1978) presented a speech at the Annual Meeting of the South African Academy, entitled 'Natural Science and Technology in the Service of Man',[7] which started with an Hegelian outline of a history of evolution as Spirit finding itself. Human development, he said, was first determined by instincts, then by intuition, that is, cognition guided by Spirit (7). It was only the development of natural science that brought liberation, for development in the meantime had progressed to the point where its further progress could be pursued purposefully (8). He trusted "that with the ever-increasing pace of development, the next 50 years, or 100 years at the most, will bring the solution to all our important material problems" (9). Diseases and nutritional problems would be solved by then. With the develop-

---

4 PV 93/1/30/1/19, f. 26, Letter by Verwoerd to C. R. Amm (Johannesburg), 8.5.1963.
5 Clark 1994:133; on the establishment of the first parastatal corporations after ISCOR, see Clark 1994: 160–165; see also Dubow 2005: 9–10.
6 The view that apartheid is a form of authoritarian modernisation has become widely accepted in recent scholarship (see for example Edwards/Hecht 2010: 620–624.)
7 Printed in *Wetenskap en Kuns*, 25.3.1945. Here offprint, apparently with its own pagination. On Mönnig's biography, see https://repository.up.ac.za/bitstream/handle/2263/15226/hc_hom%C3%B6nnig.pdf;sequence=1 (29.05.2023).

ment of Western civilisation, mankind would now be in a position to consciously engage in rational planning (9), which would also include the displacement and planned resettlement of large population groups.[8]

Verwoerd shared this emphatic belief in progress. It was therefore hardly surprising that he later entrusted Mönnig with the leadership of the Scientific Advisory Council at the moment when he embraced a comprehensive view of society, and placed it, along with economic planning, at the centre of his policy.[9]

The white South African elite as a whole was inspired by this optimistic faith in progress, as evidenced by a number of memoranda penned in various institutions during the 1950s. In 1957, Dr Moolman of the Natural Resources Development Council presented a memorandum arguing for more extensive planning and co-ordination by scientific advisory bodies. Policy was now conceivable only if it was demonstrably scientifically based, and sought to find lasting changes and solutions.[10] In special cases, the state itself carried out the economic development, as in the case of ISCOR. "Our wish in South Africa is that development should take place in a co-ordinated and planned way. In some cases, this means that new development needs to be stimulated at the right time and in the right place; in other cases, it means that development that is already underway needs to be given guidance and advice."[11] To this end, an advisory institution was required that would examine "the broad, national aspects of development" in "a systematic and comprehensive way". It must be in a position to submit "realistic, executable development plans from time to time",[12] and to "co-ordinate the various development activities within the state." The scientists had high ambitions, as Moolman demanded that the body should have the right to conduct research and develop

---

[8] Eiselen 1955b: 10–16.
[9] In 1961, Prof. D. C. Krogh was appointed as his Deputy. He was the first director of the Gefedereerde Kamers van Nywerheid van Suid–Afrika, then Professor of Economics at UNISA (Boucher 1973: 313). Verwoerd's predecessor, Prime Minister Strijdom, had previously become aware of Mönnig through the lecture summarised here. A. J. R. van Rhyn sent the Prime Minister a memorandum of Mönnig's, in which he argued that scientific research had reached a degree of complexity that necessitated reorganisation. Thus, a central organisation was to be created, which should be placed under one authority, preferably that of the Prime Minister. This would ensure that recommendations from the advisory body would reach Cabinet and "receive the necessary attention. Such an arrangement would also prevent one department from becoming involved in the affairs of others. Adequate contact with and control over medical, agricultural and industrial research would be established for the ministers by the representatives on the councils and committees of the research organisations." (PV 93/1/68/1, Letter by A. J. R. van Rhyn to Strijdom (Prime Minister), 23.8.1957).
[10] PV 93/1/68/1, f. 16, Report of Dr Moolman to the Prime Minister, 3.9.57, p. 10.
[11] Ibid., f. 9, p. 2.
[12] Ibid., f. 10, p. 3.

proposals "on its own initiative" – limited under the proviso that "departments planning major developments should consult and cooperate with the organisation".[13] Thus, the organisation itself was to formulate policy and even have some kind of authority to issue directives to the ministries. This was the beginning of a self-empowerment of the experts; but it did not take long for Verwoerd to set limits to it.

This attitude towards experts, which Verwoerd contrasted with the comprehensive competencies of the politician, is what marked the final phase of Verwoerd's political career. From the spring of 1958, Mönnig acted as Chairman of the "Adviserende Raad vir Wetenskaplike Beleid [Advisory Council on Scientific Policy]"; he proposed that this Council be given far-reaching powers. It was to be given oversight of "all scientific services", and co-ordinate these services either in the form of a new Department of Science, or as a consultative body within the Prime Minister's Office. Verwoerd considered the co-ordination in the scientific field "absolutely necessary", as there were too many overlaps and disputes. However, he left no doubt about his conviction that all decisions had to be left to the politicians, that is, the Cabinet, which is why the advisory body was to be made up of the Secretaries of the Ministries involved, along with select scientists. An "outstanding" scientist was to be appointed as advisor and Chairperson for the Advisory Board, in the office of the Prime Minister.[14]

A joint memorandum from several Broederbond organisations, drafted by economist C. G. W. Schumann, Verwoerd's old acquaintance from Stellenbosch days, supported the proposal for the establishment of an Advisory Board. In principle, the institutions involved recognised the importance of, and the need for, such a body, as times had changed and the "rather uninhibited free competition of the nineteenth century [was] no longer appropriate". Intellectual responses could no longer keep pace with technical development. "Outdated political and technical-administrative forms of thinking and control are often applied in efforts to direct a highly complex modern state machinery." Even if few people had any illusions about the transformational power that such a single body could develop, the experience of other countries showed "that more conscious efforts were made after World War II not simply to investigate and plan for the short-term

---

13 Ibid., f. 16, p. 10.
14 PV 93/1/68/1, carbon copy 'Notas samespreking op 10 November 1959 met Dr. Mönnig, Naude en Prof. Oosthuizen'. This was preceded by an exchange of letters with corresponding proposals from Mönnig (ibid., Letter by the Chairman of 'Adviserende Raad vir Wetenskaplike Beleid' (Mönnig), Pretoria, 27.5.1958, to the Private Secretary of the Prime Minister, with a memorandum. Reply, 16.6.58, stating that the Prime Minister was considering the matter and wished to discuss it in Cabinet).

prospects of economic sectors or particular government departments, but to comprehensively plan and promote the economic development of the country as a whole". Development could no longer be left to free market forces, but the state intervened much more decisively than before. Because such a body would be more globally oriented and develop a wider purview, it would have to report directly to the Prime Minister rather than to any of the departmental ministers.[15] Verwoerd explained:

> By the agency of the economic adviser and all those who assist him, certain programmes to attain our aims are being drafted. Plans, which set a certain aim in which direction the country wants to move in a fixed period of time and by which it can be determined whether or not sufficient progress is made, are of very great value. Improvements in respect of financing methods have already been made and ideas in respect of further adaptations are being obtained.[16]

A future-oriented vision was by no means a personal speciality of Verwoerd's; it was part of the political semantics of Afrikaner nationalism more generally; it is evident in the naming of places, buildings, and even newspapers, to such an extent that it has to be understood as programmatic. 'Sonop' or 'Dagbreek' were the names given to buildings at Stellenbosch University, where optimism about the future was being inculcated in young people. 'Oosterlig' and 'Dagbreek'[17] were the names of nationalist newspapers that also formed part of the programme. An orientation towards the future was a basic feature of Verwoerd's political thinking, emphatically proclaimed over and over again. It was reflected in the grandiose planning of the 1960s.

Verwoerd was the most powerful and power-hungry prime minister in South African history. During his reign, the state extended its influence immensely, reaching into the most intimate spheres of its citizens, "in[to] areas of life that had remained quite untouched during the tenures of previous prime ministers". Without the slightest self-doubt, he built on the substantial powers of the Prime Minister and even expanded them to an extent that dwarfed those of his Euro-

---

15 PV 93/1/53/3/1, ff. 33–45, Memorandum oor 'n adviserende ontwikkelingsraad, opgestel namens die Ekonomiese Instituut, die Afrikaanse Handelsinstituut en die Suid–Afrikaanse Akademie vir Wetenskap en Kuns. In that context, see also PV 93/1/34/1, f. 46, Letter by J. G. van der Merwe, n.d. [1958], to Verwoerd, stating that "a small group of leading friends in the economy" had approached the UR of the AB with the question as to whether there should not be a second congress on economic affairs.
16 Verwoerd, Annual Congress of the Afrikaans Trade Institute, Pretoria 19.9.1961 (in Pelzer 1966: 611–628, 626–627).
17 It is possible that the newspaper was named after the residence in which Verwoerd stayed during his student days in Stellenbosch (see also Booyens/Oosthuysen 1971: 27).

pean counterparts. "At the end of his life, he held more reins of government in his hands, he directly managed more major projects, down to the most astonishing detail, than even the most predominant of his predecessors, General Smuts."[18]

Verwoerd considered a policy to be truly substantiated only if it was scientifically based.[19] A policy relying on intuition was as far from his mind as demagogy was suspect to him. Since politics had to be based on criteria of objectivity and truth, that is, based on facts, it was largely dependent on scientific justification and expertise.[20] His very specific, positivist, and anti-theoretical understanding of science has to be taken into account, as does his pronounced inclination towards systematisation, which was also reflected in his self-assigned role as chief economic co-ordinator and developer: "If we want to increase our national production, if we want to set about it systematically, then we will have to build our future on this type of economic-scientific study."[21] To support the Prime Minister, a Junior Minister for Planning – J. F. W. Haak – was appointed in August 1961.[22] Verwoerd's rise from Minister to Prime Minister, tasked with tackling the constitutional problems, developed a momentum of its own, both in terms of the nature of the policies pursued, and in its ever-widening reach. The expansion of his power culminated in technical-industrial mega-projects. It offers another example, as yet largely unaccounted for, of the planning euphoria that swept through administrative and scientific circles in the period after the Second World War. As erstwhile scientist and administrator of many years' standing, Verwoerd was ide-

---

18 Cillié 1980: 55–56. On Verwoerd's obsession with detail, see also A. Boshoff 1974: 15.
19 As early as 1937, he demanded that state–appointed commissions of inquiry conduct their investigations according to scientific standards (*Die Transvaler*, 21.12.1937).
20 The variety of different research approaches "shows us all how the ordinary state administrator relies on the findings of these scientists for many of the things he has to deal with on a daily basis." (PV 93/3/4/13, f. 131, Toespraak by geleentheid van die opening van die Museum van die Geologiese Opname op 17 Mei, 1966).
21 Verwoerd, Annual Congress of the Afrikaans Trade Institute, Pretoria 19.9.1961 (in Pelzer 1966: 611–628, 627).
22 PV 93/4/1/8, ff. 17–18, Press release on scientific advisers, 2.5.1963. In the same year, Verwoerd founded a new Ministry of Planning, but kept the two advisory bodies in the Prime Minister's Office. With this decision, he emphasised that planning still enjoyed top priority. He also made it clear that the individual Ministries were to retain their planning functions, hence they would not be merged with the new Ministry. The fact that planning activities were fanning out across all Ministries reflected the growing importance of planning for his policy, which now permeated all spheres. The planning staff of hitherto decentralised units were to be integrated into the Ministry of Planning itself; the previous Adjunct Minister J. F. W. Haak was promoted upon his appointment in the new post, which now also included the Department of Mines (PV 93/1/20/1/2, ff. 124–126, Press release, 4. 6. 1964).

ally placed to tackle this task with the aim of permanently grafting the model of apartheid onto South African society.[23]

Verwoerd sought to make South Africa economically invulnerable, because he feared the increasing isolation of the country, as the first boycotts were hitting home.[24] It is significant that the Advisory Council was founded the day after the Sharpeville massacre.[25] In 1961, Mönnig addressed the Suid-Afrikaanse Genootskap vir die Bevordering van die Wetenskap (South African Association for the Advancement of Science) in Pretoria. He compared the organisation of science in various Western countries with that in South Africa and found the latter significantly wanting. In South Africa, for example, there were proportionally (taking only the white population as a basis) far too few scientists, which he attributed to inadequate research funding. As universities were traditionally teaching institutions, research was to be systematically expanded. Existing researchers would have to be better supported in their work by freeing them from teaching and administrative duties. In addition, research councils were to be established, to take over co-ordination and promotion tasks.[26] In fact, South Africa was far behind in its research performance; but the fact that it was during Verwoerd's tenure that research, both basic and applied, was recognised to be of crucial importance for the economy, was due to the political role of planning, understood as central steering mechanism for society as a whole. Thus the Council for Scientific and Industrial Research, founded in 1945, became more involved in strategic research projects.[27] Subsequently, the Scientific Advisory Council insisted that South Africa had to present herself in a better light in the international research arena.[28] The country's weak position in the international scientific community was becoming a problem, exacerbated by apartheid policies and Bantu Education. That is probably one of the reasons why Verwoerd took a combative stance when he addressed

---

23 On the diagnosis of the 20th century as the age of (state) planning, see van Laak 2008: 308–311, 322. On the intrinsic connection between order, control and planning, see Doering-Manteuffel 2008: 398, 402.
24 According to US representatives assessing the situation in 1966, South Africa was economically near–invulnerable at the time: "nothing less than an absolute blocade [sic] for 3–4 years would hurt her so badly that she would feel real pressure to recede from apartheid." (Digital National Security Archive, Ed Hamilton, White House, Memo: Assassination of Hendrik Verwoerd, 6.9.1966).
25 J. Botha 1967: 61.
26 PV 93/1/34/6, ff. 83–89, H. O. Mönnig, Die ontwikkeling van die natuurwetenskap in Suid-Afrika, Lecture, 10.5.1961. See also S. Naudé 1964: 15–16, 41.
27 Ibid, 7; on staffing and funding, see 9–10.
28 PV 93/1/68/1, f. 77, Letter by Mönnig to the Prime Minister, with attached memorandum on the conference, 26.11.1963.

Parliament on 26 March 1964, in the face of moves to exclude South Africa from the World Health Organisation. South Africa was not prepared to withdraw from the organisation, he stated, but wished to continue its participation.[29]

Under Mönnig's direction, the organisation and development of science was subordinated to national goals, in line with Verwoerd's objectives: "It is scientific work, but it is in South Africa's interest that the economic fruits of scientific work are harvested."[30] University education should generally be geared to national requirements:

> Throughout the years, the Government has realised that we in South Africa still have much to do for which we must train our own experts. Practically each country in the world suffers a shortage of scientists, experts and practical people of every description. It is, perhaps, in the field of engineering that we feel the deficiency most, and we therefore had to realise that we in South Africa would ourselves have to provide for our needs and not extend beggar's hands to other countries albeit that they have in many respects recorded greater progress than we.[31]

The aim was "to do what is also done in other countries with excellent results. Where they might have greater ability in this field than South Africa, we shall still try, within the limits of our ability, to harness science on the planning of our future life and our economic endeavours."[32]

To this end, it was necessary to start with compiling a survey of South African scientists and their main areas of work, "where exactly they work, what they have been trained in, and in what direction they could possibly move, if this were necessary in the interest of the country".[33] So far, individual departments of the state apparatus had dealt with these questions. "Now I can point to the way in

---

29 PV 93/1/4/1/10, pp. 4–5. Statement in Parliament, 26.3.64, on World Health Organisation.
30 PV 93/3/4/13, Toespraak by geleentheid van die opening van die Museum van die Geologiese Opname op 17 Mei 1966, f. 127.
31 Verwoerd, Inauguration of a Bust and Plaque at the J. G. Strijdom Building for Engineering, University of Pretoria, 15.9.1961 (in Pelzer 1966: 605–610, 605–606). Verwoerd intervened in his capacity of Prime Minister when it turned out that a bureaucratic hurdle prevented his son from transferring from a correspondence university to a residential university without losing a year of study. Verwoerd immediately recognised a mistake in a matter of principle here, for which the predicament of his son was only the occasion; if it were to be applied as a matter of principle, it could also prevent others from completing their studies without unnecessary delays. For this reason he immediately pushed for a change in the regulations (FAV 4.7.4.2, Letter by Verwoerd to Rector C. H. Rautenbach (University of Pretoria), 16.2.1965; Rautenbach's reply, 23.2.1965; Verwoerd's new reply, 3.3.1965; and the information provided by the Minister of Education, Arts and Science, Jan de Klerk, 11.3.1965).
32 Verwoerd, Annual Congress of the Afrikaans Trade Institute, held in Pretoria,19.9.1961 (in Pelzer 1966: 611–628, 618–619).
33 PV 93/4/1/10, ff. 81–96, Verwoerd before the Academy of Science and Art, 27.6.1964, p. 5.

which in recent years, the State has realised that it must establish a central co-ordinating and planning machinery that brings together all the departments of the State under one umbrella, together with the private sector, and that we need to bring this about not only in the economic sphere but also in the field of science."

The Scientific Advisory Council focused on improving the organisation of science; it was also tasked with the co-ordination of research on nuclear energy. The government sought the greatest possible degree of economic self-sufficiency, so as to be able to withstand boycotts and sanctions:

> When we initiated this policy in 1915, we did not have a programme or a "blueprint" covering all the aspects which this economic development should embrace. We did not know whether or where there would be Iscors or Sasols. We set ourselves an overall ultimate objective, namely to make South Africa as self-sufficient as possible in the economic field, and in the financial field to finance its capital requirements in our own country as far as possible because no country can strive for constitutional independence without striving to attain economic independence. To this I added that of course no country is completely independent economically, just as in the international political sphere no country is ever completely independent of the tendencies and influences making themselves felt in that sphere. But it should be our aim to achieve this independence to the extent which [sic] any country can achieve it.[34]

The new task of the Prime Minister lay in the planned management of economic development and expansion: "A new task awaits the Prime Minister and his department when certain big constitutional and other problems have been handled. This task is to take a lead in planning and co-ordinating the steps required to solve certain central problems in regard to the country's economic development and which affect the life of the country in all fields."[35]

Shortly after Sharpeville, Verwoerd first floated the idea of implementing apartheid through a Five-Year Plan, even considering a loan from the World Bank to finance it.[36] But the emphatic appeal to ideals and the will of the people stood in the foreground. Verwoerd recurred to the mobilising power of republicanism that had previously served his purposes, to redirect it towards a new goal:

> When one sees the faith in South Africa's inherent strength reaffirmed, then one wonders whether one can help encourage and whether it can be assisted in the future, not only through the work of entrepreneurs, but also through study by Government experts. The

---

34 Verwoerd, First Speech as Prime Minister, 18.9.1958 (in Pelzer 1966: 164–190, 181). Similarly FAV 4.7.2.4.5, Speech at the Natal NP Party Congress in Durban, 27.8.1963, p. 15.
35 Verwoerd, Annual Congress of the Afrikaans Trade Institute, Pretoria, 19.9.1961 (in Pelzer 1966: 611–628, 611).
36 FAV 4.7.1.5, Memorandum, Wat vorentoe gedoen moet word, p. 10.

Government believes that this is surely possible. We do not only believe that it can be done, but that it must be done. In South Africa up to now we have been very busy with short-term planning. Not enough consideration was given to planning on a long term. The principles which work against the growth of the country in the long run have not always been noticed. There was no specific and purposeful study of these principles. The Government, i.e. the Department of the Prime Minister under the supervision of an economic adviser with research officials, has started a study of the great trends in our economic life. They are also looking for the obstacles on the country's way to progress.[37]

Verwoerd's understanding of politics was strongly voluntaristic. Historian Pieter Kapp characterised him as follows: "This idealism, which reached a peak under the persuasive and charismatic leadership of Dr. H. F. Verwoerd, was based on the assumption that what seemed impossible was actually possible – through commitment, hard work, imagination and faith."[38]

Despite his enthusiastic embrace of state planning and systematic self-development for South Africa, human will remained a central factor for Verwoerd: in his view, the development of South Africa from a colony producing raw materials to an industrialised state would have been inconceivable without the exertion of will-power on the part of South Africans.[39] South Africa did not have any of its own oil reserves; her greatest vulnerability lay in the energy sector. In a near-absurd call, against all available evidence, Verwoerd appealed to the will of South African geologists to continue to search for oil, as if the mere will to find oil would yield actual results:

---

37 Verwoerd, Annual Congress of the Afrikaans Trade Institute, Pretoria 19.9.1961 (in Pelzer 1966: 611–628, 623–624).
38 Kapp 2009: 421.
39 Verwoerd, Union Show, Milner Park, Johannesburg, 9.4.1960 (in Pelzer 1966: 388–393, 393). Anton Rupert argued in a similarly voluntaristic manner in his 1950 survey of the actual and the possible share of Afrikaners in the South African economy, significantly referring to the voluntarist economic movement of Afrikaner nationalism, and to Zionism (PV 206/3/2/1, Anton Rupert, Die Afrikaner in die Nywerheid [1950], pp. 105–110). In recent times, some have tried to construe Anton Rupert retrospectively as a kind of missed alternative to Verwoerd. However, this overlooks the fact that Rupert himself came from the camp of Afrikaner nationalism, that he had a right-wing extremist past, and never developed a political alternative to Verwoerd's apartheid that would have been able to command a majority within the white population. Strikingly, Rupert gave positions to many of the extreme right–wing proponents of nationalism, such as Nicolaas Diederichs and P. J. Meyer (on the latter see P. J. Meyer 1984: 58; also Witz 2003: 124). On the other hand, Rupert was seen as a threat to Verwoerd's hegemonic position within the nationalist camp. Rupert was very well connected in the Broederbond, he was the wealthiest among the Afrikaners. As highly successful businessman, he was a role model for many; through his Rembrandt Group and his personal fortune, he had garnered great influence and, above all, an independence that an L. J. du Plessis, as salaried professor, never had.

> But there is one thing which has caused us some grief in recent years; it was in an area in which the geologist proved himself to be a pessimist, but which is where the politician, whose task drove him, is now getting ahead of the geologist again and driving him – namely the area of crude oil. . . . Well, a politician is a man who lives by kicking and pushing and if he now gets it himself, then he can also dish it out. So we started kicking and shoving the geologists and told them that it must be there and they must find it. . . . The interesting thing is that, during this time, the hope of the geologist also began to blossom again.[40]

The boost that the Scientific Advisory Council experienced during Verwoerd's reign became visible in 1962 when it was moved from the Ministry of Trade and Industry to the Office of the Prime Minister. Its members were "selected with a view to their knowledge of the whole range of different scientific disciplines", and on the basis of their expertise. In addition, members were to include staff "active in parastatal institutions and state departments in which scientific knowledge is of major importance".[41]

On 1 and 2 May, the first meeting of the Council took place in Pretoria, with Mönnig as Chairman. Prime Minister Verwoerd took the opportunity to meet the members during the lunch break, and to let them know what he expected from them. "Because the office of Prime Minister has the highest co-ordinating and planning function in the government machinery, this new body also has to have its place here, as does the Economic Advisor and the Economic Advisory Council."[42]

Planning proved to be essential in order to achieve the central goal of his policy – to permanently secure the continued existence of a white nation in Southern Africa. "By looking far ahead and planning wisely, one can achieve the preservation of European civilization. . . . It seems to us that the way in which this can happen, is by allowing the economic development to take place in such a way that there is certainty that that portion of South Africa which we know as European South Africa, remains European-controlled."[43] The idea that the economic development of South Africa could not be left to its own devices, but had to be planned and politically controlled, was nothing new in the 1960s. One of the objectives was import substitution, which was essentially designed to render the economy immune to sanctions; at the same time, it served as a kind of economic and political decolo-

---

[40] PV 93/3/4/13, Toespraak by geleentheid van die opening van die Museum van die Geologiese Opname op 17 Mei, 1966, ff. 129–130. In 1965, in an interview with the Financial Gazette, Verwoerd replied to the question about the reason for the introduction of a planning ministry, stating that the search was on for oil and that Phalaborwa, being situated close to a Bantustan and containing mineral resources, would carry the development forward (PV 93/4/1/10, ff. 150–155, Press briefing in the *Financial Gazette*).
[41] PV 93/4/1/7, ff. 123–125. Press statement, 30.11.1962.
[42] PV 93/4/1/8, Press release 2.5.1963.
[43] Verwoerd, Federated Chambers of Industry, Cape Town 25.5.1954 (in Pelzer 1966: 53–63, 55).

nisation. It was motivated not least by nationalist aims; it was Verwoerd's declared intention to reduce the colonial dependence on providing raw materials to the industrialised state of Great Britain: "There is only one method and that is to provide for sufficient compensating exports. It is, therefore, necessary to establish industries to earn income by exports and industries to replace imports.... Firstly, one must select the type of industry which will earn exports and replace imports so that on the one hand the country will obtain a steady income which will enable South Africa to pay for what must be imported and local development."[44] In a lecture presented to the Bondsraad in October 1950, Broederbond member F. S. Steyn had already pointed out the close linkages between social, political, and economic factors in shaping the future of Afrikaners. He warned against the "extreme forms of the socialist tendency"; in his view, these could turn into powerful weapons for the black population. For the Afrikaners, "controlled capitalism" was a much more viable possibility, by which he specifically meant parastatal enterprises.[45] In 1957, the Broederbond dealt with various aspects of the economy, including the relationship to the state.[46] In the 1960s, an added factor was the increasing likelihood that sanctions could be imposed on South Africa, in particular an arms embargo.[47]

The exceptionally large parastatal sector had been established during the war years under the leadership of van der Bijl.[48] In the early apartheid period, it was further expanded;[49] and during the years of Verwoerd's government, it received a strong new impetus towards a "regulated private enterprise sys-

---

[44] Verwoerd, Annual Congress of the Afrikaans Trade Institute, Pretoria 19.9.1961 (in Pelzer 1966: 611–628, 625–626).
[45] AB Archives, 2/3/18, Bondsraad, 2–3.10.1950, p. 10, TOP 14, Die Afrikanernasie en sy toekoms. In 1946, Verwoerd had firmly rejected H. J. van der Bijl's proposal to withdraw ISCOR from state control (D. Prinsloo 1979: 542).
[46] AB Archives, 2/3/34, UR meeting, 20–21.2.1957, p. 6, TOP 24, Die Afrikaner se ekonomiese strewe en die staat.
[47] PV 93/4/1/11, ff. 174–181, Speech in Pietersburg, 14.11.1964 on an arms embargo allegedly planned by the British government, with a warning about the British naval base at Simonstown. The press release, 26.11.1964 (f. 182), expressed appreciation of the promise of the British government to honour a previously announced undertaking to deliver the military planes that had been placed on order. But there was renewed disgruntlement when Prime Minister Wilson claimed that sporting rifles and ammunition would no longer be sold to South Africa because they were needed for internal purposes (f. 199, press statement 9.12.1964). The High Commissioner had then made representations to the British Foreign Office and had demanded proof. The Minister reportedly admitted that they had none.
[48] Clark 1994: 110–114.
[49] The Broederbond was also involved in the founding of Sasol (AB Archive, 2/3/15, UR meeting, 9.11.1948, p. 5, TOP 27, Vervaardiging van petrol uit steenkool; also AB Archive, 2/3/19, Verslag oor UR-Werksaamhede, 1950, p. 7).

tem".[50] Despite paying lip service to a market economy,[51] Verwoerd aimed for a kind of economic development in which the state set the central guidelines and controlled their implementation. Although there was scope for the continued existence of independent business enterprises, the state wanted to create clear frameworks for economic development.

Verwoerd assigned a prominent role to para-statal enterprises, which were to propel and pave the way for the development of private industry. "Think, for example, of the tremendous plans of Escom, Iscor, Sasol and Foskor. Within the next 10–12 years, if not sooner, according to plans that they already have, an expansion of R2,000 million will take place."[52] This was due to the fact that these companies approached infrastructural development and key industries from a long-term strategic perspective; they could not escape the direct grip of state planning. The reshaping of cities along segregationist lines, particularly in the urban mining centres of the Witwatersrand, involved planning on a grand scale.[53] This was related to the ways in which apartheid generally bolstered the state and its administrative apparatuses: the political programme of apartheid relied on planning and co-ordination, every step of the way.[54]

Verwoerd was extremely suspicious of a self-regulating market economy. He also found that co-ordination processes within the economy had so far functioned only inadequately: "That is one of the reasons why the Government instituted an economic council and appointed in my Department an economic adviser who will also be chairman of that council."[55] As in the case of white poverty, only the State was in a position to take on a steering role in the further development of the economy, especially since in a centrally planned, integrated approach, there were aspects other than purely economic ones that had to be taken into account: "All will be linked together in any future planning so that we can guide our future economic development in such a way that the social consequences of the new de-

---

50 Andrews/Gerrill/Guingand/Holloway/Meyer/van Eck 1965: 46.
51 Particularly explicit as late as June 1966 in a speech to the Johannesburg Stock Exchange (FAV 4.7.2.4.7), Address at a Banquet by the Committee of the Johannesburg Stock Exchange, 30.6.1966, esp. p. 11.
52 Verwoerd, Annual Congress of the Afrikaans Trade Institute, Pretoria 19.9.1961 (in Pelzer 1966: 611–628, esp. 621–622); see also Verwoerd, Inauguration of a Bust and Plaque at the J. G. Strijdom Building for Engineering, University of Pretoria 15.9.1961 (in Pelzer 1966:605–610, 607).
53 I. Evans 1997: ch. 4.
54 M. D. C. Nel: 1.
55 Verwoerd, Statement of Policy, 9.3.1960 (in Pelzer 1966: 340–369, 345).

velopment are taken cognisance of without interfering with the economic progress which we all value."⁵⁶

When it came to setting directions for the economy, Verwoerd displayed flexibility, because he could not completely shackle the economy; instead, he sought to achieve a balance between short- and long-term planning goals, leaving sufficient leeway for economic development:

> We cannot hold up that development pending the location of suitable areas and sites according to the longterm policy. But in permitting the laying out of industrial sites cognisance must be taken of the requirements of the long-term policy. . . . If we allow speculators to go on laying out industrial areas and sites, whether they are needed or not, vested interests will be created which will oppose the development of industry elsewhere for selfish reasons.⁵⁷

Homogenised, statistically viable data can be obtained only by disregarding and devaluing quality. The process that began about 200 years ago, by which qualitatively different and thus incomparable details were transformed into quantitatively comparable units can be considered as an aspect of political modernity. With his advocacy of psychological tests and the attempt to break down human characteristics into measurable units, Verwoerd had demonstrated his commitment to such approaches. In the 1930s, the combination of positivist data collection with formal logic, as Verwoerd espoused it, was considered the epitome of science.⁵⁸ This approach corresponds to what James Scott describes as "the view from above". The more lofty the position taken by the observer, the more life worlds are bound to disappear, while structures and systems are being rendered visible. A homogenising view from great heights often misses the most important details. The result is not only a massive reduction of complexity, but also a distortion on an elementary level, which can render the data completely useless. Although this provides the State with a basis for initiative and interventions, it can generate systematic errors leading to counterproductive results.⁵⁹ The apartheid state was excessive in its collection of data and compilation of statistics, which amounted to state-sponsored positivism. Planning and regulatory frenzy often devolved into comprehensive surveys; the bureaucrats drowned in information overload of their own making.⁶⁰ The planned surveillance state paralysed itself. The aspiration to make an all-encompassing knowledge the basis for state action

---

56 Verwoerd, Federated Chambers of Industry, Cape Town 26.5.1954 (in Pelzer 1966: 53–63, 57).
57 Ibid., 58.
58 Tayler 2010: 127.
59 Scott 1998: 57–62, ch. 9.
60 Posel 2009a.

could not be fulfilled, but this did not prevent apartheid politicians from sticking to their far-reaching plans and designs.

In the debate on the Tomlinson Report in 1956, Verwoerd was still very reserved about longer-term planning,[61] but from the beginning of the 1960s onwards, he put aside his initial scepticism, to become the protagonist of large-scale projects.[62] In September 1961, he announced the beginning of a new phase of economic development which differed from the first one in its planned character: "South Africa is beginning the second phase of its industrial development. The first one is past and the second one must be less by chance and more purposefully planned. The state machinery is being tuned for specialised planning."[63] This was a leap forward in the development of apartheid from policy to implementation: the vague ideals of former times were now becoming more concrete: "For the predecessors it was still an ideal; for us it is a project; in future it will be considered one of the great deeds accomplished in South Africa."[64] In a speech at the Convention for the Promotion of Export in the following year, he stressed

> that we look upon economic policy and economic development as the mainspring of our policy for the future. Much which we politicians felt had to be done in the constitutional field, in connection with Native policy and in other directions, has now been completed or is becoming routine. Fundamentally, just as in most other countries economic policies and economic development have become the most important government tasks. It is for that reason that I too, although Prime Minister, have had to give more attention to providing the ministers mainly concerned with Economic Affairs with the necessary support, and that within my own department an advisory body had to be developed to make it possible for me to co-ordinate such endeavours.[65]

Verwoerd's project had distinctly planned economic features; he spoke of "greater development and the preparation for much more to come, expansion planned

---

[61] Verwoerd, Commission for the Development of Bantu Areas, 14.5.1956 (in Pelzer 1966: 102–123, 105).
[62] Verwoerd, Annual Congress of the Afrikaans Trade Institute, Pretoria 19.9.1961 (in Pelzer 1966: 611–628, 626).
[63] Ibid.
[64] PV 93/4/1/9, f. 42, Verwoerd, Kaapse Middelland Ontwikkelingsvereniging, 23.10.1963.
[65] Verwoerd, Convention for the Promotion of Export Trade, Johannesburg, 16.5.1962 (in Pelzer 1966: 697–712, 712). Shortly after the announcement of the establishment of such a body after Verwoerd's assumption of office as Prime Minister in 1958, a group of representatives of the economic organisations of the Broederbond led by Verwoerd's old Stellenbosch friend C. G. W. Schumann, requested an appointment for a meeting with him (PV 93/1/34/1, f. 109, Letter by Ekonomiese Instituut to Verwoerd with attached memorandum, 8.10.1958).

systematically, even for ten years ahead".⁶⁶ He made it clear, however, that this was not a matter of a kind of development based purely on economic criteria.

In 1964, a Five-Year Plan for the years 1964–69 was in fact drawn up by the Ekonomiese Adviesraad (Economic Advisory Council) which, on the basis of previous growth figures, projected an average growth of five and a half per cent per year.⁶⁷ The Prime Minister made a point of linking the strategic planning with the sovereignty of the new Republic: "For it is a fact that this development is taking place at the beginning of our development as a republic, and it is the desire of all that the Republic should grow to real greatness – greatness not only in the political sphere, but also in the economic sphere."⁶⁸

The main task was to identify the existing weaknesses and deficits, and to address them through the targeted development of new industries: "Where the deficiencies, the gaps, are found, purposeful action will be necessary to fill them."⁶⁹ Only the state, he said, could provide the necessary scientific expertise and kickstart industrial development through investment in infrastructure. "For this reason, provision, particularly, is made for co-ordination and central planning in the gradual expansion of the Prime Minister's department."⁷⁰

Verwoerd's systematic approach, which distinguished him from all of his predecessors, was evident even in his first speech as Prime Minister, in which he announced the establishment of an economic advisory body. Again and again, he expressed his deep-seated mistrust of economic initiative independently of the State:

> The idea behind such an economic body will be to assist in the achievement of the co-ordination of the economic activities both of the state and of the private sector, not the achievement of co-ordination by throttling private enterprise, because, as has often been stated, we believe in the basic principle of private initiative in the industrial life of our country. . . . The eventual aim in establishing such an economic council is therefore not the development of some sort of central autocratic control over all economic activities, whether public or private. It envisages the proper organisation and regulation of the economic life of the country

---

66 Verwoerd, Address to the South Africa Club, London, 17.3.1961 (in Pelzer 1966:5 02–512, 503).
67 FAV, 4.7.1.5, Press release of 11.12.1964 after a meeting of the Economic Advisory Council on 30.11.1964.
68 Verwoerd, Inauguration of a Bust and Plaque at the J. G. Strijdom Building for Engineering, University of Pretoria, 15.9.1961 (in Pelzer 1966: 605–610, 606–607). See also Verwoerd, Kruger Day, Pretoria 10.0.1959 (ibid., 313–318, 317): "The country must also be independent economically to the fullest extent that a nation can be independent in the present world order."
69 Verwoerd, Annual Congress of the Afrikaans Trade Institute, Pretoria 19.9.1961 (in Pelzer 1966: 611–628, 617).
70 Ibid., 611.

in so far as this can be done through investigation, research, the dissemination of knowledge and the co-ordination of state activities.[71]

The reason for this mistrust lay in Verwoerd's integral nationalism: "It should, however, be our duty to the state, whose concerns take precedence over those of the individual, so that, while we want to do justice to the individual, we do not at the same time exploit the community, the taxpayers, in acting irresponsibly . . . ."[72] Businessmen, Verwoerd surmised, were primarily interested in profit maximisation and personal gain, which is why their commitment to nationalism could be called into question. "The prosperity of the country as a whole must be preserved in the first and final instance. The share of the individual in this will follow in one form or another, but must never be sought at the country's cost."[73] Time and again, Verwoerd appealed to the national solidarity of the business sector, precisely because it was the least willing to subordinate its own interests to those of the nation: "It is to preserve this most vital fundamental strength that everyone should cooperate in submerging understandable personal aspirations and interests in what is good for all."[74]

This explains Verwoerd's construal of different forms of economic activity in pairs of binary opposites: "The year 1965 will be a testing year. Will it prove South Africa and South Africans to be weak or strong? Energetic developers or easy-going exploiters? True patriots of self-seeking opportunists?"[75] His appeal to his compatriots to ascend from materialism to spirituality was by no means owed to his cultural conservatism alone; to him, the spiritual was the unity of the people, to which businesspeople, too, should pledge their commitment: "He who can rise above the materialistic to the spiritual enrichment of his people and those belonging to it, enriches his own works, embraces his people, and will be embraced by his people."[76]

---

[71] Verwoerd, First Speech as Prime Minister, 18.9.1958 (in Pelzer 1966: 164–190, 176–177). PV 93/1/53/3/1, f. 52, Letter by Chamber of Commerce to Verwoerd, pp. 73–75, Chamber of Commerce Memorandum: The Growth and Orientation of our Economy. See also PV 93/1/34/1, f. 115, Letter by South African Federated Chamber of Industries to Verwoerd, 11.12.1958: They had heard that an advisory body was to be established and were asking for more information.
[72] PV 93/4/1/9, Verwoerd, Kaapse Middelland Ontwikkelingsvereniging, 23.10.1963, f. 63.
[73] PV 93/4/1/11, pp. 279–283, 280, New Year's Message, 31.12.1965. See also van der Westhuizen 2007: 67–68.
[74] Ibid., f. 279.
[75] Ibid., f. 283. Nevertheless, as Prime Minister he was emphatically pro-business and appeared as a speaker at a banquet of the Johannesburg Stock Exchange (PV 93/1/60/2/13, ff. 74–75, Letter by J. A. Hyman to Verwoerd, 24.6.1966).
[76] PV 93/4/1/9, Speech at the 1963 ATKV Congress, ff. 172–187, 172.

At first, Verwoerd downplayed the importance and scope of his new venture: "All that is needed is that our industrial capacity must be properly organised, that plans must be properly co-ordinated and that the fullest initiative must be taken in the opportunities in the new directions which are opening up and on which we are embarking."[77] Two of the desired effects of the intensified scientific orientation and state control of politics were the mechanisation of agriculture, and the automation of industry, which were supposed to render the economy less dependent on cheap black labour. "This is a policy the seeds of which are being planted but which will yield its fruits to an ever-increasing extent during the new industrial development of the next 50 years."[78]

Apartheid planning served its main objective, namely to reduce the number of black workers and urban dwellers, as "mechanisation, automation and immigration have reduced the demand for black labour, or rendered it superfluous".[79] However, the systematic implementation of apartheid and economic planning interfered with each other, making co-ordination ever more urgent. Verwoerd's economic adviser composed a memorandum that foreshadowed the bureaucratic monster that was being raised. The training of skilled workers was to be organised according to demand, while being strictly divided by race. Certain branches of the economy that were training Coloureds and Indians, were supposed to entice them to move to and remain in their regions; if these businesses succeeded in doing so, they were to benefit from subsidies, just like the border industries. Similarly, black skilled workers were to be prevented from moving to the 'white' areas; instead, they were to remain in the newly established urban centres of the Bantustans, which is why the trades and vocational schools were to be located there. "If Bantu labour is kept away from the labour-intensive industries in white urban areas, this would not only accelerate the development of the border industries, but probably also reduce the unemployment rate among Coloureds and Indians."[80] All these measures involved a gamut of applications, permissions, and

---

77 Verwoerd, Convention for the Promotion of Export Trade, Johannesburg 16.5.1962 (in Pelzer 1966: 697–712, 711).
78 Verwoerd, First Speech as Prime Minister, 18.9.1958 (in Pelzer 1966: 164–190, 184–185). Verwoerd had set this as the goal of his policy as early as 1951 (PV 276/I/8/1/2, f. 128 Letter by Verwoerd to H. Dold (Howick, Natal), 8.8.1951, p. 2).
79 PV 93/1/24/10, f. 86, Letter by Verwoerd to H. W. van der Merwe (Kroonstad), 26.7.1960. In 1960, he strongly encouraged employers to "work towards paying higher wages by rationalising their business operations" (PV 276/3/1/2/1, Verklaring van die Eerste Minister namens die Regering oor verdere stappe in verband met die toepassing aan die kleurbeleid (1960), p. 6). This was not primarily about wage increases for workers, but about the reduction of their numbers.
80 PV 93/1/20/2/5, f. 47, Vakleerlingskap by die Nie–Blankes . . ., 13.11.1964, p. 15; see also f. 46, Letter by the Economic Adviser to the Prime Minister, 10.12.1964. See also Franzsen 1949: 20.

inspections, which did not make it easier for entrepreneurs to do their work. In addition, participation in business activities across the racial divide was to be prevented or at least discouraged.

In fact, the conversion of the South African economy initiated by Verwoerd, from labour-intensive to capital-intensive production methods, was showing the results that he had envisaged: from the late 1960s onwards, the number of unemployed unskilled workers increased sharply.[81] Nattrass and Seekings have identified this shift as the beginning of a fundamental change in the South African political economy,[82] which turned out to be more significant than the political revolution of the 1990s. This transition is often attributed to the government of John Vorster in the sense that it was beginning to have a concrete social impact during his tenure; but, of course, the tracks for this development had actually been set by Verwoerd in the early 1960s.

The expansion of state activities involved the new parastatal enterprises in strategically important sectors such as coal hydrogenation, initiated to reduce South Africa's dependence on oil supplies. But the government went beyond that, establishing macroeconomic management structures. In addition, the state considerably expanded its involvement in large-scale infrastructural projects such as the construction of gigantic reservoirs for artificial irrigation, water supply for the industrial centres, and power generation. Last but not least, Verwoerd was intent on securing South Africa by strengthening the military. To this end, he began to build up the country's own armaments industry during his term of office. After 1961, the purchase of arms, especially from France, increased dramatically; between 1957 and 1966, the military budget grew sevenfold.[83] In some respects, this level of control and active involvement of the State was a continuation of the expansion of its powers during Verwoerd's tenure as Minister; it followed the developmental logic of apartheid. In that sense, one could talk of a continuous process of building an interventionist state typical of "high modernism", as described by James Scott. In a manner similar to that of other "high-modernist" projects of the 20th century, Verwoerd was also concerned with industrial core areas: "I have said that there are three elements on which industry,

---

81 Jones/Muller 1992: 238–253; Posel 1997: 134–135.
82 Seekings/Nattrass 2006: 157–162.
83 Malan/Mulder 1966: 6; see also Terblanche 2001b: 24. For very instructive information on military relations, see Moukambi 2008: 84–112. On the role of Defence Minister Jim Fouché, see Sabalot 2009: 143. See also the assessment of the US Administration: "No other nation or combination of nations on the African continent is in a position to challenge South Africa militarily today." (DNSA, William Duggan, Memo on Background of the South African Problem, 10.7.1963, p. 2).

mining and agriculture all rest, namely water, power and steel."[84] Apart from the state's economic projects, planning was aimed at expanding state control over the economy and society, at reshaping South African society through the state, and at the disenfranchisement of citizens through a proliferating bureaucracy, while rhetorically professing democracy.

The identification of development goals and the efforts to achieve them in a coordinated manner were new themes for Verwoerd's constituents and supporters. He took care to elaborate on them on various occasions – at a meeting of the cultural organisation of railway employees, for instance, which was a key constituency for Afrikaner nationalism: "Economic target planning is nothing more than the determination of objectives to be achieved within a certain time; it is based on identifying and investigating the weaknesses in the economic life of the country."[85] In mentioning feedback and contingency, and being intent on keeping his programmes sufficiently open-ended to accommodate short-term shifts and changes, he was clearly arguing in the context of contemporary cybernetic thinking:

> There is never an end to such an economic target programme. As soon as someone with knowledge of the programme begins to address the full extent of the weaknesses, the picture will change. Then the programme has to be adapted to the new situation and the new needs. Other parts of the world are progressing in their development. Just as economic development takes place in other countries, or discoveries are being made, the goals shift for each country. South Africa has to persistently adjust to changing economic target programmes.[86]

The Prime Minister was enthusiastic about the new possibilities opened up by scientific and engineering research. He wanted to exploit these potentials, "including the greater role science will play when atomic energy may tap the oceans for irrigation of the land".[87] Above all, South Africa had unimagined development opportunities due to its wealth in mineral resources; technical progress opened up new possibilities for exploiting minerals that had, up to that point, been deemed less valuable.[88] In September 1961, on the occasion of the inauguration of a new

---

84 Verwoerd, Union Show, Johannesburg 9.4.1960 (in Pelzer 1966: 388–393, 390).
85 PV 93/4/1/9, Speech at the 1963 ATKV Congress, pp. 172–187, 179.
86 Ibid.
87 PV 93/4/1/12, New Year's Address 1966, ff. 157–163, 158. "And the end of our possibilities has not yet been reached, because we are also fortunately endowed with the resources required by the atomic age."
88 PV 93/3/4/13, Toespraak by geleentheid van die opening van die Museum van die Geologiese Opname, 17.5.1966, f. 129.: ". . . and then we know that we have something in South Africa that others would like to have, that they need for the development of their aeronautical industry, in the search for the outer limits of space, that this is needed in the process; and we make our contribution with what we get from our soil."

engineering building at the University of Pretoria, Verwoerd expressed himself no longer so sure

> that even this well-progressed undertaking which you have here, . . . will be able to satisfy the tremendous need. Daily one becomes more and more aware of the tremendous potential for development and of our duty towards realizing it and daily one becomes more and more aware of the great effort it will take not only in acquiring the opportunities or the financial means, but in finding the people to train for what we wish to do.[89]

Thus, in Verwoerd's view, progress could no longer be halted, even if economic growth had to be temporarily slowed down.[90] The task of state control was to steer progress for its own good, to contain the forces released by it, and to direct them towards a goal that was sure to be "the beginning of our golden age".[91]

The Orange River Dam

The Orange River Dam, one of the first large-scale economic projects, can serve as an example of Verwoerd's approach, which will be reconstructed here in some detail. The project of a dam to regulate water and generate electricity on the middle reaches of the Orange River was developed in the early 1960s. After concluding the authorisation procedures, construction was started in 1965, but the dam, named after Verwoerd, was not completed until five years after his death. The reservoir is the largest in South Africa, covering an area of 374 km^2, and drives four turbines, which jointly generate 360 megawatts of electricity.

In a speech addressing the congress of the Kaapse Middelland Ontwikkelingsvereniging (Cape Midlands Development Union) on 23 October 1963, Verwoerd made it clear to his audience right at the beginning that it was not just any dam project he was talking about, but that they were dealing with planning for the future on a large scale. "When we build a dam in the Orange River, we are talking about its volume that will last for 1000 years and longer. So today we are talking about an inexhaustible treasure that nature has given us to use, and to use for a long time to come."[92] He had thus drawn the conclusions from other projects which, due to rapidly expanding consumption data, turned out to be obsolete before they had even been completed. Nevertheless, before such a mammoth proj-

---

[89] Verwoerd, Inauguration of a Bust and Plaque at the J. G. Strijdom Building for Engineering, University of Pretoria, 15.9.1961 (in Pelzer 1966: 605–610, 606).
[90] PV 93/4/1/12, New Year's Address 1966, ff. 157–163, 158.
[91] Verwoerd 1963: 1.
[92] PV 93/4/1/9, Verwoerd, Kaapse Middelland Ontwikkelingsvereniging, 23.10.1963, ff. 40–65, 40.

ect could be tackled, it was necessary to gain sufficient experience with smaller dam constructions,

> so that when a large-scale development like this is put into practice, it will be built on a very solid foundation of water management planning for the country. You know that it was the job of previous ministers of water provision to think ahead on a large scale and thus to commission extensive studies, but at the same time to focus [in practice] on what they could do and wanted to be done.[93]

Verwoerd referred to the earlier projects to pay homage to the engineers and politicians of the past, but, more importantly, to contrast the new designs of the present with practices of the past. "... a nobler duty would be not to seek after getting one's own name and deeds associated with great ideals for the future, but rather to limit one's own ambitions, to exercise self-control and, first and foremost, to see to it that throughout the country, what is considered essential and needs to be done, actually gets done."[94]

The new project was on a completely different scale and was, for that reason alone, a symbol of the "high modernity" that Verwoerd's entire planning policy stood for. "The face of the whole of the southern part of South Africa will be changed as a result of a blueprint for development on a scale that has never before been undertaken here."[95] He managed to present himself as following a tradition of planning and dam building, while at the same time highlighting the newness that he wanted to see associated with his own reign: "But it became very clear that the whole country had to be developed before we were ready to embark on the major development that we can now undertake."[96] The ostentatious modesty with which he referred to his predecessors was factually entirely appropriate; but Verwoerd applied it to subtly indicate that, in this case, the giant stood on the shoulders of dwarves, insofar as past initiatives were only

> a necessary preparation for what is to happen now. All the more does it behove us to remember, with reverence and esteem, those who made it possible for us to move forward with this major plan, because they themselves were not destined to do it. They were the leaders of the Exodus that would eventually bring the people to the Promised Land, all the while knowing that they themselves might not behold it.[97]

Having deferred to his predecessors, Verwoerd proceeded to highlight his own contributions, which he believed could have "historical value".

---

93 Ibid., f. 42.
94 Ibid., f. 42.
95 Verwoerd 1963: 2.
96 PV 93/4/1/9, Verwoerd, Kaapse Middelland Ontwikkelingsvereniging, 23.10.1963, ff. 40–65, 43.
97 Ibid., f. 43.

The two important contributions to the project, for which he claimed credit, were cited as evidence for

> the importance of having a politician at the helm of a country's government, because he would tend to consider things from an angle different from that of other interested parties. His specific perspective may still turn out to be important for the country. These brief remarks also pay tribute to the role of political leadership in planning. This is not about the politics of a particular party, but about the value of political considerations in the broadest sense.[98]

To Verwoerd, politics was the overarching steering unit, it took the perspective 'from above', and was imbued with comprehensive competencies.

His contribution was to decide on one of two possible plans for the construction of the Dam, either on the Pongola River or on the Orange River.[99] The engineers entrusted with the feasibility study gave preference to the Pongola plan. At this point, however, the 'broader perspective' of the leading politician came into play: he was thinking not only of technical feasibility, but also of

> the importance of general development in those two parts of the country, with implications for many other people. When we looked at the future of the country from the broader perspective and moved from the purely technical issues to the human, socio-economic and political implications, we asked ourselves: is it really impossible to implement both projects at the same time? This is the one achievement with which I credit myself, that I asked this question in all its acuity at the critical moment.[100]

This actually led to the decision to undertake both projects, albeit with an extended construction period.[101]

It was in the context of these broader considerations that Verwoerd came up with his second contribution, which directly concerned the Orange River Dam.[102] Once again, he broadened the question, because he did not focus on the Dam itself, but rather on the River, that is, on the entire region.[103] The Prime Minister took the 'view from above', assessing the project from a bird's-eye view. He placed what had originally been a purely technical question in a larger context, which supposedly only the politician could adequately grasp. From the mere construction of a dam he derived a systematic project for the whole of society, by examining for

---

98 Ibid., f. 44.
99 Ibid., f. 44.
100 Ibid., f. 45.
101 Ibid., f. 46.
102 Ibid., f. 46.
103 Ibid., f. 47.

each individual step "what fits best into a comprehensive and coherent plan".[104] The message to his audience was that it was not a question of assessing such a project from a purely technical point of view; instead, the project would have to be led by politicians because only politicians had the broader perspective; only they could appreciate the need, and muster the ability, to consider additional aspects. No scope was therefore to be given to self-empowerment of experts and specialists; systematic project planning was to be reserved for politicians:

> Not only does this facilitate a proper scheme for the River; it should be the best planning not only for water use, but also for the country as a whole. In other words, because the political leaders necessarily take a view different from the purely technical one, they could commission projects and ultimately make the decisions that culminated in this truly enormous project that we are now dealing with. That is why it is always best to make sure that there are politicians at the head of the State!!![105]

Verwoerd subsequently shifted the argumentation; he no longer started from the technical requirements, but from the raw material crucial for dam construction, namely water. Following the rather trivial statement that water is "fundamental to the constitution of communities, even the most primitive communities",[106] he proceeded to talk about the possible uses to which water can be put. He built up the complexity of the problem to his audience, thereby demonstrating the need for a systematic approach. The multiple applications of water thus became more than just the means of its utilisation, they became a mark of civilisation: "Consequently the greater and the better use that is made of the water available, became a sign and a symbol of the higher development of all communities, past and present. If we in South Africa do not think basically in terms of water, then the hope of developing our civilisation in this southern tip of Africa must fall to the ground."[107] Here, as elsewhere, it became clear that his concept of civilisation was closely linked to the evolution of modern technology.

South Africa's shortage of water necessitated a particularly careful and cautious use of this scarce resource, underlining the importance of planning for the future:

> The second fundamental consideration in our basic thinking on what must be the South African attitude towards water, is that South Africa is poor in water resources. If we do not make the utmost use of all the water resources placed at our disposal, then we will be lack-

---

104 Ibid., f. 47.
105 Ibid., f. 47.
106 Ibid., f. 48.
107 Ibid., f. 48.

ing not only in our duty now but we will be making the future more difficult for the generations to come. In the conservation of water one has to think ahead.[108]

The needs of the next twenty or even forty years would have to be factored into the planning.[109] The planning of dams showed an important historical development; in stating this, he was referring not to technical, but to political aspects:

> 'The Dam' was usually an ideal propagated by those who needed more water. It was a local demand, of local value and ultimately a local scheme. . . . In the course of time this outlook changed. People started to think about irrigation schemes not as intended for the benefit of a locality but as a scheme for a nation. . . . In our country in the thinking about the Orange River scheme we have come to this modern outlook.[110]

By overcoming the local view and local needs, Verwoerd left behind what he would have called petty self-interest, and cast his eyes to the wider 'community', namely the nation, which was his central reference point. He presented his planning as something entirely new. He showcased the difference between the needs of a farmer and the interests of a businessman, between those of a regional community and those of an entire nation. His line of argumentation was thus structured by a qualitative leap.

Water was needed in three main sectors, namely in agriculture, in industry, and in the towns and villages of the region. All three were represented by different social groups whose interests the politician had to balance – and Verwoerd thought that he was the only one who would manage to do that. "Today, I would like to caution against over-emphasising one or the other of these three sectors [of water utilisation]. All three are necessary. The only question is how to balance them, and this is a question that does not necessarily need to be answered now. . . . One of the nice things about the Orange River Plan is its adaptability."[111] He thus included the possibility of contingencies; the uses of the Dam could be adapted to changing needs. This required large capacities, though, necessitating planning in huge dimensions. "Experience has always shown that what appears to be an enormous ideal today actually seems too small once future development takes off." Thus, the Dam on the Vaal River would have already proved too small.

---

108 Ibid., f. 49.
109 In a different speech, he turned the argument around, saying it was a sign of the self–confidence of South Africans to have engaged in planning that extended so far into the future (FAV 4.7.2.4.5, Speech presented to the Party Congress of the Natal NP in Durban, 27.8.1963, p. 22).
110 PV 93/4/1/9, Verwoerd, Kaapse Middelland Ontwikkelingsvereniging, 23.10.1963, ff. 40–65, 50.
111 Ibid., f. 56.

"The plan has been overtaken by itself; therefore, I repeat: one must not think in too small scales or conclude too hastily that we are going too far."[112]

This new perspective could only be taken by the politician, because only he had an overview over all relevant aspects simultaneously; it was the 'seeing state' in the sense in which James Scott characterised it. This kind of state would engage in comprehensive planning to develop a universal solution that did justice to the complexity of the problem. The Dam was to address different problems and highly differentiated needs at the same time:

> The creation of a satisfied society, with no feeling of domination by one part over the other, has political implications too. Constituencies will then be properly spread over the country. Nobody wants a whole nation to be overwhelmingly controlled by a huge number of representatives of constituencies from one urban area. It is not healthy for a nation that that should be the case. I am trying to show in fact how, when one thinks in the broader terms of the O.R. Scheme, one finds how much is at stake. The development of this part of South Africa, a fine part of South Africa, a central part of South Africa which is as yet relatively thinly populated, is necessary. It should be better populated so that we will not have a bikini-like country with top and bottom covered, and the rest denuded.[113]

What he was referring to was the fact that the middle course of the Orange River was running through a relatively dry, thinly populated area, which was adjoined by the industrial centres of the Witwatersrand in the north, and by the relatively densely populated coastal strips marked by the large cities of Port Elizabeth and East London, in the south. The Dam was to supply the local population with water and electricity, and to facilitate the decentralisation of industry, which would contribute to redressing regional imbalances,[114] as well as developing decentralised industries around the homelands, thus promising to realise Verwoerd's project and with it, a fundamental goal of territorial apartheid: "Following this way of thinking that I have just presented, there appear other principles that would need to be taken into account.... One of them implies that we have to include a major principal problem in connection with the fundamental policy: we are convinced that the well-being of the different population groups lies in their separate devel-

---

112 Ibid., f. 57.
113 Ibid., f. 53.
114 Ibid., f. 51: "One of the great needs of South Africa is the decentralisation of industry. Industry cannot remain concentrated in a few large centres. Otherwise it not only becomes strategically vulnerable but the large aggregations of people create problems which we in this country (with many races on whose future we have to decide) have to take into account.... Decentralisation of industry is not only strategically beneficial and useful for a better geographical distribution of the population, but it is also necessary for the development of under-developed portions of a country."

opment."[115] Because the Dam was located on the middle reaches of the Orange River, it remained in the 'white' area and therefore under the control of whites. However, many coloureds were living in the area. The construction of the Dam was intended to attract whites to this heartland – more than had lived there before – and thus to secure their control in the long term.[116]

In the course of his speech, Verwoerd continued to introduce new and further aspects, in order to impress the audience with the complex nature of the problems politicians were confronted with, and with the solutions envisaged. He paid due attention to the implications for tourism,[117] and included the regional administrations in the planning.[118] He calculated even the yield of agricultural products that could be produced with artificial irrigation.[119] Thus the project also entailed agricultural research and planning on a large scale.[120] Because the Dam served not least to provide electricity, it gave impetus to the mechanisation of agriculture and prevented the influx of black migrant workers, thus securing the white heartland from another side: "The farms, industries, and settlements that are being established there, must expand as white farms, white industries and white settlements."[121]

With the Dam, a Gordian knot was cut; the construction of the Orange River Dam was supposed to stimulate industrial development and remove the restraint that had hindered development up to that point. "The time when South Africa sat and hesitated, not knowing what was to become of her . . ., is over."[122] In the end, there were two messages that he wanted to drive home:

---

115 Ibid., f. 53.
116 Ibid., f. 54.
117 Ibid., f. 61: "These reservoirs will, among other things, become resorts; one of the benefits will be that they will serve tourism as well as the normal industries. . . . Therefore, when considering where to build the reservoirs, it needs to be done in consultation with those who are considering the matter from the perspective of tourism or community-building or industrial development."
118 Ibid., f. 62: "The particular provincial administration concerned must be involved at an early stage. They need to know how the development is being perceived, and what needs to be planned for."
119 Ibid., f. 62: "I can continue by pointing out that the agricultural produce that can be delivered by farmers using irrigation systems must be determined at an early stage."
120 Ibid., f. 63: "The effect of irrigation must, of course, be considered from the outset by agricultural researchers and it is, of course, already receiving the necessary attention, even if some believe that it has not been taken account of." For the positive consequences expected at the time, also for the lower reaches of the Orange River, see Jooste 1965: 117.
121 PV 93/4/1/9, Verwoerd, Kaapse Middelland Ontwikkelingsvereniging, 23.10.1963, ff. 40–65, 55.
122 Ibid., f. 57.

1. The new quality of this project, "a world-class project. It will be one of the biggest projects in Africa. . . . I am not talking here about the height of the Dam or how many cubic metres of water the reservoir will contain. I am talking about the functional importance of this plan for South Africa, taking into account its size and population. In this sense, we have before us one of the great projects of the day; something that captures the imagination, not only of South Africa, but of people beyond our borders."[123] The government, he enthused, was coming out tops in international comparison.
2. The Dam was intended to help secure the survival of whites in South Africa. "We hereby profess our conviction that our people will be here in 40 years' time, after this is completed, and even longer. This is a symbol of our will to continue to exist as a people, of our will to survive, and of our will to bequeath this land, as highly developed as it can be, to future generations."[124]

The project would mark the beginning of a new era of state action: "Co-ordination and planning are of the essence here, as . . . with no other project in the past."[125] It was multidimensional and concerned various aspects of social life.[126] The Government was thinking big, not small.[127] Because the problem was so complex, the Prime Minister, as the main thinker and helmsman of the whole thing, was establishing an interdepartmental committee:

> Because this project involves so many interests, it requires particularly careful planning and co-ordination from different angles. This requirement is being met, because the government as a whole is responsible for it. . . . But the building of community life in the broader sense involves more than half – almost three quarters – of the State departments . . ., which is why the government itself must retain central control.[128]

---

123 Ibid., ff. 64–65.
124 Ibid., f. 65.
125 Ibid., f. 58.
126 Ibid., f. 59: "Something is being tackled here which concerns many other aspects of human life."
127 Ibid., f. 58: "We envisage everything with this project, because we are not planning small, we are planning big."
128 Ibid., f. 59. Verwoerd emphasised this claim of the superiority of politics in the declaration that he dispatched from hospital after the first assassination attempt. For it was only politics that had "comprehensive knowledge" and could make decisions "after weighing up all the facts and consequences, and after consultation with experts" (PV 276/3/1/2/1, Verklaring deur die Eerste Minister namens die Regering oor verdere stappe in verband met die toepassing van die kleurbeleid (1960). Another copy is available in PV 93/1/24/12)). Because of his decisionist view of politics, Verwoerd attached little importance to commissions of inquiry led by academics, even if they were among his companions (Meiring 1990: 83, 88–92).

This Committee was not headed by a line minister, but by the Chairman of the Economic Advisory Council.[129]

At the end of his speech, Verwoerd sought to immunise himself against criticism, saying that he had only indicated the complexity of the project and of its planning "because you regularly read articles in the newspapers by clever people who claim that the Government has failed, or that its officials have failed, to take certain aspects into account. They say that our planning is incomplete. . . . That is why it must be underlined here that there is much more detailed thinking and planning than many people realise".[130] In emphasising the primacy of the state over the individual, Verwoerd's aversion to particular interests exceeding the centralising grip of the state became clear: "It should, however, be our duty to the State to give its interests priority over those of the individual; while we wish to do justice to the individual, at the same time we cannot allow the community and the taxpayers to be exploited through irresponsible actions . . . ."[131]

This text has been presented and analysed here in detail because it shows patterns of argumentation typical of Verwoerd. Apart from the self-styled superiority of the planning politician embodying modernity, he demonstrated numerous problems could be solved with a single project, but only if the complexity of the whole was taken into account which, again, only he was capable of doing. This idea of finding a solution to multiple problems at the same time recurred in his justification of apartheid and was one of the reasons for the persuasive effect with which he impressed his supporters and voters. He appeared to them as charismatic, visionary, and at the same time realistic planner who was starting from basic principles while planning with a view to the consequences, in the minutest of details.

A speech he delivered a year later, on 27.6.1964, to the South African Academy for Science and Arts was similarly structured. Verwoerd modestly presented himself as someone who had entered a "conference of highly erudite scholars" without knowing what he wanted to say. All the more baffling must have been the effect of what he had modestly announced as a "little chat [*geselsie*]". In the spirit of the Congress theme, namely the "human potential of South Africa", he unfolded the full complexity of its administrative capture and incorporation into state planning. "There is an absolutely justifiable expectation that those who shape the future of the country engage in a certain degree of centralised action, but it is not always known what problems are involved."[132] In a first step, he presented an argument

---

[129] PV 93/4/1/9, Verwoerd, Kaapse Middelland Ontwikkelingsvereniging, 23.10.1963, ff. 40–65, 60.
[130] Ibid., f. 60.
[131] Ibid., f. 63.
[132] PV 93/4/1/10, ff. 81–96. Verwoerd addressing the Academy of Science and Art, 27.6.1964, p. 1.

from psychology, stating that entrenched patterns of behaviour and habits in certain occupations and communities would have to be transformed, before other measures could be implemented. As examples, he mentioned the lack of efficiency in calculating demand, or in deploying labour.[133] The Science and Economics advisory committees set up for this purpose in the Prime Minister's Office had developed to the point where he had appointed an Adjunct Minister for Planning. The next step was to establish a proper Ministry of Planning with a comprehensive mandate.[134] In addition to racial differences, he stated, there were differences between people within a population group. An abundance of labour power was a sign of backwardness, while shortage was a sign of development. "Labour shortage acts as a stimulus. ... When labour shortages occur, when demand arises, plans are being hatched. Then all efforts go towards getting the maximum performance out of the mental and physical labour power available."[135] But the most important thing was mental acuity in relation to the community, the nation. "Human potential is secondary to the potential of the people as a whole."[136] Thus, "perseverance, diligence, trust, faith, and hard work" should be traits not only of individuals, but also of "the people (*volkskenmerke*)", that is, character traits of the people. Only once this had been achieved could one be assured that progress was underway. This would have to be taken up in basic education: the aim was to develop not only the individual, but also the potential of the people as a whole. Especially in white South Africa under threat from the black majority, the people would have to build up tenacious spiritual resilience.[137] This brought him to the "essential" aspect, that is, "the people's struggle for their survival". In order to survive, he proclaimed, dependence on non-white labour would have to be reduced. In one of his skewed comparisons, he referred to Switzerland, maintaining that apartheid was being practised there. He explained that, due to rapid economic development, Switzerland experienced a labour shortage, and therefore had to import workers from Italy and Spain. As migrant workers, they were kept separate and thus would have had to return to their countries of origin again and again.[138] He concluded with a commitment to integral nationalism: "The community is greater than the individual; it is greater than all people currently alive, and must continue to exist through the centuries." All efforts should be directed not only at present–day needs, but first and foremost

---

133 Ibid., pp. 1–4.
134 Ibid., p. 10.
135 Ibid., p. 12.
136 Ibid., p. 13.
137 Ibid., p. 14.
138 Ibid., p. 15.

at the preservation of the people in the future.[139] This example, complementary to the speech on the Orange River Dam, showed the importance that human potential held for the planning state. The human being was considered a resource that could be calculated through extensive data collection, and thus factored into comprehensive planning. The psychological typology of persons that Verwoerd had carried out in the earlier stages of his career had been aimed at the capture of individuals in a similar way. But while he granted whites all liberties as far as choice of occupation and other life choices were concerned; with regard to black South Africans, he was not bound by any democratic rules of the game and thus pursued his planning obsessions without restraint.

Many contemporaries and historians considered Verwoerd a conservative or a reactionary who adhered to a social order long outdated. His orientation towards the future and his vigorous promotion of the destruction of traditional orders were often overlooked, because he cultivated the habitus of a conservative, from his outward appearance to his commitment to the Christian order of values. This attitude was widespread within organised Afrikaner nationalism;[140] it created a conservative cultural consensus, which concealed the revolutionary nature of the modernisation programme.

---

[139] Ibid., p. 16.
[140] An example is a speech by L. I. Coertze presented to the Bondsraad 1950 (AB Archive, 2/3/19, Bondsraad 2–3.10.1950, pp. 4–5, TOP 9, Die Afrikanernasie en sy toekoms; and AB Archive, 2/3/39, UR-Agenda 18.-19.2.1960, Bylae B, Blanke integriteit en leierskap). See also PV 93/3/1/18, f .57, Letter by R. A. Haasbroek (Kroonstad) to Verwoerd, 2.12.1958, complaining that skirts were too short.

The Breath of Death

After Verwoerd had emerged victorious on all fronts from his 'crisis year' of 1960, and had silenced opponents in his own camp, he was at the height of his power; for the last years until his death, he appeared as an "almost untouchable figure",[1] which is what was reflected in the outcome of the elections in the spring of 1966.[2] The National Party won its biggest victory to date. Verwoerd could see his policies vindicated in every respect: the vast majority of whites supported him. This is why he could subsequently afford to be less circumspect in his choice of ministers whom he appointed to his cabinet. In this way, he pushed back the influence of the Cape NP. He appointed his rival Dönges to the key Ministry of Finance.[3] But it was the new Minister of Agriculture, Uys, who came from the Cape Province and until then had been a rather insignificant backbencher, who was an avowed supporter of Verwoerd's.

In 1964, when Paul Sauer resigned as Minister for Lands, Forestry and Public Works for reasons of age, Verwoerd took the opportunity to reshape his cabinet according to his own designs. The Ministry previously held by Sauer was split into its component departments, which were then distributed to other ministries. After being re-elected on 4 April 1966, he reshuffled the cabinet again, when veteran ministers de Wet Nel and Serfontein relinquished their posts.[4] The change with the greatest long-term impact was certainly the appointment of P. W. Botha as Minister of Defence. In the years that followed, he would build up his own power base.[5] The previous junior ministers (adjunct ministers) Marais Viljoen and M. C. Botha, loyal Verwoerd supporters, were made fully-fledged cabinet members; in Viljoen's portfolio Labour and Coloured Affairs were brought together. Under M. C. Botha, the two ministries – Bantu Administration and Development, and Bantu Education – were reunited, as the pressure to reshape native policy had subsided. B. Coetzee and A. H. Vosloo were appointed as adjunct ministers in M. C. Botha's ministry.

Verwoerd dominated his cabinet like no one else since Jan Smuts.[6] Piet Meiring even conjectured "that his colleagues were so weak in their association with

---

1 Barnard/Marais 1982: 159.
2 PV 34/1, Letter by Verwoerd to M. P. A. Malan, 19.4.1966, thanking him for campaigning for the election.
3 Bekker 2005: 138.
4 PV 93/1/20/2/5, f. 136, Resignation of de Wet Nel, 30.3.1966 in a letter to Verwoerd; ibid., f. 137, Resignation of Serfontein, 30.3.66.
5 PV 93/1/20/1/2, ff. 88–90, Press statement, 4.4.1966.
6 Meiring (1973b): 143) even spoke of him exceeding his powers as Prime Minister.

him, that he may very well have become a dictator if fate had not intervened".[7] The idea of a historical mission made it easier for him to stubbornly stick to his policies, and to use the temporary isolation of South Africa as a test of resilience, especially since he felt assured that future generations would vindicate his policies. "It cannot be pleasant to anyone in these difficult times to occupy this responsible position. It results in days and nights of worry and pain; it gives one no pleasure; it cannot mean anything to one personally. If I were to be selfish and consider my own comfort I would get out of here as quickly as possible."[8]

Over the years, Verwoerd's authoritarian government so shaped the political atmosphere in the country that few alternatives could be developed within the framework of the white-dominated political system. Even utopian designs – for example the 1960 book by Garry Allighan, *Verwoerd – The End. A look-back from the future* remained under the spell of the *status quo*. The influential journalist cultivated an astonishing penchant for the fictional, as can be seen from the numerous mistakes in the opening passages of his book; but this was also the case with some of his newspaper articles, such as the absurd assertion that it was Mrs Verwoerd who was the real fanatic, and who had first set her somewhat naïve and clueless husband onto the path towards radical nationalism and apartheid.[9] In his book, Allighan sketched a scenario in the immediate future in which Verwoerd, through a series of grave political mistakes, causes an unmanageable economic crisis which eventually leads to his resignation. His successor is a non-partisan expert in economics who establishes a kind of dictatorship of experts and breaks South Africa's foreign policy isolation by abolishing the offensive aspects of apartheid, while radicalising its core and completing its project by dividing the country into a black and a white state. The book reflected a widespread rejection of party politics among South Africa's whites. Even though much of the book consists of long-winded fictional parliamentary speeches, it displays a disparaging attitude towards parliamentarism as unproductive talk. The dictatorship of experts, the de facto abolition of the last democratic institutions, and governance through a state of emergency in perpetuity, amounted to a vision exceeding what Verwoerd had represented and created, just as the 'solution' was entirely consistent with apartheid thinking; with

---

[7] Meiring 1973a: 158, 170–172.
[8] Verwoerd, Budgetary Appropriation of the Prime Minister, 10.4.1961 (in Pelzer 1966: 567–575, 575).
[9] Garry Allighan, 'The Woman who MADE Verwoerd', *Sunday Times*, 9.6.1963; see also FAV, 5.5.2., handwritten by E. Verwoerd: Leuens Alleghan (ibid. 5.3.1986: 'My reaksie by die herlees van die Garry Allighan-stuk'); also *Natal Mercury*, 5.3.1966: 'I'm No Atom Bomb, Says Mrs. Betsy Verwoerd'. The family members of Betsy Verwoerd were supporters of General Botha, i.e. not cultural nationalists (A. Boshoff 1993: 13, 23).

its notions of insurmountable racial differences and differences in civilisational development, it remained entirely within Verwoerd's universe.[10]

While Verwoerd usually spliced his speeches with 'facts' and sought to convince his audiences through logic, he became impassioned and emotional when it came to "the *volk*". In an address to the Afrikaanse Taal- en Kultuurvereniging of the Railways, which had originally come up with the idea for the 1938 Symbolic Ox-Wagon Trek, he exclaimed: "As the rumbling of the ox-wagon wheels is growing larger and louder throughout South Africa, I want to honour those who went the extra mile and showed the determination to do justice to the fervour of this great event, and whose enthusiasm never waned."[11] It was precisely in connection with the Symbolic Ox-Wagon Trek that Verwoerd indulged in a rant uncharacteristic of his usual style: "Today's Afrikaner is once again engaged in a spiritual trek." The image of the black bogeyman already played a prominent role here: "In times of danger, when wild [blacks] came rushing in, the faithful ox-wagon was the fortress of the Voortrekkers."[12] This emphasis was entirely consistent with his view that values and ideals were accompanied by feelings; such ideals were to be held high and hammered into "the *volk*". The passages in his speeches that mentioned Afrikaner nationalism, especially those referring to the heroes of the Great Trek and the Boer War, were the only ones that were laced with pathos.[13]

If Afrikaner cultural nationalism demanded the incorporation and subordination of the individual (in)to the community of the people, this applied not only to poor whites or to white workers, but above all to the elite, and especially to political leaders, "the few who are called leaders but who are also only servants of their *volk*".[14] The heroes of the past, he said, deserved this designation because they had thus behaved in an exemplary manner; they were the ones "who wanted to give their all to their country and their people. It is a tribute to the unselfish national leaders of the whole period of our young history!"[15] It was precisely from those who stood at the top and were to act as role models, that humility and modesty had to be demanded. "A leader is but an ordinary person who, although he stands at the head, means nothing himself. His deeds and words count not at

---

10 Allighan 1961.
11 PV 93/4/1/9, Congress speech at the 1963 ATKV Congress, ff. 172–187, 174.
12 *Die Transvaler*, 8.8.1938, editorial.
13 'Dingaansdag' in particular was a recurring occasion for him to engage in nationalist outpourings (*Die Transvaler*, 16.12.1937).
14 PV 93/1/30/1/29, f.142, Letter by Verwoerd to J. Cloete, Elandsfontein, 17.2.1965.
15 Verwoerd, Kruger Day, Pretoria, 10.10.1959 (in Pelzer 1966: 313–318, 313).

all if the people do not take those words and deeds to heart and carry them further."[16]

Thus, Verwoerd styled himself as servant of the people, and the NP as a party in which there was no corruption.[17] In this logic, Afrikaner politicians could not be corrupt at all, since they were only tools and servants of the nation. For many Afrikaner nationalists and especially for many Afrikaner nationalist historians, Tielman Roos was the epitome of the unscrupulous party politician; he was known as someone for whom politics was just a game.[18] Political leaders unable or unwilling to carry out the will of the people would rightly be forgotten, Verwoerd said, presumably referring to Smuts: "They are like detached mountains – not forming part of the mountain range. They are persons through whose life the golden thread does not run. They are forgotten in the national life because only that which was by nature deeply attached to it sticks in the national mind. So we must also see our own national life and our own national history."[19] For Malan, Strijdom, Verwoerd and others, politics was a deadly serious matter, not to be trifled with, because – as they made it clear to their followers again and again – it was a matter of survival.[20]

Verwoerd did not only preach modesty, but he actually lived it. This was only partly a matter of deliberate self-stylisation displayed for propagandistic reasons; he was actually committed to it. Addressing the Bondsraad in 1958, Verwoerd postulated demonstrative humility in representing and carrying out the will of the people: "The top of a pyramid is only a small point. . . . A leader is such a small point. He is only an individual human being, he only has the limited power, the limited time, the limited judgement, of a single man."[21]

Politicians should make sure to render their services in publicly visible ways. "If the people can sometimes see their leaders thinking about their daily prob-

---

16 Verwoerd, Transvaal Congress of the National Party, Pretoria 12.11.1958 (in Pelzer 1966: 191–205, 191). Commemorating his predecessors in office, he stated: "In retrospect we think of them, and all who fought with them, for leaders cannot accomplish anything alone. Leaders are but the overseers of the people who actually do the work." (Verwoerd, Republican Thanksgiving Festival, Pretoria 15.10.1960, in Pelzer 1966: 423–428, 424).
17 This bubble burst with Muldergate at the latest (Marx 2018: 65).
18 Brits 1987: 113, 233; see also Koorts 2014: 161–162.
19 Verwoerd, Kruger Day, Pretoria 10.10.1959 (in Pelzer 1966: 313–318, 314). The image of the mountain was possibly an allusion to Smut's well-known eulogy to Table Mountain. Referring to Verwoerd, P. J. Meyer considered a true "people's leader" as one who embodied the people's will (P. J. Meyer 1978: 1).
20 The great store placed on moral politics, above cheap party political tricks, explains the shock waves sent through the Afrikaans–speaking public by the Muldergate Affair.
21 AB Archive, 1/1/142/1, Verwoerd se boodskap, Bondsraad 1958, pp. 7–8.

lems and worries then they will feel happier through this experience than when this always happens far away."[22] The mixture of authoritarianism, and the understanding of the political leader as a servant and executor of "the will of the people", was characteristic of the kind of Afrikaner nationalism represented by Verwoerd. He understood every form of activity as service to the nation, be it politics, research and scholarship, agriculture and industry, family life and church. "You all feel part of one community – a community with a clear-cut duty not to serve self [sic] but to serve others."[23] He underlined this when he defended himself against the opposition, which saw him as the main obstacle to a solution of South Africa's problems: "If I were convinced that I did not represent the will of the people, I would not remain in this place a moment longer."[24]

All the more striking, however, was the contrast between his demonstrative modesty and his sense of mission, and the arrogance he showed in his dealings with critics and opponents. His long-time political opponent Douglas Mitchell attested to this:

> He was a most difficult man to talk to, in the sense that he always gave the impression he knew himself to be mentally superior, and that he was only pandering to a weakness by listening patiently to someone babbling on. He was always like this, in his office or in parliament, with his own people and with the Opposition. . . . There were many in Parliament on the Government benches who didn't like being treated as mewling infants or intellectual inferiors.[25]

Verwoerd's self-image as the executor of the general will explains the contradictions in his character described by Diederichs: "On the one hand, the friendly, modest man who lived in simplicity without much outward show; on the other hand, the often implacably hard man who would fight ruthlessly against everything he regarded as detrimental to South Africa, and who would tirelessly sacrifice himself for the principles in which he believed."[26]

---

22 Verwoerd, Opening of the Transkeian Territorial Authority, 7.5.1957 (in Pelzer 1966: 149–159, 150).
23 Verwoerd, Centenary of the Municipal Administration of King William's Town, 8.2.1961 (in Pelzer 1966: 489–495, 491).
24 Verwoerd, Budgetary Appropriation of the Prime Minister, 10.4.1961 (in Pelzer 1966: 567–575, 574).
25 Wilks 1980: 153. State Department employee Don Sole similarly noted on 24.11.1961 (in Wolvaardt/Wheeler/Scholtz 2010, vol. 2: 12): "He is an amazingly dominant personality but he does not listen. He has always made up his mind and nothing you will say will move him from the essentials of his policy decisions, although he may be a little flexible on tactics."
26 Diederichs 1975: 5.

In spite of his demonstrative modesty, his friend M. E. Rothmann, who knew him well since his time as professor in Stellenbosch, concluded: "It seems to me as if Hendrik has only few friends, as if he does not have the gift of building strong friendships. And he has the character flaw of easily upsetting people."[27] The writer John Cope characterised him as follows: "Intellectually arrogant, lacking a sense of humour and intolerant of fools, he has many political admirers but few personal friends."[28] In contrast to his successor Vorster, Verwoerd was never popular; people more likely feared him.[29] Having been born in Europe, and being a member of a family who newly arrived in South Africa, he was not readily accepted there. Among Afrikaners, knowledge of family background was important for the esteem of a politician,[30] which is why the immigrant Verwoerd remained unpredictable for many: "Dr Verwoerd is less known to us than our other Prime Ministers; we do not know his family and his background as we knew that of the Steyns, the Hertzogs, the Malans and the Strydoms."[31]

Even at a young age, Verwoerd stood out as a particularly stubborn person, unwilling to reconsider decisions once they had been made. Cillié quoted his father who, like Verwoerd, had been a professor in Stellenbosch, as saying that Verwoerd was "the most stubborn man I have ever come across".[32] His stubbornness was reinforced not least by the conviction that he was far superior in intelligence to those around him – an assessment shared by many of his contemporaries. A close friend said: "I have never encountered anyone, not even among those who disagree with him, who had the slightest doubt that [Verwoerd] is particularly intelligent and particularly honest."[33] From this self-confidence, he drew the conviction that only he himself could solve South Africa's problems. Over the years, especially after 1960, more and more of his followers believed this, to the extent that he was glorified as a 'prophet' after his death.[34] This was a result of his style of logical reasoning, constructed as it was from a particular desired outcome, which in reality was never validated: the Republic did not bring about the na-

---

27 K. T. (60), Letter by M. E. Rothmann to Erika Theron, 7.2.1961. See also 55.K.T. (61), Letter by Rothmann to Theron, 14.5.1961: "It seems to me that Hendrik has hardly any friends."
28 *Rand Daily Mail*, 17.5.1954; see also Kenney 1980: 140, 154–155; similarly Burger 1961: 5–6; he called him "a strange combination of philosopher and sergeant–major" (9).
29 Swanepoel (1982: 42) and Mitchell: "Any affection the Nationalist might have had for Dr. Verwoerd before his death was waning rapidly. His personal character had not really endeared him to his followers." (qtd. in Wilks 1980: 153).
30 On the kinship reference terms, see Marx 2008: 40–44.
31 220.K 61 (14), Letter by M. E. Rothmann to Piet Cillié, 15.1.1961.
32 Cillié 1980: 12.
33 FAV 5.5.2.2, Letter by M. E. Rothmann to E. Verwoerd, 14.5.1965.
34 Grobbelaar 1966: 135.

tional unity of English and Afrikaners,[35] the rural exodus of Africans was never reversed, Africans never accommodated themselves to the homelands, international opinion never swung in South Africa's favour, and even the Orange River Dam project did not bring the desired results of a higher population density of whites around the Dam, along with a tourist and agrarian boom, both of which failed to materialise.

Helen Suzman characterised Verwoerd as "lofty" and spoke of his "divine missionary ardour".[36] Once he had arrived at decisions, he was not prepared to revise or modify them, even when valid objections were being raised. His wife characterised this form of decision-making as follows: "He only acts when he feels he has made the right and best decision and, when that decision has been made, he never wavers. Criticism never worries him because he is confident, in his own mind and heart, of the essential rightness of what he is doing."[37] British observers considered his character representative of Afrikaner nationalists: "This conviction of absolute right, the total exclusion of any possibility of error, lies at the root of all Nationalist and more especially of all Verwoerdian behaviour. To a Western European it seems to owe more to the 17th than to the 20th century – though there is an ominous Hitlerian smell about it."[38] Even Eric Louw admitted, Verwoerd "did not tolerate opposition. I would almost be inclined to say that he had dictatorial tendencies which became apparent even in cabinet meetings." Although he responded to amendments to his proposals, "he made his dissatisfaction clear when his proposal or plan was contradicted. As a result, his cabinet colleagues shied away from raising objections to, or criticism of, a proposal, or even just an opinion of the Prime Minister."[39] Cillié wrote about the attitude towards the Prime Minister: "Reverence was mixed with a considerable dose of fear. The Prime Minister was illustrious, lofty, lonely – and cold."[40]

---

35 Weber 1973: 6–7, 10.
36 Lewsen 1991: 72.
37 Interview by Dorothy Mason with E. Verwoerd (in *Natal Daily News*, 22.1.1959). Similarly Graaff 1993: 186.
38 4.7.1.2, Unnamed British Embassy staff member: South Africa's Future, additional text, with a remark on top, handwritten by Eric Louw: Top Secret. At the bottom of the page, an annotation by W. J. Verwoerd handwritten in 2015: "Hierdie geheime verslag is volgens my herinnering deur 'n Afrikaanse tikster in die Britse ambassade onderskep en aan die E.M. besorg."
39 PV 4/72, Eric Louw, 'So onthou ek hom', p. 7. See also J. Basson 2004: 145.
40 2299 Cillié 1980: 25, 52: "Sometimes one had the impression that he had such a complete command of the South African stage, as if the sweeping force of his personality and authority were so overwhelming that the initiative of others was bound to suffer and that free citizenship could be supplanted by mere allegiance." See also Kenney 1980: 223.

From early on, Verwoerd attracted the hatred of his opponents because of his dogmatism and nationalist fanaticism, his intransigence, ruthlessness and unwillingness to compromise. He was the only politician of the apartheid state to die violently. What is more, at least three assassination attempts were made on him. On 22 October 1941, there was a first attempt on his life, from which he got off lightly; it had no further consequences, which is why it usually goes unmentioned in biographical accounts. In the early evening, his wife had received a phone call from persons unknown to her; she naïvely told them when she expected her husband to be back. When Verwoerd arrived back home, the entrance to his garage was blocked. No sooner had he left his car to open it than he found himself confronted by two masked men, one of whom threatened him with a pistol. They told him to raise his hands, which he refused to do. Although other masked men joined them, he managed to reach the front door of his house, whereupon the assailants, most likely members of Ossewabrandwag, retreated.[41]

Because he had earned himself a reputation as autocrat and "architect of apartheid", he evoked violent responses, especially in his capacity of Prime Minister. His pre-eminence, and the assumption he was the person who had invented and implemented apartheid, could well have created an expectation among his political opponents that the removal of this individual would lead to the collapse of the apartheid system. On 9 April 1960, David Pratt, a white farmer, tried to shoot Verwoerd during the opening of the Union Exposition, an industrial fair in Johannesburg. He shot him twice in the head, but Verwoerd miraculously survived and was able to resume his duties a few weeks later. Pratt, on the other hand, was declared to be of unsound mind and was never tried;[42] he later took his own life in prison.

Many of his supporters, and not least the Prime Minister himself, attributed his survival to divine intervention. Admirers of German background assured him of this: "You, dear Doctor Verwoerd, miraculously escaped with your life and your wounds were healed – is this not proof of divine providence!"[43] Verwoerd himself once expressed it in these terms: "In conclusion, I trust that I will be per-

---

41 Meiring 1987: 15–157; see also D. Prinsloo 1979: 277; A. Boshoff 1993: 44; G. D. Scholtz 1974, vol. 1: 170; E. Verwoerd 2001: 47–48; and J. Botha 1967:12. Jacoba van Zyl even reported that OB members "shot at you twice" (PV 93/1/11/1, Letter by Jacoba J. van Zyl to Verwoerd, 16.11.1954). G. C. Visser (1977: 146–147) reported another plan for an assassination in 1943.
42 According to Maisels (1999: 102) Bell/Ntsebeza (2003: 24), and Bird (1992: 18), in South Africa at the time, epilepsy, the condition from which Pratt suffered, was considered a mental illness. See also B. M. Schoeman 1973: 204; also Wolf 2012.
43 PV 93/1/34/5, ff. 11–18, Letter by Walter W. K. Boehme (Nylstroom) to Verwoerd, 15.9.1960; original German.

mitted to testify to my conviction that the protection of Divine Providence was accorded me with a purpose, a purpose which concerns South Africa too."[44] While his wife was sometimes gripped by fears for the future, he remained completely undaunted: "I sometimes find my faith waning, but Hendrik's *never* does. He always sees his way clearly and manages to get people behind him."[45] Contemporaries observed that Verwoerd had become even more hard-nosed after the assassination attempt than before.[46] His self-confidence and sense of mission were boosted by the continuing economic upswing of the 1960s, which created the impression[47] that this Prime Minister could succeed at anything and everything.

After 1960, he emerged at the centre of a veritable personality cult. With his emphatically proclaimed modesty, he was somewhat embarrassed by the growing trend of naming streets, buildings, and infrastructural facilities after currently acting politicians of the National Party, such as the Hendrik Verwoerd tunnels in the Zoutpansberg mountains. He affirmed that he had "consented to my name being linked herewith, not to honour my person, not to perpetuate my name, because I do not deserve that, but rather, by using my name as present leader of the government to show that our generation has also accomplished a few great things for South Africa".[48] He also agreed to having buildings and institutions named after him.[49] Albert Hertzog, who had initially been quite critical of Verwoerd, especially because of the latter's attitude towards Hertzog's father, became an ardent admirer in the early 1960s: "In the history of a nation, it seldom happens that the whole of the future is placed in the hands of one man to the extent that the future of the Afrikaner people is placed in yours. Whether it will endure or disappear, depends on you – and never could it be in better and safer keeping."[50] Verwoerd himself was convinced "that I was saved so that we may continue to pursue, in an honest

---

44 Verwoerd, First Speech after attempted Assassination, 20.5.1960 (in Pelzer 1966: 394–397, 397); see also Kenney 1980: 195; also O'Meara 1996: 105.
45 55.K.V.16 (5), Letter by Betsie Verwoerd to M. E. Rothmann, 22.2.1960. Betsie Verwoerd also viewed his survival as "a clear indication of a providential hand from above" (55.K.V.16 (6), Letter by Betsie Verwoerd to M. E. Rothmann, 26. 4. 1961).
46 I. L.de Villiers 2009: 133–138, on the near–religious veneration of Verwoerd.
47 Houghton 1969: ch. 10.
48 Verwoerd, Opening of the Hendrik Verwoerd Tunnels, 18.11.1961 (in Pelzer 1966: 636–641, 639). The Town Clerk of Alberton also approached Verwoerd with a request to name a new white residential area after him. (PV 93/3/1/19, Letter by Town Clerk of Alberton to Verwoerd, 29.8.1958). On the proportions this took, see Hepple 1967: 199–200.
49 He even allowed a tawdry and tasteless heroic poem about him to be published in the taxpayer–funded propaganda journal *Bantu* (Lawrence 1978: 235; see also Lapping 1987: 202).
50 FAV, 4.7.2.1, Letter by Albert Hertzog to Verwoerd, 23.12.1962.

and Christian way, the course that has been developed in South Africa".[51] It was as if surviving the attempts on his life sanctified his mission. After the 1960 assassination attempt, the FAK set up a Verwoerd Trust, which awarded a prize named after him. "At first, there was wide support for the idea of a great thanksgiving service to be held at the Monument, but His Excellency Dr Verwoerd feared that this amounted to personality cult, and that thanks were due only to the Almighty. The committee representing 17 organisations of the Afrikaner people was deeply impressed by Dr Verwoerd's seriousness and respected his views."[52] The nationalists apparently did not even notice the perplexity caused by nominating Verwoerd himself as first winner of the H. F. Verwoerd Prize.[53] A lavish celebration of his birthday in 1962, revelling in a kitschy and exuberant personality cult, was embarrassing even to Verwoerd himself; it showed how the adulation had lost any and all measure.[54] Verwoerd's successful self-stylisation, as well as the dominant role in which he appeared in the party and the government, contributed to his image of being endowed with near-superhuman capabilities. Although there was not a single idea of apartheid that he himself spawned, he was posthumously praised as "our beloved visionary leader Dr Verwoerd" and "the great and wonderful statesman".[55] His successor, Balthazar Johannes Vorster, eulogised: "The history of South Africa of the past eight years and for many years to come will be found in the life and work of Dr. Hendrik Verwoerd."[56] A Party brochure commemorating him summed up his outstanding qualities. As the authors were not too particular about the truth, there was no end to the list of praises: "his tremendous capacity to work, his bright spirit, his deep religiosity, his loyalty to his colleagues, his unbending patriotism, his modesty and heart-felt humanity, his indomitable commitment to everything he believed in, his firmness of principle, his unassailable faith in the people and the youth of South Africa, his love of country, his sober logic, and so much more".[57] On the fifth anniversary of the Re-

---

51 Ibid., Letter by Verwoerd to Dr S. P. van der Walt, Gereformeerde Kerk (Potchefstroom), 15.6.1960.
52 PV 202/2/19/1/4/1, Letter, 20.10.60, Appendix, Description of the Trust. C. L. de Jager was Secretary of the Trust.
53 FAV, 4.7.2.1, Convocation of Stellenbosch University with resolution on congratulatory note to be issued on the occasion of the award to Verwoerd, 19.8.1966.
54 A. Boshoff 1974: 142.
55 However, this statement came from Jimmy Kruger, whose own visionary capacities were rather limited (PV 132/2/6/4/2/3), Letter by Jim Kruger to Vorster, 13.9.1966; for the second quote, see PV 54/2/5, Minutes of the Annual Report of the Federal Council of the NP for 1966, p. 1, item 2c.
56 PV 132/3/6/1, Radio address, 14.9.1966.
57 Malan/Mulder 1966: 4.

public in May 1966, Verwoerd viewed a parade of over 20,000 troops in Pretoria, triumphantly demonstrating the power he commanded.[58]

On 6 September 1966, South Africa's Prime Minister Hendrik Verwoerd was sitting in the government bench shortly before the start of a parliamentary session, when he was stabbed four times by a parliamentary messenger, Dimitri Tsafendas, who was alleged to be insane. The assassination was described by many eyewitnesses and reporters in minute detail.[59] Instead of reconstructing the course of events once more, I would like to adduce a lesser-known account by a visitor from what was Rhodesia at the time. She was sitting in the front row of the visitors' gallery and observed the events thus:

> One minute we could see him just sitting down, the next this man was up on the bench in front of him and appeared to be hitting, but of course, he had a long knife which we couldn't see at the time. Then there was shouting and men running, struggling, and we could see Dr. Verwoerd lying back in his seat with a face like chalk. A dozen men had grabbed the man with the knife and were dragging him along the floor – he was bleeding too by then. An official near us said something about 'a bloody Greek'. Then all visitors were asked to leave so we got out somehow, everyone so shocked and women crying. We waited outside, trying to get news – no one wanted to go away. We saw him brought out to the ambulance; he looked so pathetic, the top of his head with this white hair showing and one helpless-looking foot. He must have been dead already but we were not sure until we heard the announcement at about half-past three. I didn't feel he could possibly survive a second time but we kept hoping until there was no hope.[60]

Thus a contingent event interrupted the life of a man who, more than almost any other politician in his country, had tried to banish contingency through logical reasoning. The unpredictable had been displaced by unshakable self-assurance, and by the conviction that the future could be planned. In the end, reality caught up with him; it was the unshakeable certainty that he knew the only right way that gave his opponents the hope that they could change the course of history by eliminating him. An international commentator remarked after Verwoerd's death, "if any people had motive enough to assassinate their ruler, it would be the twelve million Africans of South Africa".[61] Yet it had always been whites who carried out the assassination attempts.

---

58 Sabalot 2009: 175.
59 E.g. J. J. J. Scholtz 1967: chs. 2, 3.
60 55.K.P.3, Letter by Eileen Pike to Anna Rothmann, 7.9.1966. See also the public statement by T. E. Dönges directly after the assassination, urging calm (FAV, 4.7.7.1, Verklaring deur Sy Edele dr. T. E. Dönges, L.V., Dinsdag, 6 September 1966); in the collection there is also a copy of the Abridged Death Certificate dated 8.11.1966. See also A. Boshoff 1993: 136–139; also Heard 1991: 126.
61 Anon. 1966: 146.

Verwoerd's assassination, and especially the circumstances surrounding it, shocked large parts of the white population.[62] On the occasion of the funeral,[63] and for several weeks afterwards, newspapers and magazines were full of tributes and eulogies to a politician who was celebrated as a "statesman". He was considered irreplaceable; because of his superior intelligence, it was believed, he had always been a few steps ahead of his supporters as well as his opponents.[64] The Afrikaans-language press covered the funeral in particularly emotionally charged terms.[65] But the speeches and sermons presented by Afrikaans-speaking preachers are of particular interest. A small anthology of sermons issued by Reformed pastors reveals astonishing aspects, shedding light on the political culture in South Africa during these years. What is striking is the large proportion of persons with higher degrees from universities, indicating the extent of the self-disenfranchisement and the intellectual conformity of a nationalist elite that had previously been open to debate. Thus the man who divided and polarised South African society like no other, miraculously came to represent the whole country.

In his foreword to the collection of these remarks published shortly after Verwoerd's funeral, ds. Corneels Hattingh stated: "The daily newspapers, the radio and other writings have made us see and hear this consternation, this dejection, these tears, these tributes as his body made its way to its final resting place, these expressions of respect from all races in a manner we shall never forget!" (1). Ds. F. J. Conradie from Stellenbosch emphasised the grief supposedly felt by other sections of the population: "Mr. Schwartz, Chairman of the Coloured Council, declared: 'We feel like a boat on a stormy sea!' The Bantus, represented by the Chairperson of the Africa Foundation, said, 'This man did not stab Dr. Verwoerd, he stabbed us!'" (110) Ds. N. van Loggerenberg from Farrarmere said: "The path of Christian service to the underprivileged chosen by Dr. Verwoerd will remain

---

62 PV 18/3/1/72, A. Neethling-Pohl to C. R. Swart, 6.9.1966. On the reaction in Potchefstroom, see E. S. van Eeden 2006: 509.

63 Verwoerd's former student, close confidant and advisor ds. J. S. Gericke, Vice-Chancellor of the University of Stellenbosch, delivered the eulogy (PV 18/4/1/2, Begrafnisrede waargeneem deur ds. J. S. Gericke tydens die staatsbegrafnis van wyle die Eerste Minister Sy Edele dr. H. F. Verwoerd, 10.9.1966). All the newspapers published extensive obituaries and illustrated special editions on Verwoerd's life and funeral. See also PV 873/5/2/1/1, Dr Hendrik Verwoerd †, handwritten, 14.9.1966.

64 See the extensive collections of newspaper articles as well as the special editions of various newspapers on the occasion of the funeral. Foreign guests also joined in the hymns of praise, eulogising Verwoerd as "one of South Africa's greatest leaders" (220.K 66 (191), Letter by J. van R. Maartens, Stellenbosch– Boerewynmakery to Piet Cillié, 14.9.1966, with attached greeting from American professor E. J. Enright).

65 Z. Adams 2011: 50–53.

ours." (124) A. P. Treurnicht was, as was to be expected, more unambiguous in his appropriation of Verwoerd primarily for the Afrikaner people:

> A people does not produce a man of his stature every day, even in every generation. The most excellent qualities of a people – its courage and perseverance, its will to freedom, its strength of thought and vision of faith, by which it transforms and masters the conditions of its time, its sense of justice towards others as well as towards itself, its sense of mission and its energy – are seldom embodied in a single person in such a fitting manner as was the case with our late Prime Minister. (23).

N. van Loggerenberg lamented: "He, our beloved Prime Minister, was torn from our hearts [. . .]" (121); he was beside himself at "the shocking tragedy, the fatal attack on our beloved leader and Prime Minister" (124). According to H. F. Heyman, "[h]e was the darling of his people and countrymen!" (29)

After his death, Verwoerd became the icon credited by large sections of the white population with unifying his country; but more than that, he was endowed with near-superhuman qualities. Thus, ds. H. F. Heyman from Paarl claimed to know that "[h]e was active in every field: – Justice, Foreign Policy, Economy, Finance, Education, Domestic Policy, Bantu, Coloured, Indian politics, etc. He was a hard worker! He had his finger on the pulse of South Africa" (31). His colleague D. T. du P. Moolman from Port Elizabeth reported (not entirely truthfully): "He was a successful businessman", but above all a "world-class statesman" (98). Ds. J. A. V. Knipe of Pietermaritzburg concurred, stating that Verwoerd was "certainly a born leader, someone in whose leadership everyone could trust" (72). Dr Geldenhuys confessed, "[w]e had boundless confidence in an infallible man at the helm" (109). Dr J. Louw from Bloemfontein also confessed his faith in authority: "We have felt so secure under his inspiring leadership – secure in spite of all the hostility of the peoples of the world –secure with a view to the future of our children and our people." (39) Dr S. J. Eloff from Potchefstroom mused self-critically, "[p]erhaps we have been all too sluggish in recent years. We knew that a great, strong, experienced helmsman was steering our people's ship." (92)

Prof Dr H. L. N. Joubert of the University of Fort Hare drew bold comparisons with Abraham Lincoln and William of Orange: "Now, for the first time, we can really comprehend the feeling of the inordinate pain that filled the soul of the Dutch people when an assassin killed its beloved Prince of Orange." (126). Several preachers even drew a comparison with the martyr of nationalist salvation history, Piet Retief. Thus, Dr J. Kemp, a youth pastor from Natal, shared his vision: "While the flag of the Republic of South Africa was set at half–mast, I looked at the statue of Piet Retief with his hand over his eyes pointing in the direction of

Dingaan's residence." (113)[66] Ds. J. du P. Malan from Brits also drew the comparison with Retief, likening both Verwoerd and Retief with the figure of Moses: "Like a Moses, he led his people, but his heart was ripped from his body by the sharp blade of a barbarian, and so his Afrikaner blood moistened our soil, so as to come into the right of ownership thus vested in this, our only fatherland." (33–34) For ds. D. Fourie from Rosettenville, Verwoerd was the "martyr leader of the Republic in its golden age" (41), thus stylising the murder as an event in salvation history.

The sermons clearly show the pastors' strenuous attempts at giving meaning to the senseless act of a mentally ill person by creating counterfactual wild conspiracy theories. Ds. H. F. Heyman called the murderer "a foreign scoundrel" (29); there really were others who were to blame, as ds. D. J. Hattingh from Stellenbosch believed:

> The foreign press, and even large parts of our own press, painted a distorted picture of Dr. Verwoerd and presented this to the readership. He was portrayed as a cruel oppressor of the Bantu, someone not to be convinced by any reasonable argument, an unapproachable person often compared to a granite rock. There were even caricatures portraying him with a whip in his hand, bending over a Bantu. It was often and repeatedly suggested that this man must be removed! (44)

Treurnicht did his usual thing, pointing at others: "The question remains as to whether the hatred and hysteria stirred up against our country have largely contributed to creating the climate that has produced an assassin." (25) His colleague P. Luckhoff from Carletonville went even further, in making it out to be the work of the devil himself:

> How eager he is to break and defile the blossom of our youth. How many of us Afrikaners do not trample on the customs, traditions, and religion of our ancestors and throw them overboard! How many have not given in to unrestrained corruption, licentiousness, and immorality. Superficial, long-haired Beatles and whimpering singers and clunkers, and immoral show-offs of the film industry have become our heroes and gods . . . And with his crooked hand, Satan raises the bloody dagger and asks mockingly, 'where is your God?' (60–61)

Murder became the proof of man's sinfulness. In true Calvinist fashion, ds. P. J. Viljoen from Verwoerd's constituency of Heidelberg called for contrition and repentance:

> The cause of murder is sin. And as long as sin remains on earth, assassination will remain, and when sin grows, assassination will flourish, too. When we weep over what has happened, we must look within and confess: I am party to this, I helped to put this dagger in

---

66 Likewise ds. F. J. Conradie, p. 111.

this man's hand. Through my sin, I was also implicated in the death of our beloved Prime Minister. (74)

Prof P. A. Verhoef from Stellenbosch even styled the deed into the murder of "someone anointed by the Lord, who led his people by God's grace, who stood up for law and order, for justice and righteousness – which make life meaningful and possible in the first place, and which are the fruits of Christ's sacrifice!" (77) Accordingly, Verwoerd had not come to power through elections, but through the grace of God, which is a peculiar way for republicans to see themselves.

"In the dark hour of our people's history", as Dr P. J. Loots from Bethlehem described the situation, murder could only be understood as punishment for sin. "But now, dear listeners, the opportunity has come to turn to the Word of God again" (95), ds. D. F. Malan from Melville said, pointing to a way out. Ds. A. P. Potgieter argued in a more secular vein, convinced

> that if our enemies had hoped to break the Afrikaner people, they missed their last chance on Tuesday, September 6, 1966; our late leader shall stand before our minds as a monument of heroism, even greater than he had been in life. From his spilt blood, our people's ideals will draw new strength; a people united by his death will be prepared, with greater determination than ever before, to live and die for South Africa. (65)

Although it was obvious that the attack had targeted Verwoerd directly and personally, Dr F. E. O'B. Geldenhuys from Pretoria claimed "that the assassination was not directed against Dr Verwoerd as a person, but against him in his capacity as an office-bearer – against him at the top of the pyramid resting on the broad foundation of the Afrikaner people; against everything that this people believes in, against all the achievements of this people in the last decades; against the particular world view and ideology by which this people lives." (106) Thus Verwoerd the splitter became the unifier; the politician who only had risen to the position of Prime Minister by dint of a contested vote, became the "anointed of God", a born leader – the man who, like no other, had contributed to the permanent division of society and to the impoverishment of the majority of the population, was stylised as a saviour, and his assassination as a hero's death. Ds. H. F. Heymann was also convinced that "[t]his event will live on in the hearts of future generations . . . as long as a civilisation exists in Southern Africa. Dr Verwoerd has taken his place among the greatest of the great" (29).[67]

---

[67] All of the church ministers' quotes can be found in Hattingh 1967 (the numbers in brackets refer to the pagination).

But it took only a few months for silence to fall upon him,[68] despite all the efforts of his supporters to keep the memory alive. Voortrekkerpers, the media group of which Verwoerd had been chairman and for which he had once worked as editor-in-chief, was planning to publish a book with the memories of celebrities, but it never appeared.[69] At times, ministers would invoke Verwoerd's concepts in order to push through their agendas.[70] Although the new government continued to follow his programme with minor changes, it was surprising to see how quickly Verwoerd was forgotten. The public remained preoccupied with the circumstances of the assassination for some time. For his part, Dimitri Tsafendas, Verwoerd's assassin, just like Pratt before him, was declared insane in a suspicious hurry.[71] The interrogation transcripts indicate that the police officers who questioned Tsafendas were posing leading questions to prove him insane.[72] Adams suspects that the reason Tsafendas was not executed was to avoid making a political martyr of him.[73] Whether Tsafendas and Pratt were declared mentally ill because an assassination attempt on Verwoerd left many Afrikaner nationalists with no other explanation, is a moot question.[74] What is plausible is that Tsafendas was not given the opportunity to explain the motives for his action, and to talk about anyone possibly backing him in his pursuit.

---

68 Thus, his successor John Vorster soon stopped mentioning him in his speeches (see PV 132/3/6/98, Speeches, 1966–67; see also PV 18/4/1/20).
69 The book was to be entitled *So onthou ons hom* (PV 132/2/6/1/1, Letter by Danie Malan (Voortrekkerpers) to B. J. Vorster, 18.10.1966 and attached synopsis of the book). Some prominent politicians wrote contributions which can still be found in their respective estates. However, a book under the above title, edited by his son, did not appear until Verwoerd's 100th birthday in 2001. This clearly shows how what had previously been public memory has become a private matter.
70 PV 132/2/6/2/1/1, Letter by Marais Viljoen to Vorster, 8.11.1966, who, referring to statements by Verwoerd, was intent on giving as many powers as possible to the new Coloured Council.
71 More recently, political scientist Dousemetzis (2018) presented a detailed report, maintaining that Tsafendas was not mentally ill and that his actions were politically motivated (see esp. the statements by Bell/Ntsebeza 2003: 56–59; also Beresford 2010: 16–17). However, Tsafendas was imprisoned for some time on Robben Island, where Kathrada saw him but could not speak to him (Kathrada 2012: 220–221); see also Sisulu 2004: 288–289. Tsafendas's life story has been retold by van Woerden (2000a, 2000 b), who has not unearthed anything new beyond the official investigation report (J. T. van Wyk 1966). Instead of admitting him to a psychiatric hospital for treatment, Tsafendas was kept in solitary confinement for 23 years in the maximum security prison in Pretoria, right next to the execution site (Z. Adams 2011: 26, 100–101).
72 Bell/Ntsebeza 2003: 57–58.
73 Z. Adams 2011: 215; see also Posel 2009b: 346.
74 Most of the information on the interrogation of Tsafendas can be found in J. J. J. Scholtz 1967: ch. 9.

The question of how a man like Tsafendas, with a long history of mental instability and, moreover, with sometime membership of the Communist Party, could have found employment in a high-security national key point such as the South African Parliament, has been repeatedly asked from various quarters.[75] In fact, security gaps had come to light earlier, when *Drum* magazine managed to get a photographer into the Prime Minister's official residence, Groote Schuur, in Cape Town. The photographs showing a black employee in the private chambers of Verwoerd's were published in the magazine.[76]

The whole affair of a Prime Minister being assassinated in the government benches was perceived by some as "a disgrace which we shall not soon be rid of".[77] Since Justice Minister John Vorster was responsible for the security of Parliament, the question as to how Tsafendas was able to slip through all the security checks, gave rise to some conspiracy theories over the decades.[78] These also in-

---

[75] PV 132/2/6/2/1/1, Letter by Elsa Wiechmann to B. J. Vorster, 16.11.1966; see also Z. Adams 2011: 34, 78–79; and J. T. van Wyk 1967: 3, §23; 6, §§31, 32.

[76] Verwoerd was highly indignant about the Report and had a police investigation carried out, as the domestic employee had made critical comments about his policies without, however, going into specific details (FAV 4.7.1.10.1, Secret letter from the Prime Minister's Department to the Police Commissioner, 23.7.1963, with copies of the article in *Drum* magazine of August 1963, and the *Sunday Times*, as well as the secret report of the Police Commissioner (5.9.1953)). The Police Commissioner conducted the investigation without questioning the domestic employee Michael Ntseto. What was seen as problematic was the fact that he chatted not only about the daily life of the Prime Minister, but also, and above all, about the security measures in Groote Schuur.

[77] 220.K 66 (96), Letter by G. P. Kempen (Victoria West lawyer) to P. Cillié, 7.9.1966.

[78] 220.K 66 (100), Letter by A. M. Schaap to Cillié, 12.9.1966, shortly after the assassination. The Herstigte Nasionale Party circulated such stories; every now and again, there were also rumours of CIA involvement in Verwoerd's assassination. In particular, the leader of the HNP, Jaap Marais, emerged as a conspiracy theorist. In a book penned by him, he suspected Vorster and Hendrik van den Bergh, as well as the Americans and, of course, the communists (J. Marais 1992: 185–193). But this raises the question of what the Americans could have expected from John Vorster. In any case, on the very day of the assassination, an internal memorandum from the White House issued the instruction, "to tell the South Africans what little we know about Tsafendakis" (DNSA: Memo by Ed Hamilton for Walt Rostow, 6.9.1966). See also the decidedly negative commentary on Vorster's election in the *New York Times*, 14.9.1966. One can read a lot into various indications, such as the fact that Vorster's 1966 diary notes all the birthdays of cabinet members except the birthday of Verwoerd (PV 132/5/1/8). However, this does not prove anything, as it could be a coincidence, and moreover, it does not reveal any motives or indications of Vorster's involvement in the killing of Verwoerd. See also the letter by J. L. van Schalkwyk, full of grammatical errors, to Vorster (8.9.1966): "Now we come to Mr Citizen Chief Parliamentary Messenger, every man has his price. How is it that he could have employed Dimitri, the murderer of our Prime Minister, as a parliamentary messenger? According to the newspapers, he can hardly speak English or Afrikaans, why did he not employ an English or an Afrikaans speaker, why [did he choose] a dubious person?" (PV 132/2/5/1/7). Completely grotesque are the fictional stories by Elsdon 2009: 76–86.

clude the fairy tale circulated by Allan Bird that his former colleague, psychiatrist Solly Jacobson, had treated both David Pratt and Dimitri Tsafendas and sent them to Verwoerd in a hypnotised state, in order to kill him.[79] Others construed connections between the assassination and a revolt in the Party, allegedly led by Cillié, to replace Verwoerd with Anton Rupert.[80] However, all these accounts cannot provide a plausible explanation as to whether and how Tsafendas was instrumentalised, and why he did not speak about it after his release in the late 1990s.[81]

'The Breath of Death'

In the early 1930s, Verwoerd wrote, among other short stories, a short piece of detective fiction entitled 'The Breath of Death' ('*Die asem van die dood*'). A prominent figure, former rugby star, later celebrated as incorruptible referee, suddenly drops dead after an altercation with his daughter. The post-mortem does not produce any significant findings until, by chance, it turns out that the coffee the referee had drunk was laced with an extremely hazardous toxin. The police officer, over-hasty in his judgement, suspects the dead man's sister and arrests her, against her insistence that her brother did not actually drink the coffee. Just as the inquiry seems settled and closed, it turns out, that there is good reason to reopen it. The story shifts when the sister's fiancé, a doctor who witnessed the whole thing, asks his professor, a famous toxicologist, for advice. When the latter learns that the referee did not exhibit any convulsions or symptoms before he fell down, the story takes a turn. A lawyer called in by the doctor has contacted the pharmacy and questioned the messenger who delivered the medicine. It turned out that the messenger, a coloured man and thus, in Verwoerd's eyes, a person oblivious to his duties, had dawdled along the way and visited his uncle, a Cape Malay specialising in herbs. The doctor, the lawyer, the policeman and the professor, in other words, the whole of supposed Western expertise, confront the uncle; the professor questions him about the "breath of death", whereupon the Cape

---

79 Bird 1992: 212–214; on Jacobson, see also 199–200; on the first assassination and Jacobson's alleged involvement, see 203–209. On Jacobson's biography, see https://www.rcpe.ac.uk/obituary/dr-solomon-solly-jacobson-frcp–edin. See also B. M. Schoeman 1974: 10. Also A. J. Sanders (2006: 25–27), who traces this story back to the South African state security service BOSS. This would also explain the noticeably antisemitic move of blaming a Jew. See also Dousemetzis 2018: 1901–1902.
80 220.K 66 (99), Letter by P. D. Basson (Rhodesia) to Cillié, 12.9.1966. See also Sabalot 2009: 182.
81 In his obituary, Robins (2000) expresses surprise that the ANC and SACP never took notice of Tsafendas after the end of apartheid.

Malay of Muslim faith falls apart and makes a confession. The professor remembers that he has heard of an extremely potent mysterious poison "from the East" that was passed down from father to son in a Cape Muslim family, but was never to be used or opened. Not only did the Muslim herbalist spike the referee's headache remedy with this poison, but he also let him take a whiff of the vial with the poison, which then developed its lethal long-term effect, on account of which it is called "breath of death". The sudden, unexpected and dramatic death of the referee stands in contrasts to the ridiculous and trivial motive of the perpetrator who killed the referee only because he did not let his favourite club win the match.

In a similar way, tragedy and triviality were strangely combined in Verwoerd's murder; the perpetrator had allegedly been acting on the orders of a tapeworm in his body. In both cases, the perpetrators were outsiders. Dimitri Tsafendas was ostracised all his life because of his dark skin colour; and the herbalist of Verwoerd's fiction was a member of a Muslim minority whose designation, "Malay", referred to their Asian background. Just as the tremendously effective poison that caused mass death in Cape Town through its invisible effect, namely through the air as "breath of death", came from Asia, the Muslim herbalist himself also came from Asia, that is, where in Verwoerd's world view, the non-assimilable came from. The putatively unassimilable outside is also reflected in the synonymous use of the term "coolie" for 'coloured'. While the Christian God infused life in man through his breath, the poison from the East, for Verwoerd, was the breath of death. While "the breath of death", in this schema, endangered the entire social order, it could be rendered innocuous by the wise intervention of the physician, the scholar, the lawyer, and the policeman.[82]

In reality, the breath of death emanated from the apartheid system itself, not only in terms of the numbers of people who fell victim to the intensifying poverty and social inequality in the country. The breath of death also paralysed the culture that was at the centre of Afrikaner nationalism. Verwoerd himself was largely responsible for the cultural paralysis that he intensified with his repeated interventions.

Verwoerd's government, his mania for control, and his authoritarianism were largely responsible for the stifling of the very things that could make Afrikaans-language culture thrive. The expansion of the state's reach during Verwoerd's tenure as Prime Minister strangled precisely those aspects that nationalism would have

---

[82] FAV, 4.4.7, typescript, Ockert Witte [Verwoerd], Die asem van die dood, 17 pp. Apparently the story was not published.

aimed to preserve and promote: artistic and scientific creativity, innovation and diversity of opinion, which alone could facilitate learning and societal development.[83]

The accusation of decadence that Verwoerd hurled at the West went further than that raised in other settler colonies, which emphatically profiled themselves as "young peoples" against tired and decadent old Europe. The censorship of "undesirable literature" and the state's interference in cultural life were due to the fact that every sphere of everyday life, such as high culture, education, sports, religion and popular culture, became vital to Afrikaner nationalists, as Verwoerd himself pointed out: "Is it not when he perpetrates crimes, becomes a juvenile delinquent, ducktail or whatever you may like to call it? Is it not when he abandons his people or even worse, when he betrays his people? Is it not when he derides his faith?"[84] From this understanding of the role of 'national culture', the state, represented by the head of government, with the backing of the Reformed Churches,[85] derived the right to interfere, to exercise censorship, to reprimand authors and artists:

> The State must often fight against the results of evil. It is often confronted with the results of decline, of downfall in the personal lives of people. It is confronted with evils that beset a whole community and sometimes spread right through the nation. Sometimes this calls for severe action, and sometimes mercy can be shown. But it must fight against the evils which can cause the downfall of the society.[86]

Even as Prime Minister, Verwoerd held on to the old cultural-nationalist convictions about the "people's own" [*volkseie*], according to which culture had to have arisen organically from its own roots, while "alien" influences were to be rejected, even if he conceded, in abstract terms, that historically, innovation was premised on international contact and collaboration.[87] To Justice Minister Swart, he therefore suggested new legislation prohibiting striptease clubs, so that "this new development from overseas can be warded off".[88] Even as a fairly young man, Verwoerd embraced the spirit of conservative Calvinism in rejecting danc-

---

[83] De Kiewiet 1956: 58–59; see also Meredith 1998: 231.
[84] Verwoerd, Inauguration of the Sunday School Buildings, Bloemfontein 1.10.1959 (in Pelzer 1966: 299–312, 305).
[85] Albertyn 1951: 91–92.
[86] Verwoerd, Centenary Celebrations of the Reformed Church at Rustenburg, 28.3.1959 (in Pelzer 1966: 258–270, 262).
[87] US, 231/2/1/2, Eerstejaar Sociologie: Algemene kursus, p. 13: "Whenever peoples came into contact with each other, social change, and usually also progress, followed." The problem of the poor whites, he stated, was partly due to isolation (ibid., p. 15).
[88] PV 93/1/69/1/1, f. 30, Letter by Verwoerd to Swart, 14.9.59.

ing.[89] Like most nationalists, he displayed a cultural conservatism, on account of which he rejected conspicuous aspects of international youth culture. In his lectures, Verwoerd had shown understanding for the problematic situation of young women who were forced into a subordinate role and often had no opportunity to develop their intellectual abilities because of their role as mothers. Nevertheless, he held on to this traditional image of women throughout his life. It is not clear whether he gave any thought to the fact that his own wife who, after all, had studied and obtained good marks for her examinations, should become active in a profession. She was always confined to the role of caring wife and mother, in which role she emphatically presented herself.[90] Equal opportunities were extremely limited, and Verwoerd did not back emancipatory aims in any respect. He was convinced "that married women with small children should stay at home to care for them. Sometimes, it is true, married women are forced into work not by their own choice, but because their financial situation compels them to work. There are certainly also cases of married women who prefer to work outside the home rather than take care of their children. That is regrettable."[91] This is how he behaved towards his older daughter Anna. When Carel Boshoff asked for her hand in marriage in the early 1950s, Verwoerd's reaction was reserved to negative. This attitude changed abruptly when the bridegroom explained to the father of the bride that he did not want Anna to stop her studies, but to finish her degree in Stellenbosch; in the meantime, he explained, he intended to take up a position as a missionary in Belfast in the Eastern Transvaal, more than 1000 km away. As far as the father was concerned, the daughter was to finish her studies and complete her intellectual formation, but not venture into professional life afterwards; instead, she was to settle into her role as wife and mother.[92] As far as the correspondence goes, Verwoerd's family bore the imprint of parental authority, as was

---

89 D. Prinsloo 1979: 549.
90 *Natal Daily News*, 21.1.1959. Apparently she also had to take criticism for this. After the death of her husband she wrote: "Yes, those of you who did not really approve of me standing with and waiting for Hendrik, would have probably also thought later that I was too submissive." (55.K.V.16 (18), Letter by Betsie Verwoerd to Anna Rothmann, 29.10.1966). On Betsie Verwoerd's studies, see FAV 5.2 for the reports and testimonials on her language skills in 1922 and 1923, and in 1925 when she was a lecturer in the Education Department of the University of Stellenbosch. She wrote her M.A. about the magazine *Die Huisgenoot*, which later acknowledged her dissertation (*Die Huisgenoot*, 12.9.1958, pp. 13–14). See also A. Boshoff 1974: 37–38; Boshoff 1993: ch. 2.
91 PV 93/3/1/36, f. 4, Letter by Verwoerd to Mrs. H. Olivier (Louis Trichardt), 2.11.1960.
92 C. Boshoff 2012: 117. This was also the attitude of the mother. *Natal Daily News*, 21.1.1959: "While Mrs. Verwoerd does not believe in married women going out to work, she does firmly believe that all women should be as highly educated as possible." Boshoff's sister Anna (Annatjie) became E. Verwoerd's private secretary. For more on her person, see C. Boshoff 2012: 54–55.

common among Afrikaner nationalist families. Thus he himself signed private letters to his children formally as 'H. F. Verwoerd'[93] and the children addressed their parents in the third person.

To Verwoerd, the fads of youth culture were the fungus that was eating away at Western civilisation from within, and was threatening to deprive it of all resilience against the communist onslaught. Fashion, hairstyles, pop music and the non-conformist behaviour of young people were therefore not a minor issue; they were bound to destroy the core of Western civilisation, its immune reaction against the communist, and ultimately Asian, subversion. This explains the intolerance of the National Party towards youth culture,[94] and its laughable claims that miniskirts, for example, were due to communist influence. Thus, on several occasions, Verwoerd appeared in public making derogatory comments about the so-called "eendsterts", the "ducktails", young men in leather jackets and with an Elvis hair style, who made their appearance in South Africa in the 1950s.[95] For Verwoerd, "eendsterts" became a general term for everything he rejected as concessions to Western decadence – facile, fashionable and psychologically immature.[96] Quite similarly to Albert Hertzog,[97] Verwoerd also saw in such phenomena a sign of the decadence, which he attested to the West in general and which, in his eyes, explained the decline of the colonial empires.

Even at the age of 21, in his Master's dissertation, Verwoerd had raised the problem of values, arguing that they derived their meaning from the community. From this, he concluded: "Two important spheres of judgement, namely Ethics and Aesthetics, therefore attain an important cultural value. Morality, virtue, art, and beauty are understood to be conducive to the happiness of society at large. A

---

93 FAV 4.7.4.1, Letter by H. F. Verwoerd to Henrik Verwoerd jnr, 12.9.1965; see also ibid., Letter by H. F. Verwoerd to Elsabet du Bois, 1.7.1966.
94 The government concerned itself with bizarre questions such as how to prevent the Beatles from entering South Africa, without their having expressed any interest in doing so (PV 93/3/1/28, Ministry of the Interior document, 'Toelating van burgers van die Vereinigde Koninkryk en kolonies tot die republiek' (21.1.1964)). Similarly, well-known right–wing extremist Rud Meyer suspected the Beatles of being behind the rebelliousness of the younger generation of blacks in particular (PV 132/2/6/2/1/1, Rud Meyer to B. J. Vorster, 26.11.1966).
95 Mooney 1998: 757–761.
96 S. Pauw, the sociologist in the Broederbond UR, in contrast, was sympathetic, attributing the phenomenon to the impulse for activity on the part of young people who no longer found a place in society (AB Archive, 2/3/36, UR meeting, 13.12.1958, p. 12, TOP 41, Eendstertbeweging). Addressing an American audience, Eric Louw stated: "You also send us 'Rock 'n Roll', Jive dances; Duck–tail fashions and methods, comics and 'pulp' magazines – all of which we could well do without!" (PV 188, South Africa reports (2.10.1956): Excerpts from Louw's speech to the American Club, Johannesburg 28.9.1956, p. 2).
97 E.g. PV 451/4/1/198, ff. 11849, 11889–11890.

foundation of ethical judgement is the prerequisite for building and consolidating human coexistence, and in society, aesthetic values receive their highest salience."[98] Accordingly, aesthetic enjoyment was not a private matter, but rather a matter subordinate to the needs of the community and its collective identity.

Psychologist Peter Lambley observed the consequences in the 1970s: corruption, abuse of power, multiple casual sexual relations.[99] Verwoerd's government cracked down on unwanted undesirable ideas in the form of publications, music recordings and films, which could have brought about innovations vital to cultural activity. This was perhaps the greatest contradiction and irony in the history of apartheid: while apartheid was meant to ensure the 'survival' of Afrikaners, yet politicians and 'cultural leaders' interpreted cultural openness to the world as cultural self-abandonment. They suppressed receptiveness and expressions of vitality, thereby cutting off resources for their own culture. This was brought about not least by Piet Meyer as head of the broadcasting station; he appointed kindred Broederbond members, such as long-standing conductor and musicologist Anton Hartman.[100] Under Meyer, the SABC was placed entirely at the service of state interests and those of the NP. The influential radio station intervened in popular music by banning its broadcasting; but the SABC never managed to manipulate the performing arts entirely to serve its interests.[101]

While Verwoerd recognised the usefulness of radio programmes for propagating his politics among "the Bantu",[102] he agreed with Albert Hertzog that television should not be introduced in South Africa. Hertzog, as the minister in charge, rejected television for culturally conservative reasons, and because he feared that it could spread alternative views on multiracial coexistence. In a memorandum, television was characterised above all as a medium that would go out to reach the greatest possible number of people, in order to generate advertising revenue, "the universal language of feeling rather than the language of discerning and circumscribing thought".[103] Ever since his doctorate, Verwoerd had not set great store on emotions because he considered them unreliable and malleable; he thus agreed with Hertzog's disdain for that medium. Television was serving the pur-

---

[98] Verwoerd 1922b: 60.
[99] Lambley 1981: 134–144.
[100] See Walton 2004: 69–70; on the cultural–nationalist narrowing of Afrikaans music, see Walton 2004: 73.
[101] S. van der Merwe 2014: 353–354.
[102] Hayman/Tomaselli 1989: 51–53.
[103] PV 93/1/59/1, Aantekeninge oor beeldradio (anon.), p. 2.

pose of advertising items of mass culture;[104] and television technology had not yet developed sufficiently to be introduced on a massive scale in South Africa. The cost of technology that would rapidly become obsolete, would amount to at least 20 million pounds. Verwoerd's annotations clearly show that he shared Hertzog's main conclusion: "So if the state decides not to introduce television in our country, it is not a question of condemning a new communication technology as such, but of the nature of this technology, which is in fact a combination of all known communications media."[105] This sounded plausible from an economic point of view, but on closer inspection, it turned out to be a matter of Verwoerd's usual sophistry, for he adduced this argument only in the discussion about television; in all other respects, he enthusiastically supported the further development of technical possibilities. Verwoerd's real motive was to buy time until apartheid had proved its worth, and the population would be immune to external criticism. He shared Hertzog's opinion that television was the medium that would directly introduce a population isolated by cultural nationalism and censorship to alternative social orders and ways of life – which would potentially deprive his policy of racial segregation of its legitimacy.[106]

The deep mistrust of subversive cultural influences from outside was also manifested in increasingly harsh censorship. Left-wing literature classified as Marxist in the broadest sense fell prey to this, as did novels and poetry by South African authors as well as cultural products from further afield that were found to express even the slightest hint of opposition to apartheid. The regime did not shy away from making a laughing stock of itself in taking actions with the avowed aim of combating pornography – such as pasting strips over the nipples of barebreasted photographic models on the covers of magazines published abroad. Once set in motion, the censorship machinery was prone to every form of paranoid xenophobia: "By 1963, there were 8,629 publications on the banned list. Many of these are pornographic; others are banned for political reasons. They include not only Communist publications, but also the writings of Dostoevsky and Tolstoy, Lawrence and Graves, Hemingway and Salinger, Faulkner and Caldwell,

---

104 As Chairman of a newspaper group, Verwoerd was possibly also motivated by fears about a loss of advertising revenue for the print media (see Corrigan 1974: 28).
105 PV 93/1/59/1, Aantekeninge oor beeldradio (anon.), pp. 3–5. W. Grünbauer, a filmmaker from Hamburg working in South Africa, complained about the fact that more and more ministries were opening their own film departments, and that he was unable to find work because of this. Verwoerd retorted that he could not expect a reversal of the decision, on which he had pinned all his hopes (PV93/1/53/14/1, f. 20, Letter by W. Grünbauer to Verwoerd, 22.5.1959; f. 21, Verwoerd's reply, 3.6.1959). The government put forward a whole range of additional reasons (Bevan 2008: 66–91); on the moral 'dangers', see ibid., 85–91.
106 Nixon 1993: 127.

and Bertrand Russell, and works by South African authors such as Peter Abrahams and Harry Bloom. South African librarians are continually engaged in recalling and destroying books that have been banned; booksellers have a difficult task in deciding what foreign publications to order."[107]

As early as 1938, the poet N. P. van Wyk Louw had complained about the presumed interpretive authority of the "cultural leaders" who canonised the cultural achievements of the past and derived norms for new artistic creations from the latter, thus congealing the whole of Afrikaans culture in a conservative bubble.[108] This also pertained to history, the discipline from which cultural nationalism and apartheid ideology sought to draw their legitimation; history was taught in a conservative mode, promising continuity and elevating the great men who made it.[109] In a contribution with the provocative title 'Kultuurleiers Sonder Kultuur' ('Cultural leaders without culture'), van Wyk Louw posed the crucial question: "Will the attempt to consolidate a culture through deliberately applied steering mechanisms not lead to the decline of culture as living force?"[110] He was certainly not referring to Verwoerd personally, but it was during this period that Verwoerd, as editor-in-chief of *Die Transvaler*, began to take on the role as guardian of what he considered the true and the good.

In his capacity as Prime Minister, Verwoerd himself acted as censor. When AB veteran William Nicol asked whether "a few Bantu could act [in a short play on Dingaansdag] instead of black-faced whites, as was the practice in the past", Verwoerd immediately expressed strong "misgivings".[111] He positioned himself in the controversy surrounding the novel *Sewe dae by die Silbersteins* [*Seven Days at the Silbersteins*] by Etienne Leroux, arguably the most important Afrikaans novelist of the 20th century, against most Afrikaans intellectuals, and vehemently denounced the award of the prestigious Hertzog Prize to the author. When Leroux nevertheless received the prize, Verwoerd made a point arriving late for the award ceremony.[112] In the spring of 1966, he used the authority of his office to publicly criticise van Wyk Louw's drama *Die Pluimsaad waai ver* [*The Plumed Seed Blows Far*], because it did not only celebrate the heroes of the Boer War, but

---

107 Thompson 1966: 129; see also Cope 1982: 75–76; also https://www.news24.com/Books/how-the-apartheid-regime-burntbooks-in-their-tens-of-thousands–20181025.
108 N. P. van Wyk Louw 1965: 2–3. S. Muller 2008: 202–203 for further information.
109 Pelzer 1966b: 48.
110 N. P. van Wyk Louw 1965: 7.
111 PV 93/1/34/9, f. 34, Letter by W. Nicol to Verwoerd, 8.2.1962; f. 36, Verwoerd's reply, 17.2.1962.
112 Steyn 1998: 986–995, esp. 993; see also Kannemeyer 2008: 383–384; also Kapp 2009: 407.

allowed cowards and collaborators to have their say, along with the heroes.[113] To Verwoerd, the artist's task was ultimately "to glorify and not to confuse".[114] This even went so far that, after watching a new film version of *Othello*, he ordered that "the film must not be shown publicly in any cinema in the country".[115] Breyten Breytenbach, at the time a renowned young poet, was driven into exile because he was not allowed to live in South Africa with his Vietnamese wife.[116] A broadcasting ban was imposed on songs if their title only contained the word 'God'; similarly, the musical *Jesus Christ Superstar* could no longer be aired after massive complaints from conservative listeners.[117] The Prime Minister himself dealt with individual incidents such as 'mixed' parties or conferences, setting in motion the entire governmental machinery to ascertain whether there were violations of the law or whether individual authorities had overstepped their powers in giving approvals for such events.[118] Towards the end of his life, his totalitarian penchant for control was pronounced – "as though he did not want to let any affairs of the country, and especially not the thinking in his country, slip from his attention".[119] One of the leading journalists of the nationalist camp, Schalk Pienaar, spoke of a pathological symptom, referring to the suspicion roused by everything and everyone who did not toe the cultural guardians' line. He did not mention Verwoerd by name, but it was clear whom he meant when he came to the defence of van Wyk Louw.[120]

The stifling of cultural life in the apartheid era, the conformism, and the twists and turns that certain individuals had to perform, were reflected in the ca-

---

[113] Steyn 1998: 1037–1045; see also Mouton 2002: 61; also Steyn 2004: 496–497; and Welsh 2010: 175–176. Verwoerd's interventions in cultural affairs had a similarly intimidating effect as Stalin's criticism of Shostakovich. Van Wyk Louw himself possibly saw it similarly (Steyn 1998: 1090). As early as 1937, Verwoerd attacked the novel *Turning Wheels* by Stuart Cloete, which had portrayed the Voortrekkers not only as pious heroes (*Die Transvaler*, 10.12.1937, 15.12.1937; see also J. Basson 2008: 67). The confrontation with van Wyk Louw had a prelude; according to Meiring (1990: 94–95), it was a late retaliatory measure by Verwoerd (see also ibid., 185).
[114] PV 72/2, Gert van der Walt, Memoirs of Verwoerd, p. 4. About other interventions of Verwoerd's in the Afrikaans literary scene of the 1960s, see Cope 1982: 153.
[115] 296.KV.32, typed note by P.A. Weber, 8. 9. 1966. See also A. Boshoff 1974: 228.
[116] His wife did not even get a visa to accompany her husband when he received a prestigious literary prize (Bekker 2005: 216–217).
[117] S. van der Merwe 2014: 354.
[118] FAV, 4.7.2.1, Letter by Verwoerd to Minister of Justice Vorster, 23.3.1965 concerning a newspaper article by B. Pogrund about a 'mixed' conference in East London; reply by Vorster, 9.4.1965 with attached detailed Report of the Police Commissioner, 30.3.1965.
[119] Cillié 1980: 56, 72.
[120] Pienaar 1975: 4–5. Yet Pienaar was no opponent of apartheid, as his response to Verwoerd's assassination shows (ibid., 9).

reer of Abraham Jonker. During the Second World War, Jonker was an acolyte of Jan Smuts, whose political line he represented when he worked as prominent journalist for the United Party-aligned newspaper *Die Suiderstem* between 1936 and 1945. In addition, he published three books in which he denounced the anti-semitism of the National Party and the extreme right-wing extra–parliamentary opposition.[121] After D. F. Malan became Prime Minister, Jonker served as an MP for the opposition United Party for several years, but joined the ruling Party in 1956. In addition to his journalistic and political activities, Jonker had a wide range of cultural interests and published several novels, which did not bring him the recognition he had hoped for. All the more disappointed was he when his daughter Ingrid, whom he had rejected, received a prestigious literary prize for her poetry. Ingrid Jonker suffered from depression, which was undoubtedly exacerbated by the stifling atmosphere that paralysed cultural creativity in Verwoerd's South Africa.[122] The fact that her father had taken a stand in Parliament denouncing her poem about a child shot by police in Langa in 1960,[123] and thus publicly turning his back on his daughter, was a severe blow to her. Abraham Jonker was enough of an opportunist to get himself elected Chairman of a parliamentary committee that was responsible for the first censorship legislation;[124] Ingrid signed a document protesting against it. Rumours had it that Abraham Jonker, upon hearing of his daughter's suicide on 19 July 1965, expressed himself extremely negatively about her.[125] Ingrid Jonker's psychological instability aside, the family tragedy can be traced back to the opportunism of her father, who had sacrificed everything he once stood for, in favour of his inclusion in the power elite. Instead, he supported the ossified conservatism that was like a leaden blanket enveloping the country.

Verwoerd's policy that did not admit of any alternatives did not allay the fears of the Afrikaner people, but actually stoked their fears. This became evident in the 1980s, when the irrationality and impracticability of apartheid became obvious to everyone and its end became foreseeable. The increase in family murders, especially among Afrikaners, in which fathers killed their families' members and then

---

[121] Jonker 1940, 1941, 1943.
[122] L. Viljoen 2012: 134.
[123] It was this poem that Nelson Mandela read on 24 May 1994 in South Africa's first democratically elected Parliament to emphasise that there was a resistant Afrikaans culture; this simultaneously contributed to the renown of Ingrid Jonker and the popularity of her work (Nicol 1995: 85–87).
[124] See also B. M. Schoeman 1973: 219.
[125] L. Viljoen 2012: 129; see also Metelerkamp/Jonker 2003: 201. On the depressing political atmosphere and the disturbed relationship with her father, see also Cope 1982: 85–92.

turned their weapons on themselves, was an indication of a sense of insecurity in the face of imminent change, and of grossly inflated role expectations of Afrikaner men, which were as violent as they were unrealistic.[126] The obsession with "survival" – the main motif of Afrikaner nationalists –, had the tragic effect of turning the violence of apartheid against its own supporters. As economist Herbert Frankel noted in 1952, "[a] civilization which is not in process of change, which can be grasped, defined, cut off and circumscribed, is a civilisation which is not living but has been, or is being, frozen to death".[127]

---

[126] S. I. du Toit 1990: 294–295.
[127] S. H. Frankel 1952: 9.

Conclusion

Contrary to the assertions of some historians that Verwoerd only became a nationalist in the latter part of his career, contemporaries who knew him were correct in their judgement: He was a political fanatic. He was a political fanatic at a young age and remained one throughout his life. This study was able to show that his political thinking was characterised by continuity, and not by ruptures, as some claim to have observed. Even in his adolescence, he had committed himself to what he later called his "principle", namely the primacy of the cultural-nationalistically conceived community over the individual. On the other hand, it is telling what he did not call a principle, that is, what did not play a role in his thinking, and what he certainly did not reflect upon: namely democracy and dialogue or accountability. It proved to be worthwhile to examine his academic career in more detail and to understand his scholarly formation as a biographical learning process. Thus, his interest in the dual task in everyday life, which he chose as the topic of his MA dissertation in Psychology, led him to orientate his own thoughts and actions along the lines of fixed principles – both in his capacity as scholar, and later, in his capacity as politician.

The link that he posited between developmental psychology and race did not amount to biological racism; it could be more accurately described as a link between civilisational development and skin colour. His developmental psychology was influenced specifically by ethnopsychology, not so much of the older version represented by Wilhelm Wundt, but of that represented by Felix Krueger and his School. The direct link with skin colour was Verwoerd's own addition, though. Apparently he did not make it clear to himself how these developmental stages were to be linked to cognitive and intellectual abilities. If all humans belonged to the genus *homo sapiens* – Verwoerd nowhere denied this – then all humans would have to have the same potential and capabilities, and the developmental gradation he posited would require justification. Above all, it would be necessary to clarify why "the Bantu" would still need a long time to catch up with the Europeans; Verwoerd himself questioned this possibility, doubting that they would be able to do so at all. Admittedly, Verwoerd's equation of "natives" with children only rehashed popular colonial ideas, and imbued them with academic credentials. This is where the logical consistency admired by his followers characteristically ceased: in this respect, Verwoerd put forward inconsistent and self-contradictory arguments.

One of the results of his psychological training was his discovery of how to manipulate people. The laboratory situation, in which the environment is set up in such a way that the psychological reactions of the test subjects can be conditioned and observed, shaped his attitude towards "the Bantu", whom he considered intellectually incapable of dialogue. Some of the essays he published in scientific journals during his time as a Professor attest to his penchant for unambiguous attributions, the systematisation of evaluative standards, and the belief that people could be 'read' through a grid of psychological traits. In his obsession with order, he abhorred everything that seemed chaotic and unregulated. For him, the epitome of chaos was communism, insofar as it supposedly dissolved "organic communities", creating, as did "liberalism", a society of atomised individuals instead. The obsession with order and manageability responded to his intention to enforce racial segregation with drastic measures; at the same time, it was the driving force behind his endeavour to separate the competencies of institutions and individuals as clearly as possible, and to regulate them without leaving any doubt or ambiguity. To Verwoerd, order was purity; apartheid, as politics of difference, was designed to maintain the 'purity' of races and nations, on which their continued existence depended.

The connection between Verwoerd's academic and political career, however, was not limited to insights on thinking processes and feelings. The connecting link was a substantive one, namely the issue of the "poor whites". Spending some time in Cape Town as a young student, he was shocked by the condition of the poor whites – which made a lasting impression on him. In his zeal, he even began to judge his contemporaries' commitment to nationalism by the extent to which they were serious in their devotion to "the despised in our midst".

Verwoerd's commitment to the "poor whites" was not owed to solidarity, but to "principle", that is, to cultural nationalism, which is what drove him into politics. Shortly after taking up the position as Professor of Applied Psychology and Psychotechnics in 1928, he was looking to work as an academic in the interests of cultural nationalism. In 1930, he proposed the establishment of a professorship for Applied Sociology and Social Work, which required some time and preparation – on account of which it stands to reason that his activity as academic psychologist soon no longer satisfied him. As Professor of Sociology since 1932, he moved onto the public stage with aplomb, while academic work clearly moved backstage. The priority that Verwoerd gave to the professional training of white social workers underlines the fact, as do the lecture notes that have been preserved, that the "poor white problem" was now at the centre of his attention and work. The preparation of the Congress on the "Poor White Problem" in Kimberley in 1934 and his chairmanship of the Continuation Committee took up a considerable amount of his time; the sources do not, however, give a clear indication as to whether and to what extent Verwoerd had been involved in the work of the Carnegie Commission before that time.

From the Psychology of Thought, above all from the work of Otto Selz, Verwoerd derived the idea of the human physiological predisposition to logical thinking, which he distorted in a racist way, claiming that Africans had a pre-logical mentality and were overpowered by feelings. With his own research, he wanted to show that feelings are fluid and unreliable, which is why he refrained from giving them any scope, or whipping them up, in his political propaganda. Rather, he attempted to convince his voters and supporters with what he considered logical reasoning, but he wielded this logic as an instrument of rhetorical persuasion.

One of Verwoerd's propagandist tricks that proved persuasive, at least to his own supporters, was to present his own measures as if they were in the interests of the victims, whom he therefore never sought to involve in decision-making. However, his ideological proximity and his exchanges with right-wing extremists, fascists, and racists gave the lie to claims that his policies were fundamentally well-intentioned, just as it made his commitment to democracy sound hollow.

Verwoerd's logic all too often exhausted itself only in construing chain reactions, from which he would then derive a policy of no compromise. In numerous instances, he did not argue logically at all, but by analogy, replete with reckless and bizarre comparisons in order to 'prove' a particular development as a necessary consequence. The analogies that he favoured in order to underline the supposedly barbaric state of "the Bantu" referred to other African countries such as Ghana, which was not even inhabited by "Bantu"-speaking peoples. Verwoerd's short-sightedness in extrapolating from one African country to all Africans provides a clear indication of his racism. His self-professed attempt to base apartheid on an ethnological foundation should have precluded this kind of argument, moreover since he always referred to the diversity of African cultures.

Even if Verwoerd never expressed himself in terms of biological racism, the connection he drew between culture and biological traits such as skin colour clearly marked him as racist. Any doubt about that can be dispelled by considering his antisemitism, to which he continued to adhere even when the more opportunist fraction of the NP around D. F. Malan officially abandoned it after the end of the Second World War. Verwoerd, for his part, just like J. G. Strydom and E. H. Louw, staunchly upheld antisemitic convictions right up to the 1960s. He was given to antisemitic outbursts on several occasions, although he took great pains not to display them openly, especially after 1960, when he pursued a form of nation-building that was to encompass all whites.

His preoccupation with academic psychology also affected his understanding and practice of propaganda. In particular, his use of logic as rhetorical instrument harks back to his dabblings in the Psychology of Thought, imbued with the racism of his own conviction. In his dealings with "the Bantu", he dispensed with logic and resorted to imagery instead, convinced that it would be easier to understand. Rhetoric based on logical reasoning, on the other hand, was reserved for his white audiences.

Verwoerd's eleven-year career as a journalist clearly indicates that he prioritised the realisation of his political programme. His sovereign disregard for journalistic standards, his self-image as a propagandist for cultural nationalism and the NP, coupled with his assiduous work in the Party and the Broederbond, are all indications that he never considered himself a professional journalist. His later dealings with journalists and newspapers, as well as his advocacy of censorship, could be adduced to further corroborate this finding. In fact, his lack of professionalism as a journalist was a manifestation of his fanaticism. From the very beginning, he used *Die Transvaler* purely as propaganda outlet rather than as a newspaper, which was also reflected in his editorials conveying the Party's points of view. Following his principle of 'community', his aim was to forge 'unity of the people' ['*volkseenheid*'], without giving any thought to how this could be reconciled with his commitment to democracy and along with it, at least implicitly, to diversity of opinion and debate.

After the end of his academic career, Verwoerd became involved in the National Party and the Broederbond, where he soon came to occupy leading positions. Here, as previously in his journalistic work, he soon acquired a reputation as implacable, intolerant, uncompromising stickler for principles. Dialogue as a principle of democratic politics was alien to him. He was certainly not a Socratic sage attempting to solve problems through dialogue. Verwoerd's version of apartheid never opened up a chance for frank discussion, consultations or even negotiations. Refusal to communicate extended to all critics of apartheid, whom Verwoerd attacked as enemies or contemptuously accused of "theorising". This contradicted his repeatedly proclaimed goal of good neighbourliness and friendly relations. To the extent that he based his politics on the general will of a suprahistorical community, he could be called a Rousseauist. Instead of questioning, he presented indisputable answers.

At the same time, these eleven years taught Verwoerd a lot in terms of networking, organisational structures and hierarchies. It was particularly the Broederbond, with its top-down authority structure, masked as bottom-up formal democratic structure, that shaped his understanding of the state and state bureaucracies, as they came to be expressed in his later work as Minister for Native Affairs and Prime Minister.

Compared to the older South African colonial state, the state that Verwoerd was instrumental in creating was a decidedly strong state with extensive ambitions. It interfered in the private lives of its citizens, even in the most intimate spheres – through the Immorality Act, for instance; and generally, it aimed at the most comprehensive surveillance possible. This, of course, took place along the lines of the racial hierarchy, so that white South Africans felt the least of the repressive measures – for as long as they did not actively object to conscription or reject apartheid in principle. The South African state's obsession with control stood in stark contrast to its disinterest in cultural life, even though apartheid ideology was harping on insurmountable cultural differences. The extent of the knowledge displayed by Verwoerd and his administration, about African history and cultures was extremely limited; it was replaced by assumptions asserted with the greatest self-confidence. This ignorance appeared to the protagonists of apartheid as certainty, to the extent that it was repeated in ever new versions within the self-referential communication framework of the power elite, never to be questioned. As politicians could rely on the consent of their voters, they did not feel pressed to check their claims. In fact, apartheid, which drew its legitimacy from cultural differences and civilisational gradations, was a "regime of ignorance".

In his capacity as Prime Minister, Verwoerd moved to comprehensive planning that was no longer restricted to the black majority, but extended to fundamentally restructuring the state and South African society as a whole. This concerned the international status of South Africa, which he wanted to craft into a 'normal' nation-state with a white majority, through exterritorialising the 'homelands'; it also pertained to the economy, which was now increasingly subject to state control. These measures, in turn, led to further planning. After 1960, Verwoerd emerged as nation-builder; during this phase, the strongly voluntaristic trait of his political thinking came to the fore. Closely related to it was the increasingly repressive character of his politics, which was also directed against internal opponents in his own base. Verwoerd was primarily interested in securing his own position of power and, along with it, the power of deciding on and interpreting the policy of racial segregation. For this reason, he moved against critics in his own camp by making examples of individuals in order to intimidate others and discourage dissent. While he succeeded with this policy, his repressive approach to Afrikaans culture reduced its vitality in such a way that by the 1960s, South Africa had become reduced to stodgy provincialism. But these repressive traits were not a late phenomenon; they only became more pronounced in the last phase of his life. His early plans for labour colonies and forced labour for the "work-shy" also point to his authoritarian character. Repression was an integral aspect of apartheid; it was not established initially as a response to resistance and opposition, but the result of an authoritarian mindset underlying the very concept of apartheid. For that reason, it would be a mistake to separate apartheid from repression.

Eric Hobsbawm has coined a formula that characterises the twentieth century, namely "the age of extremes": the hubris of creating the new man, of developing new world and social orders from fundamental ideas, and to impose these on people; of fighting for the happiness of mankind at the cost of hundreds of thousands, even millions of deaths. At the same time, however, the formula implies diametrically opposed ideologies: on the one hand, "scientific socialism", whose conception of man and society went back to the Enlightenment and whose basis was rational; on the other hand, racism, also based on claims to scientificity and progress, in the name of which the Nazi state executed millions of people; from the biologically understood formula of the superman, it derived the claim to be able to breed and exterminate people. To be sure, there are huge differences between these two extremes, which extant concepts of totalitarianism tend to blur. Nevertheless, both tendencies have something in common that distinguishes them from democracy, namely the belief in a mission, a quasi-religious understanding of history as path towards salvation, the priority of the lofty goal over individual rights, and the conviction that people are not free to shape their own lives; being biologically or socially predetermined, they always stand to be exposed as 'menaces' or 'class enemies', independently of their individual views and convictions.

Instead of designating the twentieth century "the age of extremes", it could more appropriately be called 'the age of extremists'. This epithet points to the common ground in a basic attitude to society and human nature: the assumption that there are no limits to possibilities of manipulating human individuals, groups, and populations through 'social engineering' and biopolitics. The phrase "the age of extremists" also has the advantage that, instead of focusing on ideologies and structures, it names the protagonists and responsible persons. Without getting caught up in the problematics posed by concepts of totalitarianism, it opens up a perspective beyond the two extremes of communism and National Socialism, and shows that the 20th century was, and the 21st century still is, an age of extremists in many parts of the world, not only in Europe. This age is by no means over, but today states have been replaced by large corporations such as Google and Facebook.[1] In his book, *Seeing like a state,* James Scott shows how the assumption of the unlimited possibility of manipulating people and societies gained traction, thus broadening the perspective on this kind of extremism to include foresters and bureaucrats, architects and town planners, social workers and psychologists.

The global expansion of the age of extremes also brings apartheid South Africa into focus. Here, too, extremists were at work who plastered over the monstrosity of their societal designs with the thin veneer of their cultural-political conservatism. Verwoerd's apartheid was not a reactionary adherence to a bygone order of a good old colonial era; in fact, it did not harbour the seeds of apartheid. Rather, apartheid was the template for a new social order, which could only be

---

[1] https://www.nytimes.com/2013/12/15/magazine/googles-plan-for-global-domination-dont-ask-why-ask-where.html
https://hbr.org/2015/08/digital-fairness-vs-facebooks-dream-of-world-domination

established and guaranteed by a state of a kind that had never existed in South Africa before.

This new understanding of the role of the state had already been announced by Verwoerd in his keynote speech at the Kimberley Congress in 1934; and it can be traced back to his attempts to rescue the "poor whites". This, too, is not atypical for "the age of extremes", as many of the extremists of the century have been impelled by the perceived urgency of 'the last hour' to save their world from the abyss. Verwoerd wanted to do something good, namely to help the "poor whites" to do better than that: to secure the existence of the Afrikaner nation and thus contribute to the preservation of white civilisation worldwide. Because the integration of South African society was advancing, he too was driven by a sense of urgency. This explains the tremendous dynamism of his politics, which proceeded to simultaneously transform city and country, churches, education, prisons – in short, the whole of society. Processes of decolonisation in other parts of the African continent sharpened this awareness of having caught hold of the spokes of the wheel of history. The result was the ruthlessness and callousness with which he implemented his policy. In all good conscience and bourgeois respectability, he had political opponents imprisoned, turned a blind eye to orgies of violence by the police, and perceived dangerous enemies as soon as they would no longer allow themselves to be captured by a fundamental racist consensus.

Identifying Verwoerd as a representative of the age of extremists does not imply that he should be placed on a par with Hitler and Stalin. Verwoerd was certainly nefarious, but he was neither a genocidaire nor was he a commandant of camps. If one were to compare him with another representative of "the age of extremes", the most apposite comparison would be, despite all ideological differences, with Lenin – not Stalin. Some of Verwoerd's character traits bear resemblances with some of Lenin's, especially the dogmatism, which in Lenin's case, of course, was accompanied by greater tactical flexibility; but what both of them have in common is their ideological fanaticism, coupled with a personal sense of mission, a craving for power, and with contempt for consensus, transparency and dialogue. However, Lenin was the better politician because, despite his dogmatism, he managed to retain greater freedom of action and thus had more extensive room for manoeuvre. What distinguished him from Verwoerd's more narrow-minded and inflexible adherence to blueprints derived from "principles", was his realisation, from early on, that democratic parliamentarism could best be overturned with the slogan, "all power to the soviets"; he understood that the power of the soviets, in turn, had to boil down to the power of his Party, that at a rather late stage, he had to make concessions to the 'New Economic Policy' to facilitate the country's economic recovery after the devastating civil war, and thus the survival of the communist experiment.

Verwoerd was a man of extreme opposites: friendly in his dealings with his neighbours, merciless towards opponents, whom he characteristically did not cast as 'opponents', but as 'enemies'. He surpassed his colleagues in government and Party in intelligence and at the same time, he was insipid and narrow-minded. He lacked creativity, but had a special talent for systematising the thoughts of others, which is why his followers thought him an original thinker. Verwoerd was a political fanatic, a stickler for principles and a know-it-all; he was authoritarian and showed dictatorial traits, especially in his position as Prime Minister. In his outward demeanour and in his views on culture and society, he was an old-fashioned conservative; at the same time, he was a purveyor of high modernism, believing that the future of his country was staked on comprehensive planning and centralised steering. Despite his conservatism and his commitment to cultural traditions, he had no respect for time-honoured structures, and for the emotional needs of others – as attested to by the forced resettlements he initiated, and the arbitrary severing of emotional ties between neighbours, family members, and friends. Even if apartheid cannot be simply seen as the translation of Verwoerd's dissertation into political practice, the blunting of feelings, and the bureaucratic indifference remain the hallmarks of the apartheid state – a state for which human beings were merely masses to be shifted around, objects of policies, human material. Once considered no longer useful, they were marginalised as "surplus people".

If Verwoerd's assassin reckoned that Verwoerd's death would spell the collapse of apartheid, he made a mistake. Verwoerd's successors continued to implement his programme, shifting the emphasis from racism to anti-communism, without changing the undemocratic nature of minority rule. Verwoerd's legacy is still being felt today in the widespread poverty, the culture of violence and the intransigence of many whites who still seem to remain under the sway of his suggestive propaganda. But it is also still evident in very concrete terms in the form of the black townships and squatter camps, as well as in the soil deterioration in the former 'homelands'. Hendrik Verwoerd has ensured that his memory remains alive.

Bibliography

Archives

South Africa

Bloemfontein
Archive for Contemporary Affairs, University of the Free State, Bloemfontein
PV 2 NP Transvaal
PV 4 E.H. Louw
PV 14 Marais Viljoen
PV 18 C.R. Swart
PV 34 M.P.A. Malan
PV 35 J. de Klerk
PV 42 A.H. Jonker
PV 54 NP Federale Raad / Federal Council
PV 58 J. Basson
PV 59 NP Information Service
PV 72 Piet Beukes
PV 93 H.F. Verwoerd
PV 94 E.G. Jansen
PV 97 F.C. Erasmus
PV 118 J.F.W. Haak
PV 123 J.P. van S. Bruwer
PV 132 B.J. Vorster
PV 188 W.C. du Plessis
PV 202 FAK
PV 203 P.W. Botha
PV 206 A.E. Rupert
PV 276 F. Barnard
PV 377 J.W. Rall
PV 425 Marius Swart
PV 442 F.R. Tomlinson
PV 451 A. Hertzog
PV 609 Len Verwoerd
PV 614 Tinie Vorster
PV 741 E. Verwoerd
PV 873 A. Treurnicht

Johannesburg
University of the Witwatersrand. Cullen Library, Documents
A 2628, Non-European Affairs Department, Johannesburg.

Cape Town
University of Cape Town
BC 282 Eiselen Commission (Murray Collection)

Potchefstroom
University of the North-West, Ferdinand Postma Library
Ossewabrandwag Archives
H.M. van der Westhuysen

Pretoria
National Archives
BAO
GG23_807
GGR
MEM
MHG
NTS
SAP
TES
UOD
URU
University of South Africa, Library,
United Party
Erfenisstigting / Heritage Foundation
Afrikaner Broederbond Archives

Stellenbosch
Stellenbosch University, J.S. Gericke Library
24 D.F. Malan
55 M.E. Rothmann
77 R.W. Wilcocks
191 H.B. Thom
205 G.G. Cillié
220 P.J. Cillié
231 H.F. Verwoerd
289 S.P. Cilliers
296 P.A. Weber
297 E. Theron

Stellenbosch University, University Archive
Personal File H.F. Verwoerd
Personal File Wilcocks
Raad en Senaat / Council and Senate
Studenteraad / Students Representative Council

Archives of the Nederduits Gereformeerde Kerk / Dutch Reformed Church

Germany

Berlin
Humboldt University, University Archive
Personal File Diedrich Westermann
Personal File Hans Rupp
Kaiser-Wilhelm-Institut für Erbpsychologie
Federal Archives (formerly Document Center), Personal Files Dürckheim-Montmartin und Warhold Drascher.

Koblenz
Federal Archives
Hintrager Collection

Leipzig
University of Leipzig, University Archives
F. Krueger Collection
Personal File F. Krueger
Psychological Institute

Mannheim
University of Mannheim
Otto Selz Collection

Munich
Institute for Contemporary History
Christoph Imhoff Collection

Würzburg
Julius Maximilians University
Adolf-Würth-Center for the History of Psychology
Hans Volkelt Collection

USA

Digital National Security Archive (DNSA)

Literature

Abercrombie, H. R.
1938 *Afrika se Gevaar. Ons donker probleem*, Pretoria.
Ach, Narziß
1999 'Über die Willenstätigkeit und das Denken (Ausschnitte)'. In: Ziche, Paul (Ed.): *Introspektion. Texte zur Selbstwahrnehmung des Ichs*, Wien, pp. 98–156.
Adam, Heribert
1971 'The South African Power-Élite: A Survey of Ideological Commitment'. In: *Canadian Journal of Political Science*, 4, 1, pp. 76–96.
1977 *Südafrika. Soziologie einer Rassengesellschaft*, Frankfurt am Main.
Adam, Heribert; **Giliomee**, Hermann
1979 *Ethnic Power Mobilized. Can South Africa Change?*, New Haven.
Adams, M. J.
1936 The Solution of Unemployment by the Aid of Token Money. Prepared for Submission to the National Conference of Social Work held at Johannesburg, 30th September – 3rd October, 1936.
Adams, Zuleig
2011 Demitrios Tsafendas. Race, Madness and the Archive. PhD Thesis, Bellville.
Adhikari, Mohamed
2006 *Not white enough, not black enough. Racial identity in the South African coloured community*, Athens.
Adler, Alfred
1978 'Die Individualpsychologie'. In: *Praxis und Theorie der Individualpsychologie. Vorträge zur Einführung in die Psychotherapie für Ärzte, Psychologen und Lehrer*, Frankfurt a.M, pp. 19–32.
Adler, Herman
1925 *Report of Mental Health Survey of La Salle, Peru and Oglesby*, Springfield, Ill.
Albertyn, J. R.
1934 *National Conference on the Poor White Problem, Kimberley, Oct. 2–5, 1934. Programme and Proposals*.
1951 *Die twee Volkspilare. Die Funksie van Staat en Kerk in die Volkslewe*, Cape Town – Pretoria.
Albertyn, J. R.; **Du Toit**, P.; **Theron**, H. S.
1947 *Kerk en Stad. Verslag van die Kommissie van Ondersoek van die Gefedereerde N.G. Kerke na kerklike en godsdienstige toestande in die nege stede van die Unie van Suid-Afrika*, Stellenbosch.
Alexander, Peter (ed.)
2009 *Alan Paton. Selected Letters*, Cape Town.
Allighan, Garry
1961 *Verwoerd – The End. A Look Back from the Future*, London.
Allport, Gordon W.
1923 'The Leipzig Congress of Psychology'. In: *The American Journal of Psychology*, 34, 4, pp. 612–615.
1956 *Prejudice in modern Perspective*. Hoernlé Memorial Lecture 12, Johannesburg.
1968 'The Personalistic Psychology of William Stern'. In: Wolman, Benjamin B. (ed.): *Historical roots of contemporary psychology*, New York, pp. 321–337.
Ally, Shireen; **Mooney**, Katie; **Stewart**; Paul
2003 'The state-sponsored and centralised institutionalisation of an academic discipline: sociology in South Africa, 1920–1970'. In: *Society in Transition*, 34, 1, pp. 70–103.

Alter, Peter
1985 *Nationalismus*, Frankfurt am Main.
Anderson, Benedict R. O'G
2006 *Imagined Communities. Reflections on the origin and spread of nationalism*, London.
Andrews, H. T.; **Berrill**, F. A.; **Guingand**, Francis de; **Holloway**, J. E.; **Meyer**, F.; **Van Eck**, H. J. (eds.)
1965 *South Africa in the Sixties. A Socio-Economic Survey*, Johannesburg.
Anonymous
1959 'Der weiße Traum'. In: *Der Spiegel*, 24. Juni.
1960 'Wie lange noch, Dr. Verwoerd?' In: *Sozialdemokratischer Pressedienst*, 9. April, pp. 4–5.
1961 'Verslag van die Projek vir Skakeling met Bantoe'. In: *Journal of Racial Affairs*, 12, 4, pp. 183–199.
1964 'Partners in Apartheid: U.S. Policy on South Africa'. In: *Africa Today*, 11, 3, pp. 2–17.
1966 'Apartheid Unassassinated'. In: *Economic and Political Weekly*, 1, 4, pp. 146–147.
Appel, Stephen W.
1989 '"Outstanding Individuals do not Arise from Ancestrally Poor Stock": Racial Science and the Education of Black South Africans'. In: *Journal of Negro Education*, 58, 4, pp. 544–557.
Aristoteles
1995 'Über die Seele'. In: *Philosophische Schriften*, Hamburg.
Ash, Mitchell G.
1998 *Gestalt Psychology in German Culture, 1890–1967. Holism and the Quest for Objectivity* (Cambridge Studies in the History of Psychology), Cambridge.
2002 'Psychologie'. In: Hausmann, Frank-Rutger (ed.): *Die Rolle der Geisteswissenschaften im Dritten Reich, 1933–1945* (Schriften des Historischen Kollegs. Kolloquien, Vol. 53), Munich, pp. 229–264.
2003 'Die erbpsychologische Abteilung am Kaiser-Wilhelm-Institut für Anthropologie, menschliche Erblehre und Eugenik (1935–1945) '. In: Sprung, Lothar; Schönpflug, Wolfgang (Hg.) (eds.): *Zur Geschichte der Psychologie in Berlin* (Beiträge zur Geschichte der Psychologie, Vol. 4), Frankfurt am Main, pp. 205–222.
2004 'Zeitpunkte. Geschichte eines Kongresses als Geschichte einer Disziplin'. In: *Psychologische Rundschau*, 55, 3, pp. 107–117.
2005 'The Uses and Usefulness of Psychology'. In: *Annals of the American Academy of Political and Social Science*, 600, pp. 99–114.
Auret, Abraham Josef
1965 Enkele Aspekte in die Ontwikkeling van Professionele Maatskaplike Werk in Suid-Afrika. MA Thesis, Pretoria.
Austin, Dennis
1966 'The Commonwealth Turned Upside Down'. In: *The World Today*, 22, 10, pp. 418–426.
Badenhorst, François Gerhardus
1939 Die Rassevragstuk, veral betreffende Suid-Afrika, in die lig van die gereformeerde etiek. Theol. Diss. Vrije Universiteit Amsterdam 1939, Amsterdam.
Bajohr, Frank
2015 'Der Nationalsozialismus als "Krankengeschichte der Moderne". Ein kritischer Blick zurück'. In: Hachtmann, Rüdiger; Reichardt, Sven (eds.): *Detlev Peukert und die NS-Forschung*, Göttingen, pp. 146–158.
Baker, Colin
1998 'Macmillan's 'Wind of Change' Tour, 1960'. In: *South African Historical Journal*, 38, pp. 171–182.

Bank, Andrew
2015a '"Broederbande" [brotherly bond]: Afrikaner Nationalist masculinity and African sexuality in the writings of Werner Eiselen's students, Stellenbosch University, 1930-1936'. In: *Anthropology Southern Africa*, 38, 3-4, pp. 180-197.
2015b 'Fathering volkekunde: race and culture in the ethnological writings of Werner Eiselen, Stellenbosch University, 1926-1936'. In: *Anthropology Southern Africa*, 38, 3-4, pp. 163-179.
2015c 'The Berlin Mission Society and German Linguistic Roots of Volkekunde: The Background, Training and Hamburg Writings of Werner Eiselen, 1899-1924'. In: *Kronos*, 41, 1, pp. 166-192.

Barber, James P.
1973 *South Africa's foreign policy, 1945-1970*, London.
1999 *South Africa in the twentieth century. From empire to rainbow nation*, Oxford.

Barkan, Elazar
1992 *The retreat of scientific racism. Changing concepts of race in Britain and the United States between the world wars*, Cambridge.

Barker, W. E.
1949 'Apartheid – The Only Solution'. In: *Journal of Racial Affairs*, 1, 1, pp. 24-38.
1953 'South Africa Can Do Without Native Labour'. In: *Journal of Racial Affairs*, 4, 4, pp. 24-35.
1956 'South Africa's 6-Point Claim to the Protectorates'. In: *Journal of Racial Affairs*, 8, 1, pp. 20-33.

Barnard, Fred
1967 *13 Jaar in die skadu van Dr. H.F. Verwoerd*, Johannesburg.

Barnard, S.L; **Marais**, A.H (eds.)
1982 *Die Verenigde Party. Die groot eksperiment*, Durban.

Barratt, John
1979 'South Africa in a Changing World'. In: Hellmann, Ellen; Lever, Henry (eds.): *Conflict and progress. Fifty years of race relations in South Africa*, Johannesburg, pp. 213-248.

Bartlett, F. C.
1929 *Experimental Method in Psychology*.

Baßmann, Winfried
1978 'Menschenrechtsverletzungen in Südafrika. Zur Systematik der Rassendiskriminierung unter dem Apartheid-Regime'. In: id. (ed.): *Menschenrechte in Südafrika. Perspektiven von Widerstand und Unterdrückung*, Munich, pp. 11-29.

Basson, J.L
1980 *J.G. Strijdom. Sy politieke loopbaan van 1929 tot 1948*, Pretoria.

Basson, Japie
2004 *Raam en rigting in die politiek en die storie van apartheid*, Kaapstad.
2006 *Politieke kaarte op die tafel*, Kaapstad.
2008 *Steeds op die parlementêre kolfblad. Met insigte oor die Afrikaner en Afrikaans*, Kaapstad.

Bateson, Gregory
2011 *Ökologie des Geistes. Anthropologische, psychologische, biologische und epistemologische Perspektiven*, Frankfurt am Main.

Beale, Mary
1992 'The Evolution of the Policy of University Apartheid'. In: Institute of Commonwealth Studies (ed.): *The Societies of Southern Africa in the 19th and 20th Centuries*, Vol. 18 (Collected Seminar Papers, Vol. 44), London, pp. 82-98.

Bebel, August
1910   *Aus meinem Leben*, Stuttgart.
Beckmann, Herbert
2001   'Selz in Amsterdam. Der Denkpsychologe Otto Selz (1881–1943) im niederländischen Exil'. In: *Psychologie und Geschichte*, 9, 3/4, pp. 3–32.
Beerstecher, Shan
1994   Witzieshoek. Women, Cattle and Rebellion. Master's Thesis, Cape Town.
Behrens, Peter J.
2001   Applied Psychology at Leipzig University in the Inter-War Period: The Work of Otto Klemm. Paper presented at the 20th annual conference of the European Society for the History of the Human Sciences, 14–18 August 2001, Amsterdam, Netherlands, Amsterdam.
Beinart, Peter
1996   'The Jews of South Africa'. In: *Transition*, 71, pp. 60–79.
Beinart, William
2001   *Twentieth-Century South Africa*, Oxford.
Bekker, Anton E.
1988   *Eben Dönges. Lewe en loopbaan tot 1948*, Stellenbosch.
2005   *Eben Dönges. Balansstaat: historiese perspektief*, Stellenbosch.
Bell, Morag
2000   'American Philanthropy, the Carnegie Corporation and Poverty in South Africa'. In: *Journal of Southern African Studies*, 26, 3, pp. 481–504.
Bell, Terry; **Ntsebeza**, Dumisa Buhle
2003   *Unfinished Business. South Africa, Apartheid and Truth*, London.
Benjamin, Eileen
2004   An Historical Analysis of Aspects of the Black Sash, 1955–2001. MA Thesis, Stellenbosch.
Benjamin, Walter
2015   *Zur Kritik der Gewalt und andere Aufsätze*, Frankfurt am Main.
Benson, Mary
1966   *The Struggle for a Birthright*, Harmondsworth.
Beresford, David
2010   *Truth is a strange fruit. A personal journey through the apartheid war*, Auckland Park.
Bernstein, Rusty
1999   *Memory against forgetting. Memoirs from a life in South African politics, 1938–1964*, New York.
Berridge, Geoff
1992   *South Africa, the colonial powers and "African defence". The rise and fall of the white entente, 1948–60*, New York.
Beuchelt, Eno
1974   *Ideengeschichte der Völkerpsychologie*, Meisenheim am Glan.
Bevan, Carin
2008   Putting Up Screens: A History of Television in South Africa, 1929–1976. MA Thesis, University of Pretoria, Pretoria.
Biesheuvel, Simon
1959   *Race, Culture and Personality*, Hoernlé Memorial Lecture, 15, Johannesburg.
Billig, Michael
1981   *Die rassistische Internationale. Zur Renaissance der Rassenlehre in der modernen Psychologie*, Frankfurt.

Bird, Allan
1992 *Bird on the Wing. Autobiography 1916-1992*, Simonstown.
Bittner, Christian; **Deutsch**, Werner
1990 'William Stern und die Experimentelle Psychologie'. In: *Psychologie und Geschichte*, 2, 2, pp. 59-63.
Blignaut, H.; **Burger**, A. J. V. (eds.)
1926 *Na vyftig jaar. Gedenkboek van die Unie-Debatsvereniging, Stellenbosch, 1876-1926*, Stellenbosch.
Bloom, Len
1965 'Education for Africans in South Africa'. In: *Equity and Excellence in Education*, 3, 4-5, pp. 89-94.
Bloomberg, Charles
1989 *Christian-nationalism and the rise of the Afrikaner Broderbond in South Africa*, Basingstoke.
Boehmke, B.
1928 'Some Implications of the Poor White Problem'. In: *South African Journal of Science*, 25, pp. 82-88.
Böhmke, Werner; **Tlali**, Tshepo
2008 'Bodies and behaviour: Science, psychology and politics in South Africa'. In: van Ommen, Clifford; Painter, Desmond (eds.): *Interiors. A history of psychology in South Africa*, Pretoria, pp. 125-151.
Bolton, Euri Belle
1934 'Review: The Poor White Problem in South Africa: Report of the Carnegie Commission. Part II: The Poor White by R. W. Wilcocks'. In: *The American Journal of Psychology*, 46, 4, pp. 678-679.
Bonner, P. L.; **Nieftagodien**, Noor
2008 *Alexandra. A History*, Johannesburg.
Booyens, Bun
1995 *Die Universiteit van Stellenbosch Biblioteekdiens 1895-1995*, Stellenbosch.
Booyens, Bun; **Oosthuysen**, J. J.
1971 *Dagbreek, 1921-1971. Uitgegee ter viering van Dagbreek se vyftigjarige bestaan*, Stellenbosch.
Boring, Edwin Garrigues
1929 *A History of Experimental Psychology*, New York – London.
Boshoff, Annatje
1974 *Sekretaresse vir die Verwoerds. Dankbare Herinneringe*, Cape Town – Pretoria.
1993 *Betsie Verwoerd, die vrou*, Pretoria.
Boshoff, Carel W.H.
1982 *Suid-Afrika se vraagstukke vereis 'n duidelike beleid en daadwerklike optrede*. Agste H.F. Verwoerd-Gedenklesing. gehou Pretoria 8. September 1982, Pretoria.
1996 *'n Gelate Verwoerd? En 'n vraag wat die denke van Afrikaners se vryheidstrewe onderlê*. Een-entwintigste H.F. Verwoerd-gedenklesing, Orania, 13. 9. 1996, Orania.
2012 *Dis nou ek*, Pretoria.
Botha, D. F.
1951 'Waarom is die Stadsnaturel meer onbestendig as die Stamnaturel?' In: *Journal of Racial Affairs*, 3, 1, pp. 17-24.
Botha, D.P
1960 *Die opkoms van ons derde stand*, Cape Town.
Botha, Jan
1967 *Verwoerd is dead*, Cape Town.

Botha, Marthina Elaine
1970   *Partikuliere volksorg in die Afrikaanse volkskultuur met verwysing na die ATKV (SAS en H), 1930-1964*, Potchefstroom.
Botha, M. C.
1977   *Die beleidsnalatenskap van dr. Verwoerd*. Derde H.F. Verwoerd-gedenklesing, University of Port Elizabeth, 8. 9. 1977, Pretoria.
1979   *Premiersverkiesings sedert 1910*, Johannesburg.
Botha, Pieter Willem
1948   *Aanvalle op dr. Malan oor sy kleurbeleid. Wanvoorstellings en die feite*, Cape Town.
Botha, S. P.
2001   'Leier en vriend'. In: Verwoerd, Wilhelm J.(ed.): *Verwoerd. Só onthou ons hom*, Pretoria, pp. 107-119.
Botha Commission
1967   *Report of the Commission of Enquiry into the Circumstances of the Death of the Late Dr. The Honourable Hendrik Frensch Verwoerd*, Pretoria.
Bottomley, Edward-John
2012   *Poor white*, Cape Town.
Boucher, Maurice
1973   *Spes in Arduis. 'n Geskiedenis van die Universiteit van Suid-Afrika*, Pretoria.
Boutros-Ghali, Boutros (Hg.)
1994   *The United Nations blue books series*, New York.
Branch, Daniel
2012   *Kenya. Between hope and despair, 1963-2012*, New Haven, Conn.
Breckenridge, Keith Derek
2005   'Verwoerd's Bureau of Proof. Total Information in the Making of Apartheid'. In: *History Workshop Journal*, 59, pp. 83-108.
2014   *Biometric state. The global politics of identification and surveillance in South Africa, 1850 to the present*, New York.
Brits, J. P.
1987   *Tielman Roos. Political prophet or opportunist?*, Pretoria.
1994   *Op die vooraand van apartheid. Die rassevraagstuk en die blanke politiek in Suid-Afrika, 1939-1948*, Pretoria.
2000   'The voice of the 'people'? Memoranda presented in 1947 to the Sauer commission by 'knowledgeable' Afrikaners'. In: *Kleio*, 32, pp. 61-83.
2002   'Despatching Apartheid: American Diplomats in South Africa, 1948-1953'. In: *South African Historical Journal*, 46, pp. 175-202.
Brockett, Linda
1996   'The History of Planning South African New Towns: Political Influences and Social Principles Adopted'. In: *New Contree*, 40, pp. 160-179.
Broodryk, Jacobus Johannes
1991   *Stellenbosse Academici en die politieke problematiek in Suid-Afrika, 1934-1948*. MA Thesis, Stellenbosch.
Brookes, Edgar H.
1950   *We Come of Age*. Hoernlé Memorial Lecture 6, Johannesburg.

Bruch, Rüdiger vom
1995 'Von der Sozialethik zur Sozialtechnologie. Neuorientierungen in der deutschen Sozialwissenschaft um 1900'. In: Vom Bruch, Rüdiger; Graf, Friedrich Wilhelm (eds.): *Kultur und Kulturwissenschaften um 1900*, Stuttgart, pp. 260–276.

Bruwer, A. J.
1934 *Kapitalisme, party-politiek en armoede*, Bloemfontein.

Bruwer, J. P. van S.
1953 'Grondbeginsels i.v.m. Fisiese en Kulturele Verskille'. In: *Journal of Racial Affairs*, 4, 4, pp. 36–43.
1955 'Realistiese of Kwantitatiewe Bevolkingsbeleid?' In: *Journal of Racial Affairs*, 6, 1, pp. 17–23.
1956a 'Die Kontakpatroon in Afrika. B. Interne Staatkundige Ontwikkeling en Beleids-Benadering in Afrika'. In: *Journal of Racial Affairs*, 7, 3, pp. 91–106.
1956b 'Prof. Dr. G. B. A. Gerdener Ons Huldig Sy Leierskap en Sy Lewe'. In: *Journal of Racial Affairs*, 7, 2, pp. 47–52.
1957 'Die Geboorte van 'n Onafhanklike Staat in Afrika – Ghana'. In: *Journal of Racial Affairs*, 8, 2, pp. 52–67.
1958 'Theories Based on the Concept of Race'. In: *Journal of Racial Affairs*, 9, 3, pp. 123–128.
1962 'Ons Opvoedkundige Taak in die Nuwe Staatsvorm t.o.v. Interne Rasseverhoudings'. In: *Journal of Racial Affairs*, 13, 2, pp. 85–93.
1966 'Die Staatkundige Uitbouing van 'n Selfbesturende Bantoe-volkerebeeld in Suid-Afrika'. In: SABRA (ed.): *Triomf. Jaarboek van die Suid-Afrikaanse Buro vir Rasse-Aangeleenthede*, Nr. 1, Pretoria, pp. 60–74.
1967 'Education and Political Development'. In: Duminy, P. A. (ed.): *Trends and Challenges in the Education of the South African Bantu*, Pretoria – Fort Hare, pp. 67–74.

Bruwer, J. P. van S., **Olivier**, M. J.
1964 'Hedendaagse Integrasiepoginge. Is dit Vernuwing of . . . Veraad?' In: *Journal of Racial Affairs*, 15, 1, pp. 64–78.

Bühler, Karl
1999a 'Antwort auf die von W. Wundt erhobenen Einwände gegen die Methode der Selbstbeobachtung an experimentell erzeugten Erlebnissen'. In: Ziche, Paul (ed.): *Introspektion. Texte zur Selbstwahrnehmung des Ichs*, Wien, pp. 213–236.
1999b 'Tatsachen und Probleme zu einer Psychologie der Denkvorgänge. I. Über Gedanken'. In: Ziche, Paul (ed.): *Introspektion. Texte zur Selbstwahrnehmung des Ichs*, Wien, pp. 157–212.

Bühring, Gerald
1996 *William Stern oder Streben nach Einheit*. (Beiträge zur Geschichte der Psychologie, Vol. 13), Frankfurt am Main.

Bunting, Brian Percy
1986 *The rise of the South African Reich*, London.

Burger, Martin
1961 *Dr. Verwoerd of South Africa. Architect of Doom*. A Christian Action Pamphlet, London.

Burke, Alban
2006 'Mental Health Care During Apartheid in South Africa'. In: Gozaydin, Istar; Madeira, Jody Lyneé (eds.): *Evil, Law and the State. Issues in State Power and Violence*, Oxford, pp. 117–133.
2007 Mental Health Care During Apartheid in South Africa. An Illustration of how "Science" can be Abused. Seminar-Paper, University of Johannesburg, Sociology Seminar, 11 May.

Burschel, Peter; **Marx**, Christoph
2011 'Einleitung'. In: id. (eds.): *Reinheit*, Wien, pp. 7–14.
Buss, Onko
1934 *Die Ganzheitspsychologie Felix Kruegers. Methodische Grundgedanken und grundlegende Ergebnisse*, Munich.
C. E. C.; C. M. C.
1961 'South Africa's Withdrawal and What It May Mean'. In: *The World Today*, 17, 4, pp. 135–142.
Carnegie Commission
1932 *The Poor White Problem in South Africa. Report of the Carnegie Commission*. 5 Vols., Stellenbosch.
Carrington, C. E.
1960 'Mr. Macmillan in Africa'. In: *The World Today*, 16, 3, pp. 119–125.
Cassirer, Ernst
1980 *The Philosophy of Symbolic Forms*, vol. 1: Language, New Haven – London.
Chestnut, R. W.
1972 'Psychotechnik. Industrial Psychology in the Weimar Republic 1918–1924'. In: *Proceedings of the annual convention of the American Psychological Association*, 7, pp. 781–782.
Chickering, Roger
1995 'Das Leipziger 'Positivisten-Kränzchen' um die Jahrhundertwende'. In: Vom Bruch, Rüdiger; Graf, Friedrich Wilhelm (eds.): *Kultur und Kulturwissenschaften um 1900*, Stuttgart, pp. 227–245.
Chisholm, Linda
2017 *Between Worlds. German missionaries and the Transition from Mission to Bantu Education in South Africa*, Johannesburg.
Chorover, Stephan L.
1982 *Die Zurichtung des Menschen. Von der Verhaltenssteuerung durch das Wissen*, Frankfurt.
Christie, Pam; **Collins**, Colin
1982 'Bantu Education: apartheid ideology or labour reproduction?' In: *Comparative Education*, 18, 1, pp. 59–75.
1990 'Bantu Education: Apartheid Ideology and Labour Reproduction'. In: Kallaway, Peter (ed.): *Apartheid and Education. The Education of black South Africans*, Johannesburg, pp. 160–183.
Christopher, Anthony John
1994 *The Atlas of Apartheid*, London.
Cillié, P. J.
1965 *Dawie 1946–1964. 'n Bloemlesing uit die geskrifte van Die Burger se politieke kommentator saamgestel deur Louis Louw*, Cape Town.
1980 *Tydgenote*, Kaapstad.
Cilliers, S. P.
1966 Die Kleurlingbevolking van Wes-Kaapland, unpublished paper, University of Stellenbosch.
Clark, Nancy L.
1994 *Manufacturing apartheid. State corporations in South Africa*, New Haven.
Clark, Jennifer
1998 '"The Wind of Change" in Australia. Aborigines and the International Politics of Race, 1960–1972'. In: *The International History Review*, 20, 1, pp. 89–117.
Clingman, Stephen
2000 *Bram Fischer. Afrikaner revolutionary*, Amherst.
Cloete, Andries Christof
1981 Die Ned. Geref. Kerk en die Afrikaner-Broederbond. Master Thesis Theology, Stellenbosch.

Cloete, Lucie
2001 'Broer'. In: Verwoerd, Wilhelm J. (ed.): *Verwoerd. Só onthou ons hom*, Pretoria, pp. 31–38.
Clynick, Tim
1994 A boerevolk for a boerestand? Broedertwis and Two Manuscripts of Platteland Modernity, c. 1959 (Seminar Paper), Johannesburg.
2007 'White South Africa's Weak Sons. Poor Whites and the Hartebeespoort Dam'. In: Bonner, P. L.; Esterhuysen, A.; Jenkins, Trefor (eds.): *A Search for Origins. Science, History and South Africa's Cradle of Humankind*, Johannesburg, pp. 248–273.
Cobley, Alan G. (ed.)
2016 *From cattle-herding to editor's chair. The unfinished autobiography and writings of Richard Victor Selope Thema*, Cape Town.
Coertze, P. J.
o.J. Filosofiese grondslae van die Volkekunde. Voordrag gehou voor die Filosofiese Vereniging van die Universiteit Pretoria.
1952 'Die Rol van Opvoeding en Onderwys in die Sosiale Struktur van die Bantoe'. In: *Journal of Racial Affairs*, 3, 2, pp. 11–23.
1963 'Die bio-genetiese grondslae van kulturele differensiasie'. In: Cronjé, Geoffrey (ed.): *Die westerse kultuur in Suid-Afrika*, Pretoria, pp. 156–173.
1966a "n Prinsipiele en feitlike Inleiding tot die Studie van die Bevolkingsverhoudingsvraagstuk in Suid-Afrika'. In: *Journal of Racial Affairs*, 17, 2, pp. 4–12.
1966b "n Prinsipiele en feitlike Inleiding tot die Studie van die Bevolkingsverhoudingsvraagstuk in Suid-Afrika'. In: *Journal of Racial Affairs*, 17, 3, pp. 12–19.
1975 *Die ethniese posisie van die kleurlinge*, Pretoria.
1977 *Inleiding tot die algemene volkekunde*, Johannesburg.
1979 'Die Afrikanervolk en die Nie-Blanke – ethnies- en kultuurhistories beskou'. In: Nel, Petrus Gerhardus (ed.): *Die Kultuurontplooiing van die Afrikaner*, Pretoria, pp. 245–264.
1980 *Filosofiese en metodologiese grondslae van die volkekunde*, Johannesburg.
1983 *Die Afrikanervolk en die Kleurlinge*, Pretoria.
Coertze, P. J.; **Language**, F.; **van Eeden**, B.
1943 *Die Oplossing van die Naturellevraagstuk in Suid-Afrika. Wenke ooreenkomstig die Afrikanerstandpunt van Apartheid*, Stellenbosch.
Coertze, R. D.
1991 'Aanvang van Volkekunde aan Afrikaanstalige Universiteite in Suid-Afrika'. In: *South African Journal of Ethnology*, 14, 2, pp. 25–34.
1998 'Antropologie aan die Universiteit van Pretoria. Die grondleggers en hulle invloed tot 1972'. In: *South African Journal of Ethnology*, 21, 1, pp. 1–31.
Coertze, T. F.
1950 '"Facta non Verba"'. In: *Journal of Racial Affairs*, 1, 3, pp. 23–26.
Coetzee, C. A.
1960 *The Republic – A Reasoned View*, Johannesburg – Cape Town.
Coetzee, J. Albert
1931 *Nasie-Wording in Suid-Afrika. 'n Sielkundige sleutel tot die politieke probleem van Suid-Afrika*, Potchefstroom.
1942 'Politieke organisering van die Afrikanerdom'. In: *Koers*, 9, 6, pp. 220–222.
Coetzee, J. H.; **Booysens**, J. H.; **Van Rensburg**, N. S. J.
1980 *Inleiding tot die algemene Volkekunde*. 'n Studiegids (Kursus 1), Potchefstroom.

Coetzee, John M.
1991 'The Mind of Apartheid: Geoffrey Cronjé 1907 -'. In: *Social Dynamics*, 17, 1, pp. 1–35.
Coetzer, J. P. J.
2000 *Gister se dade vandag se oordeel*, Pretoria.
Coetzer, Pieter Willem
1994 *Die Nasionale Party, Deel 5: Van Oorlog tot Oorwinning, 1940-1948*, Bloemfontein.
Coetzer, P. W.; **Le Roux**, J. H.
1986 *Die Nasionale Party, Deel 4: Die "Gesuiwerde" Nasionale Party 1934-1940*, Bloemfontein.
Cole, Josette
2012 *Behind and beyond the Eiselen line*, Cape Town.
Cooper, Saths; **Nicholas**, Lionel J.; **Seedat**, Mohamed; **Statman**, James M.
1990 'Psychology and Apartheid. The Struggle for Psychology in South Africa'. In: Nicholas, Lionel J.; Cooper, Saths (eds.): *Psychology & Apartheid*, Johannesburg, pp. 1–21.
Cope, Jack
1982 *The adversary within. Dissident writers in Afrikaans*, Cape Town.
Corrigan, Edward C.
1974 'South Africa Enters the Electronic Age: The Decision to Introduce Television'. In: *Africa Today*, 21, 2, pp. 15–28.
Coser, Lewis A.
2015 *Gierige Institutionen. Soziologische Studien über totales Engagement*, Berlin.
Coulter, Charles W.
1920 *The Lithuanians of Cleveland*, Cleveland.
1930 'Shifting the Emphasis in Social Work'. In: *The Social and Industrial Review*, pp. 6–11.
1934 'The Present Challenge'. In: *Journal of Higher Education*, 5, 7, pp. 355–364.
1935 'Problems Arising from Industrialization of Native Life in Central Africa'. In: *American Journal of Sociology*, 40, 5, pp. 582–592.
1938 'The Family as a Unit in Industrial Society'. In: *Annals of the American Academy of Political and Social Science*, 196, pp. 20–24.
1943 'Review: A History of South Africa, Social & Economic by C. W. de Kiewiet; The Native Labor Problem of South Africa by J. M. Tinley'. In: *Geographical Review*, 33, 2, pp. 336–338.
1945 'With the Technicians'. In: *Journal of Higher Education*, 16, 8, pp. 436–441.
1953 'Review: Racial Separation in South Africa: An Analysis of Apartheid Theory by Eugene P. Dvorin'. In: *Annals of the American Academy of Political and Social Science*, 285, p. 219.
1954 'Review: Report of the Ad Hoc Committee on Forced Labour by International Labour Office. United Nations'. In: *Annals of the American Academy of Political and Social Science*, 292, pp. 179–180.
1958 'Review: The Native Reserves of Natal by Edgar H. Brookes'. In: *Annals of the American Academy of Political and Social Science*, 319, pp. 175–176.
Coulter, Charles W.; **Korpi**, Orvo E.
1954 'Rehabilitation Programs in American Prisons and Correctional Institutions'. In: *The Journal of Criminal Law, Criminology, and Police Science*, 44, 5, pp. 611–615.
Cowan, L. Gray
1961 'The Current Political Status and Significance of Africa South of the Sahara'. In: *The Journal of Negro Education*, 30, 3, pp. 180–192.
Crick, Bernard
1966 *Eine Lanze für die Politik*, Munich.

Cronjé, Geoffrey
1937 *Die deterministiese standpunt in die Sosiologie*. Rede by die aanvaarding van die Professoraat in die Sosiologie aan die Universiteit van Pretoria uitgespreek op 8 September 1937, Pretoria.
1939 *Instituut vir Volkswelstand*, Pretoria.
1945 *'n Tuiste vir die Nageslag. Die Blywende Oplossing van Suid-Afrika se Rassevraagstukke*, Johannesburg.
1946a *Afrika Sonder die Asiaat. Die Blywende Oplossing van Suid-Afrika se Asiatevraagstuk*, Johannesburg.
1964b "'n Prinsipiele uiteensetting van die vennootskap van die Staat en die partikuliere welsynsorganisasies op die gebied van die maatskaplike sorg'. In: *Tydskrif vir Geesteswetenskappe*, 4, 1, pp. 20–30.
1964c 'Opvoeding vir en deur die Arbeid'. In: *Tydskrif vir Geesteswetenskappe*, 4, 4, pp. 350–360.
1968 'Persoonlikheidsteorie: 'n Kritiese Beskouing van Enkele Sieninge van die Persoonlikheid'. In: *Tydskrif vir Geesteswetenskappe*, 8, 1, pp. 27–39.
1970 *Die wysgerige antropologie en die menswetenskappe*, Pretoria.
Danziger, Kurt
1979 'The Social Origins of Modern Psychology'. In: Buss, Allan R. (ed.): *Psychology in social context*, New York, pp. 27–45.
1980 'Wundt and the Two Traditions in Psychology'. In: Rieber, Robert W. (ed.): *Wilhelm Wundt and the making of a scientific psychology*, New York, pp. 73–87.
1983 'Origins and basic principles of Wundt's Völkerpsychologie'. In: *British Journal of Social Psychology*, 22, pp. 303–313.
1993 'The social context of research practice and the priority of history'. In: *Psychologie und Geschichte*, 4, 3/4, pp. 178–186.
Davenport, Jade
2013 *Digging deep. A history of mining in South Africa, 1852–2002*, Johannesburg.
Davenport, T. R. H; **Saunders**, Christopher C.
2000 *South Africa. A modern history*, Hampshire.
Davie, T. B.
1955 *Education and Race Relations in South Africa*. Hoernlé Memorial Lecture 11, Johannesburg.
Davie, Grace
2015 *Poverty Knowledge in South Africa. A social history of human science, 1855–2005*, New York.
De Bruyn, G. F. C.
1989 *Professore: Universiteit van Stellenbosch en voorgangers*, Stellenbosch.
Degenaar, Johan J.
1978a *The roots of nationalism* (Societas 15), Pretoria – Cape Town – Johannesburg.
1978b 'The Concept of a Volksuniversiteit'. In: Van der Merwe, Hendrik W; Welsh, David (eds.): *The Future of the University in Southern Africa*, New York, pp. 148–171.
1980 *Voortbestaan in geregtigheid. Opstelle oor die politieke rol van die Afrikaner*, Kaapstad.
De Jongh, M.
1987 'Bruwer, Johannes Petrus van Schalkwyk'. In: Beyers, C. J. (ed.): *Suid-Afrikaanse Biografiese Woordeboek, Deel V*, Pretoria, pp. 106–107.
De Kiewiet, Cornelis
1956 *The Anatomy of South African Misery*, London.
De Klerk, F. W.
1999 *The Last Trek. The New Beginning*, London.

De Klerk, N. C.
1963 'Bantoe-Arbeid en Beleid in West-Kaapland'. In: *Journal of Racial Affairs*, 14, 2, pp. 115–130.
De Kock, W. J.
1970 *Die Geschichte Südafrikas*, s.l.
Delius, Anthony
1970 'Internal Argument and External Policy in South Africa'. In: *African Affairs*, 69, 277, pp. 371–374.
Delius, Peter
1996 *A lion amongst the cattle. Reconstruction and resistance in the Northern Transvaal*, Portsmouth, NH.
Delius, Peter; **Schirmer**, Stefan
2000 'Soil Conservation in a Racially Ordered Society: South Africa 1930–1970'. In: *Journal of Southern African Studies*, 26, 4, pp. 719–742.
Department of Labour and Social Welfare
1937 Report of the Department of Labour and Social Welfare for the Year ended December, 1935. U.G. 4–1937, Pretoria.
Dessoir, Max
1911 *Abriß einer Geschichte der Psychologie*, Heidelberg.
De Villiers, David
2001 'Die Wereldhofsaak in Den Haag'. In: Verwoerd, Wilhelm J. (ed.): *Verwoerd. Só onthou ons hom*, Pretoria, pp. 137–147.
De Villiers, Dirk; **de Villiers**, Johanna
1977 *Paul Sauer*, Kaapstad.
De Villiers, Johan
2004 'Sosio-ekonomiese dimensies van Suid-Afrika in die dekade 1930–1940: Arm, maar darem, of ondernemend en presterend?' In: *Tydskrif vir Geesteswetenskappe*, 44, 2 & 3, pp. 167–179.
De Villiers, I. L.
2009 *Strooidak en toring. Van mense en my tyd*, Kaapstad.
De Villiers, Marq
1990 *White tribe dreaming. Apartheid's bitter roots as witnessed by eight generations of an Afrikaner family*, London.
De Villiers, René
1945 'Nationalism's High-Priest of Rand Propaganda'. In: *Forum*, 20 Jan, p. 5.
Diederichs, Nicolaas
1975 *Eerste H.F.Verwoerd-Gedenklesing deur die Staatspresident Dr. N. Diederichs*, Stellenbosch 18. 9. 1975, Pretoria.
Diefenbaker, John
1978 *The Years of Achievement 1956–1962. One Canada. Memoirs of the Right Honourable John G. Diefenbaker, Vol. 2*, Scarborough.
Dilley, Roy; **Kirsch**, Thomas G. (eds.)
2015 *Regimes of Ignorance. Anthropological Perspectives on the Production and Reproduction of Non-Knowledge*, New York.
Dönhoff, Marion Gräfin
1965 *Welt in Bewegung. Berichte aus vier Erdteilen*, Düsseldorf.
Doering-Manteuffel, Anselm von
2008 'Ordnung jenseits der politischen Systeme: Planung im 20. Jahrhundert. Ein Kommentar'. In: *Geschichte und Gesellschaft*, 34, 3, pp. 398–406.

2015 'Konturen von „Ordnung" in den Zeitschichten des 20. Jahrhunderts'. In: Etzemüller, Thomas (ed.): *Die Ordnung der Moderne. Social Engineering im 20. Jahrhundert*, Bielefeld, pp. 41–64.

D'Oliveira, J.
1977 *Vorster – die mens*, Johannesburg.

Dommisse, Ebbe
2005 *Anton Rupert. A biography*, Cape Town.

Dooyeweerd, Herman
1931 *De Crisis in de humanistische Staatsleer in het Licht eener Calvinistische Kosmologie en Kennistheorie*, Amsterdam.

Dorsch, F.
1963 *Geschichte und Probleme der angewandten Psychologie*, Bern – Stuttgart.

Douglas, Mary
2010 *Purity and danger. An analysis of concept of pollution and taboo*, London.

Dousemetzis, Harris
2018 Report to the Minister of Justice, Advocate Tshililo Michael Masutha, in the Matter of Dr. Verwoerd's Assassination, https://www.sahistory.org.za/sites/default/files/file%20uploads%20/report_to_the_minister_of_justice_2.pdf

Dreyer, Wim
2013 'Fifty Years of Isolation. The Nederduitsch Hervormde Kerk 1960–2010'. In: Plaatjies-Van Huffel, Mary-Anne; Vosloo, Robert (eds.): *Reformed churches in South Africa and the struggle for justice. Remembering 1960–1990*, Stellenbosch, pp. 133–142.

Du Pisani, J. A.
1988 *John Vorster en die verlig/verkrampstryd. 'n studie van die politieke verdeeldheid in Afrikanergeledere, 1966–1970*, Bloemfontein.

Du Plessis, I. D.
1957 'Die Kleurling in die Raamwerk van ons Rasseverhoudings'. In: *Journal of Racial Affairs*, 8, 3, pp. 93–112.

Du Plessis, Lodewikus Johannes
1941 'Eenheid in 'n Republiek die enigste grondslag. Die Einde van die liberale beleid'. In: *Stryd*, 1, 11, pp. 10–14.
1954 'Immigrasie in Suid-Afrika. Van 'n Afrikanerstandpunt beskou'. In: *Journal of Racial Affairs*, 5, 2, pp. 35–43.

Du Preez, Max
2004 *Pale native. Memoirs of a Renegade Afrikaner*, Cape Town.

Du Raan, Lizl
1998 *Die invloed van eksterne en interne faktore op die vorming van studentekultuur aan die Universiteit van Stellenbosch 1918 – 1930*. MA Thesis, Stellenbosch.

Du Toit, André
2005 'The Legacy of Daatjie Oosthuizen: Revisiting the Liberal Defence of Academic Freedom'. In: *African Sociological Review*, 9, 1, pp. 40–61.
2008 'Afrikaander circa 1600': Reflections and Suggestions Regarding the Origins and Fate of Afrikaner Nationalism'. In: *South African Historical Journal*, 60, 4, pp. 562–578.

Du Toit, Marijke
1992 '"Die Bewustheid van Armoed": The ACVV and the Construction of Afrikaner Identity, 1904–1928'. In: *Social Dynamics*, 18, 2, pp. 1–25.

Du Toit, Pieter
1945 *Kakamas. Terwille van die waarheid*, Cape Town.

Du Toit, P. S.
1966a 'Die Victoria-Kollege, 1887-1918'. In: Thom, H.B. et al (eds.): *Stellenbosch 1866-1966. Honderd Jaar Hoër Onderwys*, Cape Town, pp. 38-61.
1966b 'Die Universiteit van Stellenbosch word 'n Werklikheid'. In: Thom, H.B. et al (eds.): *Stellenbosch 1866-1966. Honderd Jaar Hoër Onderwys*, Cape Town, pp. 62-70.
1966c 'Die Fakulteit van Lettere en Wysbegeerte'. In: Thom, H.B. et al (eds.): *Stellenbosch 1866-1966. Honderd Jaar Hoër Onderwys*, Cape Town, pp. 71-97.
1966d 'Losiesvoorsiening en Studentevoorligting'. In: Thom, H.B. et al (eds.): *Stellenbosch 1866-1966. Honderd Jaar Hoër Onderwys*, Cape Town, pp. 202-216.

Du Toit, S. I.
1990 'Family violence: familicide'. In: McKendrick, Brian; Hoffman, Wilma (eds.): *People and violence in South Africa*, Cape Town, pp. 288-300.

Dubow, Saul
1985 '"Understanding the native mind": Anthropology, cultural adaptation, and the elaboration of a segregationist discourse in South Africa, c. 1920-36'. In: Hall, Martin (ed.): *Africa Seminar Collected Papers*, Vol. 4, Cape Town, pp. 53-81.
1991 'Mental Testing and the Understanding of Race in Twentieth-Century South Africa'. In: Meade, Teresa A.; Walker, Mark (eds.): *Science, medicine and cultural imperialism*, London, pp. 148-177.
1992 'Afrikaner Nationalism, Apartheid and the Conceptualisation of "Race"'. In: *Journal of African History*, 33, 2, pp. 209-237.
1994 'Ethnic Euphemisms and Racial Echoes'. In: *Journal of Southern African Studies*, 20, 3, pp. 355-370.
1995 *Scientific racism in modern South Africa*, Cambridge.
2001 'Scientism, Social Research and the Limits of 'South Africanism': The Case of Ernst Gideon Malherbe'. In: *South African Historical Journal*, 44, pp. 99-142.
2005 'Introduction: South Africa's 1940s'. In: Dubow, Saul; Jeeves, Alan (eds.): *South Africa's 1940s. Worlds of possibilities*, Cape Town, pp. 1-19.
2006 *A commonwealth of knowledge. Science, sensibility, and white South Africa, 1820-2000*, Oxford.
2011 'Macmillan, Verwoerd, and the 1960 "Wind of Change" Speech'. In: *Historical Journal*, 54, 4, pp. 1087-1114.
2014 *Apartheid*, Oxford.
2015 'Racial Irredentism, Ethnogenesis, and White Supremacy in High-Apartheid South Africa'. In: *Kronos*, 41, 1, pp. 236-264.

Dürckheim-Montmartin, Karlfried Graf von
1954 'Gemeinschaft'. In: Klemm, Otto (ed.): *Wege zur Ganzheitspsychologie*. Festschrift zum 60. Geburtstage Felix Kruegers, Munich, pp. 195-214.
1995 *Der Weg ist das Ziel*. Gespräch mit Karl Schnelting in der Reihe "Zeugen des Jahrhunderts" (Zeugen des Jahrhunderts, Vol. 180), Göttingen.

Duerden, J. E.
1921 'Social anthropology in South Africa: Problems of race and nationality'. In: *South African Journal of Science*, 18, pp. 1-31.
1925 'Genetics and eugenics in South Africa: Heredity and environment'. In: *South African Journal of Science*, 22, pp. 59-72.

Duffy, Joanne
2003 '*Kultuur* Reclaimed: Afrikaner Nationalist Politics and the Stellenbosch District (South Africa), 1934-1939'. In: *Journal of Historical Sociology*, 16, 4, pp. 487-516.

Dunston, J. T.
1923 'Retarded and defective children. Native mentality, mental testing'. In: *South African Journal of Science*, 20, pp. 148–156.
Dux, Günter
1990 *Die Logik der Weltbilder. Sinnstrukturen im Wandel der Geschichte*, Frankfurt am Main.
Dyason, Willie
2001 'Meer as 'n werkgewer'. In: Verwoerd, Wilhelm J. (ed.): *Verwoerd. Só onthou ons hom*, Pretoria, pp. 221–232.
Eckardt, Georg
1998 'Die Thematisierung des Sozialen in der frühen Psychotechnik in Deutschland'. In: *Psychologie und Geschichte*, 8, 1/2, pp. 18–33.
Eckel, Jan
2015 *Die Ambivalenz des Guten. Menschenrechte in der internationalen Politik seit den 1940ern*, Göttingen.
Edwards, Paul N.; **Hecht**, Gabrielle
2010 'History and the Technopolitics of Identity: The Case of Apartheid South Africa'. In: *Journal of Southern African Studies*, 36, 3, pp. 619–639.
Ehrenstein, Walter
1934 *Einführung in die Ganzheitspsychologie*, Leipzig.
Ehrhardt, Adolf
1954 'Typus'. In: Klemm, Otto (ed.): *Wege zur Ganzheitspsychologie. Festschrift zum 60. Geburtstage Felix Kruegers*, Munich, pp. 151–164.
Eidelberg, Phil
1997 'South African Apartheid: The Homeland-Township Nexus, 1948–1986'. In: *South African Historical Journal*, 36, pp. 88–112.
Eiselen, Werner W. M.
1929a *Die Naturellevraagstuk*, Cape Town.
1929b *Stamskole in Suid-afrika. 'n Ondersoek oor die funksie daarvan in die lewe van die Suid-afrikaanse stamme*, Pretoria.
1946 'In Memory of Carl Meinhof'. In: *African Studies*, 5, 77–79.
1950 'Is Separation Practicable?' in: *Journal of Racial Affairs*, 1, 2, pp. 9–18.
1953 'Ons Jeug en ons Rasse-aangeleenthede'. In: *Journal of Racial Affairs*, 4, 3, pp. 18–26.
1955a 'Bantoekunde as Skoolvak'. In: *Journal of Racial Affairs*, 6, 1, pp. 24–33.
1955b 'The Coloured People and the Natives'. In: *Journal of Racial Affairs*, 6, 3, pp. 1–20.
1955c *Die Naturel in Wes-Kaapland*, Stellenbosch.
1957 'Duitse Sendingwerk in Suid-Afrika en die Bantoevolkseie'. In: *Journal of Racial Affairs*, 8, 3, pp. 113–120.
1959 *Harmonious Multi-Community Development. A Statement of South African Inter-Racial Policy*.
1961 'Die Ontvoogding van Afrikastate. Gedagtes na Aanleiding van Dr. W. Drascher se Boek "Schuld der Weissen?"'. In: *Journal of Racial Affairs*, 12, 2, pp. 103–108.
1965 'Die Aandeel van die Blanke ten Opsigte van die Praktiese Uitvoering van die Beleid van Afsonderlike Ontwikkeling-Kultureel-Maatskaplik'. In: *Journal of Racial Affairs*, 16, 1, pp. 6–24.
Eloff, Gerhard
1942 *Rasse en Rassevermenging. Die Boerevolk gesien van die standpunt van die rasseleer*, Bloemfontein – Cape Town – Port Elizabeth.

Eloff, J. F.
1959 'Tempo van Ekonomiese Ontwikkeling in die Bantoegebiede'. In: *Journal of Racial Affairs*, 10, 2, pp. 56–61.

Elsdon, Alan D.
2009 *The Tall Assassin. The Darkest Political Murders of the old South Africa*, Roggebaai.

Elstadt, Frederick
1988 Die Kerk-Staat Verhouding in Suid-Afrika in die twintigste Eeu tot en met die Einde van die Bewind van dr. H.F. Verwoerd – met besondere verwysing na die "Church of the Province of South Africa". B. Th. Thesis, Stellenbosch.

Engelbrecht, Lambert
2011 'Die ACVV as welsynspionier: Van welsyn vir armblankes tot eietydse uitdagings vir inklusiewe ontwikkelingsgerigte maatskaplike werk'. In: *Tydskrif vir Geesteswetenskappe*, 51, 4, pp. 1–16.

Engstrom, Eric J.
1997 'Kulturelle Dimensionen von Psychiatrie und Sozialpsychologie. Emil Kraepelin und Willy Hellpach'. In: Hübinger, Gangolf; Vom Bruch, Rüdiger; Graf, F. W. (eds.): *Kultur und Kulturwissenschaften um 1900*, Vol. 2: Idealismus und Positivismus, Stuttgart, pp. 164–189.

Erasmus, F. C.
1938 *Die Verskil – 'n paar van die punte. Die Nasionale Party en die Verenigde Party*, Cape Town.

Etzemüller, Thomas
2006 'Die Romantik des Reißbretts. Social Engineering und demokratische Volksmeinschaft in Schweden. Das Beispiel Iva und Gunnar Myrdal (1930–1960) '. In: *Geschichte und Gesellschaft*, 32, 4, pp. 445–466.
2015a *Auf der Suche nach dem nordischen Menschen. Die deutsche Rassenanthropologie in der modernen Welt*, Bielefeld.
2015b 'Social engineering als Verhaltenslehre des kühlen Kopfes. Eine einleitende Skizze'. In: id. (ed.): *Die Ordnung der Moderne. Social Engineering im 20. Jahrhundert*, Bielefeld, pp. 11–39.

Evans, Harold
1981 *Downing Street diary. The Macmillan years, 1957–1963*, London – Sydney – Auckland – Toronto.

Evans, Ivan
1997 *Bureaucracy and race. Native administration in South Africa*, Berkeley.

Evans, Laura
2012 'South Africa's Bantustans and the Dynamics of 'Decolonisation': Reflections on Writing Histories of the Homelands'. In: *South African Historical Journal*, 64, 1, pp. 117–137.
2014 'Resettlement and the Making of the Ciskei Bantustan, South Africa, c. 1960–1976'. In: *Journal of Southern African Studies*, 40, 1, pp. 21–40.

Eybers, E.
n.d. *Die Grey-Hersiening van die Binet-Terman Intelligensietoetse geadapteer en voorlopig gestandardiseer vir die Suid-Afrikaanse kind*, Bloemfontein.

Fabian, Reinhard
2005 'Die Grazer Schule der Gestaltpsychologie'. In: Lück, Helmut E.; Miller, Rudolf (eds.): *Illustrierte Geschichte der Psychologie*, Weinheim, pp. 71–75.

Fabre-Luce, Alfred
1961 'The Bird-Catcher and the Cage'. In: *African Affairs*, 60, 240, pp. 424–434.

Fantham, Harold Benjamin
1918 'Evolution and mankind'. In: *South African Journal of Science*, 15, pp. 287–305.
1924 'Heredity in man: Its importance both biologically and educationally'. In: *South African Journal of Science*, 21, 498–527.

1925 'Some factors in eugenics, together with notes on some South African cases'. In: *South African Journal of Science*, 22, 400-424.
1926 'Some thoughts on the social aspects of eugenics, with notes on some further cases of human inheritance observed in South Africa'. In: *South African Journal of Science*, 23, pp. 624-643.
1927 'Some Thoughts on Biology and the Race'. In: *South African Journal of Science*, 24, pp. 1-20.

Feinstein, Charles H.
2005 *An Economic History of South Africa*, Cambridge.

Fick, M. Laurence
1939 *The Educability of the South African Native*, Pretoria.

Fischer, Hans
1990 *Völkerkunde im Nationalsozialismus. Aspekte der Anpassung, Affinität und Behauptung einer wissenschaftlichen Disziplin*, Berlin.

Fitzek, Herbert
1996 'Gestalttheorie 'in nuce'. Inwiefern führt die Geschichte zum Kern gestaltpsychologischen Denkens?' In: *Psychologie und Geschichte*, 7, 3, pp. 183-199.

Flather, Horace
1977 *The way of an editor*, Cape Town – Johannesburg – London.

Fleisch, Brahm David
1995 'Social Scientists as Policy Makers. E. G. Malherbe and the National Bureau for Educational and Social Research, 1929-1943'. In: *Journal of Southern African Studies*, 21, 3, pp. 349-372.

Flight, Colin
1988 'The Bantu Expansion and the SOAS Network'. In: *History in Africa*, 15, pp. 261-301.

Floyd, T. B.
1975 *Afrikaner-nasionalisme*, Pretoria.

Foerster, Heinz von
1993 'Über das Konstruieren von Wirklichkeiten'. In: *Wissen und Gewissen. Versuch einer Brücke*, Frankfurt am Main, pp. 25-49.

Foster, Donald H.
1987 *Detention and Torture in South Africa. Psychological, Legal & Historical Studies*, Cape Town.
1991a *On racism. Virulent mythologies and fragile threads*, Inaugural lecture, University of Cape Town 161, Cape Town.
1991b 'Race and Racism in South African Psychology'. In: *South African Journal of Psychology*, 21, 4, pp. 203-210.
2008 'Critical psychology: A historical overview'. In: van Ommen, Clifford; Painter, Desmond (eds.): *Interiors. A history of psychology in South Africa*, Pretoria, pp. 92-122.

Foucault, Michel
1985 *Die Geburt der Klinik. Eine Archäologie des ärztlichen Blicks*, Frankfurt.

Fourie, J.J; **Stals**, E.L.P
1978 *Afrikaners in die Goudstad*, Pretoria.

Franke, Erich
1915 *Die geistige Entwicklung der Negerkinder. Ein Beitrag zur Frage nach den Hemmungen der Kulturentwicklung*, Leipzig.

Frankel, Glenn
2000 *Rivonia's children. Three families and the price of freedom in South Africa*, London.

Frankel, Philip
2001 *An Ordinary Atrocity. Sharpeville and its Massacre*, New Haven.

Frankel, S. Herbert
1952 *Some Reflections on Civilization in Africa* (Hoernlé Memorial Lecture 8), Johannesburg.
Franzsen, D. G.
1949 'Die Ontwikkeling van die Naturellereserwes as Deel van 'n Streekontwikkelingsprogram in die Unie'. In: *Journal of Racial Affairs*, 1, 1, pp. 16–23.
Freeman, Linda
1997 *The ambiguous champion. Canada and South Africa in the Trudeau and Mulroney years*, Toronto.
Frensch, P. A.; **Krause**, B.; **Wandke**, H.; **Zimmer**, K.; **Markner**, T.; **Franke**, R. (eds.)
2000 *100 Jahre Institut für Psychologie der Humboldt-Universität zu Berlin*, Berlin.
Friedman, Sharon Lynne
1982 Jews, Germans and Afrikaners. Nationalist Press Reaction to the Final Solution. BA Thesis, Cape Town.
Friedman, Steven
2015 *Race, class and power. Harold Wolpe and the radical critique of Apartheid*, Pietermaritzburg.
Frijda, Nico H. (ed.)
1983 *Otto Selz. His contribution to psychology*, Paris.
Froneman, J. D.
2000 'H.F. Verwoerd's student years – cradle of his political career and thought'. In: *Koers*, 65, 3, pp. 399–412.
2013 'Op soek na 'n gebalanseerde beeld van H. F. Verwoerd'. In: *Koers*, 78, 2, p. 10.
Furlong, Patrick J.
1983 *The mixed marriages act. An historical and theological study*, Rondebosch.
1991 *Between crown and swastika. The impact of the radical right on the Afrikaner nationalist movement in the fascist era*, Johannesburg.
2015 'Family ties? Afrikaner nationalism, pan-Netherlandic nationalism and neo-Calvinist "Christian nationalism".' In: *New Contree*, 74, pp. 1–24.
G. V. D.
1961 'South Africa Faces the Future'. In: *The World Today*, 17, 12, pp. 538–546.
Galliker, Mark; **Klein**, Margot; **Rykart**, Sibylle.
2007 *Meilensteine der Psychologie. Die Geschichte der Psychologie nach Personen, Werk und Wirkung*, Stuttgart.
Geldenhuys, Deon
1984 *The diplomacy of isolation. South African foreign policy making*, Johannesburg.
Gellner, Ernest
1998 *Nations and Nationalism*, Oxford.
Gerdener, G. B. A. (ed.)
1950 *Die Naturellevraagstuk*. Referate gelewer op die Kerklike Kongres van die Gefedereerde Ned. Geref. Kerke in Suid-Afrika, byeengeroep deur die Federale Sendingraad, Bloemfontein 4–6 April 1950, Bloemfontein.
1952 'Die Buiteland en die Naturellevraagstuk in Suid-Afrika'. In: *Journal of Racial Affairs*, 3, 2, pp. 4–10.
1964 *Ons taak in die nuwe Afrika*, Cape Town – Pretoria.
Gerhart, Gail M.; **Karis**, Thomas (eds.)
1991 *From Protest to Challenge. A Documentary History of African Politics in South Africa 1882-1964, Vol. 3*, Stanford, Calif.

Gesell, Arnold
1926 'A Comparative Method for Demonstration of Normal Development in Infancy'. In: *Journal of the American Medical Association*, 86, pp. 1277–1281.
Geulen, Christian
2007 *Geschichte des Rassismus*, Munich.
Geuter, Ulfried
1980 'Die Zerstörung wissenschaftlicher Vernunft. Felix Krueger und die Leipziger Schule der Ganzheitspsychologen'. In: *Psychologie Heute*, 7, pp. 35–43.
1985 'Das Ganze und die Gemeinschaft. Wissenschaftliches und politisches Denken in der Ganzheitspsychologie Felix Kruegers'. In: Graumann, Carl F. (ed.): *Psychologie im Nationalsozialismus*, Berlin, pp. 55–87.
1988 *Die Professionalisierung der deutschen Psychologie im Nationalsozialismus*, Frankfurt.
Geuter, Ulfried; **Hagemeier**, Petra; **Ash**, Mitchell G.
1986 *Daten zur Geschichte der deutschen Psychologie. Vol. 1: Psychologische Institute, Fachgesellschaften, Fachzeitschriften und Serien, Biographien, Emigranten 1879–1945*, Göttingen.
Gevisser, Mark
2015 *Thabo Mbeki. The Dream Deferred*, Jeppestown.
Geyser, O. (ed.)
1972 *Dr. H.F. Verwoerd die Republikein. Hoofartikels uit Die Transvaler 1937–1948*, Cape Town, pp. 81.
1983 *Watershed for South Africa, London, 1961*, Durban.
Gibbs, Timothy
2014 *Mandela's Kinsmen. Nationalist Elites & Apartheid's First Bantustan*, Woodbridge.
Giliomee, Hermann
1975 'Die Ontwikkeling van Selfkonsepsies by die Afrikaner'. In: van der Merwe, H.W (ed.): *Identiteit en verandering*, Cape Town, pp. 17–53.
1980 'The National Party and the Afrikaner Broederbond'. In: Price, Robert M.; Rosberg, C. G. (eds.): *The Apartheid Regime*, pp. 14–44.
1986 *The history in our politics. Inaugural lecture, University of Cape Town*, Cape Town.
1994 '"Survival in Justice": An Afrikaner Debate over Apartheid'. In: *Comparative Studies in Society and History*, 36, 3, pp. 527–548.
2003a *The Afrikaners. Biography of a people*, Charlottesville.
2003b 'The Making of the Apartheid Plan, 1929–1948'. In: *Journal of Southern African Studies*, 29, 2, pp. 373–392.
2003c '"The Weaknesses of Some": The Dutch Reformed Church and White Supremacy'. In: *Scriptura*, 83, pp. 212–244.
2004 *Piet Cillié en moontlike invloede op Die Afrikaners*, Stellenbosch.
2008 'Die enigma van Hendrik Verwoerd. 'n akademikus in die politiek'. In: *New Contree*, 56, pp. 81–103.
2009 'A Note on Bantu Education, 1953 to 1970'. In: *South African Journal of Economics*, 77, 1, pp. 190–198.
2012a *The Last Afrikaner Leaders. A Supreme Test of Power*, Cape Town.
2012b 'Bantu Education: Destructive intervention or part reform?' in: *New Contree*, 65, pp. 67–86.
2012c *Die Enigma van Hendrik Verwoerd*. Cape Town.
Gillespie, Kelly
2011 'Containing the 'Wandering Native': Racial Jurisdiction and the Liberal Politics of Prison Reform in 1940s South Africa'. In: *Journal of Southern African Studies*, 37, 3, pp. 499–515.

Glaser, Clive
2015 'Soweto's Islands of Learning: Morris Isaacson and Orlando High Schools under Bantu Education, 1958–1975'. In: *Journal of Southern African Studies*, 41, 1, pp. 159–171.
Goodwin, Geoffrey L.
1965 'The Commonwealth and the United Nations'. In: *International Organization*, 19, 3, pp. 678–694.
Goosen, Danie
1996 'Apartheid en die geskenk. 'n Dekonstruktiewe lesing van Verwoerd'. In: *South African Journal of Philosophy*, 15, 3, pp. 112–125.
Gordon, Robert J.
1988 'Apartheid's Anthropologists: The Genealogy of Afrikaner anthropology'. In: *American Ethnologist*, 15, 3, pp. 535–553.
1989 'Customary Law and Internal Pacification in South Africa'. In: Hugo, Pierre (ed.): *South African Perspectives. Essays in honour of Nic Olivier*, Cape Town, pp. 290–315.
1990 'Early Social Anthropology in South Africa'. In: *African Studies*, 49, 1, pp. 15–48.
1991 'Serving the Volk with Volkekunde – On the Rise of South African Anthropology'. In: Jansen, Jonathan D. (ed.): *Knowledge and Power in South Africa. Critical Perspectives across the Disciplines*, Johannesburg, pp. 79–97.
2004 'Anthropology in the World Court: The 1966 South-West Africa Case'. In: *History of Anthropology Newsletter*, 31, 1, pp. 3–11.
2018 'How Good People Become Absurd: J. P. van S. Bruwer, the Making of Namibian Grand Apartheid and the Decline of Volkekunde'. In: *Journal of Southern African Studies*, 44, 1, pp. 97–113.
Gould, Stephen Jay
2016 *Der falsch vermessene Mensch*, Frankfurt am Main.
Graaff, De Villiers
1993 *Div looks back. The Memoirs of Sir De Villiers Graaff*, Cape Town.
Graeber, David
2012 *Frei von Herrschaft. Fragmente einer anarchistischen Anthropologie*, Wuppertal.
Graevenitz, Gerhart von
1999 '"Verdichtung". Das Kulturmodell der Zeitschrift für Völkerpsychologie und Sprachwissenschaft'. In: *Kea*, 12, 19–57.
Graumann, Carl F.
2006 'Die Verbindung. Wechselwirkung der Individuen im Gemeinschaftsleben'. In: Jüttemann, Gerd (ed.): *Wilhelm Wundts anderes Erbe. Ein Missverständnis löst sich auf*, Göttingen, pp. 52–68.
Grobbelaar, Pieter W.
1966 *Man van die Volk. Gedenkalbum H.F. Verwoerd*, Cape Town – Pretoria.
1967 *This was a Man. A Study of Hendrik Verwoerd*, Cape Town.
Grobler, J. C. H.
1988 *Politieke leier of meeloper? Die lewe van Piet Grobler, 1873–1942*, Melville, Suid-Afrika.
Groenewald, C. J.
1987 'The Methodology of Poverty Research in South Africa: The Case of the First Carnegie Investigation 1929–1932'. In: *Social Dynamics*, 13, 2, pp. 60–74.
Grossmann, Johannes
2014 *Die Internationale der Konservativen. Transnationale Elitenzirkel und private Außenpolitik in Westeuropa seit 1945*, Munich.

Grundlingh, Albert
1987 'Sosiale Geskiedenis en die Dilemma in Afrikanergeskiedskrywing'. In: *South African Historical Journal*, 19, pp. 31-49.
2003 '"Gone to the Dogs": The Cultural Politics of Gambling – The Rise and Fall of British Greyhound Racing on the Witwatersrand, 1932-1949'. In: *South African Historical Journal*, 48, 1, pp. 174-189.
2005 'The Politics of the Past and of Popular Pursuits in the Construction of Everyday Afrikaner Nationalism, 1938-1948'. In: Dubow, Saul; Jeeves, Alan (eds.): *South Africa's 1940s. Worlds of Possibilities*, Cape Town, pp. 192-211.
Grundlingh, A. M.; **Swart**, Sandra Scott
2009 *Radelose rebellie?*, Pretoria.
Gurney, Christabel
2000 '"A Great Cause". The Origins of the Anti-Apartheid Movement, June 1959-March 1960'. In: *Journal of Southern African Studies*, 26, 1, pp. 123-144.
Guski-Leinwand, Susanne
2007 Wissenschaftsforschung zur Genese der Psychologie in Deutschland vom ausgehenden 19. Jahrhundert bis Mitte des 20. Jahrhunderts. PhD thesis, Heidelberg.
Hagemann, Albrecht
1989 *Südafrika und das "Dritte Reich". Rassenpolitische Affinität und machtpolitische Rivalität*, Frankfurt.
Haigh, Scott
1951 *Strangers may be present*, London.
Hall, Granville Stanley
1905 *Adolescence. Its Psychology and its Relations to Physiology, Anthropology, Sociology, Sex, Crime, Religion and Education*. 2 Vols., New York.
Hall, Martin
1987 *The Changing Past. Farmers, Kings and Traders in Southern Africa, 200-1860*, Cape Town.
Hallpike, Christopher Robert
1990 *Die Grundlagen primitiven Denkens*, Munich.
Halpern, Jack
1965 *South Africa's Hostages. Basutoland, Bechuanaland and Swaziland*, Harmondsworth.
Hamann, David
2011 *Gunther Ipsen in Leipzig. Die persönlich-wissenschaftliche Biographie eines "Deutschen Soziologen" 1919-1933*, Berlin.
Hammer, Steffi
1994 *Denkpsychologie – Kritischer Realismus. Eine wissenschaftshistorische Studie zum Werk Oswald Külpes*, Frankfurt am Main.
1995 'Psychologie zwischen experimentellem und hermeneutischem Ansatz. Oswald Külpe und Ludwig Klages – ein Methodenvergleich'. In: *Psychologie und Geschichte*, 7, 1, pp. 30-43.
2005 'Felix Krueger'. In: Lück, Helmut E.; Miller, Rudolf (eds.): *Illustrierte Geschichte der Psychologie*, Weinheim, pp. 103-105.
Hammond-Tooke, W. D.
1975 *Command or consensus. The development of Transkeian local government*, Cape Town.
2001 *Imperfect Interpreters. South Africa's Anthropologists, 1920-1990*, Johannesburg.
Hanekom, Marina
1969 *Hendrik Frensch Verwoerd as politikus, 1958-1966. 'n bibliografie van sy toesprake soos gerapporteer in die Burger*, Stellenbosch.

Hannaford, Ivan
1996 *Race. The History of an Idea in the West*, Baltimore – London.
Hansen, Wilhelm
1960 *Die Entwicklung des kindlichen Weltbildes*, Munich.
Harrington, Anne
2002 *Die Suche nach Ganzheit. Die Geschichte biologisch-psychologischer Ganzheitslehren, vom Kaiserreich bis zur New-Age-Bewegung*, Reinbek bei Hamburg.
Hartmann, Dirk
1993 *Naturwissenschaftliche Theorien. Wissenschaftstheoretische Grundlagen am Beispiel der Psychologie*, Mannheim.
Hattingh, Corneels
1967 *Hy was groot en gelief. 'n Geredigeerde oorsig van roudienste wat oor die land gehou is na die aanslag op dr. H. F. Verwoerd se lewe*, Johannesburg.
Hawkes, Valma Rae
1968 South Africa's Withdrawal from the Commonwealth: A Response to Multi-Racialism? MA Thesis, Hobart.
Hayes, Frank
1980 'South Africa's Departure from the Commonwealth, 1960–1961'. In: *The International History Review*, 2, 3, pp. 453–484.
Hayman, Graham; **Tomaselli**, Ruth
1989 'Ideology and Technology in the Growth of South African Broadcasting, 1924–1971'. In: Tomaselli, Ruth;Tomaselli, Keyan G.; Muller, Johan (eds.): *Broadcasting in South Africa*, London, pp. 23–83.
Heale, Jay
1981 *They made this land*, Johannesburg.
Heard, Anthony Hazlitt
1991 *The Cape of Storms. A personal history of the crisis in South Africa*, Johannesburg.
Heaton Nicholls, George
1937 *Die Naturelle-Vraagstuk in Suid-Afrika*, Pretoria.
Heese, Hans F.
1989a 'Die Wet op die Verbod van Gemengde Huwelike van 1949 en die Nürenberger Gesetze van 1935'. In: *Kronos*, 15, pp. 58–97.
1989b 'Ras en Etnisiteit: Suid-Afrikaanse perspektiewe 1938 en 1988'. In: *Kronos*, 16, pp. 42–51.
Hefer, N. F.; **Basson**, G. C.
1966 *Hendrik Frensch Verwoerd. Fotobiografie, 1901–1966*, Johannesburg.
Hegel, Georg Wilhelm Friedrich
2010 *Science of Logic* (1812) (trans. George di Giovanni), Cambridge.
Hellpach, Willy
1954 *Einführung in die Völkerpsychologie*, Stuttgart.
Hendrich, Gustav
2011 'Vereniger en opheffer: Die Nederduitse Gereformeerde Kerk in Rhodesie (1890–2007)'. In: *New Contree*, 62, pp. 155–177.
Hendricks, Fred T.
1989 'Loose Planning and Rapid Resettlement: The Politics of Conservation and Control in Transkei, South Africa, 1950–1970'. In: *Journal of Southern African Studies*, 15, 2, pp. 306–325.

Henshaw, Peter
1994 'Britain and South Africa at the United Nations: 'South West Africa', 'Treatment of Indians' and 'Race Conflict', 1946–1961'. In: *South African Historical Journal*, 31, pp. 80–102.
Hepple, Alexander
1967 *Verwoerd*, Baltimore.
Herbst, J. F.
1930 'The Administration of Native Affairs in South Africa'. In: *Journal of the African Society*, 29, 117, pp. 478–489.
HNP=Herenigde Nasionale Party of Volksparty van Transvaal
1940 *Program van Beginsels en Konstitusie*, Johannesburg.
Herrmann, Theo
1996 *Otto Selz und die Würzburger Schule*, Forschungsbericht, Mannheim.
Hexham, Irving
1981 *The Irony of Apartheid. The Struggle for National Independence of Afrikaner Calvinism against British Imperialism*, New York.
Heymans, Christiaan Stephanus
1981 *Die politieke en ideologiese strominge en aktiwiteite in en om die Afrikaanse Studentebond (1948–1980)*. MA Thesis, Stellenbosch.
Higginson, John
2014 *Collective Violence and the Agrarian Origins of South African Apartheid, 1900–1948*, Cambridge.
Hinrichs, Peter
1981 *Um die Seele des Arbeiters. Arbeitspsychologie, Industrie- und Betriebssoziologie in Deutschland. 1871–1945*, Cologne.
Hirson, Baruch
1981 *Yours for the Union. Class and Community Struggles in South Africa*, Johannesburg.
Hitzeroth, H. W.
1966 'Rasse en Raseienskappe: 'n Ontleding van teenstrydige Antropologiese Standpunte'. In: *Journal of Racial Affairs*, 17, 2, pp. 12–30.
Hobsbawm, Eric
2011 *The Age of Extremes. The Short Twentieth Century, 1914–1991*, London.
Hochgeschwender, Michael
2015 'The Noblest Philosophy and Its Most Efficient Use: Zur Geschichte des social engineering in den USA, 1910–1965'. In: Etzemüller, Thomas (ed.): *Die Ordnung der Moderne. Social Engineering im 20. Jahrhundert*, Bielefeld, pp. 171–197.
Hoernlé, A. Winifred
1948 *Penal Reform and Race Relations*. Hoernlé Memorial Lecture, 4, Johannesburg.
Hoffmann, Hermann
1926 *Das Problem des Charakteraufbaus. Seine Gestaltung durch die erbbiologische Persönlichkeitsanalyse*, Berlin.
Hoffmann, Robert R.; **Deffenbacher**, Kenneth A.
1992 'A Brief History of Applied Cognitive Psychology'. In: *Applied Cognitive Psychology*, 6, pp. 1–48.
Hofmeyr, Isabel
1987 'Building a nation from words: Afrikaans language, literature and ethnic identity, 1902–1924'. In: Marks, Shula; Trapido, Stanley (eds.), *The Politics of Race, Class and Nationalism in Twentieth-Century South Africa*, London – New York, pp. 95–123.
Hofmeyr, Jan Hendrik
1945 *Christian Principles and Race Problems*, Johannesburg.

Hofstadter, Douglas; **Sander**, Emmanuel
2014   *Die Analogie. Das Herz des Denkens*, Stuttgart.
Holleman, J. F.
1989   'The Great Purge'. In: Hugo, Pierre (ed.): *South African Perspectives. Essays in Honour of Nic Olivier*, Cape Town, pp. 34-48.
Holloway, J. E.
1964   *Apartheid - A Challenge*, Johannesburg.
Holzer, Werner
1961   *Das nackte Antlitz Afrikas*, Frankfurt.
Honikman, Alfred H.
1998   *In the Shadow of Apartheid*, Johannesburg.
Horne, Alistair
1989   *Macmillan 1957-1986*. Volume II of the official biography, London.
Horrell, Muriel
1956   *A Survey of Race Relations in South Africa, 1955-1956*, Johannesburg.
1961   *A Survey of Race Relations in South Africa, 1959-1960*, Johannesburg.
1962   *A Survey of Race Relations in South Africa, 1961*, Johannesburg.
1963   *A Survey of Race Relations in South Africa, 1962*, Johannesburg.
1964   *A Survey of Race Relations in South Africa, 1963*, Johannesburg.
1965   *A Survey of Race Relations in South Africa, 1964*, Johannesburg.
1966   *A Survey of Race Relations in South Africa, 1965*, Johannesburg.
1973   *The African homelands of South Africa*, Johannesburg.
1978   *Laws affecting Race Relations in South Africa 1948-1976*, Johannesburg.
Houghton, D. Hobart
1969   *The South African Economy*, Cape Town.
Hudson, William; **Jacobs**, Gideon Francois; **Biesheuvel**, Simon
1966   *Anatomy of South Africa. A Scientific Study of Present Day Attitudes*, Cape Town - Johannesburg.
Huffman, Thomas N.
2005   *Mapungubwe. Ancient African civilisation on the Limpopo*, Johannesburg.
Hugo, Pierre
1989   'A Journey Away from Apartheid'. In: id. (ed.): *South African perspectives. Essays in honour of Nic Olivier*, Cape Town, pp. 15-33.
1998   'The Politics of "Untruth". Afrikaner Academics for Apartheid'. In: *Politikon*, 25, 1, pp. 33-55.
Hugo, T. J.
1941   *Die Afrikaanse Universiteit en Sy Taak in die Volkslewe*, Bloemfontein - Cape Town - Port Elizabeth.
Hume, David
1939   *A Treatise of Human Nature*. 2 Vols., London - New York.
Humphrey, George
1951   *Thinking. An Introduction to its Experimental Psychology*, London - New York.
Humphries, Richard
1989   'Administrative politics and the coloured labour preference policy'. In: James, Wilmot Godfrey; Simons, Mary (eds.): *The Angry Divide. Social and Economic History of the Western Cape*, Cape Town, pp. 169-179.
Hurley, Denis E.
1964   *Apartheid: A Crisis of the Christian Conscience*. Alfred and Winifred Hoernlé Memorial Lecture, Johannesburg.

Hurter, J. A.
1981   *Die Ryke Erfenis aan Geestesgoedere wat Dr. H.F. Verwoerd nagelaat het*. Sewende H.F. Verwoerd-Gedenklesing, Pretoria 8. Sept. 1981, Pretoria.

Hutchinson, George
1980   *The last Edwardian at No. 10. An impression of Harold Macmillan*, London.

Hutschnecker, Arnold A.
1975   *Psychopolitik. Eine Kritik des Willens zur Macht*, Munich.

Huttenback, Robert A.
1976   *Racism and Empire. White settlers and colored immigrants in the British self-governing colonies, 1830-1910*, Ithaca.

Hyam, Ronald
2006   *Britain's Declining Empire. The Road to Decolonisation 1918-1968*, Cambridge.

Hyam, Ronald; **Louis**, William Roger
2000   *The Conservative Government and the End of Empire 1957-1964*. British documents on the end of the empire. Series A, Vol. 4, London.

Hyslop, Jonathan
1989   'School Boards, School Committees and Educational Politics. Aspects of the Failure of Bantu Education as a hegemonic Strategy, 1955-1976'. In: Bonner, Philip (ed.): *Holding their ground. Class, locality and culture in 19. and 20. century South Africa*, Johannesburg, pp. 201-225.
1991   'Food, Authority and Politics: Student riots in South African Schools 1945-1976'. In: Clingman, Stephen R. (ed.): *Regions and Repertoires. Topics in South African Politics and Culture*, Braamfontein, pp. 84-115.
1999   *The Classroom Struggle. Policy and Resistance in South Africa 1940-1990*, Pietermaritzburg.
2001   '"A destruction coming in": Bantu education as response to social crisis'. In: Bonner, Philip; Delius, Peter; Posel, Deborah (eds.): *Apartheid's Genesis, 1935-1962*, Braamfontein, pp. 393-410.

Israel, Jonathan I.
2013   *Democratic Enlightenment. Philosophy, Revolution, and Human Rights 1750-1790*, New York.

Jaeger, Siegfried
1987   'Wolfgang Köhler 1887-1967 zum 100. Geburtstag am 21. Januar. Biographische Daten und Publikationen'. In: *Geschichte der Psychologie*, 4, 1, pp. 5-30.
1993   'Zur Widerständigkeit der Hochschullehrer zu Beginn der nationalsozialistischen Herrschaft'. In: *Psychologie und Geschichte*, 4, 3/4, pp. 219-228.

James, William
2007   *Pragmatism*, Indianapolis.

Johnson, Walton R.
1982   'Education: Keystone of Apartheid'. In: *Anthropology and Education Quarterly*, 13, 3, pp. 214-237.

Jones, Hester Carolina
1986   Tini Vorster. Van maatskaplike werkster tot premiersvrou, Master Thesis, Bloemfontein.

Jones, Stuart; **Muller**, André
1992   *The South African economy, 1910-1990*, Basingstoke.

Jonker, Abraham H.
1940   *Israel Die Sondebok*, o.O.
1941   *Nasionaal-sosialisme as godsdiens*. Tien Radio-redes, uitgesaai vanuit Kaapstad tussen 1 April en 3 Junie, 1941, Cape Town.
1943   *Die Nazi binne ons*. 'n Boodskap aan sy mede-Suid-Afrikaners onlangs uitgesaai in Afrikaans en Engels, Cape Town.

Jooste, C. J.
1965 'Community Development in the Lower Orange River Area with special reference to the Coloured Population'. In: *Journal of Racial Affairs*, 16, 3, pp. 112–124.

Joubert, Dian (ed.)
1972 *Toe Witmense nog arm was*. Uit die Carnegie-verslag 1932, Cape Town.
1973 *Oorlogsverklaring 1939. Drama in die Volksraad*, Cape Town.

Joubert, Jurie Jacobus
1990 Die Burger se rol in die Suid-Afrikaanse partypolitiek, 1934–1948. PhD thesis, Pretoria.

Jüttemann, Gerd
2006 'Wilhelm Wundt – der missverstandene Geisteswissenschaftler'. In: id. (ed.): *Wilhelm Wundts anderes Erbe. Ein Missverständnis löst sich auf*, Göttingen, pp. 13–29.

Kallaway, Peter
2015 'Volkskirche, Volekunde and Apartheid. Lutheran Missions, German Anthropology, and Humanities in African Education'. In: Lessing, Hanns; Dedering, Tilman; Kampmann, Jürgen; Smit, Dirkie (eds.): *Umstrittene Beziehungen/Contested Relations. Protestantismus zwischen dem südlichen Afrika und Deutschland von den 1930er Jahren bis in die Apartheidzeit/Protestantism between Southern Africa and Germany from the 1930s to the Apartheid Era*, Wiesbaden, pp. 155–176.

Kannemeyer, John Christoffel
2008 *Leroux. 'n lewe*, Pretoria.

Kapp, P. H.
2004 *Verantwoorde Verlede*, 'n Historiografiese Studie. Die verhaal van die studie van Geskiedenis aan die Universiteit Stellenbosch, 1866–2000, unpublished, Stellenbosch.
2005 'Geskiedenis en kultuur. Die verhaal van 'n besondere verhouding deur onderrig en navorsing aan die Universiteit Stellenbosch se Departement Geskiedenis (1866-1985) '. In: *Suid-Afrikaanse Tydskrif vir Kultuurgeskiedenis*, 19, 1, pp. 36–64.
2009 *Draer van 'n droom. Die geskiedenis van die Suid-Afrikaanse Akademie vir Wetenskap en Kuns, 1909-2009*, Hermanus.
2013 *Maties en Afrikaans. 'n besondere verhouding, 1911–2011*, Pretoria.

Kathrada, Ahmed
2012 *Memoirs*, Cape Town.

Keet, B. B.
1955 *Suid-Afrika – waarheen? 'n Bydrae tot die bespreking van ons Rasseprobleem*, Stellenbosch.
1957 *The Ethics of Apartheid*. The Thirteenth Hornlé Memorial Lecture, Johannesburg.

Kelly, Jill E.
2015 'Bantu Authorities and Betterment in Natal: The Ambiguous Responses of Chiefs and Regents, 1955–1970'. In: *Journal of Southern African Studies*, 41, 2, pp. 273–297.

Kenney, Henry
1980 *Architect of Apartheid. H.F. Verwoerd, An Appraisal*, Johannesburg.

Kentridge, Morris
1959 *I Recall: Memoirs*, Johannesburg.

Keppel-Jones, Arthur
1949 *Friends or Foes? A Point of View and a Programme for Racial Harmony in South Africa*, Pietermaritzburg.
1968 *South Africa. A Short History*, London.

Keyter, J. de W.
1960   'Die Geestesontwikkeling van die Bantoe, met Spesiale Verwysing na Onderwys'. In: *Journal of Racial Affairs*, 11, 4, pp. 194–215.

Kgware, W. M.
1978   'The Role of Black Universities in South Africa'. In: Van der Merwe, Hendrik W; Welsh, David (eds.): *The Future of the University in Southern Africa*, New York, pp. 225–236.

Kidd, Dudley
1906   *Savage Childhood. A Study of Kafir Children*, London.

Killen, Andreas
2007   'Weimar Psychotechnics between Americanism and Fascism'. In: *Osiris*, 22, 1, pp. 48–71.

Kinghorn, Johann
1997   'Modernization and Apartheid: The Afrikaner Churches'. In: Elphick, Richard; Davenport, Rodney (eds.): *Christianity in South Africa. A political, social & cultural history*, Oxford, pp. 135–154.

Kinghorn, Johann; **Borchardt**, C. F. A (eds.)
1986   *Die NG Kerk en apartheid*, Johannesburg.

Kistner, Ulrike
2014   'Heterotopographies of a Restless Heritage: The West and the Rest of Pretoria, South Africa'. In: *Social Scientist*, 42, 5/6, pp. 81–101.

Klee, Ernst
2003   *Das Personenlexikon zum Dritten Reich. Wer war was vor und nach 1945?*, Frankfurt am Main.

Klemm, Otto
1911   *Geschichte der Psychologie*, Leipzig – Berlin.
1922   'Zur Geschichte des Leipziger Psychologischen Instituts'. In: Hoffmann-Erfurt, Arthur (ed.): *Wilhelm Wundt. Eine Würdigung*, Erfurt, pp. 105–108.

Koch, Jeroen
2006   *Abraham Kuyper. Een biografie*, Amsterdam.

Koffka, Kurt
1921   *Die Grundlagen der psychischen Entwicklung. Eine Einführung in die Kinderpsychologie*, Osterwieck am Harz.

Köhler, Wolfgang
1917   *Intelligenzprüfungen an Anthropoiden*, Berlin.
1927   'Zum Problem der Regulation'. In: *Wilhelm Roux' Archiv für Entwicklungsmechanik der Organismen*, 122, pp. 315–332.

Kondlo, Kwandiwe Merriman
2010   *In the twilight of the revolution. The Pan Africanist Congress of Azania (South Africa) 1959–1994*, Basel.

Koornhof, P. G. J.
1957   'Aparte Universiteitsopleiding vir die Bantoe'. In: *Journal of Racial Affairs*, 8, 2, pp. 77–84.

Koorts, Lindie
2014   *D.F. Malan and the rise of Afrikaner nationalism*, Cape Town.

Korf, Lindie
2010   D.F. Malan: a political biography. PhD Thesis, Stellenbosch.

Koselleck, Reinhart
1985   'Zur historisch-politischen Semantik asymmetrischer Gegenbegriffe'. In: id. (ed.): *Vergangene Zukunft. Zur Semantik geschichtlicher Zeiten*, Frankfurt, pp. 211–259.

Kotzé, C. H.
1950 'Die Ontstaan en Ontwikkeling van die Naturelleproblem in die Vrystaatse Goudgebied'. In: *Journal of Racial Affairs*, 2, 1, pp. 20–24.

Kotzé, D. J.
1966 'Stellenbosch se Bydrae'. In: Thom, H.B. et al (eds.): *Stellenbosch 1866–1966. Honderd Jaar Hoër Onderwys*, Cape Town, pp. 437–529.
1969 'Historikus'. In: id. (ed.): *Professor H.B. Thom*, Stellenbosch, pp. 17–24.

Kracauer, Siegfried
2013 *Totalitäre Propaganda*, Berlin.

Kretschmer, Ernst
1922 *Körperbau und Charakter. Untersuchungen zum Konstitutionsproblem und zur Lehre von den Temperamenten*, Berlin.

Kros, Cynthia
2010 *The seeds of separate development. Origins of Bantu education*, Pretoria.

Krueger, Felix
1913a 'Magical Factors in the First Development of Human Labor'. In: *The American Journal of Psychology*, 24, 2, pp. 256–261.
1913b 'New Aims and Tendencies in Psychology'. In: *Philosophical Review*, 22, 3, pp. 251–264.
1915 *Über Entwicklungspsychologie. Ihre sachliche und geschichtliche Notwendigkeit*, Leipzig.
1922 'Wilhelm Wundt als deutscher Denker'. In: Hoffmann-Erfurt, Arthur (ed.): *Wilhelm Wundt. Eine Würdigung*, Erfurt, pp. 1–44.
1926a 'Zur Einführung: Über psychische Ganzheit'. In: id. (ed.): *Komplexqualitäten, Gestalten und Gefühle* (Neue Psychologische Studien, Vol. 1), Munich, pp. 5–121.
1926b *Zur Entwicklungspsychologie des Rechts*. Sonderdruck aus Bruno Gutmann, Das Recht der Dschagga, Arbeiten zur Entwicklungspsychologie, Heft 7, Munich.
1929a *Das Wesen der Gefühle. Entwurf einer systematischen Theorie*, Leipzig.
1929b 'Rückblick auf die 10. Tagung der Deutschen Philosophischen Gesellschaft'. In: id. (ed.): *Philosophie der Gemeinschaft*. 7. Vorträge, gehalten auf der Tagung der Deutschen Philosophischen Gesellschaft vom 1.-4. Oktober 1928 in Leipzig, Berlin, pp. 143–168.
1931 *Die Tiefendimension und die Gegensätzlichkeit des Gefühlslebens*, Munich.
1939 'Otto Klemm und das Psychologische Institut der Universität Leipzig'. In: *Zeitschrift für angewandte Psychologie und Charakterkunde*, 56.
1940 *Entwicklungspsychologie der Ganzheit*, Cluj.
1948 *Lehre von dem Ganzen. Seele, Gemeinschaft und das Göttliche* (Beiheft zur Schweizerischen Zeitschrift für Psychologie und ihre Anwendungen, Vol. 15), Bern.
1953a 'Das Problem der Ganzheit'. In: id. (ed.): *Zur Philosophie und Psychologie der Ganzheit. Schriften aus den Jahren 1918–1940*, Berlin – Göttingen – Heidelberg, pp. 151–176.
1953b 'Erlebnisganzheit und seelische Struktur'. In: id. (ed.): *Zur Philosophie und Psychologie der Ganzheit. Schriften aus den Jahren 1918–1940*, Berlin – Göttingen – Heidelberg, pp. 146–150.
1967 'Die Tiefendimension und die Gegensätzlichkeit des Gefühlslebens'. In: id. (ed.): *Über das Gefühl. Zwei Aufsätze*, Darmstadt, pp. 3–24.

Kruger, G. J.
1985 C. R. Swart: Sy rol as minister, 1948–1959. Master Thesis, Potchefstroom.

Kruger, Jannie J.
1961 *President C.R. Swart*, Cape Town – Bloemfontein – Johannesburg.

Kühl, Stefan
1997 *Die Internationale der Rassisten. Aufstieg und Niedergang der internationalen Bewegung für Eugenik und Rassenhygiene im 20. Jahrhundert*, Frankfurt.
Külpe, Oswald
1999 'Über die moderne Psychologie des Denkens'. In: Ziche, Paul (ed.): *Introspektion. Texte zur Selbstwahrnehmung des Ichs*, Wien, pp. 44–67.
Kuper, Adam
1987 *South Africa and the Anthropologist*, London.
Kuyper, Abraham
1880 *Souvereiniteit in eigen Kring*. Rede ter Inwyding van de Vrije Universiteit den 20sten Oktober 1880 gehouden in den Koor der Nieuwe Kerk te Amsterdam, Amsterdam.
1916 *Antirevolutionaire Staatkunde*. 2 Vols., Kampen.
2007 *Lectures on calvinism*, New York.
LaFantasie, Glenn W. (Hg.)
1992 *Foreign relations of the United States, 1958-1960, Africa Vol. 14*, Washington.
Lake, Marilyn; **Reynolds**, Henry
2008 *Drawing the Global Colour Line. White Men's Countries and the International Challenge of Racial Equality*, Cambridge.
Lambert, John
2017 '"Welcome Home": White English-speaking South Africans and the Royal Visit of 1947'. In: *South African Historical Journal*, 69, 1, pp. 101–120.
Lambley, Peter
1981 *The psychology of Apartheid*, Athens.
Lambrechts, Hendrina Christina
1957 Die eerste vyftig jaar. Die ontwikkeling van die werk van die Afrikaanse Christelike Vrouevereniging (A.C.V.V.). PhD. thesis, Stellenbosch.
Language, F. J.
1950 'Native Housing in Urban Areas'. In: *Journal of Racial Affairs*, 1, 2, pp. 27–38.
1961 *Intreerede*, gehou op 27 April 1961, Bloemfontein.
Lapping, Brian
1987 *Apartheid. Südafrika am Scheideweg. Geschichte und Politik der Rassentrennung*, Munich.
Lawrence, Jeremy
1978 *Harry Lawrence*, Cape Town.
Lawrie, G. G.
1964 'South Africa's World Position'. In: *Journal of Modern African Studies*, 2, 1, pp. 41–54.
Lazar, John
1987 Conformity and Conflict. Afrikaner Nationalist Politics in South Africa, 1948–1961. PhD Thesis, Oxford.
1988 'The Role of the South African Bureau of Racial Affairs (SABRA) in the Formulation of Apartheid Ideology, 1948–1961'. In: *Collected Seminar Papers, No.37, Societies of Southern Africa, Vol. 14*, London, pp. 96–109.
2001 'Verwoerd versus the 'Visionaries': The South African Bureau of Racial Affairs (Sabra) and Apartheid, 1948–1961'. In: Bonner, Philip; Delius, Peter; Posel, Deborah (eds.): *Apartheid's Genesis, 1935-1962*, Braamfontein, pp. 362–392.
Le Bon, Gustave
2002 *The Crowd. A Study of the Popular Mind* (1895, Engl. 1896). Mineola.

Le Grange, Isak
1944   *Uit Chaos – Na Orde. Die Wording van 'n Nasional-sosialis*, Cape Town.
Le Roux, N. J
1953   *W.A. Hofmeyr. Sy Werk en Waarde*, Cape Town.
Lehmann, Alfred
1914   *Die Hauptgesetze menschlichen Gefühlslebens*, Leipzig.
Leichtman, M.
1979   'Gestalt Theory and the Revolt against Positivism'. In: Buss, Allan R. (ed.): *Psychology in Social Context*, New York. pp. 47–75.
Leipoldt, C. Louis
1988   *Bushveld Doctor*, Johannesburg.
Lekgoathi, Sekibakiba Peter
2009   '"Colonial" Experts, Local Interlocutors, Informants and the Making of an Archive on the "Transvaal Ndebele", 1930–1989'. In: *Journal of African History*, 50, pp. 61–80.
Lelyveld, Joseph
1989   *Move your shadow. South Africa, Black and White*, London.
Lever, Henry
1978   *South African Society*, Johannesburg.
Lévy-Bruhl, Lucien
1923   *Primitive Mentality*, London – New York.
Lewin, Kurt
1922   'Eine experimentelle Methode zur Erzeugung von Affekten'. In: Bühler, Karl (ed.): *Bericht über den VII. Kongreß für experimentelle Psychologie in Marburg vom 20.-23. April 1921*, Jena, pp. 146–148.
Lewis, Gavin
1987   *Between the Wire and the Wall. A history of South African "coloured" Politics*, Cape Town.
Lewsen, Phyllis (Hg.)
1991   *Helen Suzman's Solo Years*, Johannesburg.
Lifton, Robert Jay
1970   *Die Unsterblichkeit des Revolutionärs. Mao Tse-tung und die chinesische Kulturrevolution*, Munich.
Lipmann, Otto
1912   'Gedächtnis und Auffassung'. In: Institut für angewandte Psychologie und psychologische Sammelforschung (ed.): *Vorschläge zur psychologischen Untersuchung primitiver Menschen* (Beihefte zur Zeitschrift für angewandte Psychologie und psychologische Sammelforschung, Vol. 5), Leipzig, pp. 55–64.
1912   'Suggestibilität'. In: Institut für angewandte Psychologie und psychologische Sammelforschung (ed.): *Vorschläge zur psychologischen Untersuchung primitiver Menschen* (Beihefte zur Zeitschrift für angewandte Psychologie und psychologische Sammelforschung, Vol. 5), Leipzig, pp. 65–68.
1926   *Grundriß der Arbeitswissenschaft und Ergebnisse der arbeitswissenschaftlichen Statistik*, Jena.
Lipton, Merle
1989   *Capitalism and Apartheid. South Africa, 1910–1986*, Cape Town.
2007   *Liberals, Marxists, and nationalists. Competing interpretations of South African history*, New York.
Livie-Noble, F. S.
1922   'An Introductory Outline of Some of the Practical Applications of Modern Psychology'. In: *South African Journal of Science*, 19, pp. 439–448.

Lodge, Tom
1983 'The Parents' School Boycott, 1955'. In: Bozzoli, Belinda (ed.): *Town and Countryside in the Transvaal. Capitalist Penetration and Popular Response*, Johannesburg, pp. 365-395.
1990 'The Parents' School Boycott: Eastern Cape and East Rand Townships, 1955'. In: Kallaway, Peter (ed.): *Apartheid and Education. The Education of Black South Africans*, Johannesburg, pp. 265-295.
Lombard, J. A.
1964 'Die Ekonomiese Beskouingswyse t.o.v. die Beleid van Afsonderlike Ontwikkeling en die Aandeel van die Blanke daarin'. In: *Journal of Racial Affairs*, 15, 4, pp. 167-185.
Long, Wahbie; **Foster**, Don
2013 'The Changing Face of "Relevance" in South African Psychology'. In: *Psychology in Society*, 45, pp. 3-16.
Longerich, Peter
2012 *Joseph Goebbels. Biographie*, Munich.
Loosch, Eberhard
2008 *Otto Klemm (1884-1939) und das psychologische Institut in Leipzig*, Berlin.
Loram, Charles T.
1917 *The Education of the South African Native*, London.
Louw, Johan
1986 *This Is Thy Work. A contextual history of applied psychology and labour in South Africa.* PhD Thesis, University of Amsterdam.
1997 'Social Context and Psychological Testing in South Africa, 1918-1939'. In: *Theory & Psychology*, 7, 2, pp. 235-256.
Louw, Johann; **Foster**, Don
1991 'Historical perspective: psychology and group relations in South Africa'. In: Foster, Don H.; Louw-Potgieter, Johan (eds.): *Social Psychology in South Africa*, Johannesburg, pp. 57-90.
Louw, N. P. van Wyk
1958 *Liberale Nasionalisme. Gedagtes oor die Nasionalisme, Liberalisme en Tradisie vir Suid-Afrikaners met 'n kulturelle nadrup*, Cape Town - Bloemfontein - Johannesburg.
1965 *Lojale verset. Kritiese gedagtes oor ons Afrikaanse kultuurstrewe en ons literêre beweging*, Cape Town.
Lück, Helmut E.
1990 'Ein Briefwechsel zwischen William Stern und Alexius Meinong'. In: *Psychologie und Geschichte*, 1, 4, pp. 38-54.
1991 '"Noch ein weiterer Jude ist natürlich ausgeschlossen". William Stern und das Psychologische Institut der Universität Hamburg'. In: Herzig, Arno (ed.): *Die Geschichte der Juden in Hamburg, 1590-1990*, Hamburg, pp. 407-417.
2001 *Kurt Lewin. Eine Einführung in sein Werk*, Weinheim.
Lück, Helmut E.; **Bringmann**, Wolfgang G.
2005 'Hugo Münsterberg'. In: Lück, Helmut E.; Miller, Rudolf (eds.): *Illustrierte Geschichte der Psychologie*, Weinheim, pp. 178-180.
Lückhoff, A.H
1978 *Cottesloe*, Cape Town.
Luks, Timo
2015 'Die "psychognostische Schwierigkeit der Beobachtung". Industriebetriebliches Ordnungsdenken und social engineering in Deutschland und Großbritannien in der ersten

Hälfte des zwanzigsten Jahrhunderts'. In: Etzemüller, Thomas (ed.): *Die Ordnung der Moderne. Social Engineering im 20. Jahrhundert*, Bielefeld, pp. 87–107.

Luthuli, Albert
1965   *Let My People Go. An Autobiography*, London – Glasgow.

MacCrone, I. D.
1947   *Group Conflicts and Race Prejudice*. Hoernlé Memorial Lecture 3, Johannesburg.

Mack, Wolfgang
2005   'Die Würzburger Schule'. In: Lück, Helmut E.; Miller, Rudolf (eds.): *Illustrierte Geschichte der Psychologie*, Weinheim, pp. 50–53.

Mack, Wolfgang; **Kressley-Mba**, Regina A.; **Knopf**, Monika
2006   'Zum Begriff der Entwicklung in Wundts Psychologie'. In: Jüttemann, Gerd (ed.): *Wilhelm Wundts anderes Erbe. Ein Missverständnis löst sich auf*, Göttingen, pp. 69–80.

Macmillan, Harold
1972   *Pointing the way, 1959–1961*, London.

MacMillan, Hugh; **Marks**, Shula
1989   *Africa and Empire. W. M. Macmillan, Historian and Social Critic*, London.

Macmillan, William Miller
1919   *The South African Agrarian Problem and Its Historical Development*. Lectures, Johannesburg.
1930   *Complex South Africa. An Economic Footnote to History*, London.

Maisels, Isie
1999   *A life at law*, Johannesburg.

Makin, Michael
1996   'Britain, South Africa and the Commonwealth in 1960. The "Winds of Change" Re-assessed'. In: *Historia*, 41, 2, pp. 74–88.
1997   'South Africa's Departure from the Commonwealth in 1961. Postmortems and Consequences'. In: *Kleio*, 29, pp. 156–171.

Malan, Daniel François
1917   *De Achteruitgang van ons Volk. De oorzaken daarvan en de redmiddelen*, Cape Town.
1923   *Die Groot Vlug. 'n Nabetraging van die Arm-Blanke-Kongres, 1923, en van die Offisiele Sensusopgawe*, Cape Town.
1934   'Toespraak deur Dr. D. F. Malan, L.V'. In: Du Toit, Pieter (ed.): *Verslag van die volkskongres oor die Armblankevraagstuk gehou te Kimberley 2 tot 5 Oktober 1934*, Cape Town, pp. 122–125.
1959   *Afrikaner-Volkseenheid en my ervarings op die pad daarheen*, Cape Town.

Malan, M. P. A.
1957   *Apartheid. Is Beloftes uitgevoer?*, Bloemfontein.
1958   *Die Eerste Minister van S. A.* (Skietgoed; 3–1958/9), Bloemfontein.
1960   *Sal Suid-Afrika as republiek lid van die Statebond bly?*, Bloemfontein.
1964   *Die Nasionale Party van Suid-Afrika. Sy stryd en Prestasies 1914–1964*. Cape Town.

Malan, M. P. A.; **Mulder**, Cornelius Petrus
1966   *Hendrik Frensch Verwoerd, 1901–1966*, Bloemfontein.

Malherbe, Ernst Gideon (ed.)
1937   *Educational Adaptations in a Changing Society*. Report of the South African Education Conference held in Capetown and Johannesburg in July, 1934, under the auspices of the New Education Fellowship, Cape Town – Johannesburg.
1943   *The Bilingual School*, Johannesburg.

1946   *Race Attitudes and Education*, Hoernlé Memorial Lecture, 2, Johannesburg.
1973   'The Carnegie Poor White Investigation: Its Origin and Sequels'. In: *Social Work*, 9, pp. 81–90.
Mamdani, Mahmood
1996   *Citizen and Subject. Contemporary Africa and the Legacy of late Colonialism*, Princeton.
Mandela, Nelson
1995   *Long Walk to Freedom. The Autobiography of Nelson Mandela*, London.
Mannheim, Karl
2015   *Ideologie und Utopie*, Frankfurt am Main.
Mansergh, Nicholas (ed.)
1963   *Documents and speeches on Commonwealth affairs 1952 – 1962*, London.
1969   *The Commonwealth Experience*, London.
Maphalala, Jabu S. Hulumende
1996   'History and Mother-Tongue Eduation in South Africa'. In: *New Contree*, 40, pp. 102–118.
Marais, E. J.
1978   'The University and Culture – The Special Role of a Dual-medium University'. In: Van der Merwe, Hendrik W; Welsh, David (eds.): *The Future of the University in Southern Africa*, New York, pp. 196–204.
Marais, Jaap
1992   *Die era van Verwoerd*, Pretoria.
Marais, M. D.
1960   *Politieke onafhanklikheid en ekonomiese selfstandigheid*, s.l.
Marbe, Karl
1999   'Experimentell-psychologische Untersuchungen über das Urteil'. In: Ziche, Paul (ed.): *Introspektion. Texte zur Selbstwahrnehmung des Ichs*, Wien, pp. 78–97.
Marcum, John
1967   'Southern Africa and United States Policy: A Consideration of Alternatives'. In: *Africa Today*, 14, 5, pp. 5–13.
Marcuse, Herbert
1976   *Der eindimensionale Mensch. Studien zur Ideologie der fortgeschrittenen Industriegesellschaft*, Neuwied.
Maritz, Petrus Jacobus
2003   Ben Marais (1909–1999). The Influences on and Heritage of a South African Prophet during Two Periods of Transformation. PhD Thesis, Pretoria.
Marklund, Carl
2015   'Begriffsgeschichte and Übergriffsgeschichte in the History of Social Engineering'. In: Etzemüller, Thomas (ed.): *Die Ordnung der Moderne. Social Engineering im 20. Jahrhundert*, Bielefeld, pp. 199–221.
Marquard, Leo
1962   *The Peoples and Policies of South Africa*, Oxford.
Marx, Christoph
1988   "Völker ohne Schrift und Geschichte". Zur historischen Erfassung des vorkolonialen Schwarzafrika in der deutschen Forschung des 19. und frühen 20.Jahrhunderts, Stuttgart.
1994   'The Ossewabrandwag as a Mass Movement, 1939–1941'. In: *Journal of Southern African Studies*, 20, 2, pp. 195–219.
1998   *Im Zeichen des Ochsenwagens. Der radikale Afrikaaner-Nationalismus in Südafrika und die Geschichte der Ossewabrandwag*, Münster.

2000 'Folter und Rassismus. Südafrika während der Apartheid'. In: Burschel, Peter; Distelrath, Götz; Lembke, Sven (eds.): *Das Quälen des Körpers. Eine historische Anthropologie der Folter*, Cologne, pp. 257–279.
2004 'Von der Versöhnung zur Entsorgung? Die Wahrheitskommission und der Umgang mit der Vergangenheit im "neuen" Südafrika'. In: Zimmerer, Jürgen (ed.): *Verschweigen, Erinnern, Bewältigen. Vergangenheitspolitik nach 1945 in globaler Perspektive* (Comparativ, 14, 5/6), Leipzig, pp. 107–123.
2006 'Gedenken, Geschichte und Versöhnung in Südafrika und Zimbabwe'. In: *Afrika Spectrum*, 41, 2, pp. 155–174.
2007 'Die Wahrheit über die Apartheid? Geschichtswissenschaft und Wahrheitskommission in Südafrika'. In: id. (ed.): *Bilder nach dem Sturm. Wahrheitskommissionen und historische Identitätsstiftung zwischen Staat und Zivilgesellschaft* (Periplus Studien, Vol. 12), Berlin, 74–101.
2008 *Oxwagon Sentinel. Radical Afrikaner nationalism and the history of the Ossewabrandwag*, Pretoria.
2010 'From trusteeship to self-determination. L.J. du Plessis' thinking on apartheid and his conflict with H.F. Verwoerd'. In: *Historia*, 55, 2, pp. 50–75.
2011a 'Hendrik Verwoerd's Long March to Apartheid: Nationalism and Racism in South Africa'. In: Berg, Manfred; Wendt, Simon (eds.): *Racism in the modern world. Historical perspectives on cultural transfer and adaptation*, New York, pp. 281–302.
2011b 'Verwoerdian Apartheid and African Political Elites in South Africa, 1950–68'. In: Dülffer, Jost; Frey, Marc (eds.): *Elites and decolonization in the twentieth century*, Basingstoke, pp. 138–156.
2013 'Hendrik Verwoerd and the Leipzig School of Psychology in 1926'. In: *Historia*, 58, 2, pp. 91–118.
2014 'Südafrikas Austritt aus dem Commonwealth 1961'. In: Bachem-Rehm, Michaela; Hiepel, Claudia; Türk, Henning; Rausch, Dirk (eds.): *Teilungen überwinden. Europäische und Internationale Geschichte im 19. und 20. Jahrhundert. Festschrift für Wilfried Loth*, Munich, pp. 361–371.
2015a 'Wissen, Nichtwissen und Gewissheiten als Grundlage der Apartheid-Politik in Südafrika'. In: Häberlein, Mark; Paulus, Stefan; Weber, Gregor (eds.): *Geschichte(n) des Wissens. Festschrift für Wolfgang E. J. Weber zum 65. Geburtstag*, Augsburg, pp. 725–740.
2015b *Settler Colonies*. http://ieg-ego.eu/en/threads/europe-and-the-world/european-overseas-rule/christoph-marx-settler-colonies
2015c 'Bis zum bitteren Ende. Der Burenkrieg (1899–1902) als Gewalteskalation'. In: Becker, Frank (ed.): *Zivilisten und Soldaten. Entgrenzte Gewalt in der Geschichte*, Essen, pp. 103–123.
2018 '"Muldergate". Außenpolitische Propaganda und interne Machtkämpfe in Südafrika Ende der 1970er Jahre'. In: *Geschichte in Wissenschaft und Unterricht*, 69, 1/2, pp. 51–66.
2022 *Südafrika. Geschichte und Gegenwart*, 2nd edition, Stuttgart.

Mayer, A.; **Orth**, J.
1999 'Zur qualitativen Untersuchung der Association'. In: Ziche, Paul (ed.): *Introspektion. Texte zur Selbstwahrnehmung des Ichs*, Wien, pp. 68–77.

Maylam, Paul
1995 *A history of the African people of South Africa. From the early Iron Age to the 1970s*, London.

Mbeki, Govan
1984 *South Africa. The Peasants' Revolt*, London.
1992 *The struggle for liberation in South Africa. A short history*, Cape Town.

McCarthy, Thomas
2015 *Rassismus, Imperialismus und die Idee humaner Entwicklung*, Berlin.

McKay, Clare Elizabeth Anne
2015 A history of the National Union of South African Students (NUSAS), 1956–1970. PhD Thesis, Pretoria.
Meier, Wilma
1994 *Diedrich Westermann. Erforscher afrikanischer Sprachen und Kulturen*, Bremen.
Meiring, Piet
2013 'Remembering Cottesloe: Delegates to the Cottesloe Consultation tell their stories'. In: Plaatjies-Van Huffel, Mary-Anne; Vosloo, Robert (eds.): *Reformed churches in South Africa and the struggle for justice. Remembering 1960-1990*, Stellenbosch, pp. 39–51.
2015 'The Influence of the Ecumenical Movement on the Dutch Reformed Church Family (1948–1986).' In: Lessing, Hanns; Dedering, Tilman; Kampmann, Jürgen; Smit, Dirkie (eds.): *Umstrittene Beziehungen/Contested Relations. Protestantismus zwischen dem südlichen Afrika und Deutschland von den 1930er Jahren bis in die Apartheidzeit/Protestantism between Southern Africa and Germany from the 1930s to the Apartheid Era*, Wiesbaden, pp. 216–230.
Meiring, Piet G. J.
1973a *Inside information*, Cape Town.
1973b *Ons Eerste Ses Premiers. 'n Persoonlike terugblik*, Cape Town.
1973c *Tien politieke leiers. Manne na aan ons premiers*, s.l.
1979 *Vyftig jaar op die voorblad*, Johannesburg.
1985 *Die lewe van Hilgard Muller*, Pretoria.
1987 *Die Transvaler. 50 jaar*, Johannesburg.
1990 Was dit dr. Verwoerd se skuld? (Unisa manuskripte versameling).
Meischner, Wolfgang
2005 'Wilhelm Wundt'. In: Lück, Helmut E.; Miller, Rudolf (eds.): *Illustrierte Geschichte der Psychologie*, Weinheim, pp. 35–40.
Meischner, Wolfgang; **Eschler**, Erhard
1979 *Wilhelm Wundt*, Leipzig – Jena – Berlin.
Meischner-Metge, Anneros
2006a 'Die Methode der Forschung'. In: Jüttemann, Gerd (ed.): *Wilhelm Wundts anderes Erbe. Ein Missverständnis löst sich auf*, Göttingen, pp. 131–143.
2006b '"Völkerpsychologie" oder allgemeine "Entwicklungspsychologie"? Zur Wundt-Krueger-Deklarationsdiskussion'. In: Jüttemann, Gerd (ed.): *Wilhelm Wundts anderes Erbe. Ein Missverständnis löst sich auf*, Göttingen, pp. 81–87.
Meli, Francis
1989 *South Africa belongs to us. A history of the A.N.C.*, London.
Mendelsohn, Richard; **Shain**, Milton
2008 *The Jews in South Africa. An Illustrated History*, Johannesburg.
Menzies, Robert Gordon
1967 *Afternoon Light. Some Memories of Men and Events*, London.
Meredith, Martin
1998 *Nelson Mandela. A Biography*, Ringwood, Vic.
Merrett, Christopher
1995 *A Culture of Censorship. Secrecy and Intellectual Repression in South Africa*, Cape Town.
Metelerkamp, Petrovna; **Jonker**, Anna
2003 *Ingrid Jonker. Beeld van 'n digterslewe*, Vermont.

Métraux, Alexandre
2005 'Otto Selz'. In: Lück, Helmut E.; Miller, Rudolf (eds.): *Illustrierte Geschichte der Psychologie*, Weinheim, pp. 56–59.
Metzger, Wolfgang
1970 'Verlorenes Paradies. Im Psychologischen Institut in Berlin, 1922–1931'. In: *Schweizerische Zeitschrift für Psychologie*, 29, pp. 16–25.
1986 'Zur Geschichte der Gestalttheorie in Deutschland'. In: Metzger, Wolfgang; Stadler, Michael (eds.): *Gestalt-Psychologie. Ausgewählte Werke aus den Jahren 1950 bis 1982*, Frankfurt am Main, pp. 99–108.
Meyer, A.
1998 *The archaeological sites of Greefswald. Stratigraphy and chronology of the sites and a history of investigations*, Pretoria.
Meyer, Pieter Johannes
1959 *Trek Verder. Die Afrikaner in Afrika*, Cape Town – Pretoria.
1978 *Dr. H.F. Verwoerd: Afrikaner-volksman*. Vierde H.F. Verwoerd-Gedenklesing 4, Pretoria.
1984 *Nog nie ver genoeg nie. 'n persoonlike rekenskap van vyftig jaar georganiseerde Afrikanerskap*, Kaapstad.
Mildenberger, Florian
2002 'Körperbau, Charakter und Sexualität'. In: Gigi, 20. http://gigi-online.de/kretschmer20.html
Millar, David John
1988 The 1947 Consumer Boykott of Indian Retail Traders on the Transvaal Platteland. BA Honours Thesis.
Miller, Jamie
2016 *An African Volk. The Apartheid Regime and its Search for Survival*, New York.
Miller, J. D. B.
1961 'South Africa's Departure'. In: *Journal of Commonwealth Political Studies*, 1, 1, pp. 56–74.
1971 'Politicians, Officials, and Prophets'. In: *International Journal*, 26, 2, pp. 325–337.
Miller, Roberta Balstad
1993 'Science and Society in the Early Career of H.F. Verwoerd'. In: *Journal of Southern African Studies*, 19, 4, pp. 634–661.
Mills, Johan
2001 'Meesterbouer eerder as argitek'. In: Verwoerd, Wilhelm J. (ed.): *Verwoerd. Só onthou ons hom*, Pretoria, pp. 153–163.
Minnaar, Anthony
2013 'The Graaff-Reinet municipal location: Unemployment and poor relief during the Great Depression of 1929–1933'. In: *New Contree*, 66, pp. 27–53.
Mittner, M. J.
1986 Die Burger en die Kleurling-Stem 1948–1961. Master Thesis, Cape Town.
Mnaba, Victor Mxolisi
2006 The Role of the Church towards the Pondo Revolt in South Africa from 1960–1963. Master Thesis, Pretoria.
Moede, Walther
1920 *Experimentelle Massenpsychologie*, Leipzig.
1937 'Stand und Lage der angewandten Psychologie in Deutschland'. In: *The American Journal of Psychology*, 50, 1/4, pp. 307–327.

Mönnig, H. O.
1945   Natuurwetenskap en Tegniek in Diens van die Mens. Referaat gelewer op die Jaarvergadering van die S.A. Akademie, 29 Julie 1944.

Moodie, Graeme C.
1994   'The State and the Liberal Universities in South Africa: 1948-1990'. In: *Higher Education*, 27, 1, pp. 1-40.

Moodie, T. Dunbar
1975   *The Rise of Afrikanerdom. Power, Apartheid, and the Afrikaner Civil Religion*, Berkeley.
2017   'Separate Development as a Failed Project of Social Engineering: The Flawed Logic of Hendrik Verwoerd'. In: *South African Historical Journal*, 69, 2, pp. 153-161.

Mooney, Katie
1998   '"Ducktails, Flick-knives and Pugnacity": Subcultural and Hegemonie Masculinities in South Africa, 1948-1960'. In: *Journal of Southern African Studies*, 24, 4, pp. 753-774.

Morrell, Robert (ed.)
1992   *White but poor. Essays on the history of poor whites in Southern Africa 1880 - 1940*, Pretoria.

Moser, H.
1991   'Zur Entwicklung der akademischen Psychologie in Hamburg bis 1945. Eine Kontrast-Skizze als Würdigung des vergessenen Erbes von William Stern'. In: Krause, Eckart (ed.): *Hochschulalltag im "Dritten Reich". Die Hamburger Universität 1933 - 1945*, Vol. 3, Berlin, pp. 483-518.

Mostert, J.P.C
1985   'Die rol van swart verstedeliking in die algemene verkiesing van 1948'. In: *Joernaal vir eietydse geskiedenis*, 10, 3, pp. 25-57.

Moukambi, Victor
2008   *Relations between South Africa and France with Special Reference to Military Matters, 1960-1990*, Stellenbosch.

Mouton, Alex
2002   *Voorloper. Die lewe van Schalk Pienaar*, Kaapstad.
2007   'A. N. Pelzer: A Custodian of Afrikanerdom'. In: Mouton, F. A.; Southey, Nicholas; van Jaarsveld, Albert (eds.): *History, historians & Afrikaner nationalism. Essays on the History Department of the University of Pretoria, 1909-1985*, Vanderbijlpark, pp. 89-122.

Mulder, C.P; **Cruywagen**, W.A (eds.)
1964   *Die eerste skof van die Nasionale Party in Transvaal 1914-1964*, s.l.

Muller, C. F. J.
1990   *Sonop in die Suide. Geboorte en groei van die Nasionale Pers 1915-1948*, Kaapstad.

Muller, Johan
1989   'Press Houses at War: A Brief History of Nasionale Pers and Perskor'. In: Tomaselli, Keyan G.; Teer-Tomaselli, Ruth; Muller, John (eds.): *The Press in South Africa*, London, pp. 118-140.

Muller, Stephanus
2008   'Die Stem'. In: Grundlingh, A. M.; Huigen, Siegfried (eds.): *Van volksmoeder tot Fokofpolisiekar. Kritiese opstelle oor Afrikaanse herinneringsplekke*, Stellenbosch, pp. 197-205.

Muller, W.A.
1973   Dr. H.F. Verwoerd se joernalistieke bydrae tot die republikeinse idee. M.A. Thesis, Pretoria.

Munger, Edwin S.
1967   *Afrikaner and African Nationalism. South African Parallels and Parameters*, London.

Münsterberg, Hugo
1997   *Psychologie und Wirtschaftsleben*, Weinheim.

Murray, Bruce K.
1997 *Wits, The 'Open' Years. A History of the University of the Witwatersrand, Johannesburg, 1939–1959*, Johannesburg.

Mzimela, Sipo E.
1983 *Apartheid: South African Naziism*, New York.

Naiman, Joanne; **Bhabha**, Joan; **Wright**, Guy
1984 'Relations between Canada and South Africa, United Nations Centre against Apartheid'. In: *Notes and Documents*, 10, pp. 1–60.

Nash, Andrew
2009 *The Dialectical Tradition in South Africa*, New York.

Nasionale Party
n.d. *Konsep-Grondwet van die Republiek*, Johannesburg.
1935 *Nasionale Dagblad vir Transvaal*, Cape Town.
1943 *Opmars na die Republiek: Dr.Malan*, Cape Town.
1946 *'n Roekelose Regeringsplan. Onbeheerde Immigrasie bedreig Suid-Afrika*, Cape Town.
1948 *Nasionale Party se kleurbeleid. Handhawing van blanke ras as hoogste taak*, Cape Town.
1958 *Verkiesingsmanifes 1958*, Johannesburg.
1960 *Die Volkstemming 5 Oktober 1960*. Stukke uitgegee deur Die Inligtingsdiens van die Nasionale Party Bloemfontein, Bloemfontein.

Nasionale Party, Oranje Vrystaat
1930 *Beginsels, Konstitusie, Statute*, Bloemfontein.

Nasional Party, Kaapprovinsie
1937 *Die Nasionale Party en Joodse immigrasie*, Cape Town.

Nationale Partij in Transvaal
1914 *Beginsels, Konstitutie, Statuten*, Pretoria.

Nasionale Vroueparty
1927 *Nasionale Vroueparty, Kaapprovinsie – Vierde Kongres*, Gehou in die Stadsaal, Graaff-Reinet, 3–6. 12. 1926, Cape Town.

Naudé, Louis
1969 *Dr. Albert Hertzog, die Nasionale Party, en die Mynwerkers*, Pretoria.

Naudé, Stefan Meiring
1964 *Der Südafrikanische Forschungsrat für Wissenschaft und Industrie*, Cologne – Opladen.

Necker, Catharina Maria de
1998 *Die Rol van die owerheid in die voorsiening van georganiseerde maatskaplike welsynsdiens in Suid-Afrika, 1902–1995*, MA Thesis, Potchefstroom.

Nel, B. F.
1942 *Naturelle-Opvoeding en -Onderwys*. 2 Vols., Bloemfontein – Cape Town – Port Elizabeth.

Nel, M. D. C. de Wet
1956 'Die Bantoe se plek en rol in die huidige Sosiale, Ekonomiese en Politieke Struktuur van Suid-Afrika'. In: Thom, H.B. et al (eds.): *Volkskongres oor die toekoms van die Bantoe*. Bloemfontein 28–30 Junie 1956, Stellenbosch, pp. 1–12.

Ngcokovane, Cecil
1989 *Demons of Apartheid. A Moral and Ethical Analysis of the NGK, NP and Broederbond's Justification of Apartheid*, Braamfontein.

Nicol, Mike
1995   *The waiting country. A South African witness*, London.
Nixon, Rob
1993   'The Devil in the Black Box: Ethnic Nationalism, Cultural Imperialism and the Outlawing of TV under Apartheid'. In: Institute of Commonwealth Studies (ed.): *The Societies of Southern Africa in the 19th and 20th Centuries*, Vol. 19 (Collected Seminar Papers; Vol. 45), London, pp. 120–137.
Norval, Aletta J.
1996   *Deconstructing Apartheid Discourse*, New York.
Oberholzer, C. K.
1970   'Die wysgerige antropologie, die psigologie en die sosiologie'. In: Cronjé, Geoffrey (ed.): *Die wysgerige antropologie en die menswetenskappe*, Pretoria, pp. 64–80.
Oelze, Berthold
1991   *Wilhelm Wundt. Die Konzeption der Völkerpsychologie*, Münster.
Olivier, M. J.
1964   'Differensiërende Wetgewing'. In: Theron, Erika (ed.): *Die Kleurlingbevolking van Suid-Afrika*, Stellenbosch – Grahamstown, pp. 208–225.
Olivier, N. J. J.
1953   'Die Naturel in Wes-Kaapland. 'n Tentatiewe Uiteensetting'. In: *Journal of Racial Affairs*, 4, 2, pp. 1–12.
1954   'Apartheid – A Slogan or a Solution?' In: *Journal of Racial Affairs*, 5, 2, pp. 23–34.
1956a   'Die Taak van ons Afrikaanse Universiteite in verband met Rasse-Aangeleenthede'. In: *Journal of Racial Affairs*, 8, 1, pp. 33–40.
1956b   'Beleidsrigtings vir die Toekomstige Verhouding tussen Blank en Bantoe in Suid-Afrika'. In: Thom, H.B. et al (eds.): *Volkskongres oor die toekoms van die Bantoe*. Bloemfontein 28–30 Junie 1956, Stellenbosch, pp. 13–33.
1959a   'Ons Stedelike Naturellebevolking'. In: *Journal of Racial Affairs*, 10, 2, pp. 33–45.
1959b   'Ons Stedelike Naturellebevolking'. In: *Journal of Racial Affairs*, 10, 3, pp. 63–72.
1961   'The Path to African Political Maturity'. In: *Journal of Racial Affairs*, 12, 4, pp. 199–210.
1973   *Aspekte van die proses van konstitusionele ontwikkeling van die Bantoetuislande*. Rede gelewer by die jaarlikse vakskonferensie van Suid-Afrikaanse Universiteitsdosente vir Naturelle- en Bantoeontwikkelingsadministrasie en Toegepaste Volkekunde, Pretoria, 25 Mei 1973.
1984   'The Legal Status of Urban Blacks in South Africa'. In: *Koers*, 49, 3, pp. 356–384.
O'Meara, Dan
1977   'The Afrikaner Broederbond 1927–1948: Class Vanguard of Afrikaner Nationalism'. In: *Journal of Southern African Studies*, 2, pp. 156–186.
1983   *Volkskapitalisme. Class, capital, and ideology in the development of Afrikaner nationalism, 1934–1948*, Johannesburg.
1996   *Forty lost years. The apartheid state and the politics of the National Party, 1948 – 1994*, Randburg.
Oppenheimer, H. F.
1961   'South Africa's Role in a Changing Africa'. In: *African Affairs*, 60, 238, pp. 18–25.
Ovendale, Ritchie
1995   'Macmillan and the Wind of Change in Africa, 1957–1960'. In: *Historical Journal*, 38, 2, pp. 455–477.
Paine, Victor
1978   The Confrontation between the Archbishop of Cape Town, Joost de Blank, and the South African Government on Racial Policies (1957–1963). Master Thesis, Cape Town.

Pama, C.
1967   'Die afstamming van Dr. Hendrik Verwoerd'. In: *Familia. Quarterly Journal of the Genealogical Society of South Africa*, 4, 1, pp. 80–88.

Parkington, John; **Hall**, Simon
2010   'The Appearance of Food Production in Southern Africa 1,000 to 2,000 Years Ago'. In: Hamilton, Carolyn; Mbenga, Bernard K.; Ross, Robert (eds.): *The Cambridge History of South Africa, Volume 1. From Early Times to 1885*, Cambridge, pp. 63–111.

Parliament of the Union of South Africa
1960   *Souvenir of visit of The Rt. Hon. Harold Macmillan, Prime Minister of the United Kingdom to the Houses of Parliament, Cape Town, on Wednesday, 3rd February, 1960*, Cape Town.

Paton, Alan
1971   *Hofmeyr*. Abridged Edition, Cape Town.

Pauw, S.
1946   *Die beroepsarbeid van die Afrikaner in die stad*, Stellenbosch.

Peberdy, Sally
2009   *Selecting immigrants. National identity and South Africa's immigration policies, 1910 – 2008*, Johannesburg.

Pelzer, A. N.
1963   *Verwoerd aan die woord. Toesprake 1948–1962*, Johannesburg.
1963   'Die historiese grondslae van afsonderlike ontwikkeling'. In: Cronjé, Geoffrey (ed.): *Die westerse kultuur in Suid-Afrika*, Pretoria, pp. 133–155.
1966   *Verwoerd Speaks. Speeches 1948–1966*, Johannesburg.
1966b 'Geskiedenis en ons Kultuurlewe'. In: FAK (ed.): *Referate gelewer by geleentheid van die F.A.K.-Kongres op 30 September en 1 Oktober 1964 in Bloemfontein*, Johannesburg, pp. 39–52.
1979   *Die Afrikaner-Broederbond. Eerste 50 jaar*, Cape Town.
1980   *Hendrik Frensch Verwoerd*. Sesde H.F. Verwoerd-Gedenklesing, Pretoria.

Penny, H. Glenn
2002   'The Civic Uses of Science: Ethnology and Civil Society in Imperial Germany'. In: *Osiris*, 17, 228–252.

Peukert, Detlev J.K
1989   'Die Genesis der "Endlösung" aus dem Geist der Wissenschaft'. In: id. (ed.): *Max Webers Diagnose der Moderne*, Göttingen, pp. 102–121.

Pfaffe, Joachim Friedrich
1987   'Die Geschichte der an Hochschulen institutionalisierten Psychologie in Südafrika'. In: *Geschichte der Psychologie*, 4, 2, pp. 66–77.

Pfister, Roger
2005   *Apartheid South Africa and African states. From pariah to middle power, 1961–1994*, London.

Phillips, Howard
1993   *The University of Cape Town, 1918–1948. The formative years*, Cape Town.

Pick, William; **Rispel**, Laetitia; **Naidoo**, Shan
2008   'Poverty, Health and Policy: A Historical Look at the South African Experience'. In: *Journal of Public Health Policy*, 29, pp. 165–178.

Pienaar, Schalk; **Vosloo**, Ton
1975   *Schalk Pienaar. 10 jaar politieke kommentaar*, Kaapstad.

Pillay, Gerald J.
1993- *Voices of liberation, Vol. 1: Albert Lutuli*, Pretoria.

Pirie, G. H.; **Rogerson**, C. M.; **Beavon**, K.S.O.
1980   'Covert power in South Africa: The Geography of the Afrikaner Broederbond'. In: *Area*, 12, 2, pp. 97–104.

Platzky, Laurine; **Walker**, Cherryl
1985   *The Surplus People. Forced Removals in South Africa*, Johannesburg.

Plaum, Ernst
1989   'Historische Anmerkungen zum Problem eines holistischen Eklektizismus in der Psychologie'. In: *Geschichte der Psychologie*, 6, 1, pp. 34–38.
1993   'Grundlegende Aspekte holistischer Psychologien der Zwischenkriegszeit in Deutschland'. In: *Psychologie und Geschichte*, 5, 1/2, pp. 31–39.
1995   'Zur „Unwissenschaftlichkeit" Felix Kruegers'. In: *Psychologie und Geschichte*, 7, 1, pp. 3–29.
1996   '"Gestalt" und "Ganzheit" – politisch gefährliche Begriffe?' in: *Psychologie und Geschichte*, 7, 3, pp. 210–216.

Popper, Karl
1928   Zur Methodenfrage der Denkpsychologie. PhD Thesis, Wien.

Pos, Mary
1967   *Wie was Dr. Verwoerd?*, Utrecht.

Posel, Deborah
1987   'The Meaning of Apartheid before 1948: Conflicting Interests and Forces within the Afrikaner Nationalist Alliance'. In: *Journal of Southern African Studies*, 1, pp. 123–139.
1988   The Construction of Apartheid, 1948–1961. unpubl. Seminar Paper, Nr. 240.
1997   *The Making of Apartheid. 1948 – 1961. Conflict and Compromise*, Oxford.
1999   'Whiteness and Power in the South African Civil Service: Paradoxes of the Apartheid State'. In: *Journal of Southern African Studies*, 25, 1, pp. 99–119.
2001   'Race as Common Sense: Racial Classification in Twentieth-Century South Africa'. In: *African Studies Review*, 44, 2, pp. 87–113.
2009a 'A mania for measurement: statistics and statecraft in the transition to Apartheid'. In: Dubow, Saul (ed.): *Science and Society in Southern Africa*, Manchester, pp. 116–142.
2009b 'The Assassination of Hendrik Verwoerd: The Spectre of Apartheid's Corpse'. In: *African Studies*, 68, 3, pp. 331–350.
2011   'The Apartheid Project, 1948 – 1970'. In: Ross, Robert; Mager, Anne Kelk; Nasson, Bill (eds.): *The Cambridge History of South Africa*, Vol. 2, Cambridge, pp. 319–368.

Potgieter, E. F.
1956a *Die Gebied en Taak van die Volkekunde*. Intreerede gehou by geleentheid van die aanvaarding van die leerstoel in Volkekunde, Pretoria.
1956b 'Kontak in Suidelike Afrika. Enkele Gevolge en Kenmerke van die Proses'. In: *Journal of Racial Affairs*, 7, 2, pp. 52–66.
1957   'The Problem of Objectivity in the Study of Ethnic Relations in South Africa'. In: *Journal of Racial Affairs*, 8, 3, pp. 121–130.

Potgieter, F. J. M.
1958   'Veelvormige ontwikkeling die wil van God'. In: *Journal of Racial Affairs*, 10, 1, pp. 1–15.

Potgieter, M. C.
1970   Maatskaplike Sorg in Suid-Afrika. 'n Ontleding van die aard, omvang, funksieverdeling en finansiering van die dienste gelewer deur die Staat en partikuliere welsynsorganisasies. PhD Thesis, Stellenbosch.

Potgieter, P. J. J. S
1976   *L. J. du Plessis as denker oor staat en politiek*, Potchefstroom.
1981   'L. J. du Plessis as "Politieke Profeet"'. In: *Koers*, 46, 1, pp. 8–30.
Potthast, Thomas
2003   '"Rassenkreise" und die Bedeutung des "Lebensraums". Zur Tier-Rassenforschung in der Evolutionsbiologie'. In: Schmuhl, Hans-Walter (ed.): *Rassenforschung an Kaiser-Wilhelm-Instituten vor und nach 1933*, Göttingen, pp. 275–308.
Pretorius, P. J. V. E
1991   *'n Historiese beligting van die volkerebegrip van H.F. Verwoerd*. Sewentiende H.F. Verwoerd-gedenklesing, Pretoria 6 September 1991, Pretoria.
Prinsloo, C. W.
1950   'Bantoehuise vir die Bantoe'. In: *Journal of Racial Affairs*, 1, 3, pp. 12–18.
1951   'Die Opleiding van Amptenare in Naturelle-Administrasie'. In: *Journal of Racial Affairs*, 2, 2, pp. 14–21.
Prinsloo, Daan
1997   *Stem uit die wildernis. 'n Biografie oor oud-pres. P.W. Botha*, Mosselbaai.
Prinsloo, Dioné
1979   Die Johannesburg-periode in Dr. H.F. Verwoerd se loopbaan, PhD Thesis, Johannesburg.
1981   'Dr. H.F. Verwoerd as hoofredakteur van Die Transvaler'. In: *Kleio*, 13, 1, pp. 5–19.
1985   'Dr. H.F. Verwoerd en die Ossewa-Brandwag 1938–1952'. In: *Kleio*, 17, pp. 73–85.
1987   'Dr. Piet Meyer in Johannesburg, 1936–1984'. In: *Historia*, 32, 1, pp. 44–53.
1987   'H.F. Verwoerd se vriendskap met J.G. Strijdom, en die koningsbesoek van 1947'. In: *South African Journal of Cultural and Art History*, 1, 3, pp. 230–239.
Prinz, Wolfgang
1985   'Ganzheits- und Gestaltpsychologie und Nationalsozialismus'. In: Graumann, Carl F. (ed.): *Psychologie im Nationalsozialismus*, Berlin, pp. 89–111.
2000   'Ausgerechnet Krueger? Kommentar zu Ernst Plaum: „Zur Unwissenschaftlichkeit" Felix Kruegers'. In: *Psychologie und Geschichte*, 8, 3/4, pp. 410–412.
Priwitzer, Martin
2004   Ernst Kretschmer und das Wahnproblem, med. Diss., Tübingen.
Probst, Paul
1990   'Daniel Curio und Ernst Meumann. Zur Entstehung der akademischen Psychologie in Hamburg'. In: *Geschichte der Psychologie*, 7, 1, pp. 8–23.
1990   '"Den Lehrplan tunlichst noch durch eine Vorlesung über Negerpsychologie ergänzen". Bedeutung des Kolonialinstituts für die Institutionalisierung der akademisch-empirischen Psychologie in Hamburg'. In: *Psychologie und Geschichte*, 2, 1, pp. 25–36.
1992   'Angewandte Ethnopsychologie während der Epoche des Deutschen Kolonialismus (1884–1918)'. In: *Psychologie und Geschichte*, 3, 3/4, pp. 67–80.
Probst, Paul; **Bringmann**, Wolfgang G.
1993   'Ernst Meumann und William Stern. Analyse ihres Wirkens in Hamburg (1910–1933) unter Berücksichtigung biographischer und soziokultureller Hintergründe'. In: *Geschichte der Psychologie*, 10, 1, pp. 1–14.
Pugach, Sara Elizabeth Berg
2002   "He is the True Author of My Book": Carl Meinhof, Nicholas van Warmelo, and the Ordering of Africanist Knowledge, 1927–1935 (BAB Working Paper), Basel.
2004   'Carl Meinhof and the German Influence on Nicholas van Warmelo's Ethnological and Linguistic Writing, 1927–1935'. In: *Journal of Southern African Studies*, 30, 4, pp. 825–845.

2012   *Africa in Translation. A History of Colonial Linguistics in Germany and beyond, 1814–1945*, Ann Arbor.
Putnam, Carleton
1961   *Race and Reason. A Yankee View*, Washington, D.C.
Rakometsi, Mafu Solomon
2008   *The Transformation of Black School Education in South Africa, 1950–1994: A Historical Perspective*, Bloemfontein.
Rathbone, Richard
2000   *Nkrumah and the chiefs. The politics of chieftaincy in Ghana 1951–1960*, Athens, Ohio.
Rautenbach, P. S.
1965   'The Economics of Border Areas'. In: *Journal of Racial Affairs*, 16, 3, pp. 104–112.
Redaksie
1950   'Die Kerklike Kongres op Bloemfontein'. In: *Journal of Racial Affairs*, 1, 4, pp. 1–2.
Reid, B. L.
1982   'The Anti-Republican League of the 1950's'. In: *South African Historical Journal*, 14, pp. 85–94.
Reinsch, Paul S.
1900   *World Politics*, London.
Reisenzein, Rainer
2003   'Stumpfs kognitiv-evaluative Theorie der Emotionen'. In: Sprung, Lothar; Schönpflug, Wolfgang (eds.): *Zur Geschichte der Psychologie in Berlin*, Frankfurt, pp. 97–137.
Remplein, Heinz
1962   *Die seelische Entwicklung des Menschen im Kindes- und Jugendalter. Grundlagen, Erkenntnisse und pädagogische Folgerungen der Kindes- und Jugendpsychologie*, Munich – Basel.
Report of the Commission on Native Education 1949–1951
1951   U.G. No 53/1951, Pretoria.
Report on the Proceedings of the Native Representative Council
1951   Eleventh Session. U.B. 39 – 1951 Cape Town.
Rheinallt Jones, John D.
1953   *At the Crossroads*, Johannesburg.
Rhoodie, Nicolaas Johannes
1958   Die Ontwikkeling van die Apartheidsgedagte. MA Thesis, Pretoria.
1965   'n Rasse-Sosiologiese ontleding van afsonderlike volksontwikkeling en partnership, met besondere verwysing na die motiewe van hierdie beleidssisteme. PhD Thesis, Pretoria.
1966   *Apartheid en Partnership. 'n Rasse-Sosiologiese Ontleding van Afsonderlike Volksontwikkeling en Vennootskap, met Besondere Verwysing na die Motiewe vir hierdie Beleidsisteme*, Pretoria – Cape Town.
Rhoodie, N. J.; **Venter** H. J.
1960   *Die Apartheidsgedagte. 'n Sosio-historiese uiteensetting van sy ontstaan en ontwikkeling*, Cape Town – Pretoria.
Rich, Paul
1980   'The Origins of Apartheid Ideology. The Case of Ernest Stubbs and Transvaal Native Administration, c. 1902–1932'. In: *African Affairs*, 79, 315, pp. 171–194.
1983   *White Power and the Liberal Conscience*, Manchester.
1990   'Race, Science, and the Legitimization of White Supremacy in South Africa, 1902–1940'. In: *International Journal of African Historical Studies*, 23, 4, pp. 665–686.

Ringer, Fritz K.
1969   *The Decline of the German Mandarins. The German Academic Community, 1890–1933.* Cambridge (Mass.).

Roberts, Michael; **Trollip**, A.E.G
1947   *The South African Opposition 1939–1945. An Essay in Contemporary History*, London – Cape Town – New York.

Robins, Jon
2000   'The Assassin and the Tapeworm'. In: *New Statesman*, 129, 4479, p. 29.

Robinson, H. Basil
1989   *Diefenbaker's World. A Populist in Foreign Affairs*, Toronto.

Rohracher, Hubert
1988   *Einführung in die Psychologie*, Munich.

Roos, Neil
2015   'Alcohol Panic, Social Engineering, and Some Reflections on the Management of Whites in Early Apartheid Society, 1948–1960'. In: *Historical Journal*, 58, 4, pp. 1167–1189.

Ross, J. J.
1967   'Bantu Education in Historical Perspective'. In: Duminy, P. A. (ed.): *Trends and Challenges in the Education of the South African Bantu.* Golden Jubilee Lectures, Faculty of Education, University College of Fort Hare, 1966, Pretoria – Fort Hare, pp. 3–23.

Roth, Mirjana
1987   The Natives Representative Council, 1937–1951. PhD Thesis, Johannesburg.

Rothe, Katja
2013   'Spekulative Praktiken: Zur Vorgeschichte des Assessment Centers'. In: *ilinx*, 3, pp. 1–16.

Roux, Edward
1978   *Time longer than rope. A history of the black man's struggle for freedom in South Africa*, Madison, Wisc.

Rüssel, Arnulf
1943   'Über Formauffassung zwei- bis fünfjähriger Kinder'. In: Krueger, Felix; Volkelt, Hans (eds.): *Experimentelle Kindespsychologie* (Neue Psychologische Studien, Vol. 7), Munich, pp. 1–108.

Ruppenthal, Jens
2007   *Kolonialismus als "Wissenschaft und Technik". Das Hamburgische Kolonialinstitut 1908 bis 1919*, Stuttgart.

Ryan, Colleen
1990   *Beyers Naudé. Pilgrimage of faith*, Cape Town.

Saayman, Willem
2008   '"Good mission policy is good state policy in South Africa". The influence of the Tomlinson Report on racial separation in church and state at the dawn of apartheid'. In: *Studia Historiae Ecclesiasticae*, 34, 2, pp. 15–39.

Sabalot, Pierre-Olivier
2009   *Verwoerd, le prophète assassiné*, Marseille.

Sadie, Jan L.
1950   'The Political Arithmetic of the S.A. Population'. In: *Journal of Racial Affairs*, 1, 4, pp. 4–8.
1960   'The Industrialisation of the Bantu Areas'. In: *Journal of Racial Affairs*, 11, 2, pp. 57–81.
1989   'The Political Arithmethic of the South African Population'. In: Hugo, Pierre (ed.): *South African perspectives.* Essays in honour of Nic Olivier, Cape Town, pp. 150–157.

SAIRR = South African Institute of Race Relations
1961 *A Précis of the Report of the Commissions appointed to enquire into the Events occuring on March 21 1960 at Sharpeville and Langa. A Fact Paper*, Johannesburg.
Sambureni, Nelson Tozivaripi
1996 'State Labour Control Policies and African Workers of Durban, South Africa, 1960–1985'. In: *South African Historical Journal*, 34, pp. 77–105.
Sander, Friedrich
1937 'Deutsche Psychologie und nationalsozialistische Weltanschauung'. In: *Nationalsozialistisches Bildungswesen*, 2, 11, pp. 641–649.
1972 'Friedrich Sander'. In: Pongratz, Ludwig J.; Wehner, Ernst K. (Hrsg): *Psychologie in Selbstdarstellungen*, Vol. 1), Bern, pp. 309–333.
Sanders, James
2006 *Apartheid's Friends. The Rise and Fall of South Africa's Secret Service*, London.
Sanders, Mark
1999 '"Problems of Europe": N.P. van Wyk Louw, the Intellectual and Apartheid'. In: *Journal of Southern African Studies*, 25, 4, pp. 607–631.
Sapire, Hilary
1987 'The Stay-Away of the Brakpan Location, 1944'. In: Bozzoli, Belinda (ed.): *Class, community and conflict. South African perspectives*, Johannesburg, pp. 358–400.
Saron, Gustav
1940 *Nazi Models and South African Imitations*, Johannesburg.
Saron, Gustav; **Hotz**, Louis (eds.)
1955 *The Jews in South Africa. A History*, Cape Town.
Saunders, Christopher C.
1988 *The Making of the South African past. Major historians on race and class*, Cape Town.
2011 'Dag Hammarskjöld and Apartheid South Africa'. In: *Development Dialogue*, 57, pp. 61–75.
Saxinger, Robert
1902 'Dispositionspsychologisches über Gefühlscomplexionen'. In: *Zeitschrift für Psychologie und Physiologie der Sinnesorgane*, 30, pp. 391–421.
Scher, D. M.
1988 '"P.J.": The Life and Times of Senator R. D. Pilkington-Jordan'. In: *Kleio*, 20, 1, pp. 66–79.
Schlick, Moritz
2009 'Über den Begriff der Ganzheit'. In: Stöltzner, Michael; Uebel, Thomas (eds.): *Wiener Kreis. Texte zur wissenschaftlichen Weltauffassung von Rudolf Carnap, Otto Neurath, Moritz Schlick, Philipp Frank, Hans Hahn, Karl Menger, Edgar Zilsel und Gustav Bergmann*, Hamburg, pp. 616–619.
Schlögel, Karl
2004 *Im Raume lesen wir die Zeit. Über Zivilisationsgeschichte und Geopolitik*, Munich.
Schmidt, Wilfred
1991 'Sehnsucht nach Weltanschauung. William Stern um die Jahrhundertwende'. In: *Psychologie und Geschichte*, 3, 1/2, pp. 1–8.
1994 'William Stern (1871–1938) und Lewis Terman (1877–1956). Deutsche und amerikanische Intelligenz- und Begabungsforschung im Lichte ihrer andersartigen politischen und ideologischen Voraussetzungen'. In: *Psychologie und Geschichte*, 6, 1/2, pp. 3–26.
2005 'William Stern'. In: Lück, Helmut E.; Miller, Rudolf (eds.): *Illustrierte Geschichte der Psychologie*, Weinheim, pp. 124–126.

Schmidt-Durban, Wilfried
1939 *Experimentelle Untersuchungen zur Typologie der Wahrnehmung* (Neue Psychologische Studien, Vol. 15), Munich.

Schmuhl, Hans-Walter
2003 'Rasse, Rassenforschung, Rassenpolitik. Annäherungen an das Thema'. In: id. (ed.): *Rassenforschung an Kaiser-Wilhelm-Instituten vor und nach 1933*, Göttingen, pp. 7–37.

Schoeman, Beaumont M
1973 *Van Malan tot Verwoerd*, Cape Town – Pretoria.
1974 *Vorster se 1000 dae*, Kaapstad.
1977 *Parlementêre verkiesings in Suid-Afrika, 1910–1976*, Pretoria.
1982 *Die Broederbond in die Afrikaner-politiek*, Pretoria.

Schoeman, Ben
1978 *My lewe in die politiek*, Johannesburg.

Schönpflug, Wolfgang
2004 *Geschichte und Systematik der Psychologie. Ein Lehrbuch für das Grundstudium*, Weinheim.

Scholtz, Gert Daniel
1950 'Die Taak van die Pers t.o.v. ons Rasseprobleme'. In: *Journal of Racial Affairs*, 1, 3, pp. 19–22.
1960 *Die Naturellebeleid van die Nasionale Party onder Hertzog, Malan, Strijdom en Verwoerd*, Johannesburg.
1963a 'Die Afrikaner en sy pers'. In: *Koers*, 5/6, pp. 345–367.
1963b 'Die staatkundige erfenis en ontwikkeling van die Republiek van Suid-Afrika'. In: *Koers*, 1, pp. 5–25.
1970 *Die taak van die historikus*, Johannesburg.
1974 *Dr. Hendrik Frensch Verwoerd, 1901–1966*, 2 Vols., Johannesburg.
1979 *Die ontwikkeling van die politieke denke van die Afrikaner. Deel VII, 1924–1939*, Johannesburg.

Scholtz, Gert Daniel; **D'Assonville**, V. E.
1966 *Betekenis en boodskap van die jaar 1966 vir die Calvinistiese Afrikaner*, Potchefstroom.

Scholtz, J. J. J
1967 *Die moord op dr. Verwoerd*, Cape Town.

Scholtz, Magda
2002 *Geskiedenis van die Departement Sielkunde an die Universiteit van Stellenbosch 1917 tot 1979*. MA Thesis, Stellenbosch.

Schubeius, Monika
1990 *Und das psychologische Laboratorium muss der Ausgangspunkt pädagogischer Arbeiten werden! Zur Institutionalisierungsgeschichte der Psychologie von 1890–1933*, Frankfurt.

Schüler, Gerd M. K.
1956 "'n Oorsig oor die volke van Afrika'. In: *Journal of Racial Affairs*, 7, 4, pp. 168–176.
1989 'Stellenbosch en Sabra Jare: 'n Persoonlike blik'. In: Hugo, Pierre (ed.): *South African Perspectives. Essays in honour of Nic Olivier*, Cape Town, pp. 1–14.

Schulz, Wolfgang
2006 'Ansätze zu einer historisch orientierten Psychologie der Gesellschaft bei Wilhelm Wundt'. In: Jüttemann, Gerd (ed.): *Wilhelm Wundts anderes Erbe. Ein Missverständnis löst sich auf*, Göttingen, pp. 179–190.

Schumann, T. E. W.
1962 *Die abdikasie van die witman*, Johannesburg.

Schutte, G. J.
2005 *De Vrije Universiteit en Zuid-Afrika 1880–2005*, Zoetermeer.

Scott, James C.
1998 *Seeing like a state. How certain schemes to improve the human condition have failed*, New Haven.
Seebohm, Hans-Bernhard
1970 Otto Selz: ein Beitrag zur Geschichte der Psychologie. Dissertation, Heidelberg.
1971 *Der Mannheimer Philosoph und Psychologe Otto Selz*. Vortrag an d. Univ. Mannheim am 27. Mai 1971, Mannheim.
Seedat, Mohamed; **MacKenzie**, Sarah
2008 'The triangulated development of South African Psychology: Race, scientific racism and professionalisation'. In: van Ommen, Clifford; Painter, Desmond (eds.): *Interiors. A history of psychology in South Africa*, Pretoria, pp. 63–91.
Seekings, Jeremy
2008 'The Carnegie Commission and the Backlash against Welfare State-Building in South Africa, 1931–1937'. In: *Journal of Southern African Studies*, 34, 3, pp. 515–537.
Seekings, Jeremy; **Nattrass**, Nicoli
2006 *Class, Race, and Inequality in South Africa*, Scottsville, South Africa.
Sellström, Tor
2011 'Hammarskjöld and Apartheid South Africa: Mission unaccomplished'. In: *African Journal on Conflict Resolution*, 11, 1, pp. 35–62.
Selz, Otto
1913 *Über die Gesetze des geordneten Denkverlaufs. Eine experimentelle Untersuchung*, Stuttgart.
1922 *Zur Psychologie des produktiven Denkens und des Irrtums. Eine experimentelle Untersuchung. Über die Gesetze des geordneten Denkverlaufs, Zweiter Teil*, Bonn.
1924a *Die Gesetze der produktiven und reproduktiven Geistestätigkeit. Kurzgefaßte Darstellung*, Bonn.
1924b *Über die Persönlichkeitstypen und die Methoden ihrer Bestimmung*. Erweiterter Sonderabdruck aus dem Bericht über den VIII. Kongreß für experimentelle Psychologie in Leipzig (1923), Jena.
1970 Husserls Phänomenologie und ihr Verhältnis zur psychologischen Fragestellung. In: Seebohm, Hans-Bernhard, Otto Selz: ein Beitrag zur Geschichte der Psychologie. Dissertation, Heidelberg, Anhang S., pp. 73–87.
1991a 'Über genetische Ganzheitsprobleme'. In: id. (ed.): *Wahrnehmungsaufbau und Denkprozess. Ausgewählte Schriften*, Bern, pp. 25–69.
1991b 'Die Umgestaltung der Grundanschauungen vom intellektuellen Geschehen'. In: id. (ed.): *Wahrnehmungsaufbau und Denkprozess. Ausgewählte Schriften*, Bern, pp. 137–144.
1991c 'Der schöpferische Mensch'. In: id. (ed.): *Wahrnehmungsaufbau und Denkprozess. Ausgewählte Schriften*, Bern, pp. 159–172.
1991d 'Die Aufbauprinzipien der phänomenalen Welt'. In: id. (ed.): *Wahrnehmungsaufbau und Denkprozess. Ausgewählte Schriften*, Bern, pp. 173–194.
Serfontein, J. H. P.
1979 *Brotherhood of Power. An Exposé of the Secret Afrikaner Broederbond*, London.
Sevenhuysen, Karina.
2012 'Swart stedelike behuisingsverskaffing in Suid-Afrika, ca. 1923–1948: "Wanneer meer minder kos" – finansiële verliese versus welsyns- en gesondheidswinste'. In: *New Contree*, 64, pp. 105–129.
Seyfert, Robert.
2011 *Das Leben der Institutionen. Zu einer allgemeinen Theorie der Institutionalisierung*, Weilerswist.

Shain, Milton
1994   *The roots of antisemitism in South Africa*, Johannesburg.
1998   *Antisemitism and South African society. The past, the present and the future*, Inaugural lecture, Cape Town.
2015   *A perfect storm. Antisemitism in South Africa, 1930-1948*, Johannesburg
Sharp, John S.
1980   'Two Separate Developments: Anthropology in South Africa'. In: *Royal Anthropological Institute Newsletter*, 36, pp. 4-6.
1981   'The Roots and Development of Volkekunde in South Africa'. In: *Journal of Southern African Studies*, 8, 1, pp. 16-36.
Shearar, Jeremy Brown
2007   Against the World. South Africa and Human Rights at the United Nations 1945-1961. D Law Thesis, Pretoria.
Shorten, John R.
1970   *Die verhaal van Johannesburg*, Johannesburg.
Sichel, Frieda H.
1966   *From Refugee to Citizen. A Sociological Study of the Immigrants from Hitler-Europe Who Settled in South Africa*, Cape Town.
Sichler, Ralph
1998   'William Stern und das menschliche Erleben. Historische und terminologische Anmerkungen zu einem vergessenen Grundbegriff der Psychologie'. In: *Psychologie und Geschichte*, 8, 1-2, pp. 67-84.
Simson, Howard
1980   *The Social Origins of Afrikaner Fascism and Its Apartheid Policy*, Uppsala.
Sisulu, Elinor
2004   *Walter & Albertina Sisulu*, Cape Town.
Skawran, Paul
1929   *Manual of Physical and Mental Tests Standardised for South African Conditions. Part I: Physical and Sensory Tests*, Pretoria.
1930   *South African Group Intelligence Tests*, s.l.
1936   *Die sintetiese studie van die persoonlikheid*. Rede by die aanvaarding van die Professoraat in Sielkunde aan die Universiteit van Pretoria, gehou op 13 Maart 1935, Pretoria.
Skinner, Rob
2005   'Facing the Challenge of 'Young Africa': Apartheid, South Africa and British Decolonisation'. In: *South African Historical Journal*, 54, pp. 54-71.
Slabbert, Frederik van Zyl; **Welsh**, David (eds.)
1981   *South Africa's options. Strategies for sharing power*, Cape Town.
Smit, D. van Zyl
1989   'Adopting and adapting criminological ideas. Criminology and Afrikaner nationalism in South Africa'. In: *Contemporary Crises*, 13, pp. 227-251.
Smith, Kenneth Wyndham
1988   *The changing past. Trends in South African historical writing*, Johannesburg.
Smith, Nico
2009   *Die Afrikaner Broederbond. Belewinge van die binnekant*, Pretoria.
Smith, Quentin
2016   *16mm of innocence*, Kibworth.

Smuts, Jan Christian
1940   *Greater South Africa – Plans for a better world. The speeches of General The Right Honourable J. C. Smuts*, Johannesburg.
Sooryamoorthy, R.
2016   *Sociology in South Africa. Colonial, apartheid and democratic forms (Sociology transformed)*, Durban.
South African Embassy Bonn
1981   *Südafrika kontrovers*, Bonn.
Spies, F. J. du T.; **Theron**, Erika; **Scholtz**, J. J. J
1981   'Verwoerd, Hendrik Frensch'. In: Beyers, C. J. (ed.): *Suid-Afrikaanse Biografiese Woordeboek*. Deel IV, Durban – Pretoria, pp. 769–779.
Springbok Atlas
1978   *Juta's Springbok Large Print Atlas for Southern Africa*, Cape Town.
Sprung, Lothar; **Brandt**, R.
2003   'Otto Lipmann (1880–1933) und die Anfänge der angewandten Psychologie in Berlin'. In: Sprung, Lothar; Schönpflug, Wolfgang (Hg.) (eds.): *Zur Geschichte der Psychologie in Berlin*, Frankfurt, pp. 139–159.
Sprung, Lothar und Helga
2005   'Die Berliner Schule der Gestaltpsychologie'. In: Lück, Helmut E.; Miller, Rudolf (eds.): *Illustrierte Geschichte der Psychologie*, Weinheim, pp. 80–84.
Staeuble, Irmingard
1992   'Wir und die Anderen. Ethno-psychologische Konstruktionen im Wandel'. In: *Psychologie und Geschichte*, 4, 1/2, pp. 139–157.
Stallmeister, Walter; **Lück**, Helmut E.
2006   'Die Völkerpsychologie im Werk von Willy Hellpach'. In: Jüttemann, Gerd (ed.): *Wilhelm Wundts anderes Erbe. Ein Missverständnis löst sich auf*, Göttingen, pp. 116–127.
Stals, E. L. P
1986   *Afrikaners in die Goudstad*. Vol. 2, Pretoria.
1998   *Geskiedenis van die Afrikaner-Broederbond 1918 – 1994*, unpublished.
Steensland, Ann M.
2013   *Pathologizing the Bywoner: The Carnegie Commission Report's Diagnosis of "Poor White Disease" in South Africa (1932)*. Master Thesis, Fairfax, VA.
Stein, Sylvester
1999   *Who killed Mr Drum?*, Bellville.
Stern, William
1911   *Die differentielle Psychologie in ihren methodischen Grundlagen*, Bern (Reprint 1994).
1920   *Die Intelligenz der Kinder und Jugendlichen*, Leipzig.
1928a *Psychologie der frühen Kindheit bis zum sechsten Lebensjahre*, Leipzig.
1928b *Sittlichkeitsvergehen an höheren Schulen und ihre disziplinäre Behandlung*, Leipzig.
1931   'Das Psychologische Institut der Hamburgischen Universität in seiner gegenwärtigen Gestalt'. In: *Zeitschrift für angewandte Psychologie*, 39, 1–3, pp. 181–227.
Steyn, Jaap C.
1987   *Trouwe Afrikaners. Aspekte van Afrikaner-nasionalisme en Suid-Afrikaanse taalpolitiek, 1875–1938*, Kaapstad.
1998   *Van Wijk Louw. 'n lewensverhaal*, Kaapstad.
2002   *Penvegter. Piet Cillié van Die Burger*, Kaapstad.
2004   *Die 100 jaar van MER*, Kaapstad.

Stoecker, Holger
2008   *Afrikawissenschaften in Berlin von 1919 bis 1945. Zur Geschichte und Topographie eines wissenschaftlichen Netzwerkes*, Stuttgart.

Stoker, Hendrik G.
1935   'The Possibility of a Calvinistic Philosophy'. In: *The Evangelical Quarterly*, 7, 17–23.

Streminger, Gerhard
1995   *David Hume. Sein Leben und sein Werk*, Paderborn.

Strydom, Christiaan J. Scheepers
1967   *Black and White Africans. A Factual Account of South African Race Policies in the Verwoerd Era*, Cape Town.

Stubbs, E. T.
1953   'The Urgency of Separation'. In: *Journal of Racial Affairs*, 4, 2, pp. 13–19.

Stultz, Newell M.
1969   'The Politics of Security: South Africa under Verwoerd, 1961–6'. In: *Journal of Modern African Studies*, 7, 1, pp. 3–20.
1975   *Who goes to parliament?* (Occasional papers, Rhodes University. Institute of Social and Economic research, 19), Grahamstown.
1979   *Transkei's Half Loaf. Race Separatism in South Africa*, New Haven.

Stultz, Newell M.; **Butler**, Jeffrey
1963   'The South African General Election of 1961'. In: *Political Science Quarterly*, 78, 1, pp. 86–110.

Stumpf, Carl
1899   'Ueber den Begriff der Gemüthsbewegung'. In: *Zeitschrift für Psychologie und Physiologie der Sinnesorgane*, 21, pp. 47–99.
1928   *Gefühl und Gefühlsempfindung*, Leipzig.

Sussman, Gary
2006   'The Referendum as an Electoral Device in National Party Politics, 1917–60'. In: *Politikon*, 33, 3, pp. 259–275.

Suzman, Helen
1994   *In No Uncertain Terms. Memoirs*, Johannesburg.
1997   'The Real Heroes'. In: Suttner, Immanuel (ed.): *Cutting through the mountain. Interviews with South African Jewish activists*, Parktown, pp. 423–444.

Swanepoel, Johannes Jacobus
1982   *Die diplomasie van adv. B. J. Vorster*, Bloemfontein.

Swartz, Sally
2008   'Fools and ships: Psychopathology and colonial experience in South Africa, 1818–1930'. In: van Ommen, Clifford; Painter, Desmond (eds.): *Interiors. A history of psychology in South Africa*, Pretoria, pp. 261–285.

Tabata, I. B.
1980   *Education for Barbarism. Bantu (Apartheid) Education in South Africa*, London – Lusaka.

Tatz, C. M
1962   'Dr. Verwoerd's "Bantustan" Policy'. In: *Australian Journal of Politics and History*, 8, 1, pp. 7–26.

Tayler, Judith Anne
1992   '"Our poor": The Politicisation of the Poor White Problem, 1932–1942'. In: *Kleio*, 24, pp. 40–65.
2010   *With Her Shoulder to The Wheel. The Public Life of Erika Theron (1907–1990)*. PhD Thesis, Pretoria.

Tennyson, Brian Douglas
1982   *Canadian relations with South Africa. A diplomatic history*, Washington, D.C.

Teppo, Annika Björnsdotter
2004   The making of a good white. A historical ethnography of the rehabilitation of poor whites in a suburb of Cape Town. PhD Thesis, Helsinki.
ter Hark, Michel
2003   'Searching for the Searchlight Theory: From Karl Popper to Otto Selz'. In: *Journal of the History of Ideas*, 64, 3, pp. 465–487.
Terblanche, H. O.
1995   'Gemeenskapsarmoede en die Afrikaners in Port Elizabeth, 1902–1937: 'n Verkennende Studie'. In: *South African Historical Journal*, 32, pp. 138–162.
1998   *Nederland en die Afrikaner. Gesprek oor apartheid, die paginaruil tussen Trouw en Die Burger, 1963-1964*, Port Elizabeth.
2001a   'Dr. H.F. Verwoerd se Hollandse afkoms: sy Achilleshiel?' in: *Historia*, 46, 1, pp. 213–246.
2001b   '"n Biografiese skets". In: Verwoerd, Wilhelm J. (ed.): *Verwoerd. Só onthou ons hom*, Pretoria, pp. 11–28.
2010   'Die verskille tussen Nederland en Vlaandere ten opsigte van Suid-Afrika tydens die apartheidsjare: 'n Ontleding'. In: *Tydskrif vir Geesteswetenskappe*, 50, 4, pp. 447–466.
Terreblanche, Sampie
2012   *A History of Inequality in South Africa, 1652–2002*, Scottsville.
Te Water, Charles
1953   'South Africa in the Larger Africa Context. Opening address before the South African Bureau of Racial Affaris – Fourth Annual Conference 1952'. In: *Journal of Racial Affairs*, 5, 1, pp. 1–15.
Theron, Erika
1950   'Die Kleurling en die houding van die Blanke'. In: *Journal of Racial Affairs*, 1, 4, pp. 21–24.
1970   *H.F. Verwoerd as welsynbeplanner 1932-1936*, Stellenbosch – Grahamstown.
1983   *Sonder hoed of handskoen. Synde 'n klompie informele herinneringe waarin die kind (meesal) op sy naam genoem word*, Cape Town.
Theron, Erika; **Stulting**, A.A
1961   *Maatskaplike dienste in Suid-Afrika*, Stellenbosch – Grahamstown.
Theron, P. A.
1950   'Die Lae Produktiviteit in Suid-Afrikaanse Industrieë'. In: *Journal of Racial Affairs*, 1, 2, pp. 19–26.
1952   'A Psychological Approach to Separate Development'. In: *Journal of Racial Affairs*, 3, 4, pp. 10–20.
Thiermann, Werner
1981   Zur Geschichte des Leipziger psychologischen Institutes 1875–1945. PhD Thesis, Leipzig.
Thom, H. B
1965   *Universiteit en Maatskappy*. Rede gelewer op 24 Februarie 1965, Stellenbosch.
1969   'Stellenbosch as ware Volksuniversiteit'. In: Kotzé, D. J. (ed.): *Professor H. B. Thom*, Stellenbosch, pp. 77–79.
1980   *D. F. Malan*, Kaapstad.
Thomas von Aquin
2005   *Summa contra gentiles*, Darmstadt.
Thompson, Leonard M.
1966   *Politics in the Republic of South Africa*, Boston – Toronto.
1978   'Some Problems of Southern African Universities'. In: Van der Merwe, Hendrik W; Welsh, David (eds.): *The Future of the University in Southern Africa*, New York, pp. 280–296.

Thurnwald, Richard
1912 'Einleitung: Probleme der ethno-psychologischen Forschung'. In: Institut für angewandte Psychologie und psychologische Sammelforschung (ed.): *Vorschläge zur psychologischen Untersuchung primitiver Menschen*, Leipzig, pp. 1–27.
1913 *Ethno-psychologische Studien an Südseevölkern auf dem Bismarck-Archipel und den Salomo-Inseln*, Leipzig.

Tilitzki, Christian
2002 *Die deutsche Universitätsphilosophie in der Weimarer Republik und im Dritten Reich*. 2 Vols., Berlin.

Tinker, Miles A.
1932 'Wundt's Doctorate Students and Their Theses 1873–1920'. In: *The American Journal of Psychology*, 44, 4, pp. 630–637.

Tomlinson, F. R.
1939 *Die taak van die Landbou-Ekonoom in Suid-Afrika*. Rede by die aanvaarding van die professoraat in Landbou-Ekonomie aan die Universiteit van Pretoria gehou op 24 Augustus 1939, Pretoria.
1956 'Die Voorgestelde Ontwikkelingsprogram vir die Bantoegebiede'. In: Thom, H.B. et al (eds.): *Volkskongres oor die toekoms van die Bantoe*. Bloemfontein 28–30 Junie 1956, Stellenbosch, pp. 48–62.

Tomlinson-Report.
1955 *Samevatting van die verslag van die Kommissie vir die Sosio-ekonomiese Ontwikkeling van die Bantoegebiede binne die Unie van Suid-Afrika*, Pretoria.

Trapido, Stanley
1963 'Political Institutions and Afrikaner Social Structures in the Republic of South Africa'. In: *American Political Science Review*, 57, 1, pp. 75–87.

Treurnicht, Andries P.
1988 *Dr. Verwoerd oor Kleurlingverteenwoordiging*. 14. H.F.Verwoerd-gedenklesing, Pretoria.

Troup, Freda
1975 *South Africa. An Historical Introduction*, Harmondsworth.

Truscott, Ross; **Smith**, Michelle
2016 'Aftershocks: Psychotechnics in the Wake of Apartheid'. In: *Parallax*, 22, 2, pp. 248–262.

Unger, Corinna
2009 'Investieren in die Moderne. Amerikanische Stiftungen in der dritten Welt seit 1945'. In: Adam, Thomas; Lässig, Simone; Lingelbach, Gabriele (eds.): *Stifter, Spender und Mäzene. USA und Deutschland im historischen Vergleich*, Stuttgart, pp. 253–286.

United Party
1938 *The Fruits of Fusion. Five Years of Wonderful Progress and National Reconstruction – The Case for an Extended Mandate*, Pretoria.

Universiteit Stellenbosch
1960 *Die Departement van Sielkunde*, Stellenbosch.
2004 *Studenteraad 1903–2003*, Stellenbosch.

Unterhalter, Elaine
1987 *Forced removal. The division segregation and control of the people of South Africa*, London.

Uys, Stanley
1959 'Dr. Hendrik Frensch Verwoerd, Prime Minister of South Africa'. In: *Africa South*, 3, 2, pp. 1–11.

van Biljon, P.
1956 *Grensbakens tussen Blank en Swart in Suid-Afrika. 'n Historiese ontwikkeling van grensbeleid en beleid van grondtoekenning aan die Naturel in Suid-Afrika*, Cape Town – Johannesburg.

van den Berghe, Pierre L.
1967   *South Africa. A Study in Conflict*, Berkeley – Los Angeles – London.
van der Merwe, A. B.
1987   'Wilcocks, Raymond William'. In: Beyers, C. J. (ed.): *Suid-Afrikaanse Biografiese Woordeboek*, Deel V, Pretoria, pp. 941–942.
van der Merwe, Sakkie
1966   'Die Totstandkoming van die Republiek van Suid-Afrika', in: Van Jaarsveld, F. A.; Scholtz, G. D. (ed.), *Die Republiek van Suid-Afrika. Agtergrond, Ontstaan en Toekoms*, Johannesburg pp. 187–227.
van der Merwe, Schalk D.
2014   '"Radio Apartheid": Investigating a History of Compliance and Resistance in Popular Afrikaans Music, 1956–1979'. In: *South African Historical Journal*, 66, 2, pp. 349–370.
van der Merwe, Werner
1987   'Die Berlynse Sending en "Apartheid" in Suid-Afrika'. In: *Historia*, 32, 1, pp. 1–19.
1988   *Vir 'n "blanke volk". Die verhaal van die Duitse weeskinders van 1948*, Johannesburg.
van der Ross, R. E.
1978   'The Role of a Coloured University in Southern Africa'. In: Van der Merwe, Hendrik W; Welsh, David (eds.): *The Future of the University in Southern Africa*, New York, pp. 237–243.
2015   *In Our Own Skins. A Political History of the Coloured People*, Johannesburg – Cape Town.
van der Schyff, Pieter F.
1987   'Louw, Eric Hendrik'. In: Beyers, C. J.; Basson, J.L (eds.): *Dictionary of South African Biography*, Vol. 5, Pretoria, pp. 467–471.
2003   *Wonderdaad . . . ! Die PUK tot 1951: wording, vestiging en selfstandigheid*, Potchefstroom.
van der Spuy, H. I. J.
1978   'The Psychodynamics of Apartheid'. In: Van der Spuy, H. I. J; Shamley, D. A. F (eds.): *The Psychology of Apartheid. A Psychosocial Perspective on South Africa*, Washington, pp. 1–17.
van der Waal, Kees
2003   *Kultuur, mag en ongelykheid in Suid-Afrika. Die relevansie van die antropologie van ontwikkeling en organisasies*, Stellenbosch.
van der Walt, Nicolaas Gerhardus Stefanus
1968   Die Republikeinse Strewe. Dryfvere en probleem binne die Suid-Afrikaanse partypolitiek, 1902–1961. PhD Thesis, Potchefstroom.
van der Watt, P. B.
1981   'Gerdener, Gustav Bernhard August'. In: Beyers, C. J. (ed.): *Suid-Afrikaanse Biografiese Woordeboek*. Deel IV, Durban – Pretoria, pp. 186–187.
van der Westhuizen, Christi
2007   *White power & the rise and fall of the National Party*, Cape Town.
van Dyk, J. H.; **Coertze**, P. J.
1987   'Eiselen, Werner Willi Max'. In: Beyers, C. J. (ed.): *Suid-Afrikaanse Biografiese Woordeboek*, Deel V, Pretoria, pp. 247–249.
van Eck, H. J.
1951   *Some Aspects of the South African Industrial Revolution*, Hoernlé Memorial Lecture, 7, Johannesburg.
van Eeden B. I. C.
1956   'Die Tale van Afrika'. In: *Journal of Racial Affairs*, 7, 4, pp. 176–180.

van Eeden E. S.
2006 *'In U lig'. Die PU vir CHO: van selfstandigwording tot samesmelting, 1951-2004*, Potchefstroom.
van Jaarsveld, Floris Albertus
1978 *Omsingelde Afrikanerdom. Opstelle oor die toestand van ons tyd*, Kaapstad.
van Laak, Dirk
2008 'Planung. Geschichte und Gegenwart des Vorgriffs auf die Zukunft'. In: *Geschichte und Gesellschaft*, 34, 3, pp. 305-326.
van Loon, F.H.G.; **Thouless**, R. H.
1926 'Report of a Demonstration of Experiments on Hypnotism by Mr. Gustaf Wallenius (phil. mag. Upsala) at the VIIIth International Psychological Congress at Groningen (Sept. 1926)'. In: *Proceedings of the Society for Psychical Research*, 36, 102, pp. 437-454.
van Nierkerk, L. J. P.
1950 'Die Naturel in die Suid-Afrikaanse Ekonomie'. In: *Journal of Racial Affairs*, 1, 4, pp. 25-28.
van Rensburg, J. A. J.
1938 *The Learning Ability of the South African Native compared with that of the European*, Pretoria.
van Rensburg, Fanie Jansen
2006 'The first 'white' town north of the Vaal: inequality and apartheid in Potchefstroom'. In: *New Contree*, 51, pp. 131-147.
van Rooyen, Jan J
1971 *Ons politiek van naby*, Cape Town.
1976 *P. W. Botha, 40 jaar*, Kaapstad.
van Rooyen, T. B.
1962 'Van Prehistorie na Geskiedenis – Die Deurbraak in Afrika'. In: *Journal of Racial Affairs*, 13, 2, pp. 102-112.
van Schoor, A. M.
1979 *Fyfde H.F. Verwoerd-Gedenklesing*, Pretoria.
1979 *Note from my Diary*, Pretoria.
van Woerden, Henk
2000a *Domein van glas*, Kaapstad.
2000b 'The Assassin'. In: *Granta*, 69, pp. 7-79.
van Wyk, Annie Helena
2005 Die rol van die verligtes in die Nasionale Party in die politieke ontmagtiging van die Afrikaner, 1966-1994. Master's Thesis, Pretoria.
van Wyk, At
1983 *Die Keeromstraatkliek. Die Burger en die politiek van koalisie en samesmelting, 1932-1934*, Kaapstad.
van Wyk, J. T.
1966 *Report of the Commission of enquiry into the circumstances of the death of the late Dr. the Honourable Hendrik Frensch Verwoerd*, Pretoria.
van Zijl, F. D. du T.
1969 'Binne die Mure van die Universiteit'. In: Kotzé, D. J. (ed.): *Professor H. B. Thom*, Stellenbosch, pp. 48-54.
Venter, Albert
2011 'Die doodloopstraat van die Afrikanerrepubliek van 1961'. In: *Tydskrif vir Geesteswetenskappe*, 51, 4, pp. 533-550.

Venter, H. J.
1952 *Residivisme. 'n Vergelykende Kriminologiese Ondersoek*, Cape Town – Pretoria.
Venter, J. J.
1997 'Mechanistic individualism versus organistic totalitarianism'. In: *Koers*, 62, 1, pp. 91–117.
1999 'H.F. Verwoerd: Foundational aspects of his thought'. In: *Koers*, 64, 4, pp. 415–442.
Verkuyl, J.; **Gericke**, J. S; **Vorster**, J. D; **Snyman**, W. J
1970 *Die Gereformeerde Kerke en geregtigheid in Volkereverhoudings*, Johannesburg.
Verwey, J. E. M.
1966 'Hulle het die Leiding Geneem'. In: Thom, H.B. et al (eds.): *Stellenbosch 1866-1966. Honderd Jaar Hoër Onderwys*, Cape Town, pp. 239–262.
Verwoerd, Elisabeth
2001 'Eggenoot'. In: Verwoerd, Wilhelm J. (ed.) *Verwoerd. Só onthou ons hom*, Pretoria, pp. 39–51.
Verwoerd, Hendrik Frensch
1920 'Die veragterdes in ons midde'. In: *Stellenbosch University Magazine*, 21, 4, pp. 123–125.
1922a Die dubbele taak. M.A. Thesis in Psychology, Stellenbosch University, Stellenbosch.
1922b Die Probleem van die waardes. M.A. Thesis (Philosophy), Stellenbosch.
1923 ''n Sprekersburo'. In: *Stellenbosch Uniwersiteitsblad*, 24, 1, p. 2.
1924a Die afstomping van gemoedsaandoeninge. PhD Thesis in Psychology, Stellenbosch University, Stellenbosch.
1924b 'Rapport: Voorsitter Sprekersburo'. In: *Die Stellenbosse Student – The Stellenbosch Student*, 24, 2, pp. 36–37.
1924c 'Voorsittersrapport, 1923'. In: *Die Stellenbosse Student – The Stellenbosch Student*, 24, 1, pp. 3–8.
1925 *Die Afstomping van Gemoedsaandoeninge*, Annale van die Uniwersiteit van Stellenbosch, 3, B, 1, Cape Town.
1926 'A Method for the Experimental Production of Emotions'. In: *The American Journal of Psychology*, 37, pp. 357–371.
1928a 'The Distribution of "Attention" and its testing'. In: *The Journal of Applied Psychology*, 12, 5, pp. 495–510.
1928b 'Effects of Fatigue on the Distribution of Attention'. In: *The Journal of Applied Psychology*, 12, 6, pp. 595–601.
1928c ''n Bydrae tot die metodiek en probleemstellings vir die psigologiese ondersoek van koerante-advertensies'. In: *South African Journal of Science*, 25, pp. 469–480.
1929 'A Contribution to the Experimental Investigation of Testimony'. In: *South African Journal of Science*, 26, pp. 949–957.
1930a 'Oor die personlikheid van die mens en die beskrywing daarvan'. In: *South African Journal of Science*, 27, pp. 577–580.
1930b 'Oor die opstel van objektiewe personlikheidsbepalingskemas'. In: *South African Journal of Science*, 27, pp. 581–585.
1932 'Die Studie van Sociologie'. In: *Die Stellenbossche Oudstudent*, 2, 1, pp. 25–28.
1934 'Die bestryding van armoede en die herorganisasie van welvaartswerk'. In: Du Toit, Pieter (ed.): *Verslag van die volkskongres oor die Armblankevraagstuk gehou te Kimberley 2 tot 5 Oktober 1934*, Cape Town, pp. 30–39.
1935 *Eerste Jaarverslag van werksaamhede van die Voortsettingskomitee* (Volkskongres oor die Armblanke-Vraagstuk, 1934), Stellenbosch.
1936 *First Annual Report of the Activities of the Continuation Committee* (October 1934 – December 1935), Stellenbosch.

1937a   'Die Joodse Vraagstuk – Besien vanuit Die Nasionale Standpunt'. In: *Die Transvaler, 1.10.1937.*
1937b   'Maatskaplike werkers in Suid-Afrika en hulle opleiding'. In: Brümmer, F. (ed.): *Report of the National Conference on Social Work.* Held in Johannesburg, 30th September to 3rd October, 1936, Pretoria, pp. 88–99.
1938   *Let nou op die Feite insake Gemengde Huwelike,* s.l.
1941   'Ons Republiek . . . Hoe Dit Daar Moet Uitsien'. In: *Stryd,* 1, 11, pp. 7–9.
1948   *Red die Afrikaanse-Mediumskole. H.N.P bepleit moedertaalonderwys,* Johannesburg.
1950   'Waarom is ek 'n Nasionalis?' in: *Die Stellenbosse Student – The Stellenbosch Student,* 50, 4, p. 13.
1951a   'Address by the Minister of Native Affairs'. In: *Journal of Racial Affairs,* 3, 1, pp. 2–6.
1951b   'Onderhoud met Minister van Naturellesake i/s Raadsbesluite'. In: *Journal of Racial Affairs,* 2, 3, pp. 3–5.
1952   *Native Policy of the Union of South Africa.* Statement by The Hon. Dr. H. F. Verwoerd, Minister of Native Affairs, in the Senate of the Parliament of the Union of South Africa, 20th May 1952, n.b.
1954   'Joon van Rooy en die staatkundige lewe'. In: *Koers,* 22, 2, pp. 93–94.
1955   *Ontwikkeling en Vooruitgang van Bantoegemeenskappe.* Beleidsverklaring deur dr. H.F. Verwoerd, Minister van Naturellesake, in die Senaat van die Parlement van die Unie van Suid-Afrika, 20 Junie 1955, Pretoria.
1957a   'Die Akademiese Opgeleides en die Toekoms'. In: *Koers,* 24, 6, pp. 229–235.
1957b   *Local Authorities and the State.* Opening Speech delivered by the Hon. Dr. H. F. Verwoerd, Minister of Native Affairs, at the Fifth Annual Congress of the Administrators of Non-European Affairs in Southern Africa on the 17th September, 1956, Pretoria.
1958   *Aparte Ontwikkeling (Die positiewe aspek).* Toespraak deur Sy Edele Senator dr. H.F. Verwoerd, Minister van Naturellesake, by geleentheid van die opening van die Transkeise Gebiedsowerheid op 7 Mei 1957.
1959a   *Nasionale Party se Naturellebeleid.* Excerpts from a speech before the Natives Representative Council, 5.12.1950, Standerton.
1959b   *The Choice – A Racially Integrated Fatherland or A White South Africa?,* Bloemfontein.
1960a   *Die Republiek – laaste tree daarheen.* Verklaring deur sy Edele Dr. H.F. Verwoerd, Eerste Minister van Suid-Afrika, Toespraak gelewer in die Volksraad, Kaapstad, op 20 Januarie 1960, Bloemfontein.
1960b   *Prime Minister's Statement on Republic,* Pretoria.
1960c   *The Price of Appeasement in Africa.* Speech in the House of Assembly by Dr. the Hon. H.F. Verwoerd, Prime Minister of the Union of South Africa on March 10, 1960, Pretoria.
1961a   *Live and let live* (Fact Paper, 91), Pretoria.
1961b   *The Truth about South Africa.* Address by the Hon. the Prime Minister of the Union of South Africa Dr. H. F. Verwoerd before the South Africa Club in the Savoy Hotel, London, on Friday, 17th March, 1961.
1962   *A Future for the Coloured People* (Fact Paper, 101), Johannesburg.
1963   *Dr. H.F. Verwoerd on I. Crisis In World Conscience, II. The Road to Freedom for Basutoland – Bechuanaland – Swaziland* (Fact Paper, 107), Pretoria.
1964a   *Suid-Afrika vorentoe. Our View to the Future.* Toespraak gelewer deur Sy Edele, dr. H. F. Verwoerd, Eerste Minister en Hoofleier van die Nasionale Party te Johannesburg op 8 September 1964 ten tye van viering van die 50-jarige bestaan van die Nasionale Party van Transvaal, Pretoria.
1964b   '"Weltgewissen"?' in: *Nation Europa,* 14, 12, pp. 11–15.
1966   'Herinneringe op die republikeinse pad'. In: van Jaarsveld, F.A; Scholtz, G.D (eds.): *Die Republiek van Suid-Afrika. Agtergrond, Ontstaan en Toekoms,* Johannesburg, pp. 5–8.
1968   'Aan die Sy van die Ossewa'. In: *Die Taalgenoot,* Dez, p. 43.

1972 *Dr. H. F. Verwoerd die Republikein*. Hoofartikels uit Die Transvaler 1937-1948, Cape Town.
Verwoerd, H. C. Lucy
1935 Die alleenlopende moeder as 'n ontvanger van liefdadigheid. M.A. thesis, Stellenbosch.
Verwoerd, S. A. Joubert
1965 *Wilhelm Johannes Verwoerd*, Johannesburg.
Verwoerd, Wilhelm J.
1990 *Dr. H. F. Verwoerd: Vegter vir vryheid*. Sestiende H.F. Verwoerd-Gedenklesing (H.F. Verwoerd-Gedenklesing; 16e), Pretoria.
2001 'Woord vooraf'. In: id. (ed.): *Verwoerd. Só onthou ons hom*, Pretoria, pp. 7-8.
2018 *Verwoerd aan die woord II. Die laaste vier jaar. Toesprake 1963-1966*, Pretoria.
Verwoerd, Wilhem (jnr.)
1994 'Re-viewing Verwoerd's vision. Critical Reflections on the Praxis of Apartheid and the thought of its Architect'. In: Oruka, Henry Odera (ed.): *Philosophy, Humanity and Ecology. Philosophy of Nature and Environmental Ethics*, Nairobi, pp. 212-221.
2018 *Bloedbande. 'n donker tuiskoms*, Cape Town.
Verwoerd, Wilhelm, Anna, Daniel, Elsabet, Hendrik, Christiaan, Wynand
2001 'Vader'. In: Verwoerd, Wilhelm J. (ed.): *Verwoerd. Só onthou ons hom*, Pretoria, 52-104.
Vico, Giambattista
2009 *Prinzipien einer neuen Wissenschaft über die gemeinsame Natur der Völker*, Hamburg.
Viljoen, Louise
2012 *Ingrid Jonker*, Auckland Park.
Viljoen, G. van N.
1978 'The Afrikaans Universities and Particularism'. In: Van der Merwe, Hendrik W; Welsh, David (eds.): *The Future of the University in Southern Africa*, New York, pp. 172-187.
Visser, George Cloete
1977 *OB. Traitors or Patriots?*, Johannesburg.
Visser, Myda Marista
1999 Die ideologiese grondslae en ontwikkeling van die blanke fascistiese bewegings in Suid-Afrika, 1945-1995. MA Thesis, Pretoria.
Vladislavic, Ivan; **Judin**, Hilton (eds.)
1998 *Blank-. Architecture, apartheid and after*, Rotterdam
Voigt, Elizabeth A.
1983 *Mapungubwe: An Archaeological Interpretation of an Iron Age Community*, Pretoria.
Volkelt, Hans
1914 *Über die Vorstellungen der Tiere. Ein Beitrag zur Entwicklungspsychologie*, Leipzig – Berlin.
1922 *Die Völkerpsychologie in Wundts Entwicklungsgang*, Erfurt.
1925 *Über die Forschungsrichtung des Psychologischen Instituts der Universität Leipzig*. Zu seiner Fünfzigjahrfeier am 21. November 1925, Erfurt.
1926 *Fortschritte der experimentellen Kinderpsychologie*. Sonderabdruck aus dem Bericht über den IX. Kongress für experimentelle Psychologie in München, Jena.
1954 'Grundbegriffe der Ganzheitspsychologie'. In: Klemm, Otto (ed.): *Wege zur Ganzheitspsychologie. Festschrift zum 60. Geburtstage Felix Kruegers*, Munich, pp. 1-46.
1962a 'Von den Anfängen der "Ganzheitspsychologie"'. In: Sander, Friedrich; Volkelt, Hans (eds.): *Ganzheitspsychologie. Grundlagen – Ergebnisse – Anwendungen. Gesammelte Abhandlungen*, Munich, pp. 1-14.

1962b 'Grundbegriffe der Ganzheitspsychologie'. In: Sander, Friedrich; Volkelt, Hans (eds.): *Ganzheitspsychologie. Grundlagen – Ergebnisse – Anwendungen. Gesammelte Abhandlungen*, Munich, pp. 31–65.

Volkskongres oor die Toekoms van die Bantoe,
1956 *Volkskongres*, Bloemfontein 28–30 Junie 1956, Stellenbosch.

Vorster, Balthasar John
1976 *Tweede HF Verwoerd-Gedenklesing*, Pretoria.

Vorwerg, Manfred
1979 *Wilhelm Wundt – Erbe und Gegenwart. Festveranstaltung der Karl-Marx-Universität anläßlich des 100jährigen Jubiläums des von Wilhelm Wundt gegründeten Institutes für experimentelle Psychologie an der Universität Leipzig, 31. Oktober 1979*, Leipzig.
1984 *Experimentelle Psychologie in Leipzig*, Munich.

Waetjen, Thembisa
2005 'Between explanation and apology: Giliomee and the problem of the Afrikaner ethnic past'. In: *Transformation*, 58, 87–96.

Wagner, Oloff Jacobus Marais
1936 *Poverty and Dependency in Cape Town. A Sociological Study of 3,300 Dependents receiving assistance from the Cape Town General Board of Aid*. PhD Thesis, Stellenbosch.
1937 'Prof. Dr. H. F. Verwoerd'. In: *Die Stellenbossche Oudstudent*, 7, 1, pp. 9–10.

Walach, Harald
2009 *Psychologie – Wissenschaftstheorie, philosophische Grundlagen und Geschichte. Ein Lehrbuch*, Stuttgart.

Walton, Chris
2004 'Bond of Broeders. Anton Hartman and Music in an Apartheid State'. In: *The Musical Times*, 145, 1887, pp. 63–74.

Walzer, Michael
1988 *Exodus und Revolution*, Berlin.

Wannamaker, Claudia
1925 *The Recreation Program in a plan for social treatment*, Springfield.

Ward, Stuart
2011 'Run Before the Tempest. The "Wind of Change" and the British World'. In: *Geschichte und Gesellschaft*, 37, 2, pp. 198–219.

Ward, Kevin
2015 'Afrika! Mayibuye! Equality, Freedom and Humanity. The Struggle for South African Christianity in the Twentieth Century'. In: Lessing, Hanns; Dedering, Tilman; Kampmann, Jürgen; Smit, Dirkie (eds.): *Umstrittene Beziehungen/Contested Relations. Protestantismus zwischen dem südlichen Afrika und Deutschland von den 1930er Jahren bis in die Apartheidzeit/Protestantism between Southern Africa and Germany from the 1930s to the Apartheid Era*, Wiesbaden, pp. 231–242.

Weber, Phil
1973 *Nà die generaals. Republiek en nasionale eenheid. Generaal J.B.M. Hertzog-gedenklesing 3*, Stellenbosch.

Wehr, Gerhard
1988 *Karlfried Graf Dürckheim. Ein Leben im Zeichen der Wandlung*, Munich.

Weingart, Peter; **Kroll**, Jürgen; **Bayertz**, Kurt
2017 *Rasse, Blut und Gene. Geschichte der Eugenik und Rassenhygiene in Deutschland*, Frankfurt am Main.

Weisbord, Robert G.
1967   'The Dilemma of South African Jewry'. In: *Journal of Modern African Studies*, 5, 2, pp. 233-241.
Wellek, Albert
1950   *Die Wiederherstellung der Seelenwissenschaft im Lebenswerk Felix Kruegers. Längsschnitt durch ein halbes Jahrhundert der Psychologie*, Hamburg.
1953   *Das Problem des seelischen Seins. Die Strukturtheorie Felix Kruegers: Deutung und Kritik. Zugleich ein Beitrag zur Wissenschaftslehre und zur Theorie des Charakters*, Meisenheim – Wien.
1954   *Die genetische Ganzheitspsychologie*, Munich.
1972   'Albert Wellek'. In: Pongratz, Ludwig J.; Wehner, Ernst K. (eds.): *Psychologie in Selbstdarstellungen*, Vol. 1, Bern, pp. 357-388.
Welsh, David
1971   *The Roots of Segregation. Native Policy in Colonial Natal, 1845-1910*, Cape Town.
2010   *The Rise and Fall of Apartheid*, Johannesburg.
Welsh, David; **Savage**, M.
1978   'The University in Divided Societies: The Case of South Africa'. In: Van der Merwe, Hendrik W; Welsh, David (eds.): *The Future of the University in Southern Africa*, New York, pp. 130-147.
Wertheimer, Max
1967   'Über das Denken der Naturvölker'. In: id. (ed.): *Drei Abhandlungen zur Gestalttheorie*, Darmstadt, pp. 106-163.
Westphal, Ernst
1911   *Über Haupt- und Nebenaufgaben bei Reaktionsversuchen*, Leipzig.
Wiederroth, Nicole
2016   *Südafrikas Propaganda im Zweiten Weltkrieg. Zur medialen Legitimation einer kolonialen Ordnung*, St. Ingbert.
Wilcocks, Raymond William
1917   *Zur Erkenntnistheorie Hegels in der Phänomenologie des Geistes* (Abhandlungen zur Philosophie und ihrer Geschichte, Vol. 51), Halle.
1923   'Oor die "ongeldige" modi van sillogisme'. In: *Annale van die Universiteit van Stellenbosch*, 1, 1, pp. 1-23.
1924   'On the conception of intelligence'. In: *South African Journal of Science*, 21, pp. 664-675.
1925   'An Examination of Külpe's Experiments on Abstraction'. In: *The American Journal of Psychology*, 36, 3, pp. 324-341.
1928a   'On Substitution as a Cause of Errors in Thinking'. In: *The American Journal of Psychology*, 40, 1, pp. 26-50.
1928b   'Oor die metode van invalle'. In: *South African Journal of Science*, 25, pp. 491-498.
1928c   'The effect of an unexpected heterogeneity on attention'. In: *Journal of General Psychology*, 1, 1, pp. 266-319.
1929   'On the Correlation of Intelligences Scores between Siblings'. In: *South African Journal of Science*, 26, pp. 881-887.
1930   'Psigologiese aanmerkings omtrent die verhouding van arm-blanke en gekleurde'. In: *Sosiale en Bedryfsaangeleenthede / Social and Industrial Review*, Mai, pp. 1-8.
1931a   'Intelligence, Environment and Heredity'. In: *South African Journal of Science*, 28, pp. 63-76.
1931b   *The South African Group Test of Intelligence*, Stellenbosch.
1945   'Die volksaard van die Afrikaner'. In: van den Heever, C.M; Pienaar, P. de V. (eds.): *Kultuurgeskiedenis van die Afrikaner*, Vol. 1, Cape Town – Bloemfontein – Port Elizabeth, pp. 286-308.

Wilkins, Ivor; **Strydom**, Hans
1980 *The Super-Afrikaners. Inside the Afrikaner Broederbond*, Johannesburg.
Wilks, Terry
1980 *The Biography of Douglas Mitchell*, Durban.
Williams, Donovan
2001 *A history of the University College of Fort Hare, South Africa – the 1950s. The waiting years*, Lewiston, NY.
Wilson, Robert R.
1961 'International Law and Some Recent Developments in the Commonwealth'. In: *American Journal of International Law*, 55, 2, pp. 440–444.
Winckler, A. T.
1969 *Volkswelsynbeleid*, Stellenbosch.
Wirth, Wilhelm
1898 'Vorstellungs- und Gefühlscontrast'. In: *Zeitschrift für Psychologie und Physiologie der Sinnesorgane*, 18, pp. 49–90.
Wischnewski, Hans-Jürgen
1961 'Verwoerd und der deutsche Lehrer Niedermayer'. In: *Sozialdemokratischer Pressedienst*, 27. Februar.
Witz, Leslie
2003 *Apartheid's festival. Contesting South Africa's national pasts*, Bloomington.
Wolf, Loammi
2012 David Beresford Pratt: die mens agter die sluipmoordpoging. https://www.litnet.co.za/david-beresford-pratt-die-mens-agter-die-sluipmoordenaar/
Wolfradt, Uwe
2009 'Die Völkerpsychologie von Wilhelm Wundt'. In: Deimel, Claus (ed.): *Auf der Suche nach Vielfalt. Ethnographie und Geographie in Leipzig*, Leipzig, pp. 185–192.
Wolman, Benjamin B. (ed.)
1968 *Historical roots of contemporary psychology*, New York.
Wolpe, Harold
1972 'Capitalism and cheap labour-power in South Africa: from segregation to apartheid.' In: *Economy and Society*, 1, pp. 425–456.
Wolvaardt, Pieter; **Wheeler**, Tom; **Scholtz**, W. (eds.)
2010 *From Verwoerd to Mandela. South African Diplomats Remember*, Cape Town.
Wright, Harrison M.
1978 *The burden of the present. Liberal radical controversy over southern African history*, Cape Town.
Wundt, Wilhelm
1862 *Beiträge zur Theorie der Sinneswahrnehmung*, Leipzig.
1901 *Grundriss der Psychologie*, Leipzig.
1911 *Einführung in die Psychologie*, Leipzig.
1913 *Elemente der Völkerpsychologie. Grundlinien einer psychologischen Entwicklungsgeschichte der Menschheit*, Leipzig.
1914 'Die Philosophie des primitiven Menschen'. In: id. (ed.): *Reden und Aufsätze*, Leipzig, pp. 119–162.
Xuma, Alfred Bitini
2012 *A.B. Xuma. Autobiography and selected works*, Cape Town.
Yates, Anne; **Chester**, Lewis
2006 *The troublemaker. Michael Scott and his lonely struggle against injustice*, London.

Zitterbarth, Walter
2006 'War Wundt ein Konstruktivist?' In: Jüttemann, Gerd (ed.): *Wilhelm Wundts anderes Erbe. Ein Missverständnis löst sich auf*, Göttingen, pp. 102–115.
Zöllner, Linda; **Heese**, J. A.
1984 *Die Berlynse Sendelinge in Suid-Afrika en hul nageslag – The Berlin Missionaries in South Africa and their Decendants*, Pretoria.
Zungu, Yeyedwa
1977 'The Education for Africans in South Africa'. In: *Journal of Negro Education*, 46, 3, pp. 202–218.

Name Index

Albertyn, Johannes Rudolf 131, 139, 143, 144, 150, 189

Balewa, Abubakar 374
Basson, Japie 179, 246, 268, 316, 351, 377, 434
Boshoff, Carel Wilhelm Hendrik 324, 339, 429, 489
Botha, Dawid Petrus 422
Botha, Louis 21, 22, 354, 470
Botha, Michiel Coenraad 158, 256, 469
Botha, Pieter Willem 219, 220, 347, 348, 357, 422, 426, 427, 469
Botha, Stephanus Petrus "Fanie" 421
Bruwer, Johannes Petrus van Schalkwyk 180, 181, 243, 249, 305, 313, 328, 330, 332, 333, 336–338, 346, 355

Cillié, Petrus Johannes "Piet" 13, 33, 260, 274, 365, 368, 400, 417, 418, 423–428, 430, 434, 435, 437, 474, 475, 480, 485, 486
Cilliers, S. P. 418
Cloete, Lucie 27, 137, 195
Coertze, Pieter Johannes 39, 49, 117, 236, 243, 323, 329, 330, 332, 344
Coetzee, J.H. "Hennie" 213, 330, 430
Conradie, Johannes Hendrik 138
Cronjé, Geoffrey 39, 49, 128, 139, 147, 182, 189, 214, 241, 243, 255, 274, 275, 330, 411

De Klerk, Frederik Willem 316, 419
De Klerk, Jan 218, 220, 445
De Villiers Graaff, David Pieter 305, 365, 366
Diederichs, Nicholas 21, 167, 189, 210–212, 214, 216, 229, 348, 411, 412, 447, 473
Diefenbaker, John 371–375
Dönges, Ebenezer 211, 214, 215, 218, 263, 275, 347, 348, 359, 423, 425, 469, 479
Dönhoff, Christoph 172
Dönhoff, Marion 172
Drascher, Warhold 260, 261
Du Plessis, Lodewikus Johannes 81, 195, 200, 209–214, 216, 426, 429, 430, 437, 447
Du Toit, J.D. (Totius) 211
Dürckheim-Montmartin, Karlfried Graf 89, 90

Eiselen, Werner Willi Max 29, 117, 177, 191, 236, 237, 243, 280, 289, 292, 304, 306, 308, 309, 311, 319, 322, 323–330, 332, 333, 337, 338, 345, 351, 397, 413, 415, 416
Elizabeth II. 167, 359, 375
Eloff, Gerhard 256, 260
Erasmus, François Christiaan 218, 269, 270

Fischer, Abraham "Bram" 382
Fischer, Eugen 86, 97, 254–256
Fourie, Adrian Paulus Johannes 151, 153, 154

Gayre of Gayre, Robert 258–260
Gerdener, Gustav Bernhard Augustus 274, 277, 283
Gericke, Jacobus Stephanus 263, 282, 364, 432, 435–437, 480
Geyer, Albertus Lourens 34, 164, 171, 177, 197, 231, 274, 347, 365, 395, 418, 424
Geyser, Albertus Stephanus 433
Goebbels, Josef 170, 186
Gutmann, Bruno 324

Haak, Jan Friedrich Wilhelm 161, 263, 443
Havenga, Nicolaas Christiaan 193, 195, 218–221, 270
Hegel, Georg Wilhelm Friedrich 51, 52, 439
Herder, Johann Gottfried 324, 326
Hertzog, Albert 167, 181, 189, 201, 211, 215, 218, 347–349, 383, 407, 427, 477, 490–492
Hertzog, J.B.M. 10, 19, 22, 23, 42, 150–153, 188, 190, 192–196, 208, 215, 377, 378, 439, 477
Hintrager, Oskar 97, 98
Hitler, Adolf 5, 20, 33, 166, 204, 207, 253, 386, 475, 503
Hoffmann, Hermann 134, 250, 253, 254
Hofmeyr, Jan Hendrik 152, 170, 177, 258, 263, 264
Hofmeyr, Johannes Dirk Jacobs 82, 257, 259, 260, 275, 326
Hofmeyr, William Angus "Willie" 23, 161, 164, 265
Hubbard, Ron 260
Hume, David 55

Name Index

Irving, David 258

Jansen, Ernest George 28, 143, 277, 278, 288, 412, 415
Jonathan, Joseph Leabua 298, 320, 358

Kahn, Sam 382
Kant, Immanuel 51, 52, 92, 94
Keet, Barend Bartholomeus 40, 338, 351, 414, 433, 434
Kestell, John Daniel 189
Kleist, Peter 261
Klemm, Otto 88, 93, 110, 112, 222
Klopper, Henning 299, 349
Köhler, Wolfgang 61, 91, 96
Kretschmer, Ernst 134, 225, 228, 250–253, 255
Krueger, Felix 39, 56, 80, 84, 88–93, 96, 110–112, 118, 255, 497
Külpe, Oswald 56–58, 62
Kuyper, Abraham 24, 233, 241, 272, 432

Language, Francis Joseph 332
Lawrence, Harry 178
Lenin, Vladimir Ilyich 10, 155, 503
Leroux, Etienne 493
Lewin, Kurt 72, 96
Lipmann, Otto 72, 96
Lombard, Iwan Makepeace 189, 196, 411
Louw, Eric Hendrik 170, 182, 207, 220, 269, 270, 342, 356, 364, 365, 372, 375, 384, 425, 475, 490, 499
Louw, Nicolaas Petrus van Wyk 289, 338, 422, 493, 494
Luthuli, Albert 374, 402

Macmillan, Harold 122, 362, 363, 365, 370, 372–375, 385, 395, 438
Madeley, Walter 178, 218
Malan, Daniel François 22, 23, 27, 41, 126, 139, 147, 153, 154, 160, 161, 163, 166, 168, 188, 190, 194, 195, 206, 207, 209, 210, 211, 217–219, 221, 263, 268–270, 273–275, 277, 359, 365, 423, 472, 495, 499
Malan, François Stephanus 127, 131, 324
Malherbe, Ernst Gideon 127, 140, 268, 407
Mandela, Nelson 191, 280, 404, 495
Marais, Ben 433

Matthews, Zachariah Keodirelang 332, 333
Meinhof, Carl 323–328, 332, 336, 412
Meiring, Piet G. J. 13, 161, 162, 165, 171, 178, 195, 206, 230, 267, 375, 383, 417, 426, 431, 469
Mentz, Frans Engelbertus 301, 302
Menzies, Robert Gordon 368, 372–374, 438
Meyer, Pieter Johannes 179, 180, 199, 204, 212, 214, 216, 256, 268, 349, 366, 417, 436, 447, 472, 491
Mitchell, Douglas 235, 370, 377, 473, 474
Moede, Walther 86, 87, 95, 257
Moltke, Johannes Strauß von 258
Mönnig, Hermann Otto 216, 259, 439–441, 444, 445
Mosley, Oswald 258
Mühlmann, Wilhelm 243, 330

Naudé, Christian Frederick Beyers 349, 436, 437
Nel, Michiel Daniel Christiaan de Wet 209, 275, 277, 322, 327, 340, 415, 423, 424, 469
Nkrumah, Kwame 184, 353, 371, 374
Nyerere, Julius 373

Olivier, N.J.J. 284, 337, 413–416, 420, 421, 429, 437
Oppenheimer, Harry 383

Pienaar, Schalk 427, 494
Pirow, Oswald 195, 207, 208, 218
Pratt, David 364, 476, 484

Roeder, Manfred 258
Roos, Tielman 22, 472
Rothmann, Maria Elizabeth 127, 130, 141, 142, 149, 152, 154, 159, 217, 220, 313, 314, 322, 365, 391, 428, 474, 477
Rupert, Anton 33, 162, 293, 447, 486

Sampson, E. Wyatt 333, 334
Sander, Friedrich 90
Sauer, Paul 160, 161, 276–278, 280, 281, 336, 348, 364, 405, 469
Schoeman, Barend Johannes "Ben" 168, 220, 221, 347, 368
Scholtz, Gert Daniel 3, 34, 35, 42, 162, 165, 171, 177, 182, 219, 322, 341, 352, 376, 377
Schumann, Christian Gustav Waldemar 138, 161, 263, 264, 441, 452

Schumann, Theodor Eberhardt Werner 325, 355, 390
Selz, Otto 53, 58–64, 68, 72, 78, 140, 234, 498
Serfontein, J. J. 277, 408, 469
Skawran, Paul 99, 250, 251, 253
Smuts, Jan Christian 26, 42, 167, 188, 190, 193, 203–205, 271, 335, 353, 354, 443, 469, 472, 495
Stalin, Josef 5, 20, 33, 494, 503
Stern, William 87, 91, 93–96, 100–103, 114, 117, 222–224, 229, 264
Steyn, F. S. 449
Strauss, Jacobus Gideon Nel 166
Strijdom, Johannes Gerhardus "Hans" 18, 81, 160, 161, 163, 164, 167, 168, 170, 188, 189, 192, 207, 213, 217–219, 246, 269, 270, 273, 347, 359, 360, 382, 405, 415, 418, 440, 472
Stumpf, Carl 50, 80, 96
Suzman, Helen 13, 186, 404, 437, 475
Swart, Charles Robberts 165, 191, 192, 195, 207, 208, 219, 246, 270, 307, 347, 348, 395, 398, 423, 488

Tambo, Oliver 191
Theron, Erika 128, 136, 148, 150, 156, 161, 175, 179, 180, 217, 289, 331, 428, 474
Thom, Hendrik Bernardus 28, 34, 155, 157, 176, 177, 275, 328, 341, 412, 436, 437
Trollip, Alfred Ernest 381
Tsafendas, Dimitri 479, 484–487

Uys, Dirk Cornelis Hermanus 469

Van den Bergh, Hendrik 261, 485
Van der Bijl, Hendrik 449
Van der Merwe, Abraham Johannes 171
Van der Merwe, Johannes Gideon "Kaalkop" 349, 431, 442
Van der Spuy, Johannes Petrus 234, 235, 308, 370, 371, 421
Van Rensburg, Jurgens Anthonie Jansen 140, 256, 257

Van Rensburg, Johannes Frederick Janse „Hans" 195, 206–211, 217–220, 260
Van Rhyn, Albertus Johannes Roux 164, 210, 259, 440
Van Rooy, Johannes Cornelis "Joon" 43, 189, 199, 201, 203, 209, 211, 214, 411, 412, 432
Van Schalkwyk, Andries 331, 332, 342, 412
Van Schoor, Adriaan Mynhardt 172, 175, 178
Van Warmelo, Nicolaas Jacobus 325, 326, 336
Van Zyl, A. J. 163–165, 167, 220
Vedder, Heinrich 260
Verwoerd, Anje 23, 24, 27, 194
Verwoerd, Elisabeth 26, 30, 89, 97, 98, 142, 159, 314, 322, 365, 428, 477, 489
Verwoerd, Daniel 178, 179
Verwoerd, Leendert (Len) 24–28, 154, 179
Verwoerd, Wilhelm Johannes (Father) 23–25, 27, 28, 64
Verwoerd, Wilhelm Johannes (Son) 14, 17, 23, 35, 101, 157, 261, 382
Verwoerd, Wilhelm Johannes (Grandson) 3, 13
Viljoen, Marais 162, 469, 484
Volkelt, Hans 88–90, 101–103, 107, 108, 111–115, 249, 250
Vorster, Balthasar Johannes „John" 6, 136, 219, 259, 298, 348, 352, 383, 398, 403, 404, 456, 474, 478, 484, 485, 490, 494
Vorster, J. D. „Koot" 261, 436, 437

Waring, Frank 381
Weber, Phil 171, 177, 197, 231, 274, 284, 347, 405, 406, 418, 419, 423–427, 430, 435, 494
Weichardt, Louis 258
Wellek, Albert 90, 91
Wertheimer, Max 57, 96
Westermann, Diedrich 326, 342
Wilcocks, Raymond William 29, 35, 50–54, 61–63, 66, 67, 71, 75, 80, 99, 126, 127, 132, 139–141, 144, 223, 256, 265, 268
Wundt, Wilhelm 54–58, 72, 89, 92–94, 102, 109–114, 125, 224, 318, 325, 497

Location Index

Amsterdam 2, 23, 24, 33, 86, 233

Berlin 72, 85, 86, 93, 94, 96–98, 166, 257
Bloemfontein 17, 22, 131, 138, 140, 169, 207, 246, 256, 429, 481
Boston 98, 99
Botswana (Bechuanaland) 354, 355
Brandfort 25, 27, 28, 194, 407
Bulawayo 25, 26

Cape Province 22, 23, 136, 138, 148, 163, 171, 190, 197, 209, 217, 269, 275, 277, 313, 348, 359, 364, 366, 395, 405, 418, 420, 422–424, 428, 433, 436, 469
Cape Town 23–25, 29, 47, 129, 135, 137, 138, 142, 160, 218, 245, 263, 287, 400, 410, 412, 485, 487, 498
Cradock 206

Durban 287, 314, 410

East London 463, 494

Groningen 87, 223

Hamburg 84, 93–95, 116, 325, 492

Johannesburg 14, 23, 124, 150, 160–162, 174, 189, 191, 196, 197, 200, 237, 272, 281, 301, 308, 327, 363, 364, 375, 396, 416, 423–425, 438, 450, 454, 476

Kimberley 11, 12, 128, 136, 142, 143, 148, 154, 160, 168, 189, 199, 221, 265, 286, 498, 503

Leipzig 84, 86, 89, 93, 255
Lesotho (Basutoland) 298, 319, 320, 340, 351, 354–356, 358, 398
London 259, 364, 365, 370, 371, 375, 378

Malmesbury 139, 263

Natal 197, 219, 235, 271, 299, 319, 376, 377, 381, 407, 433, 481
New York 98, 100

Orange Free State 22, 27, 189, 195, 197, 206, 319, 433

Paarl 144, 481
Pietermaritzburg 352
Port Elizabeth 287, 380, 409, 463
Potchefstroom 209, 233, 302, 480
Pretoria 17, 192, 216, 259, 276, 348, 356, 357, 396, 429, 444, 448, 479, 484

Rhodesia (Zimbabwe) 25, 26, 173, 354, 479

Sharpeville 5, 231, 340, 363, 371, 395, 403, 406, 407, 409, 416, 434, 444, 446
Sophiatown 191, 301
South West Africa (Namibia) 97, 328, 337, 353, 361, 362, 386
Stellenbosch 23, 28, 75, 127, 131, 132, 156, 160–162, 165, 206, 233, 314, 342, 433, 442, 474, 489
Swaziland 354, 355

Transkei 184, 297, 300, 320, 342, 352, 354, 355, 357, 398, 413
Transvaal 18, 22, 23, 126, 160, 163, 164, 188, 189, 194, 197, 208, 209, 213, 215, 221, 222, 268, 269, 273–276, 347, 382, 405, 423, 424, 433, 436, 489

Witwatersrand 18, 160–162, 189, 197, 220, 287, 301, 302, 450, 463

https://doi.org/10.1515/9783110787313-020

Subject Index

African National Congress (ANC) 3, 191, 241, 311, 312, 332, 363, 395, 397, 402, 430, 486
Afrikaner Broederbond (AB) 8, 17–19, 23, 43, 143, 156, 176, 177, 189, 191, 193–218, 234, 235, 245, 255, 256, 266, 267, 274, 275, 289, 307–309, 322, 328, 330, 333, 336, 341, 342, 347, 349, 355, 359, 361, 363, 367, 370, 371, 375, 376, 380, 407, 411–413, 419, 429, 432, 435, 436, 439, 441, 442, 447, 449, 452, 490, 491, 500
Afrikaner Party (AP) 190, 193, 195, 218–221, 267, 270
Ambiguity 190, 222, 234, 235, 241, 298, 378, 394, 498
Anglican Church 409, 410, 431
Anti-intellectualism 155–159, 258, 285, 329, 331, 334, 345, 407, 408, 418, 419, 424, 426, 435, 480, 493, 494, 500
Anti-communism 1, 200, 230, 231, 234, 236, 246, 258, 261, 267, 319, 380, 382, 387–392, 395, 398, 403–405, 408, 409, 490, 492, 498, 504
Antisemitism 91, 160, 188, 203, 204, 258, 261–270, 292, 366, 381–384, 390, 391, 486, 495, 499
Asians 124, 125, 373, 388–392, 417, 487, 490
Association Psychology 55, 57–61, 63, 69, 72, 73, 78, 79, 92

Bantu Authorities 280, 286, 295, 298–300, 304, 306, 321, 353
Bantu Education 280, 308–315, 397, 444, 469
Boer War (South African War) 21–24, 27, 29, 42, 97, 121, 126, 192, 432, 471, 493
Border Industry 9, 172, 287, 288, 293, 295–297, 413, 455

Calvinism (Reformed Creed) 24, 25, 191, 195, 197, 198, 201, 209, 222, 232, 233, 263, 272, 277, 294, 309, 411, 430–434, 480, 482, 488
Catholicism 382, 410, 431
Censorship 406, 488, 492–494, 500
Chaos 19, 41, 124, 184, 185, 187, 222–241, 329, 340, 391, 394, 419, 498
Childhood Psychology 18, 82, 86, 89, 100–108, 111, 113, 114, 254

Churches 11, 24, 25, 48, 49, 126, 127, 143, 144, 172, 191, 197, 201, 210, 216, 234, 263, 273, 277, 281, 283, 285, 294, 310, 380, 389, 397, 409, 410–412, 415, 416, 424, 425, 430–436, 473, 488, 503
Civilisation 38, 40, 41, 43, 109–111, 115, 116, 118–123, 125, 126, 134, 144, 157, 184, 217, 231, 248, 249, 273, 291, 295, 303, 317, 318, 321, 324, 339, 342, 345, 351, 385, 391, 392, 394, 403, 422, 431, 440, 461, 471, 473, 490, 496, 497, 501, 503
Cold War 1, 384, 387, 388, 389, 390, 392, 398, 417
Coloureds 12, 30, 52, 134–137, 147, 150, 180, 181, 185, 231, 234, 235, 237, 241, 245–248, 256, 272, 275, 280, 313, 314, 329, 331, 341, 347, 349, 362, 367, 386, 395, 396, 411, 413, 416–430, 434, 435, 437, 455, 464, 484, 487
Commonwealth 2, 19, 167, 172, 194, 350, 358–360, 362–378, 384, 387, 422, 439
Communist Party 485
Cottesloe Conference 277, 416, 423, 424, 430, 433–436
Cultural Nationalism 2, 11, 19, 21–23, 27–29, 34, 38, 41, 42, 44, 46, 98, 117, 143, 154, 160, 163, 164, 188, 190, 192–194, 198, 199, 202, 206, 208, 217, 233, 242, 265, 270, 271, 314, 322, 324, 326, 328, 378, 379, 414, 430, 431, 471, 488, 492, 493, 498, 500

Decolonisation 217, 319, 321, 350, 352, 353, 355, 357, 368, 374, 378, 387, 388, 393, 430, 503
Detention without Trial 395, 404
Developmental Psychology 14, 18, 49, 82, 89, 93, 94, 100, 103, 109–113, 118–120, 222, 242, 249, 254, 320, 321, 497
Die Burger 14, 33, 141, 143, 154, 162–164, 169, 181, 197, 260, 368, 405, 411, 423, 425–427, 429, 430, 434
Die Transvaler 18, 50, 161–167, 171, 174, 176, 188, 194, 195, 199, 204, 207, 209, 219, 221, 246, 265, 267, 268, 279, 391, 425, 493, 500
Die Vaderland 165
Die Volksblad 161, 162, 164, 259

578 — Subject Index

Differential Psychology 94, 100, 103, 112, 117, 118, 130, 222, 223
Dogmatism 1, 9, 12, 13, 14, 18, 19, 34, 133, 178, 179, 281, 292, 316, 331, 373, 417, 476, 503
Double task 36, 42, 46, 47, 63-72, 173, 282

Ethnology 39, 49, 109, 110, 112, 113, 117, 118, 180, 184, 236, 243, 249, 259, 260, 272, 305, 313, 317-340, 346, 412, 430, 499
Ethnopsychology 18, 56, 82, 89, 93, 94, 100, 109-119, 122, 124, 224, 236, 249, 298, 317-321, 323, 325, 335, 344, 497

Federasie van Afrikaanse Kultuurvereniginge (FAK) 144, 189, 191, 198, 210, 212, 214, 280, 412, 478
Feelings 18, 50, 51, 63, 69-83, 85, 92, 102, 117, 135, 230, 361, 471, 491, 498, 499, 504
Forced Removal 301, 304
Foreign Policy 6, 125, 182, 364, 384, 470

Gereformeerde Kerk (Doppers) 197, 199, 209, 233, 432
Gestalt Psychology 56, 58, 61, 72, 80, 87, 92, 96, 103, 228
Greyshirts 188, 204, 220, 258, 269, 383

Harvard University 54, 95, 98, 99
High Commission Territories (Protectorates) 169, 349, 351, 354-358, 363
Holistic Psychology 80, 89-93, 102, 103, 111, 222, 228, 324
Homeland (Bantustan) 7, 9, 118, 120, 123, 124, 184, 185, 276, 278, 279, 282-297, 299, 302, 304, 313, 317, 319, 333, 342, 343, 349, 350-358, 378, 380, 383, 386, 396, 420, 434, 437, 448, 455, 463, 475, 501, 504

Indians 217, 235, 237, 248, 268, 269, 275, 305, 314, 350, 367, 389, 416, 417, 420, 428, 455, 487
Influx Control 8, 9, 174, 239, 303, 306-308, 335

Journalism (Verwoerd) 18, 35, 128, 159-169, 172, 188, 209, 219, 246, 265, 360, 368, 385, 405, 407, 423, 500

Linguistics 323-325, 328, 336, 343, 352
Logic 9, 50-52, 59, 60, 81-83, 108, 113-115, 117, 125, 158, 170, 173-175, 179-187, 229, 232, 234, 238-240, 282, 295, 298, 317, 318, 341, 360, 373, 420, 423, 451, 456, 471, 474, 478, 479, 497-499

Marxism 7, 155, 239, 240, 286, 340, 492
Military 19, 84, 208, 302, 340, 343, 392, 456
Modern, Modernising 5-7, 15, 45, 133, 145, 159, 238, 240, 276, 297, 307, 328, 342, 431, 438, 439, 441, 451, 456, 459, 462, 466, 468, 504

Nasionale Pers 160, 164, 167, 274, 405, 406, 423-425, 427
National Socialism (Nazi, NS) 5, 6, 20, 62, 85, 90, 91, 97, 98, 166, 186, 204, 207, 220, 243, 248, 253, 258-261, 273, 330, 348, 502
Native Representatives 235, 278, 350
Natives Representative Council (NRC) 238, 273, 279, 280
Nederduitse Gereformeerde Kerk (NGK=DRC) 171, 233, 327, 364, 431, 433-437
Nederduitse Hervormde Kerk (NHK) 389, 433, 434
Nuwe Orde 218

Orange River Dam 458, 460, 464, 468, 475
Ossewabrandwag (OB) 6, 168, 194, 205-212, 214-221, 256, 260, 270, 348, 404, 430, 476

Pass Laws 174, 303, 306, 308, 363, 399-402, 406
Panafricanist Congress (PAC) 231, 363
Personality Psychology 100-104, 108, 117, 223-229, 241, 250
Planning 2, 5, 6, 136, 142, 144, 147, 158, 202, 236, 239, 271, 277, 284, 288, 302, 338, 350, 401, 439-448, 450-453, 455, 457-468, 501, 504
Police 231, 246, 261, 363, 364, 396, 400, 403, 404, 406, 484, 485, 495, 503
Poor whites 2, 18, 19, 30, 33, 42, 88, 91, 105, 107, 123, 126-132, 135, 138-147, 150-152, 154, 168, 172, 189, 222, 245, 246, 250, 264, 265, 395, 396, 400, 418, 450, 471, 488, 498, 503
Positivism 15, 55, 93, 96, 109, 127, 133, 149, 157, 158, 185, 228, 317, 341, 443, 451

Potchefstroom University for Christian Higher Education 157, 195, 197–199, 209, 211–213, 233, 273, 330, 376, 414, 430, 432, 480
Pragmatism 8–10, 12–14, 34, 145, 183, 219, 225, 291, 292, 400
Press 15, 22, 32, 33, 142, 160, 164, 165, 196, 246, 248, 297, 331, 347, 351, 365, 375, 384, 389, 402, 403–406, 409, 416, 417, 423, 426, 427, 429, 480, 482
Principle 8, 13, 15, 18, 27, 30, 35–42, 46, 47, 49, 60, 71, 83, 116, 117, 133, 135, 153, 158, 159, 171, 172, 178, 179, 181–183, 185, 192, 194, 195, 203, 209, 212, 215, 219, 229, 231, 237, 238, 241, 247, 258, 270, 282–284, 286, 290, 292, 301, 303–305, 310, 316, 348, 358, 359, 365, 370, 374, 382, 392, 394, 399, 400, 412, 417, 419, 427, 433, 445, 447, 453, 463, 466, 473, 497, 498, 500, 501, 503, 504
Propaganda 2, 16, 18, 35, 78, 148, 163, 166, 168–174, 179, 186, 192, 198, 205, 209, 230, 232, 259, 260, 268, 274, 282, 297, 314, 316, 317, 342, 351–353, 357, 365, 367, 375, 376, 379, 382, 385, 391, 408–410, 412, 428, 472, 477, 499, 500, 504
Psychology of Thought 53, 54, 57, 58, 62–64, 71, 140, 234, 498, 499
Purity 19, 134, 164, 241, 242, 247, 498

Racism 6, 12, 19, 34, 91, 108, 110, 124, 134–136, 140, 141, 144, 150, 185, 236, 241–250, 255–261, 263, 265, 268, 273, 314, 326, 327, 330, 381, 390, 391, 393, 404, 413, 414, 425, 438, 497, 499, 502–504
Right Wing Extremism 6, 89, 98, 188, 195, 206, 207, 210, 211, 218, 222, 237, 241, 256, 258–261, 263, 264, 348, 366, 383, 390, 429, 447, 490, 495, 499
Reddingsdaadbond (RDB) 189, 210, 212, 214
Repression 4, 19, 20, 108, 266, 296, 340, 395, 397, 398, 403–405, 500, 501
Republic 2, 11, 15, 19, 21, 23, 81, 156, 157, 163, 167, 172, 173, 191, 192, 194, 195, 207, 216, 267, 274, 350, 352, 355, 358–363, 365–368, 370, 371, 373, 376–381, 386, 392–395, 410, 416, 419, 425, 426, 446, 453, 474, 483

Rhetoric 146, 173–175, 179, 180, 182, 186, 276, 282, 353, 365, 366, 391, 457, 499
Rhodes University 171, 407

South African Bureau of Racial Affairs (SABRA) 8, 9, 158, 234, 256, 260, 271, 274, 275, 277, 283, 287, 289, 292, 308, 330, 331, 337, 411–416, 420, 429, 434, 435
Sauer Report 277, 278, 280, 281
Social Engineering 12, 15, 149, 315, 327, 364, 418, 502
South African Institute of Race Relations (SAIRR) 127, 364, 408, 410, 411, 415
Social Darwinism 570
Socialism 10, 216, 239, 382, 449, 50
Sociology (Verwoerd) 2, 12, 18, 47, 48, 90, 108, 127, 129–134, 137, 141–143, 184, 221, 237, 250, 254, 261, 395, 418, 498
Social Work 129–132, 135–137, 140–142, 144, 145, 147, 148, 150–152, 305, 400, 418, 498, 502
Stellenbosch University 11, 17, 28, 30, 32, 33, 50, 52–54, 62, 71, 75, 98–101, 127–133, 137, 139, 145, 155–157, 161, 176, 177, 200, 206, 224, 233, 256, 257, 263, 264, 266, 268, 275, 277, 326, 328–330, 335, 337, 341, 342, 370, 395, 400, 411–414, 416, 418, 426, 433, 436, 441, 442, 452, 474, 480, 489

Territorial Segregation 271, 274, 276, 277, 286, 292, 301, 302, 350, 423
Tomlinson Report 288–294, 452
Totalitarianism 5, 15, 20, 36, 49, 186, 276, 395, 402, 494, 502
Townships 239, 276, 284, 302–304, 363, 504

United Party 17, 154, 165, 166, 170, 183, 184, 188, 190, 192, 195, 204, 221, 235, 246, 248, 348, 362, 366, 376, 381, 387, 396, 409, 417, 423, 495
University of Berlin 34, 50, 58, 61, 72, 85–87, 91, 92, 96, 103, 224
University of Cape Town 50, 318, 326, 331, 437
University of Fort Hare 31, 314, 341
University of Hamburg 85, 87, 93–96, 100–102, 117

University of Leipzig 39, 55, 80, 82, 84–93, 95, 97, 99, 101, 102, 107, 109, 112, 114, 115, 118, 222, 250, 251, 255, 324
University of Natal 407
University of the (Orange) Free State 17, 246, 256, 330–332, 342
University of Pretoria 97, 133, 147, 228, 250, 253, 255, 257, 288, 330, 344, 445, 458
University of the Witwatersrand 245, 268, 314, 434

Violence 5, 82, 184, 305, 319, 340, 345, 396, 400, 402, 403, 406, 434, 476, 496, 503, 504
Voluntarism 5, 22, 41, 67, 242, 379, 447, 501
Voortrekkerpers 160, 161, 164, 166, 167, 206, 423, 484

Wilcocks Commission 52, 286

www.ingramcontent.com/pod-product-compliance
Lightning Source LLC
Chambersburg PA
CBHW031719230426
43669CB00007B/179